abled. Plaintiffs primarily used the Rehabilitation Act of 1973 (29 U.S.C.A. § 701 et seq.), the earliest law of this type. But the Rehabilitation Act has a limited scope: it applies only to federally funded workplaces and institutions, and says nothing about those that do not receive government money.

With passage of the ADA in 1990, Congress gave broad protection to people with AIDS who work in the private sector. In general, the ADA is designed to increase access for disabled persons, and it also forbids discrimination in hiring or promotion in companies with fifteen or more employees. Specifically, employers may not discriminate if the person in question is otherwise qualified for the job. Moreover, they cannot use tests to screen out disabled persons, and they must provide reasonable accommodation for disabled workers. The ADA, which took effect in 1992, has quickly emerged as the primary means for bringing AIDS-related discrimination lawsuits.

AIDS and Health Care Closely related to work is the issue of health care. In some cases, the two overlap: health insurance, Social Security, and disability benefits for AIDS victims were often hard to obtain during the 1980s. Insurance was particularly difficult because employers feared rising costs and insurance companies did not want to pay claims. To avoid the costs of AIDS, insurance companies used two traditional industry techniques: they attempted to exclude AIDS coverage from general policies, and they placed caps (limits on benefits payments) on AIDS-related coverage.

In January 1995, the settlement in a lawsuit brought by a Philadelphia construction worker with AIDS illustrated that the ADA can be used to fight caps on coverage. In 1992, the joint union-management fund for the Laborers' District Council placed a $10,000 limit on AIDS benefits, in stark contrast to the $100,000 allowed for other catastrophic illnesses. At that time, the fund said the cap on AIDS benefits was designed to curb all health costs. In 1993, the EEOC ruled that it violated the ADA, and, backed by the AIDS Law Project of Philadelphia, the worker sued. Rather than fight an expensive lawsuit, the insurance fund settled.

AIDS and Education Issues in the field of education include the rights of HIV-positive students to attend class and of HIV-positive teachers to teach, the confidentiality of HIV records, and how best to teach young people about AIDS. A few areas have been settled in court: for instance, the right of students to attend classes was of greater concern in the early years of the epidemic, and no longer remains in dispute.

Certain students with AIDS may assert their right to public education under the Education for All Handicapped Children Act of 1975 (EAHCA), but the law is only relevant in cases involving special education programs. More commonly, students' rights are protected by the Rehabilitation Act.

Schools play a major role in the effort to educate the public on AIDS. Several states have mandated AIDS prevention instruction in their schools. But the subject is controversial: it evokes personal, political, and moral reactions to sexuality. During the 1980s, those who often criticized liberal approaches to sex education argued that AIDS materials should not be explicit, encourage sexuality, promote the use of contraceptives, or favorably portray gays and lesbians.

Civil Litigation TORT law has seen an explosion of AIDS-related suits. This area of law is used to discourage individuals from subjecting others to unreasonable risks, and to compensate those who have been injured by unreasonably risky behavior. The greatest number of AIDS-related LIABILITY lawsuits has involved the receipt of HIV-infected blood and blood products. A second group has concerned the sexual transmission of HIV. A third group involves AIDS-related psychic distress. In these cases, plaintiffs have successfully sued and recovered damages for their fear of having contracted HIV.

CROSS-REFERENCES
Disabled Persons; Discrimination; Food and Drug Administration; Gay and Lesbian Rights; Health Care; Patients' Rights; Physicians and Surgeons; Privacy.

Cross-references at end of article

ALLRED, GLORIA Gloria Allred, born July 3, 1941, in Philadelphia, is a flamboyant, widely recognized lawyer, feminist, activist, and radio talk show host. Though her critics dismiss her as a publicity monger and a dilettante, Allred has received praise from others who believe that she is a master at using the power of the news media to draw attention to the day-to-day struggles of ordinary people.

Born Gloria Rachel Bloom, Allred grew up in Philadelphia with her parents, Morris Bloom, a door-to-door salesman, and Stella Davidson Bloom, a homemaker. Her conventional middle-class childhood gave no hint of the outspoken activist to come. Allred graduated with honors from the University of Pennsylvania in 1963 with a bachelor's degree in English. She moved to New York to pursue a master's degree in teaching at New York University. Wh... interested in the CIVIL RIGHT... was beginning to gain mom... her master's degree in 19...

BIOGRAPHY

Gloria Allred

Biography of contributor to American law

GLORIA ALLRED 1941-

1925 · 1950 · 1975 · 2000

Timeline for subject of biography, including general historical events and life events

Philadelphia to teach at a high school with a predominantly black enrollment.

Allred says her interest in the struggle for equal rights arose from personal experiences. While she was in college, she married, gave birth to a daughter, and divorced. Unable to collect CHILD SUPPORT from her former husband, she was forced to return to her parents' home. She also recalls being paid less than a man for what she considered equal work. The reason given was that the man had a family to support, but at the time, Allred was the single mother of an infant.

After moving to California, Allred taught in the turbulent Watts section of Los Angeles and became the first full-time female staff member in United Teachers of Los Angeles, the union representing Los Angeles teachers. The experience stirred her interest in CIVIL RIGHTS and collective bargaining and prompted her to go to law school. She received her law degree, with honors, from Loyola Marymount University, Los Angeles, Law School in 1974. Soon after, she entered a law firm partnership with her classmates Nathan Goldberg and Michael Maroko.

Allred is probably the most flamboyant and well known member of her firm. She has achieved notoriety and name recognition through staged press conferences and demonstrations publicizing and dramatizing the cause she is championing at the time. She also accepts controversial cases that naturally attract media attention. During her years in practice, she has successfully sued Los Angeles County to stop the practice of shackling and chaining pregnant inmates during labor and delivery; put a halt on the city of El Segundo's quizzing job applicants about their sexual histories (*Thorne v. City of El Segundo*, 802 F.2d 1131 [9th Cir. 1986]); represented a client who was turned down for a job as a police officer after a six-hour lie detector exam that included questions about her sex life; and sued a dry cleaning establishment for discrimination because it charged more to launder women's shirts than men's.

Allred relishes confrontation, and her showy tactics have earned her both praise and criticism.

"THERE ARE ENOUGH HIGH HURDLES TO CLIMB, AS ONE TRAVELS THROUGH LIFE, WITHOUT HAVING TO SCALE ARTIFICIAL BARRIERS CREATED BY LAW OR SILLY REGULATIONS."

Defending what many have called self-promoting publicity stunts, Allred says she tries to use the few moments she is in the spotlight to make her point as forcefully as possible. Her detractors say that she wastes her time and energy on trivial issues that do not advance any worthwhile cause and deflect attention away from serious issues. Yet, she points out, she is often stopped on the street by people who recognize her and want to thank her for taking on the small fights that no one else wants.

Some critics say she is all show and no substance. But Allred has many supporters as well. Among them is Justice Joan Dempsey Klein, of the California Court of Appeal, who credits Allred with moving women's issues forward. Klein also points out that Allred saves her dramatics for outside the courtroom and always observes proper decorum when before the bench. According to Klein, Allred is always well-prepared and, for that reason, is quite successful.

Dressed in her trademark reds and electric blues, her striking black hair set off by deep red lipstick, Allred is a potent combination of scholarship and theatrics. Her keen intelligence and shrewd understanding of the power of the media have made her a contemporary success story in the world of law and politics.

ARBITER [*Latin, One who attends something to view it as a spectator or witness.*] Any person who is given an absolute power to judge and rule on a matter in a dispute.

Internal cross references

Quotation from subject of biography

Full cite for case

Definition enclosed in book logos with Latin translation provided

WEST'S ENCYCLOPEDIA
of
AMERICAN LAW

WEST'S
ENCYCLOPEDIA
of
AMERICAN
LAW

Volume 1

WEST PUBLISHING COMPANY
MINNEAPOLIS/SAINT PAUL   NEW YORK   LOS ANGELES   SAN FRANCISCO

This encyclopedia is the result of efforts by numerous individuals and entities from the Twin Cities and around the United States. West Group wishes to thank all who made this publication, its quality and content, a priority in their lives.

In addition to the individuals who worked on *West's Encyclopedia of American Law*, West Group recognizes Harold W. Chase (1922–1982) for his contributions to *The Guide to American Law: Everyone's Legal Encyclopedia*.

West's encyclopedia of American law.
        p.   cm.
    Includes bibliographical references and
        indexes.
    ISBN 0-314-05538-X (hard :
        alk. paper)
    1. Law—United States—Encyclopedias.
    2. Law—United States—Popular works.
    I. West Publishing Company.
    KF154.W47   1997
    348.73'03 —dc20
    [347.30803]   96-34350
                                         CIP

PRODUCTION CREDITS
Cover, interior design, and page layout: David J. Farr, ImageSmythe
Composition: Carlisle Communications
Proofreading: Maureen Meyer
Photo research: Elsa Peterson Ltd.
Art research: Nanette E. Bertaut
Editorial research: Pat Lewis
Artwork: Patricia Isaacs, Parrot Graphics
Indexing: Schroeder Indexing Services

This publication is designed to provide information on the subjects covered. It is sold with the understanding that the publisher is not engaged in rendering legal or other professional advice. If legal advice or other professional assistance is required, the services of a competent professional person should be sought.

WEST'S COMMITMENT TO THE ENVIRONMENT

In 1906, West Publishing Company began recycling materials left over from the production of books. This began a tradition of efficient and responsible use of resources. Today, 100 percent of our legal bound volumes are printed on acid-free, recycled paper consisting of 50 percent new paper pulp and 50 percent paper that has undergone a de-inking process. We also use vegetable-based inks to print all of our books. West recycles nearly 27,700,000 pounds of scrap paper annually—the equivalent of 229,300 trees. Since the 1960s, West has devised ways to capture and recycle waste inks, solvents, oils, and vapors created in the printing process. We also recycle plastics of all kinds, wood, glass, corrugated cardboard, and batteries, and have eliminated the use of polystyrene book packaging. We at West are proud of the longevity and the scope of our commitment to the environment.

West pocket parts and advance sheets are printed on recyclable paper and can be collected and recycled with newspapers. Staples do not have to be removed. Bound volumes can be recycled after removing the cover.

Production, printing, and binding by West Group.

DEDICATION

WEST'S ENCYCLOPEDIA OF AMERICAN LAW (WEAL) IS DEDICATED TO LIBRARIANS AND LIBRARY PATRONS THROUGHOUT THE UNITED STATES AND BEYOND. YOUR INTEREST IN THE AMERICAN LEGAL SYSTEM HELPS TO EXPAND AND FUEL THE FRAMEWORK OF OUR REPUBLIC.

CONTENTS

VOLUME 1

MILESTONES
IN THE LAW

PREFACE

The legal system of the United States is admired around the world for the freedoms it allows the individual and the fairness with which it attempts to treat all persons. On the surface, it may seem simple. Yet, those who have delved into it know that this system of federal and state constitutions, statutes, regulations, and common-law decisions is elaborate and complex. It derives from the English common law, but includes principles older than England, and from other lands. Many concepts are still phrased in Latin. The U.S. legal system, like many others, has a language all its own. Too often it is an unfamiliar language.

In 1983, West published *The Guide to American Law: Everyone's Legal Encyclopedia*, in response to a dearth of reference sources weaving the language of the law into the language of everyday life. *West's Encyclopedia of American Law (WEAL)*, developed with generous feedback from users of *The Guide*, replaces that set as an improved and updated legal encyclopedia. *WEAL* is a reference source devoted to the terms and concepts of U.S. law. It also covers a wide variety of persons, entities, and events that have shaped the U.S. legal system. *WEAL* contains thousands of entries, and a number of unique features and visual aids. It is the most complete reference source of its kind.

Main Features of This Set

Entries This encyclopedia contains over 4,000 entries devoted to terms, concepts, events, movements, cases, and persons significant to U.S. law. Entries on legal terms contain a definition of the term, followed by explanatory text if necessary. Entries are arranged alphabetically in standard encyclopedia format for ease of use. A wide variety of additional features, listed later in this preface, provide interesting background and supplemental information.

Definitions Every entry on a legal term is followed by a definition, which begins and ends with the symbol of an open book (📖). The appendix volume includes a glossary containing all the definitions from the *WEAL*.

Cross-References To facilitate research, *WEAL* provides two types of cross-references, within and following entries. Within the entries, terms are set in small capital letters—for example, LIEN—to indicate that they have their own entry in the encyclopedia. At the end of the entries, related entries the reader may wish to explore are listed alphabetically by title.

In Focus Pieces In Focus pieces accompany related entries and provide additional facts, details, and arguments on particularly interesting, important, or controversial issues raised by those entries. The subjects covered include hotly contested issues, such as abortion, capital punishment, and gay rights; detailed processes, such as the Food and Drug Administration's approval process for new drugs; and important historical or social issues, such as debates over the formation of the U.S. Constitution. In Focus pieces are marked by the symbol that appears in the margin.

Sidebars Sidebars provide brief highlights of some interesting facet of accompanying entries. They complement regular entries and In Focus pieces by adding informative details. Sidebar topics include the Million Man March, in Washington, D.C., and the branches of the

IN FOCUS

U.S. armed services. Sidebars appear at the top of a text page and are set in a blue box.

Biographies WEAL profiles a wide variety of interesting and influential people—including lawyers, judges, government and civic leaders, and historical and modern figures—who have played a part in creating or shaping U.S. law. Each biography includes a time line, which shows important moments in the subject's life as well as important historical events of the period. Biographies appear alphabetically by the subject's last name.

Additional Features of This Set

Milestones in the Law A special section, Milestones in the Law, appearing at the end of selected volumes, allows readers to take a close look at landmark cases in U.S. law. Readers can explore the reasoning of the judges and the arguments of the attorneys that produced major decisions on important legal and social issues. Included in the Milestones section are the opinions of the lower courts; the briefs presented by the parties to the U.S. Supreme Court; and the decision of the Supreme Court, including the majority opinion and all concurring and dissenting opinions for each case.

Enhancements Throughout WEAL, readers will find a broad array of photographs, charts, graphs, manuscripts, legal forms, and other visual aids enhancing the ideas presented in the text.

Tables and Indexes WEAL features several detailed tables and indexes at the back of each volume, as well as a cumulative index contained in a separate volume.

Appendixes An appendix volume included with WEAL contains hundreds of pages of documents, laws, manuscripts, and forms fundamental to and characteristic of U.S. law.

Citations Wherever possible, WEAL entries include citations for cases and statutes mentioned in the text. These allow readers wishing to do additional research to find the opinions and statutes cited. Two sample citations, with explanations of common citation terms, can be seen below and opposite.

Bibliography A bibliography is included at the end of each book and in the index volume.

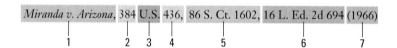

1. *Case title.* The title of the case is set in italics and indicates the names of the parties. The suit in this sample citation was between Ernesto A. Miranda and the state of Arizona.
2. *Reporter volume number.* The number preceding the reporter name indicates the reporter volume containing the case. (The volume number appears on the spine of the reporter, along with the reporter name.)
3. *Reporter name.* The reporter name is abbreviated. The suit in the sample citation is from the reporter, or series of books, called *U.S. Reports,* which contains cases from the U.S. Supreme Court. (Numerous reporters publish cases from the federal and state courts.)
4. *Reporter page.* The number following the reporter name indicates the reporter page on which the case begins.
5. *Additional reporter citation.* Many cases may be found in more than one reporter. The suit in the sample citation also appears in volume 86 of the *Supreme Court Reporter,* beginning on page 1602.
6. *Additional reporter citation.* The suit in the sample citation is also reported in volume 16 of the *Lawyer's Edition,* second series, beginning on page 694.
7. *Year of decision.* The year the court issued its decision in the case appears in parentheses at the end of the cite.

Brady Handgun Violence Prevention Act, Pub. L. No. 103-159, 107 Stat. 1536 (18 U.S.C.A. §§ 921–925A)

1   2   3   4   5   6   7   8

1. *Statute title.*
2. *Public law number.* In the sample citation, the number 103 indicates that this law was passed by the 103d Congress, and the number 159 indicates that it was the 159th law passed by that Congress.
3. *Reporter volume number.* The number preceding the reporter name indicates the reporter volume containing the statute.
4. *Reporter name.* The reporter name is abbreviated. The statute in the sample citation is from *Statutes at Large.*
5. *Reporter page.* The number following the reporter name indicates the reporter page on which the statute begins.

6. *Title number.* Federal laws are divided into major sections with specific titles. The number preceding a reference to the *U.S. Code Annotated* is the title number. Title 18 of the U.S. Code is Crimes and Criminal Procedure.
7. *Additional reporter.* The statute in the sample citation may also be found in the *U.S. Code Annotated.*
8. *Section numbers.* The section numbers following a reference to the *U.S. Code Annotated* indicate where the statute appears in that reporter.

ACKNOWLEDGMENTS

We who have had the good fortune to help create *West's Encyclopedia of American Law* (WEAL) would like to recognize the contributions of Ken Zeigler who first realized the need for a broad legal reference set and who pushed, prodded and cajoled the rest of us into understanding that need; Craig Jilk who gave support whenever support was sought; John Lindley who added his ideas and insight; and Bob Owens who presided over the final stages necessary to bring this project to completion.

We would also like to thank the many writers who contributed their work, the artists and others who gave great thought and effort to this project and various persons throughout West Group and the Thomson Corporation whose considerable talents and support have made the WEAL a flagship publication.

The Editors

WEST'S ENCYCLOPEDIA OF AMERICAN LAW

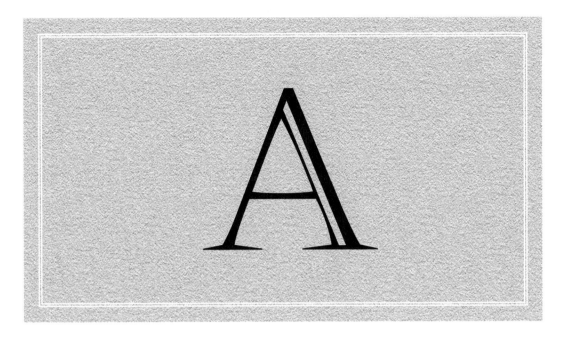

ABANDONMENT 📖 The surrender, relinquishment, DISCLAIMER, or CESSION of PROPERTY or of rights. Voluntary relinquishment of all RIGHT, TITLE, CLAIM and POSSESSION, with the intention of not reclaiming it.

The giving up of a thing absolutely, without reference to any particular person or purpose, as vacating property with the intention of not returning, so that it may be appropriated by the next comer or finder. The voluntary relinquishment of possession of thing by owner with intention of terminating ownership, but without vesting it in any other person. The relinquishing of all title, possession, or claim, or a virtual, intentional throwing away of property.

Term includes both the INTENTION to abandon and the external act by which the intention is carried into effect. In determining whether one has abandoned property or rights, the intention is the first and paramount object of inquiry, for there can be no abandonment without the intention to abandon.

Abandonment differs from SURRENDER in that surrender requires an agreement, and also from FORFEITURE, in that forfeiture may be against the intention of the party alleged to have forfeited. 📖

Property That Can Be Abandoned Various types of PERSONAL PROPERTY—such as personal and household items—contracts, copyrights, inventions, and patents can be abandoned. Certain rights and interests in REAL PROPERTY, such as easements and leases, may also be abandoned. A ranch owner, for example, gives a shepherd an EASEMENT to use a path on her property so that the sheep can get to a watering hole. The shepherd later sells his flock and moves out of the state, never intending to return. This conduct demonstrates that the shepherd has abandoned the easement, since he stopped using the path and intends never to use it again. Ownership of real property cannot be obtained because someone else abandoned it but may be gained through ADVERSE POSSESSION.

Elements of Abandonment Two things must occur for property to be abandoned: (1) an act by the owner that clearly shows that he or she has given up rights to the property; and (2) an intention that demonstrates that the owner has knowingly relinquished control over it.

The Act Some clear action must be taken to indicate that the owner no longer wants his or her property. Any act is sufficient as long as the property is left free and open to anyone who comes along to claim it.

Inaction—that is, failure to do something with the property or nonuse of it—is not enough to demonstrate that the owner has relinquished rights to the property, even if such nonuse has gone on for a number of years. A farmer's failure to cultivate his or her land or a quarry owner's failure to take stone from his or her quarry, for example, does not mean that either person has abandoned interest in the property.

The Intention A person's intention to abandon his or her property may be established by express language to that effect or may be implied from the circumstances surrounding the owner's treatment of the property, such as leaving it unguarded in a place easily accessible to the public.

The passage of time, although not an element of abandonment, may illustrate a person's intention to abandon his or her property.

ABATEMENT 📖 A reduction, a decrease, or a diminution. The suspension or cessation, in whole or in part, of a continuing charge, such as rent. 📖

With respect to ESTATES, an abatement is a proportional diminution or reduction of the monetary LEGACIES, a disposition of property by will, when the funds or assets out of which such legacies are payable are insufficient to pay them in full. The intention of the TESTATOR, when expressed in the will, governs the order in which property will abate. Where the will is silent, abatement occurs in the following order: INTESTATE property, gifts that pass by the RESIDUARY CLAUSE in the will, GENERAL LEGACIES, and SPECIFIC LEGACIES. See also WILLS.

In the context of taxation, an abatement is a decrease in the amount of tax imposed. Abatement of taxes relieves property of its share of the burdens of taxation after the ASSESSMENT has been made and the LEVY of the tax has been accomplished. See also TAXATION.

ABATEMENT OF AN ACTION 📖 An entire overthrow or destruction of a suit so that it is QUASHED and ended. 📖

The purpose of abatement is to save the time and expense of a trial when the plaintiff's suit cannot be maintained in the form originally presented. After an action abates, the PLAINTIFF is ordinarily given an opportunity to correct errors in his or her PLEADING. If the plaintiff still is unable to allege the facts necessary to state a legal CAUSE OF ACTION, then the action is terminated.

Not every possible reason for dissatisfaction with another person can be heard by a court. When the old common law FORM OF ACTION governed the procedure followed by courts (as opposed to state and federal rules of procedure, which now do), only legal wrongs that fit exactly into one of the allowed categories could be pleaded in court. If the DEFENDANT believed that the plaintiff's complaint did not fit one of these forms, the defendant could respond with a PLEA IN ABATEMENT. A plea in abatement was called a DILATORY PLEA because it delayed the time when the court would reach the merits of the plaintiff's claim, if ever.

The rigid formality of COMMON LAW pleading became less satisfactory as legal disputes became more complicated. It has been replaced in each state by a procedure that allows the plaintiff to plead facts showing his or her right to legal RELIEF. Modern systems of pleading retain a right for the defendant to seek abatement of the action when the plaintiff is not entitled to be in court. They allow a defendant to object to the court's JURISDICTION, the VENUE of the trial, the sufficiency of PROCESS, or of the SERVICE OF PROCESS, the legal sufficiency of the plaintiff's claim, or the failure to include someone who must be a PARTY. A plea in abatement is made either in the defendant's ANSWER or by MOTION and ORDER—that is, an application to the court for relief and an order that can grant it. Abatement is usually granted in the form of a DISMISSAL of cause of action, and now the term *dismissal* is used more often than the term *abatement* for this procedure.

Today, the word *abatement* is most often used for the termination of a lawsuit because of the death of a party. Under the common law, a lawsuit abated automatically whenever a party died. This rule was considered a part of the SUBSTANCE of the law involved and was not merely a question of PROCEDURE. Whether the cause of action abated depended on whether or not the lawsuit was considered personal to the parties. For example, contract and property cases were thought to involve issues separate from the parties themselves. They were not personal and did not necessarily abate on the death of a party. Personal injury cases were considered personal, however, and did abate at death. These included claims not only for physical assault or negligent injuries inflicted on the body, but also for other injuries to the person—such as libel, slander, and malicious prosecution.

Today there are statutes that permit the REVIVAL OF AN ACTION that was pending when a party died. An EXECUTOR or ADMINISTRATOR is substituted for the deceased party and the lawsuit continues. A lawsuit may not be revived unless the underlying cause of action, the ground for the suit, continues to have a legal existence after the party's death. Revival statutes vary from state to state, but today most lawsuits do not abate.

This general rule does not apply to matrimonial actions. A lawsuit for divorce or separation is considered entirely personal and therefore cannot be maintained after the death of a party. Different states do make exceptions to this rule in order to settle certain questions of property ownership. An action for the ANNULMENT of a marriage after the death of an innocent spouse may be revived by the deceased spouse's PERSONAL REPRESENTATIVE if it is clear that the marriage was induced by FRAUD and the perpetrator of the fraud would inherit property to which he or she would otherwise not be entitled.

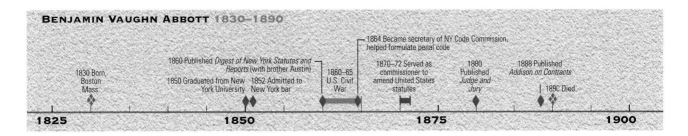

BENJAMIN VAUGHN ABBOTT 1830–1890

1830 Born, Boston, Mass.

1850 Graduated from New York University

1852 Admitted to New York bar

1860 Published *Digest of New York Statutes and Reports* (with brother Austin)

1860–65 U.S. Civil War

1864 Became secretary of NY Code Commission, helped formulate penal code

1870–72 Served as commissioner to amend United States statutes

1880 Published *Judge and Jury*

1888 Published *Addison on Contracts*

1890 Died

1825   1850   1875   1900

ABBOTT, BENJAMIN VAUGHN   Benjamin Vaughn Abbott was born June 4, 1830, in Boston, Massachusetts. He graduated from New York University in 1850 and was admitted to the New York bar in 1852.

From 1855 to 1870 Abbott, in collaboration with his brother Austin, wrote a series of law treatises and reports, including *Digest of New York Statutes and Reports* (1860). The series led to *Abbott's New York Digest*, the most recent series of which has been renamed *West's New York Digest 4th*.

In 1864 Abbott became secretary of the New York Code Commission and was instrumental in the formulation of the New York Penal Code, much of which is still in use today.

From 1870 to 1872 he served as a commissioner to amend the statutes of the United States. Abbott died February 17, 1890, in Brooklyn, New York.

As an author, Abbott wrote several publications, including *Judge and Jury* (1880); *The Travelling Law School* (1884); and *Addison on Contracts* (1888).

ABDICATION   RENUNCIATION of the PRIVILEGES and PREROGATIVES of an office. The act of a sovereign in renouncing and relinquishing his or her government or throne, so that either the throne is left entirely vacant, or is filled by a successor appointed or elected beforehand. Also, where a MAGISTRATE or person in office voluntarily renounces or gives it up before the time of service has expired. It differs from resignation, in that resignation is made by one who has received an office from another and restores it into that person's hands, as an inferior into the hands of a superior; abdication is the relinquishment of an office which has devolved by act of law. It is said to be a renunciation, quitting, and relinquishing, so as to have nothing further to do with a thing, or the doing of such actions as are inconsistent with the holding of it. Voluntary and permanent withdrawal from power by a public official or monarch.

The difference between abdicating a position and resigning one lies primarily in the irrevocability of abdication. Once an office or throne is

BIOGRAPHY

Benjamin Vaughn Abbott

© NEW YORK PUBLIC LIBRARY

abdicated, a return is not legally possible. Unlike resignation, abdication is not a matter of the relinquishment of a position to an employer or a superior. Instead, it is the absolute and final renunciation of an office created specifically by an act of law. After an abdication, the office remains vacant until a successor is named by appointment or election.

An early example of royal abdication occurred in 305 A.D., when the Roman emperor Diocletian withdrew from power after suffering a serious illness. Another sovereign, King Louis Philippe of France (the Citizen King), abdicated on February 24, 1848, because of public hostility toward the monarchy.

Perhaps the most famous abdication of power occurred on December 11, 1936, when England's King Edward VIII (1894–1972) renounced his throne in order to marry Wallis Warfield Simpson (1896–1986). Simpson was a twice-divorced socialite whose rocky marital history and American citizenship made her an unacceptable choice as wife of the British monarch. The affair between Edward and Simpson created an international scandal because it began well before her second divorce was finalized. Edward's ministers pleaded with him to sever his relationship with the woman, whom his mother, Queen Mary, dismissed as "the American adventuress." Edward could not remain king and head of the Church of England if he married Simpson, because of the church's opposition to divorce. Unhappy with many of his royal duties and transfixed by Simpson, Edward chose to renounce the monarchy and marry her.

On December 11, 1936, Edward announced his decision at Fort Belvidere, his private estate six miles from Windsor Castle. There he signed an instrument of abdication and conducted a farewell radio broadcast in which he told his subjects that he relinquished the throne for "the woman I love." The forty-two-year-old royal, who had ascended the throne on January 20, 1936, upon the death of his father, King George V, was succeeded by his younger brother, the duke of York, who became King George VI, father of Queen Elizabeth II.

INSTRUMENT OF ABDICATION

I, Edward the Eighth, of Great Britain, Ireland, and the British Dominions beyond the Seas, King, Emperor of India, do hereby declare My irrevocable determination to renounce the Throne for Myself and for My descendants, and My desire that effect should be given to this Instrument of Abdication immediately.

In token whereof I have hereunto set My hand this tenth day of December, nineteen hundred and thirty six, in the presence of the witnesses whose signatures are subscribed.

SIGNED AT
FORT BELVEDERE
IN THE PRESENCE
OF

King Edward VIII's instrument of abdication, which includes the signatures of his three brothers, Albert, Henry, and George. Edward's brother George, who was next in line to the British throne, succeeded him as king as George VI in 1936.

Edward and Simpson were married in Paris on June 3, 1937. Afterward, the former sovereign and his wife were addressed as the duke and duchess of Windsor. Except for a period during World War II spent in colonial Bahamas, the couple resided in royal exile in Paris for most of their nearly thirty-five-year marriage.

ABET To encourage or INCITE another to commit a CRIME. This word is usually applied to aiding in the commission of a crime. To abet another to commit a murder is to command, procure, counsel, encourage, induce, or assist. To facilitate the commission of a crime, promote its accomplishment, or help in advancing or bringing it about.

In relation to charge of aiding and abetting, term includes knowledge of the PERPETRATOR'S wrongful purpose, and encouragement, promotion or counsel of another in the commission of the criminal offense.

A French word, *abeter*—to bait or excite an animal.

For example, the manager of a jewelry store fails to turn on the store's silent alarm on the night she knows her cousin plans to rob the store. Her conduct is that of abetting the ROBBERY. If, however, she merely forgot to turn on the alarm, she would not have abetted the crime.

The word *abet* is most commonly used as part of the comprehensive phrase AID AND ABET.

ABETTOR One who commands, advises, INSTIGATES, or encourages another to commit a CRIME. A person who, being present, INCITES another to commit a crime, and thus becomes a PRINCIPAL. To be an *abettor*, the accused must have instigated or advised the commission of a crime or been present for the purpose of assisting in its commission; he or she must share criminal intent with which the crime was committed.

A person who lends a friend a car for use in a ROBBERY is an abettor even though he or she is not present when the robbery takes place. An abettor is not the chief actor, the principal, in the commission of a crime but must share the principal's criminal intent in order to be prosecuted for the same crime.

ABEYANCE A LAPSE in SUCCESSION during which there is no person in whom TITLE is VESTED. In the law of ESTATES, the condition of a FREEHOLD when there is no person in whom it is vested. In such cases the freehold has been said to be *in nubibus* (in the clouds), *in pendenti* (in suspension); and *in gremio legis* (in the bosom of the law). Where there is a TENANT of the freehold, the REMAINDER or REVERSION in FEE may exist for a time without any particular owner, in which case it is said to be in abeyance. A condition of being undetermined or in state of suspension or inactivity. In regard to sales to third parties of property acquired by county at TAX SALE, being held in *abeyance* means that certain rights or conditions are in expectancy.

For example, until an order of FORECLOSURE is granted by a court, a mortgagee does not have title to the property of a delinquent debtor that is the subject of a MORTGAGE in those jurisdictions that follow the LIEN theory of mortgages.

ABIDING CONVICTION A definite conviction of guilt derived from a thorough examination of the whole case. Used commonly to instruct JURIES on the frame of mind required for guilt proved BEYOND A REASONABLE DOUBT. A settled or fixed conviction. ▥

ABINGTON SCHOOL DISTRICT v. SCHEMPP In 1963, the Supreme Court banned the Lord's Prayer and Bible reading in public schools in *Abington School District v. Schempp*, 374 U.S. 203, 83 S. Ct. 1560, 10 L. Ed. 2d 844. The decision came one year after the Court had struck down, in *Engel v. Vitale*, a state-authored prayer that was recited by public school students each morning (370 U.S. 421, 82 S. Ct. 1261, 8 L. Ed. 2d 601 [1962]). *Engel* had opened the floodgates; *Schempp* ensured that a steady flow of anti-prayer rulings would continue into the 1990s. *Schempp* was in many ways a repeat of *Engel*: the religious practices it concerned were nominally different, but the logic used to find them unconstitutional was the same. This time, the majority went one step

further. Demolishing the arguments used to defend school prayer, it issued the first concrete test for determining violations of the First Amendment's Establishment Clause.

The *Schempp* ruling involved two cases: its namesake and *Murray v. Curlett*, 228 Md. 239, 179 A.2d 698 (Md. 1962). The *Schempp* case concerned a 1949 Pennsylvania law that forced public schools to start each day with a reading of ten Bible verses (24 Pa. Stat. § 15-1516). The law did not specify which version of the Bible should be used—for instance, it could be the Catholic Douay text or the Jewish version of the Old Testament. But local school officials only bought the Protestant King James Version. Teachers ordered students to rise and recite the verses reverently and in unison, or, as in Abington School District, students in a broadcasting class read the verses over a public-address sys-

Abington: U.S. Religious Bodies with Membership over Two Million

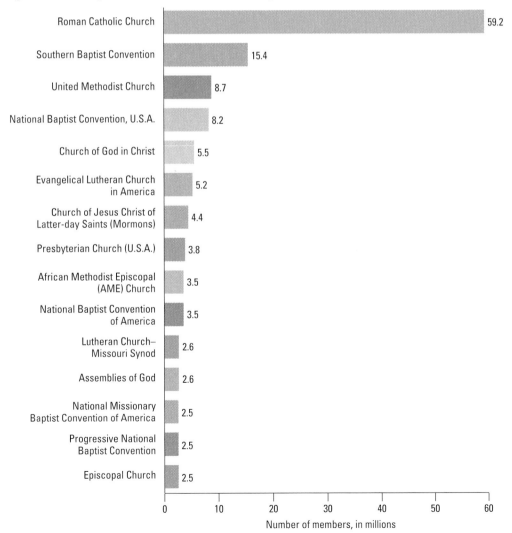

Religious Body	Number of members, in millions
Roman Catholic Church	59.2
Southern Baptist Convention	15.4
United Methodist Church	8.7
National Baptist Convention, U.S.A.	8.2
Church of God in Christ	5.5
Evangelical Lutheran Church in America	5.2
Church of Jesus Christ of Latter-day Saints (Mormons)	4.4
Presbyterian Church (U.S.A.)	3.8
African Methodist Episcopal (AME) Church	3.5
National Baptist Convention of America	3.5
Lutheran Church–Missouri Synod	2.6
Assemblies of God	2.6
National Missionary Baptist Convention of America	2.5
Progressive National Baptist Convention	2.5
Episcopal Church	2.5

Number of members, in millions

Source: Yearbook of American and Canadian Churches, 1994.

tem. Teachers could be fired for refusing to participate, and pupils occasionally were segregated from others if they did not join in the daily reading.

The Pennsylvania law brought a challenge from the Schempps, whose three children also attended Unitarian Sunday school. In 1958, a special three-judge federal court heard the case. The father, Edward L. Schempp, testified that he objected to parts of the Bible. Leviticus, in particular, upset him, "where they mention all sorts of blood sacrifices, uncleanness and leprosy. . . . I do not want my children believing that God is a lesser person than a human father." Although hardly the first lawsuit on this issue—Bible reading cases in state courts had yielded contradictory rulings since 1910—*Schempp* was the first to reach a federal court. The three-judge panel ruled that the Bible reading statute violated the First Amendment's Establishment Clause ("Congress shall make no law respecting an establishment of religion . . .") and interfered with its Free Exercise Clause ("or prohibiting the free exercise [of religion]"). Local and state officials immediately appealed to the U.S. Supreme Court.

The Supreme Court agreed to hear *Schempp* along with *Murray* as a consolidated case. Madalyn Murray and her fourteen-year-old son, William Murray, were atheists. They had challenged a 1905 Baltimore school board rule requiring each school day to start with Bible reading or the Lord's Prayer ("Our father, who art in heaven . . ."), or both. An attorney herself, Murray brought the suit only after protesting to officials, stirring up media attention, and encouraging her son to protest in a controversial strike that kept him out of school for eighteen days. The suit said the rule transgressed the Establishment Clause by requiring compulsory religious education and violated the Free Exercise Clause by discriminating against atheists. The Murrays originally lost in state courts and on appeal.

When the U.S. Supreme Court heard oral arguments for the consolidated cases on February 27 and 28, the nation was still smarting from the previous year's ruling in *Engel*. An uproar over the *Engel* decision had produced 150 proposals in Congress to amend the Constitution and had hardly diminished. *Schempp* gave advocates of school prayer a chance to argue that the Court had been wrong in *Engel*, and this they did. Attorneys representing Pennsylvania and Baltimore officials denied that Bible reading or prayer had a religious nature, and claimed that it therefore did not violate the Establishment Clause—which, in any event, they maintained, was only designed to prevent an official state religion. Their true purpose, argued attorneys, was to keep order and provide a proper moral climate for students.

The Court stood by the *Engel* decision. In an 8–1 decision, it ruled that both Bible reading and the Lord's Prayer violated the Establishment Clause. Justice Tom C. Clark's majority opinion differed in a few respects from the previous year's ruling: it admonished prayer advocates for ignoring the law, spelled out in some detail the precedents involved, and laid out the Court's first explicit test for Establishment Clause questions. Founded on the idea of state neutrality, this test had a vital standard: any law hoping to survive the prohibitions of the Establishment Clause must have "a secular purpose and a primary effect that neither advances nor inhibits religion."

The test clearly spelled out the limits. Study of the Bible or religion was acceptable, but only so long as "presented objectively as part of a secular program of education." Religious practices in public school were indefensible under the First Amendment. "While the Free Exercise Clause clearly prohibits the use of state action to deny the rights of free exercise to anyone," Justice Clark observed, "it has never meant that a majority could use the machinery of the State to practice its beliefs."

Schempp produced three concurring opinions, notably a seventy-four-page epic by Justice William J. Brennan, Jr. As in *Engel*, the sole dissent came from Justice Stewart. Again he disagreed with the majority's emphasis on the Establishment Clause's taking precedence over the Free Exercise Clause. For Stewart, the key factor was whether the states in the case had actually coerced students into praying or Bible reading. He did not think so.

Schempp concluded the initial round of the Supreme Court's prayer ban. However, the issue did not fade from public, political, and religious concern, and it came before the Supreme Court two decades later in *Wallace v. Jaffree*, 472 U.S. 38, 105 S. Ct. 2479, 86 L. Ed. 2d 29 (1985) (a one-minute period of silence for meditation or prayer had no secular purpose and was created with religious purpose).

CROSS-REFERENCES

Brennan, William J.; Clark, Tom; Constitutional Amendment; *Engel v. Vitale*; Establishment Clause; First Amendment; Free Exercise Clause; School Prayer; Stewart, Potter.

AB INITIO 📖 [*Latin, From the beginning; from the first act; from the inception.*] An agreement is said to be "void *ab initio*" if it has at no time had any legal validity. A party may be said to be a trespasser, an estate said to be good, an agreement or deed said to be VOID, or a marriage or act said to be unlawful, *ab initio*. Contrasted in this sense with EX POST FACTO, or with *postea*. 📖

The illegality of the conduct or the revelation of the real facts makes the entire situation illegal *ab initio* (from the beginning), not just from the time the wrongful behavior occurs. A person who enters property under the authority of law but who then by misconduct abuses his or her right to be on the property is considered a trespasser *ab initio*. If a sheriff enters property under the authority of a court order requiring him to seize a valuable painting, but instead he takes an expensive marble sculpture, he would be a trespasser from the beginning. Since the officer abused his authority, a court would presume that he intended from the outset to use that authority as a cloak from under which to enter the property for a wrongful purpose. This theory, used to correct abuses by public officers, has largely fallen into disuse.

ABJURATION 📖 A RENUNCIATION or ABANDONMENT by or upon OATH. The renunciation under oath of one's citizenship or some other right or privilege. 📖

ABODE 📖 One's home; habitation; place of dwelling; or RESIDENCE. Ordinarily means "domicile." Living place impermanent in character. The place where a person dwells. Residence of a legal voter. Fixed place of residence for the time being. For SERVICE OF PROCESS, one's fixed place of residence for the time being; his or her "usual place of abode." 📖

Abode: Home Ownership vs. Rentals in the U.S.

The home ownership rate was computed by dividing the number of owner-occupied households by the total number of households. Delaware had the highest home ownership rate in 1992 (73.8 percent), and New York had the lowest (53.3 percent). The rate for the District of Columbia was 35.0 percent.

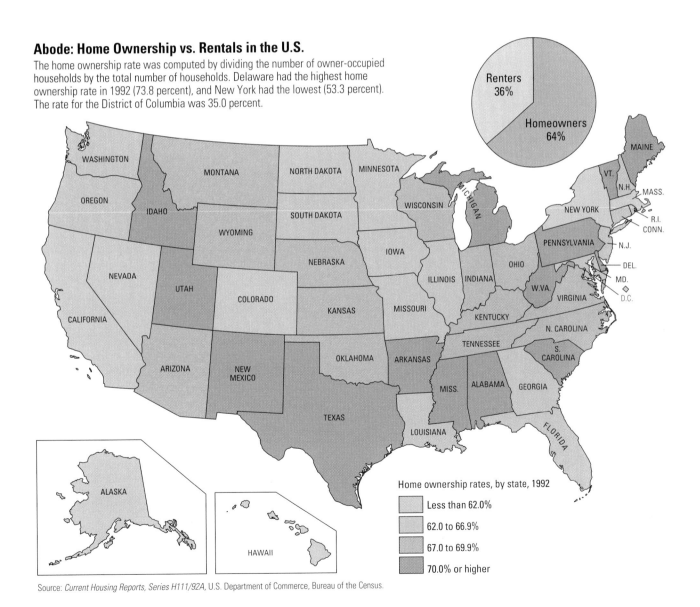

Source: *Current Housing Reports, Series H111/92A*, U.S. Department of Commerce, Bureau of the Census.

ABOLITION 📖 The destruction, annihilation, abrogation, or extinguishment of anything, but especially things of a permanent nature—such as institutions, usages, or customs, as in the abolition of slavery. 📖

In U.S. legal history, the concept of abolition generally refers to the eighteenth- and nineteenth-century movement to abolish the slavery of African Americans. As a significant political force in the pre–Civil War United States, the abolitionists had a great effect on the U.S. legal and political landscape. Their consistent efforts to end the institution of slavery culminated in 1865 with the ratification of the Constitution's Thirteenth Amendment, which outlawed slavery. The abolitionist ranks encompassed many different factions and people of different backgrounds and viewpoints, including European and African Americans, radicals and moderates. The motives of the abolitionists ran a broad spectrum, from those who opposed slavery as unjust and inhumane, to those whose objections were purely economic, focused on the effects that an unpaid Southern workforce had on wages and prices in the North.

Efforts to abolish slavery in America began well before the Revolutionary War and were influenced by similar movements in Great Britain and France. By the 1770s and 1780s, many antislavery societies, largely dominated by Quakers, had sprung up in the North. Early American leaders such as Benjamin Franklin, Alexander Hamilton, John Jay, and Thomas Paine made known their opposition to slavery.

This illustration on the frontispiece of The Child's Anti-Slavery Book *(1860) was an effort by abolitionists to alert children to the horrors of slavery. It is titled, "A Slave Father Sold Away from His Family."*

LIBRARY OF CONGRESS

The early abolitionists played an important role in outlawing slavery in Northern states by the early nineteenth century. Vermont outlawed slavery in 1777, and Massachusetts declared it inconsistent with its new state constitution, ratified in 1780. Over the next three decades, other Northern states, including Pennsylvania, New York, and New Jersey, passed gradual EMANCIPATION laws that freed all future children of slaves. By 1804, every Northern state had enacted some form of emancipation law.

In the South, where slavery played a far greater role in the economy, emancipation moved at a much slower pace. By 1800, all Southern states except Georgia and South Carolina had passed laws that eased the practice of private manumission—or the freeing of slaves by individual slaveholders. Abolitionists won a further victory in the early 1800s when the United States outlawed international trade in slaves. However, widespread smuggling of slaves continued.

During the first three decades of the 1800s, abolitionists continued to focus largely on gradual emancipation. As the nation expanded westward, they also opposed the introduction of slavery into the western territories. Although abolitionists had won an early victory on this front in 1787, when they succeeded in prohibiting slavery in the Northwest Territory, their efforts in the 1800s were not as completely successful. Under the Missouri Compromise of 1820 (3 Stat. 545), for example, it was agreed that slavery would be prohibited only in areas of the Louisiana Purchase north of Missouri's southern boundary, except for Missouri itself, which would be admitted to the Union as a slave state. Slavery in the territories remained one of the most divisive issues in U.S. politics until the end of the Civil War in 1865.

Beginning in the 1830s, evangelical Christian groups, particularly in New England, brought a new radicalism to the cause of abolition. They focused on the sinfulness of slavery and sought to end its practice by appealing to the consciences of European Americans who supported slavery. Rather than endorsing a gradual emancipation, these new abolitionists called for the immediate and complete emancipation of slaves without compensation to slaveowners. Leaders of this movement included William Lloyd Garrison, founder of the abolitionist newspaper the *Liberator*; Frederick Douglass, a noted African American writer and orator; the sisters Sarah Moore Grimké and Angelina Emily Grimké, lecturers for the American Anti-Slavery Society and pioneers for women's rights; Theodore Dwight Weld, author of an influential antislavery book, *American Slavery As It Is* (1839); and later, Harriet Beecher Stowe, whose 1852 novel *Uncle Tom's Cabin* was another important abolitionist tract.

In 1833, this new generation of abolitionists formed the American Anti-Slavery Society (AAS). The organization grew quickly, particularly in the North, and by 1840 had reached a height of 1,650 chapters and an estimated 130,000 to 170,000 members. Nevertheless, abolitionism remained an unpopular cause even in the North, and few mainstream politicians openly endorsed it.

To achieve its goals, the AAS undertook a number of large projects, many of which were frustrated by Southern opposition. For example, the organization initiated a massive postal campaign designed to appeal to the moral scruples of Southern slaveowners and voters. The campaign flooded the South with antislavery tracts sent through the mails. Although a law that would have excluded antislavery literature from the mails was narrowly defeated in Congress in 1836, pro-slavery forces, with the help of President Andrew Jackson's administration and local postmasters, effectively ended the dissemination of abolitionist literature in the South. The AAS was similarly frustrated when it petitioned Congress on a variety of subjects related to slavery. Congressional gag rules rendered the many abolitionist petitions impotent. These rules of legislative procedure allowed Congress to table and effectively ignore the antislavery petitions.

By the 1840s, the evangelical abolitionist movement had begun to break up into different factions. These factions differed on the issue of gradual versus radical change and on the inclusion of other causes, including women's rights, in their agendas. Some abolitionists decided to form a political party. The Liberty party, as they named it, nominated James G. Birney for U.S. president in 1840 and 1844. When differences later led to the dissolution of the Liberty party, many of its members created the Free Soil party, which took as its main cause opposition to slavery in the territories newly acquired from Mexico. They were joined by defecting Democrats who were disgruntled with the increasing domination of Southern interests in their party. In 1848, the Free Soil party nominated as its candidate for U.S. president Martin Van Buren, who had served as the eighth president of the United States from 1837 to 1841, but Van Buren did not win. (Zachary Taylor won the election.)

After passage of the Fugitive Slave Act of 1850 (9 Stat. 462), which required Northern states to return escaped slaves and imposed penalties on people who aided such runaways, abolitionists became actively involved in the Underground Railroad, a secretive network that provided food, shelter, and direction to escaped slaves seeking freedom in the North. This network was largely maintained by free African Americans and is estimated to have helped fifty thousand to one hundred thousand slaves to freedom. Harriet Tubman, an African American and ardent abolitionist, was one organizer of the Underground Railroad. During the 1850s, she bravely traveled into Southern states to help other African Americans escape from slavery, just as she had escaped herself.

Whereas the vast majority of abolitionists eschewed violence, John Brown actively participated in it. In response to attacks led by pro-slavery forces against the town of Lawrence, Kansas, Brown, the leader of a Free Soil militia, led a reprisal attack that killed five pro-slavery settlers in 1856. Three years later, he undertook an operation that he hoped would inspire a massive slave rebellion. Brown and twenty-one followers began by capturing the U.S. arsenal at Harpers Ferry, Virginia (now West Virginia). Federal forces under Robert E. Lee promptly recaptured the arsenal, and Brown was hanged shortly thereafter, becoming a martyr for the cause.

In 1854, abolitionists and Free Soilers joined with a variety of other interests to form the Republican party, which successfully stood Abraham Lincoln for president in 1860. Although the party took a strong stand against the introduction of slavery into the territories, it did not propose the more radical option of

Leon Coffin's farm in Indiana was a busy station of the Underground Railroad, a secret network of people who helped runaway slaves.

immediate emancipation. In fact, slavery ended as a result of the Civil War, which lasted from 1861 to 1865. Not a true abolitionist at the start of his presidency, Lincoln became increasingly receptive to antislavery opinion. In 1863, he announced the Emancipation Proclamation, which freed all slaves in areas still engaged in revolt against the Union. The proclamation served as an important symbol of the Union's new commitment to ending slavery. Lincoln later supported the ratification of the Thirteenth Amendment, which officially abolished slavery in the United States.

After the war, former abolitionists, including radical Republicans such as Senator Charles Sumner (R-Mass.), continued to lobby for constitutional amendments that would protect the rights of the newly freed slaves, including the Fourteenth Amendment, which was ratified in 1868. This amendment guaranteed citizenship to former slaves and declared that no state could "deprive any person of life, liberty, or property, without due process of law; nor deny to any person ... the equal protection of the laws." Former abolitionists also lobbied, albeit unsuccessfully, for land redistribution that would have given ex-slaves a share of their former owners' land.

CROSS-REFERENCES

Compromise of 1850; *Dred Scott v. Sandford*; Emancipation Proclamation; Fourteenth Amendment; Fugitive Slave Act of 1850; Lincoln, Abraham; Missouri Compromise of 1820; *Prigg v. Pennsylvania*; Slavery; Sumner, Charles; Thirteenth Amendment.

ABORTION The spontaneous or artificially induced expulsion of an embryo or fetus. As used in legal context, usually refers to induced abortion.

History English COMMON LAW generally allowed abortion before the "quickening" of the fetus (i.e., the first recognizable movement of the fetus in the uterus), which occurred between the sixteenth and eighteenth weeks of pregnancy. After quickening, however, common law was less clear as to whether abortion was considered a crime. In the United States, state legislatures did not pass abortion statutes until the nineteenth century. After 1880, abortion was criminalized by statute in every state of the union, owing in large measure to strong anti-abortion positions taken by the American Medical Association. Despite the illegality, many thousands of women every year sought abortions. Under a heavy cloak of shame and secrecy, women often had abortions performed in unsafe conditions, and many died or suffered complications from the procedures.

The abortion laws developed in the late nineteenth century existed largely unchanged until the 1960s and 1970s, when a number of different circumstances combined to bring about a movement for their reform. Women's rights groups, doctors, and lawyers began an organized abortion reform movement to press for changes, in part because many of them had witnessed the sometimes deadly complications resulting from illegal abortions. Women's organizations also began to see abortion reform as a crucial step toward the goal of equality between the sexes. They argued that women must be able to control their pregnancies in order to secure an equal status in American life. In addition, new concerns regarding explosive population growth and its effect on the environment increased public awareness of the need for BIRTH CONTROL. At the same time, other countries developed far more permissive laws regarding abortion. In Japan and Eastern Europe, abortion was available on demand, and in much of Western Europe, abortion was permitted to protect the mother's health.

Public awareness of the abortion issue also increased through two incidents in the early 1960s that caused a greater number of children to be born with physical defects. In 1961, the drug thalidomide, used to treat nausea during pregnancy, was found to cause serious birth defects. And a 1962–65 German measles epidemic caused an estimated fifteen thousand children to be born with defects. Pregnant women who were affected by these incidents could not seek abortions because of the strict laws then in existence.

Reacting to these and other developments, and inspired by the successes of the civil rights movement of the 1950s and 1960s, women's rights organizations—including the National Organization for Women (NOW), formed in 1966—sought to reform abortion laws through legislation and lawsuits. They hoped to educate a largely male dominated legal and judicial profession about this important issue for women. Their work, supported by such groups as the American Civil Liberties Union (ACLU), quickly began to have an effect. Between 1967 and 1970, twelve states adopted abortion reform legislation. However, the abortion activist groups began to see the abortion issue as a question of social justice and began to press for more than reform. Under the rallying cry of reproductive freedom, they began to demand an outright repeal of existing state laws and unobstructed access for women to abortion.

The increase in abortion-related cases before the courts eventually resulted in the need for clarification of the law by the Supreme Court. After considering many abortion-related appeals and petitions, on May 31, 1971, the Court accepted two cases, *Roe v. Wade*, 410 U.S. 113, 93 S. Ct. 705, 35 L. Ed. 2d 147 (1973), and *Doe v. Bolton*, 410 U.S. 179, 93 S. Ct. 739, 35 L. Ed. 2d 201 (1973), for hearing.

Roe v. Wade and Doe v. Bolton Although the two cases before the Court appeared by their titles to involve the fates of two individuals, Roe and Doe, in reality both suits were brought by many people representing many different interests. *Roe v. Wade* was argued on behalf of all women of the state of Texas—in legal terminology, it was a CLASS ACTION suit. Thirty-six abortion reform groups filed BRIEFS, or reports, with the court on Roe's behalf. These included women's, medical, university, public health, legal, welfare, church, population control, and other groups. The anti-abortion side of the case included representatives from seven different anti-abortion groups and the attorneys general of five states.

Roe involved a person using the pseudonym Jane Roe—actually Norma McCorvey, who revealed her identity in 1984. Roe, an unmarried, pregnant woman from Texas, wanted to have an abortion, but an existing abortion statute prevented her from doing so. The Texas statute, originally passed in 1857, outlawed abortion except to save the mother's life. Roe filed a lawsuit in federal district court on behalf of herself and all other pregnant women. She sought to have the abortion statute declared unconstitutional as an invasion of her right to privacy as guaranteed by the First, Fourth, Fifth, Ninth, and Fourteenth Amendments. She also sought to have an INJUNCTION, or court order, issued against the statute's enforcement so that she might go forward with the abortion. The abortion reform movement attached two other cases to Roe's in an attempt to represent a wider range of the interests involved in the issue. A physician, James Hallford, who was being prosecuted under the statute for two abortions he had performed, also filed suit against the Texas law, as did a childless couple, the Does.

The three-judge district court combined Roe's case with the cases of Hallford and the Does, but later dismissed the suit brought by the Does on the grounds that neither had violated the law and the woman was not pregnant. The district court agreed with Roe that the law was unconstitutionally vague and violated her right to privacy under the Ninth Amendment—which allows for the existence of rights, like that of privacy, not explicitly named in the Constitution's Bill of Rights—and the Fourteenth Amendment. It refused, however, to grant the injunction allowing her to go ahead with the abortion. Roe then appealed the denial of the injunction to the U.S. Supreme Court.

Doe v. Bolton involved a 1968 Georgia statute that allowed abortion if necessary to save the mother's life, in the case of pregnancy resulting from RAPE or INCEST, or if the baby was likely to be born with serious birth defects (Ga. Crim. Code § 26-1202 a,b). However, the statute also created procedural requirements that effectively would have allowed few abortions. Those requirements included hospital accreditation, committee approval, two-doctor agreement, and state residency. The case concerned Mary

Number of Abortions Performed, 1972–1990

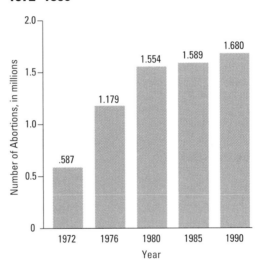

Percent of Pregnancies Ending in Abortion, 1972–1990

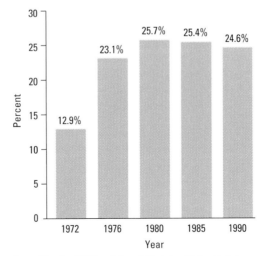

Source: "Abortions," William J. Bennett, *The Index of Cultural Indicators*, Vol 1, March 1993, p.10. Primary source: Alan Guttmacher Institute.

Doe, who had sought an abortion at Grady Memorial Hospital, in Atlanta. She claimed that she had been advised that pregnancy would endanger her health, but the hospital's Abortion Rights Committee denied her the abortion. She sought a DECLARATORY JUDGMENT holding that the Georgia law unconstitutionally violated her right to privacy as well as her Fourteenth Amendment guarantees of due process and equal protection. She also sought an injunction against the law's enforcement.

Roe and Doe were filed in March and April of 1970, and the women's pregnancies would not have lasted through December 1970. The Court heard the cases in December 1971 and October 1972, and they were not resolved until January 1973, when the Court announced its decisions.

In Roe, the Court, on a 7–2 vote, found the Texas abortion statute unconstitutional. In its opinion, written by Justice Harry A. Blackmun, the Court held that the law violated a right to privacy guaranteed by the Due Process Clause of the Fourteenth Amendment. However, the Court further held that such a right is a "qualified" one and subject to regulation by the state. The state has "legitimate interests in protecting both the pregnant woman's health and the potentiality of human life" (i.e., the life of the fetus). To specify when the state's interests emerge, the Court divided pregnancy into twelve-week trimesters. In the first trimester, the state cannot regulate abortion or prevent a woman's access to it. It can only require that abortions be performed by a licensed physician and under medically safe conditions. During the second trimester, the state can regulate abortion procedures as long as the regulations are reasonably related to the promotion of the mother's health. In the third trimester, the state has a dominant interest in protecting the "potentiality" of the fetus's life. A state may prohibit abortions during this time except in cases where they are essential to preserve the life or health of the mother. The Court also cited judicial PRECEDENT in holding that the fetus is not a "person" as defined by the Fourteenth Amendment.

In Doe, the Court found the Georgia statute to be unconstitutional as well, holding that it infringed on privacy and personal liberty by permitting abortion only in restricted cases. The Court ruled further that the statute's four procedural requirements—hospital accreditation, hospital committee approval, two-doctor agreement, and state residency—violated the Constitution. The state could not, for example, require that abortions be performed only at certain hospitals, because it had not shown that such restrictions advanced its interest in promoting the health of the pregnant woman. Such a requirement interfered with a woman's right to have an abortion in the first trimester of pregnancy, which the Court in Roe had declared was outside the scope of state regulation.

After Roe v. Wade After the Supreme Court decisions in Roe v. Wade and Doe v. Bolton, states began to liberalize their abortion laws. However, abortion quickly became a divisive political issue for Americans. Grassroots opposition to abortion—supported by such influential institutions as the Catholic Church—was strong from the start. By the early 1980s, the anti-abortion movement had become a powerful political force. President Ronald Reagan, who came to office in 1981 and served through 1989, strongly opposed abortion and used his administration to try to change abortion rulings. He appointed a surgeon general, Dr. C. Everett Koop, who opposed abortion, and he made it a top priority of his Justice Department to effect a reversal of Roe. Reagan even published a book on the subject in 1984, Abortion and the Conscience of a Nation, which contains many of the essential positions of the anti-abortion movement. Reagan argued that the fetus has rights equal to those of people who are already born. He also cited figures indicating that 15 million abortions had been performed since 1973, and he stated his belief that the fetus experienced great pain as a result of the abortion procedure. He quoted a statement by Mother Teresa, the famed nun who helped the poor of Calcutta: "[T]he greatest misery of our time is the generalized abortion of children." While abortion rights, or pro-choice, advocates argued that there were public health advantages of the new abortion laws, opponents of abortion, such as Reagan, referred to abortion as a "silent holocaust."

The anti-abortion, or pro-life, movement has challenged abortion in a number of different ways. It has sponsored constitutional amendments that would effectively reverse Roe, as well as legislation that would limit and regulate access to abortion, including government financing of abortion procedures. Some anti-abortion groups have practiced civil disobedience, attempting to disrupt and block abortion clinic activities. The most extreme opponents have resorted to violence and even murder in an attempt to eliminate abortion.

All these methods have resulted in a great deal of litigation and added to the complexity of the abortion issue. Many of the subsequent cases have come before the Supreme Court.

Observers have often expected the Court to overturn its *Roe* decision, particularly after the Reagan administration appointed three justices to the Court. However, while the Court has allowed increasingly strict state regulation of abortion since *Roe*, it has stuck to the essential finding in *Roe*, that women have a limited right to terminate their pregnancies. This right is incorporated in a right of privacy guaranteed by the Fourteenth Amendment.

Constitutional Amendments Although amending the Constitution is the most direct way to reverse *Roe v. Wade*, neither Congress nor the states have passed a CONSTITUTIONAL AMENDMENT related to the issue of abortion. The anti-abortion forces have found it extremely difficult to achieve a public consensus on this divisive issue. However, at least nineteen state legislatures have passed applications to convene a constitutional convention to propose an amendment that would outlaw abortions. Congressional representatives have also worked to bring such an amendment about. The many dozens of amendments that have been proposed can be grouped into two main categories: STATES' RIGHTS, and the right to life. The former would restore to the states the same control over abortion that they exercised prior to *Roe*. The latter would designate the fetus as a person, entitled to all the privileges and rights guaranteed under the Fourteenth Amendment.

One unsuccessful attempt at changing the Constitution was the Hatch amendment of 1983, sponsored by Senator Orrin G. Hatch (R-Utah), which stated, "A right to abortion is not secured by this Constitution." It did not receive the two-thirds majority necessary in Congress to be submitted to the states for ratification.

Congress has also sponsored legislation that would effectively reverse *Roe*. For example, the Human Life Bill (S. 158), introduced by Senator Jesse Helms (R-N.C.) in 1981, would have established that the fetus is a person, entitled to the full rights and privileges guaranteed by the Fourteenth Amendment. The bill did not pass.

Federal Financing In 1976, Representative Henry J. Hyde (R-Ill.) sponsored an amendment to the federal budget appropriations bill for the Department of Health and Human Services (HHS). His amendment denied Medicaid funding for abortion unless the woman's life is in danger or she is pregnant as a result of rape or incest, but only if the woman reports the incident at the time of its occurrence. Despite opposition from pro-abortion groups, Hyde attached this amendment every year to the same appropriations bill. The Supreme

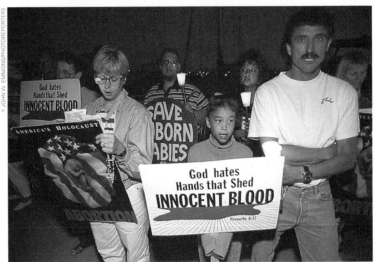

Court has upheld the constitutionality of the Hyde amendment (*Harris v. McRae*, 448 U.S. 297, 100 S. Ct. 2671, 65 L. Ed. 2d 784 [1980]; *McGowan v. Maryland*, 366 U.S. 420, 81 S. Ct. 1101, 6 L. Ed. 2d 393 [1961]). Evidence suggests that these federal actions have caused fewer women to have abortions.

In the late 1980s, with its composition having been changed by three Reagan appointees (Justices Sandra Day O'Connor, Antonin Scalia, and Anthony M. Kennedy), the Court issued a ruling related to federal financing of abortion that many perceived as a dramatic shift against abortion rights. In *Webster v. Reproductive Health Services*, 492 U.S. 490, 109 S. Ct. 3040, 106 L. Ed. 2d 410 (1989), the Supreme Court upheld a Missouri law prohibiting the use of public funds and buildings for abortion procedures and counseling, including a provision that required fetal testing for viability for abortions performed after the twentieth week of pregnancy (Mo. Rev. Stat. §§ 1.205.1, 1.205.2, 188.205,

Groups on both sides of the abortion debate have staged demonstrations and rallies in order to gain the political and emotional support of lawmakers and the public. In these photos, Patricia Ireland speaks at a National Organization for Women rally, and Operation Rescue demonstrates in Los Angeles.

188.210, 188.215). Scalia, appointed in 1986, argued in his concurring opinion that *Roe v. Wade* should be overruled and that the Court had missed an opportunity in not doing so in this case.

The *Webster* decision resulted in a flood of new state legislation related to abortion. Many states sought to reactivate old abortion laws that had never been taken off the books subsequent to *Roe*. Louisiana, for example, sought to reinstate an 1855 law making all abortions illegal and imposing a ten-year sentence on doctors and women violating it. However, in January 1990, a federal district court ruled that the 1855 law could not be reinstated and that subsequent laws allowing abortions in certain circumstances took precedence (*Weeks v. Connick*, 733 F. Supp. 1036 [E.D. La. 1990]). By mid-1991, Pennsylvania, Guam, Utah, and Louisiana had all enacted laws banning abortions except in limited circumstances. Pennsylvania became the first to approve new abortion restrictions when it amended its Abortion Control Act (Pa. Cons. Stat. Ann. § 3201) to create strict new regulations on abortion procedures (see the discussion of *Planned Parenthood of Southeastern Pennsylvania v. Casey* under "Other Major Abortion Regulations," later in this entry). In other states such as South and North Dakota, legislation that would have sharply restricted abortion was only narrowly defeated. However, some states, such as Connecticut and Maryland, reacted to the *Webster* decision by passing legislation protecting women's rights to abortion.

Before the Court ruled on Pennsylvania's Abortion Control Act, it decided a major case relating to federal funding and regulation of family planning clinics. In *Rust v. Sullivan*, 500 U.S. 173, 111 S. Ct. 1759, 114 L. Ed. 2d 233 (1991), the Court upheld a series of regulations issued in 1988 by the Reagan administration's Justice Department affecting family planning clinics that receive funds through title X of the Public Health Service Act of 1970, 42 U.S.C.A. §§ 300–300a-6. The regulations prohibited clinic personnel from providing any information about abortion, including counseling or referral. The regulations also required that the only permissible response to a request for an abortion or referral was to state that the agency "does not consider abortion an appropriate method of planning and therefore does not counsel or refer for abortion." This regulation became known to its detractors as the gag rule. The regulations also prohibited title X–funded family planning clinics from lobbying for legislation that advocated or increased access to abortion, and they required that such clinics be

"physically and financially separate" from abortion activities. Although a family planning agency could still conduct abortion-related activities, it could not use federal money to fund such activities. Chief Justice William H. Rehnquist, who wrote the Court's opinion, disagreed with the contentions of the plaintiffs—several family planning agencies—that the federal regulations violated a woman's due process right to choose whether to terminate her pregnancy. He pointed out that the Due Process Clause generally confers no affirmative right to government aid. The government has no constitutional duty to subsidize abortion and may validly choose to fund "childbirth over abortion." Rehnquist noted that a woman's right to seek medical advice outside a title X–funded agency remained "unfettered."

Justice Blackmun, author of the *Roe* majority opinion, dissented, arguing that the regulations, because they restricted speech as a condition for accepting public funds, violated the First Amendment's free speech provision. The regulations, he wrote, suppressed "truthful information regarding constitutionally protected conduct of vital importance to the listener." Blackmun saw the regulations as improper government interference in a woman's decision to continue or end a pregnancy, and he claimed that they rendered the landmark *Roe* ruling "technically" intact but of little substance.

On January 22, 1993, shortly after taking office, President Bill Clinton signed a memorandum that revoked the gag rule, maintaining that it "endangers women's lives by preventing them from receiving complete and accurate medical information." On February 5, 1993, the secretary of HHS complied with the president's decision and declared that the department would return to title X regulations that were in effect before February 1988. Title X–funded clinics would again be able to provide nondirective counseling on all options to a patient and to refer her for abortion services if she chose. However, such clinics would still be prohibited from engaging in pro-choice lobbying or litigation.

Other Major Abortion Regulations
Among the first abortion regulations to be enacted after *Roe v. Wade* were requirements for the INFORMED CONSENT of the woman seeking an abortion. Although informed consent varies according to different laws, it can generally be given only after a woman receives certain information from a doctor, medical professional, or counselor. This information can include the nature and risks of the abortion procedure, the risk of carrying the pregnancy to term,

the alternatives to abortion, the probable age of the fetus, and specific government aid available for care of a child. Related to this issue are other types of consent—including parental and spousal consent—that states have sought to require before an abortion can be performed.

In 1976, the Court reviewed a Missouri statute requiring that the following provisions be met for an abortion to be performed: that a woman in the first twelve weeks of her pregnancy give written consent; that a wife obtain her husband's consent; and that a MINOR obtain her parents' consent, unless a medical necessity exists (Mo. Ann. Stat. § 188.010 et seq.). The statute also required that physicians and clinics performing abortions keep careful records of their procedures and that criminal and civil liability be imposed upon a physician who failed to observe standards of professional care in performing abortions. Planned Parenthood, a family planning organization, initiated a lawsuit to declare the law unconstitutional. The Supreme Court, in *Planned Parenthood v. Danforth*, 428 U.S. 52, 96 S. Ct. 2831, 49 L. Ed. 2d 788 (1976), upheld the requirement that the woman give written consent in the first trimester, as well as the requirement that records of abortion procedures be kept. However, the Court ruled that a woman need not inform her husband of an abortion performed in the first trimester, because the state may not interfere in the woman's private decision concerning her pregnancy during that period. For the same reason, the Court struck down the law requiring a minor to obtain parental consent in the first trimester.

The Court clarified its position on parental consent in later rulings. In *Bellotti v. Baird*, 443 U.S. 622, 99 S. Ct. 3035, 61 L. Ed. 2d 797 (1979), it struck down a state law that required the consent of both parents or judicial approval—commonly called judicial bypass—before an unmarried minor could obtain an abortion. The Court found the law unconstitutional because it gave third parties—the child's parents or the court—absolute veto power over the minor's ability to choose abortion, regardless of her best interests, maturity, or ability to make informed decisions. In *H.L. v. Matheson*, 450 U.S. 398, 101 S. Ct. 1164, 67 L. Ed. 2d 388 (1981), the Court upheld a Utah statute requiring that a physician notify the parents of a minor before performing an abortion on her (Utah Code Ann. § 76-7-304). Since the law required only notification rather than consent, the Court reasoned that it did not give any party veto power over the minor's decision. In *Hodgson v. Minnesota*, 497 U.S. 417, 110 S. Ct.

2926, 11 L. Ed. 2d 344 (1990), the Court upheld a parental notification statute because the statute's provision for judicial bypass took into account the best interests of the minor, her maturity, and her ability to make an informed decision.

In 1982, Pennsylvania passed the Abortion Control Act, which required that the woman give "voluntary and informed" consent after hearing a number of statements, including declarations of the following: the "fact that there may be detrimental physical and psychological effects" to the abortion; the particular medical risks associated with the abortion method to be employed; the probable gestational age of the fetus; the "fact that medical assistance benefits may be available" for prenatal care and childbirth; and the "fact that the father is liable to assist" in child support. The law also required a physician to report the woman's age, race, marital status, and number of previous pregnancies; the probable gestational age of the fetus; the method of payment for the abortion; and the basis of determination that "a child is not viable."

When the Pennsylvania law came before the Court in the 1986 case *Thornburgh v. American College of Obstetricians & Gynecologists*, 476 U.S. 747, 106 S. Ct. 2169, 90 L. Ed. 2d 779, the Reagan administration's Justice Department specifically asked the Court to overturn *Roe*. In its brief, the department argued that the Court should "abandon" *Roe* because its textual and historical basis was "so far flawed" as to be a source of instability in the law. Instead, the brief urged, the Court should leave the state legislatures free to permit or prohibit abortion as they wish. However, by a narrow (5–4) vote the Court found all the provisions of Pennsylvania's Abortion Control Act to be unconstitutional, thereby reaffirming its previous decisions upholding a woman's constitutional right to abortion. "The states," wrote Justice Blackmun in the Court's opinion, "are not free, under the guise of protecting maternal health or potential life, to intimidate women into continuing pregnancies." Pennsylvania had defended itself by claiming that its procedures gave the pregnant woman information that would better inform her decision regarding abortion. Blackmun, although he agreed in principle with the idea of informed consent, found that the Pennsylvania procedures were designed not so much to inform as to encourage a woman to withhold her consent to an abortion.

The narrow margin of the Court's decision encouraged the anti-abortion movement. By the time the Court reached its next major abortion decision, in 1992—*Planned Parenthood of Southeastern Pennsylvania v. Casey*, 505 U.S. 833, 112 S. Ct. 2791, 120 L. Ed. 2d 674—many expected it to finally reverse *Roe*. Again, it did not. *Casey*, the most important abortion decision since *Roe*, concerned amendments to the same Pennsylvania Abortion Control Act of 1982. The amendments prohibited abortions after twenty-four weeks except to save the woman's life or to prevent substantial and irreversible impairment of her bodily functions; required a woman to wait twenty-four hours after giving her informed consent before receiving an abortion; allowed only a physician to give informed-consent information; required a woman to notify her spouse; and mandated that minors obtain informed consent from at least one parent or a court before receiving an abortion. The plaintiffs in the case, five family planning clinics and a physician provider of abortion services, asked the Court to declare the statutes invalid.

In a close (5–4) decision, the Court again supported the basic provisions of *Roe* and upheld a woman's right to decide to obtain an abortion. The Court did, however, uphold all the Pennsylvania statutes except for the spousal notification provision, arguing that they did not present an "undue burden" to the woman's reproductive rights. Justices O'Connor, Kennedy, and David H. Souter wrote the majority opinion, and Justices John Paul Stevens and Blackmun wrote concurring opinions. Chief Justice Rehnquist and Justices Scalia, Byron R. White, and Clarence Thomas all dissented.

Noting that the case marked the fifth time the Justice Department under the Reagan and Bush administrations had filed a report with the Court making known its desire to overturn *Roe*, the Court's opinion defended the reasoning of the *Roe* decision. The Court characterized the *Roe* ruling as having three major provisions:

> First is a recognition of the right of the woman to choose to have an abortion before viability and to obtain it without undue interference from the state. . . . Second is a confirmation of the State's power to restrict abortions after fetal viability, if the law contains exceptions for pregnancies which endanger a woman's life or health. And third is the principle that the State has legitimate interests from the outset of the pregnancy in protecting the health of the woman and the life of the fetus that may become a child.

The Court in *Casey*, as in *Roe*, found the constitutional basis of a woman's right to termi-nate her pregnancy in the Due Process Clause of the Fourteenth Amendment. As the Court stated, "It is a promise of the Constitution that there is a realm of personal liberty which the government may not enter." The Court also invoked the legal doctrine of *stare decisis*, the policy of a court to follow previously decided cases rather than overrule them.

However, the Court emphasized, more than it had in *Roe*, "the State's 'important and legitimate interest in potential life' [quoting *Roe*]." The justices also sought to better define the "undue burden" standard, originally developed by Justice O'Connor, that the Court had used to assess the validity of any possible regulations of a woman's reproductive rights. The Court more precisely defined an undue burden as one whose "purpose or effect is to place a substantial obstacle in the path of a woman seeking an abortion before the fetus attains viability."

The dissenting justices in the case restated their opinion that *Roe* was decided wrongly because no fundamental right for a woman to choose to terminate her pregnancy was written into the U.S. Constitution and because U.S. society, in the past, permitted laws that prohibited abortion. They also gave different arguments for upholding the Pennsylvania statute's restrictions. Such provisions had only to show a "rational basis," and using that test, they would have upheld all the challenged portions of the Pennsylvania law. Chief Justice Rehnquist and Justice Scalia both argued that the Court had misused the notion of STARE DECISIS in the case, because the Court did not uphold all aspects of *Roe*. Scalia also maintained that although the liberty to terminate a pregnancy may be of great importance to many women, it is not "a liberty protected by the Constitution."

The Court's decision in *Casey* was used to strike down other state laws that sharply restricted women's access to abortion. Citing the *Casey* decision, in *Sojourner v. Edwards*, 974 F.2d 27, the U.S. Court of Appeals for the Fifth Circuit in September 1992 struck down a Louisiana law that would have imposed stiff sentences on doctors performing abortions for reasons other than saving the life of the mother or in cases of rape or incest if the victim reported the crime (La. Rev. Stat. Ann. 14:87). The appeals court found the statute unconstitutional because it imposed an undue burden on women seeking an abortion before fetal viability. The Supreme Court later upheld this ruling without comment (*Sojourner*, 507 U.S. 972, 113 S. Ct. 1414, 122 L. Ed. 2d 785 [1993]).

After Planned Parenthood v. Casey
As a result of the Court's decision in *Planned*

Parenthood of Southeastern Pennsylvania v. Casey, the battle over abortion moved beyond the question of whether *Roe v. Wade* would be overturned, to focus on what conditions truly constitute an American woman's right to safe, legal abortion. After a number of incidents of violence at abortion clinics, the abortion rights movement has focused on lobbying for legislation and winning court cases guaranteeing access to abortion clinics. The anti-abortion movement, on the other hand, has continued to vigorously oppose abortion but has become increasingly split between militant and moderate factions. Behind the split are the increasingly violent actions of militant anti-abortion protesters. Between 1993 and 1994, five abortion providers were killed by anti-abortion militants. Although such killings have undermined public support for the anti-abortion movement, they have also damaged the morale of those who staff family planning clinics; some clinics have even shut down. As a result, family planning services, including abortion, remain difficult to obtain for women in many parts of the country, particularly in rural areas.

The Supreme Court has decided a number of different cases surrounding the issue of anti-abortion protests, many of which have made it more difficult for anti-abortion groups to disrupt the operations of family planning clinics. In *Madsen v. Women's Health Center,* 512 U.S. 753, 114 S. Ct. 2516, 129 L. Ed. 2d 593 (1994), the Court upheld a regulation barring abortion protesters within thirty-six feet of a Melbourne, Florida, clinic. In another 1994 decision, *National Organization for Women v. Scheidler,* 510 U.S. 249, 114 S. Ct. 798, 127 L. Ed. 2d 99, the Court upheld the use of the Racketeer Influenced and Corrupt Organizations (RICO) chapter of the Organized Crime Control Act of 1970 (18 U.S.C.A. §§ 1961–1968) against militant anti-abortion groups. RICO, which was originally designed to combat Mafia crime, gives the government a potent tool to convict those involved in violence against abortion providers and their clinics.

In May 1994, President Clinton signed into law another tool to be used against anti-abortion militants, the Freedom of Access to Clinic Entrances Act (FACE), which allows for federal criminal prosecution of anyone who, "by force or threat of force or by physical obstruction, intentionally injures, intimidates, or interferes . . . with any person . . . obtaining or providing reproductive health services" (18 U.S.C.A. § 248). The law also makes it a federal crime to intentionally damage or destroy the property of any reproductive health facility, and it permits persons harmed by those engaging in prohibited conduct to bring private suits against the wrongdoers. The law imposes stiff penalties as well for those found guilty of violating its provisions.

Ultimately, medical technology may have as much to do with the outcome of the abortion debate as politics. New drugs have been developed that induce abortion without a surgical procedure. The most well known of these is RU-486, developed by the French pharmaceutical company Roussel Uclaf. The drug blocks the action of the female hormone progesterone, preventing the implantation of a fertilized egg in the wall of the uterus. It is used with a second drug in pill form, prostaglandin, taken forty-eight hours later, which causes uterine contractions. The uterine lining is then sloughed off, along with any fertilized eggs. Widely used in Europe, RU-486 is said to be 95 percent effective. The drug is also being tested as a morning-after pill and as a possible treatment for breast cancer, endometriosis, and brain tumors. The FOOD AND DRUG ADMINISTRATION (FDA), under the Reagan and Bush administrations, banned the importation of RU-486 into the United States. However, in April 1993, the Clinton administration pressured Roussel Uclaf to license the drug for sale to the U.S. Population Council, a New York–based nonprofit organization, which said it would conduct clinical tests in the United States. Seeking to avoid the ire of anti-abortion groups, Roussel Uclaf was planning to set up a nonprofit foundation that would manufacture and distribute RU-486.

The Pro-Life Movement and the Courts Even before the Supreme Court's landmark 1973 abortion ruling in *Roe v. Wade,* 410 U.S. 113, 93 S. Ct. 705, 35 L. Ed. 2d 147, pro-life groups had begun to picket and protest at family planning clinics that perform abortions. Such groups had formed in response to an abortion reform movement that by 1970 had succeeded in liberalizing abortion laws in many states. From the start, most anti-abortion demonstrators modeled their protests on those of the civil rights movement of the 1950s and 1960s. The anti-abortion movement was led by such people as Joan Andrews, a pacifist and human rights advocate who became a hero for the movement after she spent two-and-a-half years in a Florida jail for attempting to disengage a suction machine used in abortions. The movement advocated the nonviolent approach to civil disobedience pioneered by Mohandas K. Gandhi and Martin Luther King, Jr. By 1975, two years after *Roe,* Catholic groups had begun to conduct sit-ins at family planning

THREE SIDES TO THE ABORTION DEBATE

To what extent does a woman have a right to obtain an abortion? And to what extent does a person have a right to protest the practice of abortion? These are two fundamental questions, and two conflicting rights, that have emerged in the decades following the U.S. Supreme Court's controversial decision in the 1973 case *Roe v. Wade*, 410 U.S. 113, 93 S. Ct. 705, 35 L. Ed. 2d 147. With time, the conflict between those who differ on the answers to these questions, and the interpretation of these rights, has become more and more heated, to the point of violence. The question of access to abortion clinic property—whether to obtain clinic services or to protest them—has become a pressing issue.

Three major points of view dominate the abortion debate: the pro-choice, or abortion rights, view; the moderate pro-life, or moderate anti-abortion, view; and the extremist (or militant) pro-life, or anti-abortion, view.

The pro-choice, or abortion rights, side of the debate is made up of a number of women's rights, family planning, and medical organizations, and other groups of concerned citizens and professionals. These include the National Organization for Women (NOW), the Planned Parenthood Federation of America, the National Abortion Federation, and the National Abortion and Reproductive Rights Action League (NARAL). Many religious organizations have also taken positions that endorse the right of women to seek abortions in specific situations. Most of these pro-choice groups argue that a woman's decision to carry a pregnancy to term is a private choice that should not be interfered with by the state. They also maintain that abortion, although not a preferred family planning method, has always been used by women to gain control over their pregnancies. According to this view, women must have safe and legal access to abortion; without this access, women are likely to seek unsafe, illegal abortions that may result in injury or even death. Pro-choice advocates also maintain that giving women control over their reproductive functions—what they call their reproductive rights—is a fundamental requirement for achieving equality between men and women in American society. Norma McCorvey, who sought anonymity as Jane Roe in *Roe*, spoke eloquently for the pro-choice position in a 1989 speech before a women's rally:

> Prior to *Roe v. Wade*, approximately one million women had illegal abortions each year. Approximately 5,000 of these women were killed. Another 100,000 were hospitalized from botched abortions.
>
> Obviously, abortion will continue whether it is legal or not. My concern is for the safety of millions of women should our freedom of choice be taken away from us. I want it clearly understood that I do not promote abortion. I promote personal choice.
>
> If we return to the antique methods of dealing with unwanted pregnancies that existed before *Roe v. Wade*, the women's movement will be taking an enormous step backward. We are on the verge of having our reproductive freedom taken away from us if we do not take a stand and

clinics where abortions were performed. With time, evangelical Protestant groups joined the movement, and in the mid-1990s, they accounted for a majority of anti-abortion activists.

Pro-life groups have come to call their activities direct actions or rescues, believing that they are saving unborn children from murder, and their tactics have grown increasingly complex. Typical stratagems include bringing in dozens or hundreds of volunteers and blocking clinic entrances with their bodies, often chaining themselves to doors; shouting slogans, sometimes with bullhorns; attempting to intercept women leaving or entering the building and plying them with anti-abortion literature; displaying graphic pictures of fetuses; and trailing clinic employees to and from work while shouting such things as "Baby killer!" Besides demonstrating, anti-abortion groups have sponsored "pregnancy crisis centers," where they counsel pregnant women, with the intention of persuading them to carry their pregnancies to term. By the mid-1980s, activists had created national organizations and networks that promoted civil disobedience to stop the practice of abortion. The most well known of these is Operation Rescue, which was started in the 1980s by Randall Terry, an evangelical Christian.

The aggressive strategies of the anti-abortion movement have prompted legal responses from women's and abortion rights organizations, resulting in a number of cases that have reached the Supreme Court. In several different rulings, the Court has attempted to clarify what is and is not allowed in anti-abortion demonstrations. In making these decisions, the Court has attempted to balance the rights of the demonstrators—particularly their right to free speech—with the rights of women

let our voices be heard NOW.

Pro-choice groups therefore remain committed to the constitutional right to privacy defined in *Roe*. They view anti-abortion demonstrations that prevent women from obtaining abortions as interfering with that right to privacy.

The pro-choice group also has a range of viewpoints within it. While all persons who describe themselves as pro-choice support a general right to abortion, some oppose abortions under certain circumstances, such as late term abortions.

The moderate pro-life movement consists of myriad different organizations, including the National Right to Life Committee, Human Rights Review, and Feminists for Life of America. Although its members are extremely diverse, most come from religious groups such as the Catholic Church and evangelical Protestant denominations. Generally, these groups believe that the fetus is a person with rights equal to those of other people. Many are willing to allow abortion in certain cases, usually when pregnancy threatens the health of the mother or has resulted from rape or incest. Moderates, when they support changes in abortion laws and regulations, differ from militants in their emphasis on using existing legal channels.

The militant pro-life groups share many of the views of the moderate groups, but they favor an activist use of civil disobedience to prevent abortion procedures and to save or rescue the lives of the unborn. Randall Terry and Flip Benham, of the most well known anti-abortion group, Operation Rescue, are representative of the militant views. Terry, Operation Rescue's founder and leading figure, participated in his first anti-abortion protest in 1984 and has served time in prison because of his demonstrations. As an evangelical Protestant Christian, Terry sees abortion as the work of the devil: "I believe that there is a devil, and here's Satan's agenda. First, he doesn't want anyone having kids. Secondly, if they do conceive, he wants them killed. If they're not killed through abortion, he wants them neglected or abused, physically, emotionally, sexually." Terry opposes abortion in all cases, even for pregnancies resulting from rape or incest. His group's main tactics, he says, include "rescue missions, boycotts and protests."

A minority of the militant anti-abortion activists sanction the use of physical force. A small number even regard the killing of abortion providers as justifiable homicide. When asked to explain this increasing tendency toward

violence, militant pro-life leader Joseph Scheidler, of the Pro-Life Action Network, blames it on the 1994 Freedom of Access to Clinic Entrances Act and buffer zone restrictions that keep protesters from conducting rallies at abortion clinics. Scheidler argues that making it tougher to have peaceful protests gives people a rationale to have violent protests. Benham, of Operation Rescue, has condemned the anti-abortion killings. However, after John Salvi murdered two people and wounded others in an abortion clinic shooting in late 1994, Benham commented, "There is little that federal marshals or anyone else can do to halt this murder and violence. We will not have peace outside the womb until peace is restored within the womb." Adds Terry, "We're involved in a cultural civil war."

In the end, the extremist position may do more to hurt than to help the anti-abortion cause. The growing violence of the movement appears to have alienated many of the more moderate individuals in pro-life groups, reducing the membership of those groups to a militant core and making those outside the groups less sympathetic to their cause.

seeking to use family planning clinic services. In 1988, for example, in *Frisby v. Schultz*, 487 U.S. 474, 108 S. Ct. 2495, 101 L. Ed. 2d 420, the Court upheld a Brookfield, Wisconsin, city ordinance prohibiting pickets "focused on, and taking place in front of, a particular residence." The ordinance had been created in response to anti-abortion demonstrations targeting the private home of an obstetrician who performed abortions, a tactic assumed by the protesters after picketing at the physician's clinic had not stopped its operation. Justice Sandra Day O'Connor wrote in the Court's opinion, "There is simply no right to force speech into the home of an unwilling listener."

A later Supreme Court decision gave abortion clinics further protection: it supported the constitutionality of a court INJUNCTION prohibiting protesters from going within thirty-six feet of a clinic that had been a regular target of

protests. In July 1994, in *Madsen v. Women's Health Center*, ___U.S.___, 114 S. Ct. 2516, 129 L. Ed. 2d 593, the High Court ruled 6–3 to let stand the thirty-six-foot exclusion zone for the Melbourne, Florida, abortion clinic. However, the Court did strike down other provisions of the injunction, such as a three-hundred-foot exclusion zone and restrictions on carrying banners and pictures. The ruling was considered a major defeat for the anti-abortion movement. Justice Antonin Scalia wrote a sharp dissent in which he claimed that the Supreme Court's position on abortion had claimed "its latest, greatest and most surprising victim: the First Amendment."

Increased Violence Changes the Debate Violence has been a part of the heated debate surrounding abortion ever since the 1973 *Roe v. Wade* decision that guaranteed a woman's limited right to an abortion. Bombings, arson, and even murder have been committed by anti-abortion activists in the name of their cause. The National Abortion Federation counted more than three thousand violent or threatening incidents against abortion clinics between 1976 and 1994. In the 1990s, the extremist wing of the anti-abortion movement turned even more violent, including murder as part of its tactics. Some extremists now view killing health care professionals who perform abortions as JUSTIFIABLE homicide.

Between March 1993 and the end of 1994, five staff workers at abortion clinics were murdered by anti-abortion zealots. Dr. David Gunn was fatally shot on March 10, 1993, outside an abortion clinic in Pensacola, Florida, by Michael Griffin. In August 1994, Dr. John Bayard Britton, age sixty-nine, who had replaced Gunn as circuit-riding doctor in northern Florida, and his escort, James Barrett, age seventy-four, were shot repeatedly in the face with a shotgun as their car pulled into the parking lot of the Ladies Clinic of Pensacola. Minutes later, police arrested Paul Hill, an anti-abortion extremist. President Bill Clinton called Britton's and Barrett's killings a case of domestic terrorism. In December 1994, in perhaps the most gruesome incident of all, John Salvi killed two people and wounded five more when he opened fire in two Boston-area family planning clinics.

According to the Alan Guttmacher Institute, in 1988—well before the 1993–94 wave of violence—17 percent of counties in the United States had abortion providers. The federal government cannot guarantee protection for clin-

ics; whereas there are some fifteen hundred abortion clinics nationwide, in 1995 there were only 2,100 federal marshals.

The government and abortion rights groups have responded to the increased violence in two ways: reviewing existing laws to find those that can be used to investigate and prosecute violent groups and individuals, and creating new laws that specifically address access to abortion clinics. In the late 1980s, the National Organization for Women (NOW) filed a lawsuit against long-time pro-life activist Joseph Scheidler and his Pro-Life Action Network (PLAN). Initially, NOW attempted to use the Sherman Anti-Trust Act of 1890 (15 U.S.C.A. § 1 et seq.) against PLAN, but without success. At the prompting of Chicago lawyer Fay Clayton, NOW turned to a different law, the Racketeer Influenced and Corrupt Organizations (RICO) chapter of the Organized Crime Control Act of 1970 (18 U.S.C.A. §§ 1961–1968), and broadened its attack to include Randall Terry, founder of Operation Rescue. RICO was originally drafted as a potent means to convict all members of a criminal enterprise—including those who had routinely escaped police dragnets, the Mafia bosses. The law imposes harsh penalties on those convicted under it: up to twenty years in jail for each criminal count, and triple damages in civil judgments. In early 1994, the Supreme Court, in *National Organization for Women v. Scheidler,* 510 U.S. 249, 114 S. Ct. 798, 127 L. Ed. 2d 99, upheld the use of RICO against anti-abortion groups, many of which could now be attacked as criminal enterprises. Chief Justice William H. Rehnquist, writing the Court's opinion, reasoned that to be designated a criminal enterprise under RICO, an organization need not be devoted to economic gain. Justice David H. Souter wrote a concurring opinion in which he warned that RICO could conflict with First Amendment rights regarding speech. "I think it prudent to notice," he wrote, "that RICO actions could deter protected advocacy and to caution courts applying RICO to bear in mind the First Amendment interests that could be at stake."

Women's rights groups were less successful in *Bray v. Alexandria Women's Health Clinic,* 506 U.S. 263, 113 S. Ct. 753, 122 L. Ed. 2d 34 (1993). In this case, the Supreme Court ruled that a nineteenth-century federal civil rights law (42 U.S.C.A. § 1985[3]) aimed at protecting African Americans from the Ku Klux Klan could not be used to prevent anti-abortion protesters from blockading abortion clinics. Originally enacted as part of the Ku Klux Klan

The early 1990s saw increased violence at abortion clinics. Abortion rights groups have attempted to fight this violence through the courts.

© 1993 JAMES COLBURN/PHOTOREPORTERS

Act of 1871, a law that had first been used against mob violence and vigilantism, the relevant statute had in the 1980s been applied by courts to actions of anti-abortion groups, most notably Operation Rescue. A lower-court ruling, for example, found that Operation Rescue had violated TRESPASSING and public NUISANCE laws and had conspired to violate the right to interstate travel of women seeking abortions at clinics. The court banned Operation Rescue from trespassing on or obstructing ACCESS to abortion clinics (*NOW v. Operation Rescue*, 726 F. Supp. 1483 [E.D. Va. 1989]). This decision was reversed by the Supreme Court in *Bray*, in a 6–3 ruling, when it held that women did not qualify as a class under discrimination by the provisions of the Ku Klux Klan Act.

After *Bray*, congressional supporters of abortion rights, Representative Charles E. Schumer (D-N.Y.) and Senator Edward M. Kennedy (D-Mass.), introduced the Freedom of Access to Clinic Entrances Act (FACE), which would give federal courts the authority to issue restraining orders against protesters blockading abortion clinics (18 U.S.C.A. § 248). It was signed into law by President Clinton on May 26, 1994. The law allows for federal criminal prosecution of anyone who, "by force or threat of force or by physical obstruction, intentionally injures, intimidates, or interferes . . . with any person . . . obtaining or providing reproductive health services." The law also makes it a federal crime to intentionally damage or destroy the property of any reproductive health facility, and it permits persons harmed by those engaging in prohibited conduct to bring private suits against the wrongdoers. The penalties for violation of the act include imprisonment for up to one year and a fine of $10,000 for a first offense; for each subsequent offense, penalties can be up to three years' imprisonment and $25,000. FACE is patterned after existing civil rights laws, including 18 U.S.C.A. § 245(b), which prohibits force or threat of force to willfully injure, intimidate, or interfere with any person who is voting, engaging in activities related to voting, or enjoying the benefits of federal programs. Nevertheless, FACE is not identical to previous federal civil rights laws, particularly where it prohibits acts of physical obstruction.

FACE brought on immediate challenges by anti-abortion groups who claimed that it abridged their First Amendment right to freedom of speech. Courts were unwilling to invalidate the law on this ground, reasoning that the law proscribes only conduct—as in "force," "threat of force," and "physical obstruction"—rather than speech (see *Council for Life Coalition v. Reno*, 856 F. Supp. 1422, No. 94-0843-1EG[CM], 1994 WL 363132 [S.D. Cal. 1994]).

The violence against clinics and the murder of abortion providers have given new momentum to the pro-choice, or abortion rights, side of the abortion issue. Family planning clinics that perform abortions are receiving increased protection from local, state, and federal statutes, with FACE the most prominent of these laws. However, the debate and litigation surrounding the issue of anti-abortion protests show little sign of abating, and anti-abortion protest groups are preparing to challenge the laws regulating their activities, on the grounds that such laws abridge freedom of speech.

Attitudes toward Abortion

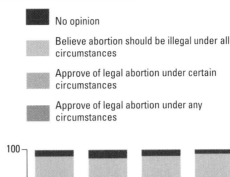

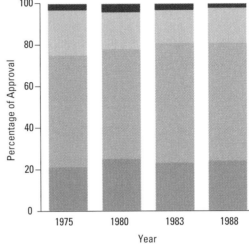

Source: *The Gallup Report* (February 1989), No. 281, p.17.

CROSS-REFERENCES

American Civil Liberties Union; Blackmun, Harry A.; Constitutional Amendment; Due Process of Law; Fetal Rights; First Amendment; Fourteenth Amendment; Freedom of Speech; Husband and Wife; Ninth Amendment; O'Connor, Sandra Day; Parent and Child; Privacy; Racketeer Influenced and Corrupt Organizations (RICO) Act; Rehnquist, William; Reproduction; *Roe v. Wade*; Scalia, Antonin; Souter, David; Wattleton, Faye; Women's Rights.

ABROGATION 📖 The destruction or annulling of a former law by an act of the legislative power, by constitutional authority, or by usage. It stands opposed to *rogation;* and is distinguished from DEROGATION, which implies the taking away of only some part of a law; from SUBROGATION, which denotes the substitution of a clause; from *dispensation*, which only sets it aside in a particular instance; and from *antiquation*, which is the refusing to pass a law. 📖

For example, the abrogation of the Eighteenth Amendment to the Constitution, which prohibited the manufacture or sale of intoxicating liquors, was accomplished by the enactment of the Twenty-first Amendment. Implied abrogation takes place when a new law contains provisions that are positively contrary to a former law, without expressly abrogating such laws, or when the order of things for which the law has been made no longer exists.

ABSCOND 📖 To go in a clandestine manner out of the JURISDICTION of the courts, or to lie concealed, in order to avoid their process. To hide, conceal, or absent oneself clandestinely, with the intent to avoid legal PROCESS. To postpone limitations. To flee from arresting or prosecuting officers of the state. 📖

ABSCONDING DEBTOR 📖 One who absconds from CREDITORS to avoid payment of DEBTS. A DEBTOR who has intentionally concealed himself or herself from creditors, or withdrawn from the reach of their suits, with intent to frustrate their just demands. Such act was formerly an *act of bankruptcy.* 📖

A person who moves out of the state may be an absconding debtor if it is that person's intention to avoid paying money that he or she owes.

It is difficult or impossible for a creditor to serve an absconding debtor with a SUMMONS in order to start a lawsuit and collect his or her money. Where a court is convinced that a debtor has absconded, it may permit the creditor to begin the lawsuit in some way other than PERSONAL SERVICE of a summons.

For example, a franchisee bought a doughnut FRANCHISE and opened up a small shop. He also bought a house for his family. Unfortunately, the business failed after a year, and he turned all of the equipment and materials back to the franchisor. The franchisor claimed that additional money was owed to him and decided to sue the former franchisee. A process server was sent to take a summons to the apartment that was listed as the address in the original application for the franchise. The landlord there told the process server that the former franchisee had moved and left no forwarding address. The franchisor applied to the court for permission to serve him as an absconding debtor. The court allowed the franchisor to publish notice of the lawsuit on three occasions in the legal section of the local newspaper. The franchisee did not see the notice and did not appear in court. The court entered a DEFAULT JUDGMENT against him without hearing his side of the story. After that, the franchisor began searching public records to see if the franchisee owned any property that could be seized to pay off the amount of the judgment. He discovered the recorded DEED for the house and went back to court, seeking an order to have the house sold. This time the franchisee, who was served personally with the court papers, appeared with his attorney. He explained at the hearing that he had never intended to conceal himself or to avoid paying the money he owed. The court found that he had never been an absconding debtor who could be served merely by PUBLICATION. The default judgment, therefore, could not be enforced, and the franchisor could not have the house seized and sold.

ABSENTEE 📖 One who has left, either temporarily or permanently, his or her DOMICILE or usual place of RESIDENCE or business. A person beyond the geographical borders of a state who has not authorized an AGENT to represent him or her in LEGAL PROCEEDINGS that may be commenced against him or her within the state. 📖

An absentee LANDLORD is an individual who leases real estate to another but who does not reside in the leased premises.

An absentee CORPORATION is one that conducts business within a state other than the place of its incorporation but has not designated an agent for purposes of SERVICE OF PROCESS, which might ensue from disputes involving its business transactions there.

ABSENTEE VOTING 📖 Participation in an election by qualified voters who are permitted to mail in their ballots. 📖

The Uniformed and Overseas Citizens Absentee Voting Act (42 U.S.C.A. § 1973ff et seq.) covers absentee voting in presidential elections, but the states regulate absentee voting in all other elections. According to Article I, Section 4, of the U.S. Constitution, "The Times, Places and Manner of holding Elections for Senators and Representatives, shall be prescribed in each state by the Legislature thereof; but the Congress may . . . make or alter such Regulations, except as to the Places of ch[oo]sing Senators."

Originally created to accommodate overseas military service personnel in World War I, absentee voting has since expanded to include all those expecting to be absent from their PRECINCTS on election day. The right to vote, even by absentee ballot, is no trifling concern. A state may restrict it only to the extent that doing so serves a compelling state interest such as preventing fraud.

Although all states allow absentee voting, the procedures and qualifications vary from state to state. For example, the amount of time that an application for an absentee ballot must precede the election can vary. In Minnesota, it is one day (M.S.A. § 203B.04[1]). In Louisiana, it depends on the voter: for example, a voter who goes in person to apply for an absentee ballot and vote must do so between twelve and six days before the election (LSA-R.S. 18:1309[a][1]); a voter who registers for an absentee ballot by mail must get the registration form to the registrar not more than sixty days and not less than ninety-six hours before the election (LSA-R.S. 18:1307[b]); military personnel must return the application not more than twelve months and not less than seven days before election day (LSA-R.S. 18:1307[c]).

Many states allow absentee voters to vote again on election day if they are present in the state. If voters so choose, they may change their votes. Officials in states that allow this practice count the absentee ballots after the poll ballots have been counted, and any duplicate absentee ballots are simply disregarded. This is the case in Minnesota (M.S.A. § 203B.13[3a]). In Louisiana, however, a person who has voted by absentee ballot may not vote again on election day (LSA-R.S. 18:1305). In 1977, Louisiana amended its law to allow absentee voters to change their votes on election day, but in 1980, it changed the law again to prohibit the practice.

In any state, to cast an absentee ballot, citizens must be eligible voters and have a reason for being unable to vote at the POLLS. If citizens know they will be absent from their voting precincts on election day, they may vote by absentee ballot. Between August 1, 1991, and November 30, 1992, Minnesota experimented with allowing voters to cast absentee ballots without explanation, but this practice was discontinued on January 1, 1994.

All states allow persons with permanent disabilities and military personnel to cast votes by absentee ballot. Other valid reasons for voting in absentia include illness, temporary disability, and religious observances or practices. In Louisiana, any person age sixty-five or older may vote by absentee ballot.

All states require that the application for an absentee ballot be requested before election day, but this rule has some exceptions. In Minnesota, for example, a health care patient who

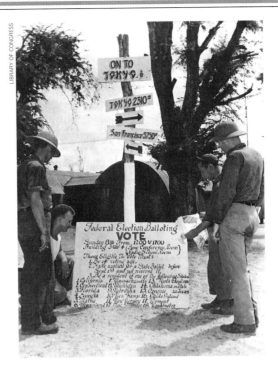

LIBRARY OF CONGRESS

During World War II military personnel voted in U.S. elections from a base in the Southwest Pacific.

becomes a resident or patient in a health care facility on the day before the election may vote by absentee ballot on election day if she or he telephones the municipal clerk by 5:00 P.M. the day before the election (M.S.A. § 203B.04[2]). Each county enlists election judges to deliver absentee ballots to hospitalized voters (M.S.A. § 203B.11[3]).

Some people have had to fight for the right to vote by absentee ballot. In *Cepulonis v. Secretary of the Commonwealth*, 452 N.E.2d 1137, 389 Mass. 930 (Mass. 1983), Richard Cepulonis and Kevin Murphy, two Massachusetts residents and long-term prisoners in the Walpole Massachusetts Correctional Institution, asserted their right to vote by absentee ballot. Cepulonis, eligible for parole in 1997, and Murphy, eligible for parole in 1985, attempted to vote from prison in 1982. City officials in Worcester told Cepulonis that he could not vote by absentee ballot without registering in person, and officials in Boston told Murphy the same.

Cepulonis and Murphy filed suit together in superior court, asking for a CLASS ACTION on behalf of Massachusetts prisoners and a judicial declaration that the class of prisoners be declared eligible to vote by absentee ballot. The judge denied the requests, holding specifically that prisoners who did not register to vote prior to their imprisonment, and prisoners who are not imprisoned in the city of their domicile, may not register to vote by absentee ballot because they must register to vote in person. The absentee voting statutes of Massachusetts contained no provision for voter registration of

Massachusetts prisoners through the postal service.

Cepulonis and Murphy asked the Massachusetts Supreme Judicial Court to review the case; on August 15, 1982, the court denied the request. On October 21, Cepulonis and Murphy moved for a court order allowing prisoners to vote in the November 2 elections; the Massachusetts high court denied this as well. Cepulonis and Murphy then filed a motion for *injunctive relief*—a court order—with the U.S. Supreme Court. Justice William J. Brennan, Jr., denied the motion without PREJUDICE, which meant that Cepulonis and Murphy were free to bring the matter before the Court in the future. Justice John Paul Stevens referred the case to the full bench of the Supreme Court, which, after consideration, refused to command Massachusetts to institute procedures enabling incarcerated residents to vote by absentee ballot.

Undaunted, Cepulonis and Murphy applied directly to the Massachusetts Supreme Judicial Court for review of the case; the court granted the application. On April 4, 1983, Cepulonis and Murphy argued that Massachusetts's failure to install an absentee registration procedure for incarcerated residents deprived those residents of their state constitutional right to vote in state elections. Although some states had chosen to prohibit convicted criminals from voting in elections, Massachusetts had not.

The court began the analysis in its opinion by discussing the CASE LAW of Massachusetts on the subject of voting. Without exception, the PRECEDENTS held that voting laws should be interpreted to facilitate voting, and not to impair or defeat the right to vote. In light of this principle, the court announced, it agreed with Cepulonis and Murphy: the Massachusetts statutory scheme was denying deserving citizens a state constitutional right.

The court then examined the Massachusetts statutory scheme and observed that some eligible prisoners could vote, whereas others could not. The absentee voting laws of Massachusetts provided that prisoners incarcerated in the municipality of their domicile, if already registered, could vote by absentee ballot. On the other hand, registered voters incarcerated in a municipality other than their own could not register for absentee ballots. Furthermore, prisoners who were adult registered voters before they were incarcerated could vote, but prisoners reaching the AGE OF MAJORITY while incarcerated could not vote. These distinctions were ARBITRARY and, according to the court, unconstitutional.

The court then cited relevant case law that held that Massachusetts must prove the existence of a compelling state interest when it denies a fundamental right such as voting. The state argued that the registration laws existed in their present form to prevent voter fraud. The court countered by pointing out that Maine, New York, Vermont, Georgia, and Pennsylvania had all seen fit to permit prisoners domiciled in their states to register as absentee voters. This showed that it was possible to create a system allowing eligible prisoners to vote by absentee ballot.

The state also argued that prisoners not registered to vote had had the opportunity to register before incarceration. Requiring the state to supply special absentee voting procedures to disinterested citizens seemed unnecessary. However, failure to register to vote before incarceration did not mean that prisoners who were otherwise eligible should be denied the right to vote, and, according to the court, no case law supported such a denial.

Ultimately, the court held that Massachusetts prisoners must be given the means to vote in state elections. The Massachusetts absentee voting statutes were unconstitutional to the extent that they prevented incarcerated, eligible Massachusetts voters from registering to vote. The court refrained from giving the vote to Cepulonis and Murphy, and instead left the job of revising the Massachusetts absentee voting laws to the legislature.

In a connected case, the Superior Court of Norfolk County awarded attorneys' fees to Cepulonis and Murphy. This decision was upheld by the Supreme Judicial Court of Massachusetts in 1986 (*Cepulonis v. Registrars of Voters*, 488 N.E.2d 1166, 396 Mass. 808).

CROSS-REFERENCES

Elections; Prisoners' Rights; Voting Rights.

ABSOLUTE 📖 Complete; perfect; final; without any CONDITION or incumbrance; as an absolute bond in distinction from a conditional bond. Unconditional; complete and perfect in itself; without relation to or dependence on other things or persons.

Free from conditions, limitations or qualifications, not dependent, or modified or affected by circumstances; that is, without any condition or restrictive provisions. 📖

Absolute can be used to describe DIVORCE, ESTATES, OBLIGATION, and TITLE.

ABSOLUTE DEED 📖 A document used to transfer unrestricted TITLE to property. 📖

An absolute deed is different from a mortgage deed, which transfers ownership back to the mortgagee when the terms of the MORTGAGE have been fulfilled.

ABSTENTION DOCTRINE

The concept under which a federal court exercises its discretion and equitable powers and declines to decide a legal action over which it has JURISDICTION pursuant to the Constitution and statutes where the state judiciary is capable of rendering a definitive ruling in the matter.

The abstention doctrine was adopted by the Supreme Court to allow the federal judiciary to refrain from ruling on constitutional questions. Because it has no explicit source in federal or state laws, it is the exception to the general rule that a litigant may sue or be sued in federal court if the federal court has *jurisdiction*, or power to hear the case. A federal court has jurisdiction over several species of cases and controversies, such as those involving a federal constitutional question, a federal statute, or litigants of different states in a dispute totaling over $50,000 (in which case, the court's power to hear is called diversity jurisdiction). Federal courts have an obligation to hear the cases properly brought before them, so abstention is an extraordinary judicial maneuver.

Also known as the Pullman doctrine, the abstention doctrine was first fashioned by the Court in *Railroad Commission of Texas v. Pullman Co.*, 312 U.S. 496 61 S. Ct. 643, 85 L. Ed. 971 (1941). At issue in *Pullman* was a Texas Railroad Commission regulation that prevented the operation of sleeping cars on trains without a Pullman conductor. Before the regulation, Texas trains used only one sleeping car in areas of light passenger traffic. When only one sleeping car was used, the trains had only Pullman porters to watch over the sleepers. When more sleeping cars were used, the trains employed Pullman conductors, who supervised the porters. The regulation eliminated a practice that deprived conductors of wages, but it also effectively decreased the earnings and eliminated the autonomy of porters. This result introduced the issue of DISCRIMINATION, since, at the time, Pullman conductors were white and porters were black.

The Pullman Company and Texas railroads objected to the regulation, and together they brought suit in federal district court to keep the commission from enforcing the order. Pullman porters joined the Pullman Company and the railroads as COMPLAINANTS, and Pullman conductors joined the commission as DEFENDANTS. The federal district court granted the request of the

This 1935 photo shows a Pullman conductor and porter helping passengers board a train. At that time Pullman conductors were white and porters were black, raising the issue of discrimination in the Pullman case.

complainants, ruling that the commission did not have the authority to make such an order. The defendants appealed directly to the U.S. Supreme Court.

The complainants argued that the regulation violated constitutional rights, namely the protections provided under the Due Process and COMMERCE CLAUSES of the U.S. Constitution. The porters specifically asserted that the order was discriminatory against "negroes," and thus violated the FOURTEENTH AMENDMENT to the Constitution. The commission answered that its authority to order such a regulation was created by Texas law. Vernon's Texas Revised Civil Statutes Annotated, article 6445, provided in part that the commission was empowered to prevent "unjust discrimination . . . and to prevent any and all other abuses" in the Texas railroad industry.

The Supreme Court acknowledged the sensitive nature of the porters' allegation of discrimination, but declared that the fate of the offending law should be decided first by the state courts. The Court then faced the question of whether a state resolution was possible.

The Supreme Court noted that a federal district court in the Fifth Circuit had ruled against the commission, but called the decision nothing more than a "forecast." According to the Court, the Texas state courts were more capable of interpreting Texas laws and determining how they should be applied. Federal courts were simply not competent to define the concept of discrimination and its prevention as understood in Texas.

Furthermore, deciding Texas law in a federal court was of little use when the ruling could later be displaced by the decision of a state court. The Court conceded that federal constitutional claims against state laws or regulations may be appealed to federal courts, but it emphasized the PUBLIC INTEREST in avoiding "needless friction with state policies." This meant that when a state had the means to resolve a constitutional issue, the first word on the meaning and constitutionality of the challenged law should be left to the state.

Texas law provided for JUDICIAL REVIEW of administrative orders in state court, so the complainants could have filed suit there. Likewise, the defendants could have brought suit in state court to enforce the order in the event of a railroad strike. Because these avenues existed and had not been traveled, the Supreme Court reversed the decision of the lower federal court and ordered the case held in the federal court pending the outcome of state proceedings.

The abstention doctrine has expanded since the *Pullman* case. The Supreme Court has identified three distinct types of cases from which a federal court should abstain: (1) If the meaning of a state law or regulation is claimed to be unconstitutional, and the meaning of the statute or regulation can be discovered in the state's court system, abstention is appropriate. (2) Abstention is also appropriate when a federal suit seeks to delay or upset an ongoing state proceeding, such as a criminal prosecution or the collection of state taxes. (3) Finally, a federal court should yield to state courts when a case presents a difficult policy question of vital importance to the state. This last justification for abstention breeds the most creative arguments.

One difficult issue of vital importance to states is domestic relations. Divorce, alimony, and child custody cases involve legitimate local policies concerning marriage and religion. Until the 1990s, domestic relations abstention has been invoked by federal courts in virtually any case concerning family members. In *Ankenbrandt v. Richards*, 504 U.S. 689, 112 S. Ct. 2206, 119 L. Ed. 2d 468 (1992), the Supreme Court put a stop to this practice.

On September 26, 1989, Carol Ankenbrandt, on behalf of her daughters, sued Jon Richards and Debra Kesler in the U.S. District Court for the Eastern District of Louisiana. Ankenbrandt, a Missouri citizen, had been married to Richards, a Louisiana citizen. After the couple divorced, Richards became romantically involved with Kesler. In her suit, Ankenbrandt claimed that Richards and Kesler had sexually and physically abused Ankenbrandt's daughters. Ankenbrandt filed the suit in federal court under diversity jurisdiction; she was able to do

so because she did not live in the defendants' home state and she was suing for over $50,000.

The federal court decided not to hear the merits of Ankenbrandt's case. The district court granted the defendants' earliest motion to dismiss, ruling that the case belonged in state court under the domestic relations exception to federal jurisdiction based on diversity. As an alternative to that holding, the court declared that its refusal to hear the case was also justified by the abstention doctrine. The court of appeals affirmed these holdings without a published opinion.

On appeal, the Supreme Court reversed the decision. The Court traced the origins of the domestic relations exception to federal diversity jurisdiction and concluded that the exception was valid. Nevertheless, the exception contemplated federal abstention only from cases such as divorce, alimony, and child custody. Ankenbrandt's action was a *tort action*, an action for monetary recovery based on the accusations of one individual against another. Ankenbrandt's previous marriage to Richards did not provide a permissible reason for the federal court to invoke the domestic relations exception.

The federal district court's alternative holding of abstention was equally erroneous. The district court had cited *Younger v. Harris*, 401 U.S. 37, 91 S. Ct. 746, 27 L. Ed. 2d 669 (1971), as support for its abstention. However, the *Younger* decision simply held that a federal court could not interfere with a PENDING state criminal prosecution. Here, no state proceeding was pending, and the defense had not alleged that any important state interest existed, so reliance on that particular reason for abstention was misplaced.

Although the argument had not been raised by Richards or Kesler, the Supreme Court anticipated another reason for abstention, to foreclose the argument in future cases. The federal district court may have sought to abstain from the *Ankenbrandt* case because the suit seemed to present a difficult state policy question of vital importance to the public. The case seemed to involve a determination of the family status of the litigants, an area of state interest that could bring the case within the domestic relations exception. This basis for abstention was not supportable, though, because the familial status of the parties had already been determined in a divorce proceeding and a parental rights proceeding.

The Supreme Court further warned that the family status of the litigants had no bearing on the underlying case. In a CIVIL ACTION for monetary damages, where sexual and physical abuse is alleged, a federal court could not refuse to hear the case because the litigants had at one time been related. Ultimately, neither the domestic relations exception nor its close relative the abstention doctrine would deprive Ankenbrandt of the right to file her complaint in federal court.

Despite its expansion since *Pullman*, federal court abstention is very rare. A federal court may refuse to hear a case over which it has jurisdiction only in unusual circumstances. When a case poses federal constitutional questions, a federal court may abstain only when the challenged state law or regulation is unclear. In addition, the methods for determining the meaning of the law or regulation must exist in the state's court system, and these methods must not have been used. Then and only then may a federal court refrain from hearing a constitutional question. The boundaries of the abstention doctrine are continually tested and stretched, but in 1992 the Supreme Court sent notice through the *Ankenbrandt* case to the federal courts that its use is limited.

CROSS-REFERENCES
Constitutional Law; Courts; Federal Courts.

ABSTRACT 📖 To take or withdraw from; as, to abstract the funds of a bank. To remove or separate. To summarize or abridge. 📖

An abstract comprises—or concentrates in itself—the essential qualities of a larger thing—or of several things—in a short, abbreviated form. It differs from a TRANSCRIPT, which is a verbatim copy of the thing itself and is more comprehensive.

See also ABSTRACT OF TITLE.

ABSTRACTION 📖 Taking from someone with an intent to INJURE or DEFRAUD. 📖

Wrongful abstraction is an unauthorized and illegal withdrawing of funds or an APPROPRIATION of someone else's funds for the taker's own benefit. It may be a CRIME under the laws of a state. It is different from EMBEZZLEMENT, which is a crime committed only if the taker had a lawful right to possession of the money when it was first taken.

ABSTRACT OF TITLE 📖 A condensed history, taken from public records or documents, of the ownership of a piece of land. 📖

An abstract of title, or title abstract, briefly summarizes the various activities affecting ownership of a parcel of land. When a person or business agrees to purchase REAL ESTATE, that person or business arranges for an examination of the history of the property's TITLE. This examination is known as a TITLE SEARCH. A title search is conducted to determine that the seller

of the property in fact owns the property and has a *free-and-clear* title. A free-and-clear title has no *clouds* on it, which means that no person or business other than the seller has an INTEREST in, or CLAIM to, the property.

The process of determining the precise ownership of a piece of land by searching an abstract is complex and laborious. Often, the title abstract does not contain every transaction or proceeding that may affect ownership of the land. The search conductor, or *abstractor*, usually a trained professional, must verify that the abstract is complete by reviewing recent certifications that the abstract is correct, checking for gaps in dates and certification numbers, and ensuring that a proper legal description appears with each entry. The abstractor conducts a credit and finances check on all the names appearing in the abstract to see if any of the parties have filed for BANKRUPTCY or have incurred other DEBTS that may have caused a CREDITOR to file a LIEN against the property toward payment of the debt.

An abstractor must refer to many different sources to verify that the title to a parcel of land is true and correct. The abstractor verifies the original government survey, which should include gaps and overlaps in land ownership. With improved technology, surveys now have a margin of error of less than one foot. The abstractor must understand the various means of describing the exact boundaries of a piece of land, and must recognize unacceptable methods.

Claims on the title to a property are subject to time limitations, but the limitations have certain exceptions. For example, the Forty-Year Law holds that no party with a potential claim that arose over forty years before can claim an interest in a property where one person or business has been the recorded owner for at least forty years. Exceptions are made, however, for those holding MORTGAGES or CONTRACTS with terms that span more than forty years, and also for prior interests claimed as school or school district lands, parkland dedications, or the property of religious corporations or associations.

To perform a title search, the abstractor must obtain a copy of the abstract from the county recorder in the county where the land is located. Then it is time to make sense of the document. The accompanying sample abstract of title illustrates typical entries.

1. Entry 1 identifies the land in question. The sample abstract is for platted land, which is land described by lots and blocks. A platted parcel spans a certain number of feet, on a

A sample abstract
of title

1. Abstract of Title to north ___500___ feet, front and rear, of Lot ___1___ ,
   Block ___2___ , in ___NW___ Addition to the City of ___New Heidelberg___ .

2. United States   Entry No. ___1___ .
         to   Dated ___Jan. 1___ , 1889.
      John Doe.   Land Office Records, page ___100___ .
                        ___North___ 1/4 of Section ___36___ , T. ___32___ , R. ___22___ .

3. United States   Patent.
         to   Dated ___Jan. 1, 1889___ .
      John Doe   Filed ___Jan. 1, 1889___ .
                      Book ___1___ of Deeds, page ___100___ .
                        ___North___ 1/4 of Section ___36___ , T. ___32___ , R. ___22___ .

4. John Doe et al.   Plat of ___Stoneybrook E___ Addition to the City
         to   of ___New Heidelberg___ .
      The Public.   Dated ___Feb. 1, 1889___ .
                      Filed ___Feb. 1, 1889___ .
                      Book ___1___ of Plats, page ___200___ .
                      ___North___ 1/4 of Section ___36___ , T. ___32___ , R. ___22___ .

5. John Doe, unmarried,   Warranty Deed.
         to   Dated ___Feb. 1, 1890___ .
      Richard Roe.   Filed ___Feb. 1, 1890___ .
                      Book ___3___ of Deeds, page ___300___ .
                      Lot ___1___ , Block ___E___ , ___Stoneybrook___ Addition
                      to City of ___New Heidelberg___ .

6. Richard Roe and   Mortgage.
   Ruth Roe, his wife,   Dated ___Feb. 1, 1890___ .
         to   Filed ___Feb. 1, 1890___ .
      John Smith.   Book ___1___ of Mortgages, page ___10___ , to secure
                      ___$10,000___ , due ___January 10, 1910___ .
                      Lot ___1___ , Block ___E___ , ___Stoneybrook___ Addition.

7. John Smith   Assignment of Mortgage No. 6.
         to   Dated ___Jan. 1, 1895___ .
      William White.   Filed ___Jan. 1, 1895___ .
                      Book ___5___ of Assignments, page ___100___ .

8. William White   Satisfaction of No. 6.
         to   Dated ___Jan. 1, 1910___ .
      Richard Roe et ux.   Filed ___Jan. 1, 1910___ .
                      Book ___3___ of Satisfactions, page ___200___ .

9. Richard Roe   Will and Probate.
         to   Dated ___July 1, 1915___ .
      Ruth Roe.   Probate ___July 1, 1915___ .
                      Filed ___Aug. 1, 1915___ .
                      Book ___10___ of Miscellaneous, page ___100___ .
                      Testator leaves all of his property, real
   and personal, to his wife, Ruth Roe.

10. Richard Roe   Final Decree.
          to   Probate Court, ___Munich___ County.
       Ruth Roe.   Dated ___Aug. 1, 1915___ .
                       Filed ___Aug. 1, 1915___ .
                       Book ___10___ of Miscellaneous, page ___300___ .
                       Adjudged and decreed that Lot ___1___ ,
                       Block ___2___ , ___NW___ Addition, is
                       hereby assigned to Ruth Roe.

11. Ruth Roe, widow,   Mortgage.
          to   Dated ___Jan. 1, 1920___ .
       Samuel Brown.   Filed ___Jan. 1, 1920___ .
                       Book ___10___ of Mortgages, page ___100___ , to secure
                       ___$20,000___ , due ___Jan. 1, 1930___ .
                       Lot ___1___ , Block ___2___ , ___NW___ Addition.

A sample abstract of title (continued)

12. Ruth Roe, widow,
    by Sheriff of _____
    County,
        to
    Samuel Brown.

Foreclosure of No. 11.
Notice of sale, _Feb. 1_ , 19_30_.
Affidavit of publication, _Feb. 1_ ,
    19_30_.
Proof of service, _Feb. 1_ , 19_30_.
Sheriff's certificate of sale, _March 1_ ,
    19_30_.
Filed _March 1_ , 19_30_.
Book _15_ of Miscellaneous, page _300_ .
Lot _1_ , Block _2_ , _NW_ Addition,
    sold _March 1_ , 19_30_, to Samuel
    Brown, for $_10,000_.

13. Samuel Brown and
    Sophy Brown, his wife,
        to
    James Jones.

Quitclaim Deed.
Date _April 1, 1940_ .
Filed _April 1, 1940_.
Book _27_ of Deeds, page _100_ .
North _250_ feet, front and rear, of Lot
    _1_ , Block _2_ , _NW_ Addition.

14. Taxes paid, except for year 1940, amounting to $15,000.

15. In re James Jones
    Bankruptcy
    No.

Petition of Debtor for arrangement
under Chapter XI of the Bankruptcy
Act, as amended (§ 301 et seq.) filed
Jan. 1, 1950 in U.S. District Court for
the District of New Hampshire.

---

certain lot, within a certain block, within a certain city. Another method of identifying a parcel of land is by METES AND BOUNDS. For metes and bounds land, a parcel is identified by its boundaries according to their terminal points and angles. Platted descriptions are used in urban areas, and metes and bounds descriptions are used mostly in rural areas.

2. Entry 2 is the original entry. It states the time and place that the U.S. government first conveyed this tract of land to a private individual. The description follows a progression from small to large. The parcel is identified first by its location within a certain section, which is located within a certain township, which is located within a certain range. Each range spans six miles and several townships, and each township contains several sections, which in turn are divided into quarters, which can also be divided into quarters. The last two lines of the right-hand column might read, for example, "Land Office Records, page 100. North ¼ of Section 36, T. [Township] 32, R. [Range] 22." The original description of any parcel of land comes from the measurements of the original government survey of the nineteenth century.

3. Entry 3 is the land PATENT, or John Doe's title defense. The land patent is issued by the government to operate as proof of title for the first governmentally recognized owner of the land. The land patent shows the date of the land transfer, the date the patent was filed with the government, the particular book of deeds containing the patent, and the land parcel as described in the original entry.

4. Entry 4 reveals that John Doe platted his quarter of section 36—that is, he subdivided the land and dedicated it to the public for sale. The beginning of the entry might read, "Plat of Stoneybrook Addition to the City of New Heidelberg." Note that township 36 has become, or has been incorporated into, what is now New Heidelberg. The entry continues with the date John Doe received approval from the city of New Heidelberg, the date the subdivision was filed with the county, the particular book of PLATS in which the subdivision is entered, and the original description of the land.

The subdivision is entered in the county's book of plats because New Heidelberg has chosen to identify its land parcels by plats, and not metes and bounds. Other means of identifying land parcels are sometimes employed. Land is sometimes identified by acres in rural areas, and by government lots for land adjacent to meandering lakes, but most of the land in the United States is identified by either plats or metes and bounds.

5. Entry 5 shows that John Doe sold a parcel of the subdivision to Richard Roe. Roe received a WARRANTY DEED, which serves as evidence of Doe's title. A warranty deed means that Doe has warranted to Roe that Doe is the rightful owner of the land. This type of deed has legal ramifications that benefit the purchaser, here Roe. There are other types of real estate deeds. A purchaser receives a TAX DEED, for example, when he or she buys real estate sold for nonpayment of taxes, and this purchase involves procedures that differ from those of other land purchases. A SHERIFF'S DEED is given to the purchaser of land sold by court order such as in a mortgage foreclosure, and this transaction also has special legal ramifications for the purchaser.

Because the land in the sample abstract is platted, the parcel is assigned a lot number, within a certain block, within the city of New Heidelberg—for example, this entry might read, "Lot 1, Block E, Stoneybrook Addition to City of New Heidelberg." The entry also contains information on when the warranty deed was signed, and when it was filed with the county.

6. Entry 6 shows that Richard Roe and Ruth Roe have mortgaged their property to John Smith. With an interest in lot 1 of block E as COLLATERAL, Smith has paid for the Roes' property, and the Roes have undertaken to repay Smith. The entry shows the date the mortgage agreement was signed and the date the mortgage was filed with the county. The remainder might read, "Book 1 of Mortgages, page 10, to secure $10,000, due January 10, 1910. Lot 1, Block E, Stoneybrook Addition."

7. Entry 7 shows that John Smith has assigned the mortgage on lot 1, block E, to William White. In other words, Smith has sold to White his mortgagee interest in lot 1, block E. An ASSIGNMENT can occur for any number of reasons, but often it is a sale made to satisfy debts. This particular action is entered in the book of assignments in the county seat.

8. Entry 8 shows that Richard Roe and Ruth Roe have paid off, or *satisfied*, the mortgage (*et ux* is Latin for "and wife"). This entry is

filed in the book of assignments in the county seat.

9. Entry 9 reveals that Richard Roe has died. This "Will and Probate" entry reports that, upon his death, Roe seeks to transfer ownership of lot 1, block E, in New Heidelberg, to his wife, Ruth Roe.

10. Entry 10 identifies Ruth Roe as the sole owner of the parcel. The PROBATE court, which tends to property matters surrounding the death of an individual, has approved the assignment of lot 1, block E, contained in Richard Roe's will.

11. Entry 11 shows that Ruth Roe has taken out a mortgage on lot 1, block E. She has borrowed money from Samuel Brown, using the real estate as collateral. The entry is identical to the first mortgage agreement with John Smith, entry 6.

12. Entry 12 reveals that Ruth Roe was unable to make her mortgage payments to Samuel Brown, and Brown has sought payment by exercising his right to force a sale of the property by foreclosing on the mortgage. The FORCED SALE was published in a newspaper. The dates of public notice, the publication AFFIDAVIT, and the SERVICE of notice to Roe are all entered in the abstract. The certificate of sale and the date the forced sale was filed with the county are also included.

This entry shows that Brown has purchased lot 1 at the resulting sheriff's sale of the property. The amount Brown paid would depend on the value of the real estate and the amount of the mortgage. The "No. 11" following "Foreclosure of" simply refers to the court document number of the foreclosure.

13. Entry 13 shows that Samuel Brown and Sophy Brown have sold a part of lot 1 to James Jones by QUITCLAIM DEED. Generally, a quitclaim deed transfers title to property without warranties that the title is free and clear. Owing to Ruth Roe's financial troubles, the Browns are probably uncertain of their title's completeness, so they have chosen to sell parts of their lot by quitclaim deed instead of warranty deed. Jones now owns a northern piece of lot 1, block E, of Stoneybrook Addition.

14. Entry 14 shows the taxes paid on the property, except for the current year. An entry of taxes paid is listed every time a tax assessment is made or paid in relation to the property of the abstract. Taxes listed in the abstract may include estate taxes, inheritance taxes, capital gains taxes, and

local government property taxes. The abstract should include the current amount of these taxes and certification that they have been paid.

15. Entry 15 reveals that, to avoid financial disaster, James Jones has filed bankruptcy. The northern piece of lot 1, block E, Stoneybrook Addition, New Heidelberg, is now being used to secure protection from creditors. Jones has given to the bankruptcy court a TRUST DEED, which the court retains until Jones has fulfilled his obligations under the financial rehabilitation plan approved by the court. Should Jones default on this arrangement, the court could order a forced sale of the property, with proceeds going to Jones's creditors.

The land covered by this particular abstract has now been defined; it is a certain northern piece of lot 1 of block E in the Stoneybrook Addition of New Heidelberg. The land to the south of this piece would have its own abstract, which would be identical to this abstract up to the point that lot 1 was divided up and part of it sold to Jones. Likewise, the abstract for the adjacent lot 2 on block E would have an abstract identical to this abstract up to the point that John Doe sold to Richard Roe the newly platted land of section 36 in township 32, range 22.

CROSS-REFERENCES

Deed; Property; Real Property; Recording of Land Titles; Torrens Title System.

ABUSE 📖 Everything that is contrary to good order established by usage. Departure from reasonable use; immoderate or improper use. Physical or mental maltreatment. Misuse. Deception.

To wrong in speech, reproach coarsely, disparage, revile, and malign. 📖

ABUSE OF DISCRETION 📖 A failure to take into proper consideration the facts and law relating to a particular matter; an arbitrary or unreasonable departure from PRECEDENTS and settled judicial custom. 📖

Where a trial court must exercise discretion in deciding a question, it must do so in a way that is not clearly against logic and the EVIDENCE. An improvident exercise of discretion is an ERROR of law and grounds for reversing a decision on APPEAL. It does not, however, necessarily amount to BAD FAITH, intentional wrong, or misconduct by the trial judge.

ABUSE OF POWER 📖 Improper use of authority by someone who has that authority because he or she holds a public office. 📖

Abuse of power is different from USURPATION of power, which is an exercise of authority that the offender does not actually have.

ABUSE OF PROCESS 📖 The use of legal PROCESS to accomplish an unlawful purpose; causing a SUMMONS, WRIT, WARRANT, MANDATE, or any other process to issue from a court in order to accomplish some purpose not intended by the law. 📖

For example, a grocer rents a small building but complains to the LANDLORD about the inadequate heating system, leaks in the roof, and potholes in the driveway. When the landlord fails to make the required repairs, the grocer decides the property is worth less and deducts $100 a month from his rent payments. The landlord starts a lawsuit to either recover the full amount of rent due or to oust the grocer and regain possession of the premises. The law in their state is fairly clear on the question: a TENANT has no right to force a landlord to make repairs by withholding a portion of the rent. The landlord knows that she has a good chance of winning her case, but she also wants to teach the grocer a lesson. On the first three occasions that the case comes up on the court calendar, the grocer closes his store and appears in court,

Number of Child Abuse and Neglect Victims Reported in 1991, by Race/Ethnicity

The total number of reports was 817,718 from 42 states.

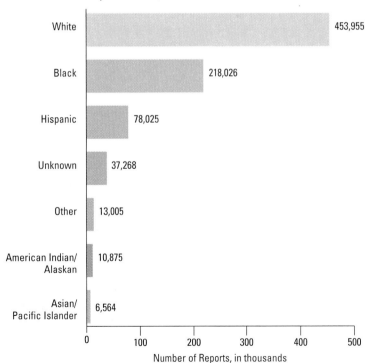

Source: U.S. Department of Health and Human Services, *National Child Abuse and Neglect Data System Working Paper 2, 1991 Summary Component.*

but the landlord does not show up. On the fourth occasion, the landlord comes to court and wins her case. The grocer, in a separate action for abuse of process, claims that the landlord is using the court's power to order him to appear simply to harass him. The court agrees and awards him money DAMAGES for lost income and inconvenience.

Abuse of process is a wrong committed during the course of LITIGATION. It is a perversion of lawfully issued process and is different from MALICIOUS PROSECUTION, a lawsuit started without any reasonable cause.

ABUSIVE 📖 Tending to deceive; practicing abuse; prone to ill-treat by coarse, insulting words or harmful acts. Using ill treatment; injurious, improper, hurtful, offensive, reproachful. 📖

Using abusive language, even though offensive, is not criminal unless it amounts to fighting words that, by their very utterance, tend to incite an immediate BREACH OF THE PEACE.

ABUT 📖 To reach; to touch. To touch at the end; be contiguous; join at a border or boundary; terminate on; end at; border on; reach or touch with an end. The term *abutting* implies a closer proximity than the term *adjacent*. 📖

When referring to REAL PROPERTY, abutting means that there is no intervening land between the abutting parcels. Generally, properties that share a common boundary are abutting. A statute may require abutting owners to pay proportional shares of the cost of a street improvement project.

ACADEMIC FREEDOM 📖 The right to teach as one sees fit, but not necessarily the right to teach evil. The term encompasses much more than teaching-related speech rights of teachers. 📖

Educational institutions are communities unto themselves with rules of their own, and when conflicts arise, the most common and compelling arguments involve freedom. As a result, the academic community is famous for blazing new trails of freedom in society, and it is often forced to confront its own concepts of freedom in the process.

Academic freedom was first introduced as a judicial *term of art* (a term with a specific legal meaning) by Supreme Court Justice William O. Douglas. In *Adler v. Board of Education*, 342 U.S. 485, 72 S. Ct. 380, 96 L. Ed. 517 (1952), the Supreme Court upheld a New York law (N.Y. Civ. Service Law § 12-a) that prohibited employment of teachers in public institutions if they were members of "subversive organizations." In a scathing dissent joined by Justice

Hugo L. Black, Douglas argued that such legislation created a police state and ran contrary to the First Amendment guarantee of free speech.

Justice Douglas equated academic freedom with the pursuit of truth. If academic freedom is the pursuit of truth and is protected by the First Amendment, reasoned Douglas, then the New York law should be struck down because it produced standardized thought. According to Douglas's dissent, the New York law created an academic atmosphere concerned not with intellectual stimulation but with such questions as "Why was the history teacher so openly hostile to Franco's Spain? Who heard overtones of revolution in the English teacher's discussion of *The Grapes of Wrath*? and What was behind the praise of Soviet progress in metallurgy in the chemistry class?" Douglas conceded that the public school systems need not become "cells for Communist activities," but he reminded the court that the Framers of the Constitution "knew the strength that comes when the mind is free."

Shortly after the *Adler* decision, a similar case began to take shape in New Hampshire that would receive very different treatment by the Supreme Court. On January 5, 1954, Paul M. Sweezy was summoned to appear before New Hampshire attorney general Louis C. Wyman for inquiries into Sweezy's political associations. Under a 1951 New Hampshire statute, the state attorney general was authorized to investigate "subversive activities" and determine whether "subversive persons" were located within the state (*Sweezy v. New Hampshire*, 354 U.S. 234, 77 S. Ct. 1203, 1 L. Ed. 2d 1311 [1957]). Wyman was especially interested in information on members of the Progressive party, an organization many politicians suspected of nurturing Communism in the United States.

Sweezy said he was unaware of any violations of the statute. He further stated that he would not answer any questions impertinent to the inquiry under the legislation, and he would not answer questions that seemed to infringe on his freedom of speech. Sweezy did answer numerous questions about himself, his views, and his activities, but he refused to answer questions about other people. In a later inquiry by the attorney general, Sweezy refused to comment about an article he had written and about a lecture he had delivered to a humanities class.

When Sweezy persisted in his refusal to talk about others and about his lecture, he was held in CONTEMPT of court and sent to the Merrimack

County jail. The Supreme Court of New Hampshire affirmed the conviction, and Sweezy appealed.

The U.S. Supreme Court reversed. The basis for the reversal was the New Hampshire statute's improper grant of broad interrogation powers to the attorney general and its failure to afford sufficient criminal protections to an accused. The Court commented strongly upon the threat such a statute posed to academic freedom.

The principal opinion, written by Chief Justice Earl Warren, questioned the wisdom of Wyman's legislative inquiry. With regard to the questions on Sweezy's lecture to the humanities class, the Chief Justice stated that "[t]o impose any strait jacket upon the intellectual leaders in our colleges and universities would imperil the future of our Nation."

Justice Felix Frankfurter wrote a separate concurring opinion. To Frankfurter, the call of the Court was to decide the case by BALANCING the right of the state to self-protection against the right of a citizen to academic freedom and political privacy. Frankfurter concluded that Wyman's reasons for questioning Sweezy on academics were "grossly inadequate" given "the grave harm resulting from governmental intrusion into the intellectual life of a university."

Neither of the PLURALITY opinions in *Sweezy* would have found all congressional inquiries into academia to be unconstitutional. However, both opinions helped free educators in later cases by recognizing and emphasizing the danger of restricting academic thought. In *Keyishian v. Board of Regents*, 385 U.S. 589, 87 S. Ct. 675, 17 L. Ed. 629 (1967), the Supreme Court finally awarded to teachers and professors the full complement of free speech and political privacy rights afforded other citizens. Political "loyalty oaths" required of New York State employees (including educators) under state civil service laws were declared void, and New York education laws against "treasonable or seditious speech" were found to violate the First Amendment right to free speech. According to the *Keyishian* decision, "[A]cademic freedom . . . is a special concern of the First Amendment, which does not tolerate laws that cast a pall of orthodoxy over the classroom."

The tension between academic oversight and academic freedom did not end with the *Keyishian* case. The Supreme Court later decided several cases that identified more precisely how much control school authorities may exercise over education. The Court held in *Board of Education v. Pico*, 457 U.S. 853, 102 S. Ct. 2799,

73 L. Ed. 2d 435 (1982), that a school board can control curriculum and book selection, but it may not remove "objectionable" books from public school libraries solely in response to community pressure. Among the books that the Island Trees Union Free School District No. 26 in New York had banned in the mid-1970s were *Slaughterhouse Five*, by Kurt Vonnegut, Jr., *Black Boy*, by Richard Wright, *Naked Ape*, by Desmond Morris, and *The Fixer*, by Bernard Malamud.

School boards and state legislatures generally control public school curriculums, but their control is not complete. A state statute will be struck down if it requires public schools to teach creationism when they present evolution, and vice versa. According to the Court in *Edwards v. Aguillard*, 482 U.S. 578, 107 S. Ct. 2573, 96 L. Ed. 2d 510 (1987), such a law undermines a comprehensive scientific education and impermissibly endorses religion by advancing the religious belief that a supernatural power created human beings. The Supreme Court has also held that if school authorities can show additional independent grounds for discharge, they may terminate a teacher for disruptive speech even if a substantial motivation for the termination was speech on issues of public concern (*Pickering v. Board of Education*, 391 U.S. 563, 88 S. Ct. 1731, 20 L. Ed. 2d 811 [1968]; *Board of Education v. Doyle*, 429 U.S. 274, 97 S. Ct. 568, 50 L. Ed. 2d 471 [1977]). This precedent seemed to give school authori-

Paul M. Sweezy, a New York magazine editor and former Harvard professor, refused to answer questions about his political associations from New Hampshire attorney general Louis C. Wyman. Sweezy was jailed for contempt of court but he won on appeal.

ties ample means to elude liability for unconstitutional terminations. However, neither of the principles helped City University of New York (CUNY) when it was sued by the chair of its black studies department.

Professor Leonard Jeffries specialized in black studies and the history of Africa, and his teaching style at CUNY was controversial. Some students felt that Jeffries discouraged classroom debate, whereas others applauded him for verbalizing the frustrations of many African Americans. Jeffries referred to Europeans as "ice people" and as "egotistic, individualistic, and exploitative." Africans, on the other hand, were "sun people" who had "humanistic, spiritualistic value system[s]."

On July 20, 1991, Jeffries spoke at the Empire State Black Arts and Cultural Festival, in Albany, New York. In his speech, he assailed perceived Jewish power, asserting that Jews controlled CUNY and Hollywood and had financed the American slave trade. The speech attracted national attention and placed CUNY on the horns of a dilemma: it could punish Jeffries and risk running afoul of the First Amendment and of academic freedom principles, or it could do nothing and risk losing expected income from offended school benefactors. For several months, the university wrestled with the problem. Then, in October, the board of trustees voted, without explanation, to limit Jeffries's current appointment as chair to one year instead of the customary three.

At the end of October, Jeffries wrote to Jeffrey Rosen, dean of social sciences, that he was declaring "war" on the faculty. In November, Jeffries scolded President Bernard Harleston as Harleston was leaving the administration building. By December, continuing performance reviews of Jeffries had become increasingly negative. On March 23, 1992, the CUNY Board of Trustees appointed Professor Edmund Gordon to the position of black studies chair. Jeffries filed suit in federal court against the CUNY trustees, Harleston, and Chancellor W. Ann Reynolds, on June 5, 1992.

Jeffries argued that the defendants violated his First Amendment free speech rights and his Fourteenth Amendment due process rights when they denied him a full three-year term as chair of black studies. The jury agreed with Jeffries that a substantial motivating factor in his dismissal was his speech in Albany. The jury also found that CUNY had not shown that Jeffries would have lost the chair had Jeffries not delivered the Albany speech. The jury further found that Jeffries had not disrupted the operation of the black studies department, the college, or the university. The jury did find, however, that CUNY had reasonably expected the speech to have a detrimental effect on the school. Despite this seemingly justifiable excuse for the school's action, the jury finally found that CUNY had deprived Jeffries of property (the position of chair) without DUE PROCESS OF LAW.

The district court judge held that Jeffries's First Amendment rights had been violated. On the issue of LIABILITY, the jury awarded Jeffries $400,000 in PUNITIVE DAMAGES: $30,000 against President Harleston, $50,000 against Chancellor Reynolds, and $80,000 against each of CUNY's four trustees. After the verdict, Harleston, Reynolds, and each of the trustees moved to overturn the award. They argued that the verdict was INCONSISTENT with the jury's findings and not supported by the evidence. The defendants also maintained that they were immune from individual liability as state officials acting in their official capacity. Jeffries filed a motion requesting a court order reinstating him as chair of CUNY's black studies department.

On August 4, 1993, the district court judge reduced Jeffries's recovery in damages by $40,000, but awarded him the black studies chair. According to the judge, it was reasonable for the jury to find that CUNY had terminated Jeffries solely because of the views he expressed in the Albany speech, without constitutional grounds. The school apparently had ample opportunity to gather and present evidence that Jeffries's speech had disrupted the efficient and effective operation of the university, but instead chose to argue that Jeffries had been terminated for tardiness, sending grades to the school by mail, and brutish behavior. The lack of evidence to buttress CUNY's defenses supported Jeffries's arguments that his free speech rights had been violated and that he deserved to be reinstated to the position of black studies chair.

Though the concept of academic freedom has traditionally been applied only to teachers, it has begun to creep into lower-court opinions involving the rights of students. Several Supreme Court cases are cited as creating a basis for such rights. In *Healy v. James*, 408 U.S. 169, 92 S. Ct. 2338, 33 L. Ed. 2d 266 (1972), the Supreme Court held that a public university may deny campus access to provably disruptive groups, but it may not deny access based on the views the students wish to express. The Supreme Court ruled in *Hazelwood School District v. Kuhlmeier*, 484 U.S. 260, 108 S. Ct. 562, 98

L. Ed. 2d 592 (1988), that a public school may censor the content of a student newspaper if the newspaper is not an entirely public forum and the reason for censure is related to a legitimate educational concern. In *Board of Education v. Mergens*, 496 U.S. 226, 110 S. Ct. 2356, 110 L. Ed. 2d 191 (1990), the Court approved the establishment of a Christian student group in a public school. The Court also held in *Mergens* that a school's refusal to permit a religious student group to meet at school and use its facilities violates the federal Equal Access Act (Education for Economic Security Act § 802, 20 U.S.C.A. § 4071 et seq. [1984]) if the school provides such access to other noncurriculum student groups.

CROSS-REFERENCES

Censorship; Colleges and Universities; Douglas, William O.; First Amendment; Frankfurter, Felix; Freedom of Speech; Loyalty Oaths; Religion; Schools and School Districts; Warren, Earl.

ACADEMIC YEAR 📖 That period of time necessary to complete an actual course of study during a school year. 📖

Social Security benefits may terminate at the end of an academic year, or a deferment from compulsory military service may continue only during an academic year.

ACADEMY OF CRIMINAL JUSTICE SCIENCES The Academy of Criminal Justice Sciences (ACJS) was founded in 1963 to foster professionalism in the criminal justice system by advancing the quality of education and research programs in the field. The academy seeks to enrich education and research programs in institutions of higher learning, criminal justice agencies, and agencies in related fields by improving cooperation and communication, by serving as a clearinghouse for the collection and dissemination of information produced by the programs, and by promoting the highest ethical and personal standards in criminal justice research and education. The academy presents numerous awards for outstanding contributions by individuals in the field. The members of the academy are individual teachers, administrators, researchers, students, and practitioners.

The academy publishes the *Journal of Criminal Justice* quarterly and a directory annually. It holds annual meetings in March.

ACCEDE 📖 To consent or to agree, as to accede to another's point of view. To enter an office or to accept a position, as to accede to the presidency. 📖

ACCELERATION 📖 A hastening; a shortening of the time until some event takes place. 📖

A person who has the right to take POSSESSION of property at some future time may have that right accelerated if the present holder loses his or her legal right to the property. If a LIFE ESTATE fails for any reason, the REMAINDER is accelerated.

The principle of acceleration can be applied when it becomes clear that one party to a CONTRACT is not going to perform his or her obligations. ANTICIPATORY REPUDIATION, or the possibility of future breach, makes it possible to move the right to REMEDIES back to the time of repudiation rather than to wait for the time when PERFORMANCE would be due and an actual breach would occur.

ACCELERATION CLAUSE 📖 The provision in a credit agreement, such as a MORTGAGE, NOTE, BOND, or DEED OF TRUST, that allows the lender to require immediate payment of all money due if certain conditions occur before the time that payment would otherwise be due. 📖

The agreement may call for acceleration whenever there is a DEFAULT of any important

A sample acceleration clause

If any default be made in the payment of the said principal sum or interest, or of any part thereof, on the day whereon the same is made payable as hereinbefore expressed, or in the performance of any of the covenants on the part of the mortgagor herein contained (and such default shall continue for the period of _____ days), then and in either or any such case the mortgagee, the mortgagee's executors, administrators, or assigns, may elect without notice that the whole of the said principal sum hereby secured and then remaining unpaid, together with the accrued interest thereon, shall become due and payable forthwith, and, in addition to the other remedies hereinbefore provided, may enforce payment thereof and of all sums expended under the terms of this mortgage by foreclosure or otherwise.

The mortgagors shall pay on the _____ day of _____ , (year), the sum of $ _____ , and a like sum of $ _____ every _____ months thereafter, together with the final installment which shall be in the amount of $ _____ , until the principal sum and interest shall have been fully paid, which payment when and as made shall be applied by the mortgagee, as holder of said notes hereby secured, as follows: first, to the payment of interest on said unpaid principal sum to the end of said _____ months' period, according to the amortization table printed on the back of the principal note secured by this mortgage [*or* according to amortization note secured hereby]; and second, to the payment and reduction of said principal sum. If the mortgagors shall fail to make payment of any amortization payment on the day it falls due, then the defaulted payment shall bear interest at the rate of _____ per cent per annum until paid, and the mortgagee may at his or her election declare all subsequent payments together with the principal sum due and payable.

obligation, such as nonpayment of PRINCIPAL or INTEREST, or the failure to pay insurance premiums.

ACCEPTANCE 📖 The taking and receiving of anything in good part as if it were a TACIT agreement to a preceding act, which might have been defeated or avoided if such acceptance had not been made. The act of a person to whom a thing is offered or tendered by another, whereby he or she receives the thing with the INTENTION of retaining it, such intention being evidenced by a sufficient act.

The exercise of power conferred by an OFFER by PERFORMANCE of some act. 📖

When a person who is offered a GIFT by someone keeps the gift, this indicates his or her acceptance of it. In the law of SALES, which governs business dealings between merchants, a buyer demonstrates his or her acceptance of goods that are not exactly what he or she had ordered from the seller by telling the seller that he or she will keep the goods even though they are not what was ordered; by failing to reject the goods; or by doing something to the goods inconsistent with the seller's ownership of them, such as selling the goods to customers of the buyer's store.

In the law of contracts, acceptance is one person's compliance with the terms of an offer made by another. Acceptance occurs in the law of insurance when an insurer agrees to receive a person's application for insurance and to issue a policy protecting the person against certain risks, such as fire or theft.

Acceptance also occurs when a bank pays a check written by a customer who has a checking account with that bank.

Types of Acceptance An acceptance may be conditional, express, or implied.

Conditional Acceptance A conditional acceptance, sometimes called a QUALIFIED ACCEPTANCE, occurs when a person to whom an offer has been made tells the offeror that he or she is willing to agree to the offer provided that some changes are made in its terms or that some condition or event occurs. This type of acceptance operates as a COUNTEROFFER. A counteroffer must be accepted by the original offeror before a contract can be established between the parties.

Another type of conditional acceptance occurs when a DRAWEE promises to pay a DRAFT upon the happening of a condition, such as a shipment of goods reaching its destination on the date specified in the contract.

Express Acceptance An express acceptance occurs when a person clearly and explicitly agrees to an offer or agrees to pay a draft that is presented for payment.

Implied Acceptance An implied acceptance is one that is not directly stated but is demonstrated by any acts indicating a person's assent to the proposed bargain. An implied acceptance occurs when a shopper selects an item in a supermarket and pays the cashier for it. The shopper's conduct indicates that he or she has agreed to the supermarket owner's offer to sell the item for the price stated on it.

ACCESS 📖 Freedom of approach or communication; or the means, power, or opportunity of approaching, communicating, or passing to and from. Sometimes importing the occurrence of sexual intercourse; otherwise as importing opportunity of communication for that purpose as between husband and wife.

In REAL PROPERTY law, the term *access* denotes the right vested in the owner of the land that adjoins a road or other highway to go and return from his own land to the highway without obstruction. *Access* to property does not necessarily carry with it POSSESSION.

For purposes of establishing element of access by defendant in COPYRIGHT infringement action, *access* is ordinarily defined as opportunity to copy.

Prisoners are entitled to have access to court. Prison officials cannot prevent prisoners from filing papers or appearing in court even if they honestly think that such prevention would help them maintain discipline and good order.

Owners of real property are entitled to some means of access to their property from a road or highway. They do not necessarily need to own a corridor of land from their property to the nearest road, but they may claim an EASEMENT of access.

In a PATERNITY SUIT, access means the opportunity to have had sexual relations. When there is a question about who is the father of a certain child, it is appropriate for a court to determine which man had access to the mother around the estimated time of conception. A man charged with being the father of an illegitimate child may plead the defense of multiple access—that the mother had several lovers at the time of conception.

ACCESSION Coming into POSSESSION of a right or office; increase; augmentation; addition.

The right to all that one's own PROPERTY produces, whether that property be movable or immovable; and the right to that which is united to it by accession, either naturally or artificially. The right to own things that become a part of something already owned.

A principle derived from the CIVIL LAW, by which the owner of property becomes entitled to all that it produces, and to all that is added or united to it, either naturally or artificially (that is, by the labor or skill of another) even where such addition extends to a change of form or materials; and by which, on the other hand, the possessor of property becomes entitled to it, as against the original owner, where the addition made to it by skill and labor is of greater value than the property itself, or where the change effected in its form is so great as to render it impossible to restore it to its original shape.

Generally, *accession* signifies acquisition of title to PERSONAL PROPERTY by bestowing labor on it that converts it into an entirely different thing or by incorporation of property into a union with other property.

The commencement or inauguration of a sovereign's reign.

For example, a person who owns property

along a river also takes ownership of any additional land that builds up along the riverbank. This right may extend to additions that result from the work or skill of another person. The buyer of a car who fails to make scheduled payments cannot get back his new spark plugs after the car is repossessed because they have become a part of the whole car. The principle of accession does not necessarily apply, however, where the addition has substantially improved the value and changed the character of the property, as when by mistake someone else's grapes were made into wine or someone else's clay made into bricks. In such cases, the original owner might recover only the value of the raw material rather than take ownership of the finished product.

In the context of a treaty, accession may be gained in either of two ways: (1) the new member nation may be formally accepted by all the nations already parties to the TREATY; or (2) the new nation may simply bind itself to the obligations already existing in the treaty. Frequently, a treaty will expressly provide that certain nations or categories of nations may accede. In some cases, the parties to a treaty will invite one or more nations to accede to the treaty.

ACCESSORY Aiding or contributing in a secondary way or assisting in or contributing to as a subordinate.

In criminal law, contributing to or aiding in the commission of a CRIME. One who, without being present at the commission of an offense, becomes guilty of such offense, not as a chief actor, but as a participant, as by command, advice, instigation, or concealment; either before or after the fact or commission.

One who aids, ABETS, commands, or counsels another in the commission of a crime.

In COMMON LAW, an accessory could not be found guilty unless the actual PERPETRATOR was convicted. In most U.S. jurisdictions today, however, an accessory can be convicted even if the principal actor is not arrested or is acquitted. The prosecution must establish that the accessory in some way instigated, furthered, or concealed the crime. Typically, punishment for a convicted accessory is not as severe as that for the perpetrator.

An accessory must knowingly promote or contribute to the crime. In other words, she or he must aid or encourage the offense deliberately, not accidentally. The accessory may withdraw from the crime by denouncing the plans, refusing to assist with the crime, contacting the police, or trying to stop the crime from occurring.

An *accessory before the fact* is someone behind the scenes who orders a crime or helps another person commit it. Many jurisdictions now refer to accessories before the fact as parties to the crime or even ACCOMPLICES. This substitution of terms can be confusing because accessories are fundamentally different from accomplices. Strictly speaking, whereas an accomplice may be present at the crime scene, an accessory may not. Also, an accomplice generally is considered to be as guilty of the crime as the perpetrator, whereas an accessory has traditionally received a lighter punishment.

An *accessory after the fact* is someone who knows that a crime has occurred but nonetheless helps to conceal it. Today, this action is often termed OBSTRUCTING JUSTICE or harboring a fugitive.

An infamous accessory after the fact was Dr. Samuel A. Mudd, the physician and Confederate sympathizer who set John Wilkes Booth's leg after it was broken when the assassin jumped from President Abraham Lincoln's box at Ford Theater. Despite Mudd's protestation of innocence, he was tried and convicted as an accessory after the fact in Lincoln's murder. He was sentenced to life imprisonment at Fort Jefferson in the Dry Tortugas off Key West, Florida. President Andrew Johnson pardoned Mudd in 1869, and the U.S. Congress gave him an official pardon in 1979.

ACCIDENT 📖 The word *accident* is derived from the Latin verb *accidere*, signifying "fall upon, befall, happen, chance." In its most commonly accepted meaning, or in its ordinary or popular sense, the word may be defined as meaning: some sudden and unexpected event taking place without expectation, upon the instant, rather than something that continues, progresses or develops; something happening by chance; something unforeseen, unexpected, unusual, extraordinary, or phenomenal, taking place not according to the usual course of things or events, out of the range of ordinary calculations; that which exists or occurs abnormally, or an uncommon occurrence. The word may be employed as denoting a calamity, CASUALTY, catastrophe, disaster, an undesirable or unfortunate happening; any unexpected personal injury resulting from any unlooked for mishap or occurrence; any unpleasant or unfortunate occurrence that causes injury, loss, suffering, or death; some untoward occurrence aside from the usual course of events. An event that takes place without one's foresight or expectation; an undesigned, sudden, and unexpected event. 📖

Accident is not always a precise legal term. It may be used generally in reference to various types of mishaps, or it may be given a technical meaning that applies when used in a certain statute or kind of case. Where it is used in a

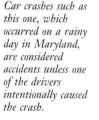

Car crashes such as this one, which occurred on a rainy day in Maryland, are considered accidents unless one of the drivers intentionally caused the crash.

general sense, no particular significance can be attached to it. Where it is precisely defined, as in a statute, that definition strictly controls any decision about whether a certain event covered by that statute was in fact an accident.

In its most limited sense, the word *accident* is used only for events that occur without the intervention of a human being. This kind of accident also may be called an ACT OF GOD. It is an event that no person caused or could have prevented—such as a tornado, a tidal wave, or an ice storm. An accident insurance policy can by its terms be limited to coverage only for this type of accident. Damage by hail to a field of wheat may be considered such an accident.

A policy of insurance, by its very nature, covers only accidents and not intentionally caused injuries. That principle explains why courts will read some exceptions into any insurance policy, whether or not they are expressly stated. For example, life insurance generally will not compensate for a suicide, and ordinary automobile insurance will not cover damages sustained when the owner is drag racing.

Accident insurance policies frequently insure not only against an act of God but also for accidents caused by a person's carelessness. An insured homeowner will expect coverage, for example, if someone drowns in his or her pool, even though the accident might have occurred because someone in the family left the gate open.

Not every unintended event is an accident for which insurance benefits can be paid; all the circumstances in a particular case must first be considered. For example, a policeman who waded into a surging crowd of forty or fifty fighting teenagers and then experienced a heart attack was found to have suffered from an accident. In another case, a man who was shot when he was found in bed with another man's wife was also found to have died in an accident because death is not the usual or expected result of adultery. However, the family of another man was not allowed to collect insurance benefits when he was shot after starting a fight with a knife. In that case, the court ruled that deadly force was a predictable response to a life-threatening attack, whether the instigator actually anticipated it or not.

Different states apply different standards when determining if an accident justifies payment of benefits under WORKERS' COMPENSATION. Some states strictly limit benefits to events that clearly are accidents. They will permit payment when a sudden and unexpected strain causes an immediate injury during the course of work but

10 Leading Causes of Death in the U.S. in 1993

Additional facts:
Total number of deaths: 2,268,000
Number of deaths not accounted for in top ten: 425,770
Percentage of deaths not in top ten: 18.8%

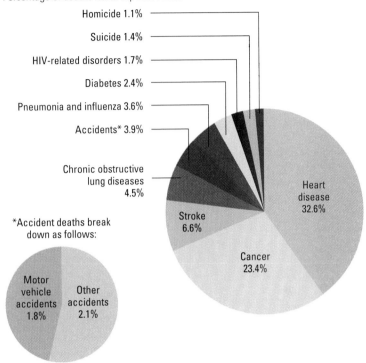

Source: National Center for Health Statistics, U.S. Department of Health and Human Services.

they will not permit payment when an injury gradually results from prolonged assaults on the body. Under this approach, a worker who is asphyxiated by a lethal dose of carbon monoxide when he goes into a blast furnace to make repairs would be deemed to have suffered in an accident. However, a worker who contracts lung cancer after years of exposure to irritating dust in a factory could not claim to have been injured in an accident. Because of the remedial purpose of workers' compensation schemes, many states are liberal in allowing compensation. In one state, a woman whose existing arthritic condition was aggravated when she took a job stuffing giblets into partially frozen chickens on a conveyor belt was allowed to collect workers' compensation benefits.

Insurance policies may set limits to the amount of benefits recoverable for one accident. A certain automobile insurance policy allowed a maximum of only $200 to compensate for damaged clothing or luggage in the event of an accident. When luggage was stolen from the insured automobile, however, a court ruled that the event was not an accident and the maximum did not apply. The owner was allowed to recover the full value of the lost property.

Sometimes the duration of an accident must be determined. For example, if a drunken driver hit one car and then continued driving until he or she collided with a truck, a court might have to determine whether the two victims will share the maximum amount of money payable under the driver's liability insurance policy or whether each will collect the full maximum as a result of a separate accident.

CROSS-REFERENCES

Automobiles: No-Fault Automobile Insurance; Automobiles: What to Do if You Are in an Auto Accident; Insurance.

ACCIDENTAL DEATH BENEFIT 📖 A provision of a life INSURANCE policy stating that if the insured—the person whose life has been insured—dies in an ACCIDENT, the beneficiary of the policy—the person to whom its proceeds are payable—will receive twice the face value of the policy. 📖

The insurance company that is liable for the payment of such a benefit will conduct a thorough investigation into the cause of death of the insured person before paying the claim.

Another name for an accidental death benefit is a DOUBLE INDEMNITY clause.

ACCIDENTAL KILLING 📖 A death caused by a lawful act done under the reasonable belief that no harm was likely to result. 📖

Accidental killing is different from INVOLUNTARY MANSLAUGHTER, which causes death by an unlawful act or a lawful act done in an unlawful way.

ACCIDENTAL VEIN 📖 An imprecise term that refers generally to a continuous body of a mineral or mineralized rock filling a seam other than the principal vein that led to the discovery of the mining claim or location. 📖

See also MINES AND MINERALS.

ACCIDENTS OF NAVIGATION 📖 Mishaps that are peculiar to travel by sea or to normal navigation; accidents caused at sea by the action of the elements, rather than by a failure to exercise good handling, working, or navigating of a ship. Such accidents could not have been avoided by the exercise of nautical skill or prudence. 📖

See also MARITIME LAW; NAVIGABLE RIVERS.

ACCOMMODATION ENDORSEMENT 📖 The act of a third person—the ACCOMMODATION PARTY—in writing his or her name on the back of a COMMERCIAL PAPER without any CONSIDERATION, but merely to benefit the person to whom the paper is payable or to enable the person who made the document—the maker—to obtain money or credit on it. 📖

An accommodation endorsement is a loan of the endorser's CREDIT up to the face amount of the paper.

ACCOMMODATION PAPER 📖 A type of COMMERCIAL PAPER (such as a bill or note promising that money will be paid to someone) that is signed by another person—the ACCOMMODATION PARTY—as a favor to the promisor—the accommodated party—so that CREDIT may be extended to him or her on the basis of the paper. 📖

Accommodation paper guarantees that the money lent will be repaid by the accommodation party on the date specified in the commercial paper if the accommodated party fails to repay it. A lender often uses an accommodation paper when the person who is seeking a loan is

A sample accommodation note of a member of a cooperative

_____ , (year)

On demand, for value received, I promise to pay to the order of _____ Cooperative Association _____ Dollars, at _____ , without interest until after demand, and then with interest at the rate of _____ per cent per annum from date of demand until paid.

This note is given to be used as collateral security only, and may be endorsed over to any bank or person making any loan to the said _____ Cooperative Association, of which association I am a stockholder, and the making of any such loan shall be sufficient consideration for my making this note. At any time any bank or person, who, having made a loan to the _____ Cooperative Association and holding this note as collateral security, may deem themselves insecure on any such loan, they may make demand on this note and enforce collection.

Demand made _____

[Signature]

considered a poor credit risk, such as a person who has a history of being delinquent in the payment of installment loans. By having a person who is a good credit risk cosign the promissory note, the lender's financial interests are protected.

An accommodation bill and an accommodation note are two types of commercial papers.

ACCOMMODATION PARTY ▥ One who signs a COMMERCIAL PAPER for the purpose of lending his or her name and CREDIT to another party to the document—the accommodated party—to help that party obtain a loan or an extension of credit. ▥

A person wanting to obtain a car loan, for example, may offer a finance company a PROMISSORY NOTE for the amount of the requested loan, promising to repay the amount over a number of years. If the company does not consider the person a good credit risk (one who will be able to repay the loan), it will request that someone else sign the note to ensure that the company will be repaid. Such a person may be an accommodation endorser, because he or she endorses the note after it has been completed, or an accommodation maker, because he or she must sign the note with the accommodation party.

An accommodation party is liable to the person or business that extended credit to the accommodation party, but not to the accommodated party. The accommodation party is liable for the amount specified on the accommodation paper. If an accommodation party repays the debt, he or she can seek reimbursement from the accommodated party.

ACCOMPANY ▥ To go along with; to go with or to attend as a companion or associate. ▥

A motor vehicle statute may require beginning drivers or drivers under a certain age to be accompanied by a licensed adult driver whenever operating an automobile. To comply with such a law, the licensed adult must supervise the beginner and be seated in such a way as to be able to render advice and assistance.

ACCOMPLICE ▥ One who knowingly, voluntarily, and with common intent unites with the principal offender in the commission of a CRIME. One who is in some way concerned or associated in commission of crime; partaker of guilt; one who aids or assists, or is an ACCESSORY. One who is guilty of complicity in crime charged, either by being present and aiding or abetting in it, or having advised and encouraged it, though absent from place when it was committed, though mere presence, acquiescence, or silence, in the absence of a duty to act, is not enough, no matter how reprehensible it may be,

to constitute one an accomplice. One is liable as an accomplice to the crime of another if he or she gave assistance or encouragement or failed to perform a legal duty to prevent it with the intent thereby to promote or facilitate commission of the crime. ▥

An accomplice may assist or encourage the principal offender with the intent to have the crime committed, the same as the chief actor. An accomplice may or may not be present when the crime is actually committed. However, without sharing the criminal intent, one who is merely present when a crime occurs and stands by silently is not an accomplice, no matter how reprehensible his or her inaction.

Some crimes are so defined that certain persons cannot be charged as accomplices even when their conduct significantly aids the chief offender. For example, a businessperson who yields to the EXTORTION demands of a racketeer or a parent who pays ransom to a kidnapper may be unwise, but neither is a principal in the commission of the crimes. Even a victim may unwittingly create a perfect opportunity for the commission of a crime but cannot be considered an accomplice because he or she lacks a criminal intent.

An accomplice may supply money, guns, or supplies. In one case, an accomplice provided his own blood to be poured on selective service files. The driver of the getaway car, a lookout, or a person who entices the victim or distracts possible witnesses is an accomplice.

An accomplice can be convicted even if the person that he or she aids or encourages is not. He or she is usually subject to the same degree of punishment as the principal offender. In the 1982 decision of *Enmund v. Florida*, 458 U.S. 782, 102 S. Ct. 3368, 73 L. Ed. 2d 1140, the Supreme Court of the United States ruled that the death penalty could not be constitutionally imposed upon an accomplice to a felony-murder, a crime leading to MURDER, if he or she had no intention to, or did not, kill the victim. Earl Enmund drove the getaway car from a robbery that resulted in the murder of its victims, an elderly married couple. Although Enmund remained in the car during the robbery and consequent killings and the trial record did not establish that he intended to facilitate or participate in a murder, the trial court sentenced him to death, along with the persons who actually killed the victims, upon his conviction for robbery in the first degree. In overturning the decision, the Supreme Court reasoned that to condemn such a defendant to death violated the Eighth and Fourteenth Amendments to the Constitution, which prohibited CRUEL AND UNUSUAL PUNISHMENT in state prosecutions. The death penalty was an excessive punishment in light of the "criminal culpability" of this accomplice.

CROSS-REFERENCES

Capital Punishment; Criminal Law; Eighth Amendment; Fourteenth Amendment; Sentence.

ACCOMPLICE WITNESS 📖 A witness to a crime who, either as principal, ACCOMPLICE, or ACCESSORY, was connected with the CRIME by unlawful act or omission on his or her part, transpiring either before, at time of, or after commission of the offense, and whether or not he or she was present and participated in the crime. 📖

Generally, there can be no conviction solely on the basis of what is said by an accomplice witness; there must be evidence from an unrelated source to corroborate the witness's testimony.

ACCORD 📖 An AGREEMENT that settles a DISPUTE, generally requiring a compromise or SATISFACTION with something less than what was originally demanded. 📖

ACCORD AND SATISFACTION 📖 A method of discharging a CLAIM whereby the parties agree to give and accept something in settlement of the claim and perform the AGREEMENT, the *accord* being the agreement and the *satisfaction* its execution or PERFORMANCE, and it is a new CONTRACT substituted for an old contract which is thereby discharged, or for an OBLIGATION or CAUSE OF ACTION which is settled, and must have all of the elements of a valid contract. 📖

To constitute an accord and satisfaction, there must have been a genuine dispute that is settled by a MEETING OF THE MINDS with an intent to compromise. Where there is an actual controversy, an accord and satisfaction may be used to settle it. The controversy may be founded on contract or TORT. It can arise from a collision of motor vehicles, a failure to deliver oranges ordered and paid for, or a refusal to finish constructing an office building, etc.

In former times, courts recognized an accord and satisfaction only when the amount of the controversy was not in dispute. Otherwise, the resolution had to be by COMPROMISE AND SETTLEMENT. The technical distinction is no longer made, however, and a compromise of amount can properly be part of an accord and satisfaction. The amount, whether disputed or not, is usually monetary, as when a pedestrian claims $10,000 in damages from the driver who struck him. The amount can be a variety of other things, however, as when a homeowner claims that she ordered a swimming pool thirty-six feet long rather than thirty-five feet or when an employee insists that he is entitled to eleven rather than ten days of vacation during the rest of the calendar year.

An accord and satisfaction can be made only by persons who have the legal CAPACITY to enter into a contract. A settlement is not binding on an insane person, for example; and an INFANT may have the right to DISAFFIRM the contract. Therefore, a person, such as a GUARDIAN, acting on behalf of a person incapable of contracting for himself or herself may make an accord and satisfaction for the person committed to his or her charge, but the law may require that the guardian's actions be supervised by a court. An EXECUTOR or ADMINISTRATOR may bind an ESTATE; a TRUSTEE can accept an accord and satisfaction for a TRUST; and an OFFICER can negotiate a settlement for a CORPORATION.

A third person may give something in SATISFACTION of a party's DEBT. In such a case, an accord and satisfaction is effected if the CREDITOR accepts the offer and the debtor authorizes, participates in, or later agrees to, the transaction.

For example, a widower has an automobile accident but is mentally unable to cope with a lawsuit because his wife has just died. He gratefully accepts the offer of a close family friend to talk to the other driver, who has been threatening a lawsuit. The friend convinces the other driver that both drivers are at fault to some extent. The friend offers to pay the other driver $500 in damages in exchange for a written statement that she will not make any claim against the widower for damages resulting from the accident. The family friend and the other driver each sign a copy of the statement for the other, and when the payment is made, the accord and satisfaction is complete. If the other driver then sues the widower for more money on account of the accident, the widower could show that he agreed to let his friend negotiate an accord and satisfaction, and the court would deny RELIEF.

An accord and satisfaction is a contract, and all the essential elements of a contract must be present. The agreement must include a definite OFFER of settlement and an unconditional ACCEPTANCE of the offer according to its terms. It must be final and definite, closing the matter it covers and leaving nothing unsettled or open to question. The agreement may call for full payment or some compromise and it need not be based on an earlier agreement of the parties. It does not necessarily have to be in writing unless it comes within the STATUTE OF FRAUDS.

Unless there are matters intentionally left outside the accord and satisfaction, it settles the entire controversy between the parties. It extinguishes all the obligations arising out of the underlying contract or tort. Where only one of two or more parties on one side settles, this ordinarily operates to discharge all of them. The reason for this is the rule that there should be only one satisfaction for a single injury or wrong. This rule does not apply where the satisfaction is neither given nor accepted with the intention that it settle the entire matter.

An accord without satisfaction generally means nothing. With a full satisfaction, the accord can be used to defeat any further claims by either party unless it was reached by FRAUD, DURESS, or MUTUAL MISTAKE.

An accord and satisfaction can be distinguished from other forms of resolving legal disputes. A payment or performance means that the original obligations were met. A RELEASE is a formal relinquishment of the right to enforce the original obligations and not necessarily a compromise, as in accord and satisfaction. An ARBITRATION is a settlement of the dispute by some outside person whose determination of an award is voluntarily accepted by the parties. A COMPOSITION WITH CREDITORS is very much like an accord but has elements not required for an accord and satisfaction. It is used only for disputes between a debtor and a certain number of his or her creditors, while an accord and satisfaction can be used to settle any kind of controversy—whether arising from contract or tort—and ordinarily involves only two parties. Although distinctions have occasionally been drawn between an accord and satisfaction and a compromise and settlement, the two terms are often used interchangeably. A NOVATION is a kind of accord in which the promise alone, rather than full performance, is satisfaction, and is accepted as a binding resolution of the dispute.

ACCOUCHEMENT The act of giving birth to a child.

The fact of accouchement may be proved by the direct testimony of someone who was present, such as a midwife or a physician, at the time of birth. It may be significant in proving parentage; for example, where there is some question about who is entitled to inherit property from an elderly person who died leaving only distant relatives.

ACCOUNT A written list of transactions, noting money owed and money paid; a detailed statement of mutual demands arising out of a CONTRACT or a FIDUCIARY relationship.

An account can simply list payments, losses, sales, debits, credits, and other monetary transactions, or it may go further and show a balance or the results of comparing opposite transactions, like purchases and sales. Businesspersons keep accounts; attorneys may keep ESCROW accounts; and EXECUTORS must keep accounts that record transactions in administering an ESTATE.

ACCOUNT, ACTION ON A civil lawsuit maintained under the COMMON LAW to recover money owed on an account.

The action on account was one of the ancient FORMS OF ACTION. Dating back to the thirteenth century, it offered a remedy for the breach of obligations owed by FIDUCIARIES. Originally, the action allowed lords to recover money wrongfully withheld by the BAILIFFS of their manors, whom they appointed to collect fines and rents. Later, statutes extended the right so that lawsuits could be brought against persons who were required to act primarily for someone else's benefit, such as guardians and partners. Eventually, the action withered away because its procedure was too cumbersome, and fiduciaries came under the jurisdiction of the special court of the king, called the CHANCERY.

An action on account is different from a modern-day ACCOUNTING, which is a settling of accounts or a determination of transactions affecting two parties, often when one party asks a court to order the other party to account.

ACCOUNTANT A person who has the requisite skill and experience in establishing and

Accouchement: U.S. Births and Birthrates

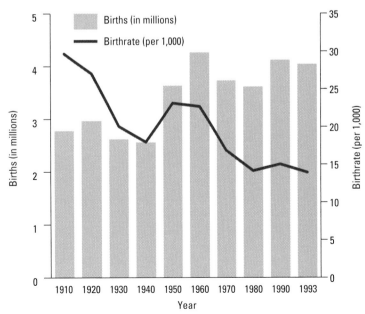

Source: National Center for Health Statistics, U.S. Department of Health and Human Services.

maintaining accurate financial records for an individual or a business. The duties of an accountant may include designing and controlling systems of records, auditing books, and preparing financial statements. An accountant may give tax advice and prepare tax returns. 📖

A *public accountant* renders accounting or auditing services for a number of employees, each of whom pays the accountant a fee for services rendered. He or she does more than just bookkeeping but does not generally have all the qualifications of a certified public accountant.

A *certified public accountant* is one who has earned a LICENSE in his or her state that attests to a high degree of skill, training, and experience. In addition to passing an accounting examination, a candidate must have the proper business experience, education, and moral character in order to qualify for the license. The letters CPA are commonly used and generally recognized to be the abbreviation for the title Certified Public Accountant.

The practice of accounting is a highly skilled and technical profession that affects public welfare. It is entirely appropriate for the state to regulate the profession by means of a licensing system for accountants. Some states do not permit anyone to practice accounting except certified public accountants, but other states use the title to recognize the more distinguished skills of a CPA while permitting others to practice as public accountants. All states limit the use of the title and the initials to those who are licensed as certified public accountants.

All accountants are held to high standards of skill in issuing professional opinions. They can be sued for MALPRACTICE if performance of their duties falls below standards for the profession.

ACCOUNTING 📖 A system of recording or settling accounts in financial transactions; the methods of determining income and expenses for tax and other financial purposes. Also, one of the remedies available to enforce a right or redress a wrong asserted in a lawsuit. 📖

There are various accounting methods. The *accrual method* shows expenses incurred and INCOME earned for a given period of time whether or not such expenses and income have been actually paid or received by that time. The *cash method* records income and expenses only when monies have actually been received or paid out. The *completed contract method* reports gains or losses on certain long-term contracts. GROSS INCOME and expenses are recognized under this method in the tax year the contract is completed. The *installment method* of account-

ing is a way regulated utilities calculate depreciation for income tax purposes.

The *cost method* of accounting records the value of ASSETS at their actual cost, and the *fair value method* uses the present MARKET VALUE for the recorded value of assets. *Price level accounting* is a modern method of valuing assets in a financial statement by showing their current value in comparison to the gross national product. See also ACCRUAL BASIS; CASH BASIS; INCOME TAX.

Where a court orders an accounting, the party against whom judgment is entered must file a complete statement with the court that accounts for his or her ADMINISTRATION of the affairs at issue in the case. An accounting is proper to show how an EXECUTOR has managed the ESTATE of a deceased person or to disclose how a partner has been handling PARTNERSHIP business.

An accounting was one of the ancient remedies available in courts of EQUITY. The regular officers of the CHANCERY, who represented the king in hearing disputes that could not be taken to courts of law, were able to serve as auditors and work through complex accounts when necessary. The chancery had the power to discover hidden assets in the hands of the defendant. Later, courts of law began to recognize and enforce regular contract claims, as actions in ASSUMPSIT, and the courts of equity were justified in compelling an accounting only when the courts AT LAW could not give relief. A plaintiff could ask for an accounting in equity when the complexity of the accounts in the case made it too difficult for a jury or when a TRUSTEE or other FIDUCIARY was charged with violating a position of trust.

Today, courts in the United States generally have JURISDICTION both at law and in equity. They have the power to order an accounting when necessary to determine the relative rights of the parties. An accounting may be appropriate whenever the defendant has violated an obligation to protect the plaintiff's interests. For example, an accounting may be ordered to settle disputes when a partnership is breaking up, when an heir believes that the executor of an estate has sold off assets for less than their fair market value, or when shareholders claim that directors of a corporation have appropriated for themselves a business opportunity that should have profited the corporation.

An accounting may also be an appropriate remedy against someone who has committed a wrong against the plaintiff and should not be allowed to profit from it. For example, a bank teller who embezzles money and makes "a killing" by investing it in mutual funds may be ordered to account for all the money taken and the earnings made from it. A businessperson who palms off a product as that of a more popular manufacturer might have to account for all the profit made from it. A defendant who plagiarizes another author's book can be ordered to give an account and pay over all the profits to the owner of the copyrighted material. An accounting forces the wrongdoer to trace all transactions that flowed from the legal injury, because the plaintiff is in no position to identify the profits.

ACCOUNT PAYABLE 📖 A DEBT owed by a business that arises in the normal course of its dealings, that has not been replaced by a note from another debtor, and that is not necessarily due or past due. 📖

Bills for materials received or obligations on an open account may be accounts payable. This kind of liability usually arises from a purchase of merchandise, materials, or supplies.

ACCOUNT RECEIVABLE 📖 A DEBT owed by a business that arises in the normal course of dealings and is not supported by a negotiable instrument. 📖

The charge accounts of a department store are accounts receivable, but income from investments usually is not. Accounts receivable generally arise from sales or service transactions. They are not necessarily due or past due. Insurance may be purchased to protect against the risk of being unable to collect on accounts receivable if records are damaged or lost.

ACCOUNT RENDERED 📖 A statement of transactions made out by a CREDITOR and presented to the DEBTOR. 📖

After the debtor has examined the account and accepted it, an account rendered becomes an ACCOUNT STATED.

ACCOUNT STATED 📖 An amount that accurately states money due to a CREDITOR; a DEBT arising out of transactions between a DEBTOR and creditor that has been reduced to a balance due for the items of account. 📖

A creditor agrees to accept and a debtor agrees that a specific sum is a true and exact statement of the amount he or she owes. The debtor may agree in words to pay the amount, or it may be understood that the debtor has accepted the account stated by failing to object within a certain period of time.

ACCREDIT 📖 To give official authorization or status. To recognize as having sufficient academic standards to qualify graduates for higher education or for professional practice. In international law: (1) To acknowledge; to receive as an envoy and give that person credit and rank accordingly. (2) To send with credentials as an envoy. This latter use is now the accepted one. 📖

ACCREDITED LAW SCHOOL 📖 A law school that has been approved by the state and the Association of American Law Schools (AALS), the American Bar Association (ABA), or both. 📖

Types of Employment for Lawyers upon Graduation
Class of 1991

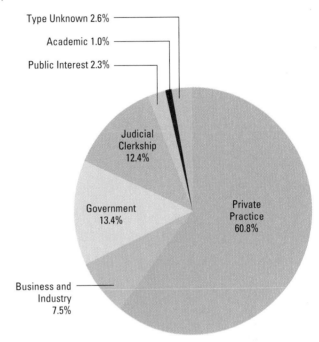

Source: National Association for Law Placement (NALP), Employment Report and Salary Survey.

In certain states—for example, California—it is acceptable for a law school to be accredited by the state and not by either the AALS or the ABA. In most states, however, only graduates of AALS or ABA accredited law schools are permitted to take the state BAR EXAMINATION. See also LEGAL EDUCATION.

ACCRETION 📖 The act of adding portions of soil to the soil already in possession of the owner by gradual deposition through the operation of natural causes.

The growth of the value of a particular item given to a person as a specific BEQUEST under the provisions of a WILL between the time the will was written and the time of death of the TESTATOR—the person who wrote the will. 📖

Accretion of land is of two types: (1) by *alluvion*, the washing up of sand or soil so as to form firm ground; and (2) by *dereliction*, as when the sea shrinks below the usual watermark. The terms *alluvion* and *accretion* are often used interchangeably, but ALLUVION refers to the deposit itself while accretion denotes the act. Land uncovered by a gradual subsidence of water is not an accretion; it is a reliction.

ACCRUAL BASIS A method of ACCOUNTING that reflects expenses incurred and INCOME earned for INCOME TAX purposes for any one year.

Taxpayers who use the accrual method must include in their TAXABLE INCOME any money they have the right to receive as payment for services once it has been earned. Any expenses that they may take as DEDUCTIONS when computing taxable income must be due at the time the deduction is taken. For example, a surgeon performed a tonsillectomy in October 1997, and on December 31, 1997, he received a bill for carpeting installed in the waiting room of his office. He was paid the surgical fee on January 3, 1998, the same day he paid for the carpeting. The surgical fee will be included in his taxable income for 1997, the year in which he earned it, regardless of the fact that he was not paid until the following year.

His expenses for the carpeting can be deducted from his 1997 income because once he received the bill, he was bound to pay it. The fact that he did not pay for the carpeting until the following year does not prevent him from taking the deduction.

The accrual method of accounting differs from the CASH BASIS method, which treats income as only that which is actually received, and expense as only that which is actually paid out. If the cash method were used in the above example, the payment of the surgical fee would be included as income for the 1998 tax year, the year in which it was received by the surgeon. The surgeon could deduct the cost of the carpeting only when he actually paid for it in 1998, although it had been installed in 1997.

Unearned income, such as interest or rent, is generally taxed in the year it is received, regardless of the method of accounting used by the taxpayer.

ACCRUE To increase; to augment; to come to by way of increase; to be added as an increase, profit, or damage. Acquired; falling due; made or executed; matured; occurred; received; vested; was created; was incurred.

To attach itself to, as a subordinate or accessory claim or demand arises out of, and is joined to, its principal.

The term is also used of independent or original demands, meaning to arise, to happen, to come into force or existence; to vest, as in the phrase, "The right of action did not *accrue* within six years." To become a present right or demand; to come to pass.

INTEREST on money that a depositor has in a bank savings account accrues, so that after a certain time the amount will be increased by the amount of interest it has earned.

A CAUSE OF ACTION, the facts that give a person a right to judicial RELIEF, usually accrues on the date that the INJURY to the PLAINTIFF is sustained. When the injury is not readily discoverable, the cause of action accrues when the plaintiff in fact discovers the injury. This occurs frequently in cases of FRAUD or MALPRACTICE. A woman, for example, has an appendectomy. Three years after the surgery, she still experiences dull pain on her right side. She is examined by another physician who discovers a piece of surgical sponge near the area of the operation. Although the injury had occurred at the time of surgery three years earlier, in this case the cause of action for medical malpractice accrues on the date that the sponge is discovered by the second doctor. This distinction is important for purposes of the running of the STATUTE OF LIMITATIONS, the time set by law within which a lawsuit must be commenced after a cause of action accrues. In cases involving injuries that cannot be readily discovered, it would be unfair to bar a plaintiff from bringing a lawsuit because he or she does not start the suit within the required time from the date of injury.

ACCUMULATED EARNINGS TAX A special tax imposed on CORPORATIONS that accumulate (rather than distribute via DIVIDENDS) their earnings beyond the reasonable needs of the business. The accumulated earnings tax is imposed on accumulated taxable income in addition to the corporate income tax.

ACCUMULATION TRUST An arrangement whereby property is transferred by its owner—the SETTLOR—with the intention that it be administered by someone else—a TRUSTEE—for another person's benefit, with the direction that the trustee gather, rather than distribute, the income of the TRUST and any profits made from the sale of any of the property making up the trust until the time specified in the document that created the trust.

Many states have laws governing the time over which accumulations may be made.

ACCUMULATIVE JUDGMENT A second or additional JUDGMENT against a person who has already been convicted and sentenced for another crime; the execution of the second judgment is postponed until the person's first SENTENCE has been completed.

ACCUMULATIVE SENTENCE 📖 A SEN-TENCE—a court's formal pronouncement of the legal consequences of a person's CONVICTION of a CRIME—additional to others, imposed on a defendant who has been convicted upon an IN-DICTMENT containing several COUNTS, each charging a distinct offense, or who is under conviction at the same time for several distinct offenses; each sentence is to run consecutively, beginning at the expiration of the previous sentence. 📖

A person must finish one sentence before being allowed to start the next one. Another name for accumulative sentence is *cumulative* or *consecutive sentence.*

The opposite of an accumulative sentence is a *concurrent sentence*—two or more prison sentences that are to be served simultaneously, so that the prisoner is entitled to be released at the end of the longest sentence.

ACCUSATION 📖 A formal criminal charge against a person alleged to have committed an offense punishable by law, which is presented before a court or a MAGISTRATE having JURISDIC-TION to inquire into the alleged CRIME. 📖

The SIXTH AMENDMENT to the Constitution provides in part that a person accused of a crime has the right " . . . to be informed of the nature and cause of the accusation." This means that in any federal criminal prosecution, the statute setting forth the crime in the accusation must define the offense in sufficiently clear terms so that an average person will be informed of the acts that come within its scope, and the charge must inform the accused in clear and unambiguous language of the offense with which he or she is being charged under the statute. An accused has the same rights when charged with violating state criminal law because the Due Process Clause of the FOURTEENTH AMENDMENT has applied the guarantees of the Sixth Amendment to the states. The paper in which the accusation is set forth—such as an INDICTMENT, INFORMATION, or a COMPLAINT—is called an *accusatory instrument.* See also CRIMINAL LAW.

ACCUSATORY BODY 📖 Body such as a GRAND JURY whose duty it is to hear evidence to determine whether a person should be accused of (charged with) a crime; to be distinguished from a TRAVERSE or PETIT JURY, which is charged with the duty of determining guilt or innocence. 📖

ACCUSED 📖 The generic name for the defendant in a criminal case. A person becomes *accused* within the meaning of a guarantee of SPEEDY TRIAL only at the point at which either formal INDICTMENT or INFORMATION has been returned against him or her, or when he or she becomes subject to actual restraints on liberty imposed by arrest, whichever occurs first. 📖

ACKNOWLEDGMENT 📖 To *acknowledge* is to admit, affirm, declare, testify, avow, confess, or own as genuine. Admission or affirmation of obligation or responsibility. Most states have adopted the Uniform Acknowledgment Act. 📖

The partial payment of a DEBT, for example, is considered an acknowledgment of it for purposes of tolling the STATUTE OF LIMITATIONS—the time set by law for bringing a lawsuit—based on a person's failure to repay a debtor. State law usually gives a CREDITOR six years from the date a debt is due, according to the creditor's contract with the DEBTOR, to sue for nonpayment. If, on the last day of the fifth year, the debtor repays any part of the loan, the statute of limitations is tolled or suspended. The creditor then has another six years from the date of partial payment to sue the debtor for the balance of the loan. The debtor's partial payment indicates acceptance of responsibility to pay the loan. If the debtor had not paid anything, he or she would have escaped liability six years after the date the loan was due.

An acknowledgment of paternity means rec-

State of _____ }
                      ss.
County of _____ }
    On this _____ day of _____ , A.D. _____ , before me _____ ,
                            (year)   (Insert title of acknowledging officer)
personally appeared _____ to me known to be the person _____ named in and who executed the foregoing instrument, and acknowledged that _____ executed the same as _____ voluntary act and deed.

                              _____
                                  Notary Public in the state of Iowa

A sample acknowledgment of an individual acting in his or her own right

A sample
acknowledgment
of an attorney

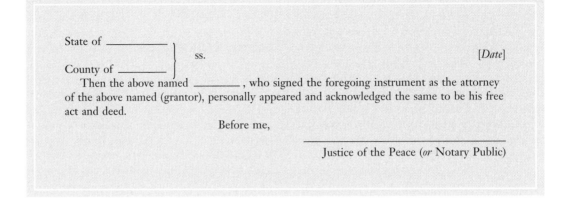

State of _____
⎫
⎬ ss.   [*Date*]
County of _____
⎭
 Then the above named _____ , who signed the foregoing instrument as the attorney
of the above named (grantor), personally appeared and acknowledged the same to be his free
act and deed.
                      Before me,

                                    _____
                                    Justice of the Peace (*or* Notary Public)

ognition of parental duties—such as financial support of an illegitimate child—by written agreement, verbal declaration, or conduct of the father toward the mother and child that clearly demonstrates recognition of paternity.

The requirement for acknowledgments on certain documents—such as DEEDS transferring the ownership of real property, WILLS giving the ownership of property to a decedent's heirs after death, or documentary evidence that is to be admitted in a legal proceeding—is established by state law. If such documents do not contain acknowledgments, they are ineffective and cannot be used in any legal proceedings.

Any or all of the parties to a document may be required to acknowledge it. Only those persons specified by law, a NOTARY PUBLIC, for example, may take an acknowledgment. Usually, a person making an acknowledgment does not have to explain the contents of the document to the person taking the acknowledgment. A person who ordinarily takes an acknowledgment might be disqualified from doing so if that person stands to gain some benefit from or has a financial interest in the outcome of the transaction. For example, state law requires a person making a will, a TESTATOR, to make an acknowledgment to a certain number of WITNESSES that the document is the genuine expression of how that person wants his or her property disposed of upon his or her death. Suppose the state requires two witnesses. If the people selected as witnesses have financial interests in the person's will, they will be disqualified for purposes of acknowledgment. This is done to deter dishonest people from fabricating a document that is beneficial to them. Such a will is legally ineffective; once the testator dies, his or her property will be transferred according to the laws of DESCENT AND DISTRIBUTION.

A certificate of acknowledgment, sometimes referred to as the acknowledgment, is evidence that the acknowledgment has been done prop-erly. Although its contents may vary from state to state, the certificate must recite: (1) that acknowledgment before the proper officer was made by the person who completed the document; (2) the place where the acknowledgment took place; and (3) the name and authority of the officer. The certificate may be on the document itself or may be attached to it as a separate instrument.

ACQUIESCENCE ▨ Conduct recognizing the existence of a transaction and intended to permit the transaction to be carried into effect; a TACIT agreement; CONSENT inferred from silence. ▨

For example, a new beer company is concerned that the proposed label for its beer might infringe on the TRADEMARK of its competitor. It submits the label to its competitor's general counsel, who does not object to its use. The new company files an application in the Patent Office to register the label as its trademark and starts to use the label on the market. The competitor does not file any objection in the Patent Office. Several years later, the competitor sues the new company for infringing on its trademark and demands an ACCOUNTING of the new company's profits for the years it has been using the label. A court will refuse the accounting, since by the competitor's acquiescence, it tacitly approved the use of the label. The competitor, however, might be entitled to an INJUNCTION barring the new company from further use of its trademark if it is so similar to the competitor's label as to amount to an INFRINGEMENT.

Acquiescence is not the same as LACHES, a failure to do what the law requires to protect one's rights, under circumstances misleading or prejudicing the person being sued. Acquiescence relates to inaction during the performance of an act. The failure of the competitor's general counsel to object to the use of the label and to the registration of the label as a trademark in the Patent Office is acquiescence. Failure to sue the company until after several years had elapsed from the first time the label had been used is laches.

ACQUIRED IMMUNE DEFICIENCY SYNDROME

Acquired immune deficiency syndrome (AIDS) is a fatal disease that attacks the body's immune system, making it unable to resist infection, and is caused by the human immunodeficiency virus (HIV), which is communicable in some bodily fluids and transmitted primarily through sexual behavior and intravenous drug use.

The United States has struggled to cope with acquired immune deficiency syndrome since the early 1980s. For a somewhat shorter length of time, U.S. law has also tried to deal with it. Only in the mid-1990s did either society in general or the law in particular begin to achieve even moderate success. Since the beginning, AIDS and its resulting epidemic in the United States have raised a great number of legal issues, which are made all the more difficult by the nature of the disease. AIDS is a unique killer, but some of its aspects are not: epidemics have been seen before; other sexually transmitted diseases have been fatal. AIDS is different because it was discovered in, and in the United States still predominantly afflicts, unpopular social groups: homosexuals and drug users. This fact has had a strong impact on the shaping of AIDS law. Law is often shaped by politics, and AIDS is a very politicized disease. The challenge of facing an epidemic that endangers everyone is complicated by the stigma attached to the people most likely to be killed by it.

Epidemics have no single answer beyond a cure. Since no cure for AIDS exists, the law must grapple with a vast number of problems. The federal government has addressed AIDS in two broad ways: by spending money on the disease and by prohibiting unfairness to people with HIV or AIDS. It has funded medical treatment, research, and public education, and it has passed laws prohibiting discrimination against people who are HIV-positive or who have developed AIDS. States and local municipalities have joined in these efforts, sometimes with federal help. In addition, states have criminalized the act of knowingly transmitting the virus through sexual behavior or blood donation. The courts, of course, are the decision makers in AIDS law. They have heard a number of cases in areas that range from employment to education and from crimes to torts. Although a body of case law has developed, it remains relatively new in most areas and controversial in all.

AIDS and the Federal Government

Political attitudes toward AIDS have gone through dramatically different phases. In the early 1980s, it was dubbed the gay disease, and as such was easy for lawmakers to ignore. No one hurried to fund research into a disease that seemed to be killing only members of a historically unpopular group. When it was not being ignored, AIDS was dismissed by some groups as a problem that homosexuals deserved, perhaps brought on them by divine intervention. Discriminatory action matched this talk as gay men lost jobs, housing, and medical care. AIDS activists complained bitterly about the failure of most U.S. citizens to be concerned. Public opinion only began to shift in the late 1980s, largely through awareness of highly publicized cases. As soon as AIDS had a familiar face, it was harder to ignore; when it became clear that heterosexuals were also contracting the disease, the epidemic took higher priority.

By the late 1980s, much of the harshness in public debate had diminished. Both liberals and conservatives lined up to support legislative solutions. President Ronald Reagan left office recommending increases in federal funding for medical research on AIDS. Already the amount spent in this area had risen from $61 million in 1984 to nearly $1.3 billion in 1988. President George Bush took a more active approach, and in 1990 signed two new bills into law. One was the Ryan White Comprehensive AIDS Resources Emergency (CARE) Act (Pub. L. No. 101-381, 104 Stat. 576), which provides much-needed money for states to spend on treatment. The other was the groundbreaking Americans with Disabilities Act (ADA) (42 U.S.C.A. §§ 12112–12117), which has proved to be the most effective weapon against the discrimination that victims of the disease routinely suffer. Bush also sped up approval by the Food and Drug Administration for AIDS-related drugs. Though he supported Americans with the disease, Bush agreed to a controversial ban by Congress on travel and immigration to the United States for people with HIV.

Like his predecessors, President Bill Clinton called for fighting the disease, rather than people afflicted with it. He also appointed the first federal AIDS policy coordinator, in 1993. He fully funded the Ryan White Care Act, increasing the government's support by 83 percent, to $633 million, and also increased funding for AIDS research, prevention, and treatment by 30 percent. These measures met most of his campaign promises on AIDS. He reneged on one: despite vowing to lift the ban on HIV-positive ALIENS, he signed legislation con-

New AIDS Cases Reported, 1988 to 1994

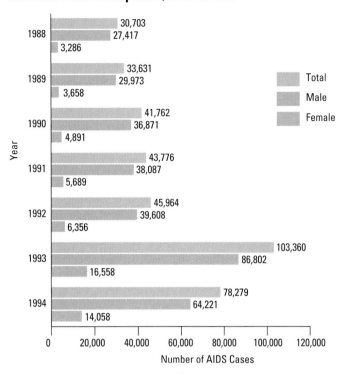

Source: U.S. Centers for Disease Control and Prevention, *Surveillance Report*, annual, also unpublished data.

Deaths Caused by AIDS-related Conditions, 1988 to 1994

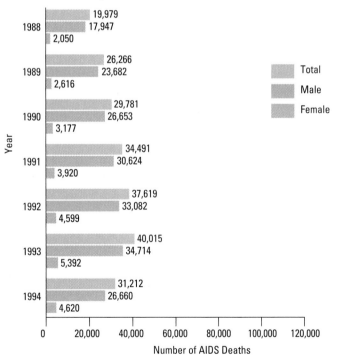

tinuing it. And he met a major obstacle on another: Congress failed to pass his health care reform package, which would have provided health coverage to all U.S. citizens with HIV, delivered drug treatment against AIDS on demand to intravenous drug users, and prohibited health plans from providing lower coverage for AIDS than for other life-threatening diseases.

AIDS and Public Life Having HIV is not a sentence to remove oneself from society. It does not limit a person's physical or mental abilities. Only later, when symptoms develop— as long as ten years from the time of infection— does the disease become increasingly debilitating. In any event, HIV-positive and AIDS-symptomatic people work, play, and participate in daily life. Moreover, their rights to do so are the same as anyone else's. The chief barrier to a productive life often comes less from HIV and AIDS than from the fear, suspicion, and open hostility of others. Because HIV cannot be transmitted through casual contact, U.S. law has moved to defend the civil rights of the afflicted.

AIDS in the Workplace The workplace is a common battleground. Many people with AIDS have lost their jobs, been denied promotions, or been reassigned to work duties that remove them from public contact. During the 1980s, this discrimination was fought through lawsuits based on older laws designed to protect the disabled. Plaintiffs primarily used the Rehabilitation Act of 1973 (29 U.S.C.A. § 701 et seq.), the earliest law of this type. But the Rehabilitation Act has a limited scope: it applies only to federally funded workplaces and institutions, and says nothing about those that do not receive government money. Thus, for example, the law was helpful to a California public school teacher with AIDS who sued for the right to resume teaching classes (*Chalk v. United States Dist. Court*, 840 F. 2d 701 [9th Cir. 1988]), but it would be of no use to the average worker in a private business.

With passage of the ADA in 1990, Congress gave broad protection to people with AIDS who work in the private sector. In general, the ADA is designed to increase access for disabled persons, and it also forbids discrimination in hiring or promotion in companies with fifteen or more employees. Specifically, employers may not discriminate if the person in question is otherwise qualified for the job. Moreover, they cannot use tests to screen out disabled persons, and they must provide reasonable accommodation for disabled workers. The ADA, which took effect in 1992, has quickly emerged as the primary means for bringing

AIDS-related discrimination lawsuits. From 1992 to 1993, more than 330 complaints were filed with the U.S. Equal Employment Opportunity Commission (EEOC), which investigates charges before they can be filed in court. Given the lag time needed for EEOC investigations, those cases started appearing before federal courts in 1994 and 1995.

AIDS and Health Care Closely related to work is the issue of health care. In some cases, the two overlap: health insurance, Social Security, and disability benefits for AIDS victims were often hard to obtain during the 1980s. Insurance was particularly difficult because employers feared rising costs and insurance companies did not want to pay claims. To avoid the costs of AIDS, insurance companies used two traditional industry techniques: they attempted to exclude AIDS coverage from general policies, and they placed caps (limits on benefits payments) on AIDS-related coverage. State regulations largely determine whether this is permissible. In New York, for example, companies that sell general health insurance policies are forbidden to exclude coverage for particular diseases. Caps have hurt AIDS patients because their treatment can be as expensive as that for cancer or other life-threatening illnesses. Insurance benefits can be quickly exhausted—in fact, AIDS usually bankrupts its victims. The problem is compounded when employers serve as their own health insurers. In *McGann v. H&H Music Co.*, 946, F. 2d 401 (5th Cir. [1991]), a federal court ruled that such employers could legally change their policies to reduce coverage for workers who develop expensive illnesses such as AIDS.

In January 1995, the settlement in a lawsuit brought by a Philadelphia construction worker with AIDS illustrated that the ADA can be used to fight caps on coverage. In 1992, the joint union-management fund for the Laborers' District Council placed a $10,000 limit on AIDS benefits, in stark contrast to the $100,000 allowed for other catastrophic illnesses. At that time, the fund said the cap on AIDS benefits was designed to curb all health costs. In 1993, the EEOC ruled that it violated the ADA, and, backed by the AIDS Law Project of Philadelphia, the worker sued. Rather than fight an expensive lawsuit, the insurance fund settled: under the agreement, it extended coverage for all catastrophic illnesses to $100,000. Hailing the settlement as a major blow against widespread discrimination in insurance coverage, the law project's executive director, Nan Feyler, told the *Philadelphia Inquirer*, "You can't single out someone based on a stereotype."

Participants in this Moms Against AIDS March carry photographs of victims of the disease.

In other respects, health care is a distinct area of concern for AIDS patients and health professionals alike. Discrimination has often taken place. State and federal statutes, including the Rehabilitation Act, guarantee access to health care for AIDS patients, and courts have upheld that right. In the 1988 case of *Doe v. Centinela Hospital*, 57 U.S.L.W. 2034 (C.D. Cal.), for example, an HIV-infected person with no symptoms was excluded from a federally funded hospital's residential program for drug and alcohol treatment because health care providers feared exposure to the virus. The case itself exposed the irrationality of such discrimination. Although its employees had feared HIV, the hospital argued in court that the lack of symptoms meant that the patient was not disabled—and thus not protected by the Rehabilitation Act. A federal trial court in California rejected this argument, ruling that a refusal to grant services based solely on fear of contagion is discrimination under the Rehabilitation Act.

More recent actions have used the ADA. In 1994, the U.S. Department of Justice reached a settlement in a lawsuit with the city of Philadelphia that ensures that city employees will treat AIDS patients. The first settlement in a health care–related ADA suit, the case grew out of an incident in 1993: when an HIV-positive man collapsed on a Philadelphia street, emergency medical workers not only refused to touch him

What Causes AIDS—and What Does Not

Since the first case was identified in 1981, acquired immune deficiency syndrome (AIDS) has grown into an epidemic that has taken more than 250,000 lives in the United States alone. The World Health Organization estimates that there are 25 million cases worldwide. No cure has been found, and existing treatment has made only small gains in prolonging life and reducing pain. Despite the limits of medical science, however, much is known about the disease. It is caused by the human immunodeficiency virus (HIV). Transmitted by bodily fluids from person to person, HIV invades certain key blood cells that are needed to fight off infections. HIV replicates, spreads, and destroys these host cells. When the body's immune system becomes deficient, the person becomes AIDS-symptomatic, developing infections that the body can no longer ward off. Ultimately, a person with AIDS dies from diseases caused by other infections. The leading killer is a form of pneumonia.

Most of the fear surrounding AIDS has to do with its most common form of transmission: sexual behavior. The virus can be passed through any behavior that involves the exchange of blood, semen, or vaginal secretions. Anal intercourse is the highest-risk activity, but oral and vaginal intercourse are dangerous too. Thus, federal health authorities recommend using a condom—yet they caution that condoms are not 100 percent effective; they can leak, and they can break. Highly accurate HIV testing is widely available, and often advisable, since infected people can feel perfectly healthy. Although the virus can be contracted immediately upon exposure to it, symptoms of full-blown AIDS may take up to ten years to appear.

Outside of sexual behavior, only a few other means of HIV transmission exist. Sharing unsterilized needles used in drug injections is one way, owing to the exchange of blood on the needle, and thus intravenous drug users are an extremely high-risk group. Several cities have experimented with programs offering free clean needles. These programs have seen up to a 75 percent reduction in new HIV cases. Receipt of donations of blood, semen, organs, and other human tissue can also transmit HIV, although here, at least, screening methods have proved largely successful. Childbirth and breast feeding are also avenues of transmission, and thus children of HIV-positive mothers may be at risk.

The medical facts about HIV and AIDS are especially relevant to the law. Unless exposed in one of a few very specific ways, most people have nothing to fear. Casual contact with people who are infected is safe. Current medical knowledge is quite strong on this point: no one is known to have caught the virus by sitting next to, shaking the hand of, or breathing the same air as an infected person. For this reason, U.S. law has moved to protect the civil rights of HIV-positive and AIDS-symptomatic persons.

but told him to get on a stretcher by himself. The man sued. In settling the case, the city agreed to begin an extensive training program for its nine hundred emergency medical technicians and fourteen hundred firefighters. In addition, officials paid the man $10,000 in compensatory damages, and apologized. The Justice Department viewed the suit as an important test of the ADA. Assistant Attorney General James Turner said the settlement would "send a clear message to all cities across the nation that we will not tolerate discrimination against persons with AIDS."

Health care professionals are not the only ones with concerns about HIV transmission. Patients may legitimately wonder if their doctors are infected. During the early 1990s, the medical and legal communities debated whether HIV-positive doctors have a duty to inform their patients of the illness. According to the Centers for Disease Control (CDC), the risk of HIV transmission from health care workers to patients is very small when recommended infection-control procedures are followed—yet this type of transmission has occurred. The first cases of patients contracting HIV during a medical procedure were reported in 1991: Dr. David J. Acer, a Florida dentist with AIDS, had apparently transmitted HIV to five patients. One was Kimberly Bergalis, age twenty-three, who died as a result. Before her death, Bergalis brought a claim against the dentist's professional liability insurer, contending that it should have known that Acer had AIDS and effectively barred him from operating by refusing to issue him a malpractice insurance policy. Bergalis's claim was settled for $1 million. A second claim by Bergalis, against the insurance company that recommended Acer to her, was settled for an undisclosed amount.

Since the Bergalis case, many U.S. dentists, physicians, and surgeons with AIDS have begun disclosing their status to their patients. *Faya v. Almaraz*, 329 Md. 435, 620 A.2d 327 (Md.

1993) illustrates the consequences of not doing so. In *Faya*, the court held that an HIV-positive doctor has the legal duty to disclose this medical condition to patients, and that a failure to inform can lead to a NEGLIGENCE action, even if the patients have not been infected by the virus. The doctor's patient did not contract HIV, but did suffer emotionally from a fear of having done so. The unanimous decision held that patients can be compensated for their fears. Although this case dealt specifically with doctor-patient relationships, others have concerned a variety of relationships in which the fear of contracting AIDS can be enough for a plaintiff to recover damages.

Routine HIV-testing in health care facilities also raises legal issues. Most people who are HIV-positive want this information kept confidential. Facilities are free to use HIV testing to control the infection, but in most states only with the patient's INFORMED CONSENT. Some states, such as Illinois, require written consent. The level of protection for medical records varies from state to state—California, for example, has broad protections; under its statutes, no one can be compelled to provide information that would identify anyone who is the subject of an HIV test. However, every state requires that AIDS cases be reported to the CDC, which tracks statistics on the spread of HIV. Whether the name of an HIV-infected person is reported to the CDC depends on state laws and regulations.

AIDS and Education Issues in the field of education include the rights of HIV-positive students to attend class and of HIV-positive teachers to teach, the confidentiality of HIV records, and how best to teach young people about AIDS. A few areas have been settled in court: for instance, the right of students to attend classes was of greater concern in the early years of the epidemic, and no longer remains in dispute.

Certain students with AIDS may assert their right to public education under the Education for All Handicapped Children Act of 1975 (EAHCA), but the law is only relevant in cases involving special education programs. More commonly, students' rights are protected by the Rehabilitation Act. Perhaps the most important case in this area is *Thomas v. Atascadero Unified School District*, 662 F. Supp. 376 (C.D. Cal. 1986), which illustrates how far such protections go. *Thomas* involved a young elementary school student with AIDS who had bitten another youngster in a fight. Based on careful review of medical evidence, the District Court for the Central District of California concluded

that biting was not proved to transmit AIDS, and it ordered the school district to readmit the girl. Similarly, schools that excluded teachers with AIDS have been successfully sued on the ground that those teachers pose no threat to their students or others, and that their right to work is protected by the Rehabilitation Act, as in *Chalk*.

Confidentiality relating to HIV is not uniform in schools. Some school districts require rather broad dissemination of the information; others keep it strictly private. In the mid-1980s, the New York City Board of Education adopted a policy that nobody in any school would be told the identities of children with AIDS or HIV infection; only a few top administrators outside the school would be informed. The policy inspired a lawsuit brought by a local school district, which argued that the identity of a child was necessary for infection control (*District 27 Community School Board v. Board of Education*, 130 Misc. 2d 398, 502 N.Y.S.2d 325 [N.Y. Sup. Ct. 1986]). The trial court rejected the argument on the basis that numerous children with HIV infection might be attending school, and instead noted that universal precautions in dealing with blood incidents at school would be more effective than the revelation of confidential information.

Schools play a major role in the effort to educate the public on AIDS. Several states have mandated AIDS prevention instruction in their schools. But the subject is controversial: it evokes personal, political, and moral reactions to sexuality. Responding to parental sensitivities, some states have authorized excused absences from such programs. The New York State Education Department faced a storm of controversy over its policy of not allowing

The AIDS quilt, on display here in Washington, D.C., has become a well known symbol of support for victims of AIDS and their families. Families and supporters of victims of AIDS create a panel to commemorate that person's life, and that panel is joined with others from around the country to create the quilt.

© MARK D. PHILLIPS/PHOTOREPORTERS

READING, WRITING, AND AIDS

Teaching young people about AIDS is an enormously popular idea. Since the late 1980s, Gallup Polls have revealed that over 90 percent of respondents think public schools should do so. Agreement ends there, however. In the 1990s, more angry debate has focused on AIDS education than on any issue facing schools since court-ordered busing in the 1970s. The core question of the debate is simple: What is the best way to equip students to protect themselves from this fatal disease? The answers may be miles apart. For one side, "equipping" means advocating the only sure means of protection, sexual and drug abstinence. For the other, it means supporting abstinence along with knowledge of sexual practices, the use of clean drug needles, and the use of prophylactics (condoms), which are distributed in some schools. Between these positions lie a great many issues of disagreement that have bitterly divided school districts, provoked lawsuits, and cost high-ranking Washington, D.C., officials their jobs.

Sex is an old battleground in public education. Liberals and conservatives argued over it in the decade following the sexual revolution of the 1960s, initially over whether sexual issues should be discussed in schools. After all, earlier generations who went to public schools learned mainly about reproductive organs. As new classes began appearing in the late 1970s, children learned about the sexual choices people make. If liberals appeared to win the "sex ed." debate, growing social problems helped: rises in teen pregnancies and sexually transmitted diseases secured a place for more explicit school health classes. The much greater threat of AIDS pushed state legislatures into action. By the mid-1990s, AIDS prevention classes had been mandated in at least thirty-four states and recommended in fourteen. But the appearance of even more explicit teaching has reinvigorated the sex ed. debate.

Supporters of a comprehensive approach say AIDS demands frankness. Originating in comprehensive sex ed theory, their ideas also come from pacesetting health authorities such as former surgeon general C. Everett Koop. Arguing in the mid-1980s that AIDS classes should be specific and detailed, and taught as early as kindergarten, Koop countered conservative arguments by saying, "Those who say 'I don't want my child sexually educated' are hiding their heads in the sand." This position holds that educators are obligated to teach kids everything that can stop the spread of the disease. "What is the moral responsibility?" Jerald Newberry, a health coordinator of Virginia schools, asked the *Washington Times* in 1992. "I think it's gigantic." Abstinence is a part of this approach, but expecting teens to refrain from having sex is considered unrealistic given some studies that show that nearly three out of four high school students have had sex before graduation. Thus, the comprehensive curriculum includes demonstrating the proper use of condoms, discussing homosexual practices, advising the sterilization of drug needles, and so on.

Abstinence-only adherents think being less frank is being more responsible. They view sexuality as a moral issue properly left to parents and children, and one in which schools have no business interfering. The conservative columnist Cal Thomas speaks for this viewpoint when he argues that parents "have lost a significant right to rear their children according to their own moral standards." Other objections come from religious conservatives who oppose any neutral or positive discussion of homosexuality. Koop, for example, was blasted for allegedly "sponsoring homosexually oriented curricula" and "teaching buggery in the 3rd grade." In addition to voicing moral objections, critics say comprehensive sex ed is generally a failure because it encourages a false sense of security among teens that leads to experimentation with sex or drugs. "We have given children more information presumably because we think it will change their behavior, and yet the behavior has gotten worse, not better," said Gary Bauer, president of the Family Research Council.

absences at parental discretion. Furthermore, at the local and the federal levels, some conservatives have opposed certain kinds of AIDS education. During the 1980s, those who often criticized liberal approaches to sex education argued that AIDS materials should not be explicit, encourage sexuality, promote the use of contraceptives, or favorably portray gays and lesbians. In Congress, lawmakers attached amendments to appropriations measures (bills that authorize the spending of federal tax dollars) that mandate that no federal funds may be used to "promote homosexuality." In response, the CDC adopted regulations that prohibit spending federal funds on AIDS education materials that might be found offensive by some members of certain communities. Despite the controversy, some communities have taken radical steps to halt the spread of AIDS. In 1991 and 1992, the school boards of New York City, San Francisco, Seattle, and Los Angeles voted to make condoms available to students in their public high school systems.

AIDS and Private Life Although epidemics are public crises, they begin with individuals. The rights of people who have AIDS and those who do not are often in contention, and seldom more so than in private life. It is no

Each side accuses the other of deepening the crisis. Comprehensive-approach supporters think abstinence-only backers are moral censors, indifferent to pragmatic solutions. The liberal People for the American Way attacks "a growing wave of censorship ravaging sexuality education" that promotes only "narrow" curricula. It mocks such abstinence-only programs as Teen Aid and Sex Respect, both of which have brought threats of legal action from the American Civil Liberties Union and Planned Parenthood. The conservative American Enterprise Institute believes that liberal programs only prod students toward bad choices, arguing, "There has been a transition from protection to preparation." Neither side can agree on any data, other than to point out that the problems of AIDS and teen sexuality appear to get worse.

Nowhere are the two sides more split than on the issue of condoms. Distribution of condoms to students has been tried in the schools of at least twenty-three cities since the mid-1990s. The assumption is that since students will have sex anyway—despite warnings not to—they had better be protected. Conservatives see this as a cop-out in two ways: it sells values short and it undermines parental authority. In 1992, in Washington, D.C., critics erupted over a decision by the Public Health Commission to hand out condoms in junior and senior high schools without parental consent. William Brown, president of the D.C. Congress of Parents and Teachers, complained, "We are looking to build and reinforce and establish family values where they have been lost,

and here we have an agency of our government that totally ignores those things we are working for." Dr. Mary Ellen Bradshaw, the commission's chief, replied, "Our whole focus is to save the lives of these children, stressing abstinence as the only sure way to avoid [AIDS] and making condoms available only after intensive education." In other cities, upset parents simply sued. By 1992, class action lawsuits had been brought against school districts in New York City, Seattle, and Falmouth, Massachusetts, arguing that condom distribution violated parents' right to privacy.

AIDS education in schools is not merely a local issue. Although most decisions are made by states and school boards, the federal government plays two important roles. First, it funds AIDS prevention programs: abstinence-based programs receive funding under the Adolescent Family Life Act of 1981, and programs that promote contraceptive use among teenagers are supported through the Family Planning Act of 1970. How these funds are spent is a matter of local control, but conservatives have sought to put limits on program content. During the early 1990s, Senator Jesse Helms (R-N.C.) twice tried to ban funding for programs that promoted homosexuality or that did not continuously teach abstinence as the only effective protection against AIDS. In response, one federal agency, the Centers for Disease Control, adopted regulations that prohibited the use of funds on any materials that are found offensive by some members of communities.

The second role of the federal gov-

ernment is largely symbolic but no less controversial. It is to guide school efforts through advice, sponsorship, and public speeches, and primarily involves the offices of the surgeon general and of the federal AIDS policy coordinator. Koop, who was a Reagan appointee, roused a fair degree of controversy, yet it was nothing compared with the upheaval that greeted statements by appointees of the Clinton administration. AIDS policy czar Kristine Gebbie and Surgeon General M. Joycelyn Elders were forced from their posts after making statements that conservatives found appalling—Gebbie promoting attitudes toward pleasurable sex, and Elders indicating a willingness to have schools talk about masturbation. Thereafter, the administration frequently stressed abstinence as its top priority for school AIDS programs.

Problems surrounding AIDS education are unlikely to go away. Communities frequently disagree on sex education itself, and compromise is often difficult on such a divisive issue of values. As the experience of the Clinton administration suggests, Washington, D.C., can easily exacerbate an already contentious area, with policy coordinators becoming lightning rods for criticism. On the matter of what to say to kids about AIDS, poll data are misleading. U.S. citizens are of three minds: say a lot, say a little, and do not say what the other side thinks.

See also Schools and School Districts.

surprise that people with HIV continue having sex, nor is it a surprise that this behavior is, usually, legal. Unfortunately, some do so without knowing they have the virus. Even more unfortunately, others do so in full knowledge that they are HIV-positive but without informing their partners. This dangerous behavior has opened one area of AIDS law that affects individuals: the legal duty to warn a partner before engaging in behavior that can transmit the infection. A similar duty was recognized by courts long before AIDS ever appeared, with regard to other sexually transmitted diseases.

A failure to inform in AIDS cases has given

rise to both civil and criminal lawsuits. One such case was brought by Mark Christian, the lover of actor Rock Hudson, against Hudson's estate. Christian won his suit on the ground that Hudson concealed his condition and continued their relationship, and the jury returned a multimillion-dollar verdict despite the fact that there was no evidence that Christian had been infected. Another case was brought in Oregon in 1991, when criminal charges were filed against Alberto Gonzalez for knowingly spreading HIV by having sex with his girlfriend. After Gonzalez pleaded no contest to third-degree ASSAULT (a felony) and to two charges of recklessly endangering others, he received an unusual sentence: the court ordered him to abstain from sex for five years and placed him under house arrest for six months. Although such convictions are increasingly common, courts have also recognized that not knowing one has HIV can be a valid defense. In *C. A. U. v. R. L.*, 438 N.W.2d 441 (1989), for example, the Minnesota Court of Appeals affirmed a trial court's finding that the plaintiff could not recover damages from her former fiancé, who had unknowingly given her the virus.

AIDS activists protest a lack of government attention to finding a cure for the disease and their signs emphasize the variety of social groups affected by AIDS.

State Legislation and the Courts To stem transmission of HIV, states have adopted several legal measures. Two states attempted to head off the virus at the pass: Illinois and Louisiana at one point required HIV blood testing as a prerequisite to getting a marriage license. Both states ultimately repealed these statutes because they were difficult to enforce; couples simply crossed state lines to be married in neighboring states. Several states have taken a less stringent approach, requiring only that applicants for a marriage license must be informed of the availability—and advisability—of HIV tests. More commonly, states criminalize sexual behavior that can spread AIDS. Michigan law makes it a FELONY for an HIV- or AIDS-infected person to engage in sex without first informing a partner of the infection. Florida law provides for the prosecution of any HIV-positive person committing PROSTITUTION, and it permits RAPE victims to demand that their attackers undergo testing. Indiana imposes penalties on persons who recklessly or knowingly donate blood or semen knowing that they are HIV-infected.

Older state laws have also been applied to AIDS. Several states have statutes that make it

a criminal offense for a person with a contagious disease—including a sexually transmitted disease—to willfully or knowingly expose another person to it, and some have amended these laws specifically to include AIDS. In addition, in many states, it has long been a crime to participate in an act of SODOMY such as anal or oral sex. The argument that punishing sodomy can stem HIV transmission was made in a case involving a Missouri sodomy statute specifically limited to homosexual conduct. In *State v. Walsh*, 713 S.W.2d 508 (1986), the Missouri Supreme Court upheld the statute after finding that it was rationally related to the state's legitimate interest in protecting public health. Other AIDS-related laws have fallen in court challenges: for instance, in 1993, U.S. district judge Aldon J. Anderson struck down a 1987 Utah statute that invalidated the marriages of people with AIDS, ruling that it violated the ADA and the Rehabilitation Act.

Sex is only one kind of behavior that has prompted criminal prosecution related to AIDS. Commonly, defendants in AIDS cases have been prosecuted for assault. In *United States v. Moor*, 669 F. Supp. 289 (D. Minn., 1987), *aff'd*, 846 F.2d 1163 (8th Cir., 1988), the Eighth Circuit upheld the conviction of an HIV-infected prisoner found guilty of assault with a deadly weapon—his teeth—for biting two prison guards during a struggle. Teeth were also on trial in *Brock v. State*, 555 So. 2d 285 (1989), but the Alabama Court of Criminal Appeals refused to regard them as a dangerous weapon. In *State v. Haines*, 545 N.E.2d 834 (2d Dist. 1989), the Indiana Court of Appeals affirmed a conviction of attempted murder against a man with AIDS who had slashed his wrists to commit suicide; when police officers and paramedics refused to let him die, he began to spit, bite, scratch, and throw blood.

Civil Litigation TORT law has seen an explosion of AIDS-related suits. This area of law is used to discourage individuals from subjecting others to unreasonable risks, and to compensate those who have been injured by unreasonably risky behavior. The greatest number of AIDS-related LIABILITY lawsuits has involved the receipt of HIV-infected blood and blood products. A second group has concerned the sexual transmission of HIV. A third group involves AIDS-related psychic distress. In these cases, plaintiffs have successfully sued and recovered damages for their fear of having contracted HIV.

CROSS-REFERENCES

Disabled Persons; Discrimination; Food and Drug Administration; Gay and Lesbian Rights; Health Care; Patients' Rights; Physicians and Surgeons; Privacy.

ACQUISITION CHARGE 📖 A fee imposed upon a borrower who satisfies a loan prior to the date of payment specified in the loan agreement. 📖

Many home MORTGAGES provide that if the persons who borrowed the money want to repay their mortgage within two years, they must pay an acquisition charge of a small percentage of the outstanding balance of the mortgage. *Prepayment penalty* is another name for acquisition charge.

ACQUIT 📖 To set free, release or discharge as from an obligation, burden or accusation. To absolve one from an obligation or a liability; or to legally certify the innocence of one charged with a CRIME. 📖

ACQUITTAL 📖 The legal and formal certification of the innocence of a person who has been charged with a CRIME. 📖

Acquittals *in fact* take place when a JURY finds a VERDICT of not guilty. Acquittals *in law* take place by OPERATION OF LAW such as when a person has been charged as an ACCESSORY to the crime of robbery and the principal has been acquitted.

ACT 📖 Something done; usually, something done intentionally or voluntarily or with a purpose. 📖

The term encompasses not only physical acts—such as turning on the water or purchasing a gun—but also refers to more intangible acts such as adopting a decree, edict, law, judgment, award, or determination. An act may be a PRIVATE act, done by an individual managing his or her personal affairs, or it may be a PUBLIC act, done by an official, a council, or a court. When a BILL is favorably acted upon in the process of legislation, it becomes an act.

ACTION 📖 Conduct; behavior; something done; a series of acts.

A case or lawsuit; a legal and formal demand for enforcement of one's rights against another party asserted in a court of justice. 📖

The term *action* includes all the PROCEEDINGS attendant upon a legal demand, its adjudication, and its denial or its enforcement by a court. Specifically, it is the LEGAL PROCEEDINGS, while a CAUSE OF ACTION is the underlying right that gives rise to them. In casual conversation, *action* and *cause of action* may be used interchangeably, but they are more properly distinguished. At one time, it was more correct to speak of actions AT LAW and of proceedings or suits in EQUITY. The distinction is rather technical, however, and not significant since the merger of law and equity. The term *action* is used more often for civil lawsuits than for criminal proceedings.

Parties in an Action A person must have some sort of legal right before starting an

Acquittal: State of New York Felony Indictments and Dispositions for 1993

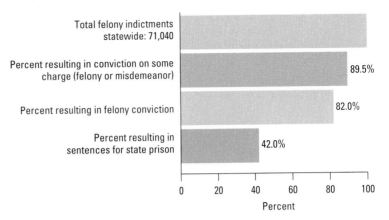

Results of Felony Trials Completed in 1993

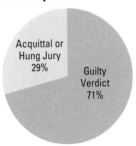

Source: *1993 Crime and Justice Annual Report,* New York City Police Department.

action. That legal right implies a DUTY owed to one person by another, whether it is a duty to do something or a duty not to do something. When the other person acts wrongfully or fails to act as the law requires, such behavior is a breach, or violation, of that person's legal duty. If that breach causes harm, it is the basis for a cause of action. The injured person may seek REDRESS by starting an action in court.

The person who starts the action is the PLAINTIFF, and the person sued is the DEFENDANT. They are the PARTIES in the action. Frequently, there are multiple parties on a side. The defendant may assert a defense which, if true, will defeat the plaintiff's CLAIM. A COUNTERCLAIM may be made by the defendant against the plaintiff or a CROSS-CLAIM against another party on the same side of the lawsuit. The law may permit JOINDER of two or more claims, such as an action for property damage and an action for personal injuries, after one auto accident; or it may require consolidation of actions by an order of the court. Where PREJUDICE or injustice is likely to result, the court may order a SEVERANCE of actions into different lawsuits for different parties.

Commencement of an Action The time when an action may begin depends on the kind of action involved. A plaintiff cannot start a lawsuit until the cause of action has accrued. For example, a man who wants to use a parcel of land for a store where only houses are allowed must begin by applying for a VARIANCE from the local zoning board. He cannot bypass the board and start an action in court. His right to sue does not ACCRUE until the board turns down his request.

Neither can a person begin an action after the time allowed by law. Most causes of action are covered by a STATUTE OF LIMITATIONS, which specifically limits the time within which to begin the action. If the law in a particular state says that an action for LIBEL cannot be brought more than one year after publication of a defamatory statement, then those actions must be initiated within that statutory period. Where there is no statute that limits the time to commence a particular action, a court may nevertheless dismiss the case if the claim is stale and if litigation at that point would not be fair.

A plaintiff must first select the right COURT, then an action can be commenced by DELIVERY of the formal legal papers to the appropriate person. Statutes that regulate proper procedure for this must be strictly observed. A typical statute specifies that an action may be begun by delivery of a SUMMONS, or a WRIT on the defendant. At one time, common-law actions had to be pleaded according to highly technical forms of action, but now it is generally sufficient simply to serve papers that state facts describing a recognized cause of action. If this SERVICE OF PROCESS is done properly, the defendant has fair notice of the claim made against him or her and the court acquires JURISDICTION over him or her. In some cases, the law requires delivery of the summons or writ to a specified public officer such as a U.S. MARSHAL, who becomes responsible for serving it on the defendant.

Acts of God, such as earthquakes, are sometimes excluded from insurance policies for property damage.

Termination of an Action After an action is commenced, it is said to be PENDING until termination. While the action is pending, neither party has the right to start another action in a different court over the same dispute or to do any act that would make the court's decision futile.

A lawsuit may be terminated because of DISMISSAL before both sides have fully argued the MERITS of their cases at TRIAL. It can also be ended because of COMPROMISE AND SETTLEMENT, after which the plaintiff withdraws his or her action from the court.

Actions are terminated by the entry of final judgments by the courts. A JUDGMENT may be based on a jury VERDICT or it may be a JUDGMENT NOTWITHSTANDING THE VERDICT. Where there has been no JURY, judgment is based on the judge's decision. Unless one party is given LEAVE—or permission from the court—to do something that might revive the lawsuit, such as amending an insufficient complaint, the action is at an end when judgment is formally entered on the records of the court.

See also CIVIL PROCEDURE.

ACTIONABLE 📖 Giving sufficient legal grounds for a lawsuit; giving rise to a CAUSE OF ACTION. 📖

An act, event, or occurrence is said to be actionable when there are legal grounds for basing a lawsuit on it. For example, an assault is an actionable tort.

ACTIONABLE PER SE 📖 Legally sufficient to support a lawsuit in itself. 📖

Words are actionable per se if they are obviously insulting and injurious to one's reputation. In lawsuits for LIBEL or slander, words that impute the commission of a crime, a loathsome disease, or unchastity, or remarks that affect the plaintiff's business, trade, profession, calling, or office may be actionable per se. No special proof of actual harm done by the words is necessary to win monetary DAMAGES when words are actionable per se.

ACT OF GOD 📖 An event that directly and exclusively results from the occurrence of natural causes that could not have been prevented by the exercise of foresight or caution; an inevitable ACCIDENT. 📖

Courts have recognized various events as acts of God—tornadoes, earthquakes, death, extraordinarily high tides, violent winds, and floods. Many insurance policies for property damage exclude from their protection damage caused by acts of God.

ACTUAL CASH VALUE 📖 The fair or reasonable cash price for which a property could be sold in the market in the ordinary course of business, and not at FORCED SALE. The price it will bring in a fair market after reasonable efforts to find a purchaser who will give the highest price. What property is worth in money, allowing for DEPRECIATION. Ordinarily, *actual cash value*, *fair market value*, and *market value* are synonymous terms. 📖

ACTUAL NOTICE 📖 Conveying facts to a person with the intention to apprise that person of a proceeding in which his or her interests are involved, or informing a person of some fact that he or she has a right to know and which the informer has a legal duty to communicate. 📖

When such notice has been given to someone personally, it is called *express actual notice* or *express notice*. If a tenant notifies a landlord that the elevator is broken, the landlord has express actual notice of the defect. Should the landlord fail to repair the elevator and another tenant is injured while riding it, the landlord would be liable for the tenant's injuries.

Actual notice can be presumed if an average person, having witness of the same evidence, should know that a particular fact exists. This is called implied actual notice or implied notice. If the landlord had been with the tenant when the tenant discovered the broken elevator, the landlord would be considered to have implied notice of the defect.

ACTUARY 📖 A statistician who computes insurance and pension rates and premiums on the basis of experience of people sharing similar age and health characteristics. 📖

ADAMS, JOHN John Adams achieved prominence as a jurist, a statesman, and as the second president of the United States.

Adams was born on October 30, 1735. A graduate of Harvard College, class of 1755, Adams was admitted to the Boston bar in 1758 and established a prestigious legal practice.

During the pre–Revolutionary War years, Adams spoke against many acts enforced by the British government, such as the TOWNSHEND ACTS, which unjustly taxed items such as glass and tea. He joined the Sons of Liberty—a group of lawyers, merchants, and businessmen who, in 1765, banded together to oppose the STAMP ACT.

"FEAR IS THE FOUNDATION OF MOST GOVERNMENTS."

BIOGRAPHY

LIBRARY OF CONGRESS

John Adams

From 1774 to 1778 Adams served as the Massachusetts representative to the Continental Congress. He entered the judiciary during this period and rendered decisions as chief justice of the Superior Court of Massachusetts from 1775 to 1777. In 1776 he signed the newly created DECLARATION OF INDEPENDENCE.

After the war, Adams entered the field of foreign service, acting as commissioner to France in 1777. In 1783 Adams went to Paris with John Jay and Thomas Jefferson to successfully negotiate the Treaty of Paris with Great Britain, which officially ended the Revolutionary War and established the United States as an independent nation. In 1785 Adams became the first U.S. minister to Great Britain.

Adams returned to the United States in 1788 and began service to the new government with his election to the office of vice president of the United States. He was the first person to serve in this office and was reelected for a second term in 1792.

In 1796 Adams was elected president of the United States. He was the second man to hold this position, following the retirement of the first president, George Washington. During his term of office, Adams advocated naval strength; approved the Alien and Sedition Acts of 1798 (1 Stat. 566, 570, 577, 596), which increased the restrictions concerning aliens and imposed harsh penalties on any person who attempted to obstruct the government system; averted war with France; and selected the eminent John Marshall as chief justice of the Supreme Court.

In 1800 Adams ran for the presidency for a second term but was defeated by Thomas Jefferson.

John Adams wrote several publications, including *Thoughts on Government* (1776) and *Defense of the Constitutions of the United States of America Against the Attacks of Mr. Turgot* (1787).

Adams was the father of four children, and his son, John Quincy, served as the sixth president of the United States. He died on July 4, 1826, in Braintree (now Quincy), Massachusetts.

See also MARSHALL, JOHN.

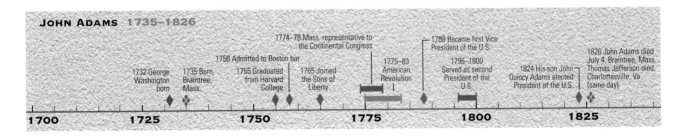

JOHN ADAMS 1735–1826

1700   1725   1750   1775   1800   1825

1732 George Washington born

1735 Born, Braintree, Mass.

1755 Graduated from Harvard College

1758 Admitted to Boston bar

1765 Joined the Sons of Liberty

1774–78 Mass. representative to the Continental Congress

1775–83 American Revolution

1788 Became first Vice President of the U.S.

1796–1800 Served as second President of the U.S.

1824 His son John Quincy Adams elected President of the U.S.

1826 John Adams died July 4, Braintree, Mass. Thomas Jefferson died, Charlottesville, Va. (same day)

ADAMS, JOHN QUINCY John Quincy Adams was more than just the United States' sixth president. He was a child of the American Revolution, having witnessed the Battle of Bunker Hill. He was the son of the nation's second president, John Adams. And he was a successful diplomat. Chosen president by the House after finishing second in the electoral college, Adams became the first president to wear long trousers, rather than breeches, at his inauguration, on March 4, 1825. After one term as president, he went on to serve with distinction for seventeen years in the House of Representatives.

Adams was born on July 11, 1767, in Braintree (now Quincy), Massachusetts. As the son of one of the nation's founders, he had many opportunities not available to other young men. Before reaching the age when young people today graduate from high school, Adams had established himself as a diplomat. He accompanied his father on diplomatic missions to Europe in 1778 and 1780, where he studied in Paris, France, and in Amsterdam and Leiden, the Netherlands. In 1781, at the age of fourteen, Adams traveled with Francis Dana, the first American minister to Russia, as Dana's private secretary and French interpreter. In 1783, the young Adams joined his father in Paris, where he served as one of the secretaries to the American commissioners in the negotiations of the peace treaty that concluded the American Revolution. Fearing alienation from his own country, Adams returned home in 1785 and, by virtue of his earlier studies, was able to enroll as a junior at Harvard College, from which he graduated in 1787.

For three years, Adams read law at Newburyport, Massachusetts, under Theophilus Parsons, and in 1790, he was admitted to the bar. While struggling to find clients, Adams engaged in political journalism. He wrote a series of eleven articles controverting some of the doctrines presented in Thomas Paine's *Rights of Man* (1791–1792). In a second series of articles, he defended President George Washington's policy of neutrality in the war between France and England in 1793. His third

BIOGRAPHY

John Quincy Adams

series of articles attacked those who wanted the United States to join France in a war against Britain. These articles impressed Washington so much that he appointed Adams U.S. minister to the Netherlands in May 1794.

President Washington thought Adams one of the ablest officers in the foreign service. In 1796, he appointed Adams minister to Portugal. However, before Adams's departure for that new post, his father became president. Both Adamses felt that it was undesirable for the son of a president to hold a post in the father's administration, but Washington urged that the younger Adams remain in the diplomatic corps, calling him the most valuable public person abroad. President Adams then appointed his son minister to Prussia.

Before taking up his new post in Prussia, Adams was married, in London, to Louisa Catherine Johnson (1775–1852), daughter of the U.S. counsel in London.

In September 1801, with a new president, Thomas Jefferson, in the White House, Adams was called back from Prussia. In 1802, he was elected to the Massachusetts Senate. One year later, the state senate elected him to the U.S. Senate. (Prior to the passage of the Seventeenth Amendment in 1913, U.S. senators were elected by the senates of the individual states.)

Adams had always considered himself a political independent, and he was given a chance to prove this in the U.S. Senate. After his election, he was set upon by forces opposed to the Federalist party, of which Adams was considered a member, and political enemies of his father. Instead of accepting his fate as a powerless and unpopular member of an unpopular political minority, Adams asserted his political independence. He began to vote with President Jefferson and the opposition Democratic-Republicans, and broke with his party completely in 1807 by supporting the EMBARGO ACT (46 App. U.S.C.A. § 328). This act, backed by Jefferson, placed an embargo on all foreign commerce. The act was opposed by the Federalists and the New England states, who wanted to encourage trade with the British. They

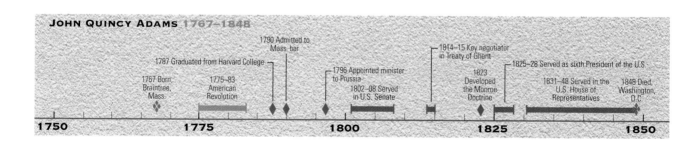

JOHN QUINCY ADAMS 1767–1848

1790 Admitted to Mass. bar

1787 Graduated from Harvard College

1814–15 Key negotiator in Treaty of Ghent

1825–28 Served as sixth President of the U.S.

1796 Appointed minister to Prussia

1823 Developed the Monroe Doctrine

1831–48 Served in the U.S. House of Representatives

1767 Born, Braintree, Mass.

1775–83 American Revolution

1802–08 Served in U.S. Senate

1848 Died, Washington, D.C.

1750　　1775　　1800　　1825　　1850

feared that the Embargo Act would stifle New England's economy. Adams voted for the Embargo Act, against the wishes of his party and region, believing that it benefited the nation as a whole.

Adams paid the price for breaking with his party. Federalist leaders in Massachusetts who felt that Adams had betrayed them elected another man to the Senate several months before the 1808 elections. Adams resigned, and later that year, in a move indicative of his political independence, attended a Democratic-Republican congressional caucus meeting, where James Madison was nominated for president, thus allying himself with that party.

Adams attempted to retire from public life and devote himself to a teaching position at Harvard College, but the lure of public service was too strong. In 1809, President Madison persuaded him to accept an appointment as minister to Russia. In 1814 and 1815, Adams played a key role in the negotiations resulting in the Treaty of Ghent, with the British, ending the War of 1812. The negotiations helped Adams gain respect as a diplomat.

In 1817, President James Monroe called Adams back to the United States to serve as his secretary of state. Adams's most important achievement in this office was the development of the MONROE DOCTRINE. It was Adams who made the first declaration of that policy in July 1823, several months before Monroe formally announced it in his annual message to Congress, on December 2, 1823. At that time, the United States feared that Russia intended to establish colonies in Alaska and, more important, that the continental European states would intervene in Central and South America to help Spain recover its former colonies, which had won their independence in a series of wars in the early nineteenth century. Adams believed that the Americas were no longer subject to any European colonial establishment, and that they should make their own foreign policies. The Monroe Doctrine set forth three basic policy statements aimed at protecting the Western Hemisphere from European intervention: North and South America were closed to further European colonization; the United States would not intervene in wars in Europe and would not interfere with European colonies and dependencies in the Americas; and the United States would regard any intervention by a European power in the independent states of the Western Hemisphere as the manifestation of an unfriendly disposition toward the United States.

Adams served as secretary of state for the entire eight years under President Monroe.

"TO FURNISH THE MEANS OF ACQUIRING KNOWLEDGE IS . . . THE GREATEST BENEFIT THAT CAN BE CONFERRED UPON MANKIND."

When the presidential election of 1824 came around, Adams was considered a favorite; after all, the previous two presidents, Madison and Monroe, had also served as secretaries of state. But 1824 was no normal year for politics in the United States. All four candidates were members of the same political party, the Democratic-Republican party, and party affiliation had given way to sectionalism. Secretary of the Treasury William Harris Crawford, of Georgia, who had recently suffered a paralytic stroke, was nominated by a congressional caucus. The Tennessee legislature nominated Andrew Jackson, and the Kentucky legislature nominated Henry Clay. Adams was nominated by an eastern faction of the party in Boston. On Tuesday, November 9, 1824, voters went to the polls and cast 153,544 votes for Jackson, 108,740 for Adams, 46,618 for Clay, and 47,136 for Crawford. (These figures are from Kane, *Facts about the Presidents* 41 [6th ed. 1993]. Figures in other sources differ.) The electoral vote results were as follows: Jackson, 99; Adams, 84; Crawford, 41; and Clay, 37. As no candidate received a majority of the electoral votes, the House of Representatives was called upon to choose the president, as set forth under Article II, Section 1, Clause 3, of the Constitution. After Clay gave his support to Adams, the House elected Adams the sixth president in February 1825.

For one who had led so accomplished a life, Adams must have viewed his presidency as a failure. He got off to a rocky start when Jackson's supporters in Congress decried what they called a corrupt bargain between Adams and Clay. Only days after the House selected Adams president, Clay was offered the office of secretary of state, which he accepted. This deal split the Democratic-Republican party, and Adams's group became known as the National Republicans. Jackson's group fought with Adams for the next four years.

Adams threw all his energies into the presidency. In his inaugural address, he called for an ambitious program of national improvements including the construction of highways, canals, weather stations, and a national university. He urged Congress to use the powers of government for the benefit of all people. Congress disagreed. Many of the programs advocated by Adams were not realized until after his death.

Despite his best efforts, Adams felt worn down by the burdens and demands of the presidency. His personal reserve, austerity, and coolness of manner prevented him from appealing to the imagination and affections of the people. He had not even tried to defend himself against the attacks of Jackson and his followers, feeling that it was below the dignity of the president to engage in political debate. Throughout Adams's presidency, Jackson gained in popularity, so much so that in the elections of 1828, he defeated Adams by 178 electoral votes to 83. Jackson won a popular vote proportionally larger than that of any other presidential candidate during the rest of the 1800s.

Once again, Adams sought to retire from public life, but the people of Massachusetts called him back. In 1830, he defeated two other candidates and was elected to the U.S. House of Representatives, representing a district from Plymouth. When it was suggested to him that his acceptance of this position would degrade a former president, Adams replied that no person could be degraded by serving the people as a representative in Congress, or, he added, as a selectman. Indeed, Adams said that his election as president was not half so gratifying as his election to the House.

Adams shone brightly from 1831 to his death in 1848. He remained independent of party politics, and held important posts in Congress, serving at times as chairman of the Foreign Affairs Committee and of the Committee on Manufactures. Adams was conspicuous as an opponent of the expansion of slavery and was at heart an abolitionist, though he never became one in the political sense of the word. He took center stage during debates over the gag rules, which resulted when abolitionists sent many petitions to Congress urging that slavery be abolished in the District of Columbia and the new territories. Southern members of Congress who did not want to discuss slave issues passed a series of rules, known as the gag rules, that kept the abolitionists' petitions from being read on the House floor, effectively blocking any discussion of slavery. Adams fought the gag rules as violations of the right of free speech and the right of citizens to petition their government as guaranteed in the First Amendment. As the leading opponent of the gag rules, Adams became the person abolitionists sent their petitions to. He, in turn, tried to have the House consider those petitions, only to run up against the gag rules. For several years, Adams tried unsuccessfully to have the rules repealed, but he was able to win supporters to his side each time he tried, and in 1844, he finally succeeded in having the rules abolished.

Another contribution of Adams to the antislavery cause was his championing of Africans on the slave ship *Amistad*. The slaves had mutinied off the coast of Cuba, capturing their masters. The slaves, unfamiliar with navigation, asked their captives to help them sail to a country where slave trade was illegal. The former masters took advantage of the slaves' navigational inexperience and directed the ship into U.S. waters near Long Island, hoping to find sympathetic U.S. authorities. Adams was one of two attorneys who argued the case of the Africans before the U.S. Supreme Court, defending the blacks as free people. President Martin Van Buren had taken the position that the slaves must be returned to their masters and to their inevitable death. Adams helped win their freedom (*United States v. Amistad*, 40 U.S. [15 Pet.] 518, 10 L. Ed. 826 [1841]).

Adams's support of the arts and sciences was evident in his battle to uphold the dying wishes of an eccentric Englishman named James Smithson. Smithson was the illegitimate son of the first duke of Northumberland. At his death in 1829, he bequeathed his entire estate to his nephew. His will further provided that if the nephew were to die without heirs, which he did in 1835, the entire estate was to be given to the U.S. government to found what Smithson asked be called the Smithsonian Institution, an establishment for the increase and diffusion of knowledge. Adams led a ten-year fight for acceptance of the endowment, which was valued at $508,000 in 1835, and the Smithsonian Institution was established on August 10, 1846.

On November 19, 1846, Adams suffered a stroke, from which he never fully recovered. However, he continued to serve in Congress until, on February 21, 1848, he suffered a second stroke and collapsed in the House of Representatives. He was carried from his seat to the Speaker's room, where he lay until his death two days later, on February 23.

ADAPTATION 📖 The act or process of modifying an object to render it suitable for a particular or new purpose or situation. 📖

In the law of PATENTS—grants by the government to inventors for the exclusive right to manufacture, use, or market inventions for a term of years—adaptation denotes a category of patentable inventions, which entails the application of an existing product or process to a new use, accompanied by the exercise of inventive faculties. Federal law provides: "Whoever invents or discovers any new and useful process, machine, manufacture, or composition of matter, or any new and useful improvement thereof, may obtain a patent therefor, subject to the conditions and requirements of this title."

The adaptation of a device to a different field can constitute an invention if inventiveness exists in the conception of new use and with modifications necessary to render the device applicable in the new field. The progressive adaptation of well-known devices to new, but similar, uses is merely a display of an expected technical proficiency, which involves only the exercise of common reasoning abilities upon materials furnished by special knowledge ensuing from continual practice. It, therefore, does not represent a patentable invention. Ingenuity beyond the mere adaptation of teachings as could be done by a skilled mechanic is required to achieve a patentable invention; inventive talent, rather than skill in adaptation, must be manifested. To entitle a party to the benefit of the patent statute, the device must not only be new, it must be inventively new. The readaptation of old forms to new roles does not constitute invention where there is no significant alteration in the method of applying it or in the nature of the result obtained. There is no invention if the new form of the result has not previously been contemplated and, irrespective of the remoteness of the new use from the old, if no modifications in the old device are necessary to adapt it to the new use.

Invention is generally not involved where an old process, device, or method is applied to a new subject or use that is analogous to the old, or to a new use, or the production of a new result, in the same or analogous field. If the new use is so comparable to the old that the concept of adapting the device to the new use would occur to a person proficient in the art and desirous of devising a method of effectuating the intended function, there is no invention even though significant alterations have been made. The application of an old device to a new use is normally patentable only if the new use is in a different field or involves a completely novel function. In addition, the physical modifications need not be extensive, as long as they are essential to the objective.

In the law of COPYRIGHTS—the exclusive right of the author of a literary project to reproduce, publish, and sell his or her work, which is granted by statute—adaptation refers to the creation of a derivative work, which is protected by federal copyright laws.

A derivative work involves a recasting or translation process that incorporates preexisting material capable of protection by copyright. An adaptation is copyrighted if it meets the requirement of originality, in the sense that the author has created it by his or her own proficiency, labor, and judgment without directly copying or subtly imitating the preexisting material. Mere minor alterations will not suffice. In addition the adapter must procure the consent of the copyright owner of the underlying work if he or she wants to copy from such work.

The copyright in a derivative work, however, extends only to the material contributed by the adapter and does not affect the copyright protection afforded to the preexisting material.

In the law of REAL PROPERTY, with respect to FIXTURES (articles that were personal property but became part of the realty through annexation to the premises), adaptation is the relationship between the article and the use that is made of the realty to which the article is annexed.

The prevailing view is that the adaptation or appropriation of an article affixed to real property for the purpose or use to which the premises are devoted is an important consideration in ascertaining its status as a fixture. According to this theory, if the article facilitates the realization of the purpose of the real property, the annexor presumably intends it to be a permanent accession. Numerous other cases, however, allude to the adaptation of an item to the use to which the premises are designated, as merely one of the tests or factors that should, or must, be evaluated in determining that it constitutes real property. Other cases view the character of the use of the article annexed as significant.

The special construction or fitting of an article for location and use on certain land or in a particular building, which mitigates against use in another location, indicates that is was intended to constitute a part of the land.

The adaptability of an annexed article for use in another location is sometimes viewed as demonstrating the retention of its character as PERSONALTY (personal property), but this characteristic is not conclusive. Articles not designed to comprise the realty retain their character as personalty.

AD DAMNUM   [*Latin, To the loss.*] The clause in a COMPLAINT that sets a maximum amount of money that the PLAINTIFF can recover under a DEFAULT JUDGMENT if the DEFENDANT fails to appear in court.

It is a fundamental principle of DUE PROCESS that a defendant must be given fair notice of what is demanded of him or her. In a CIVIL ACTION, a plaintiff must include in the complaint served on a defendant a clause that states the amount of the loss or the amount of money DAMAGES claimed in the case. This clause is the *ad damnum.* It tells a defendant how much he or she stands to lose in the case.

In some states, the *ad damnum* sets an absolute limit on the amount of damages recoverable in the case, regardless of how much loss the plaintiff is able to prove at TRIAL. The reason for this rule is that a defendant should not be exposed to greater liability than the *ad damnum* just because he or she comes into court and defends himself or herself. In states that follow this rule, a plaintiff may be given LEAVE to increase the amount demanded by amending the complaint if later circumstances can be shown to warrant this. For example, a plaintiff who sues for $5,000 for a broken leg may find out after the action has begun that she will be permanently disabled. At that point, the court may allow the plaintiff to amend her complaint and demand damages of $50,000.

In most states and in the federal courts, a plaintiff can collect money damages in excess of the *ad damnum* if proof can be made at trial to support the higher amount. A defendant may ask for more time to prepare the case in order not to be prejudiced at trial if it begins to look as though the plaintiff is claiming more money than the *ad damnum* demands. However, the defendant cannot prevent judgment for a higher amount.

ADDAMS, JANE Jane Addams (1860–1935), a pioneer in social reform, founded Hull House, the first settlement house in the United States, to serve the immigrant families who came to Chicago at the beginning of the industrial revolution. For nearly fifty years, Addams worked relentlessly for improved living and working conditions for America's urban poor, for women's suffrage, and for international pacifism.

Addams was the youngest of eight children born to John H. and Sarah Addams. Her mother died when she was two years old, and her teenage sisters, Mary, Martha, and Alice, took over her upbringing. Her family followed the Quaker faith, and valued hard work and change through peaceful efforts. Addams idolized her father, whom she described as a man of great integrity. He remained a pivotal figure in her life until his death in 1881.

Addams's first exposure to urban poverty occurred when she was six years old, during a trip with her father to Freeport, Illinois. Upon seeing the city's garbage-filled streets and slum housing, she asked her father why the people lived in such horrid houses. After her father

BIOGRAPHY

THE BETTMANN ARCHIVE

Jane Addams

told her the people were too poor to have nicer homes, she announced that she would buy a big house when she was grown, where poor children could come and play whenever they liked.

Addams suffered throughout her life from a painful curved spine that caused her to walk pigeon-toed. As a result, she was always self-conscious about her appearance. She was a good student and often helped classmates who were having difficulties with their studies. After graduating from high school in 1877, she attended nearby Rockford Female Seminary, one of the oldest institutions for female education in the area. Rockford encouraged its students to become missionaries, but Addams, who struggled with her religious beliefs all her life, refused to consider that vocation. While at Rockford, she met Ellen Gates Starr, who would later help her found Hull House. Reflecting Addams's emerging concern about the place of women in America, she and Starr attempted to convince the seminary to offer coursework equivalent to that of men's colleges. Eventually, the seminary did become Rockford College.

Addams graduated from Rockford in 1881. Several months later, she was devastated when her father died of a ruptured appendix while on a family vacation in Wisconsin. His death left her a wealthy woman, and she decided to fulfill her plan to attend the Women's Medical College of Philadelphia. Addams began her studies that fall, but almost immediately the back pain she had suffered all her life flared up, forcing her to undergo back surgery.

During her lengthy recovery, Addams toured Europe with her stepmother, Anna Haldeman Addams. Throughout her trip, Addams was struck by the poverty of the industrialized countries she visited. At a fruit and vegetable auction in London, she watched as starving men and women fought over decayed and bruised produce. As she wrote in her autobiography, her impression was of "myriads of hands, empty, pathetic, nerveless and workworn, . . . clutching forward for food that was already unfit to eat." She was also appalled at the lack of

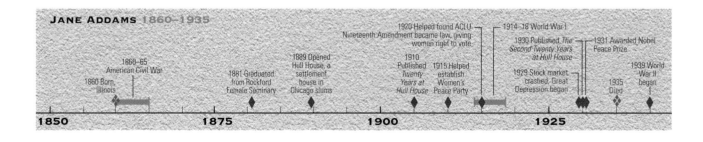

JANE ADDAMS 1860–1935

1860 Born, Illinois

1860–65 American Civil War

1881 Graduated from Rockford Female Seminary

1889 Opened Hull House, a settlement house in Chicago slums

1910 Published *Twenty Years at Hull House*

1915 Helped establish Women's Peace Party

1920 Helped found ACLU. Nineteenth Amendment became law, giving women right to vote

1914–18 World War I

1929 Stock market crashed. Great Depression began

1930 Published *The Second Twenty Years at Hull House*

1931 Awarded Nobel Peace Prize

1935 Died

1939 World War II began

1850   1875   1900   1925

concern for poor people shown by better-off Europeans.

On her return home in 1885, Addams found herself exhausted, depressed, and unsure of her life's purpose. On a second trip to Europe, she visited Toynbee Hall, an experimental Oxford-based project in London's poverty-stricken East End. Educated young men had moved into the area and were offering literacy classes, art lessons, and other activities to residents. Because the men actually settled in the area and lived with the residents, Toynbee was called a settlement house.

Addams decided to use Toynbee as a model and establish a similar facility in the slums of Chicago. With over a million residents, that city was home to hundreds of thousands of immigrants—from Germany, Ireland, Sweden, Italy, Russia, Greece, and many other countries. These desperate people were a ready source of cheap labor for the Chicago factories, and their poor wages forced them to live in overcrowded, rat-infested tenements, surrounded by filthy, garbage-filled streets. Journalist Lincoln Steffens described the Chicago of that time as violent, foul smelling, and lawless.

Addams enlisted the aid of her former schoolmate, Starr, in her new venture. The women first had to overcome the adamant objections of friends and relatives who were horrified that two educated, unmarried women would consider living in the city's slums. But Addams and Starr soon found a house where they could begin their work, the former mansion of Charles J. Hull. Once a stately country home, the house was now surrounded by run-down, noisy city tenements. In the beginning, Addams was able to rent only a few rooms in the house, but eventually, Hull's heir, Helen Culver, gave her the entire house and some surrounding land.

After several months of cleaning and refurbishing, Addams and Starr opened Hull House in September 1889. Initially, the two were met with great suspicion by the area's residents. Local priests warned their parishioners the women might try to convert them to a new religion, and street children threw garbage and rocks at the house. But Addams and Starr continued to greet their neighbors in a friendly manner, and the residents soon discovered that the women were concerned about their well-being. They also found that the women would sell them nourishing food for just a few pennies, and they soon came to depend on Hull House.

In the first few years of the settlement house, Addams established a kindergarten, a women's boarding house, the nation's first public play-

"PRIVATE BENEFICENCE
IS TOTALLY
INADEQUATE TO DEAL
WITH THE VAST
NUMBERS OF THE
CITY'S DISINHERITED."

ground, and a day care center for mothers forced to leave their children alone for as long as ten hours each day in order to work. Hull House offered evening college extension courses, English and art classes, a theater group, and books and magazines for children and adults. Observing the long hours and dangerous working conditions that the neighborhood children were forced to endure, Addams and her friends soon began working for state regulation of child labor, and went on to lobby in Washington, D.C. At home, when city garbage collectors continually ignored overflowing garbage bins, Addams applied for and was appointed to the position of ward garbage inspector, and forced the trash collectors to remove the filth.

Addams described her work at Hull House as an effort to conserve and push forward the best of the community's achievements. She strove to respect and preserve the immigrants' cultures, and the holidays of their various nations were always celebrated at Hull House.

Among the volunteers who flocked to Hull House to work with Addams were several women who later brought about important social reform. Julia C. Lathrop helped establish Chicago's first juvenile court. Dr. Alice Hamilton worked in industrial medicine and conducted studies that helped improve factory conditions. Florence Kelley investigated sweatshops for the Illinois State Bureau of Labor and helped establish child labor laws. Although Addams developed a wide circle of influential supporters because of her work, such as socialist Eugene V. Debs and journalist Steffens, she also occasionally lost admirers for the same reason. Addams never wavered in her belief that the same activities that caused her to lose some supporters would help her to gain others.

In the first decade of the twentieth century, Addams established herself as a prolific writer, publishing *Democracy and Social Ethics* (1902), *Newer Ideals for Peace* (1907), *The Spirit of Youth and the City Streets* (1909), and the best-selling first volume of her autobiography, *Twenty Years at Hull House* (1910). During these years, she began to turn her attention more and more to women's issues—particularly the right to vote. In 1913, seven years before the NINETEENTH AMENDMENT to the U.S. Constitution granted women the right to vote in all elections, she helped secure the vote for women in Chicago.

Addams's work continued to expand beyond Hull House and WOMEN'S RIGHTS. In 1909, she supported the founding of the National Association for the Advancement of Colored People and served on its executive committee. In 1915, she helped establish the Women's Peace Party, and traveled to Europe to attend the International Women's Peace Conference in the Netherlands and carry the message of peace to the countries fighting in World War I. Addams continued to hold to her pacifist views even when the United States entered the war in 1917, and she was blacklisted as a result. The Daughters of the American Revolution, a group that had once honored Addams for her colonial ancestry, expelled her, and she was shunned by many other supporters. She continued her humanitarian work during the war, however, helping the U.S. Department of Food Administration to distribute food to European allies.

Following the war, Addams also worked to have food sent to the starving civilians in the defeated countries, setting off yet another round of criticism. In 1920, in response to increasing attempts to stifle unpopular opinion in the United States, Addams helped found the AMERICAN CIVIL LIBERTIES UNION, dedicated to protecting the individual's right to believe, write, and speak whatever he or she chooses.

By the 1930s, the public's bitterness toward Addams had abated. In 1931, she was awarded the Nobel Peace Prize, an achievement that Addams felt justified her pacifist work to the world. Frederick Stang, of the Nobel Committee in Norway, said Addams had clung to her idealism during a difficult time in which peace was overshadowed. Addams went on to receive fourteen honorary degrees, among them one from Yale, the first honorary degree that school had ever awarded to a woman.

In 1930, Addams completed her autobiography with the publication of *The Second Twenty Years at Hull House*. A few years later, surgery revealed that Addams was suffering from advanced cancer. She died in May 1935. Shortly before her death, Addams was honored at an event marking the twentieth anniversary of the Women's International League for Peace and Freedom. In response to the many tributes she received, she said she was driven by the fear that she might give up too soon and fail to make the one effort that might save the world.

ADDICT Any individual who habitually uses any narcotic drug so as to endanger the public morals, health, safety, or welfare, or who is so drawn to the use of such narcotic drugs as to have lost the power of self-control with reference to his or her drug use.

Addiction to narcotics is not a CRIME in itself, but that does not excuse violation of related statutes. It may be an offense to be under the influence of an illegal drug in a public place, even though being an addict is not illegal.

Addiction to narcotics is not a crime in itself, but this man, who has been sniffing heroin, may be arrested on another charge related to his drug use.

While such a statute is intended to protect society from the dangers of drug abuse and the antisocial conduct of drug abusers, it generally is not necessary for conviction to prove that the defendant was disturbing the peace when arrested. See also DRUGS AND NARCOTICS.

ADDITIONAL EXTENDED COVERAGE A provision added to an INSURANCE policy to extend the scope of coverage to include further risks to dwellings.

The provision may cover water damage from the plumbing or heating systems, VANDALISM or MALICIOUS MISCHIEF, glass breakage, falling trees, damage from ice or snow storms, or additional risks not otherwise covered by the liability policy.

ADDITIONAL INSTRUCTIONS A charge given to a JURY by a judge after the original INSTRUCTIONS to explain the law and guide the jury in its decision making.

Additional instructions are frequently needed after the jury has begun deliberations and finds that it has a question concerning the evidence, a point of law, or some part of the original charge.

ADDITUR The power of the trial court to assess DAMAGES or increase the amount of an inadequate award made by JURY verdict, as a condition of a denial of a motion for a new trial, with the consent of the DEFENDANT whether or not the PLAINTIFF consents to such action. This is not allowed in the federal system.

Damages assessed by a jury may be set aside when the amount is shocking to the judicial conscience—so grossly inadequate that it constitutes a MISCARRIAGE OF JUSTICE—or when it appears that the jury was influenced by PREJUDICE, corruption, passion, or mistake.

For example, a sixty-one-year-old woman was mugged in a hallway of her apartment building after the landlord failed to replace a broken lock on the back service entrance. She sustained a broken shoulder, a broken arm, and numerous cuts and bruises. Her medical bills amounted to more than $2,500. She sued the landlord for his negligent maintenance of the building, and the jury returned a verdict in her favor but awarded damages of only $2,500. Her attorney immediately moved for a new trial on the ground that the verdict was shockingly inadequate. The trial judge ruled that the jury could not possibly have calculated compensation for the woman's pain and suffering, an item that should have been included under state law. The trial judge, therefore, awarded an additur of $15,000. The effect of this order was to put the defendant on notice that he must either pay the $15,000 in addition to the verdict of $2,500 or a new trial would be held. The defendant weighed the disadvantages of investing time and money in a new trial and the risk of an even higher award of monetary damages by a sympathetic jury. He consented to the additur.

An additur is not justified solely because the amount of damages is low. For example, damages of $10,000 certainly will not compensate the family of a forty-four-year-old man who had been steadily employed as a plumber until he was permanently disabled in an auto accident. In such a case, however, the jury could have found that the plaintiff's NEGLIGENCE contributed to the cause of the accident and reduced the damages proportionately, as is permitted in most states.

An award of additur is not permitted in every state, nor is it allowed in the FEDERAL COURTS. Under the rules that govern procedure in the federal courts, a trial judge has the power to set aside a verdict for a plaintiff on the ground that the damages awarded are clearly inadequate, but then the judge's only recourse is to grant a new trial.

CROSS-REFERENCES

Civil Procedure; Trial.

ADD-ON 📖 A purchase of additional goods before payment is made for goods already purchased. 📖

An add-on may be covered by a clause in an INSTALLMENT payment contract that allows the seller to hold a security interest in the earlier goods until full payment is made on the later goods.

ADDUCE 📖 To present, offer, bring forward, or introduce. 📖

For example, a BILL OF PARTICULARS that lists each of the plaintiff's demands may recite that it contains all the evidence to be adduced at trial.

ADEMPTION 📖 The failure of a gift of personal property—a BEQUEST—or of real property—a DEVISE—to be distributed according to the provisions of a decedent's WILL because the property no longer belongs to the TESTATOR at the time of his or her death or because the property has been substantially changed. 📖

There are two types of ademption: by extinction and by satisfaction.

Extinction   Ademption by extinction occurs when a particular item of PERSONAL PROPERTY or specially designated REAL PROPERTY is substantially changed or not part of the testator's ESTATE when he or she dies. For example, a testator makes a will giving her farm to her nephew and a diamond watch to her niece. Before she dies, she sells the farm and loses the watch. The proceeds of the sale of the farm are traced to a bank account. After the testator's death, the nephew claims the proceeds from the sale and the niece claims that the executor of the estate should pay her the value of the diamond watch. Neither claim will be upheld. Once the farm is sold, the specific devise is adeemed by extinction. The proceeds from its sale are not its equivalent for INHERITANCE purposes. In some states, however, if all of the proceeds had not yet been paid, the nephew would be entitled to receive the unpaid balance.

Since the testator no longer owns the diamond watch when she dies, that specific bequest is also adeemed by extinction.

Satisfaction   Ademption by SATISFACTION takes place when the testator, during his or her lifetime, gives to his or her HEIR all or a part of the gift he or she had intended to give by his or her will. It applies to both specific bequests and devises as well as to a general bequest or LEGACY payable from the general assets of the testator's estate. If the subject of the gift made while the testator is alive is the same as the subject of a provision of the will, many states presume that it is in place of the TESTAMENTARY gift if there is a parent-child or grandparent-grandchild relationship. Otherwise, an ademption by satisfaction will not be found unless there is independent evidence, such as express statements or writings, that the testator intended this to occur. A father makes a will leaving his ski house to his daughter and $25,000 to his son. Before death, he gives the daughter the deed to the ski house and he gives the son $15,000 with which to complete medical school. After the father's death, the daughter will get nothing, while the son will get $10,000.

After the son received the $15,000 from his father, there was an ademption by satisfaction of the general legacy of $25,000 to the extent of the size of the lifetime gift, $15,000. The son is entitled to receive the remaining $10,000 of the original general legacy. Since there was a parent-child relationship, there was no need for independent proof that the $15,000 gift was intended to adeem the gift under the will.

ADEQUATE 📖 Sufficient; equal to what is required; suitable to the case or occasion. 📖

A law that requires public utilities to provide adequate service does not create a right for customers to sue the electric company whenever the meat in their freezers spoils because of a power outage in the absence of NEGLIGENCE. Service does not have to be perfect in order to meet a standard of adequacy.

ADEQUATE REMEDY AT LAW 📖 Sufficient compensation by way of monetary DAMAGES. 📖

Courts will not grant equitable remedies, such as SPECIFIC PERFORMANCE or INJUNCTIONS, where monetary damages can afford complete legal relief. An equitable remedy interferes much more with the defendant's freedom of action than an order directing the defendant to pay for the harm he or she has caused, and it is much more difficult for a court to supervise and enforce judgments giving some relief other than money. Courts, therefore, will compensate an injured party whenever possible with monetary damages; this remedy has been called the remedy at law since the days when courts of EQUITY and courts at law were different.

ADHESION CONTRACT 📖 A type of CONTRACT, a legally binding agreement between two parties to do a certain thing, in which one side has all the bargaining power and uses it to write the contract primarily to his or her advantage. 📖

An example of an adhesion contract is a standardized contract form that offers goods or services to consumers on essentially a "take it or leave it" basis without giving consumers realistic opportunities to negotiate terms that would benefit their interests. When this occurs, the consumer cannot obtain the desired product or service unless he or she acquiesces to the form contract.

There is nothing unenforceable or even wrong about adhesion contracts. In fact, most businesses would never conclude their volume of transactions if it were necessary to negotiate all the terms of every CONSUMER CREDIT contract.

INSURANCE contracts and residential LEASES are other kinds of adhesion contracts. This does not mean, however, that all adhesion contracts are valid. Many adhesion contracts are UNCONSCIONABLE; they are so unfair to the weaker party that a court will refuse to enforce them. An example would be severe penalty provisions for failure to pay loan installments promptly that are physically hidden by small print located in the middle of an obscure paragraph of a lengthy loan agreement. In such a case a court can find that there is no MEETING OF THE MINDS of the parties to the contract and that the weaker party has not accepted the terms of the contract.

AD HOC 📖 [Latin, *For this; for this special purpose.*] An attorney ad hoc, or a GUARDIAN or curator ad hoc, is one appointed for a special purpose, generally to represent the client or infant in the particular action in which the appointment is made. 📖

AD HOMINEM 📖 [Latin, *To the person.*] A term used in debate to denote an argument made personally against an opponent, instead of against the opponent's argument. 📖

AD INTERIM 📖 [Latin, *In the meantime.*] An officer *ad interim* is a person appointed to fill a position that is temporarily open, or to perform the functions of a particular position during the absence or temporary incapacity of the individual who regularly fulfills those duties. 📖

ADJACENT 📖 Lying near or close to; neighboring. 📖

Adjacent means that objects or parcels of land are not widely separated, though perhaps they are not actually touching; but adjoining implies that they are united so closely that no other object comes between them.

ADJECTIVE LAW 📖 The aggregate of rules of procedure or practice. Also called adjectival law, as opposed to that body of law that the courts are established to administer (called *substantive law*), it means the rules according to which the SUBSTANTIVE LAW is administered, e.g., Rules of Civil Procedure. That part of the law that provides a method for enforcing or maintaining rights, or obtaining redress for their invasion. Pertains to and prescribes the practice, method, procedure, or legal machinery by which substantive law is enforced or made effective. 📖

See also CIVIL PROCEDURE.

ADJOINING LANDOWNERS 📖 Those persons, such as next-door and backyard neighbors, who own lands that share common BOUNDARIES and therefore have mutual rights, duties, and liabilities. 📖

The reciprocal rights and obligations of adjoining landowners existed at COMMON LAW but have been modified by various state laws and court decisions.

Rights, Duties, and Liabilities Landowners are expected to use their PROPERTY reasonably without unduly interfering with the rights of the owners of contiguous land. Anything that a person does that appropriates adjoining land or substantially deprives an adjoining owner of the reasonable enjoyment of his or her property is an unlawful use of one's property. A man buys a house in a residentially zoned area and converts it into an office building. He paves the backyard for a parking lot, but encroaches two feet beyond his property into the lot of the adjoining landowner. His use of the property is unlawful for a number of reasons. He has appropriated his neighbor's land and substantially interfered with his neighbor's right to use it. His neighbor may sue him in a TORT action for the NUISANCE created and, if successful, the neighbor will be awarded DAMAGES and an INJUNCTION to stop the unlawful use of the land. In addition, the purchaser has violated ZONING laws by using residential property for commercial purposes without seeking a VARIANCE.

Property owners have the right to grade or change the level of their land or to build foundations or embankments as long as proper precautions are taken, such as building a retaining wall to prevent soil from spilling upon adjoining land. If permitted by law, landowners may blast on their own property but will be liable for damages caused by the flying debris thrown onto adjoining land.

Lateral Support A landowner has a legally enforceable right to LATERAL SUPPORT from an adjoining landowner. Lateral support is the right to have one's land in its natural condition held in place from the sides by the neighboring land so that it will not fall away. Land is considered in its natural condition if it has no artificial structures or buildings on it. A landowner can enforce the right to lateral support in court. A lawsuit for the removal of lateral support accrues when the damage occurs, not when the excavation is done.

An adjoining landowner who excavates close to his or her boundary line has a duty to prevent injury arising from the removal of the lateral support of a neighbor's property. Because the right to lateral support is considered an absolute property right, an adjoining landowner will be liable for damages to the natural condition of the land regardless of whether or not he or she acted negligently.

When, however, a landowner has erected buildings on the land, his or her right to

recover for deprivation of the lateral support is different. Since additional weight has been placed on the land, thus increasing the burden on the lateral support, the landowner can be awarded damages for injuries to the building caused by excavation only if his or her neighbor has been negligent. Sometimes local ORDINANCES require that persons planning to excavate on their own property give notice to neighboring adjoining landowners so that neighbors may take preventive measures to protect their property. The failure of landowners who receive notice to take precautions does not necessarily absolve the excavator of liability for NEGLIGENCE. If, however, the excavator does not notify neighboring landowners, courts have treated this failure as negligence, and the excavator will be responsible for damages even though the excavating itself was not done negligently.

When evidence establishes that an adjoining landowner has removed the lateral support of a neighbor's land, the neighbor will recover damages in the amount of either the cost of restoring the property to its value before its support was removed or the cost of restoring the land to its former condition, whichever is less. An injunction prohibiting further excavation may be granted if it poses a clear danger to contiguous lands and if it will cause irreparable damage.

Subjacent Support A landowner is entitled to subjacent support, the absolute right to have one's land supported from beneath its surface. If one person owns the surface of the land while another owns the subjacent surface, the owner of the surface is entitled to have it remain in its natural condition without subsidence caused by the subsurface owner's withdrawal of subjacent materials. An adjoining landowner who, during excavation, taps a subterranean stream, causing

Suburban housing is encroaching on prime farmland in California's San Joaquin Valley.

the soil of the neighbor's land to subside, will be liable for any injuries that result. The surface owner's right to sue the subsurface owner for deprivation of subjacent support arises when the land actually subsides, not when the excavation is made.

The construction of buildings on the surface of the land does not lessen a person's right to subjacent support. It does, however, change the circumstances under which that person may recover for the removal of subsurface support. If such buildings are damaged, their owner must show that the removal of the support was done negligently.

Light, Air, and View No landowner has an absolute right to light and air from or passing over adjoining property or to a view over adjoining lands. Zoning laws imposed by localities may, however, require that any construction undertaken by an individual not deprive an adjoining landowner of adequate air, light, and view. Similarly, many agreements such as RE-STRICTIVE COVENANTS in DEEDS or EASEMENTS affect a person's duty toward his or her next-door neighbor's right to air, light, and view. In the absence of zoning laws or agreements, therefore, a person may build on his or her own property without regard to the fact that he or she is depriving the next-door neighbor of the light, air, and view that was enjoyed before the building was erected. An exception is a structure that blocks air, light, and view for the sole purpose of injuring a neighbor—such as a "spite" fence—and which is of no beneficial use or pleasure to the owner. Courts will generally not permit such structures.

Encroachments An ENCROACHMENT is an intrusion upon the property of another without that person's permission. No person is legally entitled to construct buildings or other structures so that any part, regardless of size, extends beyond that person's property line and intrudes upon adjoining lands. An encroaching owner can be required to remove the eaves of a building that overhang an adjoining lot. If he or she refuses to do so, the owner of the contiguous lot may personally remove as much of the encroachment that deprives him or her of the complete enjoyment of his or her land, but if negligent, he or she will be liable for damages. Should any expenses be incurred in the removal of the encroachment from the adjoining land, the person whose property was encroached upon can sue the owner to recover damages.

The person whose property has been encroached upon may sue the encroacher under either the theory of nuisance or the theory of TRESPASS to obtain monetary damages, or instead, may seek an injunction against continuation of the encroachment or to force its removal.

Trees and Shrubs Landowners should not permit trees or hedges on their property to invade the rights of adjoining landowners. If an individual knows, for example, that a tree on his or her property is decayed and may fall and damage the property of another, that individual has a duty to eliminate the danger. A tree on the boundary line of contiguous land belongs to both adjoining landowners. Each owner has an interest identical with the portion standing on his or her land. Each can sever intruding tree branches or roots at the boundary line of his or her property, whether or not any injuries have been sustained by the intrusion, but reasonable care must be exercised so as not to kill the entire tree.

See also LAND USE CONTROL.

ADJOURNED TERM ◫ A CONTINUANCE of a previous or regular court session that results from postponement. ◫

When a term is adjourned, it is actually prolonged due to a temporary putting off of the business being conducted.

ADJOURNMENT ◫ A putting off or postponing of proceedings; an ending or dismissal of further business by a court, legislature, or public official—either temporarily or permanently. ◫

If an adjournment is final, it is said to be sine die, "without day" or without a time fixed to resume the work. An adjournment is different from a RECESS, which is only a short break in proceedings.

ADJUDGE ◫ To determine by a judge; to pass on and decide judicially. ◫

A person adjudged guilty is one who has been convicted in court.

ADJUDICATION ◫ The legal process of resolving a dispute. The formal giving or pronouncing of a JUDGMENT or DECREE in a court proceeding; also the judgment or decision given. The entry of a decree by a court in respect to the parties in a case. It implies a hearing by a court, after notice, of legal evidence on the factual issue(s) involved. The equivalent of a DETERMINATION. It indicates that the claims of all the parties thereto have been considered and set at rest. ◫

Three types of disputes are resolved through adjudication: disputes between private parties, such as individuals or corporations; disputes between private parties and public officials; and disputes between public officials or public bodies. The requirements of full adjudication include NOTICE to all interested parties (all parties with a legal interest in, or legal right affected by, the dispute) and an opportunity for all parties to present EVIDENCE and ARGUMENTS. The adjudicative process is governed by formal rules of evidence and procedure. Its objective is to reach a reasonable settlement of the controversy at hand. A decision is rendered by an impartial, passive fact finder, usually a judge, JURY, or administrative tribunal.

The adjudication of a controversy involves the performance of several tasks. The trier must establish the FACTS in controversy, and define and interpret the applicable law, or, if no relevant law exists, fashion a new law to apply to the situation. Complex evidentiary rules limit the presentation of proofs, and the Anglo-American tradition of STARE DECISIS, or following PRECEDENTS, controls the outcome. However, the process of applying established rules of law is neither simple nor automatic. Judges have considerable latitude in interpreting the statutes or case law upon which they base their decisions.

An age-old question that still plagues legal theorists is whether judges "make" law when they adjudicate. Sir William Blackstone believed that judges do nothing more than maintain and expound established law (*Commentaries on the Laws of England*); other writers vehemently disagree. Some legal analysts maintain that the law is whatever judges declare it to be. Echoing those sentiments, President Theodore Roosevelt asserted that "the chief lawmakers in our country may be, and often are, the judges, because they are the final seat of authority. Every time they interpret . . . they necessarily enact into law parts of a system of social philosophy; and as such interpretation is fundamental, they give direction to all law-making" (Message to Congress [Dec. 8, 1908]). Supreme Court Justice Benjamin N. Cardozo, writing in *The Nature of the Judicial Process*, argued that the law is evolutionary and that judges, by interpreting and applying it to specific sets of facts, actually fashion new laws.

Whether judges are seen as making law or merely following what came before, they are required to operate within narrow strictures. Even when they are deciding a case of FIRST IMPRESSION (a question that has not previously been adjudicated), they generally try to analogize to some existing precedent. Judges often consider customs of the community; political and social implications; customs of the trade, market, or profession; and history when applying the law. Some, such as Justice Oliver Wendell Holmes and Justice Cardozo, thought that considerations of social and PUBLIC POLICY are the most powerful forces behind judicial decisions.

A HEARING in which the parties are given an opportunity to present their evidence and arguments is essential to an adjudication. Anglo-American law presumes that the parties to the dispute are in the best position to know the facts of their particular situations and develop their own proofs. If the hearing is before a court, formal rules of procedure and evidence govern; a hearing before an ADMINISTRATIVE AGENCY is generally less structured.

Following the hearing, the decision maker is expected to deliver a reasoned OPINION. This opinion is the basis for review if the decision is appealed to a higher tribunal (a court of appeals). It also helps ensure that decisions are not reached arbitrarily. Finally, a well-reasoned opinion forces the judge to carefully think through his or her decision in order to be able to explain the process followed in reaching it.

Adjudication of a controversy generally ensures a fair and equitable outcome. Because courts are governed by evidentiary and procedural rules, as well as by stare decisis, the adjudicative process assures litigants of some degree of efficiency, uniformity, and predictability of result.

CROSS-REFERENCES

Blackstone, Sir William; Cardozo, Benjamin; Holmes, Oliver Wendell; Judiciary.

ADJUDICATIVE FACTS

Factual matters concerning the parties to an administrative proceeding as contrasted with LEGISLATIVE FACTS, which are general and usually do not touch individual questions of particular parties to a proceeding. FACTS that concern a person's motives and intent, as contrasted with general policy issues. Those facts that must be found BEYOND A REASONABLE DOUBT by the trier of fact before there can be a conviction.

Adjudicative facts, of which a trial court may take notice if a fact is not subject to reasonable dispute, are those to which law is applied in the process of adjudication; they are facts that, in a jury case, normally go to the jury.

The role of a U.S. court is to resolve the dispute that has brought the parties before it. Determining what happened to whom, when and how it happened, and what the result is or will be, is part of the adjudicative process by which the court reaches that resolution. These determinations establish the adjudicative facts of the dispute.

Adjudicative facts differ from ordinary facts in that they are considered facts only if the court recognizes and accepts them. For ex-

Adjudicative facts are specific to a particular case and are the kinds of issues decided by juries.

ample, a witness may testify that she saw the defendant's car parked at a specific place at a specific time. These are the facts as she recalls them. However, the court may reject her account and instead accept another witness's testimony that the defendant was driving that same car in another part of town at the same time. The second witness's account will therefore become part of the adjudicative facts of the case, and the first witness's recollection will be considered IMMATERIAL.

Adjudicative facts are specific and unique to a particular controversy. For this reason, the fact determination in one case is not controlling in other similar cases, even if all the cases arose from the same incident. Adjudicative facts differ from legislative facts, which are general and can be applied to any party in a similar situation. For example, the facts used by a court to determine the legality of a tax increase levied against a single taxpayer would be adjudicative facts particular to that taxpayer's case. By contrast, the facts used to determine the legality of a general tax increase levied against all the residents of a city would be legislative in nature. Because facts can be perceived and interpreted differently by different people, the skillful lawyer is careful about what facts to present and how to present them at trial.

Adjudicative facts re-create the course of events that led to the dispute. They may also predict what will happen as a result. For example, where one party is suing another for personal injury, adjudicative facts will determine what happened, who was at fault, and what redress is appropriate for pain and suffering. Adjudicative facts will further establish what lasting consequences, such as lost future wages, the plaintiff is likely to suffer and what compensation is fitting.

Adjudicative facts found by the court are final and will not be reviewed on appeal except in cases where it can be shown that the findings were made on insubstantial evidence or were clearly erroneous.

ADJUNCTION Attachment or affixing to another. Something attached as a dependent or auxiliary part.

Under the CIVIL LAW system which prevails in much of Europe and Latin America, adjunction is the permanent union of a thing belonging to one person to something that belongs to someone else.

A branch agency, for example, is an adjunct of the main department or administrative agency.

ADJURATION A swearing; taking an OATH to be truthful.

To adjure is to command solemnly, warning that penalties may be invoked.

ADJUST To settle or arrange; to free from differences or discrepancies. To bring to a satisfactory state so that parties are agreed, as to adjust amount of loss by fire or controversy regarding property or estate. To bring to proper relations. To determine and apportion an amount due. The term is sometimes used in the sense of pay, when used in reference to a liquidated claim. Determination of an amount to be paid to insured by insurer to cover loss or damage sustained.

ADJUSTED GROSS INCOME The term used for INCOME TAX purposes to describe GROSS INCOME less certain allowable deductions such as trade and business deductions, moving expenses, alimony paid, and penalties for premature withdrawals from term savings accounts, in order to determine a person's taxable income.

The rules for computing adjusted gross income for federal income tax may differ from the rules in a state that imposes a state income tax.

ADJUSTER A person appointed or employed to settle or arrange matters that are in dispute; one who determines the amount to be paid on a CLAIM.

An INSURANCE adjuster determines the extent of the insurance company's liability when a claim is submitted. A public adjuster is a self-employed person who is hired by litigants to determine or settle the amount of a claim or debt.

ADJUSTMENT SECURITIES STOCKS and BONDS of a new CORPORATION that are issued to stockholders during a corporate REORGANIZATION in exchange for stock held in the original corporation before it was reorganized.

AD LITEM 📖 [*Latin, For the suit; for the purposes of the suit; pending the suit.*] A GUARDIAN AD LITEM is a guardian appointed to prosecute or defend a suit on behalf of a party who is legally incapable of doing so, such as an infant or an insane person. 📖

ADMINISTER 📖 To give an OATH, as to administer the oath of office to the president at the inauguration. To direct the transactions of business or government. Immigration laws are administered largely by the Immigration and Naturalization Service. To take care of affairs, as an EXECUTOR administers the ESTATE of a deceased person. To directly cause the ingestion of medications or poisons. To apply a court decree, enforce its provisions, or resolve disputes concerning its meaning. 📖

School teachers generally are not authorized to administer medicines that pupils take to school, for example.

When divorced parents cannot agree on how to administer a visitation provision in a judgment granting child custody to one of them, they might have to return to court for clarification from the judge.

ADMINISTRATION 📖 The performance of executive duties in an institution or business. The Small Business Administration is responsible for administration of some disaster-relief loans. In government, the practical management and direction of some department or agency in the executive branch; in general, the entire class of public officials and employees managing the executive department. The management and distribution of the ESTATE of a

decedent performed under the supervision of the surrogate's or PROBATE court by a person duly qualified and legally appointed. If the decedent made a valid WILL designating someone called an EXECUTOR to handle this function, the court will issue that person LETTERS TESTAMENTARY as authority to do so. If a person dies INTESTATE or did not name an executor in his or her will, the court will appoint an ADMINISTRATOR and grant him or her LETTERS OF ADMINISTRATION to perform the duties of administration. 📖

An executor or administrator must carry out the responsibilities of administration, including collection and preservation of the decedent's assets; payment of debts and claims against the estate; payment of estate tax; and distribution of the balance of the estate to the decedent's heirs.

ADMINISTRATION, OFFICE OF The Office of Administration was established within the Executive Office of the President (EOP) by Reorganization Plan 1 of 1977 (implemented by Executive Order 12, 028, 42 Fed. Reg. 62, 895 [1977], issued on December 12, 1977, by President Jimmy Carter). The office was created to help centralize the activities of all EOP offices into a single agency. The director of the Office of Administration, who is appointed by and reports directly to the president, is responsible for, according to Executive Order 12,028, "ensuring that the Office of Administration provides units with the Executive Office of the President common administrative support and services."

The Office of Administration provides administrative support services to all EOP offices

Office of Administration

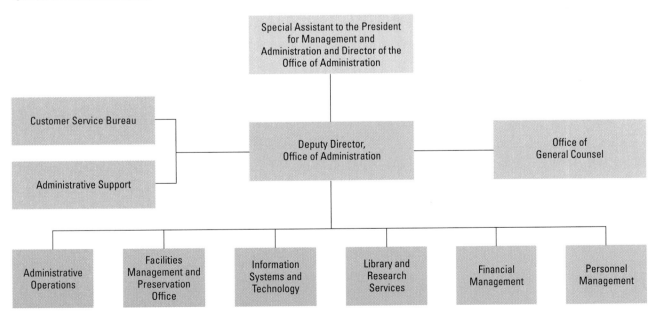

in the White House, except services that are in direct support of the president. The Office of Administration may, however, at the request of the president, help the White House provide administrative services in direct support of the president. The services provided by the Office of Administration include personnel management; financial management; data processing; library; and office operations, including the handling of mail (except for presidential mail), messenger service, printing and duplication, graphics, word processing, procurement, and supply. The office also oversees three libraries (not open to the general public): a general reference library located in the New Executive Office Building, and a reference library and a law library in the Old Executive Office Building.

The Office of Administration consists of nearly two hundred full- and part-time employees who maintain accounts for all EOP offices; recruit employees (except for those who will staff the Office of Policy Development and the White House, all of whom are political appointees); and maintain official records, including those of the White House. In addition to the director and an assistant director, the office is managed by three deputy assistant directors, who provide supervision in the areas of general services, information management, and resources management.

Since its creation, the Office of Administration has developed sophisticated computer systems to respond to the increasingly complex needs of the White House and the EOP.

ADMINISTRATIVE ACTS 📖 Whatever actions are necessary to carry out the intent of STATUTES; those acts required by legislative policy as it is expressed in laws enacted by the legislature. 📖

If a city commission votes to create the position of park superintendent, that is a LEGISLATIVE ACT that can take effect only if the commission follows all the steps required for formal legislation. When the same commission votes to rezone a parcel of real property from single-family residential to business uses, however, that is an administrative act that does not require the same formality as legislation. It is administrative because it is carrying out the zoning laws already in effect.

ADMINISTRATIVE ADJUDICATION 📖 The process by which an ADMINISTRATIVE AGENCY issues an ORDER, such order being affirmative, negative, injunctive, or declaratory in form. 📖

Most formal proceedings before an administrative agency follow the process of either rule making or ADJUDICATION. Rule making formulates policy by setting RULES for the future conduct of persons governed by that agency. Adjudication applies the agency's policy to the past actions of a particular party, and it results in an order for or against that party. Both methods are strictly regulated by the law of administrative procedure.

See also ADMINISTRATIVE LAW AND PROCEDURE.

ADMINISTRATIVE AGENCY 📖 An official governmental body empowered with the authority to direct and supervise the implementation of particular LEGISLATIVE ACTS. In addition to *agency*, such governmental bodies may be called commissions, corporations (e.g., F.D.I.C.), boards, departments, or divisions. 📖

Administrative agencies are created by the federal Constitution, the U.S. Congress, state legislatures, and local lawmaking bodies to manage crises, redress serious social problems, or oversee complex matters of governmental concern beyond the expertise of legislators. Although Article I, Section 1, of the federal Constitution plainly states that "[a]ll legislative Powers herein granted shall be vested in a Congress of the United States," the "necessary-and-proper" clause, in the eighth section of the same article, states that Congress shall have power "[t]o make all Laws which shall be necessary and proper for carrying into Execution the foregoing Powers, and all other Powers . . . in any Department or Officer thereof." With this language, many have argued that the Framers of the Constitution expected, indeed encouraged, the creation of powerful administrative agencies. This argument currently prevails, and courts have therefore allowed the U.S. Congress—and other legislative bodies—to make laws that delegate limited lawmaking authority to administrative agencies. The substance of an administrative agency's powers must be intelligible, and a system of controls must be in place to limit those powers, but courts almost always find that administrative agencies meet these requirements.

Administrative agency RULES and regulations often have the force of law against individuals. This has led many critics to charge that the creation of agencies circumvents the constitutional directive that laws are to be created by elected officials. According to these critics, administrative agencies constitute an unconstitutional, bureaucratic fourth branch of government with powers that exceed those of the three recognized branches (the legislative, executive, and judiciary). In response, supporters of administrative agencies note that agencies are created and overseen by elected officials or the president. Agencies are created by an ENABLING STATUTE, which is a state or federal law that gives birth to the agency and outlines the procedures for the agency's rule making. Furthermore, agencies include the public in their rulemaking processes. Thus, by proxy, agencies are the will of the electorate.

Supporters of administrative agencies note also that agencies are able to adjudicate relatively minor or exceedingly complex disputes more quickly or more flexibly than can state and federal courts, which helps preserve judicial resources and promotes swift resolutions. Opponents argue that swiftness and ease at the expense of fairness are no virtues, but while the debate continues, administrative agencies thrive.

Governmental representation in an administrative capacity of any kind can be considered administrative agency. The PRESIDENT is an administrative agent whose enabling statute is the federal Constitution. The thirteen executive departments reporting to the president are administrative agencies. For example, the Department of Justice is a cabinet-level executive department, but it functions as the administrative agency that addresses the legal concerns of the U.S. government and its people. The departments housed within the Department of Justice, such as the Drug Enforcement Administration and the Federal Bureau of Investigation, are also administrative agencies, and they have procedures and rules of their own.

Administrative agencies are made up of experts in the field in which the agency operates. For example, the Maritime Administration employs experts in the areas of sea commerce and navigation to set its rules on merchant marine activities. Many agencies have the power to assess fines or otherwise deprive persons of liberty in HEARINGS conducted by their own judicial bodies, or ADMINISTRATIVE BOARDS. Given the specialized knowledge within administrative agencies, administrative law judges (ALJs), who hear agency claims and disputes, are loath to overturn the legal conclusions reached by administrative boards. Determinations and sanctions made by ALJs are subject to review by state or federal courts, but a party must exhaust all appeals within the agency before suing in civil court.

An agency's actions must be in accordance with its enabling statute, and courts will examine the agency records to determine whether the agency exceeded its lawmaking or judicial powers. Rigorous judicial oversight of agencies would defeat a cherished feature of administrative agency by eliminating agency flexibility in resolving conflicts. To avoid this, most enabling

THE BETTMANN ARCHIVE

statutes are worded vaguely, in such a way as to allow the agencies broad discretion in determining their rules and procedures. To keep agencies from wielding unbridled power, the Administrative Procedure Act of 1946 (APA) (5 U.S.C.A. § 551 [1982]) sets standards for the activities and rule making of all federal regulatory agencies. The APA provides federal courts with a framework for reviewing the rules made and procedures used by administrative agencies. Individual states have similar statutes to guide their own courts.

History of Administrative Agency

The first administrative agency was created by Congress in 1789 to provide pensions for wounded Revolutionary War soldiers. Also in the late 1700s, agencies were created to determine the amount of duties charged on imported goods, but it was not until 1887 that the first permanent administrative agency was created. The Interstate Commerce Commission (ICC), created by the Interstate Commerce Act (49 U.S.C.A. § 10101 et seq. [1995]), was invented by Congress to regulate commerce among the

The National Recovery Administration was created in the early 1930s to ensure fair market competition. It was one of numerous agencies created by Congress during the Great Depression in an effort to regulate the production and marketing of goods.

states, especially the interstate transportation of persons or property by carriers. The ICC was designed to ensure that carriers involved in interstate commerce provided the public with fair and reasonable rates and services. To buttress the Interstate Commerce Act, the Federal Reserve System was established by the Federal Reserve Act of 1913 (12 U.S.C.A. § 221) to serve as the United States' central bank and execute U.S. monetary policy. One year later, the Federal Trade Commission was established by Congress to promote free and fair competition in interstate commerce by preventing unfair methods of competition.

In 1908, the Federal Bureau of Investigation (FBI) was established to investigate violations of federal laws not assigned to other federal agencies. The FBI is charged with solving crimes such as kidnapping, espionage, sabotage, bank robbery, extortion, interstate transportation of stolen property, civil rights violations, interstate gambling violations, fraud against the government, and the assault or killing of a federal officer or the president. As an agency concerned with criminal apprehension, the FBI is considered an arm of the government, and its directorship is subject to presidential approval. However, the FBI carries out its investigations independent of political influence. It can, for example, probe the actions of presidents and legislators, the very persons responsible for its existence.

Administrative agencies are usually created in response to a felt public need. Some older agencies, for example, were created after the Civil War to address economic matters critical to the United States' expanding government. After the stock market crash of October 1929, and during the Great Depression of the 1930s, Congress created numerous agencies in an effort to regulate the production and marketing of goods. Agencies such as the Social Security Administration (created by the Social Security Act of 1935 [42 U.S.C.A. § 301 et seq.]), the Federal Savings and Loan Insurance Corporation (established by a 1933 amendment to the Federal Reserve Act, 12 U.S.C.A. § 264, and now codified at 12 U.S.C.A. §§ 1811–1831) helped provide financial security for many Americans. The National Industrial Recovery Act (NIRA) (48 15 U.S.C.A. § 701 et seq., 40 U.S.C.A. § 401 et seq.) created the National Recovery Administration to ensure fair market competition. However, the NIRA gave the president limitless authority to impose sanctions, and it was declared invalid by the Supreme Court in the "sick chicken" case, *Schechter Poultry v. United States*, 295 U.S. 495,

55 S. Ct. 837, 79 L. Ed. 1570 (1935). The National Labor Relations Board (created by the National Labor Relations Act of 1935 [29 U.S.C.A. § 151 et seq.], later amended by acts of 1947 and 1959) also helped to ease the devastating effects of the Depression, by protecting employees' rights to organize, preventing unfair labor practices, and promoting collective bargaining between employers and labor unions.

Congress installed the Federal Radio Commission (FRC) in 1927 after entrepreneurs discovered the commercial potential of radio airwaves. In 1934, the FRC was merged into the Federal Communications Commission (FCC), which was created by the Communications Act of 1934 (47 U.S.C.A. § 151 et seq.) to tackle the myriad issues presented by the sudden widespread use of radio waves. In the wake of television's popularity, the Communications Satellite Act of 1962 (47 U.S.C.A. §§ 701–744) was enacted by Congress to broaden the FCC's powers to include regulation of television broadcasting; telephone, telegraph, and cable television operation; two-way radio and radio operation; and satellite communication.

When the United States entered World War II, more agencies were created or enlarged to mobilize human resources and production, and to administer price controls and rationing. The social upheaval of the 1960s spawned agencies designed to improve urban areas, provide opportunities to people who were historically disadvantaged and marginalized, and promote artistic endeavors. In the 1970s, 1980s, and 1990s, pressing issues such as human and environmental health were addressed through the creation of agencies such as the Environmental Protection Agency and a new, enlarged Department of Energy.

Federal Administrative Agencies On the federal level, business and individual matters are addressed by such agencies as the Farm Credit Administration, Small Business Administration, Commodity Futures Trading Commission, Federal Trade Commission, Federal Deposit Insurance Corporation, Office of Thrift Supervision, Internal Revenue Service, Department of Commerce, Interstate Commerce Commission, and Securities and Exchange Commission.

Governmental money matters are overseen and assisted by the General Accounting Office, Office of Management and Budget, Office of the Comptroller of the Currency, Treasury Department, General Services Administration, Congressional Budget Office, and Federal Reserve Board.

Public services are handled by administrative agencies that include the Department of Education, Department of Transportation, Environmental Protection Agency, Food and Drug Administration, Department of Health and Human Services, Department of Housing and Urban Development, Department of Interior, Immigration and Naturalization Service, and National Highway Traffic Safety Administration.

Work-related administrative agencies include the Tennessee Valley Authority, Office of Technology Assessment, Occupational Safety and Health Administration, Occupational Safety and Health Review Commission, National Labor Relations Board, Mine Safety and Health Administration, Mine Safety and Health Review Commission, Merit Systems Protection Board, Department of Labor, Equal Employment Opportunity Commission, and Office of Personnel Management.

Police and military functions are served by the Central Intelligence Agency, Department of Defense, Department of Justice, Department of Veterans Affairs, Federal Bureau of Investigation, and National Security Council.

The administrative agency that directly affects the most U.S. citizens is the Social Security Administration (SSA). The SSA collects contributions from workers and pays out cash benefits when a worker retires, dies, or becomes disabled.

State and Local Administrative Agencies State and local administrative agencies often mirror federal agencies. Thus, the individual states have agencies that control transportation, public health, public assistance, education, natural resources, labor, law enforcement, agriculture, commerce, and revenue. Any regulation established by such an agency that conflicts with a federal regulation will not be legally valid, but this does not keep state agencies from developing regulations that differ from those promulgated by their federal counterparts. In the spirit of administrative agency, state and local governments also create additional agencies that help address compelling, peculiarly local concerns.

Just like federal agencies, state and local administrative agencies are often empowered to hold hearings. These hearings are conducted by their administrative boards, which are obligated to represent the PUBLIC INTEREST. By contrast, courts must remain impartial to the two parties before them. A parole board, for example, holds informal hearings where prisoners are allowed to offer evidence of their suitability for early release from incarceration. The strict rules observed in a courtroom do not apply to these

hearings, and the board's decisions must account for the public interest as well as the rights of the prisoners.

CROSS-REFERENCES

Administrative Conference of the United States; Administrative Law and Procedure; Bureaucracy; National Industrial Recovery Act; *Schechter Poultry Corp. v. United States;* individual entries for specific federal agencies.

ADMINISTRATIVE BOARD ▯ A comprehensive phrase that can refer to any ADMINISTRATIVE AGENCY but usually means a public agency that holds HEARINGS. ▯

An administrative board is usually obligated to represent the PUBLIC INTEREST; courts, in contrast, must remain impartial between the two parties before them. A parole board, for example, holds informal hearings where prisoners are allowed to offer evidence of their suitability for early release from prison. The strict rules observed in a courtroom do not apply to board hearings like these, and the board's decision must take into account the public's interest as well as the prisoner's rights.

ADMINISTRATIVE CONFERENCE OF THE UNITED STATES The Administrative Conference of the United States (ACUS) is the administrative agency that helps guide federal administrative agencies. The purpose of ACUS is to recommend improvements in the procedures by which federal agencies administer regulatory, benefit, and other government programs. It has no power to enact its recommendations into law, but it does carry great weight in the formulation of procedures and policies of federal administrative agencies.

ACUS is made up of heads of administrative agencies, private lawyers, university professors, various federal officials, and other experts in administrative law and government. These experts collectively conduct continuing studies of selected problems that exist in the procedures of federal administrative agencies. The specific charge of ACUS is to harness the experience and judgment of the administrative agency specialists to improve the fairness and effectiveness of administrative procedures.

CROSS-REFERENCES

Administrative Agency; Administrative Law and Procedure.

ADMINISTRATIVE DISCRETION ▯ The exercise of professional expertise and judgment, as opposed to strict adherence to regulations or statutes, in making a decision or performing official acts or duties. ▯

A discretionary action is informal and, therefore, unprotected by the safeguards inherent in formal procedure. A public official, for example, has administrative discretion when he or she has the freedom to make a choice among potential courses of action. ABUSE OF DISCRETION is the failure to exercise reasonable judgment or discretion. It might provide a CAUSE OF ACTION for an unconstitutional invasion of rights protected by the Due Process Clause of the Constitution.

ADMINISTRATIVE LAW AND PROCEDURE

Administrative law is the body of law that allows for the creation of public regulatory agencies and contains all the statutes, judicial decisions, and regulations that govern them. It is the body of law created by administrative agencies to implement their powers and duties in the form of rules, regulations, orders, and decisions. *Administrative procedure* constitutes the methods and processes before administrative agencies, as distinguished from judicial procedure, which applies to courts.

The Administrative Procedure Act (5 U.S.C.A. §§ 551–706 [Supp. 1993]) governs the practice and proceedings before federal administrative agencies. The procedural rules and regulations of most federal agencies are set forth in the Code of Federal Regulations.

The fundamental problem of administrative law is trying to design a system of checks that will minimize the risks of bureaucratic arbitrariness and overreaching, while preserving for the agencies the flexibility they need to act effectively. Administrative law thus seeks to limit the powers and actions of agencies and fix their place in our scheme of government and law. It contrasts with traditional notions that the three branches of the U.S. government must be kept separate, that they must not delegate their responsibilities to bureaucrats, and that the formalities of due process must be observed.

Separation of Powers The U.S. Constitution established a three-part system of government consisting of the legislative branch, which makes the laws, the executive branch, which carries out or executes the laws, and the judicial branch, which enforces and interprets the laws. This system of checks and balances is designed to keep any one branch from exercising too much power. Administrative agencies do not fit neatly into any of the three branches. They are frequently created by the legislature and are sometimes placed in the executive branch, but their functions reach into all three types of government.

For example, the Securities and Exchange Commission administers laws governing the registration, offering, and sale of securities, like stocks and bonds. The SEC formulates laws like a legislature, by writing rules spelling out what disclosures must be made in a prospectus describing shares of stock offered for sale. The SEC enforces its rules the way the executive branch of government does, by prosecuting violators. It can bring disciplinary actions against brokers-dealers, or it can issue STOP ORDERS against corporate issuers of securities.

The Securities and Exchange Commission administers laws governing the actions of these traders on the floor of the Chicago Mercantile Exchange. The SEC is an independent agency that enforces its rules without need for approval from Congress or the executive branch of the government.

The SEC acts as judge and jury when it conducts adjudicatory HEARINGS to determine violations or prescribe punishment. Although SEC commissioners are appointed by the president subject to the approval of the Senate, the SEC is an independent agency. It is not part of Congress, nor is it part of any executive department.

Combining the three functions of government allows an agency to tackle a problem and get the job done most efficiently, but this combination has not been accepted without a struggle. Some have taken the position that the basic structure of the administrative law system is an unconstitutional violation of the principle of the separation of powers.

Delegation of Authority The first question encountered in the study of administrative law is, how can Congress effectively delegate its legislative power to an administrative agency? Article I, Section I, of the Constitution provides that all legislative power is vested in Congress. Despite early resistance, the delegation of legislative authority was gradually accepted by the U.S. Supreme Court so long as Congress set clear standards for the administration of the duties in order to limit the scope of agency discretion. With this basic principle as their guide, courts have invalidated laws granting too much legislative power to an administrative agency. President Franklin D. Roosevelt learned just how far the Supreme Court would go in allowing the delegation of authority, in two cases stemming from his administrative agency actions to support his New Deal program.

The National Industrial Recovery Act (15 U.S.C.A. § 701 et seq., 40 U.S.C.A. § 401 et seq. [1933]) authorized the president to prohibit interstate shipments of oil produced in violation of state board rules that attempted to regulate crude oil production to match consumer demand. The Panama Refining Company sued to prevent federal officials from enforcing the prohibition, known as the "hot oil" law (*Panama Refining Co. v. Ryan*, 293 U.S. 388, 55 S. Ct. 241, 79 L. Ed. 446 [1935]). The Supreme Court found the law unconstitutional. Congress could have passed a law prohibiting interstate shipments of hot oil, but it did not do that; instead, it gave that power to the president. This has been called a case of delegation run riot because the law had no clear standards defining when and how the president should use the authority the statute delegated to him.

Four months later, the Supreme Court invalidated a criminal prosecution for violation of the Live Poultry Code, a fair competition law

approved by President Franklin D. Roosevelt in 1934 pursuant to another section of the National Industrial Recovery Act. This was the case of *Schechter Poultry v. United States*, 295 U.S. 495, 55 S. Ct. 837, 79 L. Ed. 1570 (1935). The problem in this case was not that the delegation of authority was ill defined but that it seemed limitless. The president was to "formulate codes of fair competition" for any industry if these codes would "tend to effectuate the policy" of the law. Comprehensive codes were created establishing an elaborate regulation of prices, minimum wages, and maximum hours for all kinds of businesses. But there were no procedural safeguards from arbitrariness or abuses by enforcement agencies. Someone charged with a violation was not given the right to notice of the charges, the right to be heard at an agency hearing, or the right to challenge the agency's determination in a lawsuit. The Court struck down this law, stating that the unfair procedures helped strong industrial groups use these codes to improve their commercial advantage over small producers.

As a result of *Panama Refining* and *Schechter Poultry*, when Congress delegates authority to agencies, it also sets out important provisions detailing procedures that protect against arbitrary administrative actions.

Due Process of Law An administrative agency may not deprive anyone of life, liberty, or property without a reasonable opportunity, appropriate under the circumstances, to challenge the agency's action. People must be given fair warning of the limits an agency will place on their actions. Very broad delegations of authority are upheld by federal courts all the time. When reviewing administrative agency actions, courts ask whether the agency afforded those under its jurisdiction DUE PROCESS OF LAW as guaranteed in the U.S. Constitution. The Fifth and Fourteenth Amendments guarantee that the federal government and the state governments, respectively, will not deprive a person of her or his life, liberty, or property without due process of law.

For example, the Supreme Court has held that it is improper for a state agency to deny welfare benefits to applicants who meet the conditions for entitlement to those benefits as defined by the legislature. The state must afford due process, in this case an oral hearing, before it can terminate benefits (*Goldberg v. Kelly*, 397 U.S. 254, 90 S. Ct. 1011, 25 L. Ed. 2d 287 [1970]). Likewise, when a state grants all children the right to attend public schools, and establishes rules specifying the grounds for suspension, it cannot suspend a given student for alleged misconduct without affording the student at least a limited prior hearing (*Goss v. Lopez*, 419 U.S. 565, 95 S. Ct. 729, 42 L. Ed. 2d 725 [1975]).

Political Controls Over Agency Action—Legislative and Executive Oversight Government institutions that set and enforce public policy must be politically accountable to the electorate. When the legislature delegates broad lawmaking powers to an administrative agency, the popular control provided by direct election of decision makers is absent—but this does not mean that administrative agencies are free from political accountability. In many areas, policy oversight by elected officials in the legislature or the executive branch is a more important check on agency power than is judicial review.

Federal agencies are dependent upon Congress and the president for their budgets and operating authority. An agency that loses the support of these bodies or oversteps the bounds of political acceptability may be subjected to radical restructuring. In the 1970s, the Atomic Energy Commission (AEC) took the politically unpopular position of promoting nuclear power, while underemphasizing safety and environmental protection. It paid the price when some of its promotional functions were transferred to a newly created Department of Energy, and the AEC was restructured into the Nuclear Regulatory Commission, which was responsible for the former agency's regulatory duties.

Federal administrative agencies must be responsive to legislative and executive oversight mechanisms. During the 1970s, many members of Congress began to feel that the normal process of legislation was too cumbersome for effective control of administrative action. They devised a solution called the legislative veto. Legislative vetoes took a variety of forms, but most of them directed agencies to transmit final administrative rules to Congress for review before they became effective. Just as this approach was gaining in popularity and use, the Supreme Court stepped in and declared the legislative veto unconstitutional. This ruling involved the Immigration and Nationality Act (8 U.S.C.A. § 1101 et seq. [1995]), which allowed either house of Congress to nullify a decision by the attorney general suspending DEPORTATION of an alien. When the House of Representatives exercised this power in the case of Jagdish Rai Chadha, he brought suit. The Supreme Court held, in *INS v. Chadha*, 462 U.S. 919, 103 S. Ct. 2764, 77 L. Ed. 2d 317 (1983), that the legislative veto was essentially a one-house veto, and

therefore it violated Article I, Section 7, of the Constitution, which states that no legislation is valid unless passed by both houses of Congress and signed by the president (or, if the president vetoes it, repassed by two-thirds of each house). The Court said that in *Chadha*, the House veto of the attorney general's decision was a legislative action, and therefore Article I, Section 7, applied. The *Chadha* decision invalidated all of the nearly two hundred legislative veto provisions that were on the books.

Another important legislative oversight mechanism is the annual appropriations process. Congress determines the budget and appropriates money for the various administrative agencies. An administrative agency that angers Congress, or a key member, may find less money to work with next year, or even see certain programs eliminated. A legislature may also enact a SUNSET PROVISION, which provides for automatic termination of an agency after a stated time unless the legislature is convinced that the need for the agency continues. Sometimes a sunset provision is written into the statute that creates a particular agency, but a general sunset law may terminate any agency that cannot periodically demonstrate its effectiveness. A useful agency can always be revived or retained by the enactment of a new statute.

Like Congress, the president uses a variety of powers and techniques to oversee and influence the operations of administrative agencies. The Appointments Clause of the Constitution (art. II, § 2, cl. 2) states that the president may generally appoint all "officers of the United States," with the advice and consent of the Senate. Under the authority of this provision, presidents often appoint agency heads who share their political agenda. The president's power to remove an agency head depends on whether the agency is an independent agency or a CABINET department. Independent agencies tend to be multimember boards and commissions, like the Securities and Exchange Commission, Federal Communications Commission, and National Labor Relations Board (NLRB), which are run by officials appointed for a fixed period that does not correspond with the president's term of office. There may also be statutes protecting the commissioners from arbitrary removal during their terms of office. The heads of cabinet-level agencies, called secretaries, serve at the pleasure of the president and may be removed at any time. (Appointments of cabinet secretaries must be confirmed by the Senate.)

The president also reviews agency budgets, through the Office of Management and Budget.

A president's disapproval of agency initiatives can block appropriations in Congress. The president may also use an EXECUTIVE ORDER, a formal directive, to direct federal agencies or officials. One technique that has been used frequently is the president's authority to modify the organizational structure of the bureaucracy. Under the Executive Reorganization Act (5 U.S.C.A. §§ 901–912 [Supp. 1993]), the president may submit a REORGANIZATION PLAN to Congress, transferring functions from one department to another. This law recognizes that although responsibility for the organization and structure of the executive branch is vested in Congress, the president needs flexibility to carry out executive duties.

Public opinion is another forceful weapon against unbridled agency action. A few jurisdictions of the United States have created special public offices to investigate complaints about administrative misconduct. Investigators holding these offices, called OMBUDSPERSONS, usually have broad authority to evaluate individual complaints, to intercede on behalf of beleaguered victims of red tape, and to make reports or recommendations.

The Development of Administrative Procedure Law Administrative agencies were established to do the government's work in a simpler and more direct manner than if the legislature did the job by enacting a law and the courts applied that law in various cases. Because they pursue their actions less formally, agencies do not follow the civil procedure set up for courts; instead, the law of administrative procedure has developed to ensure that agencies do not abuse their authority even though they use simplified procedures.

Although administrative agencies have existed since the founding of the United States, the early twentieth century saw a growth in the number of agencies designed to deal with new problems. During the Great Depression, a host of new agencies sprang up to meet economic challenges. Antagonism toward bureaucracy increased as existing dissatisfactions were multiplied by the number of new bureaucrats. In 1939, President Franklin D. Roosevelt appointed a committee to investigate the need for procedural reform in the field of administrative law. Although the comprehensive and scholarly report of that committee was not enacted into law, a later version of it was enacted in 1946 when Congress unanimously passed the Administrative Procedure Act (5 U.S.C.A. §§ 551–706). The act made the methods used by agencies more fair so that there would be less reason to object to them; it also limited the power of the courts to review agency actions and overturn them.

JUDICIAL REVIEW of agency action furnishes an important set of controls on administrative behavior. Unlike the political oversight controls, which generally influence entire programs or basic policies, judicial review regularly operates to provide relief for the individual person who is harmed by a particular agency decision. Judicial review has evolved over a period of years into a complex system of statutory, constitutional, and judicial doctrines that define the proper boundaries of this system of oversight. The trend of judicial decisions and the Administrative Procedure Act is to make judicial review more widely and easily available.

How far can a court go in examining an agency decision? The reviewing court may be completely precluded from testing the merits of an agency action, or it may be free to decide the issues DE NOVO, that is, without deference to the agency's determination. In general, administrative agencies make either informal or formal decisions, and courts have different standards for reviewing each type.

Informal Agency Action Most of the work done by agencies is accomplished with informal procedures. For example, a person applying for a driver's license does not need or want a full trial in court in order to be found qualified. So long as the motor vehicle department follows standard fair procedures and processes the application promptly, most people are happy. Agencies take informal action in a variety of settings. The Social Security Administration reviews over four million claims for benefits annually, holding hearings or answering challenges to their decisions in only a small number of cases. Most transmitter applications before the Federal Communications Commission are approved or disapproved without any formal action. The Internal Revenue Service processes most tax returns without formal proceedings. It will also provide informal opinions to help people avoid making costly mistakes in their financial planning.

Anyone who objects to the informal decisions made by a government agency can invoke more formal procedures. Someone may believe that standards are unclear and should be promulgated through formal agency rule making. Or someone may feel that the decision in a particular case is unfair and demand a formal adjudicatory hearing. If one of these formal procedures does not satisfy a party, the agency's decision can be challenged in court.

Formal Agency Action Most formal action taken by administrative agencies consists of RULE

These employees of the Internal Revenue Service process tax returns using informal procedures, which makes their jobs easier and less time-consuming. If a taxpayer objects to a decision made in this way, he or she may initiate more formal procedures.

making or ADJUDICATION. Rule making is the agency's formulation of policy that will apply in the future to everyone affected by the agency's activities. Adjudication is for the agency what a trial is for the courts: it applies the agency's policies to some act already done so that an ORDER is issued for or against a party appearing for a decision. Rule making looks to the future; adjudication looks at the past. Where either of these formal procedures is used, the agency will usually give interested or affected persons notice and an opportunity to be heard before a final rule or order is issued.

Rule making Three types of rules are promulgated by administrative agencies: procedural, interpretative, and legislative. Procedural rules identify the agency's organization and methods of operation. Interpretative rules are issued to show how the agency intends to apply the law. They range from informal policy statements announced in a press release to authoritative rules that bind the agency in the future and are issued only after the agency has given the public an opportunity to be heard on the subject. Legislative rules are like statutes enacted by a legislature. Agencies can promulgate legislative rules only if the legislature has given them this authority.

The Administrative Procedure Act sets up the procedures to be followed for administrative rule making. Before adopting a rule, an agency generally must publish advance notice in the *Federal Register*, the government's daily publication for federal agencies. This gives persons who have an interest in, or are affected by, a proposed rule the opportunity to participate in the decision making by submitting written data or by offering views or arguments orally or in writing. Before a rule is adopted in its final form, and thirty days before its effective date,

the agency must publish it in the *Federal Register*. Formally adopted rules are published in the *Code of Federal Regulations*, a set of paperback books published by the government each year so that rules are readily available to the public.

Adjudication The procedures used by administrative agencies to adjudicate individual claims or cases are extremely diverse. Like trials, these hearings resolve disputed questions of fact, determining policy in a specific factual setting and ordering compliance with laws and regulations. Although often not as formal as courtroom trials, administrative HEARINGS are extremely important. Far more hearings are held before agencies every year than are trials in courts. Adjudicative hearings deal with a variety of subjects, such as individual claims for workers' compensation, welfare, or Social Security benefits, in addition to multimillion-dollar disputes about whether business mergers will violate antitrust rulings. These proceedings may be called hearings, adjudications, or adjudicatory proceedings. Their final disposition is an administrative order.

Many administrative proceedings appear to be just like courtroom trials. Most are open to the public and conducted in an orderly and dignified manner. Typically, a proceeding begins with a COMPLAINT filed by the agency, much as a civil trial begins with a complaint prepared by the plaintiff. After the RESPONDENT answers, each side may conduct DISCOVERY of the other's evidence and prehearing conferences. A HEARING EXAMINER, sometimes called an administrative law judge, presides over the hearing, giving rulings in response to a party's applications for some sort of relief. The agency presents its evidence, usually through counsel, either by a written report or in the question-and-answer style of a trial, then the respondent offers his or her case. Witnesses may be called and cross-examined. The examiner gives a decision, usually with written findings and a written opinion, shortly after the hearing.

Unlike a trial, an administrative hearing has no jury. The hearing examiner, or administrative law judge, is usually an expert in the field involved and is likely to be more concerned with overall policies than with the particular merits of one party's case. The Administrative Procedure Act affords parties appearing in administrative hearings involving federal agencies the right to notice of the issues and proceedings, the right to counsel, and the right to confront and cross-examine witnesses.

Judicial Review of Agency Actions

When someone believes that she or he is the victim of administrative error or wrongdoing and seeks to have the actions of the responsible agency reviewed in a court of law, the reviewing court is faced with two questions: Does the court have a right to review the agency action? And if it does, what is the scope of that court's review?

The Right to Have a Court Review an Agency's Decision Whether someone has the right to ask a court to review the action taken by an agency depends on the answers to several questions. The first question is whether the person bringing the action has STANDING, or the legal right, to bring the suit. Section 702 of the Administrative Procedure Act allows court review for any person adversely affected or aggrieved by agency action within the meaning of a relevant statute. When the Supreme Court reviewed section 702 in *Association of Data Processing Service Organizations v. Camp*, 397 U.S. 150, 90 S. Ct. 827, 25 L. Ed. 2d 184 (1970), the Court said that for the plaintiff to have standing to seek judicial review of administrative action, two questions must be answered affirmatively: (1) has the complainant alleged an "injury in fact"; and (2) is the interest sought to be protected by the complainant "arguably within the zone of interests to be protected or regulated by the statute or constitutional guarantee in question"?

Even though an agency's decision is reviewable and the plaintiff has standing to litigate, the plaintiff may still be unable to get judicial review if he or she has brought the action at the wrong time. The aggrieved person must exhaust all other avenues of relief before the dispute is ripe for judicial determination. The doctrines of EXHAUSTION OF REMEDIES and RIPENESS require a person dealing with an agency to follow patiently all the steps available within the agency's procedures before resorting to court action. These rules are essential to prevent overloading the courts with questions that may not even be disputes by the time the agencies determine what their final orders or rulings will be.

The Scope of a Court's Review If an aggrieved person can convince a court that she or he has standing, that all available administrative remedies have been exhausted, and that the case is ripe for judicial review, the court will hear the case, but the scope of its review is limited. The law seeks to give agencies enough freedom of action to do their work, while ensuring that individual rights will be protected. The Administrative Procedure Act provides that courts may not second-guess agencies when the agencies are exercising discretion that has been granted to them by statute. A court is generally limited to asking whether the agency went

outside the authority granted to it, whether it followed proper procedures in reaching its decision, and whether the decision is so clearly wrong that it must be set aside. The court usually will accept the agency's findings of fact but is free to determine how the law shall be applied to those facts. It will look at the whole record of the administrative proceeding and take into account the agency's expertise in the matter. The court will not upset agency decisions for HARMLESS ERRORS that do not change the outcome of the case. If the question at issue has been committed to agency discretion, the court may consider whether the agency has exercised its discretion. If it has not, the court can order the agency to look at the situation and make a decision. The court can also set aside an agency decision that is clearly wrong. The Administrative Procedure Act allows courts to overrule agency action that is found to be "arbitrary, capricious, an abuse of discretion, or otherwise not in accordance with law."

CROSS-REFERENCES

Administrative Agency; Administrative Conference of the United States; Bureaucracy; Code of Federal Regulations; Federal Bugdet; Federal Register; National Industrial Recovery Act; Roosevelt, Franklin D.; Separation of Powers; *Schechter Poultry Corp. v. United States;* Veto; individual entries for specific federal agencies.

ADMINISTRATIVE OFFICE OF THE UNITED STATES COURTS The Administrative Office of the United States Courts is the administrative headquarters of the federal court system. It was created by congressional act on August 7, 1939 (28 U.S.C.A. § 601), and since November 6, 1939, it has tended to the nonjudicial business of the U.S. courts. The Administrative Office helps Congress monitor the state of affairs within the federal judiciary. It arranges clerical and administrative support to federal district courts and their subdivisions, and it provides for the various benefits available to the federal judiciary. Furthermore, by gathering and analyzing statistics and data and reporting the findings to Congress and the Judicial Conference of the United States, the Administrative Office plays an important part in determining the extent and character of the very support it provides.

The director of the Administrative Office is the administrative officer of all the federal courts except the Supreme Court. The Judicial Conference of the United States—the federal agency charged with overseeing federal judicial matters—supervises and guides the director's work. The director and the deputy director are appointed by the Supreme Court of the United States.

The director is required to perform a variety of tasks. First and foremost, the director must supervise all administrative matters relating to the offices of clerks and other clerical and administrative personnel of the federal courts. These administrative matters can range from performance policies and pay scales to guidelines on clerical procedures.

The director is charged with providing many reports to various governmental bodies. With the aid of the deputy director and the Audit Office and other operatives, the director must examine court dockets, determine the needs of the various courts, and report the results four times a year to the chief judges of the circuits. This allows the federal courts to analyze and plan for their own clerical and administrative costs. This information is also used when the director prepares and submits to Congress the budget of the federal courts.

The director must submit a report of the Administrative Office to the annual meeting of the Judicial Conference of the United States. At least two weeks before the conference, the director prepares an overview of the activities of the Administrative Office and the state of the business of the courts, together with certain statistical data submitted to the chief judges of the circuits. This report also contains the director's recommendations on administrative efficiency. The director submits the report, data, and recommendations to Congress, and makes all these materials available to the public.

The director is responsible for many financial matters of the federal courts. The director must fix the compensation of employees of the courts whose compensation is not otherwise fixed by law, regulate and pay annuities to the surviving spouses and dependent children of judges, disburse monies appropriated for the maintenance and operation of the federal courts, examine accounts of court officers, regulate travel of judicial personnel, and provide accommodations and supplies for the courts and their clerical and administrative personnel.

The director must also establish and maintain programs for the certification and utilization of court interpreters and the provision of special interpretation services in the courts. Other duties may be assigned to the director by the Supreme Court or the Judicial Conference of the United States.

Probation Officers The Probation Division of the Administrative Office supervises the accounts and practices of the federal PROBATION offices. However, primary control of probation practices and procedures is left to the district courts served by the probation offices. The Probation Division establishes pretrial services in the federal district courts according to the Pretrial Services Act of 1982 (18 U.S.C.A. § 3152). The pretrial service offices report to their respective courts with information on the pretrial release of persons charged with federal offenses. These offices also supervise criminal defendants released to their custody.

With the Bureau of Prisons of the Department of Justice, the Administrative Office publishes a magazine entitled *Federal Probation*. The magazine, issued four times a year, is a journal "of correctional philosophy and practice."

Bankruptcy Act The Administrative Office has special responsibility for BANKRUPTCY courts. The Bankruptcy Amendments and Federal Judgeship Act of 1984 (28 U.S.C.A. § 152) established bankruptcy judges as distinct units of the federal district courts. Under the Bankruptcy Amendments Act, all cases under title 11 of the United States Code and all proceedings related to federal statute 28 U.S.C.A. § 1334 are to be brought before federal district courts. Such a case arises when a person seeks to discharge his or her debts through judicial proceedings. When a suit is filed under title 11, the federal district court will refer the case to its bankruptcy judges, as authorized by 28 U.S.C.A. § 157.

The bankruptcy judges are appointed by the federal courts of appeals and serve a fourteen-year term as judicial officers of the district courts. The number of bankruptcy judges is controlled by Congress, but the bankruptcy courts are overseen by the Administrative Office.

The director of the Administrative Office has specific duties related to the bankruptcy courts. The director must make recommendations to the Judicial Conference on logistical concerns such as the geographic placement of bankruptcy courts. The director must consider whether additional bankruptcy judges should be recommended to Congress, and the director is also in charge of determining the staff needs of bankruptcy judges and clerks.

Federal Magistrates Under the Federal Magistrates Act as amended in 1979 (28 U.S.C.A. § 631), the director of the Administrative Office must answer to Congress and the Judicial Conference on the affairs of federal magistrates. Federal magistrates are appointed by federal district court judges, and their job is to whittle each case to its essence before it reaches the district courts. Federal proceedings are expensive; by ruling on pretrial motions and issuing various orders at the pretrial stage, federal magistrates help preserve judicial resources.

Federal magistrates do not have the full range of judicial powers available to other federal judges. For example, they cannot preside over felony trials. Federal magistrates may conduct civil or misdemeanor criminal trials, but they normally conduct pretrial proceedings in both criminal and civil cases. Owing to their special function, federal magistrates operate separately from the district courts and maintain a separate budget.

With the guidance of the Judicial Conference, the director supervises the administrative matters of federal magistrates through the Magistrate Division of the Administrative Office. The director prepares legal and administrative manuals for the use of the magistrates. In addition, the Administrative Office must conduct surveys of the federal judiciary to ask questions on court conditions. With these surveys, the director makes recommendations as to the number, location, and salaries of magistrates. The expansion of magistrate offices depends significantly on the availability of funds appropriated by Congress.

The director of the Administrative Office compiles and evaluates information on the magistrate offices and reports the findings to the Judicial Conference. The director must also report to Congress every year on the general affairs of federal magistrates.

Federal Defenders The Administrative Office also assists and oversees the offices of federal PUBLIC DEFENDERS. Under the Criminal Justice Act (18 U.S.C.A. § 3006A [1964]), the federal district courts are required to appoint counsel to criminal defendants who are unable to afford adequate representation. The act also authorizes the district courts to establish federal public defender and federal community defender organizations. This can be done in districts where at least two hundred persons annually require the appointment of counsel. Two adjacent districts may be combined to reach this total.

Each defender organization submits to the director of the Administrative Office an annual report of its activities along with a proposed budget. Because they rely on grants and not regular funding, community defender organizations submit grant proposals to the Administrative Office for the coming year. The director then submits the proposed budgets and grants to the Judicial Conference of the United States for approval. After budgets are determined, the director pays the defender organizations. The director also compensates private counsel appointed to defend individuals charged in federal court.

CROSS-REFERENCES
District Court; Federal Courts; Judicial Conference of the United States; Magistrate.

ADMINISTRATOR 📖 A person appointed by the court to manage and take charge of the assets and liabilities of a decedent who has died without making a valid WILL. 📖

When such a person is a male, he is called an administrator, while a woman is called an administratrix. An administrator c.t.a. (*cum testamento annexo*, Latin for "with the will annexed") is appointed by the court where the TESTATOR had made an incomplete will without naming any executors or had named incapable persons, or where the executors named refuse to act. A public administrator is a public official designated by state law to perform the duties of administration for persons who have died INTESTATE.

An EXECUTOR differs from an administrator in that he or she is named in the decedent's will to manage the estate. If an executor dies while performing these duties, a court will appoint an administrator *de bonis non cum testamento annexo* (Latin for "of the goods not (already) administered upon with the will annexed") to complete the distribution of the decedent's estate. This term is often abbreviated: administrator d.b.n.c.t.a.

ADMIRALTY AND MARITIME LAW 📖 A field of law relating to, and arising from, the practice of the admiralty courts (tribunals that exercise jurisdiction over all contracts, torts, offenses, or injuries within maritime law) that regulates and settles special problems associated with sea navigation and commerce. 📖

History of Admiralty and Maritime Law The life of the mariner, spent far away from the stability of land, has long been considered an exotic one of travel, romance, and danger. Stories of pirates, mutinies, lashings, and hasty trials—many of them true—illustrate the peculiar, isolated nature of the maritime existence. In modern times, the practice of shipping goods by sea has become more civil, but the law still gives maritime activities special treatment by acknowledging the unique conflicts and difficulties involved in high-seas navigation and commerce.

The roots of maritime law are traced as far back as 900 B.C., which is when the Rhodian Customary Law is believed to have been shaped by the people of the island of Rhodes. The only concept in the Rhodian Laws that still exists is the law of jettison, which holds that if goods must be thrown overboard (*jettisoned*) for the safety of the ship or the safety of another's property, the owner of the goods is entitled to compensation from the beneficiaries of the jettison.

Codes enacted by medieval port cities and states have formed the current U.S. maritime law. The eleventh-century Amalphitan Code, of the Mediterranean countries; the fourteenth-century Consolato del Mare, of France, Spain, and Italy; the twelfth-century Roll of Oleron, from England; and the thirteenth-century Law of Visby all drew on the customs of mariners and merchants to create the unique substantive law of admiralty that still exists today. Procedural differences existed between maritime cases and other civil proceedings until 1966, when the U.S. Supreme Court approved amendments to the Federal Rules of Civil Procedure that brought admiralty and maritime procedural rules into accord with those used in other civil suits. The substantive maritime law, however, has remained intact.

Current Admiralty and Maritime Law

The terms *admiralty* and *maritime law* are sometimes used interchangeably, but *admiralty* originally referred to a specific court in England and the American colonies that had jurisdiction over torts and contracts on the high seas, whereas substantive maritime law developed through the expansion of admiralty court jurisdiction to include all activities on the high seas and similar activities on navigable waters.

Because water commerce and navigation often involve foreign nations, much of the U.S. maritime law has evolved in concert with the maritime laws of other countries. The federal statutes that address maritime issues are often customized U.S. versions of the convention resolutions or treaties of international maritime law. The United Nations organizes and prepares these conventions and treaties through branches such as the International Maritime Organization, and the International Labor Organization, which prepares conventions on the health, safety, and well-being of maritime workers.

The substance of maritime law considers the dangerous conditions and unique conflicts involved in navigation and water commerce. Sailors are especially vulnerable to injury and sickness owing to a variety of conditions, such as drastic changes in climate, constant peril, hard labor, and loneliness. Under the Shipowners' Liability Convention (54 Stat. 1693 [1939]), a shipowner may be liable not only for the main-

tenance and cure of sailors injured on ship, but also for injuries occurring on land. Courts have construed accidents occurring during leave as being the responsibility of the shipowner because sailors need land visits in order to endure the long hours of water transportation.

Assigning responsibility for onboard NEGLIGENCE was a long-standing problem, but the Jones Act of 1920 (46 U.S.C.A. § 688 et seq.) solidifies the right of sailors to recover from an employer for injuries resulting from the negligence of the employer, a master, or another crew member. The 1920 Death on High Seas Act (46 App. U.S.C.A. § 761 et seq.) allows recovery by the decedents of a sailor's estate when the sailor dies by negligence, DEFAULT, or wrongful act on the high seas "beyond a marine league from the shore of any state [territory or dependency]." A marine league is one-twentieth of a degree of latitude, or three miles.

Accidents suffered by nonmaritime persons on docks, piers, wharfs, or bridges do not qualify for the application of maritime law principles. However, personal injuries suffered while aboard a ship or as a result of an air-to-water airplane crash will be considered within the jurisdiction of admiralty law.

The Longshoremen's and Harbor Workers' Compensation Act (33 U.S.C.A. § 901 et seq. [1927]) sets up a federal system to compensate injured maritime workers who do not sail. Through the Federal Office of Workers' Compensation Programs, employees such as *stevedores* (workers who load and unload ships) and ship service operators can receive compensation for injuries suffered in the course of their employment. U.S. sailors benefit from title 46 of the United States Code, which sets a schedule for sailors' earnings and the conditions of their contracts. Title 46 also lists the qualifications for sailor employment (§§ 7301 et seq.), the hours and conditions of the employment (§§ 8104 et seq.), and the living conditions that must be provided (§§ 11101 et seq.).

Federal laws also address the problems that beset ships and the life-or-death decisions made by carriers. The Carriage of Goods by Sea Act (46 U.S.C.A. §§ 1300–1315 [1936]) regulates the rights, responsibilities, liabilities, and immunities regarding the relationship between shippers and carriers of goods. The Salvage Act (46 U.S.C.A. §§ 727–731 [1912]) provides for compensation to persons who help save a ship or cargo from danger, or help recover a ship or cargo from actual loss. To qualify for salvage remuneration, a person must not be acting in service of the ship or in performance of a contract, and the help given must have contrib-

UPI/BETTMANN NEWSPHOTOS

Admiralty law concerns personal injuries or loss of cargo suffered during accidents such as this one, where the Trans Hawaii *hit the* Republic of Colombia.

uted at least in part to a wholly or partially successful salvage of the ship or goods.

The CASE LAW of the United States is rich in the areas of sailors' rights respecting the unseaworthiness of vessels, compensation for vessel suppliers and servicers, and the liabilities arising from collisions, towage, pilotage, and groundings. The Maritime Lien Act (46 U.S.C.A. §§ 31341–31343 [1920]) gives a LIEN to any person who, upon the order of the shipowner, furnishes repairs, supplies, towage, use of dry dock or marine railway, or other necessaries to any vessel, without allegation or proof that credit was given. The Ship Mortgage Act (46 U.S.C.A. §§ 31301–31330 [1920]) regulates the MORTGAGES on ships registered in the United States, and also provides for enforcement of the maritime liens obtained through the Maritime Lien Act.

In case of collision or other damage to a vessel, an in rem proceeding is often used to recover damages. An IN REM action is a lawsuit brought against an offending thing (in admiralty, usually the ship), whereas an IN PERSONAM action is a suit brought against a person. Rule C of the Supplemental Rules for Certain Admiralty and Maritime Claims (1985) provides necessary details for the seizure of an offending owner's vessel or property if a defendant vessel owner does not live in the state in which a suit is brought. The practical effect of Supplemental Rules B to E is to make it easier for a plaintiff to bring actions against out-of-state and foreign vessel owners, and to provide for the attachment and garnishment of the offending vessel.

An important consideration in any lawsuit is VENUE. Under Article III, Section 2, of the U.S. Constitution, federal courts have the power to try "all Cases of admiralty and maritime Jurisdiction" (art. III, sec. 2). However, state courts can also hear admiralty and maritime cases by virtue of the "saving-to-suitors" clause of 28 U.S.C.A. § 1333(1). This clause allows a plaintiff to sue in state court through an ordinary civil action when the court's COMMON LAW is competent to give a remedy. In such actions, the state court must apply the federal law of admiralty to the admiralty claims. Nevertheless, if a plaintiff believes he or she will fare better before a local tribunal, the option is available.

Where no applicable federal statute exists, the governing law of a maritime case will be the uniform laws as expounded by the U.S. Supreme Court and applicable to all TORTS and CONTRACTS, whether the case is tried in federal or state court. Maritime case law—not the general common law—will govern a contract dispute only if the subject matter of the contract pertained to water commerce. Maritime precedents will govern a tort claim only if the negligent or reckless actions involved commercial activity on navigable waters.

Charter parties are often a topic of concern in maritime law. A *charter party*, or *charter*, is an agreement between a shipowner, a crew (the charterer), and the owner of the goods to be transported. Charter parties come in three types: time, voyage, and demise. A *time charter* is the lease of a ship to a charterer for a specified period of time. A *voyage charter* is the lease of a ship for a specific number of voyages. A *demise charter* (so called because the ship-owner effectively relinquishes ownership for a certain period, causing a "demise" in ownership interest) is usually a bareboat charter, which means that the charterer supplies the master and crew for the ship. Other demise charters provide that the shipowner's master and crew take charge of the vessel.

In contrast to the usual contract practice of providing risk-of-loss INSURANCE for one party, charters utilize what is called a general average. *General average* is the traditional, primitive form of maritime risk allocation whereby all participants in a charter agree to share any damages resulting from an unsuccessful voyage. Most parties to a charter obtain insurance to cover their portion of risk. However, because a charter involves multiple parties, and because insurance policies are subject to interpretation, insurance coverage does not always prevent disputes over damages.

Risk of loss is sometimes decided according to a BILL OF LADING. This document confirms a carrier's receipt of goods from the owner (*consignor*), verifies the voyage contract, and shows rightful ownership of the goods. In *Lekas & Drivas, Inc. v. Goulandris*, 306 F.2d 426 (2d Cir. 1962), the SS *Ioannis P. Goulandris* had chartered to carry olive oil, cheese, and tobacco from the western Greek port of Piraiévs to the United States via the Strait of Gibraltar. On October 28, 1940, with the *Ioannis* docked in Piraiévs, Italy attacked Greece, and the *Ioannis* was requisitioned by the Greek government for a military mission.

On November 10, 1940, the *Ioannis* finally set sail with its cargo for the United States via the Suez Canal and the Red Sea, and around Cape Horn. After an arduous journey that included two crossings of the equator, hull damage, and lengthy repairs, the *Ioannis* limped into port at Norfolk, Virginia, on May 3, 1941. En route, the tobacco had been damaged, much of the olive oil had leaked from its drums, and the cheese was " '[m]elted with a terrible stench, and worthless.' "

Despite the *Ioannis*'s brave participation in wartime activities, the intended recipients (*consignees*) of the tobacco and olive oil sued the *Ioannis* and were able to recover for the losses suffered as a result of the damage. However, on the subject of the cheese, the court refused to allow recovery by Lekas and Drivas, which had consigned the cheese to itself.

Lekas argued that the crew of the *Ioannis* was negligent in storing the cheese in the structure at the stern above the main deck, known as the poop. According to Lekas, it was inappropriate for the cheese to be in the poop. The poop lacked ventilation, and it was not refrigerated. However, according to the bill of lading between Lekas and the *Ioannis*, special cooling was not necessary and had not been contracted for. The cheese was also stored on *lighters* (large, flat-bottomed barges used for loading and unloading ships) during the thirty-five days needed for repairs of the *Ioannis*, and Lekas claimed that this storage was improper. But, because wartime conditions were responsible for the length of repairs and the lack of proper storage space for the cheese, the court ultimately held that the *Ioannis* was not negligent in its handling of the cheese.

In addition to the state and federal governments, municipalities can affect the private enjoyment of maritime activity. In *Beveridge v. Lewis*, 939 F.2d 859 (9th Cir. 1991), appellants Richard Beveridge, Peter Murray, Gregory Davis, and Peter Eastman challenged a Santa Barbara city ordinance (Santa Barbara Municipal Code § 17.13.020) that prohibited the anchoring or mooring of boats within three hundred feet of Stearns Wharf from December to March. Santa Barbara had acquired ownership of Stearns Wharf in 1983, passed the ordinance in 1984, and started issuing citations for noncompliance shortly thereafter. Beveridge, Murray, Davis, and Eastman all owned boats moored or anchored within three hundred feet of Stearns Wharf, and the four, represented by Eastman, brought suit against the city in 1989, seeking injunctive relief against enforcement of the ordinance.

At trial, Eastman argued that the Santa Barbara ordinance conflicted with the Ports and Waterways Safety Act of 1972 (PWSA) (33 U.S.C.A. §§ 1221 et seq.), a federal act designed to reduce the loss of vessels and cargo, protect marine environment, prevent damage to structures on or adjacent to navigable waters, and ensure compliance with vessel operation and safety standards. The trial court dismissed the case, reasoning that the ordinance was neither preempted by, nor in conflict with, the federal statute.

On appeal, the Ninth Circuit Court of Appeals agreed that the Santa Barbara ordinance was not in conflict with the PWSA, because the federal act was not intended to limit a municipality's control over its local shores. The appeals court also rejected the proposition that the enactment of the PWSA implicitly foreclosed the enactment of similar ordinances by municipalities, and Santa Barbara's control over the Stearns Wharf was complete.

Admiralty and maritime matters will always deserve laws carefully crafted to suit the complexity and urgency of maritime endeavors. The international nature of high-seas navigation and its attendant perils demand no less. Federal, state, and local control of navigable waters can affect everyone from the largest charter party to a private boat owner.

CROSS-REFERENCES

Carriers; Environmental Law; Maritime Law; Navigable Rivers; Piracy; Salvage; Shipping Law; Territorial Waters.

ADMISSIBLE

A term used to describe information that is relevant to a determination of issues in any judicial proceeding so that such information can be properly considered by a JUDGE or JURY in making a decision.

Evidence is admissible if it is of such a character that the court is bound to accept it during the trial so that it may be evaluated by the judge or jury. Admissible evidence is the foundation of the deliberation process by which a court or jury decides upon a judgment or verdict.

The Federal Rules of Evidence regulate the admissibility of evidence in federal courts. State rules of evidence determine evidence that is admissible in state court proceedings.

ADMISSION

A voluntary acknowledgment made by a party to a lawsuit or in a criminal prosecution that certain facts that are inconsistent with the party's claims in the controversy are true.

In a lawsuit over whether a defendant negligently drove a car into the plaintiff pedestrian, the defendant's apology to the plaintiff and payment of the plaintiff's medical bills are admissions that may be introduced as evidence against the defendant.

An admission may be EXPRESS, such as a written or verbal statement by a person concerning the truth, or it may be IMPLIED by a person's conduct. If someone fails to deny certain assertions which, if false, would be denied by any reasonable person, such failure indicates that the person has accepted the truth of the allegations.

An admission is not the same as a CONFESSION. A confession is an acknowledgment of guilt in a criminal case. Admissions usually apply to civil matters; in criminal cases they apply only to matters of fact that do not involve criminal intent.

Admissions are used primarily as a method of discovery, as a pleading device, and as evidence in a trial.

Once a COMPLAINT is filed to commence a lawsuit, the parties can obtain facts and information about the case from each other to assist their preparation for the trial through the use of DISCOVERY devices. One type of discovery tool is a request for admission: a written statement submitted to an opposing party before the trial begins, asking that the truth of certain facts or the genuineness of particular documents concerning the case be acknowledged or denied. When the facts or documents are admitted as being true, the court will accept them as such so that they need not be proven at trial. If they are denied, the statements or documents become an issue to be argued during the trial. Should a party refuse to answer the request, the other party can ask the court for an order of PRECLUSION that prohibits denial of these facts and allows them to be treated as if they had been admitted.

By eliminating undisputed facts as issues in a case, requests for admissions expedite trials. Matters that are admitted are binding only for the pending case and not for any other lawsuit.

Judicial admissions—made in court by a party or the party's attorney as formal acknowledgments of the truth of some matter, or as STIPULATIONS—are not considered evidence that may be rebutted but are a type of PLEADING device. AVERMENTS in a pleading to which a RESPONSIVE PLEADING is required are admitted if they are not denied in the responsive pleading. If a party has made an admission in a pleading that has subsequently been amended, the pleading containing the admission will be admissible as evidence in the case. In civil actions any offers to settle the case cannot be admitted into evidence.

A PLEA of GUILTY in a criminal case may usually be shown as an admission in a later civil or criminal proceeding, but it is not conclusive. The defendant may explain the circumstances that brought it about, such as a PLEA BARGAINING deal. Any admissions or offers to plead guilty during the plea-bargaining process are inadmissible as evidence. Many courts refuse to admit a guilty plea to a traffic offense as evidence since many people plead guilty to avoid wasting their time and money by appearing in traffic court. A guilty plea that has subsequently been withdrawn and followed by a plea of not guilty cannot be used as an admission in either a criminal or civil case. It is considered an unreliable admission that has a potentially prejudicial effect on the opportunity of the defendant to get a fair trial.

Admissions are used as a type of EVIDENCE in a trial to bolster the case of one party at the expense of the other, who is compelled to admit the truth of certain facts. They may be made directly by a party to a lawsuit, either in or out of court; or implicitly, by the conduct of a party or the actions of someone else which bind the party to a lawsuit. When an admission is made out of court, it is hearsay because it was not made under oath and not subject to cross-examination. Although hearsay cannot be used as evidence in a trial because of its unreliable nature, admissions can be introduced as evidence because they are considered trustworthy. An admission by a party can be used only to prove the existence of the fact admitted and to IMPEACH the credibility of the party. An admission by a witness can be introduced as evidence only to discredit the witness's testimony.

An admission against interest is a statement made by a party to a lawsuit, usually before the suit, that contradicts what he or she is now alleging in the case. Because the statements tend to establish or disprove a MATERIAL fact in the case, they are considered admissions against interest. The truth of such statements is presumed because people do not make detrimental statements about themselves unless they are true.

Such an admission is considered an exception to the hearsay rule and, therefore, can be used as evidence in a lawsuit.

ADMISSION TO THE BAR 📖 The procedure that governs the authorization of attorneys to practice law before the state and federal courts. 📖

Statutes, rules, and regulations governing admission to practice law have been enacted to protect the PUBLIC INTEREST, in terms of preventing the victimization of clients by incompetent practitioners. The courts have inherent power to promulgate reasonable rules and regulations for admission to the bar. Although this authority is vested exclusively in the courts, the legislature can, subject to constitutional limitations, issue reasonable rules and regulations governing bar admission provided they do not conflict with judicial pronouncements.

The highest state court administers the admission of applicants to the state bar, usually requiring successful completion of a bar examination and evidence of good moral character. With respect to admission to the federal bar,

federal district courts are empowered to issue requirements for admission separately from those of the state courts. If, however, a federal district court, pursuant to a rule, derivatively admits to its bar those admitted to the state bar, it cannot arbitrarily deny admission to an applicant who is a member in good standing of the state bar. In most instances, the federal district courts have considerable latitude in establishing requirements for admission to practice before them, but their rules must not contravene federal law.

In terms of the federal bar, an attorney is also eligible for admission to the bar of a court of appeals, if he or she has been admitted to practice before the Supreme Court, or the highest court of a state, or another federal court, and if the lawyer is of good moral and professional character. The attorney must comply with the procedural requirements and take and subscribe to the following oath: "I, [name], do solemnly swear (or affirm) that I will demean myself as an attorney and counselor of this court, uprightly and according to law; and that I will support the Constitution of the United States."

In order to gain admission to the bar of the Supreme Court, an attorney must have practiced for three years in the highest court of a state, territory, district, commonwealth, or possession. The person must be of good character in terms of both his or her private and professional lives, and complete the specified procedures, including taking or subscribing the following oath: "I, [name], do solemnly swear (or affirm) that as an attorney and as a counsellor of this court I will conduct myself uprightly, and according to law, and that I will support the Constitution of the United States."

In some instances, a particular board is empowered to promulgate rules pertaining to applicants seeking to practice before it as attorneys. For example, the Securities and Exchange Commission has implied authority under its general statutory power to determine qualifications for attorneys practicing before it. Under federal law, the Commissioner of Patents and Trademarks, subject to the approval of the secretary of commerce, can promulgate regulations governing the recognition and conduct of attorneys appearing before the Patent and Trademark Office.

Qualifications for admission to the bar must be rationally related to the applicant's fitness to practice law; therefore, a state cannot prevent a person from practicing law for racial, political, or religious reasons. Good moral character is a prerequisite to the right to admission to prac-

Rates of Female Law School Graduation and Bar Membership, 1960 to 1991

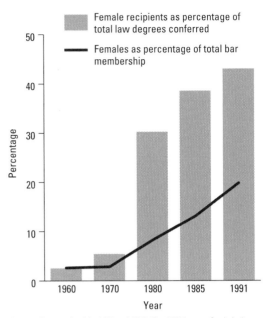

Female recipients as percentage of total law degrees conferred

Females as percentage of total bar membership

Sources: Bar membership: 1960 and 1970, *The 1971 Lawyer Statistical Report,* 1971 (copyright); 1980, *The Lawyer Statistical Report, A Statistical Profile of the U.S. Legal Profession in the 1980s,* 1985 (copyright); 1985, *Supplement to the Lawyer Statistical Report: The U.S. Legal Profession in 1985;* 1991, *1991 Lawyer Statistical Report: The U.S. Legal Profession in the 1990s,* 1994 (copyright); graduation rates: U.S. National Center for Education Statistics, *Digest of Education Statistics,* annual.

tice law and, at a minimum, consists of honesty. Lack of good moral character is demonstrated by an immutable dishonest and corrupt nature and not in radical political beliefs or membership in lawful but controversial political parties.

In regard to the effect of criminal conduct upon the evaluation of an applicant's character, a conviction for the commission of a FELONY is not, per se, sufficient to demonstrate a lack of good moral character. It will be incumbent upon the applicant, however, to prove complete rehabilitation. Although a conditional PARDON is insufficient to remove objections to bar admission, a felony CONVICTION will not prevent an applicant from practicing law if he or she has received a full pardon and is otherwise qualified.

MISDEMEANOR convictions do not necessarily result in a finding of lack of good moral character, but mere conduct that does not culminate in a conviction might present an insurmountable obstacle to admission if it indicates a lack of moral fitness. In some cases, an applicant has been rejected for want of good moral character because he or she has made false statements or concealed material facts in the application for admission or in other legal documents. In other cases, the withholding or falsification on the application of minor matters has been viewed as of no effect on an evaluation of character; the same principle applies to unintentional concealment of information.

Admission to the bar cannot be denied because the applicant is not a United States citizen, but the states can impose reasonable residency requirements upon all applicants prior to, or during, the time a license is sought. This requirement enables the state examining authority to investigate the character of the applicant, but it must be rationally related to the attainment of this objective. While a majority of states have some form of residency requirement for admission to the bar, the emerging trend is to nullify durational residency requirements, which mandate that an attorney live in a state for a prescribed period as a prerequisite to certification to practice law.

Applicants for admission to practice law must take a bar examination, unless they are exempted from this requirement by statute or court rule. Attorneys from other states can be admitted to practice in the state without examination upon providing the required proof of practice in another state that has reciprocity provisions, pursuant to which an attorney licensed in one state can be admitted to the bar of another state, if the first state grants RECIPROCAL rights to attorneys admitted to practice in the other state. Under the device of PRO HAC VICE, an attorney can be admitted to practice in a JURISDICTION without having to take the bar examination, but only on a limited basis and only for a particular case. Such an attorney must be a member of a bar in good standing of other states or countries.

In order to practice law, an attorney must obtain a CERTIFICATE or LICENSE, which is a PRIVILEGE rather than a PROPERTY RIGHT. Attorneys must also comply with the court rules or statutes governing the registration system, which is used to maintain a current list of all attorneys authorized to practice law in the state. Generally, admission by court order constitutes sufficient registration, but in some states, attorneys sign the roll or file a certificate with the CLERK of the court to establish that they have been duly admitted to practice.

An applicant for admission to the bar is entitled to NOTICE of, and a HEARING on, the grounds for rejection either before the committee on character and fitness or the court. The courts can review the decision of bar examiners denying an applicant admission to the bar and ascertain whether the examiners acted after a fair investigation and hearing, exercised their discretion impartially and reasonably, and conducted their proceedings in compliance with the requirements of procedural DUE PROCESS.

CROSS-REFERENCES

Attorney; Bar Association; Bar Examination; Courts; Federal Courts; Residency Laws.

ADMONITION ▯ Any formal verbal statement made during a TRIAL by a JUDGE to advise and caution the JURY on their duty as jurors, on the admissibility or nonadmissibility of EVIDENCE, or on the purpose for which any evidence admitted may be considered by them. A reprimand directed by the court to an attorney appearing before it cautioning the attorney about the unacceptability of his or her conduct before the court. If the attorney continues to act in the same way, ignoring the admonition, the judge will find him or her in CONTEMPT of court, punishable by a fine, imprisonment, or both. In criminal prosecution, before the court receives and records the PLEA of the accused, a statement made by a judge informing the accused on the effect and consequences of a plea of GUILTY to criminal charges. ▯

ADOPT ▯ To accept, appropriate, choose, or select, as to adopt a child. See also ADOPTION. To consent to and put into effect, as to adopt a constitution or a law. ▯

ADOPTION ▯ A two-step judicial process in conformance to state statutory provisions in which the legal obligations and rights of a child toward the biological parents are terminated and new rights and obligations are created in the acquired parents. ▯

Adoption involves the creation of the relation of parent and child between individuals who are not naturally so related. The adopted child is given the rights, privileges, and duties of a child and heir by the adoptive family.

Since adoption was not recognized at COMMON LAW, all adoption procedures in the United States are regulated by statute. Adoption statutes prescribe the conditions, manner, means, and consequences of adoption. In addition, they specify the rights and responsibilities of all parties involved.

DE FACTO adoption is a VOIDABLE agreement to adopt a child, based on a statutory proceeding in a particular state, which becomes lawful when the PETITION to adopt is properly presented.

Equitable adoption, sometimes referred to as *virtual adoption*, is treated by the law as final for certain purposes in spite of the fact that it has not been formally executed. When adoption appears to comply with standards of fairness and justice, some states will grant a child the rights of one who has been adopted even though the adoption procedure is incomplete. An equitable adoption might be enforced by the court for the benefit of a child in order to determine INHERITANCE rights, for example. Similarly, adoption by ESTOPPEL is the equitable adoption of a child by promises and acts that prevent the adoptive parents and their ESTATES from denying the child adoptive status.

Who May Adopt To be entitled to adopt a child, an individual must meet the qualifications under the laws of her or his state, since the state has sole power to determine who may become an adoptive parent. Unless otherwise provided by state statute, U.S. citizenship is not a prerequisite for adoption.

A child may be jointly adopted by a husband and wife. If not contrary to statutory provision, either may adopt without being joined by the other. Unmarried people may adopt unless prohibited by law.

A growing area of controversy by the courts is whether adoption by a child's grandparents is a viable alternative. Such adoption might be considered in the child's best interests if the natural parents die or if the custodial parent is found unfit. A legal GUARDIAN may adopt a child but is not ordinarily given preference in the court proceedings.

The best interests of the child are of paramount importance in policy considerations toward adoption. Although legislative policy prefers such conditions as adoption by people of the same religion as the prospective adoptee, an interfaith adoption is allowed when it does not adversely affect the welfare of the child.

Elements in determining who will be suitable adoptive parents include race, religion, economic status, home environment, age, and health. Most of these criteria are taken into consideration in placements by agencies or in private placements where state law requires that adoptive parents be investigated.

Who May Be Adopted Since the status of an adopted person is regulated by state statutes that authorize the adoption, state law determines whether an individual is a proper candidate for adoption. In addition, to be subject to adoption in a particular state, the individual must be living within that state.

Children may be adopted in situations where their natural parents are living, dead, or unknown, or where they have been abandoned. An adoption will not be prevented by the fact that a child has a legal guardian.

Some statutes expressly limit adoption to MINORS, and others expressly provide for adoption of ADULTS. The adoption of adults is regarded by statutes and the courts in a manner similar to the adoption of children. Practically, however, the adoption of adults differs greatly, since it serves different purposes and creates few of the difficulties arising out of the adoption of children. In most cases, the purpose of adult adoption is to facilitate a device for inheritance. One may designate an HEIR by adopting an adult. Generally, the adoptee would not otherwise be entitled to inherit but for the adoption.

Social Considerations In the past, adoption was viewed primarily as a means for a childless married couple to "normalize" their relationship. The focus has switched, however; now, adoption is ordinarily seen as an institution that exists to help place children into improved environments.

A number of states have, in recent years, enacted statutes that permit subsidization of adoptions. The adoption procedure thereby became a social instrument for the improvement of the lives of underprivileged children. Subsidized adoption tends to encourage adoption of children by suitable individuals who would otherwise be unable to afford it. This type of adoption has a significant effect upon placement of children labeled hard-to-place. Such children, who are frequently either physically or mentally handicapped, might have no other alternative except protracted institutionalization.

State law may require that the adopting parent have CUSTODY of a child for a certain period before obtaining an adoption DECREE. This requirement is designed to prevent premature action and to establish whether the best interests of the child will be furthered by the adoption.

Transracial Adoption In recent years, the issue of transracial adoption has come under close scrutiny by courts, legislatures, and the public. Americans are sharply divided on this issue. Is it a positive way to create stable families for needy children and well-meaning adults? Or is it an insidious means of co-opting members of racial minorities and confusing their sense of identity?

In 1972, when the number of African American children adopted annually by white families rose to fifteen thousand, the National Association of Black Social Workers (NABSW) issued its opinion on the subject. Igniting a furious national debate that continued in the mid-1990s, the association equated transracial adoption with cultural genocide for African Americans.

The NABSW and other minority groups opposed to the adoption of African American

U.S. Adoption Statistics, 1980–1987
Child's Country of Birth
Percent of total adoptions

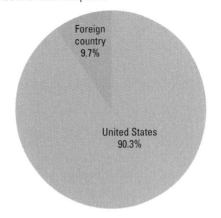

How Adoption Arranged
Percent of total adoptions

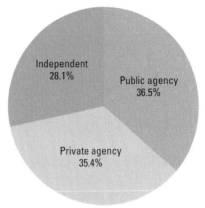

Source: "Number of unrelated children ever adopted by women 20–54 years of age and percent distribution by selected characteristics, according to year of adoption: National Health Interview Survey, 1987," Christine A. Bachrach, Ph.D., et al., *Adoption in the 1980's*, Advance Data from Vital and Health Statistics of the National Center for Health Studies, No. 181, Jan. 5, 1990, Table 2, p.5.

children by whites claim that the children are deprived of a true appreciation and understanding of their culture. Their childhood is skewed toward white values and assimilation. Without a sense of racial identity and pride, these children cannot truly belong to the African American community; yet, by the same token, racism prevents their full inclusion in the white world.

Despite these arguments, some African Americans applaud the unconditional love and permanence offered by transracial adoptions. Transracial adoption supporters argue that it is much worse to grow up without any family at all than to be placed with parents of a different race. Because a disproportionate number of African American children are placed in foster care, mixed-race adoptions may be necessary to ensure permanent homes for some African

American children. Transracial adoption may also be viewed as an opportunity to achieve integration on the most basic level.

Controversies involving transracial adoption soon found their way to the courts. In 1992, the Minnesota Supreme Court upheld a district court's order to transfer a three-year-old African American girl from her suburban Minneapolis foster home to her maternal grandparents' home in Virginia (*In re Welfare of D. L.*, 486 N.W.2d 375 [Minn. 1992]). Referred to as Baby D in court records, the child had been raised since birth by white foster parents who had been married for twenty-four years and had already raised three grown children. Baby D's birth mother placed her in foster care almost immediately after delivery and had not seen the child since. When no relatives could be found to claim the child, the foster parents decided to adopt the girl, whom they had grown to love.

When Baby D's grandparents learned that their daughter had delivered a baby, they set out to find their grandchild and to obtain custody. (The couple was already raising their daughter's three other children.) When the foster parents' petition to adopt Baby D surfaced, the grandparents vigorously opposed it.

The Minnesota Minority Heritage Preservation Act mandated a preference for placing children with relatives and adoptive parents of the same race (Minn. Stat. Ann. § 259.57(2)). An intermediate appeals court and the Minnesota Supreme Court agreed with the lower court that under the law, the Virginia grandparents must be granted custody. Despite the white foster parents' argument that they had provided security and loving care for the child, the grandparents' claim to Baby D was superior. Although many African Americans applauded the decision, some critics questioned the constitutionality of a law favoring same-race adoption.

A similar case in Lexington, Texas, produced a different result in 1995. Two foster parents, Scott Mullen and Lou Ann Mullen, who are white and Native American, respectively, applied to adopt two African American boys in their care. Initially, social workers for the Texas Department of Protective and Regulatory Services denied the Mullens' request, stating that departmental policy required them to seek adoptive parents of the same race as the children.

A civil liberties group called the Institute for Justice filed suit against the department on behalf of the Mullens. The institute also filed suits in other states, arguing that adoption decisions based on race are unconstitutional.

The Texas department reconsidered and allowed the Mullens to adopt the boys despite race differences.

Another statute affecting transracial adoptions is the Indian Child Welfare Act of 1978 (25 U.S.C.A. § 1901 et seq.) (ICWA), a federal law giving special preference to family and tribal adoptions of Native American children. Prior to its enactment, nearly one quarter of all Native American children were removed from their parents' care and placed in foster care, through which some were adopted. ICWA's sponsors argued that the adoption of Native American children by white parents was not necessarily in the children's best interests and was unquestionably harmful to tribal membership. The law was intended to preserve Native American culture and to support an Indian child-rearing philosophy that relies heavily upon the extended family.

Under the 1978 law, tribes have jurisdiction over the proposed adoption of any Native American child living on a reservation. Extended families or tribal placements are given automatic priority over all other applicants.

Another law covering transracial adoptions is the Multiethnic Placement Act of 1994 (42 U.S.C.A. §§ 622, 5115a, 5115a note). Sponsored by Senator Howard M. Metzenbaum (D-Ohio), the law prevents federally assisted child welfare agencies from screening prospective adoptive parents on the basis of race, color, or national origin. Although agencies may still consider the cultural or racial identity of children when making permanent placements, the law is intended to prevent discrimination and to speed the adoption process. The intention of the law is to give thousands of minority foster children who are eligible for adoption a greater chance of finding permanent homes.

Consent Virtually all statutes make parental CONSENT to adoption an indispensable condition. Most statutes set forth detailed requirements for the form and procedure of such consent. Ordinarily, statutes dispense with the parental consent requirement only when a parent has reached a serious level of unfitness that would be so significant as to terminate parental rights, or when such rights have already been judicially terminated.

In addition to parental consent, most states require a child to consent to the adoption if the child has reached a certain age, generally between ten and fourteen years.

The increasing number of DIVORCES has resulted in deemphasis of the necessity of consent to adoption by noncustodial parents, the purpose being to ease integration of children of a former marriage into the family created by a subsequent marriage. Some statutes allow adoption without the consent of the noncustodial parent if that parent has been unable to or has failed to contribute to the support of a child for a certain period of time. Grounds for termination of noncustodial parental rights are generally more easily provable than those governing normal severance of such rights. Courts are more inclined to find ABANDONMENT—a common ground for termination of parental rights—in cases involving noncustodial divorced parents.

Unmarried Father's Consent Historically, if a child was illegitimate, most jurisdictions required only the consent of the child's natural mother to the adoption of the child. The right to grant or withhold such consent was not extended to the fathers of illegitimate offspring, since they were not considered to have sufficient interest in the benefits and obligations of raising a child to determine whether the child should be released for adoption.

In 1979, this trend was reversed in *Caban v. Mohammed*, 441 U.S. 380, 99 S. Ct. 1760, 60 L. Ed. 2d 297 (1979). The key issue was whether the consent of an unwed biological father need be obtained before an adoption could be finalized.

In *Caban*, a mother of illegitimate children and her husband filed a PETITION for adoption. The children's natural father filed a cross petition to adopt. The New York Surrogate's Court granted the mother's petition, and the natural father appealed. The decision was affirmed by the Supreme Court, Appellate Division, and subsequently affirmed by the New York Court of Appeals.

On appeal, the U.S. Supreme Court ruled that a law depriving all unwed fathers of the right to decide against adoption, whether or not they actually took care of the children in question, was unconstitutional and a form of SEX DISCRIMINATION. The unwed father in *Caban* had lived with the mother of the children for five years prior to the birth of the children. The Court held that he had the right to block their adoption by a man who subsequently married the mother.

Consents that are signed by the parents either immediately before or after the birth of the child may be particularly subject to challenge by the natural mother. Owing to the mother's weakened physical and mental condition, findings of involuntary consent frequently have been handed down in such cases.

A parent can FORFEIT the right to give or deny consent for the adoption of his or her child in certain instances. *Abandonment*, the nonperformance of the natural obligations of caring for the child, including support, is one such case. The parent and child will ordinarily be kept together by the courts when the parent exhibits a continuing interest in the child's welfare.

A finding of abandonment may terminate a parent's rights and free the child for adoption with or without parental consent. A parent's rights may also be severed in cases of serious CHILD ABUSE or NEGLECT. Some statutes provide that a noncustodial parent cannot veto an adoption; however, that parent is generally entitled to be heard when a court considers the case. This is particularly true when the parent has established some kind of family tie with the child, either by having been married to, or having lived with, the custodial parent or by taking the child into her or his home.

State law may require that if a child has been placed in the custody of an agency, the agency's consent is a prerequisite for an adoption. Similarly, consent of a guardian having custody of a child is necessary. The consent of the natural mother's parents may also be required if she is under eighteen years of age and unwed.

Invalid Consent If COERCION or deception plays any part in the decision to terminate parental rights, the birth parent's consent may be ruled invalid. In the wake of the highly publicized battle over "Baby Jessica," it appears that regardless of the length of time or quality of a child's placement, the consent rights of the birth parents outweigh the best interests of the child.

In an agonizing case that divided the adoption community, Michigan couple Roberta DeBoers and Jan DeBoers lost custody in 1993 of Jessica, the two-and-a-half-year-old child they had raised from birth (*In re Clausen*, 442 Mich. 648, 502 N.W.2d 649 [1993]). Courts in both Iowa and Michigan concluded that the necessary consent by Iowa birth parents Cara Schmidt and Daniel Schmidt was flawed. After a protracted legal battle, Jessica was ordered to return to Iowa to live with her biological parents.

Shortly after Jessica's birth on February 8, 1991, the DeBoers filed a petition in Iowa juvenile court to adopt her. The couple, who for ten years had tried to conceive or adopt a child, were named her temporary guardians and custodians. When Jessica was less than four weeks old, however, birth mother Cara Clausen sued to have her maternal rights restored. The birth father, Dan Schmidt, also sought custody.

Unmarried at the time, Clausen had signed a release-custody form, terminating her parental rights, approximately forty hours after giving birth to Jessica. (Iowa law requires a seventy-two-hour waiting period before waiving parental rights.) The man Clausen identified as the child's father—not Schmidt—also signed a release form. Seventeen days later, Clausen informed Schmidt that she had lied on the release form and that Schmidt was actually the father.

On March 6, 1991, Clausen sought to revoke the custody agreement, naming Schmidt as the child's father. Upon learning that he was the baby's father, Schmidt filed an affidavit of paternity and asked for a court intervention to prevent the adoption proceedings. Clausen and Schmidt were married shortly thereafter.

The district court and subsequent courts determined that Dan Schmidt was indeed the biological father and that he had not agreed to have his parental rights terminated. Because he had not abandoned the baby, it was not clearly in the best interests of Jessica to remain with the DeBoers. Also, the parental rights waiver signed by Cara Schmidt was invalid because the statutorily imposed waiting period had not been observed. Therefore, early in the legal skirmish, the court ordered the baby returned to the Schmidts.

The DeBoers continued to fight Jessica's removal from their custody. With the legal maneuvering and delays, the case stretched out over a twenty-nine-month period. By the end, the DeBoers had developed a close bond with Jessica, even though they knew from the time Jessica was an infant that their claim to her might not hold up in court. But with the passage of time, the DeBoers could make a powerful claim that Jessica needed them more than the Schmidts. After all, they were the only parents she knew. The DeBoers argued that it was in Jessica's best interests to remain with them, or she could face possible emotional and psychological damage.

After Iowa courts refused to change position on the custody, the DeBoers took their case to Michigan, hoping that the best-interests-of-the-child argument would be persuasive. However, Michigan courts also agreed that Jessica should be returned to her Iowa birth parents. She was delivered to the Schmidts on August 2, 1993, and renamed Anna.

Methods of Adoption There are several types of adoption placement procedures. Foreign adoptions are affected by the policies and procedures of the adoptees' countries. Agency placement and independent placement are governed by statute, as is adoption by contract or by deed. Some people adopt through illegal purchase of a child or arrange to have a child by a surrogate mother.

Foreign Adoption Because of the scarcity of healthy babies for adoption in the United States, many U.S. citizens are pursuing adoption of orphaned and abandoned babies from foreign countries.

Most U.S. parents with children in foster care do not relinquish their parental rights. Foster children in the U.S. may also be difficult to place because many are older and carry the emotional scars of physical or sexual abuse.

Since the 1950s, U.S. couples have adopted thousands of Korean children. The number of Korean adoptions is declining, however, reportedly because the Korean government is uncomfortable with its reputation as a baby exporter. On the other hand, children from South America are being adopted in greater numbers by U.S. citizens, as are children from China, Romania, and Russia. In these countries, poverty, natural disasters, abandonment, war, and collapsed governments have resulted in an increased population of needy children.

Each country has different adoption policies regarding the age, income level, and marital status of prospective parents. Often, foreign adoptions are handled privately. Countries may allow children to be escorted to the United States or may require adoptive parents to come and stay for days or even months to complete the adoption paperwork. The costs of adoption also vary from nation to nation.

Agency Placement In agency placement of a child, the arrangements are made by a licensed public or private agency. Such agencies exist solely for the placement of children, and part of their responsibility involves a thorough investigation of the suitability of the potential adoptive parents. Such an investigation is ordinarily quite detailed and takes into consideration the background of both child and prospective parents.

Statutes generally provide for agencies that are operated or licensed by the government to act in an intermediary role between natural and adoptive parents. The method by which a child is transferred to an adoption or placement agency is by the execution of a formal SURRENDER agreement that the natural parents sign. By surrendering a child to an agency, the parent relinquishes all rights to the child. The agency is then given complete authority to arrange for adoption. In arranging for an adoption, agencies must take into consideration such issues as whether a particular child is a proper subject for adoption, whether the proposed home is a suitable one, and whether the adoption is in the child's best interests.

Agency placement has three basic advantages: (1) It minimizes such risks as the adoption of nonhealthy children, the discovery of the adoptive parents' identity by the natural mother, and the natural mother's changing her mind about the adoption. (2) The suitability of adoptive parents is determined by a stringent investigation, which minimizes the risk that a child will be adopted by unfit parents. (3) Adoption through an agency minimizes fees incidental to the adoption.

One essential disadvantage of agency placement is that it involves a long, detailed process. The adoptive parents might be forced to wait for many months while they are being investigated as to their suitability. A second disadvantage of agency placement is that only a limited number of children are available for adoption through agencies.

Independent Placement In independent placement, or private adoption, a child is directly transferred from the natural mother, or her representative, to the parents seeking to adopt. This type of placement is ordinarily arranged by the natural mother's family or doctor. Generally, neither the natural nor the adoptive parents are thoroughly investigated. The adoptive parents often arrange to pay all medical bills incidental to the pregnancy and birth, in addition to legal expenses. Private adoptions are lawful in most states.

Like agency placement, independent placement has both advantages and disadvantages. Private placement facilitates the adoption of a child by parents who might otherwise be forced to endure an extended waiting period or who might be unable to find a child through agency channels because of stringent requirements or mere nonavailability of adoptable children. As with all adoptions, there is an inherent risk that the natural mother might change her mind and never complete the adoption procedure. With some private adoptions, the natural mother remains anonymous. With others, her identity is known to the adoptive parents at the outset.

Independent placement aids mothers who do not have financial resources, by arranging for the payment of medical expenses by the adoptive parents. Such a procedure can, however, lead to a black market if not carefully monitored.

Other disadvantages of private placements are the risks of adoption of an unhealthy child or of nonsuitability of the adoptive parents.

Some states prohibit lawyers from obtaining babies for adoption by clients under any circumstances. Attorneys, however, are ordinarily permitted to accept fees for handling the legal aspects of adoption.

Surrogate Motherhood During the 1980s, many infertile couples turned to surrogate motherhood as an alternative to traditional adoption. A surrogate mother was paid a fee to bear a child conceived through artificial insemination. Once the child was born, the surrogate mother agreed to terminate her parental rights in favor of the sperm donor, typically the husband of the woman unable to have children. For public policy reasons, paid surrogate motherhood has been denounced as an unacceptable means of buying and selling babies.

The wrenching "Baby M" case proved to be the ultimate downfall of surrogate motherhood contracts. In *In re Baby M*, 109 N.J. 396, 537 A.2d 1227 (1988), Mary Beth Whitehead entered a written agreement to bear the child of William Stern, whose wife, Elizabeth Stern, was unable to have children. Whitehead was to be paid $10,000 for her services. When the baby girl was born in 1985, Whitehead refused to give her up and fled with the infant to Florida. Four months later, she was apprehended by authorities, who gave the baby over to the Sterns.

Despite Whitehead's efforts to regain the child, the New Jersey Superior Court stripped her of parental and visitation rights and allowed the Sterns to adopt the baby, whom they had named Melissa. The decision had little to do with adoption policy but centered primarily on contract enforcement. The court ruled that Whitehead was obligated to honor her contract with the Sterns.

The New Jersey Supreme Court reversed the lower-court decision, declaring that surrogate motherhood contracts are unenforceable because they violate public policy. The Sterns were allowed to maintain custody of Baby M, although the adoption was voided and some of Whitehead's parental and visitation rights were restored. After the decision, most states passed legislation to prohibit surrogate motherhood contracts altogether.

Adoption by Contract or Agreement Generally, an adoptive relationship cannot be formed by private CONTRACT, either EXPRESS or IMPLIED. Although adoption contracts are not usually considered to be injurious to public welfare, they are discouraged on the basis of the principle that a parent should not be permitted to trade away her or his child.

A court may, however, choose to treat a contract of adoption as an agreement to be enforced, with the outcome being equivalent to a formal adoption. The courts have upheld contracts between parents and institutions. In addition, in a number of states, an adoption contract between a natural parent and an institution that provides that the parent is not to be informed of the child's location is enforceable.

A sample petition
for adoption

FAMILY COURT OF THE STATE OF _____
COUNTY OF _____

In the Matter of the
Adoption by

of   Index No.

a minor having the first
name of
                                                                              PETITION
                                                                              (Agency)

whose last name is contained
in the Schedule annexed to
the Petition herein.

TO THE FAMILY COURT:

1. (a) The name and place of residence of the petitioning adoptive mother is:
     Name:
     Address: (include county)
She is (of full age) (a minor), born on
She is (unmarried) (married to
and they are living together as husband and wife).
Her occupation is
and her approximate annual income is $
   (b) The name and place of residence of the petitioning adoptive father is:
     Name:
     Address:(include county)
He is (of full age) (a minor), born on
He is (unmarried) (married to
and they are living together as husband and wife).
His occupation is
and his approximate annual income is $
2. As nearly as the same can be ascertained, the full name, date and place of birth of the
(male) (female) adoptive child are set forth in the Schedule annexed to this Petition and verified by a duly constituted official of an authorized agency.
3. The manner in which the adoptive parents obtained the adoptive child is as follows:
4. The adoptive child has resided continuously with the adoptive parents since
5. The name by which the adoptive child is to be known is
6. The consent of the above-mentioned authorized agency has been duly executed and is
filed herewith. The consent of the natural parents of the adoptive child is not required because
7. No previous application has been made to any court or judge for the relief sought
herein, except
8. The adoptive child has not been previously adopted, except
9. To the best of petitioners' information and belief, there are no persons other than those
hereinbefore mentioned interested in this proceeding except
10. WHEREFORE, your Petitioners pray for an order approving the adoption of the aforesaid adoptive child by the above named adoptive parents and directing that the said adoptive
child shall be regarded and treated in all respects as the child of the said adoptive parents
and directing that the name of the said adoptive child be changed as specified in paragraph 6
above and henceforth (s)he shall be known by that name.

Since courts are not eager to deprive natural parents of the right to care for a child, adoption contracts are not enforced when they are in conflict with the welfare of the child. Some states provide that a contract made by one parent alone, absent a showing of clear consent by the other, is not valid. The procedure for adoption by a written declaration or deed is permitted in some states. Ordinarily, it must be properly recorded before the adoption will be valid.

Revocation A court will allow an agreement for the adoption of a child to be broken by a natural parent if the circumstances warrant it, such as when a parent was forced into an adoption agreement.

The court has discretion over whether to permit REVOCATION of an adoption agreement. In such cases, the court will scrutinize the circumstances under which the parent gave consent as well as the parent's reasons for revoking the contract.

Consequences of Adoption Adoption ordinarily terminates the rights and responsibilities of the natural parents to the child. The death of an adoptive parent does not restore the rights of the natural parents.

Adoption creates the same rights and responsibilities between a child and adoptive parents as existed between natural parent and child. An adopted child is entitled to the same rights as a natural child. When an adult is adopted, however, the adoptive parent does not assume the usual duty of support.

State law governs whether or not the name of a child will be affected by adoption. When a minor child is adopted, his or her legal residence is changed from that of the natural parent to that of the adoptive parent.

Inheritance A state legislature has the authority to impart or remove inheritance rights of adopted children or adoptive parents. Statutes usually provide that adopted children can inherit from adoptive parents in the same capacity as natural children and, conversely, adoptive parents can inherit the property of an adopted child who predeceases them.

Revocation of Adoption If an adoption decree is acquired by FRAUD, it may be revoked. In addition, in the absence of the requisite consent of all concerned parties, an order of adoption is VOID. After a decree is revoked, a child assumes the status she or he had prior to the adoption proceedings.

Summary of Adoption Procedure The formal steps in adoption of a child are generally uniform in all states.

Notice NOTICE of adoption proceedings is given to all parties who have a legal interest in the case except the child. In the case of illegitimacy, both natural parents should be given notice if they can be located.

Some statutes provide that a parent who has failed to support a child is not entitled to notice. Ordinarily, a parent who has lost custody of a child in a divorce or separation case is, however, entitled to notice. Similarly, an adoption agency that has custody of the child is entitled to notice.

Petition The parents seeking to adopt must file a petition in court that supplies information about their situation as well as the situation of the child. The filing of a proper petition is ordinarily a prerequisite to the court's jurisdiction.

The petition indicates the names of the adoptive parents, the child, and the natural parents, if known. In addition, the child's gender and age are stated, and some states mandate that a medical report on the child must also accompany the petition. An example of such a petition is found on page 98.

Consent Written consent of the adoption agency or the child's natural parents accompanies the petition for adoption. Consent of the natural parents is not required if their parental rights have been involuntarily terminated as a result, for example, of abandonment or abuse of the child.

Hearing A HEARING is held so that the court may examine the qualifications of the prospective parents and either grant or deny the petition. There must be an opportunity for the parties to present testimony and to examine witnesses at such a hearing.

Adoption proceedings are confidential, so the hearing is conducted in a closed courtroom.

Ordinarily, the records of an adoption hearing are available for inspection only by court order. Confidentiality is thought to promote a sense of security for the child with his or her new family.

Probation Most states require a period of PROBATION in adoption proceedings. During this period, the child lives with the adoptive parents, and the appropriate state agency monitors the development of the relationship. The agency's prime concern is the ability of the adoptive parents to properly care for the child. If the relationship is working well for all concerned parties, the state agency will request that the court issue a permanent decree of adoption.

If the relationship is unsatisfactory, the child is either returned to her or his previous home or is taken care of by the state.

Decree An adoption decree is a judgment of the court and is given the same force and effect as any other judgment.

Birth Certificate Following the adoption proceedings, a certificate of adoption is issued for the adopted child, to replace the birth certificate. It lists the new family name, the date and place of the child's birth, and the ages of the adoptive parents at the time the child was born.

Generally, the certificate of adoption does not indicate the names of the child's natural parents or the date and place of adoption. A child may never know that he or she was adopted unless the adoptive parents reveal the information, since the old birth certificate is sealed away and may be opened only by court order.

Right to Information on Natural Parents Ordinarily, all information concerning an adopted child's origins is sealed, in compliance with the court adoption proceedings, to facilitate development of a relationship between the adoptive parents and child free from the natural parents' influence.

Most state statutes deny adoptees access to records that disclose information about the natural parents. Often, the natural parents make their consent to the adoption contingent upon the condition that no information about them should ever be revealed.

In recent times, because of a growing public interest in tracing ethnic and family backgrounds, many adoptees, as adults, have been calling for the right to obtain access to sealed adoption records.

The adult adoptees recognize that a disclosure of this kind of information could be traumatic to minor adoptees, but they contend that lack of access could cause serious psychological trauma to them as adults. In addition, they cite medical problems or misdiagnoses that could be caused by absence of genetic history, lack of religious identity, and fear of unwitting INCEST.

Adult adoptees contend that most adoption statutes do not make a distinction between adoptees as minors and later as adults, which causes the adults to be deprived of the right to trace their background. In addition, the adults allege that they have been denied EQUAL PROTECTION of law because their status precludes them from receiving medical information readily available to nonadoptees.

Various approaches are being used to resolve this problem. One approach involves the enactment of a legislative requirement that public and private adoption agencies be required to open their records upon request to adults who were adopted as children, with certain limitations. For example, if the child had been placed by the natural parents prior to the effective date of the legislation, the natural parents could prevent the adoptee from seeing the records.

The issue of right to access to adoption records by adoptees when they reach adulthood also encompasses the legal consideration of the natural parents' right to PRIVACY, which could be violated if free access to sealed court records were given to adult adoptees. The adult adoptees' right to know must be balanced against their natural parents' right to privacy. The way to achieve such a balance, however, has never been clearly determined.

CROSS-REFERENCES

Child Custody; Children's Rights; Child Support; Family Law; Illegitimacy; Infants; Parent and Child; Surrogate Motherhood.

ADULT A person who by virtue of attaining a certain age, generally eighteen, is regarded in the eyes of the law as being able to manage his or her own affairs.

The age specified by law, called the legal AGE OF MAJORITY, indicates that a person acquires full legal CAPACITY to be bound by various documents, such as contracts and deeds, that he or she makes with others and to commit other legal acts such as voting in elections and entering marriage. The age at which a person becomes an adult varies from state to state and often varies within a state, depending upon the nature of the action taken by the person. Thus, a person wishing to obtain a license to operate a motor vehicle may be considered an adult at age sixteen, but may not reach adulthood until age eighteen for purposes of marriage, or age twenty-one for purposes of purchasing intoxicating liquors.

Anyone who has not reached the age of adulthood is legally considered an INFANT.

ADULTERATION Mixing something impure with something genuine, or an inferior article with a superior one of the same kind.

Adulteration usually refers to mixing other matter of an inferior and sometimes harmful quality with food or drink intended to be sold. As a result of adulteration, food or drink becomes impure and unfit for human consumption. The federal Food and Drug Administration prohibits transportation of adulterated foods, drugs, and cosmetics in interstate commerce, as provided under the Food, Drug and Cosmetic Act (21 U.S.C.A. § 301 et seq. [1938]). State and local agencies, acting under the authority of local laws, do the same to ban the use of such impure goods within their borders.

ADULTERY Voluntary sexual relations between an individual who is married and someone who is not the individual's spouse.

Adultery is viewed by the law as an offense injurious to public morals and a mistreatment of the marriage relationship.

Statutes attempt to inhibit adultery by making such behavior punishable as a CRIME and by allowing a blameless party to obtain a DIVORCE against an adulterous spouse.

Although adultery has ordinarily been regarded as a legal wrong, it has not always been considered a crime. Historically it was punishable solely in courts created by the church to impose good morals. In the ECCLESIASTICAL COURTS, adultery was any act of sexual intercourse by a married person with someone not his or her spouse. The act was considered wrongful regardless of whether or not the other person was married. At COMMON LAW, adultery was wrongful intercourse between a married woman and any man other than her husband.

Criminal Laws Several state legislatures have statutorily defined adultery as a crime. The PUBLIC POLICY reason for this classification is to further peace and order in society by preservation of the sanctity of family relationships and to proscribe conduct that undermines such relationships.

Under some statutes, both parties to an adulterous relationship are guilty of a crime if either of them is married to someone else. Other statutes provide that the act is criminal only if the woman is married.

Under the law of some states, one act of adultery constitutes a crime, whereas in others, there must be an ongoing and notorious relationship. The punishment set by statute may be greater for an individual who engages in repeated acts of adultery than for one who commits an isolated act.

Defenses An individual who has been charged with committing adultery may have a valid legal defense, such as the failure or physical incapacity to consummate the sex act.

A woman is not guilty of adultery if the sex act resulted from RAPE. Some states recognize ignorance of the accused regarding the marital status of his or her lover as a defense. In some states, only the married party can be prosecuted for adultery. If the other party to the relationship is not married, he or she may be prosecuted for FORNICATION instead of adultery.

Initiation of Criminal Proceedings Under some statutes, a prosecution for adultery can be brought only by the spouse of the accused person although technically the action is initiated in the name of the state. Other states provide that a husband or wife is precluded from commencing prosecution for adultery since those states have laws that prohibit a husband or wife from testifying against his or her spouse. In such states, a complaint can be filed by a husband or wife against the adulterous spouse's lover.

Evidence Customary rules prescribe the types of EVIDENCE that can be offered to prove guilt or innocence. There must be a showing by the prosecutor that the accused party and another named party had sexual relations. Depending on state statutes, the prosecutor must show that either one or both parties to the adultery were wed to someone else at the time of their relationship.

Evidence of a chance to have sexual relations coupled with a desire, or *opportunity* and *inclination*, might be sufficient to prove guilt. Photographs, or the testimony of a witness who observed the couple having sexual intercourse, is not necessary. The fact that a married woman accused of adultery became pregnant during a time when her husband was absent might be admissible to demonstrate that someone, other than her spouse, had access to her for the opportunity of engaging in illicit sex. In addition, evidence that an accused woman gave birth to an illegitimate child might also be admissible.

Letters in which the accused parties have written about their amorous feelings or clandestine encounters may be introduced in court to support the assertion that the parties had the inclination to engage in sexual relations. Character evidence indicating the good or bad reputation of each party may be brought before the jury. Although evidence of a woman's sexual relationships with men other than the party to the adultery generally cannot be used, if her reputation as a prostitute can be demonstrated, it may be offered as evidence.

Suspicious activities and incriminating circumstances may be offered as circumstantial evidence.

Enforcement of Statutes Although adultery is a crime in many states, the prosecution of offenders is rare. The legal system of the United States is currently reevaluating crimes such as adultery in light of the question of whether or not it is expedient to use jail time and fines to punish consenting adults for their sexual activities, even when family stability is threatened.

As a Defense Occasionally, adultery has been successfully asserted as a defense to the crime of MURDER by an individual charged with killing his or her spouse's lover. Courts are loath, however, to excuse the heinous crime of murder on the ground that the accused party was agitated about a spouse's adulterous activities, unless the spouse acted in HEAT OF PASSION.

Divorce Based on the state's interest in the marital status of its residents, all legislatures had traditionally assigned statutes enumerating the grounds on which a divorce would be granted. These grounds, listed separately in the laws of each jurisdiction, generally included DESERTION, NONSUPPORT, and adultery.

The basis of adultery as a ground for divorce has been discussed in various cases. There is an overriding public policy in favor of preserving the sanctity of marital relationships and family unity, and a fear that adultery will serve to undermine these societal objectives.

Recent changes in divorce laws, primarily the enactment of no-fault divorce statutes in many states, have made it easier for couples seeking divorce to end their marriages without having to prove adultery or any other ground. In the past many unhappy couples resorted to trickery to attempt to obtain a divorce through staging the discovery of allegedly adulterous conduct.

CROSS-REFERENCES
Family Law; Husband and Wife; Marriage.

AD VALOREM 📖 According to value. 📖

The term *ad valorem* is derived from the Latin *ad valentiam*, meaning "to the value." It is commonly applied to a tax imposed on the value of property. REAL PROPERTY taxes that are imposed by the states, counties, and cities are the most common type of *ad valorem* taxes. *Ad valorem* taxes can, however, be imposed upon PERSONAL PROPERTY. For example, a motor vehicle tax may be imposed upon personal property such as an automobile.

An article of commerce may be subjected to an *ad valorem* tax in proportion to its value, which is determined by assessment or appraisal.

Duties, taxes on goods imported or brought into this country from a foreign country, are either *ad valorem* or specific. An *ad valorem* duty is one in the form of a percentage on the value of the property, unlike a specific duty that is a fixed sum imposed on each article of a class, such as all Swiss wristwatches, regardless of their individual values.

See also TAXATION.

ADVANCE 📖 To pay money or give something of value before the date designated to do so; to provide capital to help a planned enterprise, expecting a return from it; to give someone an item before payment has been made for it. 📖

ADVANCEMENT 📖 A gift of money or property made by a person while alive to his or her child or other legally recognized HEIR, the value of which the person intends to be deducted from the child's or heir's eventual share in the ESTATE after the giver's death. 📖

An advancement is not the same as a GIFT or a loan because the person intends that the "advance" of the heir's share of the estate be applied against what the heir would normally inherit. Although sometimes used to describe situations involving both people who have died INTESTATE (without leaving a valid WILL) and people who have left a will, the term *advancement* should be used only when there is no valid

will. The laws of DESCENT AND DISTRIBUTION regulate the distribution of an intestate's property. The term ADEMPTION applies to lifetime gifts that reduce a beneficiary's share under a will.

ADVANCE SHEETS 📖 Pamphlets containing recently decided OPINIONS of FEDERAL COURTS or state COURTS of a particular region. 📖

Cases appearing in advance sheets are subsequently published in bound volumes containing several past pamphlets, usually with the same volume and page numbers as appeared in the advance sheets. Sometimes a court will publish an individual opinion soon after it has been rendered by the court. This is called a slip opinion, which later may appear in an advance sheet.

Advance Sheets in the National Reporter System The National REPORTER System, published by West Publishing Company, St. Paul, Minnesota, is the most comprehensive collection of the decisions of the appellate courts of the states and of the United States. There are eighteen reporters in the National Reporter System. Eight of the units cover federal courts and ten units cover the fifty states and the District of Columbia.

Advance sheets are published fifty times each year (weekly, except for the last week of September and the first week of October) for the regional units reporting state cases. Three units report federal cases fifty-two times per year. Of the remaining units, one publishes advance sheets biweekly, one monthly, and one semimonthly, during the term of the SUPREME COURT OF THE UNITED STATES.

All DECISIONS, opinions, and MEMORANDA of the United States Supreme Court are published in the *Supreme Court Reporter* (cited as S. Ct.). The advance sheets are issued semimonthly during the term of the Court. At the end of the term, two or three hardbound volumes are published, depending on the number of cases decided.

The *Federal Reporter* (F.), *Federal Reporter, Second Series* (F.2d) and *Third Series* (F.3d) contain the reported cases of the United States Courts of Appeal, Court of Claims, Court of Customs and Patent Appeals, and Temporary Emergency Court of Appeals. The *Federal Supplement* (F.Supp.) reports decisions of the United States District Courts, the United States Court of International Trade, and the Judicial Panel on Multistate Litigation. *Federal Rules Decisions* (F.R.D.) contains District Court opinions construing the Federal Rules of Civil Procedure. *Military Justice Reporter* (M.J.) carries the cases of the Court of Military Appeals and Courts of Military Review. *Bankruptcy Reporter* (Bankr.) reports decisions of the United States Bankruptcy Courts and bankruptcy decisions of other federal courts.

The regional units of the National Reporter System report the opinions of the highest courts of all fifty states and the District of Columbia. In addition, these reporters contain opinions of state intermediate appellate courts that are selected by the courts for publication. Many of the states have designated the unit of the National Reporter System in which their cases appear as their official reports.

The regional units of this system are the *Atlantic Reporter, Second Series* (A., A.2d); *North Western Reporter, Second Series* (N.W., N.W.2d); *Pacific Reporter, Second Series* (P., P.2d); *South Eastern Reporter, Second Series* (S.E., S.E.2d); *Southern Reporter, Second Series* (So., So.2d); and *South Western Reporter, Second Series* (S.W., S.W.2d). Because of the large volume of reported cases, three states have their own reporter units. They are the *California Reporter* (Cal. Rptr.); *Illinois Decisions* (Ill. Dec.); and *New York Supplement* and *New York Supplement, Second Series* (N.Y.S., N.Y.S.2d).

ADVERSARY PROCEEDING Any action, HEARING, investigation, INQUEST, or inquiry brought by one party against another in which the party seeking relief has given legal NOTICE to and provided the other party with an opportunity to contest the claims that have been made against him or her.

A court trial is a typical example of an adversary proceeding.

ADVERSARY SYSTEM The scheme of American jurisprudence wherein a judge renders a decision in a controversy between PARTIES who assert contradictory positions during a judicial examination such as a TRIAL or HEARING.

U.S. courtrooms have often been compared to battlefields or playing fields. The adversary system by which legal disputes are settled in the United States promotes the idea that legal controversies are battles or contests to be fought and won using all available resources.

The contemporary Anglo-American adversary system has gradually evolved over several hundred years. Early English jury trials were unstructured proceedings in which the judge might act as inquisitor or even prosecutor as well as fact finder. Criminal defendants were not allowed to have counsel, call witnesses, conduct cross-examination, or offer affirmative defenses. All types of evidence were allowed, and juries, although supposedly neutral and passive, were actually highly influenced by the judge's remarks and instructions. In fact, before

1670, jurors could be fined or jailed for refusing to follow a judge's directions.

The late 1600s saw the advent of a true adversarial system in both England and America. Juries took a more neutral stance, and appellate review, previously unavailable, became possible in some cases. By the eighteenth century, juries assumed an even more autonomous position as they began functioning as a restraint on governmental and judicial abuse and corruption. The Framers of the Constitution recognized the importance of the jury trial in a free society by specifically establishing it in the SIXTH AMENDMENT as a right in criminal prosecutions.

The independent judiciary was somewhat slower in developing. Before the 1800s, English judges were still biased by their ties with the Crown, and U.S. judges were often politically partisan. U.S. Supreme Court Chief Justice JOHN MARSHALL, who served from 1801 to 1835, established the preeminence and independence of the Supreme Court with his opinion in *Marbury v. Madison*, 5 U.S. (1 Cranch) 137, 2 L. Ed. 60 (1803). *Marbury* established "the basic principle that the federal judiciary is supreme in the exposition of the law of the Constitution" (*Cooper v. Aaron*, 358 U.S. 1, 78 S. Ct. 1401, 3 L. Ed. 2d 5 [1958]). By the early 1800s, ATTORNEYS had risen to prominence as ADVOCATES and presenters of EVIDENCE. Procedural and evidentiary rules were developed, which turned the focus of litigation away from arguments on minute points of law and toward resolution of disputes. The basic parameters of the United States' modern legal system had been established.

In the Anglo-American adversary system, the parties to a dispute or their advocates square off against each other and assume roles that are strictly separate and distinct from that of the decision maker, usually a judge or jury. The decision maker is expected to be objective and free from bias. Rooted in the ideals of the American Revolution, the modern adversary system reflects the conviction that everyone is entitled to a day in court before a free, impartial, and independent judge. Adversary theory holds that requiring each side to develop and present its own proofs and arguments is the surest way to uncover the information that will enable the judge or jury to resolve the conflict.

In an adversary system, the judge or jury is a neutral and passive fact finder, dispassionately examining the evidence presented by the parties with the objective of resolving the dispute between them. The fact finder must remain uninvolved in the presentation of arguments so as to avoid reaching a premature decision.

THE ADVERSARY SYSTEM: WHO WINS? WHO LOSES?

The legal system in the United States is known as an adversary system. In this system, the parties to a controversy develop and present their arguments, gather and submit evidence, call and question witnesses, and, within the confines of certain rules, control the process. The fact finder, usually a judge or jury, remains neutral and passive throughout the proceeding.

Critics pose some disturbing questions about the adversary system: Is justice served by a process that is more concerned with resolving controversies than with finding the ultimate truth? Is it possible for people with limited resources to enjoy the same access to legal services as do wealthy people? Does a system that puts a premium on winning encourage chicanery, manipulation, and deception?

The 1995 trial of O. J. Simpson, an actor, sportscaster, and professional football player accused of murdering his former wife and her friend, cast unprecedented scrutiny on the criminal justice system, and left many people wondering whether truth or justice play any role in its operation. Each day for over a year, the trial was televised in the homes of millions of people, most of whom had never seen the inside of a courtroom. They were fascinated and repelled by prosecutors and defense attorneys who argued relentlessly about seemingly trivial points. Even more disturbing to some viewers was the acrimonious name-calling that went on between the two sides as each attempted to discredit the other's evidence and witnesses. Likewise, the 1994 trials of Eric and Lyle Menendez, wealthy brothers who admitted killing their parents but whose first trials ended in hung juries, left

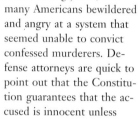

IN FOCUS

many Americans bewildered and angry at a system that seemed unable to convict confessed murderers. Defense attorneys are quick to point out that the Constitution guarantees that the accused is innocent unless found guilty in a court of law, and it is impossible to protect the innocent without occasionally protecting the guilty. Lawyers are obligated to challenge the evidence against their clients, even if that means impugning the police or attacking a victim's or witness's character. It is their job to win an acquittal by whatever legal and ethical means within their power.

Disparaging the legal system has become something of a national pastime. Indeed, criticism of the system comes from all corners of the landscape, including the top of the system itself. The late Chief Justice Warren E. Burger was outspoken in his lambasting of the system and of lawyers, asserting that they are too numerous and too zealous, that they file too many frivolous lawsuits and motions, and that there is general failure within the system to encourage out-of-court settlements. Burger was a vocal proponent of alternative dispute resolution (ADR). He advocated the use of nonlitigious solutions such as mediation or arbitration as a means of reducing court congestion. Supporters of the adversary system point out that it is not clear that the savings reaped from ADR always outweigh the costs. In situations where the parties are not at equal bargaining strength, questions arise as to whether settlements are extracted through duress. Some attorneys and litigants have noted that ADR is often as adversarial in nature as litigation, with evidence presented and slanted by counsel. They further complain that there is no guarantee that an arbitrator will be informed about the subject matter of the dispute, and therefore no guarantee of a fair outcome.

Without doubt, during the 1980s and 1990s, the United States experienced tremendous growth in the number of civil suits filed. The results were clogged courts, trial delays, and increased legal costs. However, the experts disagree on how to solve these problems. Critics of the system clamor for reforms to address what they perceive as its deficiencies, whereas many commentators, particularly those within the legal profession, feel that the sys-

The Anglo-American requirement of an impartial and passive fact finder contrasts with the requirements of other legal systems. For example, most European countries employ the inquisitorial system, in which a judge investigates the facts, interviews witnesses, and renders a decision. Juries are not favored in an inquisitorial court, and the disputants are minimally involved in the fact-finding process. The main emphasis in a European court is the search for truth, whereas in an Anglo-American courtroom, truth is ancillary to the goal of reaching the fairest resolution of the dispute. It has been suggested that the inquisitorial system, with its goal of finding the truth, is a more just and equitable legal system. However, proponents of the adversary system maintain that the truth is most likely to emerge after all sides of a controversy are vigorously presented. They also point out that the inquisitorial system has its own deficiencies, including abuse and corruption. European judges must assume all roles in a trial, including those of fact finder, evidence gatherer, interrogator, and decision maker. Because of these sometimes conflicting roles, European judges may tend to prejudge a case in an effort to organize and dispose of it. Inquisitorial courts are far less sensitive to individual rights than are adversarial courts, and inquisitorial judges, who are government bureaucrats (rather

tem, although imperfect, is actually working the way it is designed to work and should not be altered.

One criticism of the adversary system is that it is slow and cumbersome. The judge, acting as a neutral fact finder, can do little to accelerate a trial, and procedural and evidentiary rules further slow the process. Likewise, the wide availability of appellate review means that a final determination can take years. However, at least one study has shown that in courts where adversarial trials were discouraged and settlements actively encouraged, litigants still encountered substantial delays in resolution. And supporters of the adversary system maintain that a methodical, albeit cumbersome, system is necessary for protection of individual rights.

It is fair to challenge the ethics of a legal system that places a higher value on winning than on truth seeking. At least one commentator has characterized the system as one in which lawyers spend more time avoiding truth than seeking it. But proponents argue that the vigorous clash of opposing viewpoints eventually yields the truth, and that allowing the sides to fight it out under specific rules that guarantee fair play allows the truth to surface on its own.

Many other complaints have been leveled against the United States' adversary system. Some feel that because the parties control the litigation, they are encouraged to present only the evidence that is favorable to them and to suppress evidence that is unfavorable.

Criticism of attorneys abounds. Some feel that the lawyers' ethics code encourages zealous representation at the expense of truth, making attorneys, in the words of Burger, "hired guns" (*In re Griffiths*, 413 U.S. 717, 93 S. Ct. 2851, 37 L. Ed. 2d 910 [1973]). Others complain that lawyers file too many frivolous lawsuits and have become too dominant in the adversary process. Some even say that the rules of evidence, designed to guarantee fairness to all parties, actually work against fairness by preventing important information from being presented to the fact finder.

Defenders of the adversary system are quick to refute each criticism lobbed at it. They contend that it is necessary for the parties to control the litigation in order to preserve the neutrality of the judge and jury. They point out that lawyers, although as susceptible to corruption as any other group, are governed by a code of ethical conduct that, when enforced, deals effectively with instances of overreaching. And, while conceding that evidentiary rules may be subject to manipulation, they vigorously maintain that such rules are the only means by which to ensure fairness and prevent judicial abuse.

The criticism of the U.S. legal system that may be most difficult to refute has to do with accessibility. It cannot be plausibly argued that an average criminal defendant has the same access to legal representation as O. J. Simpson or the wealthy Menendez brothers, nor can it be argued that an injured plaintiff in a civil suit is in an equal bargaining

position with a huge corporation. Yet, supporters of the adversary system counter that unequal access to legal services is the result of economic and social conditions, not the structure of the legal system, and that changing the way legal services are delivered would do nothing to address the root causes of the disparity. They also point out that the much-criticized contingency fee arrangement, by which an attorney is paid a percentage of the award her or his client receives, opens the courts to members of the population who could not otherwise afford legal representation.

Most legal experts agree that, in the long run, the adversary system results in societal benefits that outweigh its inherent shortcomings. By allowing all sides of a controversy to be heard, the system protects against abuse of power, and forces those with the most at stake to focus on the issues in dispute. At its worst, it can be manipulated to the benefit of those least deserving, but at its best, it offers every injured party a forum for relief, sometimes against powerful odds. No doubt, the arguments about whether and how to change the system will go on into the twenty-first century. As a system that has evolved over three hundred years, it probably will undergo some changes. But the basic values at its heart, such as presumption of innocence, the right to trial by jury, and protection of individual rights, appear to be firmly cemented as the cornerstones of U.S. jurisprudence.

---

than part of an independent judiciary), may identify more with the government than with the parties. Critics of the inquisitorial system say that it provides little, if any, check on government excess and invites corruption, bribery, and abuse of power.

The parties to an Anglo-American lawsuit are responsible for gathering and producing all the evidence in the case. This forces them to develop their arguments and present their most compelling evidence, and also preserves the neutrality and passivity of the fact finder. The adversary process is governed by strict rules of evidence and procedure that allow both sides equal opportunity to argue their cases. These

rules also help ensure that the decision is based solely on the evidence presented. The structure of this legal system naturally encourages zealous advocacy by lawyers on behalf of their clients, but the code of ETHICS governing the conduct of lawyers is designed to curb the tendency to attempt to win by any means.

The adversarial system has staunch defenders as well as severe critics. The image of the courtroom as a battleground or playing field where contestants vie for victory is evident in the news media's preoccupation with who is "winning" or "losing" or "scoring points" in such highly visible cases as the 1995 trial of O. J. Simpson, an actor, sportscaster, and former professional football player accused of killing his former wife Nicole Brown Simpson and her friend Ronald Goldman.

The emphasis on "winning at all costs" without commensurate concern for truth seeking dismays some U.S. citizens, and a growing number are demanding reforms in the legal system. During the 1980s and 1990s, the use of alternative forms of dispute resolution such as MEDIATION and ARBITRATION grew dramatically. However, defenders of the adversary system note that these alternatives have actually been used all along, in the form of settlement conferences, minitrials, and summary jury trials, and that the vast majority of lawsuits are already settled before the parties ever appear in court.

When a dispute cannot be resolved without a trial, the adversary system is the established method of adjudication in the United States. Indeed, the organized bar remains committed to the notion that vigorous advocacy by both sides of a legal controversy ultimately leads the judge or jury to the facts needed for a fair resolution and is the process best calculated to elicit the truth and protect individual rights. Although many concede that the adversary system is imperfect and that it may be subject to abuse and manipulation, the majority still believe that, by giving all parties and their advocates the opportunity to present evidence and arguments before an impartial judge, it provides a free and pluralistic society with the best available means of settling disputes.

CROSS-REFERENCES

Alternative Dispute Resolution; Civil Law; Common Law; Inquisitorial System; Judge; Judiciary; Jury.

ADVERSE INTEREST 📖 The legal right or liability of a person called to TESTIFY as a WITNESS in a lawsuit that might be lost or impaired if the party who called him or her to testify wins the case. 📖

This interest against the interest of the party calling a witness to the stand makes him or her an adverse or HOSTILE WITNESS. Although usually the party calling a witness to testify cannot IMPEACH that person's CREDIBILITY, if the person has an adverse interest, the TESTIMONY may be discredited by the party who called that witness to the stand.

ADVERSE POSSESSION 📖 A method of gaining LEGAL TITLE to REAL PROPERTY by the actual, open, hostile, and continuous POSSESSION of it to the exclusion of its true owner for the period prescribed by state law. PERSONAL PROPERTY may also be acquired by adverse possession. 📖

Adverse possession is similar to PRESCRIPTION, another way to acquire TITLE to real property by occupying it for a period of time. Prescription is not the same, however, because title acquired under it is presumed to have resulted from a lost grant, as opposed to the expiration of the statutory time limit in adverse possession.

Real Property Title to land is acquired by adverse possession as a result of the lapse of the STATUTE OF LIMITATIONS for EJECTMENT, which bars the commencement of a lawsuit by the true owner to recover possession of the land. Adverse possession depends upon the intent of the occupant to claim and hold real property in opposition to all the world and the demonstration of this intention by visible and hostile possession of the land so that the owner is or should be aware that adverse claims are being made.

The legal theory underlying the vesting of title by adverse possession is that title to land must be certain. Since the owner has, by his or her own fault and NEGLECT, failed to protect the land against the hostile actions of the adverse possessor, an adverse possessor who has treated the land as his or her own for a significant period of time is recognized as its owner.

Title by adverse possession may be acquired against any person or CORPORATION not excepted by statute. Property held by the federal government, a state, or a MUNICIPAL CORPORATION cannot be taken by adverse possession. As long as the property has a public use, as with a highway or school property, its ownership cannot be lost through adverse possession.

Anyone, including corporations, the federal government, states, and municipal corporations, can be an adverse possessor.

Elements In order that adverse possession ripen into legal title, nonpermissive use by the adverse claimant that is actual, open and notorious, exclusive, hostile, and continuous for the statutory period must be established. All of these elements must coexist if title is to be acquired by adverse possession. The character, location, present state of the land, and the uses to which it is put are evaluated in each case. The adverse claimant has the burden of proving each element by a PREPONDERANCE OF THE EVIDENCE.

Actual Adverse possession consists of actual occupation of the land with the intent to keep it solely for oneself. Merely claiming the land or paying taxes on it, without actually possessing it, is insufficient. Entry on the land, whether legal or not, is essential. A TRESPASS may commence adverse possession, but there must be more than temporary use of the property by a trespasser for adverse possession to be established. Physical acts must show that the possessor is exercising the DOMINION over the land that an average owner of similar property would exercise. Ordinary use of the property—for example, planting and harvesting crops or cutting and selling timber—indicates actual possession. In some states acts that constitute actual possession are found in statute.

Open and notorious An adverse possessor must possess land openly for all the world to see, as a true owner would. Secretly occupying another's land does not give the occupant any legal rights. Clearing, fencing, cultivating, or improving the land demonstrates open and notorious possession, while actual residence on the land is the most open and notorious possession of all. The owner must have actual knowledge of the adverse use, or the claimant's possession must be so notorious that it is generally known by the public or the people in the neighborhood. The notoriety of the possession puts the owner on notice that the land will be lost unless he or she seeks to recover possession of it within a certain time.

Exclusive Adverse possession will not ripen into title unless the claimant has had EXCLUSIVE possession of the land. Exclusive possession means sole physical occupancy. The claimant must hold the property as his or her own, in opposition to the claims of all others. Physical improvement of the land, as by the construction of fences or houses, is evidence of exclusive possession.

An adverse claimant cannot possess the property jointly with the owner. Two people may, however, claim title by adverse possession as joint tenants if they share occupancy of the land. When others or the general public have regularly used or occupied the land with the adverse claimant, the requirement of exclusive possession is not satisfied. Casual use of the property by others is not, however, inconsistent with exclusive possession. Generally, EASEMENTS do not affect the exclusive possession by an adverse possessor. In some jurisdictions easements exercised by the public or railroad rights of way will destroy exclusive possession.

Hostile Possession must be hostile, sometimes called adverse, if title is to mature from adverse possession. Hostile possession means that the claimant must occupy the land in opposition to the true owner's rights. There need not be a dispute or fighting over title as long as the claimant intends to claim the land and hold it against the interests of the owner

and all the world. Possession must be hostile from its commencement and must continue throughout the statutory period.

One type of hostile possession occurs when the claimant enters and remains on land under COLOR OF TITLE. Color of title is the appearance of title as a result of a DEED that seems by its language to give the claimant valid title but, in fact, does not because some aspect of it is defective. If a person, for example, was suffering from a legal disability at the time he or she executed a deed, the grantee-claimant does not receive actual title. But the grantee-claimant does have color of title because it would appear to anyone reading the deed that good title had been conveyed. If a claimant possesses the land in the manner required by law for the full statutory period, his or her color of title will become actual title as a result of adverse possession.

Continuous Adverse possession must be continuous for the full statutory period if title is to VEST. Continuity means regular, uninterrupted occupancy of the land. Mere occasional or sporadic use is not enough. Continuity is sometimes explained as the daily control of the land by the adverse claimant for the length of the statutory period. If a person has continuously occupied only a part of all the land claimed under adverse possession, he or she will acquire title only to the occupied portion.

While continuous possession is required for the acquisition of title by adverse possession, it is not necessary that only one person hold the land continuously for the statutory period. The time periods that successive adverse occupants have possessed the land may be added together to meet the continuity requirement if PRIVITY exists between the parties. The addition of these different periods is called TACKING. Privity refers to the giving of possession of the land from one owner to the next so that it is continuously occupied by a possessor. Privity exists between different persons whose interests are related to each other by a sale or INHERITANCE of the land or by OPERATION OF LAW, as possession by a TRUSTEE in BANKRUPTCY.

Tacking is permitted only when the possession by the prior occupant had been adverse or under color of title. If any time lapses between the end of one owner's possession and the start of another's occupation, there is no continuity, so tacking will not be allowed.

Interruption of continuous possession deprives the adverse possessor of the legal effect of his or her prior occupancy. The statute of limitations will begin to run again from the time he or she starts actual, open, hostile, notorious, and exclusive possession. The length of the interruption is insignificant as long as it disturbs continuous possession. At that time the law restores constructive possession of the land to the true owner.

The commencement of a lawsuit by the owner against the occupant over the right of ownership and possession of the land is one way to interrupt continuous possession. It may be an action to QUIET TITLE, for trespass, for an INJUNCTION involving possessive rights, or to file a PETITION for REGISTRATION OF LAND TITLE. Such lawsuits will destroy the continuity of possession only if successfully pursued to final judgments. If the owner chooses to abandon or settle a suit, or if a court dismisses it, the continuity of possession is not breached.

The entry of the owner upon the land with the intent to repossess it is a clear exercise of ownership that disturbs possession. A survey of the land made at the request of the true owner does not interrupt possession unless the purpose is to help the true owner take possession. The owner's actions must be notorious and open so there can be no doubt as to what is intended. An accidental, casual, secret, or permissive entry is ineffective. While the entry must be notorious, it must also be peaceable to prevent violence and warfare, which might otherwise result.

The payment of real estate taxes by the owner, while demonstrating that he or she has not abandoned land, is not considered to have any impact on continuous possession.

The adverse claimant may destroy his or her continuous possession by abandoning the land or giving it to someone else, even the owner, before the time at which title to it would vest. It does not matter how long or brief the abandonment is as long as it was intentional. A temporary absence from the land is not the same as an abandonment and has no effect on the occupancy, provided it is for a reasonable period of time.

Statutory period   The time period of the statute of limitations that must expire before title can be acquired by adverse possession varies from state to state. No statute will begin to run until the adverse claimant actually possesses the property in question under color of title or claim of right, where necessary. As of that time, the landowner is entitled to bring a lawsuit against the possessor to recover the property.

The adverse possessor must occupy the property for the full statutory period. In jurisdictions that also require color of title, it must coexist with possession for the complete period.

If the statute of limitations has been suspended—for example, because there is a lawsuit pending between the owner and the claimant or the owner is insane, an INFANT, or serving in the armed services—that amount of time will not be counted toward the time necessary for the acquisition of title.

Acquired Title   Once adverse possession is completed, the claimant has full legal title to the property. The expiration of the statutory period eliminates any CAUSE OF ACTION or liability for ejectment or trespass regarding the new owner's prior unlawful possession of the property. Once the time period is satisfied, the adverse possessor is considered the original owner of the land. He or she may use the land any way he or she sees fit provided it is lawful.

Personal Property   Ownership of personal property may be acquired by adverse possession if the same requisites are met. The claimant must possess the property actually, openly, notoriously, exclusively, hostilely, under claim of right, and uninterrupted for the statutory period.

ADVISE 📖 To give an opinion or recommend a plan or course of action; to give notice; to encourage, inform, or acquaint. 📖

Advise does not mean the same as instruct or persuade. If a statute authorized a trial court to acquit, the court has no power to instruct the jury to acquit. The court can only counsel, and the jury is not bound by the advice.

ADVISEMENT 📖 Deliberation; consultation. 📖

A court takes a case *under advisement* after it has heard the arguments made by the counsel of opposing sides in the lawsuit but before it renders its decision.

ADVISORY OPINION 📖 An OPINION by a court as to the legality of proposed legislation or conduct, given in response to a request by the government, legislature, or some other interested party. 📖

Advisory opinions are issued in the absence of a case or controversy. Although they are not binding and carry no precedential value, they are sometimes offered as persuasive evidence in cases where no PRECEDENT exists.

FEDERAL COURTS will not issue advisory opinions. This rule, based on the constitutional guarantee of SEPARATION OF POWERS, was established in 1793 when JOHN JAY, the first chief justice of the Supreme Court, refused to provide legal advice in response to requests by President George Washington and Treasury

Secretary Alexander Hamilton. Washington asked the Court for advice relating to his Neutrality Proclamation in regard to the French Revolution. Hamilton asked Jay for an opinion on the constitutionality of a resolution passed by the Virginia House of Representatives. In both instances, the Court diplomatically but firmly refused to supply an opinion.

The Supreme Court has steadfastly resisted subsequent efforts to elicit advisory opinions, even when these efforts appear under the guise of an actual lawsuit. Thus, in *Muskrat v. United States*, 219 U.S. 346, 31 S. Ct. 250, 55 L. Ed. 246 (1911), the Court struck down an act of Congress that authorized the plaintiffs to sue the United States to determine the validity of certain laws. The Court found the lawsuits authorized by the act to be thinly veiled attempts to obtain advisory opinions, since the constitutional requirements of JUSTICIABILITY and an actual case or controversy were not satisfied. Justice WILLIAM R. DAY, writing for the Court, predicted that if the justices rendered a judgment in the case,

> the result will be that this court, instead of keeping within the limits of judicial power and deciding cases or controversies arising between opposing parties, as the Constitution intended it should, will be required to give opinions in the nature of advice concerning legislative action, a function never conferred upon it by the Constitution.

Echoing the convictions expressed in *Muskrat*, Supreme Court Justice FELIX FRANKFURTER, writing on advisory opinions, said, "Every tendency to deal with constitutional questions abstractly, to formulate them in terms of barren legal questions, leads to . . . sterile conclusions unrelated to actualities."

Unlike their federal counterpart, a number of state constitutions authorize their courts to issue advisory opinions. However, even in those states, courts usually restrict advisory opinions to pending legislation and refuse requests for opinions on abstract or theoretical questions of law. In any event, the opinions are not binding authority in future cases.

Advisory opinions have their greatest effect as guides to policy making for the executive and legislative branches of state government. They are most often sought in the areas of intergovernmental relations, taxation, and finance.

Advisory opinions contrast with DECLARATORY JUDGMENTS, which determine the rights of litigants in an actual controversy and involve specific individuals who are at least nominally adverse to each other. Declaratory judgments are allowed by courts at both the federal and state levels. Although the line between advisory opinions and declaratory judgments is a fine one, the Supreme Court has consistently reiterated the necessity of keeping it intact. In *Ashwander v. Tennessee Valley Authority*, 297 U.S. 288, 56 S. Ct. 466, 80 L. Ed. 688 (1936), the justices insisted that the Federal Declaratory Judgment Act, which gives federal courts the power to issue declaratory judgments, "does not attempt to change the essential requisites for the exercise of judicial power." An actual, not theoretical, case or controversy between specific parties must still be shown. In another case, the Court stated specifically that the Declaratory Judgment Act cannot be invoked to "obtain an advisory decree upon a hypothetical state of facts" (*Electric Bond & Share Co. v. Securities & Exchange Commission*, 303 U.S. 419, 58 S. Ct. 678, 82 L. Ed. 936 [1938]).

ADVOCACY ▥ The act of pleading or arguing a case or a position; forceful persuasion. ▥

ADVOCATE ▥ To support or defend by argument; to recommend publicly. An individual who presents or argues another's case; one who gives legal advice and pleads the cause of another before a court or tribunal; a counselor. A person admitted to the practice of law who advises clients of their legal rights and argues their cases in court. ▥

AERONAUTICS ▥ The science and art of flight, encompassing the functioning and ownership of aircraft vehicles from balloons to those that travel into space. ▥

Aviation is travel by means of an aircraft that is heavier than air. *Aerospace* is a term used in reference to the atmosphere and the area beyond, such as the *aerospace industry*, which is involved with the planning and building of vehicles operating in both air and space.

Airspace is the region that extends above real property. *Air transportation*, as set forth by federal statute, refers to interstate and distant conveyance of people, cargo, and mail by U.S. and foreign aircraft vehicles.

Airspace Rights The federal government has JURISDICTION over airspace within its domain, and each state has authority over the space above the grounds within its borders except in places within the domain of federal regulation. An aircraft is subject to the authority of the federal government and to the authority of a particular state while traveling over it. Landowners have air rights that extend upward beyond their PROPERTY, the boundaries of which are delineated by local ZONING ordinances.

These air rights ordinarily may be used to the extent that they are connected to the enjoyment of the property.

Since the general public has a right to freedom of travel in the navigable airspace of the United States, an aircraft may have legal access to airspace above private property. A landowner might have a civil CAUSE OF ACTION for TRESPASS or NUISANCE, however, where an aircraft enters his or her airspace in such manner as to constitute an infringement on the landowner's right to the use and possession of the property. In some instances the landowner is entitled to an INJUNCTION to prohibit unlawful intrusion of his or her airspace.

Air Transportation Regulation The Federal Aviation Administration (FAA) is the agency with the authority to govern air commerce. The intent of such regulation is to advance the growth and safety of air travel while simultaneously satisfying national defense needs. The director of the FAA has the power to engage in, or monitor, work and testing that will bring about the production of advanced aircraft; to set forth prescribed rules and regulations for the planning and servicing of airplanes; and to administer stringent sanctions if the regulations are not observed. The FAA is also responsible for air traffic control at airports. The National Transportation Safety Board (NTSB) is charged with the responsibility of investigating the circumstances surrounding, and the causes of, accidents involving aircraft.

Certificate Requirements An airplane must have a valid airworthiness certificate in order for it to be lawfully operated. The airworthiness of a plane is determined by an inspector authorized by the FAA. The inspector may neither delegate this duty to inspect the aircraft nor depart from procedures for inspection that have been prescribed by the administrator of the FAA.

The FAA administrator is empowered to create minimum standards for the inspection, maintenance, and repair of air carrier equipment as well as for safe operation of the vehicle. Another important function of the administrator is to issue certificates to eligible aeronautical personnel: that includes pilots, navigators, and people who inspect, maintain, overhaul, and repair aircraft. The administrator specifies the particular function that each of these individuals is qualified to perform.

Certain prerequisites exist for an airline pilot rating, including a great degree of technical skill, medical fitness, care, judgment, and emotional stability. If public safety is endangered,

Active Pilot Certificates Held, 1970 to 1993

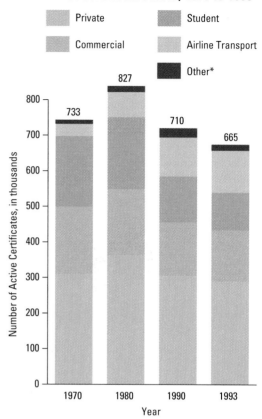

* Includes pilots who hold only a helicopter, glider, or lighter than air certificate.

Source: Federal Aviation Administration, *FAA Statistical Handbook of Aviation,* annual.

the FAA administrator will either revoke or suspend a pilot's LICENSE. A pilot is entitled to NOTICE and a fair HEARING before the revocation or suspension of his or her certification, absent an emergency that warrants such immediate action. The pilot may appeal the order of suspension or revocation to the NTSB, and subsequent appeals may be brought to the usual appellate channels of federal courts.

Regulation on the State and Local Level A state or municipality has the authority to regulate the air traffic that affects it. This power, however, is limited by the condition that the regulation must not interfere or conflict with either interstate commerce or federal restraints. State or municipal regulations on noise precipitated by aircraft engines may not, for example, conflict with federal rules governing noise pollution.

Airport Operation The state can give a local legislature the power to regulate airports and their connected facilities. States may join together to form a regional airport authority to operate an airport. An airport may also be built and maintained by a private party or a corporation, subject to the requirement that use and enjoyment of neighboring landowners' property is not unreasonably disrupted.

Airports that are not properly constructed and operated might amount to nuisances. A private homeowner can sue for DAMAGES in the event that an improperly run airport constitutes a nuisance, and can attempt to have the court suspend its operation pursuant to the provisions of an injunction. Notice must be given to the municipality before such a cause of action may be commenced against it. In considering the need for intervention concerning the building and operation of airports, courts examine the interests of the concerned parties in light of prevailing PUBLIC POLICY in favor of encouraging quiet use and enjoyment of one's land compared to the interests of society at large in accessible and convenient air travel.

The creation and maintenance of airports are subject to zoning regulations. In certain jurisdictions a public agency is empowered by the state to adopt zoning laws that limit the use of adjacent property. Such ordinances are designed to reduce interference with the operation of the airport.

The owner of a public airport may arrange leases for its use, and a municipality that owns an airport may charge reasonable fees for the right to do business there. A public airport owner has the power to govern its ground transportation, to give exclusive privileges to transport passengers to and from the airport to qualified individuals and companies, and to run an automobile rental company on airport grounds.

Use and Ownership of Aircraft Vehicles The legality of the sale or conveyance of an aircraft is regulated by the statute of the jurisdiction where the document of conveyance or sale is transferred.

Federal law mandates the registration of aircraft and the proper recording of any paper that affects its title, such as a mortgage. Such recording must take place at the administration and records branch of the FAA. In addition, documents creating security interests in the aircraft must be recorded to provide notice to prospective purchasers of prior claims to the vehicle.

General principles of CONTRACT law govern aircraft rental and parties to the agreement are ordinarily bound by its terms. The renter of a defective vehicle might, however, have the right to terminate the contract since the individual

offering the aircraft for rent is obligated to provide a vehicle in satisfactory operating condition.

Duties in Aircraft Operation An individual who is injured as a result of the operation of an aircraft usually has a legally enforceable right to damages for any injuries or losses sustained.

Manufacturers A manufacturer is under a duty to exercise reasonable care and proficiency in the design, production, and assembly of an aircraft vehicle. LIABILITY for a departure from this duty may be extended to the manufacturer regardless of whether that company was directly involved in the manufacture of the parts. The law will imply a WARRANTY of proper design and manufacture of an aircraft. A manufacturer of parts will also be held responsible for damage caused by the product and must use a high degree of care in their production, although they need not be made accident-proof. A manufacturer is not relieved of a continuing obligation to improve the component parts of an air vehicle when there is continuing risk to safe travel.

Pilots The pilot of a private aircraft is subject to ordinary NEGLIGENCE standards in the absence of a special law. The pilot is required to exercise ordinary, but not extreme, care and caution regarding its operation. Negligence rules, however, impose a greater standard of care when applied to aviation, because of the severity and magnitude of potential harm posed by improper operation of an aircraft.

Owners Generally ownership of an aircraft vehicle is insufficient to render an owner liable for damage resulting from its unreasonable operation by another. In certain jurisdictions, however, an owner who lends a plane to an individual he or she knows to be reckless or incompetent will be held responsible. Similarly, the federal or state government cannot evade liability for damage arising out of the improper operation of its aircraft by government employees.

Passengers Passengers in a private aircraft have the obligation to exercise reasonable care for their own well-being. They must subscribe to the REASONABLE PERSON standard and refrain from going on a particular flight that would be an obvious danger, such as a flight during a hurricane.

Passengers on airlines and other air common carriers must observe safety precautions by obeying instructions of flight attendants, such as by fastening their seatbelts.

Operators of Airplanes An airport operator has the duty to exercise ordinary care in protecting aircraft on its premises and the people who use airport facilities. Neglecting to maintain the airport premises in a reasonably safe condition results in tort liability for resulting injuries to persons present.

Air Traffic Control The federal government has responsibility for air traffic control. Air traffic controllers have a duty to keep aircraft from colliding with each other by guiding their paths. Liability can be extended to the federal government for the negligence of its air traffic controllers. Contributory negligence by the individual harmed might, however, block recovery against the United States for damage caused only partially by the negligence of controllers.

Airlines An airline has the duty to employ the greatest degree of care possible to protect its passengers. Liability might be imposed for harm to a passenger resulting from wrongful behavior of its employees. It must also take steps to guard passengers against misconduct of fellow passengers.

Companies that accept goods for air transport must exercise a high degree of care to properly handle and deliver such goods. Liability for loss or damage may be restricted to a prearranged amount, which must be listed on the passenger's ticket in the case of baggage or on the bill of lading regarding the goods shipped.

Flying Schools A flying school that maintains facilities that interfere with the customary use and enjoyment of property by neighboring landowners can be liable for nuisance or trespass. A student pilot flying with a flight instructor is considered legally to be a passenger, and, therefore, the school owes the same duty of care to the student as a commercial airline owes to its passenger. A trainee, however, assumes certain risks while being taught to fly and the school can successfully assert the defense of assumption of the risk in tort cases. A member of a flight club, as an owner of an airplane that belongs to the club, may be held personally liable for accidents that might occur while he or she is piloting the craft. Statutes that govern the liability of a flight club member should be consulted.

Air Piracy Aircraft piracy or an attempt to hijack an airplane is a federal offense, punishable by either death or imprisonment. Airlines can deny an individual passage on an airplane if a magnetometer (an instrument used to measure magnetic intensity) indicates the presence of a metal object, such as a weapon, on that person by registering a positive reading and the person refuses to surrender to the appropriate officials any metal object that might have energized the instrument.

Aerospace The National Aeronautics and Space Administration (NASA) was established by Congress to organize, direct, and carry out research into difficulties attached to flight within and beyond the atmosphere of the earth and to facilitate the development and functioning of aeronautical vehicles.

CROSS-REFERENCES
Airlines; Carriers; Federal Aviation Administration; Hijacking; National Transportation Safety Board; Pilots.

AFFIDAVIT ▣ A written statement of facts voluntarily made by an affiant under an OATH or AFFIRMATION administered by a person authorized to do so by law. ▣

Distinctions An affidavit is voluntarily made without any CROSS-EXAMINATION of the affiant and, therefore, is not the same as a DEPOSITION, a record of an examination of a witness or a party made either voluntarily or pursuant to a SUBPOENA, as if the party were testifying in court under cross-examination. A PLEADING—a request to a court to exercise its judicial power in favor of a party that contains allegations or conclusions of facts that are not necessarily verified—differs from an affidavit, which states facts under oath.

Basis An affidavit is based upon either the personal knowledge of the affiant or his or her information and belief. Personal knowledge is the recognition of particular facts by either direct observation or experience. Information and belief is what the affiant feels he or she can state as true, although not based on firsthand knowledge.

The Affiant Any person having the intellectual capacity to take an oath or make an affirmation and who has knowledge of the facts that are in dispute may make an affidavit. There is no age requirement for an affiant. As long as a person is old enough to understand the facts and the significance of the oath or affirmation he or she makes, the affidavit is valid. A criminal CONVICTION does not make a person incapable of making an affidavit, but an adjudication of incompetency does.

Someone familiar with the matters in question may make an affidavit on behalf of another, but that person's authority to do so must be clear. A GUARDIAN may make an affidavit for a MINOR or insane person incapable of doing so. An attorney may make an affidavit for a client if it is impossible for the client to do so. When necessary to the performance of duties, a PERSONAL REPRESENTATIVE, AGENT, or corporate officer or partner may execute an affidavit that indicates the capacity in which the affiant acts.

A sample affidavit

UNITED STATES DISTRICT COURT
EASTERN DISTRICT OF NEW YORK

-----------------------------------x

IN THE MATTER OF THE APPLICATION OF
        JOHN DOE   SPONSORING AFFIDAVIT

TO BE ADMITTED AS AN ATTORNEY, PROCTOR,
COUNSELLOR, SOLICITOR AND ADVOCATE

-----------------------------------x

STATE OF NEW YORK   )   ss:
COUNTY OF NASSAU   )

    FREDERICK ROE, being duly sworn, deposes and says:

    FIRST: I reside at 200 Valentines Road, Westbury, New York, and maintain offices and official address for the general practice of law at 44 Court Street, County of Nassau, State of New York.

    SECOND: I am an attorney at law having been admitted to practice in the Supreme Court, Appellate Division of the Second Department of New York during the May, 1993 Term, and the United States District Court for the Eastern District of New York, July 14, 1995. That I am now a member of the New York State Bar in good standing.

    THIRD: I have known the petitioner since January 14, 1985, and have visited with him on numerous occasions.

    FOURTH: I know that the petitioner has practiced law in all of its branches in the various courts of the State of New York for more than five years; that petitioner is a man of good moral character and fully qualified to be admitted to practice in this court.

    FIFTH: I know that the petitioner has been attorney in actions on contracts and breach of contract, commercial actions and proceedings, matrimonial, negligence, Surrogate's and injunction proceedings. He has also drafted certificates of incorporation, copartnership agreements and various contracts and has been engaged in the general practice of law.

    SIXTH: In my opinion petitioner believes in the fundamental principles of the Constitution of the United States and will make an honorable and capable member of the bar of this Court.

                                        FREDERICK ROE

                                          (signed)

SIGNED TO BEFORE ME THIS
_____ day of _____ , _____

A court cannot force a person to make an affidavit, since, by definition, an affidavit is a voluntary statement.

The Taker of the Affidavit Any public officer authorized by law to administer oaths and affirmations—such as city recorders, court clerks, notaries, county clerks, commissioners of deeds, and court commissioners—may take affidavits. Justices of the peace and magistrates are sometimes authorized to take affidavits.

Unless restricted by state law, judges may take affidavits involving controversies before them.

An officer cannot take affidavits outside of the particular JURISDICTION in which he or she exercises authority. The source of this authority must appear at the bottom of the affidavit. A NOTARY, for example, would indicate the county in which he or she is commissioned and the expiration date of the commission.

An official seal is not essential to the validity of the affidavit but may be placed on it by the proper official.

The Oath or Affirmation Unless otherwise provided by statute, an oath is essential to an affidavit. The statement of the affiant does not become an affidavit unless the proper official administers the oath.

When religious convictions prevent the affiant from taking an oath, he or she may affirm that the statements in the affidavit are true.

Contents There is no standard form or language to be used in an affidavit as long as the facts contained within it are stated clearly and definitely. Unnecessary language or legal arguments should not appear. Clerical and grammatical errors, while to be avoided, are inconsequential.

The affidavit usually must contain the address of the affiant and the date that the statement was made, in addition to the affiant's signature or mark. Where the affidavit has been made is also noted. When an affidavit is based on the affiant's information and belief, it must state the source of the affiant's information and the grounds for the affiant's belief in the accuracy of such information. This permits the court to draw its own conclusions about the information in the affidavit.

An affiant is strictly responsible for the truth and accuracy of the contents of the affidavit. If false statements are made, the affiant can be prosecuted for PERJURY.

Functions Affidavits are used in business and in judicial and administrative proceedings.

Business Generally affidavits are used in business whenever an official statement that others might rely upon is needed. Statements of the financial stability of a corporation, the pedigree of animals, and the financial conditions of a person applying for credit are examples of affidavits used in the commercial world.

Judicial Proceedings Affidavits serve as EVIDENCE in civil actions and criminal prosecutions in certain instances. They are considered a very weak type of evidence because they are not taken in court, and the affiant is not subject to cross-examination. Their use is usually restricted to times when no better evidence can be offered. If a WITNESS who has made an affidavit is not available to TESTIFY at a TRIAL, his or her affidavit may be admitted as evidence. If the witness is present, his or her affidavit is inadmissible except when used to IMPEACH the witness's testimony, or to help the witness with past recollection of facts.

Affidavits are also used as evidence in EX PARTE proceedings such as a hearing for the issuance of a TEMPORARY RESTRAINING ORDER or an order to SHOW CAUSE. The expeditious nature of such proceedings is considered to substantially outweigh the weak probative value of the affidavits. In addition, there is normally a subsequent opportunity in the course of litigation for the opposing party to refute the affidavits or cross-examine the affiants.

An affidavit based on the knowledge of the affiant is accorded more weight than one based on information and belief. When admissible, affidavits are not conclusive evidence of the facts stated therein.

Administrative Proceedings Affidavits are frequently used in administrative and quasi-judicial proceedings as evidence when no objection is made to their admission and there is an opportunity for cross-examination.

AFFILIATION PROCEEDING 📖 A court hearing to determine whether a man against whom the action is brought is the father of an illegitimate child and thus legally bound to provide financial support for the child. 📖

AFFINITY 📖 The relationship that a person has to the blood relatives of a spouse by virtue of the MARRIAGE. 📖

The doctrine of affinity developed from a maxim of CANON LAW that a HUSBAND AND WIFE were made one by their marriage. There are three types of affinity. *Direct affinity* exists between the husband and his wife's relations by blood, or between the wife and the husband's relations by blood. *Secondary affinity* is between a spouse and the other spouse's relatives by marriage. *Collateral affinity* exists between a spouse and the relatives of the other spouse's relatives. The determination of affinity is important in various legal matters, such as deciding whether to prosecute a person for INCEST or whether to disqualify a juror for bias.

AFFIRM 📖 To ratify, establish, or reassert. To make a solemn and formal declaration, as a substitute for an OATH, that the statements contained in an AFFIDAVIT are true or that a witness will tell the truth. In the practice of APPELLATE COURTS, to declare a judgment, decree, or order valid and to concur in its correctness so that it must stand as rendered in the lower court. As a matter of PLEADING, to allege or aver a matter of fact. 📖

A judgment, decree, or order that is not

affirmed is either REMANDED (sent back to the lower court with instructions to correct the irregularities noted in the appellate opinion) or REVERSED (changed by the appellate court so that the decision of the lower court is overturned).

AFFIRMANCE 📖 A declaration by an APPELLATE COURT that a judgment, order, or decree of a lower court that has been brought before it for review is valid and will be upheld. 📖

AFFIRMATION 📖 A solemn and formal declaration of the truth of a statement, such as an AFFIDAVIT or the actual or prospective TESTIMONY of a WITNESS or a party that is in place of an OATH. 📖

An affirmation is used when a person cannot take an oath because of religious convictions.

AFFIRMATIVE ACTION 📖 Employment programs required by federal statutes and regulations designed to remedy discriminatory practices in hiring minority group members; i.e. positive steps designed to eliminate existing and continuing discrimination, to remedy lingering effects of past discrimination, and to create systems and procedures to prevent future discrimination; commonly based on population percentages of minority groups in a particular area. Factors considered are race, color, sex, creed, and age. 📖

The idea of affirmative action was foreshadowed as early as the Reconstruction era, which followed the U.S. Civil War. When that conflict had ended, the former slave population throughout the South owned virtually nothing with which they could make a living. To help these newly emancipated citizens sustain a minimal economic base, the victorious General William T. Sherman proposed to divide up the land and goods from the sizable plantations of southeastern Georgia that were under his command and grant to each family of color "forty acres and a mule." The proposal ran into powerful political opposition, however, and it was never widely adopted.

Nearly a century later, this idea of assisting whole classes of individuals to gain access to the goods of U.S. life reemerged in U.S. law and society through a series of court decisions and political initiatives interpreting the civil rights guarantees within the Equal Protection Clause of the Fourteenth Amendment. These decisions and initiatives came to be known as affirmative action.

The term itself refers to both mandatory and voluntary programs intended to *affirm* the civil rights of designated classes of individuals by taking positive *action* to protect them from, in the words of Justice William J. Brennan, Jr., "the lingering effects of pervasive discrimination" (*Local 28 of the Sheet Metal Workers' Int'l*

Assoc. v. EEOC, 478 U.S. 421, 106 S. Ct. 3019, 92 L. Ed. 2d 344 [1986]). A law school, for example, might voluntarily take affirmative action to find and admit qualified students of color. An employer might recruit qualified women where only men have worked before, such as to operate heavy equipment.

Affirmative action developed during the four decades following the decision in *Brown v. Board of Education*, 347 U.S. 483, 74 S. Ct. 686, 98 L. Ed. 873 (1954). In *Brown*, the Supreme Court held that public school segregation of children by race denied minority children equal educational opportunities, rejecting the doctrine of "separate but equal" in the public education context. During the 1960s and early 1970s, the civil rights movement as well as the Vietnam War inspired members of minorities and women to advocate collectively for increased equality and opportunity within U.S. society. These groups appealed for equal rights under the Fourteenth Amendment, and they sought opportunity in the public arenas of

UPI/BETTMANN

Affirmative action programs are designed to increase the numbers of women and minorities in nontraditional professions. Toni McIntosh was the first woman fire fighter in Pittsburgh, Pennsylvania.

Degrees Earned by Women

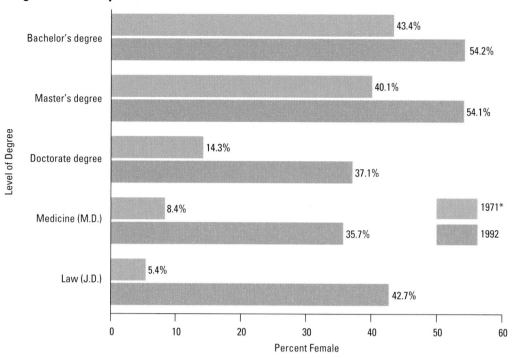

Percent Female

*Percent statistics for women earning degrees in medicine and law are for 1970 and 1992.

Source: U.S. National Center for Education Statistics, *Digest of Education Statistics,* annual.

education and employment. In many ways, they were successful. As affirmative action grew, however, it drew increasing criticism, often from men and whites, who opposed what they viewed as "reverse discrimination."

While the *Brown* decision declared segregated schools unlawful, it did not create affirmative action to remedy discriminatory practices. A decade after *Brown*, little had changed to integrate the nation's schools. The Court acted ahead of business executives and legislatures when it mandated, in *Green v. County School Board*, 391 U.S. 430, 88 S. Ct. 1689, 20 L. Ed. 2d 716 (1968), that positive actions must be taken to integrate schools. There followed the adoption of an array of devices such as redistricting, majority-to-minority transfers, school pairings, magnet schools, busing, new construction, and abandonment of all-black schools.

The first major legal setback for voluntary affirmation action was *Regents of the University of California v. Bakke*, 438 U.S. 265, 98 S. Ct. 2733, 57 L. Ed. 2d 750 (1978), in which the Supreme Court struck down an admission plan at the University of California, Davis, medical school. The plan, which had set aside sixteen places for minority applicants, was challenged by white applicant Allan Bakke, who had been refused admission even though he had higher test scores than some of the minority appli-

cants. The Court held that by setting aside a specific number, or quota, of places by race, the school had violated Bakke's civil rights. By denying the "set-aside" practice of an affirmative action plan, the decision seemed to threaten the principle underlying affirmative action as well.

The following year, however, the Court found in *United Steelworkers v. Weber*, 443 U.S. 193, 99 S. Ct. 2721, 61 L. Ed. 2d 480 (1979), that the voluntary plan of Kaiser Aluminum Company to promote some of its black workers into a special training program ahead of more senior white workers did *not* violate the latter's civil rights when it did not involve quotas. The Court also found in *Local 28 of Sheet Metal Workers' International Ass'n v. EEOC*, 478 U.S. 421, 106 S. Ct. 3019, 92 L. Ed. 2d 344 (1986), that rights were not being violated by a court-ordered membership goal of 29.23 percent minorities. Writing for the plurality, Justice Brennan said title VII of the Civil Rights Act of 1964 does not prohibit courts from ordering "affirmative race-conscious relief as a remedy for past discrimination" in appropriate circumstances. Such circumstances might include "where an employer or labor union has engaged in persistent or egregious discrimination, or where necessary to dissipate the lingering effect of pervasive discrimination."

How Much Affirmative Action Is Enough Affirmative Action?

In the combustive debate over affirmative action, fairness is the hottest issue of all. Most people agree that employers should hire and promote people fairly. Does affirmative action make this happen? Americans disagree sharply: a July 1995 Associated Press poll found that 39 percent think it does, but 48 percent said giving preference to women and minorities produces even greater unfairness. These numbers barely scratch the surface of the antagonisms in a debate now more than thirty years old. Proponents argue that the benefits of affirmative action policies are tangible, deserved, and necessary. Opponents reply that these benefits hide the real harm done by affirmative action: rewarding the wrong people, devaluing the idea of merit, and punishing white men. The two sides disagree on what should be done, yet there is no shortage of ideas. In the 1990s, a flurry of arguments have come from politicians, academics, civil rights leaders, and reformers that are aimed at preserving, modifying, or ending affirmative action.

History has drastically rewritten the terms of this debate. In the years of great advances in federal civil rights, Presidents John F. Kennedy and Lyndon B. Johnson could easily frame the issue as a purely moral one. Johnson put it this way in 1965:

> Freedom is not enough. . . . You do not take a man who for years has been hobbled by chains, liberate him, bring him to the starting line of a race, saying, "you are free to compete with all the others," and still justly believe you have been completely fair. Thus it is not enough to open the gates of opportunity.

Thirty years later, Senate majority leader Bob Dole (R-Kan.) made this widely quoted attack: "The race-counting game has gone too far." Polls indicate that both Johnson and Dole spoke for a majority of citizens of their time. Johnson captured the essence of a nation willing to move beyond the legacy of Jim Crow laws. Dole summoned the resentment of white males who had seen the affirmative action net expand to hold not only minorities but also women and immigrants. But white men are hardly the only complainers: according to a March 1995 *Washington Post*–ABC News poll, 79 percent of middle-class white women oppose preferences for women.

For affirmative action's strongest supporters, explaining the new harshness in the policy's politics is a matter of going back to the beginning. They point out that affirmative action was never supposed to be painless. Making room for groups that have historically suffered discrimination means that the very group that did not suffer—white males—now has to do so. This can be characterized as the sins-of-the-fathers argument, illustrated in a 1995 briefing paper from the American Civil Liberties Union (ACLU): "[W]hile it's true that white males in any given era may not all have been responsible for excluding people of color and women, all white males have benefited unjustly from that historical exclusion . . . [thus enjoying] privileged status and an unfair advantage." This position is supported by statistics: in 1995 white males held nearly 95 percent of senior management positions in major corporations, earned 25 to 45 percent more than women and minorities, and held well over 80 percent of the seats in Congress. On the other hand, from 1973 to 1993, black poverty increased from 31.4 to 33.1 percent. Without doubt, discrimination continues; from the perspective of supporters of affirmative action, the sins of the fathers are far from paid for.

Because equality still eludes the beneficiaries of affirmative action, supporters dismiss attacks on the policies as part of a backlash. Three decades of advances for affirmative action's beneficiaries have meant diminished dominance for white men, a group whose income has been falling in real terms since 1973. But, supporters say, the reason white men earn less today than their fathers did is not the fault of affirmative action. They point to long-term changes in the U.S. economy and job market as the real explanations for stagnating incomes, diminishing buying power, and decreasing job security. Yet affirmative action gets the blame. "We are the ultimate scapegoat for whatever goes wrong," Mary Frances Berry, chairwoman of the U.S. Commission on Civil Rights, told the *Boston Globe* in 1995. Dwindling support from middle-class white women also draws the ire of affirmative action's advocates. "In the 1970s and 80s, white women had no problem hitching up to the affirmative action banner of 'women and minorities,' " journalist Derrick Z. Jackson wrote. "If they now want to rip down the banner, it will confirm the dirtiest little secret of all about affirmative action"—that white women supported it only to the extent that it benefited themselves.

Dismissing these explanations as excuses, critics of affirmative action denounce it as "reverse discrimination." They either reject outright the idea that historical wrongs can be redressed through contemporary means, or believe that the cost to those who must pay for such redress is too high. Conservative think tanks such as the Institute for Justice and the Heritage Foundation regularly lead this prong of the attack. Clint Bolick, the Institute for Justice's vice president, told *Congressional Quarterly*, "If you add up the number of people who have encountered reverse discrimination in college admissions, scholarships, public school magnet programs, government contracts and jobs in the private and public sectors, you have a pretty sizable population." The charge strikes the strongest advocates of affirmative action as insupportable. According to the research of law professor Alfred Blumrosen, of Rutgers University, only a few dozen such cases reached the federal courts in the early 1990s, and in most, the plaintiff failed. Other advocates see the reverse

HOW MUCH AFFIRMATIVE ACTION IS ENOUGH AFFIRMATIVE ACTION?
(CONTINUED)

discrimination argument as sour grapes; the ACLU goes so far as to call it a smoke screen "for retention of white male privilege."

Critics frequently argue that affirmative action does an injustice to the idea of merit. Organizations representing police officers and firefighters, such as the national Fraternal Order of Police, complain that qualifications and standards have fallen to accommodate affirmative action candidates. This criticism is popular not only with whites, who have long claimed that better-qualified candidates lose out as a result of affirmative action, but also with two leading conservative African American critics. "What we've had to do for 25 years to pull off affirmative action," the author Shelby Steele said, "is demean the idea of merit." The economist Thomas Sowell advances much the same argument in his claim that the policy hurts African Americans. Like other conservatives, Sowell ties the rise of affirmative action in the 1970s to the development of the black economic underclass. Steele and Sowell have argued that affirmative action sets up its beneficiaries for failure, corrupting the value of achievement for blacks and reinforcing racist stereotypes for whites. Viewing affirmative action as antidemocratic, they conclude that individual qualities alone should determine who is hired or accepted into an academic program.

Advocates are highly suspicious of the merit argument. In the first place, they deny that creating opportunities ignores the value of personal merit. Voluntary affirmative action merely gives people who traditionally have been excluded a leg up, they assert; and when it is court ordered to redress a pattern of workplace discrimination, the question of merit misses the point. More crucially, supporters think the merit line is superficial. Political commentator Michael E. Kinsley quipped

that critics "seem to imagine that everyone in America can be ranked with scientific precision, from No. 1 to No. 260,000,000, in terms of his or her qualification for any desirable career opportunity." He and other supporters consider the argument specious in a society in which merit is often the last reason for success and other variables that give advantages to certain groups are deemed perfectly natural—the children of the rich attend the best schools regardless of their abilities, for example, and military veterans receive preferences whether or not they have personally sacrificed anything for the nation. The United States was never a meritocracy, asserts Laura Murphy Lee, director of the ACLU's national legislative office: "Affirmative action didn't come along to taint a process that never existed."

Proposals for reforming affirmative action became increasingly popular in the mid-1990s. At one extreme, politicians have called for dumping it altogether. This idea has been urged in Congress chiefly by ultraconservative Republicans such as Senators Phil Gramm (R-Tex.) and Jesse Helms (R-N.C.). Although no action has been taken on the congressional level, similar proposals in the states of California and Florida have gained ground. California reformers scored two victories in 1995: First, in July, regents of the University of California dropped gender- and race-based admissions, hiring, and contracting. Then, reformers succeeded in having an anti–affirmative action referendum—the California Civil Rights Initiative, a measure that would outlaw gender- and race-based preferences in government programs—placed on the November 1995 ballot.

Less radical and perhaps more politically feasible, another proposal calls for preserving affirmative action while shifting its emphasis. The idea would aban-

don race and gender as yardsticks and match preferences solely with economic need. Conservatives again lead this campaign, but it draws some support even from moderates: President Bill Clinton, declaring that his administration was against quotas and guaranteed results, ordered a review of federal employment policies in 1995 to ensure that they were being applied fairly. Critics of affirmative action believe that this kind of reform would ensure opportunity for disadvantaged people while ending what they see as egregious abuses, such as the awarding of contracts to rich minority-owned businesses. Traditional supporters agree that affirmative action benefits do not always help the people who most need them. But they believe that substantial gains should not be reversed, and that any need-based measurement should only augment—not replace—existing policies.

The journey of affirmative action from its heyday to the present reflects great changes in the United States. Between the administration of President Johnson and the Republican-controlled Congress elected in 1994 lies a thirty-year experience with Great Society initiatives that has left many citizens soured on the idea of government assistance. Radical changes in the nation's economy and workforce have surely not made the journey any easier. Bridging this gap seems unlikely, given the vastly different history of white males on the one hand, and women and people of color on the other. From these two poles of experience, two opposing ideas of necessity emerge. Critics say the time is ripe to overhaul affirmative action, a well-intentioned policy gone bad. Supporters, perceiving a playing field that is still far from level, maintain that the real work of affirmative action has scarcely begun.

The Court later found, in *City of Richmond v. J. A. Croson Co.*, 488 U.S. 469, 109 S. Ct. 706, 102 L. Ed. 2d 854 (1989), that the Minority Business Utilization Plan of Richmond, Virginia, violated the rights of private contractors. The plan, which required 30 percent of all subcontracts to be awarded to minority-owned companies, was struck down because this municipality had failed to show compelling state interest for such a measure. The Court applied the compelling interest test after holding that race-based action by state and local government was subject to strict scrutiny. The Court extended this to the federal government in *Adarand Constructors, Inc. v. Pena*, 115 S. Ct. 2097, 132 L. Ed. 2d 158 (1995).

In *Johnson v. Transportation Agency*, 480 U.S. 616, 107 S. Ct. 1442, 94 L. Ed. 2d 615 (1987), the Court ruled that a county agency had not violated title VII of the Civil Rights Act when, as part of an affirmative action plan, it took a female employee's gender into account in promoting her ahead of a male employee with a slightly higher test score. The Court held that a "manifest imbalance" existed in this workforce because of an underrepresentation of women, and that the employer had acted properly in using a "moderate, flexible, case-by-case approach to effecting a gradual improvement in the representation of minorities and women."

At issue in affirmative action cases is whether the Equal Protection Clause of the Fourteenth Amendment can be employed to advance the welfare of one class of individuals for compelling social reasons even when that advancement may infringe in some way upon the life or liberty of another. The continuing existence of affirmative action laws and programs suggests that so far, the Supreme Court's answer has been yes.

Affirmative action plans may be undertaken voluntarily, as in the case of a private school's admissions goals; imposed by the courts to protect civil rights; or required by law to qualify for federal contracts. Plans required to qualify for federal contracts are enforced by the Office of Federal Contract Compliance Programs (OFCCP), an agency of the U.S. Department of Labor. The OFCCP defines its mission with its critics in mind: "Affirmative action is not preferential treatment. Nor does it mean that unqualified persons should be hired or promoted over other people. What affirmative action does mean is that positive steps must be taken to provide equal employment opportunity" (EEOC, U.S. Department of Labor, Pub. No. 2850, *Making EEO and Affirmative Action Work* 8 [1993]). One ranking OFCCP adminis-

trator defended the program even more sharply by saying, "Affirmative action is not about goals and has nothing to do with preferences. It is about inclusion versus exclusion: people who have been excluded from participation in the process for years are now to be included."

Affirmation action plans are subject to mandatory compliance procedures, which may include monitoring by review, conciliation of disputes, exclusion from federal contract work, or even suit by the Justice Department.

Criticism of affirmative action has taken many forms, and calls to abolish or significantly constrain it have gained momentum. Although civil rights and women's organizations, among others, have risen to defend affirmative action, many observers believe that the focus of the policy will change, to designate economic class rather than race or gender as the primary eligibility standard.

CROSS-REFERENCES

Brennan, William; Civil Rights; Civil Rights Acts; Discrimination; Equal Employment Opportunity Commission; Equal Protection; Fourteenth Amendment; *Regents of the University of California v. Bakke*; Seniority; Sex Discrimination; *United Steelworkers of America v. Weber*.

AFFIRMATIVE DEFENSE 📖 A new fact or set of facts that operates to defeat a CLAIM even if the facts supporting that claim are true. 📖

A PLAINTIFF sets forth a claim in a CIVIL ACTION by making statements in the document called the COMPLAINT. These statements must be sufficient to warrant relief from the court. The DEFENDANT responds to the plaintiff's claims by preparing an answer in which the defendant may deny the truth of the plaintiff's allegations or assert that there are additional facts that constitute a defense to the plaintiff's action. For example, a plaintiff may demand compensation for damage done to his or her vehicle in an automobile accident. Without denying responsibility for the accident, the defendant may claim to have an affirmative defense, such as the plaintiff's contributory NEGLIGENCE or expiration of the STATUTE OF LIMITATIONS.

An affirmative defense is also allowed under rules of CRIMINAL PROCEDURE. For example, a defendant accused of ASSAULT may claim to have been intoxicated or insane, to have struck out in self-defense, or to have had an alibi for the night in question. Any one of these affirmative defenses must be asserted by showing that there are facts in addition to the ones in the indictment or information charging the defendant and that those additional facts are legally sufficient to excuse the defendant.

The rules that govern PLEADING in most courts require a defendant to raise all affirmative defenses when first responding to the civil claim or criminal charges against him or her. Failure to do so may preclude assertion of that kind of defense later in the trial.

AFFRAY 📖 A criminal offense generally defined as the fighting of two or more persons in a public place that disturbs others. 📖

The offense originated under the COMMON LAW and in some jurisdictions has become a statutory crime. Although an agreement to fight is not an element of the crime under the common-law definition, some statutes provide that an affray can occur only when two or more persons agree to fight in a public place.

An affray is a type of DISORDERLY CONDUCT and a BREACH OF THE PEACE since it is conduct that disturbs the peace of the community. It is punishable by a fine, imprisonment, or both.

AFORESAID 📖 Before, already said, referred to, or recited. 📖

This term is used frequently in deeds, leases, and contracts of sale of REAL PROPERTY to refer to the property without describing it in detail each time it is mentioned; for example, "the aforesaid premises."

AFORETHOUGHT 📖 In criminal law, intentional, deliberate, planned, or premeditated. 📖

MURDER in the first degree, for example, requires MALICE aforethought; that is, the murder must have been planned for a period of time, regardless how short, before it was committed.

A FORTIORI 📖 [*Latin, With stronger reason.*] This phrase is used in logic to denote an argument to the effect that because one ascertained fact exists, therefore another which is included in it or analogous to it and is less improbable, unusual, or surprising must also exist. 📖

AFTER-ACQUIRED PROPERTY CLAUSE 📖 A phrase in a MORTGAGE (an interest in land that furnishes SECURITY for payment of a DEBT or PERFORMANCE of an OBLIGATION) that provides that any holdings obtained by the borrower subsequent to the date of the loan and mortgage will automatically constitute additional security for the loan. 📖

AFTER-ACQUIRED TITLE 📖 A legal doctrine under which, if a GRANTOR conveys what is mistakenly believed to be good TITLE to land that he or she did not own, and the grantor later acquires that title, it VESTS automatically in the GRANTEE. 📖

AFTER-BORN CHILD 📖 A child born after a WILL has been executed by either parent or after the time in which a class gift made according to a trust arrangement expires. 📖

The existence of an after-born child has significant legal ramifications upon GIFTS made under wills and trusts. Under the law of wills,

A sample after-acquired property clause

_____ of _____ (herein called Debtor) and _____
     Name   No. and Street City County State   Name
of _____ (herein called Secured Party) agree as follows:
   No. and Street City County State

Debtor hereby grants a security interest in the following property (herein called Collateral):

Equipment. One new 1997 Drillmaster drill, Model B, Manufacturer's Serial No. X51810, complete with standard catalogue attachments and accessories.

Consumer Goods. All household furniture, including but not limited to a living room suite (5 pieces), a bedroom suite (4 pieces), one 1989 9 cu. ft. General Electric refrigerator and one 1992 36 in. Tappan gas range.

Farm Products. All crops of every name, nature and description, which are sown, growing, grown, or to be planted within one year from the date of this Security Agreement on the Debtor's farm located at _____

[Portions omitted for purposes of illustration.]

. . . including property, goods and chattels of the same classes as those listed above acquired by the Debtor subsequent to the execution of this agreement and prior to its termination, proceeds of the Collateral, and all increases, substitutions, replacements, additions and accessions to the Collateral.

the birth of an after-born child after the parent makes a will does not revoke it but has the effect of modifying its provisions. Generally, the after-born child must be given the share of the parent's ESTATE that the child would have been entitled to if the parent had died without leaving a will, according to the law of DESCENT AND DISTRIBUTION. The beneficiaries of the will must contribute a proportionate share of what they inherited to make up the after-born child's share.

Under the law of TRUSTS, a gift to a class is one in which the creator of the trust, the SETTLOR, directs that the principal of the trust should be distributed to a specifically designated group of persons, such as to grandchildren, who are alive at a certain time, such as at the settlor's death. Any child born after this time would not be entitled to a proportionate share of the trust principal unless conceived before the settlor died. An after-born child born eleven months after the settlor's death, therefore, would not share in the principal, since the class had closed nine months after the settlor's death.

AGE DISCRIMINATION As the baby boom generation, the largest demographic group in U.S. history, reached middle age and looked toward retirement, laws governing the treatment of older U.S. citizens took on greater importance than ever before. Between 1970 and 1991, the number of workers over the age of forty in the U.S. workforce rose from 39,689,000 to 53,940,000. It is no surprise, then, that major developments, both legislative and judicial, occurred in the area of age discrimination in employment.

Congress outlawed discrimination by employers against employees or applicants over the age of forty, with the Age Discrimination in Employment Act of 1967 (ADEA) (29 U.S.C.A. § 621 et seq.). Amendments to the act in 1974, 1978, and 1986 (29 U.S.C.A. § 623 et seq.) raised and then eliminated the mandatory retirement age for most workers and extended the act's coverage to most employers. The ADEA does permit employers to set maximum age limits for employees if the employer can show that age is a bona fide occupational qualification (BFOQ) and is reasonably necessary for the operation of the business. Although the ADEA did not originally apply to government employers, Congress extended the act to cover federal, state, and local governments in 1974.

The Equal Employment Opportunity Commission (EEOC) is charged with enforcing the ADEA. Complainants must first file a claim with the EEOC or their state's employment or human rights commission, before pursuing a lawsuit. The EEOC attempts to resolve the dispute through voluntary compliance on the part of the employer, conciliation, or other persuasive measures. If the EEOC decides to bring an action against the employer, the employee's right to sue is extinguished. However, the employee need not exhaust his or her administrative remedies—that is, wait for a final determination from the EEOC—before filing suit.

A number of landmark cases have interpreted the ADEA since its passage. *Western Air Lines v. Criswell*, 472 U.S. 400, 105 S. Ct. 2743, 86 L. Ed. 2d 321 (1985), set out the guidelines for defending an age limit based on the BFOQ exception. Western required flight engineers, who are members of the flight crew but generally do not operate flight controls, to retire at age sixty. When this policy was challenged, the airline maintained that the age limit was a BFOQ necessary to ensure safety. The Supreme Court disagreed, and in a unanimous decision announced a two-pronged test to be applied when evaluating a BFOQ based on safety: (1) whether the age limit is reasonably necessary to the overriding interest in public safety; and (2) whether the employer is justified in applying the age limit to all employees rather than deciding each case on an individual basis.

In another case the same year, the Supreme Court found TWA guilty of age discrimination for refusing to transfer pilots to the position of flight engineer after they reached age sixty, the Federal Aviation Administration's (FAA's) mandatory retirement age for pilots (*Trans World Airlines v. Thurston*, 469 U.S. 111, 105 S. Ct. 613, 83 L. Ed. 2d 523 [1985]). TWA had allowed younger pilots who had become disabled to transfer automatically to the position of flight engineer, but did not allow pilots and copilots past the age of sixty to do the same. The Court held that the airline must give the same opportunity to retiring pilots and copilots as it had given to younger disabled pilots. However, the Court denied the pilots' request for double DAMAGES, which are allowed in cases of "willful violation" of the ADEA, stating that a violation is willful only if the employer knew that its conduct was prohibited by the ADEA or showed a "reckless disregard" for whether the act applied.

Older workers seeking redress under the ADEA received mixed opinions in 1989. *Public Employees Retirement System of Ohio v. Betts*, 492 U.S. 158, 109 S. Ct. 2854, 106 L. Ed. 2d 134 (1989), overturned a series of courts of appeals decisions as well as EEOC and Labor Department regulations that required employers to justify any age-based distinctions in employee benefit plans by showing a "substantial business purpose." *Betts* shifted the burden of proof to the plaintiff to show that the disputed plan was a "subterfuge" for discrimination.

Congressional response to *Betts* was a compromise between employee advocates and business interests. A 1990 amendment to the ADEA known as the Older Workers Benefit Protection Act (OWBPA) (29 U.S.C.A. § 626) prohibits discrimination against older employees in the provision of fringe benefits unless the benefit differences are due to age-based differences in cost.

Shortly after the *Betts* decision, the Supreme Court relaxed the procedural rules governing CLASS ACTIONS alleging age discrimination, in *Hoffmann-LaRoche v. Sperling*, 493 U.S. 165, 110 S. Ct. 482, 107 L. Ed. 2d 480 (1989). The *Sperling* decision made it easier for plaintiffs to join a class action suit against an employer after the suit has been filed.

During the late 1980s and early 1990s, businesses trying to survive in a sluggish economy began reducing their workforces, a practice known as downsizing. When layoffs or early retirements affected older workers disproportionately, age discrimination claims escalated.

Many companies offered attractive early-retirement packages in return for an employee's WAIVER of rights to any legal claims. During the 1980s, courts generally allowed such waivers as long as the employee's acceptance was knowing and voluntary and the employee received valuable consideration in return. In *Cirillo v. Arco Chemical Co.*, 862 F.2d 448 (1988), for example, the U.S. Court of Appeals for the Third Circuit held that because the plaintiff had knowingly and voluntarily signed a waiver of his right to sue, and in return had received a higher-than-average severance package, the waiver did not violate the ADEA. Likewise, in *Lancaster v. Buerkle Buick Honda Co.*, 809 F.2d 539, *cert. denied*, 482 U.S. 928, 107 S. Ct. 3212, 96 L. Ed. 2d 699 (1987), the U.S. Court of Appeals for the Eighth Circuit found that the plaintiff, by virtue of his years of business experience, was well equipped to understand the waiver he signed. Similar reasoning prevailed in *Runyan v. National Cash Register Corp.*, 787 F.2d 1039 (6th Cir. 1986) (en banc), *cert. denied*, 479 U.S. 850, 107 S. Ct. 178, 93 L. Ed. 2d 114 (1986), where the court upheld a waiver because the employee who signed it was an experienced labor lawyer.

The ADEA specifically recognizes the validity of waivers, in the OWBPA, and establishes strict guidelines for employers to follow in executing them. The waiver must use simple, understandable language that clearly delineates the terms of the agreement and leaves no question that the employee is giving up any right to pursue a lawsuit (29 U.S.C.A. § 626[f]). Several cases in 1993 and 1994 that invalidated waiver agreements illustrate the importance to the employer of following the guidelines to the letter. *Oberg v. Allied Van Lines, Inc.*, 11 F. 3d 679 (7th Cir. 1993), *cert. den.* __U.S. __, 114 S. Ct. 2104, 128 L. Ed. 2d 665 (1994), held that a waiver agreement that did not meet the requirements of the OWBPA was void and could not be ratified even though the employee accepted and retained the severance package offered in exchange for the waiver. The same reasoning applied to invalidate the waiver agreement in *Soliman v. Digital Equipment Corp.*, 869 F. Supp. 65 (D. Mass. 1994).

Two 1991 cases further clarified the application of the ADEA. In *Gilmer v. Interstate/Johnson Lane Corp.*, 500 U.S. 20, 111 S. Ct. 1647, 114 L. Ed. 2d 26 (1991), the Supreme Court upheld compulsory ARBITRATION under the ADEA. When Robert Gilmer was hired by Interstate/Johnson Lane Corporation, he was required to register with the New York Stock Exchange, which compelled him to agree to arbitrate any controversy regarding employment or termination. He was fired at age sixty-two and filed a COMPLAINT with the EEOC. He then filed an age discrimination suit against Interstate, which moved to compel arbitration of the dispute. In a decision that seems to reflect the Court's growing encouragement of ALTERNATIVE DISPUTE RESOLUTION, Justice Byron R. White dismissed Gilmer's arguments that compulsory arbitration was inconsistent with the purposes of the ADEA and that he was in an unequal bargaining position with Interstate. The Court held that an ADEA claim can be subjected to compulsory arbitration without triggering any "inherent conflict" with the ADEA's underlying purposes. The Court further pointed out that Gilmer was a professional businessman who signed the arbitration agreement voluntarily and with full knowledge.

Stevens v. Department of the Treasury, 500 U.S. 1, 111 S. Ct. 1562, 114 L. Ed. 2d 1 (1991), clarified the statutory time limits for federal employees to file an age discrimination claim. Charles Z. Stevens, III, an Internal Revenue Service (IRS) employee, filed an age discrimination complaint with the IRS's administrative unit. His complaint was rejected because it had not been filed within 30 days of the alleged discriminatory conduct. His subsequent complaint filed with the Department of Treasury was also dismissed, and the EEOC affirmed that dismissal. Stevens filed suit in U.S. district

treatment" because of his age. In a claim of disparate treatment, the employee must prove that the employer intended to discriminate against the employee based on an impermissible criterion, here age. Biggins alleged that, since the firing occurred just weeks before his ten-year anniversary, when he would have been fully VESTED in the company's PENSION plan, the dismissal was due to his age. The company maintained that Biggins's outside activities created a risk of exposing TRADE SECRETS and that his refusal to sign a nondisclosure, noncompetition agreement prompted its decision to fire him.

The district court jury found that Biggins had proved his case of age discrimination and that the employer's reason for his dismissal was a pretext. It further stated that a termination for the purpose of avoiding pension rights violates the ADEA. Finally, the jury ruled that Hazen Paper Company had acted willfully, thus allowing an award of LIQUIDATED DAMAGES (damages in an amount fixed by statute or contract). On a posttrial motion by Hazen, the court struck the "willfulness" finding. On appeal to the Court of Appeals for the First Circuit, the finding of age discrimination was affirmed and the willfulness finding reinstated (*Biggins*, 953 F.2d 1405 [1992]).

The Supreme Court attempted to address several questions presented by the case. Did Biggins prove a case of disparate treatment based on age? Is discrimination based on pension status necessarily equivalent to discrimination based on age? What constitutes willfulness under the ADEA?

On the first issue, the Court found that the element of intent to discriminate because of age, necessary to prove a claim of disparate treatment, was absent. A decision to fire Biggins because he was close to vesting in the pension plan did not satisfy the proof requirements because it was not motivated by the prohibited presumptions about older workers, namely, that they are less productive and less competent than younger employees. Biggins failed to show that these stereotypes "had a determinative influence" on Hazen's decision.

Next, the Court found that Biggins did not prove that Hazen's reason for terminating him was a pretext for age discrimination. Justice Sandra Day O'Connor, writing for a unanimous Court, stated that "an employer does not violate the ADEA just by interfering with an older employee's pension benefits that would have vested by virtue of the employee's years of service." The Court found that pension status is not the same as age under the ADEA and that employers may make business decisions based

court, only to have his suit dismissed on the ground that it was not timely, a decision that was affirmed by the U.S. Court of Appeals for the Fifth Circuit. The Supreme Court disagreed with the lower courts' interpretation of the statute and held that the ADEA requires federal employees to give the EEOC notice of intent to sue *not less than* 30 days before the suit is filed, rather than *within* 30 days, and within 180 days of the alleged discriminatory conduct. These small but significant clarifications of statutory interpretation made it easier for federal employees to seek redress under the ADEA.

In 1993, the Supreme Court clarified the standards by which a business decision will be found to be a "pretext" for discrimination, and what conduct constitutes "willful" violation of the ADEA. In *Hazen Paper Co. v. Biggins*, 507 U.S. 604, 113 S. Ct. 1701, 123 L. Ed. 2d 338 (1993), a sixty-two-year-old employee, Walter Biggins, sued his employer and its two owners, alleging age discrimination in the decision to fire him after almost ten years of employment. Biggins sought relief by claiming "disparate

Employers may not require the retirement of a worker unless they can demonstrate that the employee's age is relevant to the operation of the business.

on an employee's years of service without necessarily violating the ADEA. Biggins did prove that his firing was a pretext for discrimination because of his pension status. It did not follow, however, that he was fired because of his age. Age and pension status, according to the Court, are "analytically distinct" factors in determining a claim under the ADEA. The Court concluded that proof of discrimination based on an employee's pension status is not, absent further evidence, the legal equivalent of proof of discrimination based on age.

Addressing the question of whether Hazen acted willfully so as to incur liquidated damages under the ADEA, the Court reaffirmed its position that a violation is WILLFUL only if the employer knew or showed reckless disregard for whether its actions violated the act. Using this test, the employer will not incur liquidated damages if it makes an age-based decision that it believes, in good faith and nonrecklessly, is permitted.

Biggins makes it more difficult for an ADEA plaintiff to prevail. The plaintiff must now show direct evidence of age discrimination. Indirect, empirical correlations, such as pensions and seniority, will not be enough to prove the claim.

Other Developments in Age Discrimination in Employment In an interesting twist, the New York office of the EEOC announced in 1994 that it was investigating several law firms for age discrimination. Because the firms advertised for lawyers from a specific graduating class, or with a certain range of years of experience, they may have been artificially eliminating older attorneys from their pools of applicants. The agency was investigating whether this practice violated the ADEA.

Studies have shown that older applicants do face discrimination in finding a job. In one study conducted by the American Association of Retired Persons, identical résumés, in which the only difference was the applicant's age, were sent to 775 large corporations. The study found that the companies discriminated against the fictional older applicant 26.5 percent of the time.

Age Discrimination Outside Employment Age discrimination is not limited to the workplace, nor is it experienced only by those over age forty. In 1994, the state of New York successfully sued five car rental agencies for refusing to rent vehicles to licensed drivers between the ages of eighteen and twenty-five (*People by Koppell v. Alamo Rent A Car, Inc.*, 162 Misc. 2d 636, 620 N.Y.S.2d 695 [1994]). A few months earlier, New York City had become the first city in the United States to prohibit discrimination against the young in public places; a violation of the new law could bring a fine of up to $100,000.

Reverse Age Discrimination? In January 1994, coverage of the ADEA was extended to TENURED faculty (at COLLEGES AND UNIVERSITIES). The result was that many tenured professors continued to teach after the age of seventy, the typical mandatory retirement age before ADEA. With enrollments shrinking and fewer faculty positions opening up, younger people found it more and more difficult to obtain teaching positions in higher education, raising the specter of a "reverse discrimination" challenge.

CROSS-REFERENCES

Affirmative Action; Discrimination; Equal Employment Opportunity Commission; Seniority.

AGENCY Under the law of agency, if a person is injured in a traffic accident with a delivery truck, the truck driver's employer may be liable to the injured person even if the employer was not directly responsible for the accident. That is because the employer and the driver are in a relationship known as principal-agent, in which the driver, as the AGENT, is authorized to act on behalf of the employer, who is the PRINCIPAL.

The law of agency allows one person to employ another to do her or his work, sell her or his goods, and acquire property on her or his behalf as if the employer were present and acting in person. The principal may authorize the agent to perform a variety of tasks or may restrict the agent to specific functions, but regardless of the amount, or scope, of authority given to the agent, the agent represents the principal and is subject to the principal's control. More important, the principal is liable for the consequences of acts that the agent has been directed to perform.

A voluntary, GOOD FAITH relationship of trust, known as a FIDUCIARY relationship, exists between a principal and an agent for the benefit of the principal. This relationship requires the agent to exercise a duty of loyalty to the principal and to use reasonable care to serve and protect the interests of the principal. An agent who acts in his or her own interest violates the fiduciary duty and will be financially liable to the principal for any losses the principal incurs because of that breach of the fiduciary duty. For example, an agent who accepts a bribe to purchase only the goods from a particular seller breaches his fiduciary duty by taking the money, since it is the agent's duty to work only for the best interests of the principal.

An agency relationship is created by the consent of both the agent and the principal; no one can unwittingly become an agent for another. Although a principal-agent relationship can be created by a CONTRACT between the parties, a contract is not necessary if it is clear that the parties intend to act as principal and agent. The intent of the parties can be expressed by their words or implied by their conduct.

Perhaps the most important element of a principal-agent relationship is the concept of control: the agent agrees to act under the control or direction of the principal. The extent of the principal's control over the agent distinguishes an agent from an INDEPENDENT CONTRACTOR, over whom control and supervision by the principal may be relatively remote. An independent contractor is subject to the control of an employer only to the extent that she or he must produce the final work product that she or he has agreed to provide. Independent contractors have the freedom to use whatever means they choose to achieve that final product. When the employer provides more specific directions, or exerts more control, as to the means and methods of doing the job—by providing specific instructions as to how goods are to be sold or marketed, for example—then an agency relationship may exist.

The agent's authority may be actual or apparent. If the principal intentionally confers EXPRESS and IMPLIED powers to the agent to act for him or her, the agent possesses *actual authority*. When the agent exercises actual authority, it is as if the principal is acting, and the principal is bound by the agent's acts and is liable for them. For example, if an owner of an apartment building names a person as agent to lease apartments and collect rents, those functions are express powers, since they are specifically stated. To perform these functions, the agent must also be able to issue receipts for rent collected and to show apartments to prospective tenants. These powers, since they are a necessary part of the express duties of the agent, are implied powers. When the agent performs any or all of these duties, whether express or implied, it is as if the owner has done so.

A more complicated situation arises when the agent possesses *apparent authority*. In this case, the principal, either knowingly or even mistakenly, permits the agent or others to assume that the agent possesses authority to carry out certain actions when such authority does not, in fact, exist. If other persons believe in good faith that such authority exists, the principal remains liable for the agent's actions and cannot rely on the defense that no actual authority was granted. For instance, suppose the owner of a building offers it for sale and tells prospective buyers to talk to the rental agent. If a buyer enters into a purchase agreement with the agent, the owner may be liable for breaching that contract if she later agrees to sell the building to someone else. The first purchaser relied on the apparent authority of the agent and will not be penalized even if the owner maintains that no authority was ever given to the agent to enter into the contract. The owner remains responsible for acts done by an agent who was exercising apparent authority.

The scope of an agent's authority, whether apparent or actual, is considered in determining an agent's LIABILITY for her or his actions. An agent is not personally liable to a third party for a contract the agent has entered into as a representative of the principal so long as the agent acted within the scope of her or his authority and signed the contract as agent for the principal. If the agent exceeded her or his authority by entering into the contract, however, the agent is financially responsible to the principal for violating her or his fiduciary duty. In addition, the agent may also be sued by the other party to the contract for FRAUD. The principal is generally not bound if the agent was not actually or apparently authorized to enter into the contract.

With respect to liability in TORT (i.e., liability for a civil wrong, such as driving a car in a negligent manner and causing an accident), the principal is responsible for an act committed by an agent while acting within his or her authority during the course of the agent's employment. This legal rule is based on *respondeat superior*, Latin for "let the master answer." The doctrine of respondeat superior, first developed in England in the late 1600s and adopted in the United States during the 1840s, was founded on the theory that a master must respond to third persons for losses negligently caused by the master's servants. In more modern terms, the employer is said to be *vicariously liable* for injuries caused by the actions of an employee or agent; in other words, liability for an employee's actions is IMPUTED to the employer. The agent can also be liable to the injured party, but because the principal may be better able financially to pay any judgment rendered against him or her (according to the "deep-pocket" theory), the principal is almost always sued in addition to the agent.

A principal may also be liable for an agent's criminal acts if the principal either authorized or consented to those acts; if the principal directed the commission of a crime, she or he can be prosecuted as an ACCESSORY to the crime. Some state and federal laws provide that a CORPORATION may be held criminally liable for the acts of its agents or officers committed in the transaction of corporate business, since by law a corporation can only act through its officers.

An agent's authority can be terminated only in accordance with the agency contract that first created the principal-agent relationship. A principal can revoke an agent's authority at any time but may be liable for DAMAGES if the termination violates the contract. Other events—such as the death, insanity, or bankruptcy of the principal—end the principal-agent relationship by OPERATION OF LAW. (Operation of law refers to rights granted or taken away without the party's action or cooperation, but instead by the application of law to a specific set of facts.) The rule that death or insanity terminates an agent's authority is based on the policy that the principal's estate should be protected from potential fraudulent activity on the part of the agent. Some states have modified these common-law rules, allowing some acts of the agent to be binding upon other parties who were not aware of the termination.

CROSS-REFERENCES

Master and Servant; Respondeat Superior; Vicarious Liability.

AGENT One who agrees and is authorized to act on behalf of another, a PRINCIPAL, to legally bind an individual in particular business transactions with third parties pursuant to an AGENCY relationship.

AGE OF CONSENT The age at which a person may marry without parental approval. The age at which a female is legally capable of agreeing to sexual intercourse, so that a male who engages in sex with her cannot be prosecuted for STATUTORY RAPE.

A person below the age of consent is sometimes called an INFANT or MINOR.

AGE OF MAJORITY The age at which a person, formerly a MINOR or an INFANT, is recognized by law to be an ADULT, capable of managing his or her own affairs and responsible for any legal obligations created by his or her actions.

A person who has reached the age of majority is bound by any contracts, deeds, or legal relationships, such as marriage, which he or she undertakes. In most states the age of majority is eighteen, but it may vary depending upon the nature of the activity in which the person is engaged. In the same state the age of majority for driving may be sixteen while that for drinking alcoholic beverages is twenty-one.

Another name for the age of majority is legal age.

Age of Consent Laws for U.S. States, Puerto Rico, and the District of Columbia

State	Age with Parental Consent		Age without Consent	
	Male	Female	Male	Female
Alabama*	14a	14a	18	18
Alaska	16h	16h	18	18
Arizona	16h	16h	18	18
Arkansas	17b	16b	18	18
California	None	None	18	18
Colorado*	16h	16h	18	18
Connecticut	16h	16h	18	18
Delaware	18b	16b	18	18
Florida	16a, b	16a, b	18	18
Georgia*	16b, h	16b, h	16	16
Hawaii	15	15	16	16
Idaho*	16h	16h	18	18
Illinois	16	16	18	18
Indiana	17b	17b	18	18
Iowa*	18h	18h	18	18
Kansas* #	18h	18h	18	18
Kentucky	18b, h	18b, h	18	18
Louisiana	18h	18h	18	18
Maine	16h	16h	18	18
Maryland	16b, d	16b, d	18	18
Massachusetts	14f	12f	18	18
Michigan	16	16	18	18
Minnesota	16h	16h	18	18
Mississippi	17	15	17	15
Missouri	15c, 18h	15c, 18h	18	18
Montana ##	16	16	18	18
Nebraska ##	17	17	19	19
Nevada	16h	16h	18	18
New Hampshire	14f	13f	18	18
New Jersey	16b, h	16b, h	18	18
New Mexico #	16b, c	16b, c	18	18
New York	16h	16h	18	18
North Carolina	16b, e	16b, e	18	18
North Dakota	16	16	18	18
Ohio*	18b, h	16b, h	18	18
Oklahoma*	16b	16b	18	18
Oregon	17	17	18	18
Pennsylvania*	16c	16c	18	18
Puerto Rico #	18b, c, h	16b, c, h	21	21
Rhode Island*	18c	16c	18	18
South Carolina*	16b	14b	18	18
South Dakota	16b	16b	18	18
Tennessee	16c	16c	18	18
Texas* #	14f, g	14f, g	18	18
Utah*	18a	18a	18i	18i
Vermont	16h	16h	18	18
Virginia	16a, b	16a, b	18	18
Washington	17c	17c	18	18
West Virginia	18b	18b	18	18
Wisconsin	16c	16c	18	18
Wyoming	16c	16c	18	18
District of Columbia*	16a	16a	18	18

*Indicates 1987 common-law marriage recognized; in many states, such marriages are only recognized if entered into many years before.
Marriages by proxy are valid.
Proxy marriages are valid under certain circumstances.
(a) Parental consent not required if minor previously married.
(b) Younger parties may obtain license in case of pregnancy or birth of child.
(c) Younger parties may obtain license in special circumstances.
(d) If parties are at least 16 years of age, proof of age and the consent of parents in person is required. If a parent is ill, an affidavit by the incapacitated parent and a physician's affidavit to that effect required.
(e) Unless parties are 18 years of age or more, or female pregnant, or applicants are the parents of a living child born out of wedlock.
(f) Parental consent and/or permission of judge required.
(g) Below age of consent parties need parental consent and permission of judge.
(h) Younger parties may marry with parental consent and/or permission of judge.
(i) Authorizes counties to provide for premarital counseling as a requisite for issuance of license to persons under 19 and persons previously divorced.
Source: Gary N. Sokoloff, Sokoloff & Wolfe, Livingston, NJ; as of Sept. 1, 1994

AGE OF REASON 📖 The age at which a child is considered capable of acting responsibly. 📖

Under COMMON LAW, seven was the age of reason. Children under the age of seven were conclusively presumed incapable of committing a CRIME because they did not possess the reasoning ability to understand that their conduct violated the standards of acceptable community behavior. Those between the ages of seven and fourteen were presumed incapable of committing a crime, but this PRESUMPTION could be overcome by evidence, such as the child having possession of the gun immediately after the shooting. The rebuttable presumption for this age group was based on the assumption that, as the child grew older, he or she learned to differentiate between right and wrong. A child over the age of fourteen was considered to be fully responsible for his or her actions. Many states have modified the age of criminal responsibility by statute.

All states have enacted legislation creating JUVENILE courts to handle the ADJUDICATION of young persons, usually under eighteen, for criminal conduct rather than have them face criminal prosecution as an ADULT. However, a child of thirteen who commits a violent crime may be tried as an adult in many jurisdictions.

AGE REQUIREMENT FOR HOLDING OFFICE The Framers of the Constitution of the United States as well as the drafters of constitutions for most of the individual states set a minimum age for a person to be eligible for elective office. As a result, voters may not always be able to evaluate and elect candidates for public office on whatever criteria they choose, or on no criteria at all.

With respect to the states, the minimum age required to serve as a house representative ranges from eighteen to twenty-five, with about half the states requiring a minimum age of twenty-one. Only about a third of the states allow eighteen-year-olds to serve in the state senate, and twenty have set a minimum age of twenty-five. In five states, the minimum age required to serve as a state senator is thirty.

For governor, most states require a minimum age of thirty. Oklahoma has a minimum age of thirty-one, six states have no age qualification, three allow a minimum age of eighteen, and six specify a minimum age of twenty-five.

Although many states, over the years, have voluntarily changed their age qualification laws to allow more people to run for elective office, court challenges to these statutes have largely failed. In 1971, the Supreme Court of the United States held that the Twenty-Sixth Amendment to the U.S. Constitution, which forbids the states to deny the vote to anyone eighteen years or older, had no effect on the constitutionality of age requirements for holding office. Those challenging age restrictions have argued that such laws deny people under the required age EQUAL PROTECTION of the law. These challenges have not been successful. Courts have found that holding office is not a fundamental right that states may not restrict. They have determined that age is a reasonable basis of discrimination to ensure that those serving in government possess the necessary maturity, experience, and competence to perform as effective representatives.

The Framers of the U.S. Constitution set forth a number of reasons for requiring a minimum age for election to office, beliefs that are still held today. James Madison successfully argued that a minimum age of thirty should be required to serve in the U.S. Senate. He cited as his reason "the Senatorial trust," requiring a "stability of character" that could only be realized with age (*Federalist* No. 62). George Mason, of Virginia, suggested that twenty-five be set as the minimum age for the House of Representatives, a proposal that was adopted. He maintained that twenty-one-year-olds did not possess sufficient maturity to serve in the House, as their political beliefs were "too crude and erroneous to merit an influence on public opinions" (1 Records of the Federal Convention of 1787). James Wilson, a drafter from Pennsylvania, countered, unsuccessfully, that age requirements would "damp the effects of genius and of laudable ambition" and added that there was "no more reason for incapacitating youth than age" (1 Records of the Federal Convention of 1787). In the mid-1990s, the average member of Congress was in her or his middle fifties, but the number of younger members elected to serve was on the increase.

The Framers also considered the minimum age that should be required for individuals seeking the presidency of the United States, and settled on thirty-five—the highest age qualification for any office in the United States. John F. Kennedy, who became president at the age of forty-three, was the youngest person to be elected to that office.

Although the Framers of the U.S. Constitution and the individual states were careful to set minimum age requirements for office, upper age limits have not been established. President Ronald Reagan was the oldest individual to assume the office of president; he was almost seventy when he was sworn in, and served two terms before leaving office at nearly seventy-eight.

Constitution; Constitution of the United States; Discrimination.

AGGRAVATED ASSAULT 📖 A person is guilty of aggravated ASSAULT if he or she attempts to cause serious bodily injury to another or causes such injury purposely, knowingly, or recklessly under circumstances manifesting extreme indifference to the value of human life; or attempts to cause or purposely or knowingly causes bodily injury to another with a deadly weapon. In all jurisdictions statutes punish such aggravated assaults as assault with intent to murder (or rob or kill or rape) and assault with a dangerous (or deadly) weapon more severely than "simple" assaults. 📖

Number of Aggravated Assaults Committed and Rate per 100,000, 1983–1992

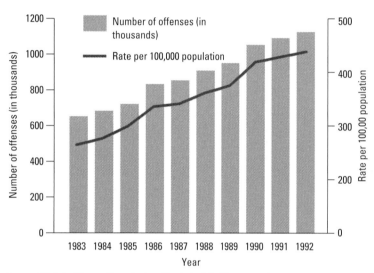

Sources: U.S. Federal Bureau of Investigation, *Crime in the United States,* annual.

AGGRAVATION 📖 Any circumstances surrounding the commission of a CRIME that increase its seriousness or add to its injurious consequences. 📖

Such circumstances are not essential elements of the crime but go above and beyond them. The aggravation of a crime is usually a result of intentional actions of the PERPETRATOR. Such crimes are punished more severely than the crime itself. One of the most common crimes that is caused by aggravation is AGGRAVATED ASSAULT.

AGGRESSION 📖 Unjustified planned, threatened, or carried out use of force by one nation against another. 📖

The key word in the definition of aggression is "unjustified"—that is, in violation of INTERNATIONAL LAW, TREATIES, or agreements. It was the basic charge leveled against Nazi Germany at the NUREMBERG TRIALS in 1946.

AGGRESSIVE COLLECTION 📖 Various legal methods used by a CREDITOR to force a DEBTOR to repay an outstanding OBLIGATION. 📖

ATTACHMENT of the debtor's property and GARNISHMENT of his or her salary are common kinds of aggressive collection.

AGGRIEVED PARTY 📖 An individual who is entitled to commence a lawsuit against another because his or her legal rights have been violated. 📖

A person whose financial interest is directly affected by a decree, judgment, or statute is also considered an aggrieved party entitled to bring an action challenging the legality of the decree, judgment, or statute.

AGREEMENT 📖 A MEETING OF MINDS with the understanding and acceptance of RECIPROCAL legal rights and duties as to particular actions or obligations, which the parties intend to exchange; a mutual assent to do or refrain from doing something; a CONTRACT.

The writing or document that records the meeting of the minds of the parties. An oral COMPACT between two parties who join together for a common purpose intending to change their rights and duties. 📖

An agreement is not always synonymous with a contract because it might lack an essential element of a contract, such as CONSIDERATION.

AGRICULTURAL LAW 📖 The body of law governing the cultivation of various CROPS and the raising and management of livestock to provide a food and fabric supply for human and animal consumption. 📖

The law as it relates to agriculture is concerned with farmers, ranchers, and the consuming public. Agricultural law is designed to ensure the continued, efficient production and distribution of foods and fibers. Through a vast system of regulations that control the various aspects of agricultural practice, federal and state governments are able to provide for the needs of both agriculturalists and consumers.

History of Agricultural Law Agricultural law is a relatively new phenomenon. Farmers have always been subject to established CONTRACT, REAL PROPERTY, and ESTATE laws, but it wasn't until the mid-1980s that federal and state governments began treating the production of food and fiber as a calling worthy of special legal treatment.

State regulations concerning the inspection, promotion, and improvement of farm production were in place at the United States' infancy, but the federal government's first foray into the promotion of farming was the HOMESTEAD ACT OF 1862 (ch. 75, 12 Stat. 392 [repealed 1976]). This act encouraged the westward expansion of European Americans by selling federally owned lands for farming. Another method of sale was *land debt*, a financial arrangement in which farmers agreed to pay the federal government a certain amount from their yearly profits in exchange for the land. Congress passed subsequent legislation concerning land ownership for farming purposes, but federal lands were eventually exhausted, and in 1976, these late-nineteenth- and early-twentieth-century acts became unnecessary and were repealed.

The colonial and pioneer families that practiced farming generally raised a variety of animals and crops, depending on what the soil would yield. This seminal arrangement came to be known as the family farm. The family farm community was rich in resources derived from land, not money, and from this unique prosperity grew a lifestyle with a status all its own. Expendable income was not a priority for farm families. The values attached to their way of life placed a higher premium on plentiful food, vast land ownership, and a spiritual fulfillment derived from farming. Farmwork was difficult, and the farmer was different from the rest of society; it was against this backdrop that federal and state legislators began to work when addressing the pressing issues that farmers would come to face.

The years following the Civil War were especially fruitful for farming communities. World War I saw an increase in the value of farm products, and in the Roaring Twenties, robust prices were maintained by a general public capable of buying food and clothing. However, in the months before the stock market crash of October 1929, the value of farmland and its products began to decrease. This was due in part to high TARIFFS on manufacturing equipment essential to farming, which allowed U.S. manufacturers to price farming equipment without foreign competition. It was also due in part to a new emphasis on mass productivity inspired by the industrial revolution. The ability of farmers to increase production on less land led to lower prices and, eventually, fewer family farms.

The Great Depression of the 1930s eliminated many family farms. As the general public became less able to buy such basic farm products as food and clothing, food prices dropped drastically, and farmers found themselves without the profits for their MORTGAGE payments. FORECLOSURES became routine. Farm families considered foreclosures a breach of the government's promise to allow productive farm families to keep their land, and vast numbers of farmers organized to withhold food from their markets in an effort to force product prices higher. A smaller number of farmers resorted to

Armed with rifles, Iowa National Guard members stand ready to put down any disturbance as Sheriff Hugo J. Willy begins a farm auction in Crawford County in 1933.

© UPI/BETTMANN

violence to prevent other farmers from delivering their goods to market. Several foreclosures were also prevented by force.

The unrest of the early 1930s in the Great Plains states eventually led to widespread state legislation that limited the rights of banks to foreclose on farms with undue haste. Action was also taken on the federal level. To avoid a national farmers' strike planned for May 13, 1933, President Franklin D. Roosevelt signed the Agricultural Adjustment Act (7 U.S.C.A. § 601 et seq.) on May 12. This act was the first in a series of federal laws that provided compensation to farmers who voluntarily reduced their output. Parts of the act were declared unconstitutional by the Supreme Court in 1936, in part because the Court considered agriculture a matter of local concern. Congress and President Roosevelt continued to press the issue, with the amended Agricultural Adjustment Act of 1938, which contained more federal control of production, benefit payments, loans, insurance, and soil conservation.

The test case for the new Agricultural Adjustment Act was *Wickard v. Filburn*, 317 U.S. 111, 63 S. Ct. 82, 87 L. Ed. 122 (1942). In *Wickard*, Ohio farmer Roscoe C. Filburn sued Secretary of Agriculture Claude R. Wickard over the part of the act concerning wheat acreage allotment. Under the act, the Department of Agriculture had designated 11.1 acres of Filburn's land for wheat sowing and established a normal wheat yield for this acreage. Filburn defied the department's directive by sowing wheat on more than 11.1 acres and exceeding his yield. This constituted farm marketing excess, and Filburn was penalized $117.11 by the department. When Filburn refused to pay the fine, the government issued a LIEN against his wheat and the Agriculture Committee denied him a marketing card. This card was necessary to protect Filburn's buyers from liability for the fine, and to protect buyers from the government's lien on Filburn's wheat.

Filburn sued to invalidate the wheat acreage allotment provision, arguing in part that it was beyond the power of the federal government to enforce such farming limitations. Even though Filburn did not intend to sell much of the wheat, the Supreme Court reasoned that because all farm product surplus had a substantial effect on interstate commerce, it was within the power of the U.S. Congress to control it. This decision affirmed the power of Congress to regulate all things agrarian, and the U.S. farmer, for better or worse, was left with a meddlesome lifetime friend in the federal government.

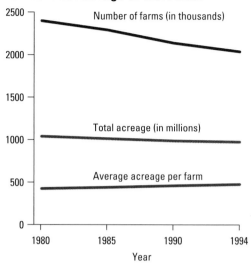

Number and Acreage of U.S. Farms

Source: U.S. Department of Agriculture, National Agricultural Statistics Service, *Farm Numbers and Land in Farms,* July releases.

As the United States enjoyed economic prosperity through the 1950s and 1960s, the number of family farms remained relatively stable. Farm families learned to work with the federal government and its dizzying stream of agencies, regulations, and paperwork. Nevertheless, the mid-1980s saw another farm crisis. Widespread financial difficulty led to the loss of hundreds more family farms and prompted further federal action.

In response to this crisis, Congress passed an extensive credit-relief package in 1985, over the protest of President Ronald Reagan's agriculture secretary, John R. Block. The several bills in this package provided for additional federal monies for loan guarantees, reduction of lender interest rates, and loan advancements.

This farm crisis was triggered by a combination of natural disasters, market shifts, lower prices, and production improvements. Furthermore, the onset of *corporate farming*, which involves mass production of farm products, forced farm families to consistently reckon with the harsh realities of the financial world.

Most farmers are now trained in business and keep abreast of farming trends, technological and manufacturing improvements, and the stock market. Many family farms have adapted by specializing in the mass production of one or two particular foods or fibers, like corporate farms. Other farmers have formed what is called a COOPERATIVE, a group of farmers dedicated to the most profitable sale of their products. By pooling their resources and producing a variety of goods, cooperative farmers are able to weather low-price periods and postpone sales until a product price reaches a high level.

Agriculture has become a powerful lobbying group in state capitals across the country, and the political issues are myriad. The agriculture industry is split into competing special interests, according to product. Family farms and cooperatives are pitted against each other, and together against massive corporate farming. Farming interests are sometimes opposed by advocates for the environment and food purity. The government does not always seem to act in the best interests of farmers, and farmers and their creditors continually struggle for leverage. Federal and state regulations seek to provide some predictability for the players in these struggles.

Federal Law According to the *Wickard* case, the U.S. Congress has the power to regulate agricultural production under Article I, Section 8, of the federal Constitution, and Congress has left virtually nothing to chance. The numerous programs and laws that promote and regulate farming are overseen by the secretary of agriculture, who represents the U.S. Department of Agriculture (USDA) in the president's cabinet. The USDA is the government agency that carries out federal agricultural policy, and it is the most important legal entity to the farmer.

Usually, some two dozen agencies are housed within the USDA, all charged with carrying out the various services and enforcing the numerous regulations necessary for the efficient, safe production of food and fiber. Other administrative agencies can affect a farmer's legal rights, such as the Food and Drug Administration, Department of the Environment, Department of the Interior, and Department of the Treasury, but the USDA is the single department to which every farmer must answer. In the early 1990s, the USDA contemplated a restructuring of its services to provide farmers with "one-stop shopping." Such a program would reduce to one the number of visits required of a farmer to transact financial business with the government.

The Agricultural Adjustment Acts establish and maintain prices for crops by preventing extreme fluctuations in their availability. These acts empower the secretary of agriculture to allot a certain amount of farmland for the production of a specific crop, and to apportion the land among the states capable of producing the crop. State agricultural committees then assign a certain amount of the land to various counties, and the counties in turn assign the land to local farms. This system guards against crop surpluses and shortages, and preserves economic stability by preventing extreme fluctuations in crop prices.

The Commodity Credit Corporation (CCC) exists within the USDA to further the goal of stabilizing food prices and farmers' incomes. The CCC provides disaster relief to farmers, and it controls prices through an elaborate system of price support. Loans to farmers and governmental buyouts of farm products allow the CCC to maintain reasonable price levels. The secretary of the CCC is also authorized to issue subsidies, or governmental grants, to farmers as another means of controlling prices by maintaining farmers' incomes. By encouraging or discouraging the production of a particular food or fiber through financial reward, subsidies promote price stability in the markets.

Several federal programs help serve the same purpose of price stability. The secretary of agriculture may set national quotas for the production of a certain farm product. *Set-aside conditions*, also established by the secretary of agriculture, require farmers to withhold production on a certain amount of cropland during a specified year. *Diversion payments* are made to farmers who agree to divert a percentage of their cropland to conservation uses, and the Payment in Kind Program allows farmers to divert farmland from production of a certain commodity in exchange for a number of bushels of the commodity normally produced on the diverted land. Federal crop insurance, emergency programs, and indemnity payment programs protect farmers against unforeseen production shortfalls. The Farm Credit Administration, established by Congress as an independent agency in the executive branch of government, provides funds for farmers who are unable to purchase feed for livestock or seed for crops, and the USDA's Farmers Home Administration (FmHA) makes direct mortgage loans to farmers.

Also in place are federal programs and regulations that provide for the coordination of farm cooperatives, standardization of marketing practices, quality and health inspections, the promotion of market expansion, the reporting of farm statistics, and the administration of soil conservation efforts. For example, the Soil Conservation and Domestic Allotment Act (16 U.S.C.A. §§ 590 et seq. [1936]) directs the secretary of agriculture to help farmers and ranchers acquire the knowledge and skill to preserve the quality of their soil. The federal Food Stamp Program helps to support domestic food consumption and economic stability for consumers and farmers alike by subsidizing the food purchases of people with low incomes.

Under title VII of the United States Code, the secretary of agriculture is charged with coordinating educational outreach services. The Morrill Act (7 U.S.C.A. §§ 301-05, 307, 308), passed by Congress in 1863, granted public land to institutions of higher education for the purpose of teaching agriculture. In 1887, the Hatch Act (7 U.S.C.A. § 361a et seq.) created agricultural experiment stations for colleges of agriculture, and in 1914, the Smith-Lever Act (7 U.S.C.A. § 341 et seq.) created the Extension Service, which allowed agriculture colleges to educate farmers not enrolled in school.

In the Extension Service, agents are hired by an agriculture college to help farmers address a variety of farming issues, and to promote progress in farming by providing farmers with information on technological advances. Many farm families have been helped by the land-grant programs, but some critics have argued that this college system too often emphasizes increased productivity and frenzied technological advancement at the exclusion of small-scale farm operations. In the mid-1990s, the Extension Service began to branch out. The Minnesota Extension Service, for example, has begun to address issues such as teen drug abuse and child neglect. This use of agricultural monies for social services has disappointed some and pleased others.

One high-profile controversy involves the Bovine Somatatropin (BST) bovine growth hormone. The BST hormone increases the milk output of dairy cows. The Milk Labeling

Act bills passed by Congress in April 1993 regulate the use of the drug by requiring the secretary of agriculture to conduct a study of its economic effect on the dairy industry and on the federal price support program for milk. The act also requires the producers of the milk from cows treated with BST to keep records on its manufacture and sale. Proponents of the drug extol its production benefits, but opponents argue that increasing productivity is less important than ensuring food purity.

Homestead protection is another form of federal relief, which helps keep farms out of foreclosure. *Schmidt v. Espy*, 9 F.3d 1352 (8th Cir. 1993) was a suit brought by the Schmidt family to stop the FmHA from calling in the Schmidts' farm loan.

To qualify for HOMESTEAD protection, farmers must show that they have received a gross farm income that is comparable to that of other local farmers, and that at least 60 percent of their income has come from farming. The USDA had ruled that because the Schmidt farm had suffered net losses, it could not qualify for homestead protection. The Schmidts took their case to the U.S. district court, which affirmed the USDA's decision.

The Eighth Circuit Court of Appeals reversed. According to the appeals court, the statutory definition of income for purposes of homestead protection is GROSS INCOME, not gross profits. The court reasoned that because homestead protection is normally sought by finan-

The number of independent family farms was relatively stable throughout the 1950s and 1960s, but today agriculture constitutes a powerful lobbying group and the political issues are myriad.

UPI/BETTMANN

cially distressed farmers, limiting the protection to profitable farmers would run contrary to the purpose of homestead protection.

State Law   The TENTH AMENDMENT grants states the right to pass laws that promote the general safety and well-being of the public. Because courts have found that agricultural production and consumption directly affect public health and safety, states are free to enact their own agricultural laws, provided those laws do not conflict with federal laws and regulations.

Many state laws provide for financial assistance to farmers. By issuing loans or providing emergency aid, states are able to ensure the survival of family farms and continued agricultural production. The states also have the power to impose agricultural liens, which are claims upon crops for unpaid debts. If a farmer is unable to make timely payments on loans for services or supplies, the state may sue the farmer to gain a security interest in the farmer's crops. States also enact laws to supervise the inspection, grading, sale, and storage of grain, fertilizer, and seed.

Municipalities can also set regulations that ostensibly control agricultural production. The subject of wetlands, for example, is within the ambit of local governing bodies. In *Ruotolo v. Madison Inland Wetlands Agency*, No. CV 93-0433106, 1993 WL 544699 (Conn.Super., Dec. 23, 1993), Michael Ruotolo, a farmer in Madison, Connecticut, challenged a municipal regulation that prevented him from filling in wetlands located on his property. Ruotolo had sought to plant nursery stock on the area after moving earth to raise the ground level, but the Madison Wetlands Regulation precluded the filling in of any wetlands. According to a state statute, though, farming was permitted on some wetlands of less than three acres.

Ruotolo asserted a right to farm, and argued that since the state law and the local regulation were in conflict, the state law should prevail. However, in previous proceedings between Ruotolo and the Madison Inland Wetlands Agency, the agency had found that the wetland on Ruotolo's property had "continual flow," and was therefore subject to more protection than standing-water wetlands. Because the state statute prevented even farmers with less than three acres from filling in wetlands with continual flow, Ruotolo was prevented from farming the wetlands on his property.

CROSS-REFERENCES

Agriculture Department; Agriculture Subsidies; Commodity Credit Corporation; Environmental Law; Farm Credit Administration; Land Use Control; Zoning.

AGRICULTURE DEPARTMENT   The U.S. Department of Agriculture (USDA) is an executive, cabinet-level department in the federal government. It is directed by the secretary of agriculture, who reports to the president of the United States. Its primary concern is the nation's agriculture industry, and it addresses this concern through numerous economic, regulatory, environmental, and scientific programs. The USDA provides financial aid to farmers through loans, grants, and a system of price supports that delicately balances the nation's agriculture markets, and its international efforts to promote domestically grown products abroad. It regulates the quality and output of the grain, meat, and poultry industries. Through various conservation programs, the department helps protect soil, water, forests, and other natural resources. The USDA also administers the federal Food Stamp Program, one of the WELFARE system's largest services.

The USDA has a long history. It was created by an act of May 15, 1862 (12 Stat. 387, now codified at 7 U.S.C.A. § 2201), and was administered by a commissioner of agriculture until 1889 (25 Stat. 659). In 1889, Congress enlarged the department's powers and duties (7 U.S.C.A. §§ 2202, 2208). It made the USDA the eighth executive department in the federal government, and the commissioner became the secretary of agriculture. Federal lawmakers have tinkered with the department ever since. Notably, programs providing economic aid to farmers were established during the Great Depression, and they have since become a firmly entrenched part of federal law. Important contemporary reforms have included federal welfare services such as the Food Stamp Program, administered through the Food and Nutrition Service since the 1970s, and the Food, Agriculture, Conservation, and Trade Act of 1990 (7 U.S.C.A. § 1421 note et seq.), enacted to maintain the income of farmers.

The secretary of agriculture sits above an elaborate bureaucracy. The assistant secretary for administration runs day-to-day operations, serving as the secretary's principal adviser. Reporting to the assistant secretary are five departmental staff offices, which also help provide staff support to top policy officials and program agencies. These are the Office of Personnel, the Office of Finance and Management, the Office of Information Resources Management, the Office of Advocacy and Enterprise, and the Office of Operations. These offices coordinate the USDA's personnel management program; equal opportunity and civil rights activities; safety and health activities; management improvement programs; accounting, fiscal, and financial activities; automated data processing administration; procurement and contracts; and management of real and personal property.

Legal affairs are handled in various branches of the USDA. The judicial officer serves as the final deciding officer, in the place of the secretary, in regulatory proceedings and APPEALS of a QUASI-JUDICIAL nature where a HEARING is required by law. Two quasi-judicial agencies, the Office of Administrative Law Judges and the Board of Contract Appeals, adjudicate cases and decide contract disputes. Additional input to the secretary comes from the general counsel, who is both the principal legal adviser and the chief law officer of the department. All audits and investigations are conducted by the Office of the Inspector General, established by the Inspector General Act of 1978 (5 U.S.C.A. § 2 et seq.). The Office of Congressional Relations informs Congress of administrative policy.

The USDA is divided into seven divisions, each of which operates a number of programs. These are Small Community and Rural Development, Marketing and Inspection Services, Food and Consumer Services, International Affairs and Commodity Programs, Science and Education, Natural Resources and Environment, and Economics. The USDA also runs a graduate school.

Small Community and Rural Development   The Small Community and Rural Development Division includes four programs that provide financial help to farmers and rural communities. The Farmers Home Administration (FHA) provides loans to buy, operate, and improve farms and guarantees loans from commercial lenders. The Rural Development Administration (RDA) provides loans and grants to help rural communities become more economically competitive and to improve their standard of living. The Rural Electrification Administration (REA) is a credit agency that helps rural electric and telephone utilities obtain financing. The Federal Crop Insurance Corporation (FCIC) insures crops against loss from natural dangers.

Marketing and Inspection Services   Two of the six programs in the Marketing and Inspection Services Division address the role of marketing in agriculture; five of the six programs are concerned with inspections. The Agricultural Cooperative Service (ACS) provides technical assistance and research to farmers' cooperative organizations. The Agricultural Marketing Service (AMS) administers standardization, grading, inspection, market news, marketing orders, research, promotion, and regula-

tory programs. The Animal and Plant Health Inspection Service conducts programs pertaining to quarantine, environmental protection, the humane treatment of animals, and the reduction of crop and livestock losses. The Federal Grain Inspection Service regulates grain and other commodities; similarly, the Food Safety and Inspection Service regulates the meat and poultry industry. The Packers and Stockyards Administration enforces ANTITRUST LAWS to ensure fair competition in the meat industry.

Food and Consumer Services   The Food and Consumer Services Division includes two social welfare programs and one consumer information service. The Food and Nutrition Service administers federal assistance programs to needy people, including the Food Stamp Program, special nutrition programs, and supplemental food programs. The Human Nutrition Information Service (HNIS) conducts research to improve professional and public understanding of diets and eating, and develops the national Dietary Guidelines for Americans. The Office of the Consumer Advisor focuses on consumer advocacy by helping USDA policy makers, representing the department before Congress, monitoring USDA programs, and conducting consumer outreach. See also CONSUMER PROTECTION.

International Affairs and Commodity Programs   Two of the International Affairs and Commodity Programs Division's four programs help maintain a stable market for farm COMMODITIES, thus ensuring a steady income for farmers. The Agriculture Stabilization and Conservation Service (ASCS) administers programs of the COMMODITY CREDIT CORPORATION (CCC). These programs include so-called price supports: farmers who agree to limit their production of specially designated crops can sell them to the CCC or borrow money at support prices. The ASCS also furnishes emergency financial aid to farmers, operates a grain reserve program, provides milk producers refunds of the reduction in the price received for milk during a calendar year, and provides payments to dairy farmers if their milk is removed from the market because of contamination. It has responsibility for plans relating to food production and conservation in preparation for a national security emergency, and provides incentives for preserving and protecting agricultural resources.

The division also has an international focus. The Foreign Agricultural Service (FAS) has primary responsibility for the USDA's overseas market information, access, and development

Agriculture Department

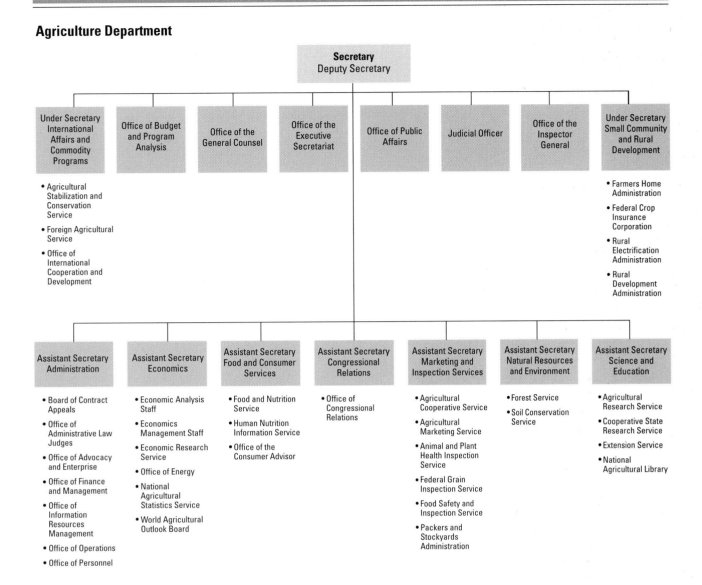

programs. Maintaining a worldwide agricultural intelligence and reporting system, it also administers the USDA's export assistance and foreign food assistance programs. The Office of International Cooperation and Development (OICD) helps other USDA agencies and U.S. universities enhance U.S. agricultural competitiveness globally. Through utilizing the technical expertise of the U.S. agricultural community, it seeks to increase income and food availability in developing nations.

Science and Education The Agricultural Research Service of the Science and Education Division conducts studies in the United States and overseas to improve farming. The Cooperative State Research Service (CSRS) administers acts of Congress that authorize federal appropriations for agricultural research carried out by the State Agricultural Experiment Stations. The Extension Service is the educa-

tional agency of the USDA. The National Agricultural Library provides information services to everyone from research scientists to the general public, and maintains the electronic Agricultural Online Access (AGRICOLA) database, available over the Internet and on compact disc.

Natural Resources and Environment

Two programs in the Natural Resources and Environment Division address environmental resources. The Forest Service oversees the national forests. It manages 156 national forests, nineteen national grasslands, and fifteen land-utilization projects on 191 million acres in forty-four states, the Virgin Islands, and Puerto Rico. It provides national leadership and financial and technical assistance to owners and operators of nonfederal forestland, processors of forest products, and urban forestry interests. The Social Conservative Service (SCS) has responsibility for developing and carrying out a national soil and water conservation program in cooperation with landowners, developers, communities, and federal, state, and local agencies. It also assists in agricultural pollution control, environmental improvement, and rural community development. See also ENVIRONMENTAL LAW.

Economics The Economic Research Service (ERS) of the Economic Division analyzes economic and other social science data in order to improve agricultural performance and rural living. The National Agricultural Statistics Service prepares estimates and reports on production, supply, price, and other economic information. The Economic Analysis Staff makes analyses of recommendations by USDA agencies, task forces, and study groups to be used as a basis for short-term agricultural policy. The Office of Energy develops and coordinates all USDA energy policies, and works with other federal agencies on energy activities that may affect agriculture and the rural United States. The World Agricultural Outlook Board coordinates the USDA's worldwide gathering of economic intelligence. The Economics Management Staff provides management services to all these programs within the department.

USDA Graduate School The Graduate School, U.S. Department of Agriculture, is a continuing education school offering career-related training to adults. Not directly funded by Congress or the USDA, it is self-supporting, with a mostly part-time faculty drawn from government and industry. The graduate school, administered by a director and governed by a general administration board appointed by the secretary of agriculture, was established on September 2, 1921, pursuant to act of May 15, 1862 (7 U.S.C.A. § 2201); joint resolution of April 12, 1892 (27 Stat. 395); and the Deficiencies Appropriation Act of March 3, 1901 (20 U.S.C.A. §. 91).

CROSS-REFERENCES
Agricultural Law; Agriculture Subsidies.

AGRICULTURE SUBSIDIES Agriculture subsidies are government programs providing benefits to farmers for the purpose of stabilizing food prices, ensuring plentiful food production, and guaranteeing farmers' basic incomes.

The premises behind agriculture subsidies are that the nation's food supply is too critical to the nation's well-being to be governed by uncontrolled market forces and that to keep a steady food supply, farmers' incomes must be somewhat stable, or many farms would go out of business during difficult economic times. These premises are not accepted by all lawmak-

ers and are the subject of continual debate. Critics argue that the subsidies are exceedingly expensive and do not achieve the desired market stability.

The U.S. government first initiated efforts to control the agriculture economy during the Great Depression of the late 1920s and early 1930s. During this period, farm prices collapsed, and farmers became increasingly desperate in attempts to salvage their livelihood, sometimes staging violent protests. President Herbert Hoover made several failed attempts to shore up prices and stabilize the market, including the disastrous Hawley-Smoot Tariff Act of 1930, 6 U.S.C.A. § 1, 19 U.S.C.A. § 6 et seq., which created a limited TARIFF to protect farmers from competition from foreign products. The tariff set in motion a worldwide wave of protective tariffs, greatly exacerbating the global economic panic and resulting in drastically decreased export markets for U.S. commodities.

After the Hawley-Smoot Tariff Act of 1930, tariffs were not a widely supported method of subsidizing most agricultural products. The model for post–Hawley-Smoot farm subsidies is the Agricultural Adjustment Act of 1933 (AAA), 7 U.S.C.A. § 601 et seq., passed by President Franklin D. Roosevelt and the New Deal Congress. The AAA implemented some ideas that became staples of agriculture subsidy programs to the present day, including provisions allowing the government to control production by paying farmers to reduce the number of acres in cultivation; purchase surplus products; regulate the marketing of certain crops; guarantee minimum payments to farmers for some products; and make loans to farmers using only their unharvested crops as COLLATERAL.

The government also has attempted to stabilize agricultural markets by subsidizing the export of U.S. agricultural products and by signing international agreements designed to promote agricultural exports. In the 1950s and 1960s, the government took major steps to increase exports, including the adoption of the Agricultural Trade Development and Assistance Act of 1954, 7 U.S.C.A. § 1427 et seq., and the General Agreement on Tariffs and Trade (GATT). Such measures resulted in widened markets for U.S. agricultural products.

The GATT, a multination agreement intended to reduce international trade impediments and decrease the potential for tariff-based trade wars, has undergone several revisions during its history. Agriculture subsidies and tariffs have often been a source of great debate in these revisions. During the Uruguay round of modifications, GATT members could not agree on this issue. The stalemate nearly resulted in a renewed tariff war and the abandonment of the agreement during the 1980s and 1990s. At one point, farmers in France staged violent demonstrations when that country agreed to lower its subsidies and open its markets to imports.

Some export-based policies have had drawbacks. In 1972, the Nixon administration announced a monumental agreement with the Soviet Union whereby the Soviet Union would purchase virtually all surplus grain produced in the United States. U.S. grain and food prices escalated rapidly owing to this new demand, causing great public skepticism about the deal, except in the rural United States, where farm values and incomes escalated.

Another method used by the government to subsidize agricultural products is the combination of target prices, deficiency payments, and mandatory acreage reduction. This approach is used primarily for corn and wheat, the main U.S. grain crops. Under this method, the government sets an ideal price, or target price, for a commodity. If the market price falls below that target price, the government pays the farmer the difference—that is, makes a deficiency payment to the farmer. This prevents the farmer from being forced to sell the product at a price deemed unfairly low by the government, and supports the farmer's income during difficult economic periods. Programs using this method are not mandatory, so the farmer must enlist in one to be involved. In return for a guaranteed minimum income and price stability, the farmer normally is required to take a specified portion of land out of production—that is, make a mandatory acreage reduction—at least for program commodities.

In any given year, it is impossible to predict how expensive the deficiency payment programs will be, because weather conditions and uncontrolled market forces often greatly affect prices. These types of agriculture subsidies often have been quite expensive, especially during years when market prices are low owing to high production and low exports. To reduce the government's cash payments to farmers during one particularly disastrous market swing, the Reagan administration implemented the Payment in Kind (PIK) Program in 1983. Under the PIK Program, instead of paying farmers with cash, the government paid them with certificates good for federal surplus grain. Farmers could then exchange the certificates for actual grain or trade them like stock certificates. PIK, combined with a drought in 1983, succeeded in reducing the cash cost of the defi-

Government Payments to Farmers, 1983 to 1993

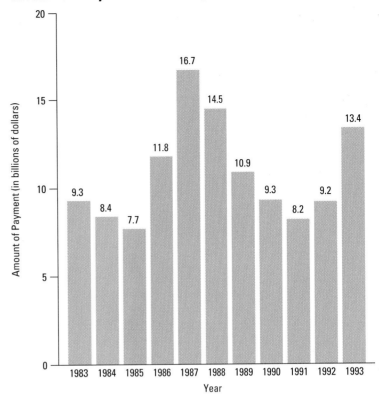

Source: U.S. Department of Agriculture, Economic Research Service, *Economic Indicators of the Farm Sector: National Financial Summary,* annual.

ciency payment programs and the excessive grain surplus.

In the dairy industry, the government subsidizes milk production by agreeing to purchase milk from processors at a predetermined price. Dairy farmers receive no direct deficiency payments; rather, they receive from their processor a milk check that includes the federal money.

The international community often attacks the U.S. dairy subsidy programs as predatory, although similar and even greater subsidies are given to many dairy farmers in European communities. U.S. dairy producers claim that until the other producing nations drop their subsidies, it would be economic suicide for the United States to lower subsidies.

The government also subsidizes agriculture through nonrecourse loans. With this type of subsidy, the government loans money to farmers using the farmers' future harvest as collateral. The government sets a per-bushel loan rate at which farmers can borrow money prior to harvest, so that they can hold their crops for later sale when the market price rises. The government determines how much a farmer can borrow by multiplying the loan rate (which is usually equal to the government target price for the crop) by the farmer's base acreage (which is

Restrictive tariffs protect sugar growers from foreign imports.

be unable to support themselves through market lows and weather catastrophes. Supporters often state that government support for family farms keeps farm monopolies from dominating production and raising prices. Supporters cite the great advances in per capita production since the New Deal revisions in farm policy as evidence of the success of agriculture subsidies.

Supporters also point out that the government has encouraged soil conservation through subsidies. They point to laws such as the Soil Conservation and Domestic Allotment Act of 1936, 7 U.S.C.A. § 608-1 et seq., 16 U.S.C.A. § 590 et seq., which required that farmers who received income subsidies plant soil-conserving crops like legumes rather than soil-depleting crops such as corn, and that farmers use contour crop-stripping methods to hinder soil erosion resulting from water runoff.

Opponents of agriculture subsidies say the farm economy is overly dependent on government, and that market forces would be a more efficient and inexpensive method of regulating production and market price. They contend that in the 1970s and 1980s, up to 30 percent of farmers' incomes were made up of government payments, primarily during years when guaranteed deficiency payments ballooned, and that farm programs have become the third largest federal program expense, behind Social Security and Medicare.

Another primary criticism of farm commodity programs, especially corn and wheat programs, is that they encourage farmers to expand their operation in order to acquire more base acres and higher guaranteed government payments. Opponents believe that this leads to a concentration of production in the hands of fewer and fewer farm corporations, and actually undermines the concept of family farms. Opponents also state that although a primary goal of agriculture subsidies always has been to control production, most programs have had little success in doing so because farmers who are paid to keep part of their land out of production tend to remove the least productive acres.

The Republican Congress of 1994–95 proposed large cuts in farm subsidies as a means to reduce the federal deficit. In March 1996 Congress passed the Federal Agriculture Improvement and Reform Act, which provides for agriculture subsidies to be phased out by 2003.

Many environmentalists opposed farm subsidies for different reasons. Corn and wheat programs came under attack by environmental groups. These groups claimed that the base acreage and deficiency payment system encouraged farmers to produce soil-depleting and

determined by calculating the number of acres the farmer planted of a target crop over several years, and multiplying that total by the farmer's average yield). The crop is the collateral for the loan, and the farmer can either repay the loan in cash and sell the crop, or DEFAULT and FORFEIT the crop to the government. If the market price is lower than the loan rate or target price, or if the farmer's actual production rate is below the farmer's base acreage rate, the government's only recourse for recouping part of its loan is to take the collateral crop. This subsidy is used primarily for corn and wheat, with a modified form of the program applying to soybeans, rice, and cotton.

The government still enforces restrictive tariffs to subsidize certain domestic crops, especially sugar, for which the U.S. tariff virtually eliminates all foreign imports. The tariff protects U.S. sugar producers and costs the government little, but opponents argue that the cost of this domestic monopoly is passed on to consumers, who are forced to pay sugar prices almost four times higher than the world market rates, to the benefit of a few large sugar manufacturers.

For peanuts and tobacco, the government allows legal monopolies for a few government-licensed growers, and imposes large tariffs on imports of these products. Also, cigarette companies are allowed to help determine the price of tobacco and the volume of foreign imports, creating a dual-monopoly relationship between tobacco growers and the cigarette industry.

Supporters of subsidies attribute the relatively low cost of food and the stability of food production to the assistance of the federal government. They say that if agriculture subsidies did not exist, food prices would vary wildly from year to year, and that many farmers would

erosion-prone crops such as corn year after year, even if the market offered a better price for a different crop. Soil depletion and the need to increase average yields led to heavy use of chemical fertilizers, which in turn added to soil and water pollution.

Over the past few decades, agriculture subsidies were a significant and controversial part of the federal budget. Often, the subsidy programs had disparate and contradictory goals. On one hand, the federal government wanted to ensure an adequate, inexpensive food supply. On the other, it wanted to provide farmers with a degree of market certainty and a decent price for their goods. Overriding these goals were mounting pressures to keep the federal budget in check and to promote the export of U.S. products in an ever more intertwined world economy. This delicate balancing act caused much debate and discussion, as well as intensive lobbying efforts by various interest groups.

CROSS-REFERENCES

Agricultural Law; Agriculture Department; General Agreement on Tariffs and Trade.

AID AND ABET ▣ To assist another in the commission of a CRIME by words or conduct. ▣

The person who aids and abets participates in the commission of a crime by performing some OVERT act or by giving advice or encouragement. He or she must share the criminal intent of the person who actually commits the crime, but it is not necessary for the aider and abettor to be physically present at the scene of the crime.

An aider and abettor is a party to a crime and may be criminally liable as a PRINCIPAL, an ACCESSORY before the fact, or an accessory after the fact.

AID AND COMFORT ▣ To render assistance or counsel. ▣

Article 3, Section 3, Clause 1 of the Constitution specifies that the giving of aid and comfort to the enemy is an element in the crime of TREASON.

Aid and comfort may consist of substantial assistance or merely attempting to provide some support. Actual help or the success of the enterprise is not necessary. Any act that deliberately strengthens or tends to strengthen enemies of the United States or that weakens or tends to weaken the power of the United States to resist and attack such enemies is characterized as aid and comfort.

AIDING THE ENEMY ACTS The outbreak of war normally ends all forms of normal relations between belligerent states. In support of the war effort municipal laws may be implemented to prevent citizens and other persons within a belligerent state's jurisdiction from assisting an enemy state through trade or other forms of contact. In the United States, for example, the Trading with the Enemy Act (40 Stat. 411 as amended [1917]) suspends all forms of trade or communication with persons in enemy territory. The statutory or executive restrictions imposed under the Trading with the Enemy Act are limited to formal periods of war, although other authority exists permitting the president to impose restrictions on trade or communications with a country without a declaration of war. See also RULES OF WAR; WAR.

AIRLINES During the 1980s and 1990s, the airline industry underwent significant change. The industry, which had been heavily regulated and controlled, was liberated from governmental oversight and released to the vagaries of the marketplace in 1978. What followed was a period of evolution and metamorphosis that changed the nature of flying forever. At the same time, serious safety questions arose.

Deregulation When the first airlines appeared after World War I, fewer than six thousand passengers a year traveled by air. By the 1930s, the Big Four—Eastern Air Lines, United Air Lines, American Airlines, and Trans World Airlines (TWA)—dominated commercial air transport. These companies had garnered exclusive rights from the federal government to fly domestic airmail routes, and Pan American (Pan Am) held the rights to international routes. The hold of these four airlines on their lucrative contracts was virtually unchallenged until deregulation in 1978. Even after the formation of the Civil Aeronautics Board (CAB) in 1938, formed to license new airlines, grant new routes, approve MERGERS, and investigate accidents, the Big Four and Pan Am continued to be guaranteed permanent rights to these routes. In fact, no new major scheduled airline was licensed for the next four decades.

In October 1978, Congress passed the Airline Deregulation Act (49 U.S.C.A. § 334 et seq.), ending the virtual MONOPOLY held by the Big Four and Pan Am. The government's goal was to promote competition within the industry. The act gave airlines essentially unrestricted rights to enter new routes without CAB approval. The companies could also exit any market and raise and lower fares at will.

The immediate effect of deregulation was a drop in fares and an increase in passengers. New cut-rate, no-frills airlines, such as People Express Airlines and New York Air, offered travelers the lowest fares ever seen in the industry. Forced to compete to fill their planes, the larger companies lowered their prices as well. Then the oil-producing countries in the Middle East formed a CARTEL and raised the price of jet fuel 88 percent in 1979 and an additional 23 percent in 1980. Combined with tumbling fares and increased passenger loads, the higher cost of jet fuel caused airlines' profits to drop.

Labor strife also affected the industry in the early days following deregulation. In 1981, after years of working under stressful conditions made worse by deregulation, the Professional Air Traffic Controllers Organization (PATCO) called a STRIKE, demanding shorter working hours and higher pay. The union expected support and cooperation from the Reagan administration because of a sympathetic letter President Ronald Reagan had sent to PATCO when he was campaigning for the presidency. In the letter, he pledged to do whatever was necessary to meet PATCO's needs and ensure the public's safety. But Reagan ordered the strikers to return to work within three days or be fired. Most did not return. The Federal Aviation

Administration (FAA) ordered all carriers to temporarily reduce their number of flights by one-third. Newer and smaller carriers found themselves increasingly unable to gain access to lucrative routes. Rebuilding the air traffic controller force took years, during which landing slots at the largest airports remained restricted, and small carriers, unable to compete, simply abandoned their attempts to break into the larger markets.

To some extent, competitive pricing actually had the opposite effect of what the deregulators intended. When the small "upstart" companies offered extremely low fares, the larger companies responded aggressively. For example, in 1983, People Express announced a $99 round-trip fare between Newark, New Jersey, and Minneapolis–St. Paul. Northwest Airlines, which had always dominated the Twin Cities market, undercut People by instituting a $95 fare for the same destination and scheduling extra departures around People's. As a result, People decided it could not compete and with-

U.S. Airline Industry, 1985 to 1993

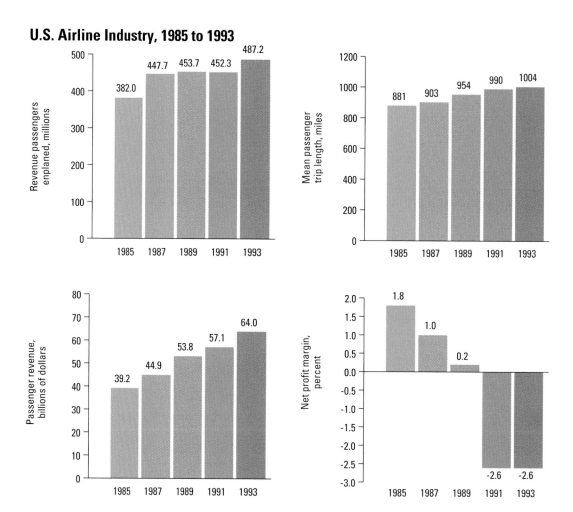

Source: Air Transport Association of America, Washington, D.C., *Air Transport,* annual and *Air Transport, Facts and Figures,* annual.

drew from the market. Passengers enjoyed the benefit of lower fares, but only for a short time before the competitive effect faded and high fares returned.

When deregulation brought competitive pricing, the large carriers began to realize that it was not profitable for them to do business the way they had in the past. The first major change they made was to abandon the practice of crisscrossing the continent with nonstop flights to many different cities. Instead, the major airlines scheduled most of their flights into and out of a central point, or hub, where passengers might need to change to a different flight to complete their journey. One airline controlled most of the reservation desks and gates at a particular hub—for instance, United in Chicago, Northwest in Minneapolis–St. Paul, American in Dallas–Fort Worth, and Delta in Atlanta. For this reason, and because passengers tend to dislike changing carriers in the middle of a trip, the dominant company in a hub had a tremendous advantage over the competition in influencing what carrier a passenger would choose. By 1990, two-thirds of all domestic passengers traveled through a hub city before arriving at their final destination. Of those passengers, eight out of ten remained on the same airline throughout their journey. By 1992, there were at least twelve "fortress hubs," or airports where one airline controlled more than 60 percent of the traffic. Passengers who flew out of these hubs paid over 20 percent more than they would have for a comparable trip out of an airport that was not a hub.

After deregulation, the airlines also came to realize that they needed a more efficient way to book reservations and issue tickets. It is difficult to imagine, in these days of highly sophisticated computers and split-second communications, that until the late 1970s and early 1980s, airline schedules were contained in large printed volumes, reservations were taken over the telephone and tallied manually at the end of each day, and tickets were written by hand. To streamline this process the large companies initially proposed a joint computer system, listing schedules and fares. The Justice Department objected on the grounds that such a system would be anticompetitive and would violate the Sherman Anti-Trust Act (15 U.S.C.A. § 1 et seq. [1890]). Instead, each airline developed its own computer system and entered data in a manner that unfairly biased travel agents' choices in favor of the carrier that owned the system. Through skillful manipulation of the data, the airlines were able to put competitors at a disadvantage. For example, the airline that owned the system might enter the data so that all its flights to a particular destination appear on the screen before any flights of a competitor.

In a further attempt to win loyalty from passengers, the large airlines instituted frequent-flier programs, which awarded free tickets to travelers after they logged a certain number of miles flown with the company.

The combination of hubs, central computer reservation systems, and frequent-flier programs made the major airlines almost invulnerable in large markets.

Deregulation also brought a period of financial upheaval and an epidemic of "merger fever." A number of companies ceased doing business between 1989 and 1992, and still others merged with stronger, more aggressive companies. Among the companies that disappeared from the skies were Eastern, Pan Am, Piedmont, and Midway Airlines. Continental and TWA sought the shelter of Chapter Eleven BANKRUPTCY reorganization. USAir and Northwest required cash infusions through cooperative arrangements with foreign airlines. Even financially strong carriers such as United and American laid off employees and abandoned plans to purchase new aircraft, which added to the woes of the depressed aerospace industry.

By 1993, the industry began to rebound. Continental Airlines and TWA emerged from bankruptcy, and a few small carriers, such as Kiwi International, formed by former Eastern pilots, responded to the public's demand for low fares and began to make incursions into the established markets, although they generally shied away from directly challenging the giants. Older carriers for the most part chose to stay with their hub-and-spoke systems, and several, including Northwest, Continental, and TWA, gained concessions from their unions that helped them emerge from apparently imminent financial ruin.

The mergers and buyouts of the 1980s were often accomplished in an atmosphere of hostility and distrust. Charges of predatory pricing and other unfair business practices were leveled by one carrier against another. During the 1980s, the Justice Department's Antitrust Division made a number of GRAND JURY investigations into alleged anticompetitive activity by the major airlines, but no INDICTMENTS were handed down. However, the companies that survived did not emerge unscathed. Many of the acquisitions were highly leveraged buyouts that left the reconstituted companies heavily in debt. With profits insufficient to cover their enormous debt loads, the companies frantically competed for business, engaging in fare wars that produced a dizzying array of pricing plans with equally numerous and confusing restrictions. Some of the tactics were questionable, but, again, not clearly illegal. In 1993, American Airlines was sued by Continental and Northwest for alleged predatory pricing during a 1992 fare war. The jury took just over two hours to return a verdict in favor of American.

By 1993, a creative new solution to the airlines' financial woes began to emerge. Northwest avoided bankruptcy when its unions agreed to wage concessions in return for part ownership of the airline. Then, in 1994, after seven years of negotiating, employees of United gained majority control of their company in return for deep pay and benefits cuts. Secretary of Labor Robert B. Reich commented that other financially troubled companies would undoubtedly follow suit: "From here on in, it will be impossible for a board of directors to not consider employee ownership as one potential business strategy." However, some industry analysts doubted that employee ownership would be effective in the long run because of inherent conflicts between labor and management, or between different labor groups. "It can't work," declared former Chrysler chairman Lee A. Iacocca. "What do you think will happen when it's a choice between employee benefits and capital investment?"

Proponents of deregulation are confident that the changes accompanying it will result in a stronger, more stable, and efficient industry, better equipped than ever to serve the needs of the flying public. Others maintain that at least some degree of regulation is needed to guarantee safety and fair competitive practices.

Safety One troubling criticism of deregulation is that aggressive competition has forced airlines to cut corners, resulting in safety lapses. In 1990, Eastern Airlines was handed a sixty-count federal indictment charging it with shoddy and dishonest maintenance practices. The indictments came after years of complaints by mechanics for the financially troubled airline who claimed that pressures to cut costs led to maintenance shortcuts and falsification of maintenance records. In January 1991, Eastern ceased operation.

Critics contend that Eastern was hardly alone in its cavalier approach to safety. They charge that the FAA is understaffed and poorly managed and that money shortages have caused all the airlines to relax safety standards. They point not only to increased pressures on the labor force but also to companies' reluctance to replace their aging fleets, the congestion of

airspace caused by increased air travel, crowded hub airports that create security risks, and overworked and sometimes poorly trained air traffic controllers. Yet, statistically, passengers are no more likely to die in a plane crash since deregulation than they were before it. Still, critics maintain that, despite the airlines' and the government's efforts to assure the traveling public to the contrary, air safety is in need of substantial improvements.

Many critics feel that at least part of the problem lies in the dual role of the FAA. Charged simultaneously with promoting the economic health of the aviation industry and fostering safety, the agency is often at odds with itself. In addition, the FAA's budget was cut and the number of inspectors reduced in the 1980s, the same period during which the number of passengers multiplied and the number of air traffic controllers was reduced. Furthermore, unions, which stand to benefit from the increased scrutiny and higher standards imposed by the FAA, continue to be major instigators for change. However, even neutral commentators have suggested that it is time to impose some degree of regulation, in the form of stronger FAA oversight, on the industry. In fact, the FAA has been accused of suffering from a "tombstone mentality" that causes the agency to delay acting on safety concerns until negative publicity generated by a crash forces the issue. Even after safety measures are recommended by the National Transportation Safety Board (NTSB), the agency charged with investigating accidents, the FAA has been criticized for not always following through.

Aging aircraft became a major concern during the late 1980s and early 1990s. In 1988, an Aloha Airgroup Boeing 737-200, purchased in 1969, lost the top of its fuselage while flying at twenty-four thousand feet. A flight attendant was immediately sucked out of the plane and plunged to her death. The plane made a harrowing emergency landing, but not before sixty-five passengers suffered injuries, some serious. Congress responded in 1991 by passing the Aging Aircraft Safety Act (49 App. U.S.C.A. 1421 note), which requires airlines to demonstrate that their older planes are airworthy. Critics claim that enforcement of the law has been lax and that it ignores other compelling reasons to replace aging aircraft, such as the availability of newer fire-retardant seat materials and of updated seats designed to be more resistant to the impact of a crash.

Concerns over airline safety became even more acute in the early 1990s with a series of fatal crashes. The Boeing Company, a major

Police and fire rescue units search the tail section of a plane after it crashed into the East River from a runway of New York's La Guardia airport. Concerns over airline safety increased in the early 1990s.

producer of aircraft, predicts that the number of jet crashes worldwide could double by the year 2010 if accident rates of the early 1990s continue. Such a projection strikes fear into the hearts of the flying public. However, according to David R. Hinson, the federal aviation administrator, flight safety "is not a simplistic science that lends itself to easy solutions." Flight safety experts point out that all the most obvious causes of crashes have been addressed with technological advances that include such safeguards as early warning systems for wind shear.

Many experts feel that not enough research has been devoted to the study of the human elements that contribute to crashes. Boeing reports that flight crews have been the primary cause in more than 73 percent of jet crashes since 1959. In 1990, a federal jury in Minneapolis convicted three Northwest Airlines crewmen—a flight captain, a copilot, and a flight engineer—of flying a jet aircraft while under the influence of ALCOHOL. Although this was the first flying-while-intoxicated conviction involving professional pilots, many claim that the problem of alcohol and drug abuse among flight crews is widespread and well hidden. Yet it is difficult to convince companies to focus on the issue of human elements that contribute to accidents. According to Clay Foushee, vice president of flight operations for Northwest Airlines, "It's a lot easier to convince someone to fund a fancy new piece of technology than research into social sciences."

In 1994, five fatal crashes, three involving commuter airlines, brought safety concerns to light once again. After the fifth crash, transportation secretary Federico Peña ordered a safety audit of the entire airline industry. As a result, commuter airlines, which had previously been held to a lower standard of safety than major carriers, were placed under new operating rules that required them to bring their safety standards up to those of the other companies by the end of 1996. Industry experts said the elimination of the two-tier safety standards was "the most important decision affecting the industry since it was deregulated in 1978."

Several other safety and health issues have been publicized. The quality of air aboard an airplane has been questioned by some. As a result of intense lobbying by passenger groups and flight attendants, most airlines now prohibit smoking on all domestic flights and on many international flights as well. Air quality was again questioned in 1993 when it was revealed that, as a cost-saving measure, many airlines were circulating fresh air into their aircraft less frequently than they had in the past. This led to complaints by passengers and crew of headaches, nausea, and the transmission of respiratory illnesses. Although the FAA conceded that circulating more fresh air would be beneficial, it backed off from requiring airlines to do so, because of the cost involved.

The safety of babies and toddlers on airplanes was investigated after it was shown that a number of them suffered injuries, some serious or fatal, during incidents that did not injure their parents. Unlike adults and their luggage, children under age two are not required to be secured on an airplane but rather may be held on an adult's lap. These "lap babies" are often ripped from the adult's grasp during turbulence or crashes. In 1994, Representatives Jolene Unsoeld, D-Wash., and Jim Ross Lightfoot, R-Iowa, introduced a bill that would have required the use of child safety restraints on commercial flights. However, the measure, which was supported by the Association of Flight Attendants, NTSB, Air Transport Association, Aviation Consumer Action Project, and Air Line Pilots Association, was opposed by the FAA and eventually defeated. An FAA spokesperson, testifying in opposition to the bill, said the FAA's research indicated that if all children who needed them were placed in child safety seats, the airlines would save approximately one life over a ten-year period, and the children's families would save about $2.5 billion. A study conducted at Harvard Medical School estimated that one infant a year could be saved through the use of safety seats. The sponsors of the bill vowed to continue to press for more stringent safety standards for babies.

Safety concerns will continue to plague the airline industry, even though the FAA assures the flying public that, statistically, at least, flying a major airline in the United States is far safer than driving on an interstate highway. Questions persist about the FAA's effectiveness in overseeing air safety. And financially strapped airlines, which posted $12.8 billion in losses from 1990 to 1994, must make difficult risk-benefit analyses when contemplating new safety measures.

Some critics such as RALPH NADER, who initially supported deregulation, are now calling for limited government intervention to ensure safety. However, experts warn that the U.S. airline system, which is already extremely safe, probably can never be completely without risk. According to Stuart Matthews, president of the Flight Safety Foundation, "If the public absolutely demands that flying be totally safe, you are going to have to ban flying." Given the choice between taking a calculated risk and not flying at all, Americans, who take their lives into their hands each time they drive, will probably continue to trust the statistics and take their chances. What form the industry will assume when the deregulation dust finally settles remains an open question.

CROSS-REFERENCES

Aeronautics; Carriers; Federal Aviation Administration; Labor Union; National Transportation Safety Board; Sherman Anti-Trust Act; Unfair Competition.

AIR POLLUTION Air pollution has plagued communities since the industrial revolution and even before. Airborne pollutants, such as gases, chemicals, smoke particles, and other substances, reduce the value of and ability to enjoy affected property and cause significant health and environmental problems. Despite the long history and significant consequences of this problem, effective legal remedies are relatively recent. Though some cities adopted air quality laws as early as 1815, air pollution at that time was seen as a problem best handled by local laws and ordinances. Only as the United States' cities continued to grow, and pollution and health concerns with them, did federal standards and a nationwide approach to air quality begin to emerge.

The earliest cases involving air pollution were likely to be brought because of a noxious smell, such as from a slaughterhouse, animal herd, or factory, that interfered with a landowner's ability to enjoy his or her property. These disputes were handled through the application of the NUISANCE doctrine, which provides that the possessor of land has a duty to make a reasonable use of his or her property in a manner that does not harm other individuals in the area. A person who polluted the air and caused harm to others was liable for breaching this duty and was required to pay DAMAGES or was ENJOINED (stopped through an INJUNCTION issued by a court) from engaging in the activities that created the pollution. In determining whether to enjoin an alleged polluter, courts balanced the damage to the plaintiff landowner's property against the hardship the defendant polluter would incur in trying to eliminate, or abate, the pollution. Courts often denied injunctions because the economic damage suffered by the defendant—and, by extension, the surrounding community, if the defendant was essential to the local economy—in trying to eliminate the pollution often outweighed the damage suffered by the plaintiff. Thus, in many cases, the plaintiff was left only with the remedy of money damages—a cash payment equal to the estimated monetary value of the damage caused by the pollution—and the polluting activities were allowed to continue.

Using the nuisance action to control widespread air pollution proved inadequate for other reasons as well. At COMMON LAW, only the attorney general or local prosecutor could sue to abate a *public nuisance* (one that damages a large number of persons) unless a private individual could show "special" damage that was

© UPI/BETTMANN

distinct from and more severe than that suffered by the general public. The private plaintiff with special damage had the necessary STANDING (legally protectible interest) to seek injunctive relief. The problem of standing has been corrected in some states through laws that allow a private citizen to sue to abate public nuisances such as air pollution, though these laws are by no means the norm. Yet another difficulty with the nuisance doctrine is the plaintiff's burden of showing that the harm she or he has experienced was caused by a particular defendant. Pollutants can derive from many sources. As a result, it can be difficult, if not impossible, to prove that a particular polluter is responsible for a particular problem. Lastly, nuisance law was useful only to combat particular polluters; it did not provide an ongoing and systematic mechanism for the regulation and control of pollution.

Early in the nineteenth century, a few U.S. cities recognized the shortcomings of common-law remedies and enacted local laws that attempted to address the problem of air pollution. Pittsburgh, in 1815, was one of the first to institute air quality laws. Others, like Chicago and Cincinnati, passed smoke control ordinances in 1881, and by 1912, twenty-three U.S. cities with populations of over two hundred thousand had passed smoke abatement laws.

Though the early court cases usually addressed polluted air as an interference with the ENJOYMENT of property, scientists quickly discovered that air pollution also poses significant health and environmental risks. It is believed to contribute to the incidence of chronic diseases such as emphysema, bronchitis, and other respiratory illnesses and has been linked to higher mortality rates from other diseases, including cancer and heart disease.

The shortcomings associated with the common-law remedies to control air pollution and increasing alarm over the problem's long-range effects finally resulted in the development of state and federal legislation. The first significant legislation concerning air quality was the Air Pollution Control Act, enacted in 1955 (42 U.S.C.A. § 7401 et seq. [1955]). Also known as the Clean Air Act, it gave the secretary of health, education, and welfare the power to undertake and recommend research programs for air pollution control. Amendments passed during the 1960s authorized federal agencies to intervene to help abate interstate pollution in limited circumstances, to control emissions from new motor vehicles, and to provide some supervision and enforcement powers to states trying to control pollution. By the end of the 1960s, when it became clear that states had made little progress in combating air pollution, Congress toughened the Clean Air Act through a series of new laws, which were known as the Clean Air Act Amendments of 1970 (Pub. L. No. 91-604, 84 Stat. 1676 [Dec. 31, 1970]).

The 1970 amendments greatly increased federal authority and responsibility for addressing the problem of air pollution. They provided for, among other things, uniform national emissions standards for the hazardous air pollutants most likely to cause an increase in mortality or serious illness. Under the amendments, the states retained some regulatory authority, having "primary responsibility for assuring air quality within the entire geographic area comprising such state." Thus, states could not "opt out" of air pollution regulation and for the first

Temperature inversions in Denver often cause pollution to settle over the city, and on days like this the city issues a pollution alert. Air quality on this December day was considered extremely poor.

time were required to attain certain air quality standards within a specified period of time. In addition, the amendments directed the administrator of the Environmental Protection Agency (EPA), which was also established in 1970, to institute national standards regarding ambient air quality for air pollutants endangering public health or welfare, in particular sulfur dioxide, carbon monoxide, and photochemical oxidants in the atmosphere. The EPA was also granted the authority to require levels of harmful pollutants to be brought within set standards before further industrial expansion would be permitted.

Despite the ambitious scope of the 1970 legislation, many of its goals were never attained. As a result, the Clean Air Act was extensively revised again in 1977 (Pub. L. No. 95-95, 91 Stat. 685 [Aug. 7, 1977]). One signifi-

cant component of the 1977 amendments was the formulation of programs designed to inspect, control, and monitor vehicle emissions. The 1977 revisions also sought to regulate parking on the street, discourage automobile use in crowded areas, promote the use of bicycle lanes, and encourage employer-sponsored carpooling. Unlike the goals of several of the 1970 amendments, many of the 1977 reforms have become reality. Many states, with the help of federal funding, have developed programs that require automobiles to be tested regularly for emissions problems before they can be licensed and registered. The 1977 amendments also directed the EPA to issue regulations to reduce "haze" in national parks and other wilderness areas. Under these regulations the agency has sought to improve air quality in a number of areas, including the Grand Canyon in Arizona.

During the 1980s and 1990s, several environmental issues, including acid rain, global climate change, and the depletion of the ozone layer, gave rise to further federal regulation. Acid rain, which has caused significant damage to U.S. and Canadian lakes, is created when the sulfur from fossil fuels, such as coal, combines with oxygen in the air to create sulfur dioxide, a pollutant. The sulfur dioxide then combines with oxygen to form sulfate, which, when washed out of the air by fog, clouds, mist, or rain, becomes acid rain, with potentially catastrophic effects on vegetation and water. Amendments to the Clean Air Act in 1990 (Pub. L. No. 101-549, 104 Stat. 2399 [Nov. 15, 1990]) sought to address the challenges posed by acid rain by commissioning a number of federally sponsored studies, including an analysis of Canada's approach to dealing with acid rain and an investigation of the use of buffering and neutralizing agents to restore lakes and streams. The 1990 laws also directed the EPA to prepare a report on the feasibility of developing standards related to acid rain that would "protect sensitive and critically sensitive aquatic and terrestrial resources." In addition, the amendments provided for a controversial system of "marketable allowances," which authorize industries to emit certain amounts of sulfate and which can be transferred to other entities or "banked" for future use.

The problem of global climate change is linked to the accumulation of gases, including carbon dioxide and methane, in the atmosphere. Scientists disagree over the net effect of this pollution on the global climate: some argue that it produces global warming; others maintain that it gradually cools global temperatures.

Urban Air: Soot** in Selected Cities, 1990

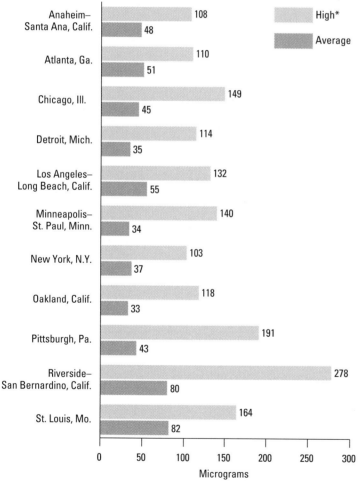

*The EPA treats the reading from the highest day as a statistical anomaly and reports the reading for the second highest day of the year.

**Soot is defined as: Micrograms per cubic meter of air of suspended particles that are 10 microns or less in diameter.

Source: Environmental Protection Agency.

Scientists do agree that a sustained climate change in either direction could significantly affect the environment.

The 1990 amendments implemented a number of strategies to address changes in the global climate, including the commissioning of studies on options for controlling the emission of methane. The amendments also contain provisions to deal with the depletion of the ozone layer, which shields the earth from the harmful effects of the sun's radiation. Though the long-term consequences are hard to determine at this time, damage has already been seen in the form of a "hole" in the ozone layer over Antarctica. The destruction of the ozone layer is believed to be caused by the release into the atmosphere of chlorofluorocarbons (CFCs) and other similar substances. The 1990 laws include a ban on "nonessential uses" of ozone-depleting chemicals, and the placement of conspicuous warning labels on certain substances, indicating that their use harms public health and the environment by destroying the ozone in the upper atmosphere.

In the 1990s, the battle to control air pollution moved indoors, into homes and businesses. Studies have shown that people are exposed to higher concentrations of air pollution for longer periods of time inside buildings than out-of-doors. Furthermore, evidence indicates that this exposure is contributing to a rapidly increasing incidence of illness, thus costing businesses, taxpayers, and the government billions of dollars in health care costs and lost work time. The typical U.S. home contains many hazardous chemicals and substances, including radon, which has been linked to lung cancer and other ailments. Congress has responded to public concern about indoor air quality by requiring the EPA, with the Superfund Amendments and Reauthorization Act (SARA), to establish a program to study the problem and make appropriate recommendations (Superfund Amendments and Reauthorization Act of 1986, Pub. L. No. 99-499, 100 Stat. 1613 [codified as amended in scattered sections of 10 U.S.C.A., 26 U.S.C.A., 29 U.S.C.A., 33 U.S.C.A., and 42 U.S.C.A.]).

One contentious air pollution issue is the effect of smoking in public places, especially as it concerns the rights and health of nonsmokers. Many states have enacted legislation designed to protect nonsmokers in public places, and the battle between smokers and nonsmokers is also making its way into the courts. An increasing number of restaurants, airlines, and other public facilities have dealt with the problem by banning smoking completely.

CROSS-REFERENCES

Automobiles; Environmental Law; Environmental Protection Agency; Pollution; Surgeon General; Tobacco.

BIOGRAPHY

COURTESY GEORGIA DEPT. OF ARCHIVES AND HISTORY

Amos Tappan Akerman

AKERMAN, AMOS TAPPAN Amos Tappan Akerman, born in 1819 in New Hampshire, served as attorney general of the United States from 1870 to 1872 under President Ulysses S. Grant.

A graduate of Dartmouth College, Akerman was admitted to the bar in 1841. He opened his first practice at Elberton, Georgia, in 1850. He was a well-established attorney by the outbreak of the Civil War. Akerman supported Georgia's decision to secede from the Union in 1861, and he served the Confederate government in the quartermaster's department during the war. (A quartermaster is charged with procuring and dispensing uniforms, weapons, and other supplies for the troops.) After the war, Akerman developed ties with the Republican party and the Reconstructionists. He was appointed district attorney for Georgia in 1866. Four years later, he was named attorney general of the United States.

Akerman's tenure as attorney general coincided with the Grant administration's early attempts to enforce civil rights laws in the South during Reconstruction. Initially, Akerman believed prosecutions for violations of criminal civil rights acts should be left to state and local authorities. However, he soon changed his mind and advocated a more aggressive federal role in the prosecution of crimes related to civil rights.

His change of mind can be attributed to the growth of the Ku Klux Klan in the South, and the results of a congressional investigation. In-

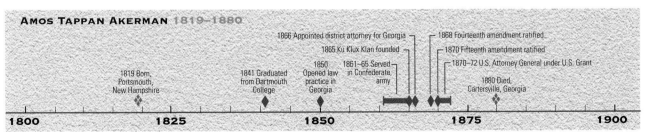

AMOS TAPPAN AKERMAN 1819–1880

1866 Appointed district attorney for Georgia
1865 Ku Klux Klan founded
1868 Fourteenth amendment ratified
1870 Fifteenth amendment ratified
1819 Born, Portsmouth, New Hampshire
1841 Graduated from Dartmouth College
1850 Opened law practice in Georgia
1861–65 Served in Confederate army
1870–72 U.S. Attorney General under U.S. Grant
1880 Died, Cartersville, Georgia

1800   1825   1850   1875   1900

vestigators found that state and local legal systems in the South were inadequate to protect the rights of free blacks or to prosecute the increasingly violent actions of the Klan.

Akerman agreed that the federal government should step in, and he wrote extensively on the subject. In his opinion, some Southerners would never acknowledge the rights of free blacks and government attempts to "conciliate by kindness" were a waste of time. He noted that Southern klansmen and other malcontents "take all kindness . . . as evidence of timidity, and hence are emboldened to lawlessness by it." He concluded that the federal government should "command their respect by the exercise of its powers."

With Akerman's leadership—and his successful effort to obtain a financial commitment from Congress—attorneys from the newly created Department of Justice worked with local U.S. attorneys to bring hundreds of indictments under the Enforcement Act of 1870 (16 Stat. 140 [codified as amended at 42 U.S.C.A. § 1981 et seq.]) and the Ku Klux Klan Act of 1871 (§ 2, 17 Stat. 13 [current version at 42 U.S.C.A. § 1985(3) (Supp. V 1976)]).

Together, these government officials prosecuted, convicted, and imprisoned hundreds of Klan members from 1870 to 1872, and, for a short time, criminal civil rights acts were successfully enforced in the South. Though he "rejoiced" at the suppression of the Klan, Akerman wrote, "I feel greatly saddened by this business. It has revealed a perversion of moral sentiment among the Southern whites, which bodes ill to that part of the country for this generation."

Akerman was also saddened—and frustrated—by fiscal circumstances that combined to slow his efforts. Concerned by the growing financial burden of the actions, and pressured to allocate funds for other priorities, Congress and the Grant administration eventually brought Akerman's prosecutions to a standstill. The violence resumed, and Akerman resigned.

Akerman's resignation as attorney general can also be attributed to his discouragement with the pace of federal civil rights enforcement, and to political issues as well. Akerman had angered President Grant by refusing to execute a deed conveying western lands to the railroads, and he had antagonized many congressional Republicans with his lack of support for other business and railroad projects.

After his resignation, Akerman returned to private life and the practice of law. He died in 1880.

"IT CONCERNS US MORE TO ASCERTAIN WHAT IS THE CONSTITUTIONAL RULE THAN TO LEARN WHETHER THAT RULE HAS ALWAYS BEEN OBSERVED. NINETEEN VIOLATIONS OF THE CONSTITUTION DO NOT JUSTIFY A TWENTIETH."

CROSS-REFERENCES
Civil Rights Acts; Grant, Ulysses S.; Ku Klux Klan Act; Railroads.

ALCOHOL

A Congressman was once asked by a constituent to explain his attitude toward whiskey. "If you mean the demon drink that poisons the mind, pollutes the body, desecrates family life, and inflames sinners, then I'm against it," the Congressman said. "But if you mean the elixir of Christmas cheer, the shield against winter chill, the taxable potion that puts needed funds into public coffers to comfort little crippled children, then I'm for it. This is my position, and I will not compromise."

The legal history of alcohol in the United States closely parallels the economic and social trends that shaped the country. The libertarian philosophy that ignited the Whiskey Rebellion was born in the American Revolution. Shifting concerns about morality and family harmony that were characteristic of the industrial revolution inspired the temperance movement and brought about Prohibition, which began with the passage of the Eighteenth Amendment to the Constitution in 1919 and ended with its repeal in 1933. The return of legalized drinking in the United States led to renewed discussion of the many health and safety issues associated with alcohol consumption. Over the years, the states have addressed these issues through a variety of laws, such as those dealing with a minimum age for the purchase or consumption of alcohol, the labeling of alcoholic beverages, and drunk driving. Private litigants have expanded protections against harm from alcohol through TORT actions, and various groups, both national and local, continue to lobby for increased legislation and higher penalties for alcohol-related acts that lead to injury.

Historical Background of Alcohol in the United States

Drink is in itself a good creature of God, and to be received with thankfulness, but the abuse of drink is from Satan, the wine is from God, but the Drunkard is from the Devil.

(Increase Mather, Puritan clergyman, *Wo to Drunkards* [1673])

Alcoholic beverages have been consumed in the United States since the days of Plymouth Rock. Beer and wine were staples on the ships carrying settlers to the New World. However, debate and controversy have surrounded alcohol consumption throughout the nation's history.

In colonial times, water and milk were scarce and susceptible to contamination or spoilage, and tea and coffee were expensive. The Pilgrims turned to such alternatives as cider and beer, and, less frequently, whiskey, rum, and gin. In 1790, per capita consumption of pure alcohol, or absolute alcohol, was just under six gallons a year. (Pure alcohol constitutes only a small percentage of an alcoholic drink. For example, if a beverage contains 10 percent alcohol by volume, one would have to drink ten gallons of it to consume one gallon of pure alcohol.)

Although the majority of the colonists drank alcohol regularly, strong community social strictures curbed any tendency toward immoderation. Drunken behavior was dealt with by emphasizing the need to restore community harmony and stability, rather than by imposing punishment.

Alcohol consumption continued without much controversy until after the Revolutionary War when whiskey and other distilled spirits became valuable commercial commodities. When Congress imposed an excise tax on the farmers who produced liquor in the 1790s, they resisted paying the tax. Their resistance became known as the Whiskey Rebellion, a protest movement of farmers who felt the tax placed an undue burden on their commercial activities.

Before the nineteenth century, farming was the predominant occupation, and although it involved grueling work, it did not demand precision or speed. The industrial revolution brought millions of workers into factories where efficiency, dexterity, and rigid scheduling were necessary. With these economic changes came a shift in societal attitudes toward alcohol. Gone was the time when people considered the midday liquor break a benign diversion.

The Temperance Movement

'Mid pleasures and palaces, though we may roam,
Be it ever so humble, there's no place like home.
But there is the father lies drunk on the floor,
The table is empty, the wolf's at the door,
And mother sobs loud in her broken-back'd chair,
Her garments in tatters, her soul in despair.

(Nobil Adkisson, *Ruined by Drink* [c. 1860])

As the United States entered the industrial age, attitudes about alcohol consumption gradually changed. A moralistic and punitive view of alcohol replaced the laissez-faire attitudes of earlier times. What had been the "good creature of God" in the eighteenth century became the "demon rum" of the nineteenth.

The U.S. temperance movement emerged around 1826 with the formation of the American Society for the Promotion of Temperance, later called the American Temperance Society. In the 1840s, the society began crusading for complete abstinence from alcohol. Dissemination of the temperance message caused a fall in per capita consumption of pure alcohol from a high of over seven gallons a year in 1830 to just over three in 1840, the largest ten-year drop in U.S. history. By the outbreak of the Civil War, thirteen states, beginning with Maine in 1851, had adopted some form of prohibition as law.

Other temperance organizations became prominent during the middle to late 1800s. In 1874, the Woman's Christian Temperance Union (WCTU) was founded. The only temperance organization still in operation, the WCTU has worked continuously since its inception to educate the public and to influence policies that discourage the use of alcohol and other drugs. In 1990, the group was nominated for a Nobel Peace Prize.

In 1869, the antialcohol movement created its own political party—the National Prohibition party—devoted to a single goal: to inspire legislation prohibiting the manufacture, transportation, and sale of alcoholic beverages. The party made modest showings in state elections through the 1860s and 1870s, and reached its peak of popular support in 1892 when John Bidwell won almost 265,000 votes in his bid for the presidency. The Prohibition party's main effect was its influence on public policy. It succeeded in placing Prohibition planks into many state party platforms and was a potent impetus behind passage of the Eighteenth Amendment.

One of the most powerful forces in the Prohibition movement was the Anti-Saloon League, a nonpartisan group founded in 1893 by representatives of temperance societies and evangelical Protestant churches. The Anti-Saloon League, unlike the Prohibition party, worked within established political parties to support candidates who were sympathetic to the league's goals. By 1916, the league, with the help of the Prohibition party and the WCTU, had sent enough sympathetic candidates to

Alcoholics Anonymous

The courts have long struggled with the problem of what sanctions to impose on people who violate the law while under the influence of liquor. Punishing these offenders fails to address the root cause of the behaviors, the uncontrolled consumption of alcohol. Many judges order offenders to undergo alcohol-dependency treatment or counseling as part of a sentence or as a condition of probation.

One of the most popular programs for treating alcoholism is Alcoholics Anonymous (AA). AA was founded in 1935 by New York stockbroker Bill Wilson and Ohio surgeon Robert Smith. Wilson and Smith recognized their inability to control their drinking and were determined to overcome their problem. They developed the Twelve Steps, on which AA is based and which have become the foundation for similar self-help and recovery programs. AA comprises ninety thousand local groups in 141 countries. Participation is voluntary, and there are no dues or other requirements. Members attend meetings run by nonprofessionals, many of whom are recovering alcoholics. The meetings offer fellowship, support, and education to those with a desire to stop drinking.

Participants in AA declare that they cannot control their drinking alone, and invoke a higher power to help them overcome their dependence on alcohol. AA's Twelve Steps require a fundamental change in personality and outlook. Members admit their powerlessness over alcohol to themselves, to God, and to their friends and families. They attempt to make amends for any wrongs they have committed because of alcohol abuse. Finally, through prayer, meditation, and daily self-evaluation, AA members strive for a radical transformation or spiritual awakening, which results in changed perceptions, thought processes, and actions. Finally, participants share their experiences with others.

Although AA's Twelve Steps speak of God, a higher power, and spiritual awakening, AA maintains that it is not a religious organization. However, the group's religious underpinnings and the tone of its meetings, which may begin with the Serenity Prayer and generally end with group recitation of the Lord's Prayer, are objectionable to some. Courts have split over the issue of whether forced participation in AA violates the First Amendment religion clauses.

See also First Amendment; Religion.

Congress to ensure action on a Prohibition amendment to the Constitution.

Prohibition

Prohibition is an awful flop.
We like it.
It can't stop what it's meant to stop.
We like it.
It's left a trail of graft and slime
It don't prohibit worth a dime
It's filled our land with vice and crime,
Nevertheless, we're for it.

(Franklin P. Adams,
quoted in *Era of Excess*)

In December 1917, the temperance movement achieved its goal when Congress approved the Eighteenth Amendment, which prohibited the manufacture, sale, transportation, importation, or exportation of intoxicating liquors from or to the United States or its territories. The amendment was sent to the states, and by January 1919 it was ratified. In January 1920, the United States became officially dry.

The demand for liquor did not end with Prohibition, however. Those willing to violate the law saw an opportunity to fill that demand and become wealthy in the process. Illegal stills produced the alcohol needed to make "bathtub

gin." Rum and other spirits from abroad were commonly smuggled into the country from the east and northwest coasts, and illegal drinking establishments, known as speakeasies or blind pigs, proliferated. The illicit production and distribution of alcohol, called bootlegging, spawned a multibillion-dollar underworld business run by a syndicate of criminals.

Perhaps the most famous of the bootleggers was Al Capone, who ran liquor, prostitution, and racketeering operations in Chicago—one of the wettest of the wet towns. At the height of his power in the mid-1920s, Capone made hundreds of millions of dollars a year. He employed nearly a thousand people and enjoyed the cooperation of numerous police officers and other corrupt public officials who were willing to turn a blind eye in return for a share of his profits. For years, Capone and others like him evaded attempts to shut down their operations. Capone's reign finally ended in 1931 when he was convicted of income tax evasion.

Historians differ about the success of Prohibition. Some feel that the effort was a ludicrous failure that resulted in more severe social problems than had ever been associated with alcohol consumption. Others point to ample evidence that Prohibition, although never succeeding in making the country completely dry, dramatically changed U.S. drinking habits. Per capita consumption at the end of Prohibition had fallen to just under a gallon of pure alcohol a year, and accidents and deaths attributable to alcohol had declined steeply.

Although Prohibition enjoyed widespread popular support, a substantial minority of U.S. citizens simply ignored the law. Also, although Prohibition unquestionably fostered unprecedented criminal activity, many people were concerned that the government's enforcement efforts unduly intruded into personal privacy. In cases such as *Carroll v. United States*, 267 U.S. 132, 45 S. Ct. 280, 69 L. Ed. 543 (1925), the Supreme Court indicated its willingness to stretch the limits of police power in order to enforce Prohibition. In *Carroll*, the Court held that federal agents were justified in conducting a warrantless search of an automobile, because they had PROBABLE CAUSE to believe it contained illegal liquor.

Concerns over diminished liberties led to feelings that Prohibition was too oppressive a measure to impose upon an entire nation. This sentiment was bolstered by arguments that the production and sale of alcohol were profitable enterprises that could help bolster the nation's depressed economy. By the beginning of the 1930s, after little more than a decade as law, Prohibition lost its hold on the U.S. conscience. The promise of jobs and increased tax revenues helped the anti-Prohibition message recapture political favor. The Twenty-first Amendment, repealing Prohibition, swept through the necessary thirty-six-state ratification process, and the "noble experiment" ended on December 5, 1933.

Post-Prohibition Regulation and Control   The repeal of Prohibition forced states to address once more the dangers posed by excessive alcohol consumption. The risks are well documented: figures compiled in 1990 indicate that as many as 10.5 million U.S. citizens are alcohol dependent and an additional 7.2 million drink heavily enough to cause impaired health and social functioning. Mothers against Drunk Driving (MADD) reported in 1995 that over eighteen thousand alcohol-related traffic deaths occur each year in the United States. Alcohol is the most widely used drug among teenagers and is linked to juvenile crime, health problems, suicide, date rape, and unwanted pregnancy. Alcohol-related traffic accidents are the leading cause of death among fifteen- to twenty-four-year-olds.

In the face of rising concerns about liquor consumption and personal injury, many states chose to regulate alcohol through dramshop laws. A dramshop is any type of drinking establishment where liquor is sold for consumption on the premises. Dramshop statutes impose LIABILITY on sellers of alcoholic beverages for injuries caused by an intoxicated patron. Under such statutes, a person injured by a drunk patron sues the establishment where the patron was served. The purpose of dramshop laws is to hold responsible those who enjoy economic benefit from the sale of liquor, thereby ensuring that a loss is not borne solely by an innocent victim (as when the intoxicated person who caused the injuries has no assets and no insurance).

The first dramshop law, enacted in Wisconsin in 1849, required saloons or taverns to post a bond for expenses that might result from civil lawsuits against their patrons. Many states followed Wisconsin's lead, and dramshop laws were prominent until the 1940s, 1950s, and 1960s, when most were repealed. However, the 1980s brought renewed concern over the consequences of overindulgence in alcohol, and public pressure led to the passage of new dramshop statutes. By 1993, thirty-six states had imposed some form of liability on purveyors of alcoholic beverages for injuries caused by their customers.

All states and the District of Columbia also regulate the sale of liquor to MINORS or to individuals who are intoxicated. Challenges to the age restriction on equal protection grounds have been unsuccessful.

Along with statutory measures, most courts have also recognized a common-law cause of action against alcohol vendors for the negligent sale of alcohol. In *Rappaport v. Nichols*, 31 N.J.

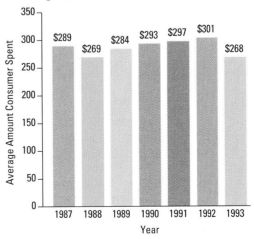

U.S. Consumer Spending on Alcoholic Beverages, 1987–1993

Source: U.S. Bureau of Labor Statistics, *Consumer Expenditures in 1993.*

188, 156 A.2d 1 (1959), the court held that a tavern could be held liable for the plaintiff's husband's death after the tavern served an intoxicated minor who caused the accident that killed the man. The court relied on the PUBLIC POLICY concerns underlying liquor control laws. Such laws are intended to protect the general public as well as minors or intoxicated persons, the court reasoned, and therefore the tavern should be held liable if its NEGLIGENCE was a SUBSTANTIAL factor in creating the circumstances that led to the husband's death. Under *Rappaport*, serving as well as consuming alcohol can be construed to be the PROXIMATE CAUSE of an injury. A majority of jurisdictions now follow the *Rappaport* court's reasoning.

In determining the extent of an alcohol vendor's liability, a growing number of courts apply comparative negligence principles. Comparative negligence assesses partial liability to a plaintiff whose failure to exercise reasonable care contributes to his or her own injury. In *Lee v. Kiku Restaurant*, 127 N.J. 170, 603 A.2d 503 (1992), and *Baxter v. Noce*, 107 N.M. 48, 752 P.2d 240 (1988), the plaintiffs sued under dramshop statutes for injuries suffered when they rode with drunk drivers. The courts in both cases recognized the importance of dramshop statutes in protecting innocent victims of drunk behavior. However, they also recognized the need to hold individuals responsible to some degree for their own safety. Under comparative negligence, which divides liability among the parties in accordance with each party's degree of FAULT, both goals are achieved.

A few courts have extended liability for injuries to social hosts who serve a minor or an intoxicated guest. In *Kelly v. Gwinnell*, 96 N.J. 538, 476 A.2d 1219 (1984), the New Jersey Supreme Court found both the host and the guest jointly liable when the guest had an accident after drinking at the host's house. The court based the host's liability on his continuing to serve alcoholic beverages to the guest when he knew the guest was intoxicated and likely to drive a car. Similarly, in *Koback v. Crook*, 123 Wis.2d 259, 366 N.W.2d 857 (1985), the Wisconsin Supreme Court held that a social host was negligent for serving liquor to a minor guest at a graduation party. The guest was later involved in a motorcycle accident in which the plaintiff was injured. However, the Ohio Supreme Court refused to extend liability to the social host in *Settlemyer v. Wilmington Veterans Post No. 49*, 11 Ohio St. 3d 123, 464 N.E.2d 521 (1984). The court in *Settlemyer* held that assigning liability to a social host is a matter better left to the legislature.

All states and many local governments regulate the sale of alcohol through the issuance of LICENSES. These licenses limit the times and locations where liquor sales can take place. The government also regulates alcohol through TAXATION. Current taxes on liquor serve the same dual purpose as did the first excise tax on liquor when it was proposed by Alexander Hamilton in 1791: they provide a source of revenue for the government and, theoretically, discourage overindulgence. Enforcement of the laws regulating and taxing alcohol is carried out by the Bureau of Alcohol, Tobacco, and Firearms (ATF), an agency of the U.S. Department of the Treasury. The collection of alcohol revenues is important to the federal government: in 1993, liquor taxes exceeded $7.2 billion.

During the 1980s and 1990s, public awareness of the dangers of alcohol led to a number of changes in the law. Groups such as MADD and Students against Drunk Driving (SADD) pressured state legislatures to greatly increase enforcement and penalties for driving while intoxicated. Likewise, increased knowledge about the physical consequences of alcohol consumption led to the imposition of a duty on the part of liquor manufacturers to warn consumers that their product may be hazardous.

Before 1987, manufacturers of alcoholic beverages were immune from civil liability for injuries resulting from the use of liquor. *Garrison v. Heublein, Inc.*, 673 F.2d 189 (7th Cir. 1982), held that the defendant did not have a DUTY to warn the plaintiff of the dangers of its product. The court stated that the dangers inherent in the use of alcohol are "common knowledge to such an extent that the product cannot objectively be considered to be unreasonably dangerous." *Garrison* was followed by other jurisdictions until 1987 when *Hon v. Stroh Brewery*, 835 F.2d 510 (3d Cir. 1987), signaled a shift in judicial sentiment. In *Hon*, the plaintiff's twenty-six-year-old husband died of pancreatitis attributable to his moderate consumption of alcohol over a six-year period. The plaintiff alleged that the defendant's products were "unreasonably dangerous" because consumers were not warned of the lesser-known dangers of consumption. The court, relying on the Restatement (Second) of Torts § 402A, held that a product is defective if it lacks a warning sufficient to make it safe for its intended purpose. Since the general public is unaware of all the health risks associated with liquor consumption, the court found the defendant liable for failing to warn the plaintiff. The reasoning in *Hon* has been followed in other cases, including *Brune v. Brown-Forman Corp.*, 758 S.W.2d 827 (Tex. Ct. App. 1988), where the court found that the defendant's product was unreasonably danger-

DRINKING ON CAMPUS:
A RITE OF PASSAGE OUT OF CONTROL?

Alcohol has always had its advocates and its critics, particularly on college campuses, where the desires of students to enjoy the rights and freedoms of adults collide with the concerns of parents, university officials, and the police. Although some widely publicized studies from the late 1980s and early 1990s indicated that student drinking is at an all-time high, threatening students' health and academic careers, others indicate that the problem of student drinking is overblown and on the decline. Those concerned about the problem propose a variety of solutions, with some suggesting that lowering the drinking age might diminish the lure of alcohol as a forbidden fruit.

During the 1980s and 1990s, attention focused increasingly on alcohol use by college students. An article published in the December 7, 1994, issue of the *Journal of the American Medical Association* reported the findings of a study conducted by Dr. Henry Wechsler, director of the Alcohol Studies Program at the Harvard School of Public Health. Wechsler and his team surveyed more than seventeen thousand students, first-year students to seniors, at 140 colleges in forty states. They concluded that college students were drinking more than ever before.

In Wechsler's study, 44 percent of the students surveyed reported binge drinking, defined as having five drinks in a row for men or four in a row for women, on at least one occasion in the two weeks before the survey. (Wechsler defined binge drinking at a lower level of consumption for women because women's bodies take longer to metabolize alcohol, causing them to be affected by lesser amounts in a given time period.) Nineteen percent of all the surveyed students were found to be frequent binge drinkers, meaning they had at least three recent binges.

Similar findings were reported in 1994 by the Commission on Substance Abuse at Colleges and Universities, a group established by the Center on Addiction and Substance Abuse at Columbia University. Its report, titled *Rethinking Rites of Passage: Alcohol Abuse on America's Campuses,* stated that white males were the biggest drinkers on campus. However, the commission noted a sharp rise in the percentage of college women who drank to get drunk, from 10 percent in 1977 to 35 percent in 1994. Unlike women students in earlier studies, those in 1994 reported that they felt little or no social stigma attached to their drinking. At the same time, they felt pressure to succeed, and consuming alcohol was one way they chose to relieve some of that pressure.

College administrators were not surprised by the findings of the two studies. The Harvard study reported that an overwhelming majority of the supervisors of security, deans of students, and directors of health services at the colleges surveyed considered heavy alcohol use a problem on their campuses. And a survey by the Carnegie Foundation revealed that college presidents considered alcohol abuse their most pressing dilemma.

College presidents and administrators have practical reasons to be concerned about student drinking. Reports of drunken brawls, sexual assaults, even deaths attributable to alcohol create public relations nightmares for schools competing for students. There is also the issue of liability: is a college responsible for injuries inflicted by a drunk student? In addition, much of the drinking on campus is done illegally by students who are under the minimum drinking age.

Academic administrators find the increases in drinking among women particularly disturbing. According to women students, the desire to compete with men in all arenas, including social, is one reason they feel the need to demonstrate their equality by drinking as much as or more than their male peers. A study conducted by Virginia's College of William and Mary indicated that the number of women at the college who had five or more drinks at one sitting increased from 27 percent to 36 percent during the early 1990s.

Both men and women students cite intense peer pressure to join the partying that takes place on college campuses, which may begin as early as Wednesday or Thursday night and last through the weekend. At some schools, alcohol-centered gatherings can readily be found any night of the week. Administrators acknowledge that partying may have been just as hearty in the past, but note that before the late 1980s, it was generally confined to the weekend.

The fallout from uncontrolled drinking is felt throughout campus life. According to the report issued by the Commission on Substance Abuse at Colleges and Universities, 95 percent of violent crimes and 53 percent of injuries on campus are alcohol related. In 90 percent of all campus rapes, the assailant, the victim, or both had been drinking. Sixty percent of college women who acquire sexually transmitted diseases, including herpes and AIDS, report that they were drunk at the time they were infected. The financial costs are high as well. Students spend $5.5 billion on alcohol each year, more than they spend on books, coffee, tea, sodas, and other drinks combined. Although athletes might be expected to take fewer risks with their health than other students, the commission concluded that they were equally affected by alcohol abuse.

The commission also found that students who belong to fraternities and sororities drink three times more than their non-Greek counterparts, averaging fifteen drinks a week. Indeed, fraternity drinking has been blamed in several disciplinary actions and at least one death. In July 1994, the national office of Alpha Tau Omega (ATO) announced it was closing eleven of its chapters for violating rules against hazing and alcohol abuse. ATO had already closed its chapter at Wittenberg University, in Springfield, Ohio, after a newly recruited pledge was hospitalized in Janu-

DRINKING ON CAMPUS: A RITE OF PASSAGE OUT OF CONTROL?
(CONTINUED)

ary 1994 for alcohol poisoning. Similarly, the national office of Beta Theta Pi (BTP) announced in 1994 that it would intensify enforcement of rules against hazing and alcohol use in its chapters. According to Erv Johnson, director of communications for the national office, BTP was concerned not only about the legal issues involved but also about the image of the fraternity and the national office's desire to emphasize that the primary purpose of college is to learn.

Excessive drinking has a direct effect on academic performance. Students with an A average generally have 3.6 drinks a week, C students average 9.5 drinks a week, and D and F students consume almost eighteen drinks a week. According to college officials, alcohol is implicated in almost half of all academic problems and is an issue for more than one-fourth of dropouts.

Excessive drinking has obvious negative consequences for the students who engage in it, but it also affects those who do not partake. During the early 1990s, some students and school officials began to speak out against the damage and disorder that binge drinkers cause. Just as nonsmokers brought awareness of the effects of secondhand smoke, moderate and nondrinking students called attention to the results of "secondhand bingeing." Likewise, administrators, who had traditionally tried to downplay the severity of the problem, began to acknowledge it and tried several approaches to controlling it. One method involved having peer counselors educate students about the dangers of excessive drinking and about the effects of their actions on others. Another program provided students with recreational options that did not include alcohol. Some schools offered houses or sections of dorms where residents pledged not to drink or smoke. In 1994, the University of Pittsburgh considered requiring first-year students to take a one-credit course on responsible drinking. The action came after a premed student died after drinking sixteen shots of liquor and some beer in less

than an hour. However, most administrators stopped short of preaching abstinence, acknowledging that most students have begun to drink before they enter college.

Some college officials advocate lowering the legal drinking age, on the theory that if alcohol is readily available to students it may lose some of its appeal. Susan Vaughn, coordinator of judicial affairs at Miami University, of Ohio, says that laws setting the minimum drinking age at twenty-one are unenforceable. She contends that the higher drinking age entices students to drink to excess in order to prove their maturity, and that lowering the legal age would bring drinking "out of the closet," where it can be properly supervised.

Others who have studied college drinking vehemently dispute the wisdom of lowering the minimum age. Joseph A. Califano, Jr., former health secretary and president of the Center on Addiction and Substance Abuse, contends that lowering the minimum drinking age would encourage more drinking and that drinking by college students should no longer be thought of as a rite of passage but rather should now be considered a stumbling block to success. His sentiments are echoed by the Reverend Edward A. Malloy, president of the University of Notre Dame, who considers heavy alcohol use an unhealthy trend that runs counter to the goals of an educational institution. Still, some people believe that learning how to drink is part of the college experience, essential to growing up and breaking away from home and parental control.

Some evidence suggests that drinking on college campuses is declining. A 1994 survey of three hundred thousand students nationwide found that nearly half abstained from virtually all alcohol; in 1971, only one in four abstained. Another 1994 study indicated that, although binge drinking remained a problem, light to moderate drinkers were consuming fewer drinks a week than their counterparts in a 1982 sur-

vey. Some experts speculate that these students were following the lead of their parents, who drank less in the 1990s than they had in the 1970s and 1980s. Others felt that the trend reflected an increased awareness of health and safety issues.

Additional evidence that student drinking may not be as big a problem as some surveys suggest is found in a 1994 study conducted by Dr. David Hanson and Dr. Ruth Engs, of the State University of New York College at Potsdam. The Hanson and Engs study contradicted the findings of the Center on Addiction and Substance Abuse and indicated that student drinking had declined from that in previous years. Furthermore, Hanson questioned the center's statistics on an increase in binge drinking among college women, stating that if such behavior had actually increased 250 percent between 1977 and 1994, other studies conducted during that time would have shown the same rise.

Some who note a decrease in college drinking speculate that it may be because college students of the 1990s grew up with a higher minimum drinking age and stricter drunk driving laws. They assert that it takes a number of years for changes in the law to affect the targeted population. With those changes finally having the desired effect, they maintain, it would be counterproductive to return to a lower minimum age.

The only certain conclusion to be drawn from the research is that excessive drinking among college students may lead to a wide range of social and academic problems. These problems are not new; in fact, they date back to the earliest days of the country's history. The graduation procession at Harvard University is still led by a sheriff, a tradition that harkens to colonial days when a sheriff's presence was required to quell disruptions caused by drunken students.

See also Colleges and Universities.

ous because it bore no warning about the dangers of excessive consumption. The plaintiff's daughter, a college student, died after consuming fifteen shots of tequila over a short period of time.

The duty of liquor manufacturers to warn consumers of the hazards of drinking was codified when Congress passed the Alcoholic Beverage Labeling Act of 1988 (27 U.S.C.A. § 215). The act requires all alcoholic beverage containers to bear a clear and conspicuous label warning of the dangers of alcohol consumption.

The United States' long history of ambivalence toward the consumption of alcoholic beverages shows no sign of abating. At the same time that manufacturers are required to warn consumers about the health risks inherent in liquor, some medical studies indicate that some health benefits may be associated with moderate imbibing.

CROSS-REFERENCES

Alcohol, Tobacco and Firearms, Bureau of; Automobiles; Automobile Searches; Capone, Alphonse; Dramshop Acts; Eighteenth Amendment; Organized Crime; Product Liability; Prohibition; Temperance Movement; Twenty-First Amendment; Whiskey Rebellion.

ALCOHOL, TOBACCO AND FIREARMS, BUREAU OF
The Bureau of Alcohol, Tobacco and Firearms (ATF) is an agency of the U.S. Department of the Treasury. The ATF was established in its present form and with its present name on July 1, 1972, but it traces its roots to the days of Prohibition. The legendary Eliot Ness and his Untouchables, famous U.S. revenue agents remembered for their dramatic surprise raids on illegal alcohol operations, were predecessors of today's ATF agents. The Untouchables earned their name because of their reputation for high moral integrity and resistance to corruption.

The ATF has a long and somewhat confusing history. With the passage of the Eighteenth Amendment, the manufacture, sale, transportation, importation, and exportation of "intoxicating liquors" from or to the United States or its territories became illegal. This amendment ushered in Prohibition, an era of organized crime and underworld syndicates that controlled an illicit liquor business with violence and intimidation. In an attempt to stanch the flow of weapons to these criminals, Congress passed several laws to regulate the firearms and ammunition industries. Originally, the Bureau of Prohibition was responsible for administering these laws. In 1942, the Alcohol Tax Unit (ATU), a forerunner of the ATF, formally took over the bureau's job when the bureau was disbanded following repeal of the Eighteenth

Amendment. In 1952, the ATU added enforcement of tobacco tax laws to its list of responsibilities and changed its title to the Alcohol and Tobacco Tax Division (ATTD) of the Internal Revenue Service (IRS).

During the 1960s, Congress recognized the need to control destructive devices other than firearms. The Omnibus Crime Control and Safe Streets Act of 1968 and the Gun Control Act of 1968, 18 U.S.C.A. § 921 et seq., superseded earlier firearms control laws and placed bombs and other explosives as well as firearms under the strict control of the government. The ATTD was given jurisdiction over the criminal use of explosives and was renamed the Alcohol, Tobacco and Firearms Division (ATFD) of the IRS.

In 1970, the Organized Crime Control Act, 18 U.S.C.A. 841-848, which included the Explosives Control Act, 18 U.S.C.A. § 842, provided for close regulation of the explosives industry and established certain arsons and bombings as federal crimes. With the additional responsibility of enforcing these new laws, the ATFD's mission was redefined and distinguished from that of the IRS. On July 1, 1972, the ATFD was given full bureau status within the Treasury Department and acquired its present name, the Bureau of Alcohol, Tobacco and Firearms.

The ATF is responsible for enforcing and ensuring compliance with the following laws:

Federal Alcohol Administration Act, 27 U.S.C.A. § 201 et seq. (1935);

Internal Revenue Code of 1954, as it relates to distilled spirits, tobacco products, and firearms;

Gun Control Act of 1968, as amended, 18 App. 26 U.S.C.A. § 5801 et seq.;

Title XI of the Organized Crime Control Act (1970) (Explosives Control Act);

Portions of the Arms Export Control Act (1976);

Trafficking in Contraband Cigarettes Act (1978) 18 U.S.C.A. 2341–2346;

Anti-Arson Act of 1982 (amended title XI of the Organized Crime Control Act), 18 U.S.C.A. §§ 841 note, 844;

Armed Career Criminal Act of 1984, 18 App. U.S.C.A. §§ 1201, 1202.

In the area of alcohol and tobacco regulation, the ATF controls production, labeling, advertising, and the relationships between producers, wholesalers, and retailers. The agency's efforts are directed mainly at protecting consumers against products that are impure or mislabeled or otherwise potentially harmful.

During the 1980s, the ATF's alcohol-related

activities focused on the promulgation and enforcement of labeling regulations. For example, in March 1994, the Miller Brewing Company replaced an advertisement for one of its beers in response to concerns raised by ATF officials. The advertisement showed the beer's label, which listed the product's alcohol content, a violation of the Federal Alcohol Administration Act (FAAA), 27 U.S.C.A. § 201 et seq., one of the laws the ATF enforces. However, the strength of that act was diluted later by a 1995 Supreme Court decision declaring the restriction unconstitutional. In *Rubin v. Coors Brewing Co.*, ___U.S. ___, 115 S. Ct. 1585, 131 L. Ed. 2d 532 (1995), the Court held that the subsection of the act that prohibits brewers from advertising the alcohol content of their beers was unnecessarily broad and violated the FIRST AMENDMENT. The Court stated further that the government's legitimate interest in preventing manufacturers from competing by increasing the alcohol content of their beers could be accomplished through less restrictive means, such as by directly limiting the alcohol content of beer or by banning the advertisement of alcohol content of high-alcohol brews.

During the 1980s and 1990s, the ATF's enforcement duties were increasingly focused on firearms as alcohol and tobacco regulation became mainly a matter of TAXATION. As of 1991, an estimated 270,000 dealers, importers, and manufacturers of firearms, ammunition, and explosives were licensed in the United States. Approximately 140 million to 200 million firearms were in circulation. It is the ATF's job to oversee enforcement of the laws regulating these items.

The ATF functioned with relative anonymity until February 28, 1993, when it became involved in an ill-fated raid that tainted its reputation and called its future into question. Acting on reports of stockpiled weapons and explosives at the headquarters of a religious sect, the Branch Davidians, of Waco, Texas, ATF agents executed a military-style raid of the compound. The agents proceeded with the raid even after discovering that the Branch Davidians had been tipped off by an informant. In the ensuing gunfight, four ATF agents were killed and fifteen wounded. The Davidians refused to surrender, and the agents refused to back down. The standoff continued until April 19, when ATF agents again moved to take the compound by force. The raid turned into a shoot-out and conflagration in which eighty-five members of the cult, including seventeen children, perished.

The bureau was widely criticized for its actions at Waco. A report on the incident issued by the Treasury Department concluded that the decision to proceed was wrong, and that those in charge of the operation knew it was a mistake to proceed with the raid because the element of surprise was missing. The report found that bureau officials unwisely insisted on carrying out the February 28 raid even though the critical element of surprise had been lost. The bureau's director, Stephen E. Higgins, retired early from his position, and two agents, Phillip J. Chojnacki and Charles D. Sarabyn, were suspended for their roles in the botched raid. Chojnacki and Sarabyn appealed their suspensions, and, in December 1994, they were reinstated with full back pay and benefits, although they were demoted to lower level positions. In addition, the incident was removed from their personnel files.

The incident at Waco aroused the ire of many U.S. citizens, particularly right-wing militia groups who saw the raid as an example of government intrusion into their right to keep and bear arms. A letter distributed to members of the National Rifle Association in 1995 described ATF agents as "jack-booted government thugs." Many believe that an April 1995 bombing of a federal building in Oklahoma City, which took place exactly two years after Waco, was planned in retaliation for the ATF raid on the Branch Davidians.

Controversy continues to surround the ATF. Some critics say that its agents are not sufficiently trained to carry out the types of operations its administrators seem to favor. Others contend that it lacks a coherent mission and that many of its duties, such as enforcement of alcohol regulations, are better suited to other agencies.

CROSS-REFERENCES

Alcohol; Explosives; Gun Control; Treasury Department; Weapons.

ALDERMAN OR ALDERWOMAN 📖 A public officer of a town or city council or a local legislative body who is elected to the position by the persons he or she represents. 📖

ALEATORY CONTRACT 📖 A mutual agreement between two parties in which the PERFORMANCE of the contractual obligations of one or both parties depends upon a fortuitous event. 📖

The most common type of aleatory CONTRACT is an INSURANCE policy in which an insured pays a premium in exchange for an insurance company's promise to pay damages up to the face amount of the policy in the event that one's house is destroyed by fire. The insurance company must perform its obligation only after the fortuitous event, the fire, occurs.

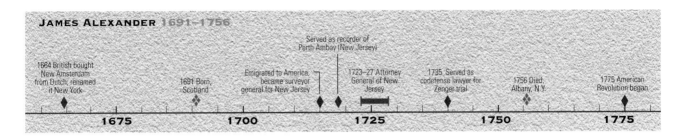

Served as recorder of
Perth Amboy (New Jersey)

1664 British bought
New Amsterdam
from Dutch; renamed
it New York

1691 Born,
Scotland

Emigrated to America;
became surveyor
general for New Jersey

1723–27 Attorney
General of New
Jersey

1735 Served as
codefense lawyer for
Zenger trial

1756 Died,
Albany, N.Y.

1775 American
Revolution began

1675   1700   1725   1750   1775

ALEXANDER, JAMES

James Alexander, born in 1691 in Scotland, was an eminent lawyer who became famous for his support of FREEDOM OF THE PRESS.

In 1715, Alexander immigrated to America, and began a career of public service to New York and New Jersey. He performed the duties of surveyor general for the Province of New Jersey in 1715, and three years later served as recorder of Perth Amboy.

Alexander participated in the Council of New York from 1721 to 1732 but continued to be active in New Jersey. He was admitted to the New Jersey Provincial bar in 1723, and joined the Council of New Jersey in that same year, serving until 1735. From 1723 to 1727 Alexander performed the duties of New Jersey attorney general.

In 1735, journalist John Peter Zenger was on trial, accused of libelous attacks on the administration of New York Governor William Cosby. Alexander served as codefense lawyer at this trial, and Alexander Hamilton pleaded the case. Zenger was acquitted, and the success of this defense was a triumph for the principles of a free press.

Alexander died in Albany, New York, on April 12, 1756.

ALIAS

[*Latin, Otherwise called.*] A term used to indicate that a person is known by more than one name.

Alias is a short and more popular phrase for *alias dictus.* The abbreviation a.k.a., *also known as,* is frequently used in connection with the description of a person sought by law enforcement officers to disclose the names that the person has been known to use. A fictitious name assumed by a person is popularly termed an alias.

ALIAS WRIT

A second WRIT, or court ORDER, issued in the same case after an earlier writ of that kind has been issued but has not been effective.

ALIENABLE

The character of PROPERTY that makes it capable of sale or transfer.

ALIENATE

To voluntarily convey or transfer TITLE to REAL PROPERTY by GIFT, disposition

BIOGRAPHY

James Alexander

"... I THINK IT ABSOLUTELY NECESSARY THAT SOME PERSON BE HERE TO DEFEND ZENGER."

During World War II, the U.S. government moved thousands of Japanese Americans to detention camps because it considered them alien enemies while the country was at war with Japan.

by WILL or the laws of DESCENT AND DISTRIBUTION, or by SALE.

ALIENATION CLAUSE

A provision in a document permitting or forbidding a person from transferring property that is the subject of the document.

In a fire INSURANCE policy, an alienation clause prohibits the alienation of the insured premises while the policy is in effect. If the insured violates this provision, the policy is void.

ALIENATION OF AFFECTION

The removal of love, companionship, or aid of an individual's spouse.

Historically, alienation of affection furnished grounds for an ACTION against the individual who interloped in a MARITAL relationship. The harm caused was viewed as a deprivation of an individual's rights of CONSORTIUM.

The elements of the action generally included wrongful conduct by the interfering party with the complainant's spouse, the loss of affection or consortium, and a nexus between the conduct of the defendant and the impairment or loss of consortium, which included a deprivation of such rights as services, assistance, and sexual relations.

Today, the action has fallen into disuse and no longer constitutes a ground for a lawsuit in most states.

ALIEN ENEMY

In INTERNATIONAL LAW, a foreign born citizen or subject of a nation or power that is hostile to the United States.

An alien enemy is an individual who, due to permanent or temporary allegiance to a hostile power, is regarded as an enemy in wartime. The term is used to describe any and all subjects of a foreign nation that is at war with the United States.

ALIENS ◫ Foreign-born persons who have not been naturalized to become U.S. citizens under federal law and the Constitution. ◫

The federal immigration laws determine whether a person is an alien. Generally, a person born in a foreign country is an alien, but a child born in a foreign nation to parents who are U.S. citizens is a U.S. citizen. The term *alien* also refers to a native-born U.S. citizen who has relinquished U.S. citizenship by living and acquiring citizenship in another country. Aliens are categorized in several ways: resident and nonresident, immigrant and nonimmigrant, documented and undocumented ("illegal").

Overview The United States welcomes a large number of aliens every year. Millions of foreign-born persons travel, work, and study in the country, and hundreds of thousands more choose to immigrate and become U.S. citizens. All of them are subject to federal immigration law. At the simplest level, the law serves as a gatekeeper for the nation's borders: it determines who may enter, how long they may stay, and when they must leave. In totality, of course, its scope far exceeds this simple purpose. Immigration law is concerned not only with borders but with what goes on inside them. It has much to say about the legal rights, duties, and obligations of aliens in the United States, which, in some respects, are different from those of citizens. Ultimately, it also provides the means by which certain aliens are naturalized as new citizens with all the rights of citizenship.

Congress has total authority over immigration. In the legislative branch of government, this power has no equal. The U.S. Supreme Court has determined that "over no conceivable subject is the legislative power of Congress more complete" (*Fiallo v. Bell*, 430 U.S. 787, 97 S. Ct. 1473, 52 L. Ed. 2d 50 [1977]). With a few notable exceptions concerning the right of aliens to constitutional protections, the courts have rarely intruded. Presidents have no inherent say; their influence is limited to policies on REFUGEES. Moreover, congressional authority preempts all state laws and regulations, and even addresses the rights of aliens during wartime. In practical terms, these circumstances mean that immigration law is entirely the domain of federal lawmakers, whose say is usually final. Congress alone decides who will be welcomed or turned away, as well as what aliens may and may not do in the United States.

This authority has a long and controversial past. The first laws date to 1875, and their history is rife with discrimination. Lawmakers have always created barriers that favor some aliens over others. At one time, Chinese were not wanted, at others, Japanese; the list goes on and on. Only in the last half of the twentieth century were these widely divergent policies codified under a primary federal statute, the Immigration and Nationality Act (INA) (Pub. L. No. 414, ch. 477, 66 Stat. 163, codified as amended in scattered sections of 8 U.S.C.A., 18 U.S.C.A., 22 U.S.C.A., 49 U.S.C.A., 50 App. U.S.C.A.), since 1952 the basic source of immigration law. For decades, the INA was easily tinkered with through amendments and bills. A dazzling number of political reasons made Congress create a patchwork of preferences, exceptions, and quotas, each reflecting who was wanted and who was not. Although somewhat less frequently toward the end of the twentieth century, national origin has often decided whether the United States admitted an alien.

Modern legislation has introduced great changes. Reform has followed two distinct lines of thought: the need to stem illegal immigration, and the desire to make the law more fair for legal immigrants. Congress tackled the first issue in the Immigration Reform and Control Act of 1986 (IRCA) (Pub. L. No. 99-603, 100 Stat. 3359, codified as amended in scattered sections of the U.S.C.A.). The IRCA toughened criminal sanctions for employers who hire illegal aliens, denied these aliens federally funded WELFARE benefits, and legitimized some aliens through an AMNESTY program. Related legislation, the Immigration Marriage Fraud Amendments of 1986, 8 U.S.C.A. § 1101 note et seq., cracked down on the popular illegal practice of marrying to obtain citizenship. Fairness issues helped influence the second major reform, the Immigration Act of 1990, Pub. L. No. 101-649, 104 Stat. 4978 (codified in scattered sections of the U.S.C.A.). Thoroughly revamping the INA, the 1990 act allocated visas more evenly among foreign nations, eliminated archaic rules, and increased the level of worldwide immigration by 35 percent, to an annual level of 675,000. Congress slightly modified the 1990 act with the Technical Amendments of 1991.

Admission Procedures Normally, aliens wishing to enter the United States first apply for a VISA at one of the over two hundred U.S. consulates and embassies abroad. Visas are documents required for travel to most nations in the world. For example, U.S. citizens may not simply cross the borders of Germany or Zaire without a visa. Aliens, likewise, may not simply cross the borders into the United States; they have no inherent right to enter the country. A visa is the only legal means of entry. In a larger sense, it is the key to understanding the goals and practices of immigration law.

Two types of visas exist: immigrant visas and nonimmigrant visas. It is much easier to obtain nonimmigrant visas, which are primarily issued to tourists and temporary business visitors. In 1993, the INS admitted 21,447,000 nonimmigrants to the United States. Nonimmigrant visas are divided into eighteen main categories ranging from vacationers and diplomatic personnel to athletes, temporary workers, and students. Most categories do not have any numerical limitation. The reasoning is simple: nonimmigrants generally spend a short time and a lot of money in the United States, with obvious benefits for the nation's economic, social, and cultural life, and relatively few demands on its resources. The most significant issue in nonimmigrant visas is whether the alien may work in the United States without violating the terms of the visa.

Immigrants find visas much harder to obtain. Millions of aliens want to live and work in the United States and enjoy the benefits of U.S. citizenship, but only a fraction of them can. Congress sets numerical limits on most types of immigrant visas, under the theory that the country can realistically absorb only so many new people. The 1995 annual ceiling was 675,000, with flexibility for some categories. In addition, many immigrant visas are subject to per-country caps—roughly 25,000 per country, though some countries receive special allowances.

In law, aliens granted visas are said to have obtained entry. The term *entry* has a special meaning that is different from a mere "physical presence in the United States." An alien might cross the border, but still be determined by authorities not to have entered the country. Entry means legal admittance and the freedom from official restraint. Its benefits are tangible: generally, aliens recognized by law to have gained entry have more rights than those who have not gained entry.

Denial of entry is called *exclusion*. Dating from the earliest attempts to control immigration, this controversial concept holds that it is not in the national interest to admit some persons. Far-reaching grounds bar applicants for reasons related to health, crime, national security, and other variables. As part of reviewing applications for visas, consular officials decide whether any of the grounds for exclusion apply. If the officials decide that none do, a visa may be granted, but entry is still not certain.

Immigrant Aliens Admitted into the United States, 1985 to 1993

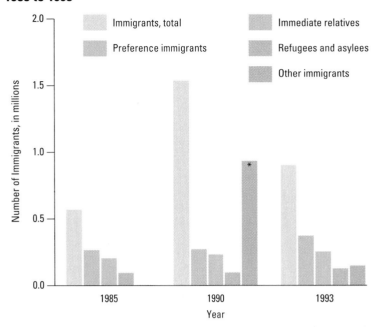

Nonimmigrant Aliens Admitted into the United States, 1985 to 1993

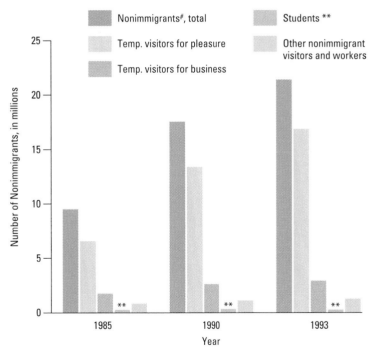

*Includes over 880,000 legalization adjustments as a result of the Immigration Reform and Control Act of 1986.
** Nonimmigrants include nonresident aliens admitted to the U.S. for a temporary period. The official numbers do NOT include border crossers, crew members, or insular travelers.
#Includes spouses and children of students.

Source: U.S. Immigration and Naturalization Service, *Statistical Yearbook*, annual.

The Immigration and Naturalization Service (INS) can decide otherwise when the alien actually attempts to cross the border. In practice, exclusion occurs every day.

Excluded aliens can argue their case in an *exclusion hearing*. This procedure differs greatly from a *deportation hearing*, which involves an alien who has already entered the United States. Deportation hearings are actually more advantageous: unlike exclusion proceedings, deportation hearings only follow from specific allegations and aliens subject to deportation have more forms of legal relief. In an exclusion hearing, the burden is always on the alien to prove his or her right to enter the United States. The alien is entitled to many attributes of procedural due process, and aliens who lose may also seek *asylum* (refuge or protection, usually for political reasons) in some instances.

Excluded applicants seeking to cross the border may be kept in detention facilities until their hearings have been held. In some cases, INS officers may choose to release an alien on *parole* pending further review. Parole allows an alien to travel away from the border and detention facilities temporarily, for reasons such as preventing the separation of families. As a limited right, parole is not equivalent to entry.

Nonimmigrant Visas Each applicant for a nonimmigrant visa must demonstrate that she or he has no intention of immigrating. Generally, the application requires detailed information about the alien's native residence, place of employment, reason for traveling to the United States, and destination. Most nonimmigrant visas do not have annual numerical limits, but the INA does restrict those for professionals to 65,000; temporary agricultural workers to 66,000; and performing athletes, artists, and entertainers to 25,000.

Nonimmigrant aliens apply for a visa from one of eighteen categories, each assigned a letter, as follows:

A. Career diplomats;
B. Temporary visitors for business and pleasure;
C. Aliens in transit;
D. Crew members;
E. Treaty traders and investors;
F. Students;
G. International organization representatives;
H. Temporary workers;
I. Foreign media representatives;
J. Exchange program visitors;
K. Fiancées, fiancés, or children of U.S. citizens;
L. Intracompany transferees;
M. Students in nonacademic institutions;
N. Parents and children of special immigrants;
O. Aliens with extraordinary abilities;
P. Entertainers;
Q. Participants in cultural exchange programs;
R. Religious workers.

The visas are further categorized by numbers—for example, A-1, A-2, and so forth.

Aliens use specific procedures for the particular visa sought. Broadly speaking, these fall into three classes: (1) applications that do not require contact with anyone in the United States (visas A, B, C, D, E, G, I, and O); (2) applications that require proof of acceptance in an authorized program (visas F, J, M, and Q, and visas for special education trainees); and (3) applications that require approved petitions which provide the basis for the alien's presence in the United States (visas H, K, L, P, and R). Over half of all visas require supporting documents at the time of application. For example, an alien hoping to work temporarily in the United States as a registered nurse needs an employer's petition to obtain an H-1A visa. Similarly, an alien planning to study at a university must present proof of acceptance at the university for an F-1 visa. An alien engaged to a U.S. citizen will never see a K visa—let alone the altar—unless the citizen has filed a petition. In all cases, consular officials make the final decision. Generally, no judicial review is available.

Once admitted into the United States, aliens are inspected by INS officers, who give them a form I-94 indicating the length and terms of their stay. Most aliens ultimately return to their country of origin. Some wish to stay and immigrate. Generally, all nonimmigrant visa holders who are in the United States may apply to have their visa status adjusted to permanent-resident status, with the exception of crew member visa (visa D) holders. To qualify, the alien must have been inspected and admitted or paroled into the United States, and must meet standard eligibility requirements for obtaining an immigrant visa, and an immigrant visa must be immediately available at the time the application is filed. In addition, the alien must not have been in an unlawful status or, with few exceptions, have accepted any unauthorized employment.

Immigrant Visas Immigrant visas come in two main categories: visas subject to numerical limitation and visas not subject to numerical limitation. The term *numerical limitation* means several things. First, it refers to the overall limits on immigrants set by Congress. Second, it involves the use of per-country caps. Third, and most important, numerically limited visas are organized along a system of preferences that favors certain aliens over others. Every immigrant wants the best shot at a visa, but qualifying for the easiest category—visas not subject to numerical limitation—is quite difficult. Congress has reserved this category for immediate relatives of U.S. citizens, resident aliens returning from temporary visits abroad, and former U.S. citizens. Consequently, for the vast majority of aliens who want to immigrate, demand is much higher than the relatively short supply prescribed by law.

Though having no numerical limitation makes it easier to obtain, the immediate-relative visa still carries strict limitations. Generally, the term *immediate relatives* means children, spouses, and parents, but unique rules apply to children and spouses. To qualify as a child, the person must be unmarried and under twenty-one years of age. The law is also concerned with how the parent came to have the child, and it applies special age restrictions to legitimate and illegitimate children, stepchildren, adopted children, and orphans. Spouses of U.S. citizens must pass the most demanding tests. The law requires the alien to have a "valid and subsisting marriage" with the citizen under the laws of the country where the marriage took place, and considers a wide variety of marriages insufficient for granting the visa. This severity is an answer to the common abuse of marriage to obtain citizenship. The Immigration Marriage Fraud Amendments of 1986 impose criminal penalties for violations. The Fraud Amendments also impose a two-year conditional residency requirement before alien spouses and their sons and daughters may petition for permanent-resident status.

Three categories exist for visas subject to numerical limitation: family sponsored, employment related, and so-called diversity immigration. The last is a special category created to reverse the drastic reductions in immigration from European countries, particularly Ireland. Effective from 1995 on, a formula is used to determine whether in the previous five years a country has been "underrepresented." If so, an alien from that country is eligible for one of 55,000 visas annually allocated to diversity immigrants. Aliens may apply once a year in a lottery, making this a highly uncertain way to obtain a visa. Not everyone is eligible; applicants must generally have a high school education and two years of work experience. Different goals make more visas available to Hong Kong: because of uncertainty over an impending transfer of the country to China, the law allots 20,000 visas annually to certain Hong Kong citizens who are employees of U.S. businesses, their spouses, and their children.

With zero days left for legalization in May of 1988, illegal aliens wait in line outside an immigration office in Georgia.

FOR LEGALIZATION

0

The primary types of numerically limited visas—family sponsored and employment related—are organized into preference categories. *Preference* means that the law allocates visas to certain aliens over others in order to promote such goals as preserving families, protecting U.S. jobs, and admitting immigrants most likely to benefit the nation. How the law ranks aliens can be seen from the numerical limits on each category. Families are allotted 226,000 visas annually, with a somewhat flexible maximum of 465,000 in four preference categories. Only 140,000 employment-related visas are allotted, in five preference categories. Unused visas from higher preference categories are reallocated to the lower categories.

Preference in family-sponsored visas is decided by the nature of an alien's relationship to the petitioner:

First preference–Unmarried sons and daughters of U.S. citizens, who are too old to qualify (age twenty-one or older) for the nonnumerically limited immediate-relative visa: 23,400 visas plus any unused visas from the other family-sponsored preference classes.

Second preference–Spouses, children, and unmarried sons and daughters of aliens who are lawful permanent residents: minimum of 114,200 visas. Spouses and children are allocated 77 percent of the visas; unmarried sons and daughters (at least twenty-one years old), 23 percent.

Third preference–Married sons and daughters of U.S. citizens: 23,400 plus any unused visas from the first- and second-preference classes.

Fourth preference–Brothers and sisters of U.S. citizens, if the citizen is at least twenty-one years old: 65,000 plus any unused visas from the three higher classes.

Employment-related preferences are not based on any familial relationship. They focus on educational attainment, stressing occupations that are highly specialized. Their levels are set as percentages of the worldwide maximum of 140,000.

First preference–Priority workers: 28.6 percent. These are persons of "extraordinary ability" in the sciences, arts, education, business, or athletics; outstanding professors and researchers; and multinational executives and managers.

Second preference–Professionals holding advanced degrees, or persons of exceptional ability in the sciences, arts, or business: 28.6 percent.

Third preference–Skilled workers in short supply, professionals holding baccalaureate degrees, and other workers in short supply: 28.6 percent.

Fourth preference–Certain special immigrants: 7.1 percent. These are mainly religious workers, as well as former employees of the U.S. government and international organizations.

Fifth preference–Employment creation immigrants: 7.1 percent. These are investors who will create at least ten U.S. jobs by investing in a new commercial enterprise benefiting the U.S. economy, especially in areas of low employment. Generally, the minimum required investment is $1 million.

Though all potential immigrants face rigorous application requirements, certain categories are more exacting. Petitions are needed for visas based on the immediate-relative, family-sponsored, and employment-related preference categories. These must be filed in the United States by citizens or resident aliens on behalf of the applicant, and then approved by the INS. (Under a significant exception, anyone may petition on behalf of Amerasian children of U.S. servicemen.) Many of the employment-related preference categories also need an employer's petition. As a safeguard intended to protect U.S. jobs, the employer is first required to seek an official form of permission called *labor certification.* This is approved only if (a) sufficient qualified workers are not available and (b) employment of the alien will not adversely affect wages or working conditions of similarly employed U.S. workers. The Department of Labor defines the occupations for which employers may seek certification in two groups: the professions and unskilled labor. Only rarely is an unskilled labor application approved. Furthermore, the job for which the employer seeks labor certification must also be permanent in nature.

After approval of the labor certification or preference petition, or both, the actual visa application process begins for an alien who resides outside the United States. This process takes place at the appropriate U.S. consulate, where authority to approve or deny an application belongs exclusively to consular officials. If eligible, the alien must submit considerable documentation. The required documents include biographical reports; police, court, prison, and military records; birth and marriage certificates; passports; photographs; and evidence that the alien will not become a public charge while

WELFARE AND IMMIGRATION

Dissatisfaction with immigration is much older than the Statue of Liberty. Half a century before the famous monument was erected in New York harbor in 1924, the United States had begun, in 1875, passing the first of many restrictive laws intended to keep out certain aliens. A powerful force behind federal legislation has always been widespread hostility toward some new arrivals. Disliking everything from skin color to habits of speech, appearance, and worship, citizens have dependably opposed certain immigrants: the Irish in the 1800s, Jews and Slavs in the early twentieth century, and Southeast Asians most recently. Illegal aliens have upset many U.S. citizens for decades. Since the late 1980s, a new theme has entered public discussion: opposing welfare benefits to legal immigrants. Currently, aliens who immigrate legally are entitled to many of the same state and federal benefits that citizens receive, but, increasingly, popular arguments demand that they should be cut off.

The argument is related only in part to traditional anti-immigration sentiment. When Congress barred the Chinese from immigrating in 1882, for example, it did so in response to complaints that they depressed wage scales and refused to assimilate; few would deny that racism was a factor. Similar economic and cultural arguments resulted in immigration quotas based on national origin, which lasted from the end of World War I until 1965. Modern immigration reform has increasingly stressed fairness, emphasized family unity, and reduced discrimination. But since the mid-1960s, the United States has undergone an economic revolution, giving increasingly vast financial assistance to poor people and thus creating a welfare state. Many liberals, moderates, and conservatives think this situation is not good, and so it is not surprising that calls for reform of the welfare system have branched out to include the issue of immigration.

Some opponents of immigrants receiving welfare start their case with an all-out attack on the welfare system in general. The influential conservative author George Will argues that aliens are brainwashed in much the same way as a poor U.S. citizens—into believing that welfare is a normal way of life. "Today immigrants are received in a welfare culture that encourages an entitlement mentality," Will wrote. The notion of an "entitlement mentality" is well-established in the antiwelfare camp, where it is believed that government has erred by creating a mind-set of casual acceptance among recipients of benefits. This view does not discriminate between citizens and aliens. It holds that welfare is equally wrong for both because it creates dependence over several generations and leads, as the prominent critic Charles Murray has asserted, to social ills such as crime, drug addiction, and illegitimate births. Moderates, such as President Bill Clinton, have embraced this analysis to a substantial degree, yet remain less willing than conservatives to eliminate welfare completely.

Welfare is a jumping-off point for a broader attack on federal immigration law. If welfare is a mistaken policy, it follows that any immigration policy that creates new dependents is itself flawed. Does current policy create new dependents? The major emphasis of the 1990 Immigration Act (Pub. L. 101–649, Nov. 29, 1990, 104 Stat. 4978) is on family unification: it stresses immigration by relatives of U.S. citizens and resident aliens, the majority of whom are generally granted visas as long as they will not become "public charges," that is, welfare recipients. That requirement is easily met if the immigrant has a sponsor family that will help feed, clothe, and care for him or her, but federal data support the contention that many immigrants become public charges anyway. In early 1995, the General Accounting Office (GAO) reported

that 6 percent of legal immigrants receive assistance, as opposed to only 3.4 percent of citizens.

To the most outspoken critics, the United States is clearly welcoming the wrong immigrants. Instead of opening its doors to just anyone, they argue, the nation should be more selective. "Today's laws," *Investor's Business Daily* editorialized in 1995, ". . . perversely favor immigrants from the Third World over others with higher skills and greater understanding of Western culture." The newspaper bemoaned this "low-skilled tide" for "push[ing] down the wages of poorer Americans." Not only the conservative financial press makes this argument; the left-wing magazine of opinion the *Nation* also repeats it, with a slightly different emphasis on race. Immigrants have "pushed blacks out of the marketplace altogether," the writer Wanda Coleman asserted in 1993. The economist Simon Kuznets and the author Peter Brimelow have tied the relative economic progress of African Americans to the dramatic decline in immigration between 1920 and 1965.

Ironically, immigrants are criticized for receiving welfare if they do not work, and for stealing jobs and cheapening wages if they do. As an alternative to economic dependency on the one hand and economic injury on the other, some reformers want to revise the Immigration and Nationality Act (INA). The American Enterprise Institute, a neoconservative think tank, calls for dumping the family-reunification goal for a system based on "designer immigration": admitting better-educated immigrants. This case is made in detail in a 1995 book called *The Immigration Wave: A Plea to Hold It Back*, by Brimelow, himself an immigrant from England. Brimelow contended that the future is bleak: by the year 2050, the U.S. population will be nearly 400 million, and over one-third of it will be low-skilled immigrants who arrived after 1970. Unlike the one-third of the immigrant population that came during the great wave between 1890 and 1920

WELFARE AND IMMIGRATION
(CONTINUED)

and then returned home, these men, women, and children will have stayed because of the welfare system. "The failures are no longer winnowed out," Brimelow wrote. "Instead, they are encouraged to stay—at the expense of the American taxpayer." Only a designer approach can prevent a "bureaucratically-regulated racial spoils system."

The opposite side of the debate stands on traditional pro-immigration, pro-welfare ground. Reviewing *The Immigration Wave*, the author Richard Bernstein criticized Brimelow for ignoring "the genuinely moving spectacle of millions of people making better lives for themselves in this country than they could in the countries they came from." Writing in the *New York Times*, Nathan Glazer expressed regret over an increasingly agitated tone in the debate: "[W]e will all have to keep our heads and remember that we all came from someplace else." Such sentiments have long informed arguments in favor of immigration—namely, that it is generous and humanitarian.

In a different spirit, sharper attacks on the reformers come the further one looks to the political left. In 1993, the *New Left Review* defended immigration by blasting public selfishness in the form of "the fiscal constraints on public spending imposed by conservative, suburban voters." Instead of restricting immigration, the *Progressive* magazine urged President Clinton to "try to ease the economic deprivations and political persecutions the United States has fos-

tered around the globe, which themselves have propelled much of the immigration to this country."

At the state and federal levels, politicians have largely disagreed. California is a prime example: in 1994, nearly two-thirds of the state's voters passed Proposition 187 (CA Prop. 187 [1994], 1994 Cal. Legis. Serv. Prop. 187 [WEST]), a law intended to deny education and public assistance to illegal aliens. Although it was not aimed at legal immigrants, its success with voters prompted some observers to regard it as a symptom of increasing intolerance toward immigration in general; by early 1995, only court challenges to its constitutionality had prevented it from going into effect. The biggest appeal of Proposition 187 is saving tax dollars. Concerns about heavy state expenditures prompted California and Florida to bring unsuccessful lawsuits in the early 1990s, demanding reimbursement from the federal government, alleging that Washington, D.C.'s, failure to enforce immigration laws has saddled the states with incredible debt.

Federal reform efforts against welfare for *legal* immigrants follow the same money-saving logic. The Republican party made denying such benefits part of its successful 1994 platform, The Contract with America, claiming that reform would save an estimated $20 billion in federal spending over five years. In March 1995, the House of Representatives passed the measure

(H.R. 4) in a welfare reform bill, but the legislation's future seemed doomed by President Clinton's promise of a veto on the grounds that it would too severely hurt all welfare recipients. However, seen as part of an anti-immigrant backlash that includes Proposition 187, the House bill touched off a wave of panic among legal immigrants who rushed to apply for citizenship. The Immigration and Naturalization Service (INS) reported unprecedented numbers of applications in the Southwest and Midwest. In the Southern California INS District alone, officials said the rate of twenty-five hundred applications a day was creating a backlog that would take eight months to process.

As current debate shows, attitudes toward immigration and welfare are inextricably linked in the political imagination. Immigrants have long suffered from nativist resentment that found its way into federal law, but the contemporary demand for welfare reform has generated unique pressures on them. These pressures will probably result in new federal welfare or immigration laws, or even both. In light of a 1995 ABC News–Washington Post poll finding that 65 percent of U.S. citizens want spending cuts on welfare, and broad bipartisan support for welfare reform, Congress will likely ultimately adopt some changes that affect citizens and legal immigrants alike.

See also Welfare.

in the United States. The alien gives the consul these documents and the results of a medical examination. If all is in order, the applicant signs a formal application under oath.

The consul usually rules on the application the same day. The principal consular officer reviews any refusal to issue a visa, but no formal review is available after that. The Department of State has only limited authority over visa denials. The applicant has one year to overcome the objection to the visa on which a refusal was based, or the entire visa application process must be started anew. The burden of

proof is always on the applicant to establish eligibility. If the applicant passes, the CONSUL issues an immigrant visa. Under certain circumstances, immigrants unable to travel immediately may receive new visas later.

Once the immigrant actually arrives in the United States, an immigration officer again independently examines the alien's visa eligibility. This officer may exclude the alien in spite of the visa. In that case, the alien may be temporarily detained, either aboard the vessel of arrival or in the United States pending a ruling. If the officer finds the visa in order and admits the alien, the visa is retained by the INS as a permanent record of admission. The alien is then issued a form I-151, commonly known as a GREEN CARD (even though its color is now off-white), and becomes a permanent-resident alien. Although it is most often thought of as an employment permit, the green card was originally designed to serve as evidence of the alien's status as a permanent resident of the United States.

Rights of Aliens Aliens enjoy many of the rights accorded to citizens. They can claim general protections under the Constitution and the Bill of Rights. On the other hand, aliens cannot vote or hold federal elective office—rights belonging solely to citizens. Further legal rights depend on an alien's status: use of the courts, ownership of land, an education, and federal welfare benefits are each to a varying degree restricted to lawful resident aliens. Similarly, the liability of an alien to pay taxes depends on resident or nonresident status. Resident aliens pay taxes in much the same way that citizens do; nonresident aliens may qualify for special exemptions. Aliens can also be required to obtain a so-called exit permit to ensure that all taxes owed are paid before leaving the country.

In addition to following laws generally, aliens also have special duties. Some visas impose additional requirements such as notifying the INS of changes of address and refraining from engaging in paid employment. Criminal penalties apply to some misconduct of aliens and citizens who abet them, including MISREPRESENTATION or FRAUD in obtaining immigration status, unlawful entry, and transporting or concealing an undocumented alien. For aliens who violate the law, the penalty is commonly DEPORTATION. Citizens who bring aliens into the country illegally may face a fine, imprisonment for up to five years, or both, for each alien they have illegally transported.

Although the Supreme Court has held that Congress alone makes immigration law, historically, states have placed harsh restrictions on aliens. In 1886, the Supreme Court struck down a San Francisco ordinance effectively banning Chinese laundries, in the landmark case *Yick Wo v. Hopkins*, 118 U.S. 356, 6 S. Ct. 1064, 30 L. Ed. 220. *Yick Wo* established that the Fourteenth Amendment's Equal Protection Clause applied to aliens. But states simply ignored it, and for decades, the Supreme Court found numerous ways to uphold discriminatory restrictions.

In state cases, the modern turning point came in 1971, and it was brief. In *Graham v. Richardson*, 403 U.S. 365, 91 S. Ct. 1848, 29 L. Ed. 2d 534, the Supreme Court held that aliens could not be denied state welfare benefits. Most important, the *Graham* decision struck a blow against state discrimination in general: it said that EQUAL PROTECTION cases involving aliens would be subject to the same "STRICT SCRUTINY" applied in racial discrimination cases. In a series of decisions that followed, the Court removed numerous state barriers—laws that barred all aliens from competitive civil service employment, engineering licenses, and licenses to practice law. Nonetheless, through the late 1970s and 1980s, it backed away from the strict scrutiny standard: it upheld New York's limitations on the certification of alien public school teachers (*Ambach v. Norwick*, 441 U.S. 68, 99 S. Ct. 1589, 60 L. Ed. 2d 49 [1979]), for example, and California's restriction of peace officer jobs to citizens (*Cabell v. Chavez-Salido*, 454 U.S. 432, 102 S. Ct. 735, 70 L. Ed. 2d 225 [1982]). One key exception was *Plyler v. Doe*, 457 U.S. 202, 102 S. Ct. 2382, 72 L. Ed. 2d 786 (1982), granting the children of undocumented aliens the right to attend public schools.

Naturalization and Citizenship Resident aliens become citizens through naturalization. To apply for naturalization, most aliens must meet several requirements. They must (1) reside continuously in the United States for five years as lawfully admitted permanent residents; (2) be physically present in the United States for at least half of the time before filing the petition for naturalization; and (3) reside for at least three months within the district in which the petition is filed. Aliens must generally be at least eighteen years of age, although parents who are citizens can file on behalf of younger children. Literacy and educational standards must be met: unless physically unable to do so, aliens must be able to speak, understand, read, and write simple English. They have to show "good moral character"—an ambiguous term that includes not being a drunkard, gambler, or convict jailed for 180 days or more. They must exhibit an attachment to constitutional principles, essentially proved through a belief in representative democracy, the Bill of Rights, and political processes.

To ascertain an applicant's fitness for naturalization, a naturalization examiner conducts an informal hearing. The examiner questions the applicant and witnesses who can testify on her or his behalf, and then renders a decision. If denied, the applicant may reapply with legal representation; in some cases, federal district courts may determine naturalization or remand the matter to the INS with instructions. Finally, if approved, the applicant is granted citizenship at a hearing in open court after taking an oath of allegiance to the United States.

Deportation Deportation is the expulsion of an alien from the United States. In theory, it is a civil proceeding rather than a punishment, though those who are deported may certainly see it as a punishment. It is designed to remove undesirables as defined under the INA. As in most aspects of immigration law, the Supreme

Nearly ten thousand new U.S. citizens were sworn in during this ceremony at Florida's Orange Bowl stadium.

Court has left total authority over deportation to Congress. Merely allowing aliens to enter the country "is a matter of permission and tolerance," the Court has said, leaving the government free rein "to terminate hospitality" (*Harisiades v. Shaughnessy*, 343 U.S. 580, 72 S. Ct. 512, 96 L. Ed. 586 [1952]). Deportation provisions apply to all aliens whether they have legally or illegally entered the country, with several specific exceptions ranging from ambassadors to employees of international organiza-

tions such as the United Nations. Citizens cannot be deported, but denaturalization proceedings can be brought against a naturalized citizen and can then lead to deportation.

Five major broad categories of grounds for deportation cover (1) being excludable at the time of entry or adjustment of status; (2) committing criminal offenses; (3) failing to register and falsifying documents; (4) posing a security risk and related grounds; and (5) becoming a public charge of the state. Many more grounds for deportation follow from these; the first category alone establishes nine classes of aliens excludable at the time of entry. Since the Technical Amendments Act of 1991, these grounds have expanded with the addition of attempting or conspiring to commit a crime. Deportation is far-reaching in additional ways: frequently, the INS applies the statutes retroactively, so that aliens may be deported for conduct that was not a ground for deportation at the time they committed the act. Many of the provisions also depend on when the alien entered the United States, and still others make aliens deportable for acts they committed prior to entry.

The mechanism of deportation involves broad official powers. INS officers have considerable power to investigate without search warrants, arrest, and detain suspects within one hundred miles of the U.S. border. Aliens then receive a deportation hearing conducted by an immigration judge. They are entitled to legal counsel—though not at government expense—and the basic rights of DUE PROCESS, as well as the rights to examine evidence, present new evidence, and cross-examine witnesses. If the judge finds an alien deportable, various avenues of relief are available, including administrative and judicial appeals. Furthermore, several forms of discretionary relief may entitle the alien to leave voluntarily, claim suspension of deportation, apply for an adjustment of status, seek asylum as a refugee, or pursue numerous other options.

Deportation often causes the U.S. citizen children of aliens to leave the United States. These children are not technically deported, and may ultimately choose to return.

Deportation Remedies Aliens generally want to avoid DEPORTATION at all costs. Even if an immigration judge rules that an alien is deportable, the alien may still fight the deportation order. This is called seeking relief from deportation. Broadly speaking, two kinds of options exist: filing an APPEAL, and seeking "discretionary" RELIEF. Whichever method the alien chooses, time is of the essence. She or he usually must seek relief before the INS begins executing the deportation order.

Appeals from deportation rulings operate on three levels. First, the alien's attorney may file a *motion to reopen* the case, also called a motion to reconsider. It is used chiefly to present new evidence, and strict rules govern its usage. Courts frown on such MOTIONS because of the potential for unnecessarily delaying deportation, and the judge may deny the motion if the alien has previously failed to establish a sufficient case. In any event, the motion will not stop a pending deportation order. Second, aliens may go to the higher authority of the Board of Immigration Appeals (BIA). Filing a so-called *administrative appeal* with the BIA automatically delays the execution of a pending deportation order. The BIA's decision to uphold the deportation order, throw it out, or send the case back to the immigration judge is final. Within six months, however, the alien may appeal a decision of the BIA to a federal court for *judicial review*. Courts may hear the case if there have been violations of the alien's constitutional rights.

As the name implies, discretionary relief is granted at the discretion of a judge. If granted, it will eliminate or postpone the execution of a deportation order. Generally, the alien must apply for discretionary relief during the deportation hearing, although some forms of relief may be sought before the hearing begins. In a two-part process, the judge first determines whether the alien is eligible under statutory requirements, and then at the judge's discretion decides whether to grant it. Mere eligibility is not a guarantee of relief.

Several forms of discretionary relief exist. One very popular form is *voluntary departure*, which permits the alien to leave the United States under his or her own power, seek a destination, and even return to the selected country immediately, thus avoiding the stigma and penalties of deportation. *Suspension of deportation* helps the alien who has been in the United States for a long period of time and for whom deportation would result in harsh consequences. Qualifying for suspension relief is difficult: the alien must have been continuously present in the United States for seven to ten years, depending on the nature of the conduct that rendered the alien deportable—for example, overstaying a VISA versus committing a FELONY; must have been a person of good moral character during that time; and must demonstrate that he or she or the alien's U.S. citizen spouse, parent, or child would suffer extreme hardship (under the seven-year rule) or exceptional and extremely unusual hardship (under the ten-year rule) if the alien were deported. Another form of relief, *adjustment of status*, is available to an alien whose status would otherwise let him or her remain in the United States: if an alien is admissible for permanent residence, he or she may seek this relief to avoid having to go abroad while an immigrant visa is processed.

Asylum, available only to aliens who qualify as refugees, differs from other forms of discretionary relief. First, it does not guarantee an alien permanent residence but merely grants the right to reside and work in the United States temporarily, for as long as the alien is entitled to REFUGEE status. Under the INA, a refugee is an alien unwilling or unable to return to her or his nation because of a well-founded fear of persecution on the ground of race, religion, nationality, membership in a particular social group, or political opinion, or an alien whose nationality has been given refugee status by the president of the United States. Asylum may be sought at any time during a deportation or exclusion hearing and can sometimes lead within one year to the granting of permanent residence.

Closely related to asylum is *withholding of deportation*. Although the grounds for withholding are similar to those for asylum, this form of relief may only be sought during a deportation hearing, and its duration is always temporary. Aliens granted asylum or withholding of deportation may qualify for adjustment of status and thereby become lawful permanent residents or citizens.

Finally, a few kinds of discretionary relief are used in exceptional circumstances. A *stay of deportation* is a temporary hold on a deportation order, commonly used in connection with a motion to reopen a case or pending an application for permanent residence. *Registry*, available only to aliens who entered the United States before January 1, 1972, is used to create a lawful record of admission when no record is available. Further relief includes *deferred action status*, a nonstatutory guideline contained within INS instructions to district directors; it amounts to an indefinite hold on any deportation action based on sympathetic factors. Rarely used is *estoppel*, in which courts stop deportation orders because of government misconduct.

CROSS-REFERENCES

Citizens; Immigration.

ALIMONY Payment that a family court may order one person in a couple to make to the other person when that couple separates or divorces.

The purpose of alimony is to avoid any unfair economic consequences of a divorce, even after property is divided and child support, if any, is awarded. Courts set few specific guidelines to attaining this broad goal: instead of telling judges how and when to award alimony, most courts simply grant them broad discretion to decide what is fair in each case. Consider this scenario:

A couple who married in 1985 agree in 1995 to divorce. The husband now earns $63,000 a year, after seven years at a large company where the top pay for his specialty is $80,000. When they married, he was in graduate school and the wife was earning $22,000. The wife worked for three more years, supporting the husband while he completed his coursework and graduated.

When their first child was born, they agreed that the wife would care for the child at home. At the time of divorce, the wife had been working full-time for one year since the couple's children, ages seven and six, had entered school. She was earning $23,000 a year and would have custody of the children.

A judge in this case would certainly award child support and would probably divide marital property equally between the couple. But it might not seem fair to the judge to allow the husband to leave the marriage with the sole possession of the couple's most valuable asset—his earning potential—when the wife contributed to his education by supporting him.

Unlike the family's home or station wagon, the husband's earning power has not yet reached its full value, but promises to grow. It seems especially unfair for the wife not to receive a share of it since after helping the husband attain his education, she agreed to forfeit her earning power to invest time in the family. The several years she spent out of the workforce continue to handicap her earnings. Alimony is the only means available to the court to avoid a potentially unjust division of assets.

The judge in this case may award alimony, or may award a token amount—such as $1 a year—so that the wife has the option to request an increase later on (modifying an award is easier than winning one after the divorce). Or the judge may award no alimony; judges are not required to award alimony.

The husband and wife in this example are unlikely to find a single solution they both consider equitable. In trying to reach an order

that is fair, judges must balance spouses' contributions and decisions during the marriage with their needs after the divorce. Although the result may not match both spouses' ideas of what is fair, one of alimony's biggest virtues is its flexibility: it can always be changed.

Alimony can be modified or eliminated as the former spouses' needs change, if those needs are the result of decisions they made as a married unit. Awards and increases in alimony are meant to address only needs that are caused by the divorce itself, not unrelated needs. If the wife's elderly mother becomes ill and dependent on her after the divorce, for example, the wife's need increases, but the increase is unrelated to the divorce and will not increase her eligibility for alimony. However, a significant change in circumstances—such as a rise in the recipient's income or a drop in the payer's income—can cause the court to reduce or end alimony. Occasionally, courts increase alimony to keep up with inflation.

Many courts have indicated that situations such as maltreatment are not valid triggers for alimony. Courts have clarified that allegations of physical or other harm done by one spouse must be brought in a civil lawsuit, to be heard and decided by a jury. In successful cases, compensatory and punitive DAMAGES would be awarded, not alimony.

Even in less egregious cases, alimony is not awarded as a punishment, especially in states that have adopted no-fault divorce laws—that is, laws providing that neither spouse has to prove wrongdoing on the part of the other.

Gaps in earning power that favor men over women in general create another situation that many courts believe they cannot resolve using alimony. Such gaps are often the reason married couples decide that if it is appropriate for only one spouse to be the wage earner, it should be the husband. But courts do not base individual alimony awards on this trend alone, in part because an individual spouse cannot be held responsible for social injustices.

In fact, state laws specifying the gender of the paying spouse and of the receiving spouse have been ruled unconstitutional. In deciding *Orr v. Orr* (440 U.S. 268, 99 S. Ct. 1102, 59 L. Ed. 2d 306) in 1979, the U.S. Supreme Court ruled that Alabama state law, which specified that husbands may be ordered to pay support to wives, but not vice versa, violated the Equal Protection Clause of the FOURTEENTH AMENDMENT. The case arose when William Orr, who had been ordered to pay alimony, was taken to court by his ex-wife for failure to pay. Orr's defense included a motion requesting that the Alabama alimony statute be declared unconstitutional. Although Orr was not seeking alimony from his ex-wife, he argued that the award to her would decrease if his circumstances were considered in addition to hers.

The Supreme Court decision supporting Orr meant that gender could not be considered in awarding alimony (although even in the mid-1990s very few alimony awards are made in favor of men).

Modern underpinnings for alimony have little to do with gender, but this was not always so. The U.S. model of alimony is based on ecclesiastical law (guidelines of the Christian religion), dating from a time in England's history when divorce did not exist. Unhappily married couples could live separately, but the husband was still obliged to support the wife financially. This arrangement was known as a divorce A MENSA ET THORO ("from bed and board," in Latin), and was not really a termination of the marriage. This limited divorce did not allow the parties to remarry, for example, and did not affect INHERITANCE rules. The wife remained her husband's dependent, and alimony was seen as his ongoing marital obligation to her.

When full divorce became available, the idea of alimony continued, but with some important differences. Today's alimony awards are made based not on men's and women's roles, but on relative needs arising from decisions made during the marriage. Alimony is not an aspect of marriage, as it was in divorce *a mensa et thoro*, but only becomes necessary—and available— from the time of divorce.

Because the considerations that enter into a divorce award are sometimes complex, courts usually clarify the award's purpose and may place a time limit on it.

No mathematical guidelines exist to tell courts how to calculate alimony. In addition, each state legislature sets its own policy regarding whether and when alimony may be awarded.

The Uniform Marriage and Divorce Act (UMDA), which many states use as a model, recommends that courts consider the following factors:

The financial condition of the person requesting alimony;

The time the recipient would need for education or job training;

The standard of living the couple had during the marriage;

The length of the marriage;

The age, physical condition, and emotional state of the person requesting alimony;

The ability of the other person to support the recipient and still support himself or herself.

Courts have at times awarded alimony when an unmarried couple separates, if the relationship closely resembled marriage or in other circumstances, such as in keeping with the couple's intentions and verbal agreements. Awards of this type are informally called palimony. Private separation agreements negotiated between a divorcing couple also can contain alimony provisions. For these reasons, it is difficult to estimate accurately the size and frequency of awards through the most common method, U.S. census data.

The divorce case of Donald and Ivana Trump, one of the richest couples in the United States, raised questions of how much alimony Trump would pay his former wife.

If awards are hard to estimate, compliance with awards is nearly impossible to gauge. Alimony enforcement is unlike child support enforcement, which has the "teeth" of wage GARNISHMENT, LIENS, and other mechanisms. Returning to court with contempt-of-court charges is usually the only option a would-be recipient has to enforce an existing alimony order.

If the divorce decree does not specify an ending date, an order to pay alimony usually remains effective until the court that awarded it changes or ends it. Alimony usually ends when the recipient remarries; this is known as terminable alimony. In the case of the recipient's remarriage, the payer sometimes must return to court to have the court change the alimony order, but often the termination is automatic.

The payer's death is not necessarily enough to end payments: some orders allow the recipient to inherit funds from the payer's estate, or require the payer to maintain a life INSURANCE policy that will continue to support the recipient after the payer's death. These provisions, when made, often involve a recipient whose age or health makes it too difficult for the recipient to enter or reenter the workforce.

CROSS-REFERENCES

Child Support; Divorce; Family Law; Husband and Wife; Marriage; Sex Discrimination.

ALLEGATION  The assertion, claim, declaration, or statement of a party to an action, setting out what he or she expects to prove.

If the allegations in a plaintiff's COMPLAINT are insufficient to establish that the person's legal rights have been violated, the defendant can make a motion to the court to dismiss the complaint for failure to state a CAUSE OF ACTION. If the allegations in the defendant's answer do not contradict the allegations in the complaint, the plaintiff can make a motion for SUMMARY JUDGMENT.

ALLEGE To state, recite, assert, or charge the existence of particular facts in a PLEADING or an INDICTMENT; to make an allegation.

ALLEGIANCE In English law, the duty of loyalty and obedience owed by all persons born within the king's realm that attaches immediately upon their birth and that they cannot be relieved of by their own actions.

In U.S. law, the obligation of fidelity and obedience that is owed by native born and naturalized American CITIZENS to the United States that cannot be relinquished without the consent of the government expressed by a statutory enactment.

ALL FOURS Identical; similar.

All fours specifically refers to two cases or decisions that have similar fact patterns and raise identical legal issues. Since the circumstances leading to their individual determinations are virtually the same, the decision rendered by the court in each case will be similar. Such cases or decisions are said to be on *all fours* with each other.

ALLOCATION The apportionment or designation of an item for a specific purpose or to a particular place.

In the law of TRUSTS, the allocation of cash DIVIDENDS earned by a STOCK that makes up the principal of a trust for a beneficiary usually means that the dividends will be treated as income to be paid to the beneficiary. The allocation of stock dividends generally means that such dividends will be added to the shares of stock held as principal, thereby increasing its size.

ALLOCUTION The formal inquiry by a judge of an accused person, CONVICTED of a crime, as to whether the person has any legal cause to show why JUDGMENT should not be pronounced against him or her or as to whether the person has anything to say to the court before being SENTENCED.

ALLODIAL Free; not subject to the rights of any lord or superior; owned without obligation of vassalage or fealty; the opposite of feudal.

After these naturalized citizens have been sworn in, they will pledge allegience to the United States.

UPI/BETTMANN NEWSPHOTOS

A description given to the outright owner-ship of land that did not impose upon its owner the performance of feudal duties. *See also* FEUDALISM.

ALLOGRAPH A writing or signature made by one person for another.

When a PRINCIPAL gives his or her AGENT the power to pay creditors, the checks written by the agent are allographs for the principal.

An autograph is the opposite of an allograph.

ALLONGE Additional paper firmly attached to COMMERCIAL PAPER, such as a PROMISSORY NOTE, to provide room to write endorsements.

An allonge is necessary when there is insufficient space on the document itself for the endorsements. It is considered part of the commercial paper as long as the allonge remains affixed thereto.

ALLOTMENT A portion, share, or division. The proportionate distribution of shares of STOCK in a corporation. The partition and distribution of land.

ALLRED, GLORIA Gloria Allred, born July 3, 1941, in Philadelphia, is a flamboyant, widely recognized lawyer, feminist, activist, and radio talk show host. Though her critics dismiss her as a publicity monger and a dilettante, Allred has received praise from others who believe that she is a master at using the power of the news media to draw attention to the day-to-day struggles of ordinary people.

Born Gloria Rachel Bloom, Allred grew up in Philadelphia with her parents, Morris Bloom, a door-to-door salesman, and Stella Davidson Bloom, a homemaker. Her conventional middle-class childhood gave no hint of the outspoken activist to come. Allred graduated with honors from the University of Pennsylvania in 1963 with a bachelor's degree in English. She moved to New York to pursue a master's degree in teaching at New York University. While there, she became interested in the CIVIL RIGHTS MOVEMENT, which was beginning to gain momentum. After earning her master's degree in 1966, she returned to Phila-

delphia to teach at a high school with a predominantly black enrollment.

Allred says her interest in the struggle for equal rights arose from personal experiences. While she was in college, she married, gave birth to a daughter, and divorced. Unable to collect CHILD SUPPORT from her former husband, she was forced to return to her parents' home. She also recalls being paid less than a man for what she considered equal work. The reason given was that the man had a family to support, but at the time, Allred was the single mother of an infant. Perhaps the experience that most galvanized her commitment to equal rights was being raped and then having to undergo an ABORTION at a time when the operation could not legally be performed by a doctor. She nearly died after the operation. According to Allred, the experience made her realize the need for safe and legal abortions and precipitated her lifelong commitment to the fight for reproductive freedom.

Allred moved to Los Angeles and married her second husband, Raymond Allred, in 1968. They were divorced in 1987. She taught in the turbulent Watts section of Los Angeles and became the first full-time female staff member in United Teachers of Los Angeles, the union representing Los Angeles's teachers. The experience stirred her interest in CIVIL RIGHTS and collective bargaining and prompted her to go to law school. She received her law degree, with honors, from Loyola Marymount University, Los Angeles, Law School in 1974. Soon after, she entered a law firm partnership with her classmates Nathan Goldberg and Michael Maroko. Allred, Maroko, Goldberg and Ribakoff grew during the 1970s and 1980s into a thirteen-lawyer firm with annual revenues exceeding $2.5 million. The firm's caseload ranges from family and constitutional law to business litigation and personal injury suits.

Allred is perhaps the most flamboyant and well known member of her firm. She has achieved notoriety and name recognition through staged press conferences and demon-

BIOGRAPHY

Gloria Allred

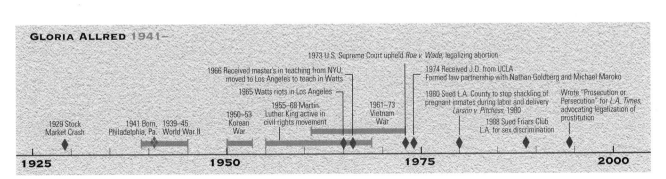

strations publicizing and dramatizing the cause she is championing at the time. She also accepts controversial cases that naturally attract media attention. During her years in practice, she has successfully sued Los Angeles County to stop the practice of shackling and chaining pregnant inmates during labor and delivery; put a halt on the city of El Segundo's quizzing job applicants about their sexual histories (*Thorne v. City of El Segundo*, 802 F.2d 1131 [9th Cir. 1986]); represented a client who was turned down for a job as a police officer after a six-hour lie detector exam that included questions about her sex life; and sued a dry cleaning establishment for discrimination because it charged more to launder women's shirts than men's. She also successfully sued on behalf of two lesbians who had been denied entrance to the "romance booth" at a Los Angeles restaurant (*Rolon v. Kulwitsky*, 153 Cal. App. 3d 289, 200 Cal. Rptr. 217 [Cal. App. 2 Dist. 1984]). The owner of the restaurant vowed to close the booth if Allred's clients won. They did, and he made good on his promise.

Allred relishes confrontation, and her showy tactics have earned her both praise and criticism. Defending what many have called self-promoting publicity stunts, Allred says she is aware of the impression she makes, and contends that it is exactly the effect she wants. She tries to use the few moments she is in the spotlight to make her point as forcefully as possible. Her detractors say that she wastes her time and energy on trivial issues that do not advance any worthwhile cause and deflect attention away from serious issues. Yet, she points out, she is often stopped on the street by people who recognize her and want to thank her for taking on the small fights that no one else wants. Allred contends that what she is really doing is tackling issues that are symbolic of the day-to-day struggles people face. It is her way of educating the public and the legal establishment to move beyond stereotypes.

Asked whether she is an activist or a lawyer, Allred replied that she is an "activist lawyer." She added that she believes in seeking change and winning rights through the legal process, but that she does not shrink from utilizing the political process when legal remedies prove inadequate. She once held a press conference in the office of Governor Jerry Brown, of California, to cast media attention on his threat to veto a bill authorizing payroll deductions for child support payments. When the news media arrived, Allred and a group of women and children had hung diapers across the governor's office. Brown reversed his position and signed the bill. In another case that drew media atten-

"THERE ARE ENOUGH HIGH HURDLES TO CLIMB, AS ONE TRAVELS THROUGH LIFE, WITHOUT HAVING TO SCALE ARTIFICIAL BARRIERS CREATED BY LAW OR SILLY REGULATIONS."

tion, she held a press conference at the door of the all-male Friars Club, of New York, to dramatize her lawsuit challenging the club's policy of not allowing women members and not allowing women to enter, even as guests, before 4:00 P.M. She won her suit on the grounds that the club did not meet the "substantially private" requirement under New York law that would have allowed it to legally exclude women. Possibly her most famous politically motivated demonstration was presenting California state senator John Schmitz (R-Corona del Mar) with a chastity belt at a hearing on a bill to limit abortion and birth control. Schmitz retaliated in a press release in which he called Allred "a slick butch lawyeress." Allred sued for LIBEL and won a damage award and an apology.

Allred has earned a reputation as a champion of those who have been sexually victimized. She represented a woman who won a $5 million civil suit against an accused rapist the district attorney declined to prosecute; represented a boy who claimed to have been sexually abused by a famous rock singer (although she abruptly and without explanation withdrew from the case before it was settled); and tackled the thorny issue of clergy sexual abuse. She says she wants the public to know that even if the criminal justice system fails them, they are entitled to file a civil suit.

Allred is an ardent feminist who believes that all attorneys and all judges should be feminists, because she feels anyone who is not a feminist is a bigot. Some critics say she is all show and no substance. She has been compared to legal showmen such as Melvin M. Belli ("the King of Torts") and Marvin Mitchelson, who gained notoriety through a series of celebrity palimony suits. However, even Mitchelson, not one to shrink from publicity himself, describes her style as rough. But Allred has many supporters as well. Among them is Justice Joan Dempsey Klein, of the California Court of Appeal, who credits Allred with moving women's issues forward. Klein also points out that Allred saves her dramatics for outside the courtroom and always observes proper decorum when before the bench. According to Klein, Allred is always well-prepared and, for that reason, is quite successful.

In 1994, Allred wrote an editorial for the December 6 issue of the *Los Angeles Times*, titled "Prosecution or Persecution," in which she asserted that laws prohibiting PROSTITUTION are sexist and victimize women. She advocated legalization and regulation of the sex trade in order to reduce sexually transmitted diseases and drug abuse. According to Allred, "Unprotected, uninsured sex workers are the real victims who deserve legal status and an end to government-funded harassment."

Dressed in her trademark reds and electric blues, her striking black hair set off by deep red lipstick, Allred is a potent combination of scholarship and theatrics. Her keen intelligence and shrewd understanding of the power of the media have made her a contemporary success story in the world of law and politics. Though her antics do not appeal to everyone, they do seem to have the result she desires. As the world becomes more complex and moves at a faster pace, as people depend more on sound bites for news and opinions, Allred may become a role model for the new breed of "performance lawyers."

ALLUVION See TERRITORY.

ALTERATION 📖 Modification; changing a thing without obliterating it. 📖

An alteration is a variation made in the language or terms of a legal document that affects the rights and obligations of the parties to it. When this occurs, the alteration is MATERIAL and the party who did not consent to the change can be released from his or her duties under the document by a court.

When an essential part of a writing has been cut, torn, burned, or erased, the alteration is also known as a MUTILATION.

The alteration of a document by someone other than a party to it is called a SPOLIATION.

ALTERATION OF INSTRUMENTS 📖 A change in the meaning or language of a legal document, such as a contract, deed, lease, or commercial paper, that is made by one party to the document without the consent of the other after it has been signed or completed. 📖

If such a change is made by a third party without the consent of either party to the instrument, it is called a SPOLIATION or MUTILATION.

Method The face of an instrument is changed by its alteration. A difference in handwriting, a change in words or figures, an erasure, and the striking out of particular words are some methods used to alter an instrument. Since there must be a change in the meaning or language of a document, retracing an original writing—as when a figure written in pencil is retraced in ink—is not an alteration.

Material Changes The alteration of an instrument materially changes it. The document no longer reflects the terms that the parties originally intended to serve as the basis of their legal obligation to each other. To be MATERIAL, the change must affect an important part of the instrument and the rights of the

parties to it. Any material alteration relieves the nonconsenting party of any obligation to perform according to the terms of the instrument. If the altered instrument is a CONTRACT, then the original contract is void. The nonconsenting party cannot be legally obligated by the new contract since he or she never agreed to it. A document that has been materially altered does not regain its original validity if it is restored to its original form by erasing or deleting unauthorized words.

The date of an instrument is often considered a material provision when it establishes the time within which the parties to a document must perform their obligations under it. An unauthorized change of date that shortens the time of payment or extends the time of performance so that more interest will become due is a material alteration.

An alteration of a signature that changes the legal effect of an instrument is material. Erasing words that show that the signer is acting as an AGENT, for example, changes the signer's liability under the instrument and, therefore, is a material alteration. However, when a signature that was improperly placed on a document is erased, there is no material alteration since the legal meaning of the document is not changed.

Any change in the terms of the instrument that affects the obligations of the parties is material. In a contract to sell land on commission, a change in the rate of commission is material. A change in a description in a DEED so that it transfers a smaller piece of land, a change in the name of a purchaser in a sales contract, or an alteration in the terms of financing set forth in a MORTGAGE is also material.

Time of Alteration A modification in a document before its completion is not an alteration. The parties are bound to review the document and to have agreed upon its terms before executing it. In order for an alteration to nullify the legal effect of an instrument, the change must be made after its completion.

Intention A material change must be intentionally made. The motive behind the alteration is unimportant. If a mistake or accident causes a change, this is not considered a material alteration, but the document may be reformed or rescinded.

The Person Making the Change The change to the instrument must be made by a party or someone authorized by him or her to do so. No change made by a third person without the consent of either party to the document will invalidate it if its original terms can be learned. When a material alteration is made by a party to COMMERCIAL PAPER, such as a

CHECK or PROMISSORY NOTE, the paper will be enforced as originally written against the party who made the changes.

Consensual Alteration A change in an instrument made with the consent of the parties is binding upon them. Such CONSENSUAL ALTERATION is usually evidenced by the signing by each party of his or her initials and the date that the agreement to the changes to the instrument was reached.

ALTER EGO 📖 A doctrine used by the courts to ignore the corporate status of a group of stockholders, officers, and directors of a CORPORATION in reference to their limited LIABILITY in order to hold them personally liable for their actions when they have acted fraudulently or unjustly, or when to refuse to do so will deprive an innocent victim of redress for an injury caused by them. 📖

A corporation is considered the alter ego of its stockholders, directors, or officers when it is used merely for the transaction of their personal business for which they want IMMUNITY from individual liability. A parent corporation is the alter ego of a SUBSIDIARY corporation if it controls and directs its activities so that it will have limited liability for its wrongful acts.

The alter ego doctrine is also known as the instrumentality rule because the corporation becomes an instrument for the personal advantage of its parent corporation, stockholders, directors, or officers. When a court applies it, the court is said to pierce the corporate veil.

ALTERNATIVE DISPUTE RESOLUTION
📖 Procedures for settling disputes by means other than LITIGATION; e.g., by ARBITRATION, MEDIATION, or minitrials. Such procedures, which are usually less costly and more expeditious than litigation, are increasingly being used in commercial and labor disputes, divorce actions, in resolving motor vehicle and medical malpractice tort claims, and in other disputes that would likely otherwise involve court litigation. 📖

In the late 1980s and early 1990s, many people became increasingly concerned that the United States' traditional method of resolving legal disputes, through conventional litigation, had become too expensive, too slow, and too cumbersome for many civil lawsuits (cases between private parties). This concern has led to the growing use of ways other than litigation to resolve disputes. These other methods are commonly known as alternative dispute resolution (ADR).

ADR techniques are being used more and more, as parties and lawyers and courts realize that these techniques can often help them resolve legal disputes faster and cheaper and more privately than can conventional litigation. Moreover, many people prefer ADR approaches because they see these methods as being more creative and more focused on problem solving than litigation, which has always been based on an adversarial model.

The term *alternative dispute resolution* is somewhat of a misnomer. In reality, fewer than five percent of all lawsuits filed go to trial; the other 95 percent are settled or otherwise concluded before trial. Thus, it is more accurate to think of *litigation* as the alternative and ADR as the norm. Despite this, the term *alternative dispute resolution* has become such a well-accepted shorthand for the vast array of nonlitigation processes that its continued use seems assured.

Although certain ADR techniques are well established and frequently used—for example, mediation and arbitration—alternative dispute resolution has no fixed definition. The term *alternative dispute resolution* includes a wide range of processes, many with little in common except that each is an alternative to full-blown litigation. Litigants, lawyers, and judges are constantly adapting existing ADR processes, or devising new ones, to meet the unique needs of their legal disputes. The definition of alternative dispute resolution is constantly expanding to include new techniques.

The directors of a large corporation must consider that the parent company can be the alter ego of a subsidiary corporation in terms of liability.

© TONY FREEMAN/PHOTOEDIT

Sixty State Street
THE SHERATON CORPORATION
WORLD HEADQUARTERS

ADR techniques have not been created to undercut the traditional U.S. court system. Certainly, ADR options can be used in cases where litigation is not the most appropriate route. However, they can also be used in conjunction with litigation when the parties want to explore other options but also want to remain free to return to the traditional court process at any point.

Of the many ways to resolve a legal dispute other than formal litigation, mediation, arbitration, mediation-arbitration, minitrial, early neutral evaluation, and summary jury trial are the most common.

Mediation Mediation—also known as conciliation—is the fastest growing ADR method. Unlike litigation, mediation provides a forum in which parties can resolve their own disputes, with the help of a neutral third party.

Mediation depends upon the commitment of the disputants to solve their own problems. The mediator, also known as a facilitator, never imposes a decision upon the parties. Rather, the mediator's job is to keep the parties talking and to help move them through the more difficult points of contention. To do this, the mediator typically takes the parties through five stages.

First, the mediator gets the parties to agree on procedural matters, such as by stating that they are participating in the mediation voluntarily, setting the time and place for future sessions, and executing a formal confidentiality agreement. One valuable aspect of this stage is that the parties, which often have been unable to agree on anything, begin a pattern of saying yes.

Second, the parties exchange initial positions, not by way of lecturing the mediator but in a face-to-face exchange with each other. Often, this is the first time each party hears the other's complete and uninterrupted version of its position. The parties may begin to see that the story has two sides and that it may not be so unreasonable to compromise their initial positions.

Third, if the parties have agreed to what is called a caucusing procedure, the mediator meets with each side separately in a series of confidential, private meetings and begins exploring settlement alternatives, perhaps by engaging the parties in some "reality testing" of their initial proposals. This process, sometimes called shuttle diplomacy, often uncovers areas of flexibility that the parties could not see, or would have been uncomfortable putting forward officially.

Fourth, when the gap between the parties begins to close, the mediator may carry offers and counteroffers back and forth between them, or the parties may elect to return to a joint session to exchange their offers.

Finally, when the parties agree upon the broad terms of a settlement, they formally reaffirm their understanding of that settlement, complete the final details, and sign a settlement agreement.

Mediation permits the parties to design and retain control of the process at all times and, ideally, eventually strike their own bargain. Evidence suggests that parties are more willing to comply with their own agreements, achieved through mediation, than with adjudicated decisions, imposed upon them by an outside party such as a judge.

An additional advantage is that when the parties reach agreement in mediation, the dispute is over—they face no appeals, delays, continuing expenses, or unknown risks. The parties can begin to move forward again. Unlike litigation, which focuses on the past, mediation looks to the future. Thus, a mediated agreement is particularly valuable to parties that have an ongoing relationship, such as a commercial or employment relationship.

Arbitration Arbitration more closely resembles traditional litigation in that a neutral third party hears the disputants' arguments and imposes a final and binding decision that is enforceable by the courts. The difference is that in arbitration, the disputants generally agreed to the procedure before the dispute arose; the disputants mutually decide who will hear their case; and the proceedings are typically less formal than in a court of law. One extremely important difference is that, unlike court decisions, arbitration offers almost no effective AP-PEAL process. Thus, when an arbitration decision is issued, the case is ended.

Final and binding arbitration has long been utilized in labor-management disputes. For decades, unions and employers have found it mutually advantageous to have a knowledgeable arbitrator—whom they themselves have chosen—resolve their disputes in this cheaper and faster fashion. One primary advantage for both sides has been that taking disputes to arbitration has kept everyone working by providing an alternative to strikes and lockouts, and has kept everyone out of the courts. Given this very successful track record, the commercial world has become enthusiastic about arbitration for other types of disputes as well.

Now a new form of arbitration, known as court-annexed arbitration, has emerged. Many variations of court-annexed arbitration have developed throughout the United States. One can be found in Minnesota, where, in the mid-1990s, the Hennepin County District Court adopted a program making civil cases involving less than $50,000 subject to mandatory non-binding arbitration. The results of that experimental program were so encouraging that legislation was later enacted expanding the arbitration program statewide. Now, most cases are channeled through an ADR process before they can be heard in the courts. A growing number of other federal and state courts are adopting this or similar approaches.

Mediation-Arbitration As its name suggests, mediation-arbitration, or med-arb, combines mediation and arbitration. First, a mediator tries to bring the parties closer together and help them reach their own agreement. If the parties cannot compromise, they then proceed to arbitration—before that same third party or before a different arbitrator—for a final and binding decision.

Minitrial The minitrial, a development in ADR, is finding its greatest use in resolving large-scale disputes involving complex questions of mixed law and fact, such as product liability, massive construction, and antitrust cases. In a minitrial, each party presents its case as in a regular TRIAL, but with the notable difference that the case is "tried" to the parties themselves, and the presentations are dramatically abbreviated.

In a minitrial, lawyers and experts present a condensed version of the case to top management of both parties. Often, a neutral adviser—sometimes an expert in the subject area—sits with management and conducts the hearing. After these presentations, top management representatives—by now more aware of the strengths and weaknesses of each side—try to negotiate a resolution of the problem. If they are unable to do so, they often ask for the neutral adviser's best guess as to the probable outcome of the case. They then resume negotiations.

The key to the success of this approach is the presence of both sides' top officials and the exchange of information that takes place during the minitrial. Too often, prelitigation work has insulated top management from the true strengths and weaknesses of their cases. Minitrial presentations allow them to see the dispute as it would appear to an outsider and set the stage for a cooperative settlement.

Early Neutral Evaluation An early neutral evaluation (ENE) is used when one or both parties to a dispute seek the advice of an experienced individual, usually an attorney, concerning the strength of their cases. An objective evaluation by a knowledgeable outsider can sometimes move parties away from unrealistic positions, or at least provide them with more insight into their cases' strengths and weaknesses. Of course, the success of this technique depends upon the parties' faith in the fairness and objectivity of the third-party neutral, and their willingness to compromise.

Summary Jury Trial Summary jury trials have been used primarily in the FEDERAL COURTS, where they provide parties with the opportunity to "try" their cases in an abbreviated fashion before a group of jurors, who then deliberate and render an advisory opinion.

Like an early neutral evaluation, an advisory opinion from a summary jury trial can help the parties assess the strengths and weaknesses of their cases and sometimes can facilitate the settlement of the dispute. Another advantage of the summary jury trial, as well as the minitrial, is that it can be scheduled much sooner than a trial. When early evaluations help the parties settle their cases, the parties typically avoid much of the delay, expense, and anxiety that occurs in litigation.

ALTERNATIVE RELIEF 📖 REMEDIES sought in a lawsuit in various forms or in the alternative, such as a demand for SPECIFIC PERFORMANCE of a contract or monetary DAMAGES to compensate for the failure to perform the obligation, or both. 📖

Modern rules governing PLEADING in courts now specifically permit a party to demand relief in the alternative. This eliminates the harsh consequences of the rule of common-law pleading that required a party to make one demand for one type of relief and to lose the case if a different remedy were more appropriate. Today, a party can ask for alternative forms of relief and recover what is later proved to be most appropriate at trial.

ALTERNATIVE WRIT 📖 An order, issued originally by the king in England but more recently by a court, commanding a person to do a specific thing or to appear and explain why he or she should not be compelled to do it. 📖

Under the COMMON LAW, the WRITS of PROHIBITION and MANDAMUS were alternative writs. In modern systems of court procedure, an order to SHOW CAUSE serves the same purpose. It commands a person to do something or come into court and show cause why he or she should not be made to do it.

AMBASSADOR See DIPLOMATIC AGENTS.

AMBASSADORS AND CONSULS 📖 An *ambassador* is the foreign diplomatic representative of a nation who is authorized to handle political negotiations between his or her country

Pamela Harriman served as U.S. ambassador to France from 1993 until her death in 1997.

and the country where the ambassador has been assigned. A *consul* is the commercial agent of a nation, who is empowered only to engage in business transactions, and not political matters in the country where he or she is stationed. 📖

The president with the consent of the Senate appoints ambassadors and consuls whereas the secretary of state appoints staff officers and other subordinate employees.

Powers and Duties   The powers of an ambassador are specified in his or her credentials, or documents of introduction, which the ambassador submits to the foreign government. In addition to responsibility for political negotiations, an American ambassador may initiate legal proceedings on behalf of the United States and defend suits instituted against it. A foreign ambassador in the United States has similar duties regarding his or her government.

In general, a consul is authorized to safeguard the legal rights and property interests of the citizens of his or her country and to appear in court to ascertain that the laws of the nation where he or she is assigned are administered impartially to all of the ambassador's compatriots. A U.S. citizen who has legal difficulties in a foreign country should consult the United States consul.

Consuls are also empowered and obligated to protect the ESTATES of their countrymen and -women who die within their consular districts. This duty terminates when the decedent's HEIRS are represented by an attorney.

Diplomatic Immunity   The development of harmonious international relations and protection against arrest, harassment, or other unjustified actions taken against diplomatic representatives constitute the objectives of diplomatic immunity. The Vienna Convention on Diplomatic Relations, which became effective as part of the federal law in 1972, governs diplomatic immunity by granting various degrees of immunity from civil and criminal liability to the members of diplomatic missions.

Diplomatic Agents   The supervisor of a mission, such as an ambassador, and members of the mission staff who possess diplomatic rank are diplomatic agents. Such an agent is immune from criminal liability in the nation in which he or she serves, but the commission of a crime may result in a recall request to the ambassador's country. His or her expulsion may ensue upon the refusal of any such request.

In addition, a diplomatic agent is immune from civil lawsuits, except for actions involving estates, when he or she is the executor, administrator, or beneficiary; actions concerning REAL PROPERTY held by the diplomatic agent for personal, not official functions; and actions relating to professional or business activities that are beyond the scope of diplomatic duties. A diplomatic agent is not required to TESTIFY as a WITNESS; and the family members living in the agent's household enjoy the same immunities.

Due to the hardship imposed on the victims of motor vehicle accidents in the United States caused by foreign diplomats who have diplomatic immunity, federal law mandates that mission members and their families insure their personal motor vehicles, boats, and airplanes. If the mission has similar vehicles registered in its name, it also must purchase liability INSURANCE. An action for DAMAGES for property loss, PERSONAL INJURIES, or WRONGFUL DEATH can be maintained directly against the diplomat's insurance company and is tried by the court, presiding without a jury.

Staff Members   The administrative and technical staffs and families and household members of the mission are completely immune from criminal liability, but are immune from civil liability only for official acts. Similar rules apply to members of the service staff employed as domestics, but their families and private servants employed by staff members are not so protected against liability.

Consuls   Consuls are not diplomatic agents and, therefore, they are usually amenable to civil lawsuits and criminal prosecution in the country where they are assigned. Federal law, however, extends immunity to consuls from all suits and proceedings in state courts. This prevents any embarrassment to foreign nations that might ensue from such proceedings.

Other Exemptions Diplomatic agents in the United States and the members of their households are generally exempt from federal, state, and municipal taxes. They are responsible, however, for indirect taxes that are part of the price of goods, taxes on property inherited from a citizen, taxes on any real property they own privately, or capital gains taxes on profits from personal investments. Diplomatic agents have no obligation to serve in the U.S. armed forces. These exemptions also apply to the administrative and technical staffs of the mission and their families. The service staff and private servants are exempt from taxes on wages received from their employment with the mission or its members.

CROSS-REFERENCES
Consuls; Diplomatic Agents; Diplomatic Immunity; International Law; State Department.

AMBIGUITY ◻ Uncertainty or doubtfulness of the meaning of language. ◻

When language is capable of being understood in more than one way by a reasonable person, ambiguity exists. It is not the use of peculiar words or of common words used in a peculiar sense. Words are ambiguous when their significance is unclear to persons with competent knowledge and skill to understand them.

There are two categories of ambiguity: LATENT and PATENT. Latent ambiguity exists when the language used is clear and intelligible so that it suggests one meaning but some extrinsic fact or evidence creates a need for INTERPRETATION or a choice among two or more possible meanings. In a classic case, *Raffles v. Wichelhaus*, 159 Eng. Rep. 375 (Ex. 1864), a contract was made to sell 125 bales of cotton that were to arrive on a ship called Peerless that sailed from Bombay, India. Unknown to the parties to the contract, two ships of the same name were to arrive from the same port during different months of the same year. This extraneous fact necessitated the interpretation of an otherwise clear and definite term of the contract. In such cases, EXTRINSIC or PAROL EVIDENCE may be admitted to explain what was meant or to identify the property referred to in the writing.

A patent ambiguity is one that appears on the face of a document or writing because uncertain or obscure language has been used.

In the law of CONTRACTS, ambiguity means more than that the language has more than one meaning upon which reasonable persons could differ. It means that after a court has applied rules of interpretation, such as the PLAIN MEANING, COURSE OF DEALING, COURSE OF PERFORMANCE, or TRADE USAGE rules to the unclear terms, the court still cannot say with certainty what meaning was intended by the parties to the contract. When this occurs, the court will admit as evidence extraneous proof of prior or contemporaneous agreements to determine the meaning of the ambiguous language. Parol evidence may be used to explain the meaning of a writing as long as its use does not vary the terms of the writing. If there is no such evidence, the court may hear evidence of the subjective intention or understanding of the parties to clarify the ambiguity.

Sometimes, courts decide the meaning of ambiguous language on the basis of who was responsible or at fault for the ambiguity. When only one party knew or should have known of the ambiguity, the unsuspecting party's subjective knowledge of the meaning will control. If both parties knew or should have known of the uncertainty, the court will look to the subjective understanding of both. The ambiguity no longer exists if the parties agree upon its meaning. If the parties disagree and the ambiguous provisions are MATERIAL, no contract is formed because of lack of mutual assent.

Courts frequently interpret an ambiguous contract term against the interests of the party who prepared the contract and created the ambiguity. This is common in cases of ADHESION CONTRACTS and INSURANCE contracts. A drafter of a document should not benefit at the expense of an innocent party because the drafter was careless in drafting the agreement.

In constitutional law, statutes that contain ambiguous language are VOID FOR VAGUENESS. The language of such laws is considered so obscure and uncertain that a reasonable person cannot determine from a reading what the law purports to command or prohibit. This statutory ambiguity deprives a person of the notice requirement of DUE PROCESS OF LAW, and, therefore, renders the statute unconstitutional.

AMBIT ◻ A BOUNDARY line that indicates ownership of a parcel of land as opposed to other parcels; an exterior or enclosing line. The limits of a POWER or JURISDICTION. The delineation of the scope of a particular subject matter. ◻

AMBULANCE CHASER ◻ A colloquial phrase that is used derisively for a person who is hired by an ATTORNEY to seek out NEGLIGENCE cases at the scenes of accidents or in hospitals where injured parties are treated, in exchange for a percentage of the DAMAGES that will be recovered in the case.

© TONY FREEMAN/PHOTOEDIT

An auto accident may attract what is called an ambulance chaser: someone who works for an attorney to find victims of accidents who may become clients of the attorney.

Also used to describe attorneys who, upon learning of a PERSONAL INJURY that might have been caused by the negligence or the wrongful act of another, immediately contact the victim for consent to represent him or her in a lawsuit in exchange for a CONTINGENT FEE, a percentage of the judgment recovered. 📖

AMBULATORY 📖 Movable; revocable; subject to change; capable of alteration. 📖

An *ambulatory court* was the former name of the Court of KING'S BENCH in England. It would convene wherever the king who presided over it could be found, moving its location as the king moved.

An *ambulatory disposition* is a judgment, decree, or sentence that is subject to change, AMENDMENT, or REVOCATION.

A WILL is considered ambulatory because as long as the person who made it lives, it can always be changed or revoked.

AMENDMENT 📖 The modification of materials by the addition of supplemental information; the deletion of unnecessary, undesirable, or outdated information; or the correction of errors existing in the text. 📖

In practice, a change in the PLEADINGS—statements of the ALLEGATIONS of the parties in a lawsuit—may be achieved if the parties agree to the amendment or if the court in which the proceeding is pending grants a MOTION for the amendment made by one party. A JUDGMENT may be altered by an amendment if a motion to do so is made within a certain time after its

entry and granted by the court. The amendment of pleadings and judgments is regulated by state codes of CIVIL PROCEDURE and the rules of federal civil procedure.

A constitution or a statute may be changed by an amendment. See also CONSTITUTIONAL AMENDMENT.

A WILL, TRUST, corporate charter, and other legal documents are also subject to amendment.

A MENSA ET THORO 📖 *Latin, From table and bed*, but more commonly translated as "from bed and board." 📖

This phrase designates a DIVORCE which is really akin to a SEPARATION granted by a court whereby a HUSBAND AND WIFE are not legally obligated to live together, but their MARRIAGE has not been dissolved. Neither spouse has the right to remarry where there is a divorce *a mensa et thoro;* only parties who have been awarded a divorce *a vinculo matrimonii,* the more common type of divorce, can do so.

AMERICAN BAR ASSOCIATION The American Bar Association (ABA) is a nationwide organization to which qualified attorneys voluntarily belong.

The American Bar Association was founded in 1878 to improve legal education, to set requirements to be satisfied to gain admittance to the bar, and to facilitate the exchange of ideas and information among its members. Over the years, the ABA has been responsible for the further development of American jurisprudence, the establishment of formal education requirements for persons seeking to become attorneys, the formulation of ethical principles that govern the practice of law, and the creation of the American Law Institute and the Conference of Commissioners on Uniform State Laws, which advance the fair administration of justice through encouraging uniformity of statutes and judicial decisions whenever practicable. In recent years, the ABA has been prominently involved in the recommendation and selection of candidates for the federal judiciary, the accreditation of law schools, and the refinement of rules of legal and judicial ethics.

An applicant for membership in the ABA must meet certain criteria. One must be a member in good standing of the bar of a state, territory, or possession of the United States. One must have good moral character and pay the designated dues. Law students qualify to be members of the Law Student Division of the ABA if they attend an ABA-approved law school and pay the specified dues.

The ABA provides various forums through which attorneys continue their legal education during their careers. Its national institutes are held frequently in areas of law that have become topical or have undergone sweeping reform. In conjunction with the American Law Institute (ALI), the ABA holds seminars in order to continue the professional education of interested members.

Within the ABA, members may participate in the activities of numerous sections, which are organized according to specialized areas of law. Various committees exist that deal with such topics as judicial selection, professional responsibility and discipline, lawyer referral services, and the unauthorized practice of law. Other committees are concerned with topical areas, such as prepaid legal services, malpractice, legal problems of the elderly, and public-interest law.

The ABA is involved in the political process through its seven-person Governmental Affairs Office (GAO), a LOBBYING effort that serves as the "eyes, ears and voice" of the organized bar at the seat of the national government in Washington, D.C. The GAO staff is housed with about 170 other ABA staffers in the ABA's District of Columbia office. (The ABA's main offices are in Chicago, with more than 500 staff members.) The lobbying group in Washington, D.C., headed by the ABA's associate executive director, testifies on Capitol Hill more often than any other trade association. The ABA's lobbyists offer detailed information and analysis on various technical issues, such as tax or antitrust legislation. And on issues such as abortion, which many ABA members and leaders con-

sider as having an effect on the legal system, the ABA offers its voice along with those of other interested groups.

Equal access for all to the justice system has become an increasingly important theme in the ABA's mission. The association has sought for a number of years to increase and improve free legal services to needy persons by practicing lawyers. These lawyers donate some of their work *pro bono publico* ("for the good of the public"). In 1981, the ABA created the Private Bar Involvement Project, now called the Pro Bono Project, which acts as a national clearinghouse of information and resources for various pro bono programs around the United States. When it began, there were 66 organized projects nationwide; by 1995, there were more than 950.

The ABA holds annual conventions and midyear meetings to discuss designated legal topics and ABA matters. It publishes the monthly *American Bar Association Journal*, an annual directory, and various journals and newsletters reporting the work of its sections and committees. The ABA also supports the activities of affiliated organizations—such as the American Bar Foundation, which sponsors research activities in law.

The ABA also provides a social outlet for its members through which members meet to freely exchange ideas and experiences that add to the human dimension in the practice of law.

The ABA has eleven goals:

1. Promote improvement in the U.S. system of justice;
2. Promote meaningful access to legal representation and the U.S. system of justice for all persons regardless of their economic or social condition;
3. Provide ongoing leadership in improving the law to serve the changing needs of society;
4. Increase public understanding of and respect for the law, the legal process, and the role of the legal profession;
5. Achieve the highest standards of professionalism, competence, and ethical conduct;
6. Serve as the national representative of the legal profession;
7. Provide benefits, programs, and services that promote professional growth and enhance the quality of life of the members;
8. Advance the rule of law in the world;
9. Promote full and equal participation in the legal profession by members of minorities and women;
10. Preserve and enhance the ideals of the legal profession as a common calling and its

dedication to public service;

11. Preserve the independence of the legal profession and the judiciary as fundamental to a free society.

CROSS-REFERENCES

Attorney; Bar Association; Bar Examination; Ethics; Judiciary; Legal Education; Pro Bono.

AMERICAN CIVIL LIBERTIES UNION

Since 1920, the American Civil Liberties Union (ACLU) has fought energetically for the rights of individuals. The private, nonprofit organization is a multipurpose legal group with three hundred thousand members committed to the freedoms in the Bill of Rights. Although these liberties—free speech, equality, due process, and privacy—are guaranteed to each citizen, they are never completely secure. Governments and majorities can easily weaken them or even take them away. The ACLU has had enormous success fighting such cases: many of the most important Supreme Court decisions of the twentieth century have been won with its involvement, and it continues to fight thousands of lawsuits in state and federal courts each year. The ACLU also lobbies lawmakers and speaks out on a wide variety of civil liberties and civil rights issues. Its passionate devotion to these concerns makes it highly controversial.

The ACLU dates to World War I, a dark era for civil liberties. War fever gripped the United States, and official hostility toward dissent ran high. Attorney General A. Mitchell Palmer orchestrated much of this hostility from Washington, D.C., by ordering crackdowns on protesters, breaking strikes, prosecuting conscientious objectors, and deporting thousands of immigrants. One group in particular stood up to him: the American Union against Militarism (AUAM), led by social reformers and radicals. Among its founders was the pacifist Roger Baldwin, a former sociology teacher. In 1917, as the United States prepared to enter the war, Baldwin gave the group a broader mission by transforming it into the Civil Liberties Bureau, dedicated to the defense of those the government saw fit to crush and corral. Anti-Communist hysteria worsened the civil liberties picture between 1919 and 1920, and the upstart bureau had its hands full as Palmer, and his assistant, J. Edgar Hoover, staged massive police raids that netted thousands of alleged subversives at a time.

In 1920, the Civil Liberties Bureau became the ACLU. Joining Baldwin in launching the new organization were several distinguished social leaders, including the author Helen A. Keller, the attorney and future Supreme Court justice Felix Frankfurter, and the socialist clergyman Norman Thomas. The ACLU quickly joined the U.S. Congress and the American Bar Association in denouncing Attorney General Palmer for his raids—and the outcry helped end his tyrannical career. Weighing the effectiveness of public activism, Baldwin reflected, in the first annual ACLU report, "[T]he mere public assertion of the principle of freedom . . . helps win it recognition, and in the long run makes for tolerance and against resort to violence." In its weekly "Report on Civil Liberties Situation," the group watched over a torrent of abuses: a mob forcing a Farmer-Labor party delegation in Washington State to salute the U.S. flag; a Russian chemist being arrested in Illinois for distributing "inflammatory" handbills; and the lynching and burning of six black men in Florida after a black man attempted to vote.

From the beginning, strict political neutrality was the ACLU's rule. The group did not oppose political candidates, and declared itself neither liberal nor conservative. This position had an important consequence: the ACLU would defend the civil liberties of all people—including those who were weak, unpopular, and despised—without respect to their views. This principle made for strange bedfellows. As the *Boston Globe* recalled in its eulogy for Baldwin,

> [A]t one point Mr. Baldwin was engaged simultaneously in defending the rights of the Ku Klux Klan to hold meetings in Boston, despite the orders of a Catholic mayor; of Catholic teachers to teach in the schools of Akron, despite the opposition of the Ku Klux Klan; and of Communists to exhibit their film, "The Fifth Year," in Providence, despite the opposition of both the Catholics and the Ku Klux Klan.

Consequently, while carving out a unique place for the ACLU in U.S. law, these defenses also won the organization enemies.

Within a few years, the ACLU was widely known. Its first victory before the Supreme Court came in the landmark 1925 case *Gitlow v. People of New York*, 268 U.S. 652, 45 S. Ct. 625, 69 L. Ed. 1138, in which the Court threw out the defendant's conviction under New York's "criminal anarchy" statute (New York Penal Law § 160, 161, Laws 1909, C. 88; Consol. Laws 1909, C. 40), for advocating the overthrow of the U.S. government in a printed flyer. *Gitlow* established that the Fourteenth Amendment, which applies to the states, includes freedom of speech in its liberty guarantee. By 1926, the ACLU was involved in the debate over

WHOSE CIVIL LIBERTIES, ANYWAY?
THE ACLU AND ITS CRITICS

Since 1920, the American Civil Liberties Union (ACLU) has stood at the forefront of every great legal battle over personal freedom. The *C* in *ACLU* might easily stand for *Controversial*: although the ACLU's role as a major institution in U.S. law is indisputable, its effect on the law and on the lives of citizens is frequently in dispute. Political debate over the group yields very little middle ground and a great amount of passionate disagreement. Supporters agree with its self-styled epithet, "the guardian of liberty." To them, the ACLU is often all that stands between freedom and tyranny. Opponents think it is simply a liberal establishment bent on imposing its views on society. They fault its reading of the law, despise its methods, and rue its results. At the heart of this debate is a fascinating irony: how does an organization that fights for the very foundations of the nation's commitment to liberty inspire so much conflict?

Even from the start, the idea of a group devoted to defending liberty (the right of each person to be free from the despotism of governments or majorities) made some observers angry. In 1917, members of the Civil Liberties Bureau, which was soon renamed the ACLU, got this welcome from the *New York Times* editorial page: "Jails Are Waiting for Them." Although World War I was a period of government heavy-handedness, the *Times* proved to be both right and wrong. The next three-quarters of a century, the ACLU became a vastly powerful force in shaping law, and it won many more enemies

than friends. By the 1988 presidential election, candidate George Bush could make political hay in campaign speeches by attacking the ACLU as "the criminal's lobby." Other critics said the ACLU was anti-God, anti-American, antilife, and so on. In the end, no jails held ACLU members (at least for long), but no small number of people would have liked to lock them away.

The case against the ACLU is actually many cases. Every time the organization goes into court, it naturally has to displease someone; litigation is hardly about making friends. Although its mandate is abstract—freedom—it must oppose the will of very specific, very real people if it is to be carried out. Take, for example, one of the ACLU's many civil liberties battles: religious freedom. For some, religious freedom means the First Amendment's guarantee that "Congress shall make no law respecting an establishment of religion"—in other words, that people will be free from government-imposed religious worship; for many others, religious freedom implies just the opposite First Amendment assurance—that Congress shall not prohibit the free exercise of religion. In a 1962 court battle, the ACLU won a point for the former, an end to prayer in public schools, a victory that polls indicate was unwanted and unsupported by most U.S. citizens (*Engel v. Vitale*, 370 U.S. 421, 82 S. Ct. 1261, 8 L. Ed. 2d 601). Equally stymied by ACLU activism are people who want to display religious crèches on govern-

ment property at Christmastime. They have their holiday hopes dashed every time the ACLU wins a court order blocking such a display on First Amendment grounds. Each victory for the organization in such cases is another disaster in local public relations.

In response, scorn heaped on the ACLU seldom fails to question its motives. The ACLU's "yuletide work" was attacked by the conservative commentator John Leo in an essay in the *Washington Times* entitled "Crushing the Public Crèche." "While others frolic, the grinches of the ACLU tirelessly trudge out each year on yet another creche-patrol, snatching Nativity scenes from public parks and rubbing out religious symbols." Leo's point is shared by many conservatives: the government, far from remaining neutral in religious matters, is actually engaging in hostility toward religion—at the behest of ACLU "zealots." In this view, the defense of an abstract principle has taken hold of the senses of its defenders; they have become inflexible, rigid absolutists. The conservative attorney and author Bruce Fein took this complaint much further, discovering something insidious: "A partial sketch of the ACLU's vision of America reveals a contempt for individual responsibility, economic justice and prosperity and moral decency." Fein meant that the ACLU defends welfare.

Ascribing suspicious aims to the ACLU moves the debate into a more complicated area. The ACLU is not opposed simply because it has fought to block government-sanctioned religious displays, causing local upset and anger.

church-state separation. It joined the so-called Scopes Monkey Trial, arguing against a Tennessee law that forbade teaching the theory of evolution in public schools (*Scopes v. State*, 152 Tenn. 424, 278 S.W. 57 [1925]; 154 Tenn. 105 289 S.W. 363 [1927]). Besides bringing the group to national and worldwide attention, *Scopes* set it on a course from which it never veered: fighting government interference in re-

ligious matters. It staged this fight with equanimity, opposing official help and hindrance to religion, and it soon backed the Jehovah's Witnesses in a series of key Supreme Court cases. This involvement laid the groundwork for the Supreme Court's ruling, in a 1962 challenge originally brought by the ACLU, that school prayer is unconstitutional (*Engel v. Vitale*, 370 U.S. 421, 82 S. Ct. 1261, 8 L. Ed. 2d 601).

Similarly, it is not opposed merely because it defends the rights of some of society's most unpopular groups—Nazis, for example, or homosexuals. The deeper issue is civil liberties themselves. Here we have a new question: why does an organization that fights for the very foundations of the nation's commitment to liberty even have to exist?

The ACLU's answer is rather simple. Civil liberties, it argues, exist only when everyone enjoys them. In other words, there is no such thing as freedom for some without freedom for all, including those individuals whom society hates or whom the government seeks to silence. Loren Siegel, ACLU director of public education, wrote that the United States

> was founded upon not one, but two great principles. The first, democracy, is the more familiar: The majority rules. The second principle, liberty, is not as well understood. Even in our democracy, the majority's rule is not unlimited. There are certain individual rights and liberties, enshrined in the Bill of Rights, that are protected from the "tyranny of the majority." Just because there are more whites than blacks in this country does not, for example, mean that whites can vote to take the vote away from blacks. And just because there are more heterosexuals than homosexuals should not mean that the majority can discriminate with impunity against the minority.

But civil liberties "are not self-enforcing," Siegel adds. Moreover, Nadine Strossen, ACLU president, points out that victories in civil liberties need to be continually rewon. It is not the habit of enemies to grant their opponents the same constitutional rights that they themselves enjoy; plainly, it is the habit of enemies to ignore, restrict, or even crush those rights. Not by accident, the government or a majority of voters can do this; the weak and the few cannot. Thus, the ACLU's commitment is precisely to those whose purchase on freedom is slim—not because the ACLU is necessarily in favor of their cause, but because it is in favor of upholding their rights.

That argument sounds nice on paper, opponents say, but it is neither practical nor sensible at all times in real life. Indeed, they ask, what about the majority—why must it suffer to please the few in its midst who cause trouble, such as criminals? This is the point that Bush wanted to make with his famous "criminal's lobby" blast: the civil liberties of criminals should not be upheld at the expense of the civil liberties of law-abiding citizens. Bush, like other critics, turned this charge into a broader indictment of the ACLU: in his 1988 campaign for the presidency, he accused Democratic presidential candidate Michael Dukakis of being a "card-carrying member of the ACLU." The term *card-carrying* resonates in U.S. political history; it comes from the era of anti-Communist witch-hunts and implies anti-Americanism. Ira Glasser, the ACLU's executive director, indignantly replied to Bush in the *Boston Globe*, "The vice president feels it is politically expedient to beat up on us, and if the only way that he can carry it off is by engaging in McCarthyism and distorting our record, then he is willing to do it."

Despite the conservative claim that the ACLU is a liberal group, the political left also has taken shots at it. In the 1980s and 1990s, some feminists opposed the ACLU's absolute defense of free speech. They were particularly distressed by the organization's standing behind the speech rights of pornographers. Others on the left, notably academics, resent the ACLU's opposition to so-called hate-speech codes that colleges and universities have imposed on campuses to protect members of minorities from abusive expression. Such issues have caused dissent even among the ranks of the ACLU itself, leading some to argue that the organization should emphasize civil rights over civil liberties—that is, jettison its traditional mission in order to focus more specifically on the rights of women and racial minorities. In the ACLU's 1992–93 annual report, Strossen dismissed this argument. Liberty and equality, she wrote, are not mutually exclusive. "How can individual liberty be secure if some individuals are denied their rights because they belong to certain societal groups? How, on the other hand, can equality for all groups be secure if that equality does not include the exercise of individual liberty?"

Liberty rights, which are always fragile and susceptible to circumstance, have rarely enjoyed widespread support. In fact, they are generally the first casualty of any public policy dispute, as the thousands of court cases joined by the ACLU illustrate. Just how trivial these rights—hard-won in the first place, and harder won ever since—can appear to people may be seen from a 1991 American Bar Association poll. Only one-third of respondents knew what the Bill of Rights is—but more than half were willing to give up some of their freedoms to fight "the war on drugs." The ACLU exists to remind both groups—all groups—that liberty is the law, even when people do not want it to be so.

Between the 1930s and the mid-1990s, the ACLU won (as counsel) or helped to win (through amicus briefs) several Supreme Court cases that profoundly changed U.S. law and life. Among these were *Brown v. Board of Education*, 347 U.S. 483, 74 S. Ct. 686, 98 L. Ed. 873 (1954) (declaring racially segregated schools unconstitutional); *Mapp v. Ohio*, 367 U.S. 643, 81 S. Ct. 1684, 6 L. Ed. 2d 1081 (1961) (severely limiting the power of police officers and prosecutors to use illegally obtained evidence); *Griswold v. Connecticut*, 381 U.S. 479, 85 S. Ct. 1678, 14 L. Ed. 2d 510 (1965) (invalidating a state law that banned contraceptives and, for the first time, locating the concept of privacy in the Bill of Rights); *Miranda v. Arizona*, 384 U.S. 436, 86 S. Ct. 1602, 16 L. Ed. 2d 694 (1966) (requiring the police to advise suspects of their rights before interrogation); *Loving v. Virginia,* 388 U.S. 1, 87 S. Ct. 1817, 18 L. Ed. 2d 1010 (1967) (striking down the laws of Virginia and fifteen other states that made interracial marriage a criminal offense); *Brandenburg v. Ohio,* 395 U.S. 444, 89 S. Ct. 1827, 23 L. Ed. 2d 430 (1969) (invalidating state sedition laws aimed at radical groups); and *Roe v. Wade,* 410 U.S. 113, 93 S. Ct. 705, 35 L. Ed. 2d 147 (1973) (recognizing a woman's constitutional right to an abortion).

Rarely did these victories endear the ACLU to its opponents. Liberals often—though not always—applauded the effort and the result. They praised, for instance, the ACLU fight against the Customs Bureau for banning James Joyce's novel *Ulysses,* and its battle to secure publication of the Pentagon Papers during the Vietnam War. Conservatives often found the ACLU meddlesome and the results of its meddling ruinous. Southerners denounced its war on segregation, antiabortion groups blamed it for legal abortion, and Vice President George Bush even labeled it "the criminal's lobby" for its insistence on combating police illegality. At times, the organization outraged nearly everyone, as when it went to court to win the right of Nazis to march in public in Skokie, Illinois. Yet throughout its many controversies, the ACLU seldom seemed to go against its charter. Especially in the early 1990s, it did not avoid cases even when taking them on meant clashing with such traditional allies as feminists and university professors over its support of the freedom to publish pornography and opposition to campus speech codes.

The ACLU is often called the nation's foremost advocate of individual rights. With dozens of Supreme Court cases and thousands of state and federal rulings behind it, it is a firmly established force in U.S. law. Its reach goes beyond the courts. Watchful of lawmakers, it frequently issues public statements on pending national, state, and local legislation, campaigning for and against laws. It also pursues special projects on women's rights, reproductive freedom, children's rights, capital punishment, pris-

oners' rights, national security, and civil liberties. In these areas, its goal is not merely the defense of existing liberties but also their expansion into quarters where they are not generally enjoyed.

The ACLU's national headquarters is in New York City. The group maintains a legislative office in Washington, D.C., and a regional office in Atlanta, along with chapters in each state. These state chapters follow the decisions of the national executive board, yet are also free to pursue cases on their own.

CROSS-REFERENCES

Baldwin, Roger; Bill of Rights; *Brown v. Board of Education of Topeka, Kansas;* Civil Rights; *Engel v. Vitale;* Frankfurter, Felix; *Gitlow v. New York; Griswold v. Connecticut;* Palmer, Alexander Mitchell; *Roe v. Wade;* Scopes, John T.; Strossen, Nadine.

BIOGRAPHY

CULVER PICTURES

James Barr Ames

"AN IMMORTAL RIGHT TO BRING AN ETERNALLY PROHIBITED ACTION IS A METAPHYSICAL SUBTLETY THAT THE PRESENT WRITER CANNOT PRETEND TO UNDERSTAND."

AMES, JAMES BARR James Barr Ames was born June 22, 1846, in Boston. He achieved prominence as an educator and concentrated his career efforts at Harvard University.

A graduate of Harvard College in 1868, Ames earned a master of arts degree in 1871 and attended Harvard Law School in 1872. He received several doctor of laws degrees from various universities, including the University of Pennsylvania in 1899, Northwestern University in 1903, and Harvard in 1904.

In 1868, Ames began his teaching career as an instructor for a private school in Boston. Three years later he began his professional association with Harvard, acting as a tutor in French and German until 1872 and continuing as an instructor in medieval history for the next year. From 1873 to 1877 he was an associate professor of law; in 1877, he became a professor of law. From 1895 to 1910 he performed the duties of dean of the law school. In 1897, he participated in the establishment of the *Harvard Law Review.*

Ames distinguished himself as a teacher of law by utilizing the CASE METHOD introduced by legal educator and former Harvard Dean CHRISTOPHER COLUMBUS LANGDELL. Langdell's approach presented principles of law in relation to

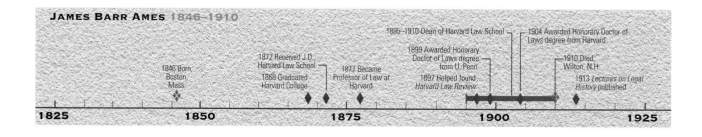

JAMES BARR AMES 1846–1910

1846 Born, Boston, Mass.

1868 Graduated Harvard College

1872 Received J.D. Harvard Law School

1877 Became Professor of Law at Harvard

1895–1910 Dean of Harvard Law School

1897 Helped found *Harvard Law Review*

1899 Awarded Honorary Doctor of Laws degree from U. Penn.

1904 Awarded Honorary Doctor of Laws degree from Harvard

1910 Died, Wilton, N.H.

1913 *Lectures on Legal History* published

1825 1850 1875 1900 1925

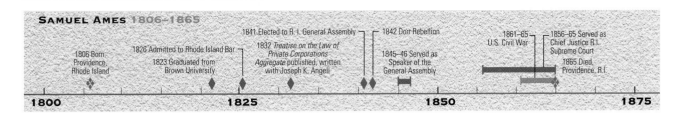

SAMUEL AMES 1806–1865

1841 Elected to R. I. General Assembly — 1842 Dorr Rebellion

1832 Treatise on the Law of
Private Corporations
Aggregate published, written
with Joseph K. Angell

1826 Admitted to Rhode Island Bar

1806 Born,
Providence,
Rhode Island

1823 Graduated from
Brown University

1845–46 Served as
Speaker of the
General Assembly

1861–65
U.S. Civil War

1856–65 Served as
Chief Justice R.I.
Supreme Court

1865 Died,
Providence, R.I.

1800   1825   1850   1875

actual cases to which they were applied. By studying the cases, a student of law was given an accurate example of the law at work.

Ames extended his talents to the field of legal literature. He is the author of *Lectures on Legal History*, which was published in 1913. He died January 8, 1910, in Wilton, New Hampshire.

See also LEGAL EDUCATION.

AMES, SAMUEL
Samuel Ames was born September 6, 1806. He graduated from Brown University in 1823 and was admitted to the Rhode Island bar in 1826.

From 1841 to 1851 Ames represented Providence in the Rhode Island general assembly. During his tenure, he was a prominent supporter of state authority in the "Dorr Rebellion." This insurrection occurred in 1842 as a protest against the limited voting rights that existed in Rhode Island. The protest resulted in a more liberal interpretation of the right to suffrage.

Beginning in 1856 Ames served as chief justice of the Rhode Island Supreme Court. In 1861, he was the representative from Rhode Island during a series of unsuccessful negotiations to effect a peace between the North and South during the Civil War. Ames died December 20, 1865, in Providence, Rhode Island.

See also DORR, THOMAS WILSON.

AMICABLE ACTION
An action commenced and maintained by the mutual consent and arrangement of the parties to obtain a judgment of a court on a doubtful QUESTION OF LAW that is based upon facts that both parties accept as being correct and complete.

The action is considered amicable because there is no dispute as to the facts but only as to the conclusions of law that a judge can reach from consideration of the facts. An amicable action is considered a JUSTICIABLE controversy because there is a real and substantive disagreement between the parties as to the appropriate relief to be granted by the court.

Other names for an amicable action are a CASE AGREED ON, a CASE STATED, or a FRIENDLY SUIT.

AMICUS CURIAE
Literally, friend of the court. A person with strong interest in or views on the subject matter of an ACTION, but not a

BIOGRAPHY

Samuel Ames

"IT IS DIFFICULT TO

DRAW AND APPLY THE

PRECISE LINE

SEPARATING THE

DIFFERENT POWERS OF

GOVERNMENT."

PARTY to the action, may petition the court for permission to file a BRIEF, ostensibly on behalf of a party but actually to suggest a rationale consistent with its own views. Such amicus curiae briefs are commonly filed in appeals concerning matters of a broad public interest; e.g., civil rights cases. They may be filed by private persons or the government. In appeals to the U.S. courts of appeals, an amicus brief may be filed only if accompanied by written consent of all parties, or by leave of court granted on motion or at the request of the court, except that consent or leave shall not be required when the brief is presented by the United States or an officer or agency thereof.

An amicus curiae educates the court on points of law that are in doubt, gathers or organizes information, or raises awareness about some aspect of the case that the court might otherwise miss. The person is usually, but not necessarily, an ATTORNEY, and is usually not paid for her or his expertise. An amicus curiae must not be a party to the case, nor an attorney in the case, but must have some knowledge or perspective that makes her or his views valuable to the court.

The most common arena for amici curiae is in cases that are under APPEAL (are being reconsidered by the court) and where issues of public interest—such as social questions or civil liberties—are being debated. Cases that have drawn participation from amici curiae are those involving civil rights (such as 1952's *Brown v. Board of Education*), capital punishment, environmental protection, gender equality, infant adoption, and affirmative action. Amici curiae have also informed the court about narrower issues, such as the competency of a juror; or the correct procedure for completing a deed or will; or evidence that a case is collusive or fictitious—that is, that the parties are not being honest with the court about their reasons for being there.

The PRIVILEGE that friends of the court are granted to express their views in a case is just that: amici curiae have no RIGHT to appear or to file briefs. Unless they represent the government, amici curiae must obtain leave (permission) to do so from the court, or consent of all parties in the case, before filing. No court is obligated to follow or even to consider the advice of an amicus curiae, even one it has invited.

The principle that guides the appropriate role of a friend of the court is that he or she should serve the court without also acting as "friend" to either of the parties. Rules of court and CASE LAW (past court decisions) have attempted to spell out the sometimes tricky specifics of how an amicus curiae should—and should not—participate in a case.

For example, Missouri's supreme court in 1969 distinguished the role of amicus curiae from the normal role of the attorney in assisting the court. In this case, the court requested the attorney who had formerly represented the parties in the case to help elicit testimony and cross-examine witnesses. The lawyer also made objections and argued objections against the city, which was defending the lawsuit over zoning. In seeking the payment of attorney fees for his services, the attorney argued that he had served as amicus curiae due to his acting at the court's request. The supreme court found that "in the orderly and intelligent presentation of the case, he rendered assistance to the court, the same as any attorney who contributes to the orderly presentation of a case. He was appearing, however, not as an adviser to the court but as a representative of private litigants . . . advancing their partisan interests . . . and is not entitled to have the fee for his admittedly valuable and competent professional services taxed as costs" (*Kansas City v. Kindle*, 446 S.W.2d 807 [Mo. 1969]).

The amicus curiae walks a fine line between providing added information and advancing the cause of one of the parties. For instance, she or he cannot raise issues that the parties themselves do not raise, since that is the task of the parties and their attorneys. If allowed by the court, amici curiae can file briefs (called *briefs amicus curiae* or *amicus briefs*), argue the case, and introduce evidence. However, they may not make most MOTIONS, file PLEADINGS, or manage the case.

Whether participating by leave or by invitation, in an appearance or with a brief amicus curiae, a friend of the court is a resource person who has limited capacity to act.

AMNESTY The action of a government by which all persons or certain groups of persons who have committed a criminal offense—usually of a political nature that threatens the SOVEREIGNTY of the government (such as SEDITION or TREASON)—are granted IMMUNITY from prosecution.

Amnesty allows the government of a nation or state to "forget" criminal acts, usually before prosecution has occurred. Amnesty has traditionally been used as a political tool of compromise and reunion following a war. An act of amnesty is generally granted to a group of people who have committed crimes against the state, such as treason, rebellion, or DESERTION from the military. The first amnesty in U.S. history was offered by President George Washington, in 1795, to participants in the Whiskey Rebellion, a series of riots caused by an unpopular excise tax on liquor; a conditional amnesty, it allowed the U.S. government to forget the crimes of those involved, in exchange for their signatures on an oath of loyalty to the United States. Other significant amnesties in U.S. history were granted on account of the Civil and Vietnam Wars.

Because there is no specific legislative or constitutional mention of amnesty, its nature is somewhat ambiguous. Its legal justification is drawn from Article 2, Section 2, of the Constitution, which states, "The President . . . shall have Power to grant Reprieves and Pardons for Offences against the United States, except in Cases of Impeachment." Because of their common basis, the difference between amnesty and PARDON has been particularly vexing. In theory, an amnesty is granted before prosecution takes place, and a pardon after. However, even this basic distinction is blurry—President Gerald R. Ford, for example, granted a pardon to President Richard M. Nixon before Nixon was charged with any crime. Courts have allowed the two terms to be used interchangeably.

The earliest examples of amnesty are in Greek and Roman law. The best documented case of amnesty in the ancient world occurred in 403 B.C. A long-term civil war in Athens was ended after a group dedicated to reuniting the city took over the government and arranged a general political amnesty. Effected by loyalty oaths taken by all Athenians, and only later made into law, the amnesty proclaimed the acts of both warring factions officially forgotten.

In other nations in which amnesties are accepted parts of the governing process, the power to grant amnesty sometimes lies with legislative bodies. In the United States, granting amnesties is primarily a power of the executive branch, though on some occasions Congress may also initiate amnesties as part of legislation. The Immigration Reform and Control Act of 1986 (100 Stat. 3359, 8 U.S.C.A. § 1101) attempted to reduce the number of ALIENS illegally entering the United States by punishing employers who knowingly hired them. However, because of concerns voiced by both employers and immigrant community leaders, the act compromised: it contained provisions for an amnesty giving citizenship to illegal immigrants who had been residents for a set period of time.

Though the Supreme Court has given the opinion that Congress can grant an independent amnesty, it has never expressly ruled on the issue. However, the president's power to grant amnesty autonomously has never been in serious question. The president always has recourse to the pardoning powers granted the office by the Constitution.

During the Civil War period, President Abraham Lincoln offered a series of amnesties without congressional assent to Union deserters, on the condition that they willingly rejoin their regiments. After the war, Lincoln issued a proclamation of amnesty for those who had participated in the rebellion. Though Congress protested the leniency of the plan, it was helpless to alter or halt it. Lincoln's amnesty was limited, requiring a loyalty oath and excluding high-ranking Confederate officers and political leaders. Lincoln hinted at but never offered a broader amnesty. It was not until President Andrew Johnson's Christmas amnesty proclamation of 1868 that an unconditional amnesty was granted to all participants in the Civil War. Amnesty used in this way fosters reconciliation—in this case, by fully relinquishing the Union's criminal complaints against those participating in the rebellion.

Amnesty was used for a similar purpose at the conclusion of the Vietnam War. In 1974, President Ford attempted reconciliation by declaring a conditional amnesty for those who had evaded the draft or deserted the armed forces. The terms of the amnesty required two years of public service (the length of a draft term), and gave evaders and deserters only five months to return to the fold. Many of those whom the amnesty was designed to benefit were dissatisfied, viewing the required service as punishment. On the other hand, many U.S. citizens agreed with President Nixon that *any* amnesty was out of the question. It was left to President Jimmy Carter, in 1977, to issue a broad amnesty to draft evaders. Carter argued the distinction that their crimes were forgotten, not forgiven. This qualification makes clear the purpose of an amnesty: not to erase a criminal act, nor to condone or forgive it, but simply to facilitate political reconciliation.

Though an amnesty can be broad or narrow, covering one person or many, and can be seriously qualified (as long as the conditions are not

With a portrait of Abraham Lincoln as a background, President Gerald Ford signed the order of conditional amnesty for thousands of Vietnam era draft evaders and military deserters. During the U.S. Civil War, Lincoln offered a series of amnesties to Union deserters.

unconstitutional), it cannot grant a license to commit future crimes. Nor can it forgive crimes not yet committed.

CROSS-REFERENCES

Carter, James Earl; Civil War; Ford, Gerald; Johnson, Andrew; Lincoln, Abraham; Nixon, Richard; Vietnam War; Washington, George; Whiskey Rebellion.

AMORTIZATION 📖 The reduction of a DEBT incurred, for example, in the purchase of STOCKS or BONDS, by regular payments consisting of interest and part of the principal made over a specified time period upon the expiration of which the entire debt is repaid. A MORTGAGE is amortized when it is repaid with periodic payments over a particular term. After a certain portion of each payment is applied to the interest on the debt, any balance reduces the principal.

The allocation of the cost of an INTANGIBLE ASSET, for example, a PATENT or COPYRIGHT, over its estimated useful life that is considered an expense of doing business and is used to offset the earnings of the ASSET by its declining value. If an intangible asset has an indefinite life, such as GOOD WILL, it cannot be amortized. 📖

Amortization is not the same as DEPRECIATION, which is the allocation of the original cost of a TANGIBLE asset computed over its anticipated useful life, based on its physical wear and tear and the passage of time. Amortization of intangible assets and depreciation of tangible assets are used for tax purposes to reduce the yearly income generated by the assets by their decreasing values so that the tax imposed upon the earnings of assets is less. Amortization differs from depletion, which is a reduction in the book value of a natural resource, such as a mineral, resulting from its conversion into a marketable product. Depletion is used for a similar tax purpose as amortization and depreciation—to reduce the yearly income generated by the asset by the expenses involved in its sale so that less tax will be due.

AMOTION 📖 Putting out; removal; taking away; dispossession of lands. 📖

Amotion essentially means the deprivation of POSSESSION. The term has been used to describe a wrongful seizure of personal CHATTELS.

The most common legal use of the word is in CORPORATION law. In that context, amotion is the ousting of an OFFICER from his or her post in the corporation prior to the end of the term for which the officer was appointed or elected, without taking away the person's right to be a member of the corporation. It can be distinguished from DISFRANCHISEMENT, which is the total expulsion of a corporation's officer or official representative.

AMOUNT IN CONTROVERSY 📖 The value of the RELIEF demanded or the amount of monetary DAMAGES claimed in a lawsuit. 📖

Some courts have JURISDICTION, or the power to hear cases, only if the amount in controversy is more or less than an amount specified by law. For example, federal district courts can hear lawsuits concerning questions of federal law and controversies between citizens of different states, but they can do this only if the amount in controversy is more than $50,000. Some lower-level state courts, such as those that hear small claims, have no authority to hear controversies involving more than certain maximum amounts.

When the amount in controversy determines the court's authority to hear a particular case, it may also be called the jurisdictional amount.

ANALOGY 📖 The inference that two or more things that are similar to each other in some respects are also similar in other respects. 📖

An analogy denotes that similarity exists in some characteristics of things that are otherwise not alike.

In a legal argument, an analogy may be used when there is no PRECEDENT (prior CASE LAW close in facts and legal principles) in point. Reasoning by analogy involves referring to a case that concerns unrelated subject matter but is governed by the same general principles and applying those principles to the case at hand.

ANARCHISM 📖 The theory espousing a societal state in which there is no structured government or law or in which there is resistance to all current forms of government. 📖

Anarchists promote the absence of rules, which leads to the absence of any identifiable social structure beyond that of personal autonomy. When anarchy becomes defined by one anarchist, other anarchists may feel bound to change it.

Anarchism thus means different things to different believers. Anarchists do not hold common views on subjects such as desirable levels of community cooperation and the role of large industry in society. Another matter of continuing debate is whether anarchy is an end unto itself or simply the best means to a better government. To all anarchists, though, anarchy is the best refuge from political dogma and authority. And most anarchists agree that anarchism begins with the notion that people are inherently good, or even perfect, and that external authority—laws, governments, institutions, and so forth—limits human potential. External authority, they suggest, brings a corruption of the innocent human spirit and a ceiling on achievement.

William Godwin (1756–1836) is widely regarded as the first to give anarchy a comprehensive intellectual foundation. Godwin, the son of a Calvinist minister, argued that the state and its laws were enslaving people instead of freeing them. According to Godwin, government was necessary only to prevent injustice and external invasion. With every person educated in sincerity, independence, self-restraint, and seriousness, any more governmental activity would be unnecessary.

Godwin opposed the rise of liberal democracy in the late 1700s. In the wake of the American and French Revolutions, he observed, "Electioneering is a trade so despicably degrading, so eternally incompatible with moral and mental dignity that I can scarcely believe a truly great mind capable of the dirty drudgery of such vice." Godwin's observations and proposals were largely ignored during his lifetime, but they informed anarchists several decades later, when the brutal working conditions and "wage slavery" of industrialism began to present new reasons for revolt.

Two well-known anarchists, Emma Goldman (1869–1940) and Alexander Berkman (1870–1936), gained recognition in the 1890s. Goldman, the daughter of Jewish merchants, immigrated to the United States from Russia in 1885 at the age of sixteen. In Rochester, New

UPI/BETTMANN

Emma Goldman spoke about birth control at this May 1916 rally. Goldman was well known for her ideas on sexuality, free love, and family structures, and she was once jailed for distributing illegal birth control information.

York, Goldman worked in a sweat shop—a large, unsafe factory that paid low wages and demanded long hours. The experience radicalized Goldman, and with her natural flair for public speaking, she soon became a spokeswoman for anarchism. Goldman worked extensively for the Industrial Workers of the World (IWW), an organization dedicated to *anarcho-syndicalism*, which seeks to use the industrial union as the basis for a reorganization of society. Goldman's cross-country lecture tours, in which she addressed a broad range of social topics in German and English, earned her a reputation as a witty speaker and provocative thinker. A voracious reader and a magazine publisher, Goldman gave voice to ideas on sexuality, free love, birth control, and family structures that shocked members of her generation, including fellow anarchists.

Like many devout anarchists, Goldman had trouble with the law. She was imprisoned for a year for allegedly inciting a riot during a New York City hunger demonstration in 1893. Goldman also served a two-week sentence for distributing illegal birth control information. She was jailed on suspicion of complicity in the ASSASSINATION of President William McKinley, in 1901. In 1917, she was arrested with Berkman for participating in antiwar protests, and both were charged with violating the Selective Service Act of 1917 (40 Stat. 76) by inducing young men to resist the draft. Goldman and

Berkman were convicted, and, despite appeals to the Supreme Court, both served prison terms. Upon release in 1919, they were deported to Russia.

Berkman, Goldman's ally, shared Goldman's passion for breaking social barriers and inspiring creative thought. He also possessed a violent streak. In 1892, he was arrested for attempting to assassinate steel magnate Henry Clay Frick during a steel strike. After serving a fourteen-year prison sentence, Berkman devoted the rest of his life to freeing imprisoned political radicals and promoting workers' rights. He remained a close companion of Goldman until his death in 1936.

Goldman and Berkman cut dashing figures as romantic, intellectual anarchists, and they played no small part in a modest rise of anarchism in the early 1900s. Although anarchism still gains followers in colleges and universities and among self-styled intellectuals, it has been mostly dormant as a social force since the Great Depression, of the 1930s.

Many anarchists have suffered the bemusing fate of being convicted for breaking laws in which they do not believe. However, the justice system does occasionally protect the anarchist. In *Fiske v. Kansas*, 274 U.S. 380, 47 S. Ct. 655, 71 L. Ed. 1108 (1927), Harold B. Fiske was charged in Rice County, Kansas, with violating the Kansas Criminal Syndicalism Act (Laws Sp. Sess. 1920, c. 37). Fiske had been arrested for

Alexander Berkman addressed a meeting of the Industrial Workers of the World in New York in 1914. He and Emma Goldman (who may appear right below Berkman) were allies in the cause for anarchy. They promoted workers' rights and encouraged young men to avoid the draft in 1917.

promoting the Workers' Industrial Union (WIU), an organization devoted in part to establishing worker control of industry and the abolition of the wage system.

Under the syndicalism statute in Kansas, any person advocating "the duty, necessity, propriety or expediency of crime, criminal syndicalism, or sabotage . . . is guilty of a felony" (1920 Kan. Sess. Laws ch. 37, § 3). Criminal syndicalism was defined as the advocation of crime, physical violence, or destruction of property "as a means of effecting industrial or political revolution, or for profit" (§ 1). Kansas authorities charged Fiske with criminal syndicalism, citing only the preamble to the constitution of the IWW, the parent organization of Fiske's WIU. This preamble stated, in part, that "a struggle must go on until the workers of the World organize as a class, take possession of the earth, and the machinery of production and abolish the wage system" (*Fiske*).

The U.S. Supreme Court found insufficient evidence against Fiske to warrant conviction of criminal syndicalism. According to the Court, there was no suggestion that "getting possession of the machinery of production and abol-

ishing the wage system, was to be accomplished by other than lawful means." The Court confirmed that a state may enact legislation to protect its government from insurrection, but it may not be arbitrary or unreasonable in policing its citizens who advocate changes in the social order.

CROSS-REFERENCES

Chicago Eight; Freedom of Speech; Goldman, Emma; Industrial Workers of the World; Rousseau, Jean Jacques.

ANCIENT LIGHTS ⬛ A doctrine of English COMMON LAW that gives a landowner an EASEMENT or right by PRESCRIPTION to the unobstructed passage of light and air from adjoining land if the landowner has had uninterrupted use of the lights for twenty years. ⬛

Once a person gains the right to ancient lights, the owner of the adjoining land cannot obscure them, such as by erecting a building. If the neighbor does so, he or she can be sued under a theory of NUISANCE, and damages could be awarded.

The doctrine of ancient lights has not been adopted in the United States since it would greatly hinder commercial and residential growth and the expansion of towns and cities.

ANCIENT WRITING 📖 An original document affecting the TRANSFER of REAL PROPERTY, which can be admitted as EVIDENCE in a lawsuit because its aged condition and its location upon discovery sufficiently establish its authenticity. 📖

Under COMMON LAW, an ancient writing, sometimes called an ancient document, could be offered as evidence only if certain conditions were met. The document had to be at least thirty years old, the equivalent of a generation. It had to appear genuine and free from suspicion. For example, if the date of the document or the signatures of the parties to it appeared to have been altered, it was not considered genuine. When found, the document must have been in a likely location or in the possession of a person who would logically have had access to it, such as a deed found in the office of the county clerk or in the custody of the attorney for one of the parties to the writing. An ancient writing must also have related to the transfer of real property, for example, a WILL, a DEED, or a MORTGAGE. When all these requirements were met, an ancient writing was presumed to be genuine upon its presentation for admission as evidence without any additional proof.

Today various state rules of evidence and the Federal Rules of Evidence have expanded the admissibility of ancient writings. An ancient writing can now be offered as evidence if its condition does not suggest doubt as to its authenticity, if it is found in a likely place, and if it is at least twenty years old at the time it is presented for admission into evidence.

Some states still adhere to the requirement that a document be at least thirty years old before it comes within the ancient writing exception to the HEARSAY rule. A few states recognize ancient documents only if, in addition to these basic requirements, the person seeking the admission of the ancient writing has taken possession of the property in question.

An ancient writing is admissible in a trial as an exception to the rule that prohibits hearsay from being used as evidence in a trial. In a case where no other evidence exists, the legitimacy of the writing must be considered if the case is to be determined on its merits. The probability that such a document is trustworthy is determined by its condition and location upon discovery. These factors permit a court and a jury to presume the authenticity of an ancient writing.

ANCILLARY 📖 Subordinate; aiding. A legal proceeding that is not the primary dispute but which aids the JUDGMENT rendered in or the outcome of the main ACTION. A descriptive term that denotes a legal CLAIM, the existence of which is dependent upon or reasonably linked to a main claim. 📖

For example, a plaintiff wins a judgment for a specified sum of money against a defendant in a NEGLIGENCE action. The defendant refuses to pay the judgment. The plaintiff begins another proceeding for a WRIT of ATTACHMENT so that the judgment will be satisfied by the sale of the defendant's property seized under the writ. The attachment proceeding is ancillary, or subordinate, to the negligence suit. An ancillary proceeding is sometimes called an ancillary suit or bill.

A claim for ALIMONY is an ancillary claim dependent upon the primary claim that there are sufficient legal grounds for a court to grant a DIVORCE.

ANCILLARY ADMINISTRATION 📖 The settlement and distribution of a decedent's property in the state where it is located and which is other than the state in which the DECEDENT was domiciled. 📖

Ancillary administration occurs in a state to enable an EXECUTOR or ADMINISTRATOR to collect assets or to commence litigation on behalf of the ESTATE in that jurisdiction.

ANIMAL RIGHTS By the end of the 1980s, membership in animal advocacy organizations had reached 10 million people in the United States and opposition to the use of animals in laboratory experiments was rapidly growing. By 1990, seventy-six medical schools claimed that demonstrations and break-ins by animal rights advocates had cost them more than $4.5 million, according to a report from the Association of American Medical Colleges.

As the conflict between animal rights activists and medical and scientific researchers has grown, federal and state regulation of activities involving animal research has also expanded. At the federal level, the Animal Welfare Act (7 U.S.C.A. § 2131 et seq. [1994]) regulates the treatment of animals used in federally funded research. Under amendments added to the act in 1985, the secretary of agriculture was required to promulgate standards to govern the humane handling, care, treatment, and transportation of animals by dealers, research facilities, and exhibitors. These standards were to include minimum requirements for housing, feeding, watering, sanitation, ventilation, shelter from extremes of weather and temperature, adequate veterinary care, and separation by species where necessary; for exercise of dogs, as determined by an attending veterinarian; and for a physical environment adequate to promote the psychological well-being of primates. In addition, the standards were to include requirements for animal care, treatment, and practices in experimental procedures in research facilities.

In February 1991, the secretary of agriculture issued final regulations under the act (56 Fed. Reg. 6426; 9 C.F.R. § 3). Shortly thereafter, two animal rights organizations, the Animal Legal Defense Fund and the Society for Animal Protective Legislation, along with several individuals, sued the U.S. Department of Agriculture (USDA), claiming that the final regulations were ARBITRARY and capricious, in violation of the Administrative Procedure Act (APA) (5 U.S.C.A. § 551 et seq. [1994]). Under the APA, a court can compel agency action that is unlawfully withheld or unreasonably delayed, and can set aside agency action that is arbitrary and capricious, an abuse of discretion, or otherwise in violation of the law.

The plaintiffs challenged the USDA on several grounds, including the lack of minimum requirements regarding exercise for dogs and the psychological well-being of primates; the amount of delay permitted under the regulations in complying with new cage requirements; and the loophole in the regulations' provision for special cage designs, which permitted facilities to evade the existing minimum requirements for cage sizes.

In February 1993, a federal district court found that the USDA's treatment of laboratory animals waiting to be used in biomedical experiments violated federal statutes providing for the humane treatment of such animals. In *Animal Legal Defense Fund v. Secretary of Agriculture*, 813 F. Supp. 882 (1993), the U.S. District Court for the District of Columbia ruled that the regulations enacted by the secretary of agriculture and the USDA failed to comply with the mandate of Congress to ensure the well-being and humane treatment of animals, notwithstanding the importance of research.

The defendants appealed the district court's decision. In *Animal Legal Defense Fund v. Espy*, 29 F.3d 720 (1994), the U.S. Court of Appeals for the District of Columbia Circuit ruled that the animal rights organizations and other plaintiffs did not have STANDING to challenge the USDA. (*Standing* is a legal requirement that the plaintiff must have been injured or threatened with injury by the action complained of, and focuses on the question of whether the plaintiff is the proper party to bring the lawsuit.) Because the plaintiffs lacked standing, the court ordered that the case be dismissed.

Whereas the Animal Welfare Act governs the general treatment of research animals, other federal statutes govern the testing procedures that may be used on animals in the course of scientific and commercial research and in product testing. The Toxic Substances Control Act (15 U.S.C.A. § 2601 et seq. [1994]) authorizes the use of two procedures that have been particularly controversial: the Draize test and the lethal dose 50 (LD50) test.

The Draize test measures the irritancy of a substance such as a cosmetic or pesticide by applying it to the eyes of live rabbits for twenty-four hours. The LD50 test is used to calculate the median lethal dose of a substance by feeding it to a defined population of animals until 50 percent of them die. Some product manufacturers, such as Avon Products, Revlon, Faberge, Amway Corporation, Mary Kay Cosmetics, and Noxell Corporation, have discontinued some or all animal testing in the face of continued protests over the use of these tests.

During the late 1980s, the Federal Bureau of Investigation reported more than fifty incidents of vandalism annually at research facilities and attacks on researchers themselves. In response, the U.S. Congress and numerous state legislatures enacted protective legislation. In August 1992, Congress passed the Animal Enterprise Protection Act (18 U.S.C.A. § 43 [1994]), which provides, in part, that anyone who

> intentionally causes physical disruption to the functioning of an animal enterprise by intentionally stealing, damaging, or causing the loss of, any property (including animals or records) used by the animal enterprise, and thereby causes economic damage exceeding $10,000 to that enterprise, or conspires to do so shall be fined under this title or imprisoned not more than one year, or both.

If serious bodily injury or death to another person occurs in the course of the prohibited activity, the statute provides for imprisonment up to a life term. The act defines an animal enterprise as "(A) a commercial or academic enterprise that uses animals for food or fiber production, agriculture, research, or testing; (B) a zoo, aquarium, circus, rodeo, or lawful competitive animal event; or (C) any fair or similar event intended to advance agricultural arts and sciences."

By 1995, over twenty states had passed similar legislation, including Alabama, Arizona, Arkansas, Colorado, Georgia, Idaho, Illinois, Louisiana, Massachusetts, Minnesota, Missouri, Montana, Nebraska, New York, North Caro-

WELCOME TO THE MONKEY LAB: THE BATTLE OVER ANIMAL RESEARCH

In May 1981, Alex Pacheco, cofounder of an animal rights organization called People for the Ethical Treatment of Animals (PETA), went to work as a volunteer at the Institute for Behavioral Research, a private research center in Silver Spring, Maryland. Pacheco told the institute's chief research scientist, Edward Taub, that he was fascinated by animal research. Taub's research involved the surgical crippling of monkeys using a procedure called deafferentation, in which the spinal cord is opened and various nerves leading to arms and legs are sliced away, causing numbness.

At the time Pacheco joined his lab, Taub had performed the procedure on seventeen macaques, attempting to show that function could be restored to limbs by forcing new nerve growth. He had destroyed the nerves to only one arm on some of the monkeys, and then used straitjackets, binding up their good arms to force them to use their damaged arms, and had also applied electric shock to restrained monkeys if they did not move their numbed limbs. Taub planned to kill the monkeys after a year in order to determine whether this forced movement had stimulated nerve growth.

After receiving permission from Taub to work at night, Pacheco set to work documenting the filthy, cramped conditions of the lab, and the stressed behavior of the monkeys, many of which were chewing their numbed limbs open. With his PETA cofounder, Ingrid Newkirk, stationed outside with a walkie-talkie, Pacheco took photographs and brought in sympathetic veterinarians and scientists to provide affidavits about the lab conditions. Several months later, he took his documentation to the local police department, which seized the lab's monkeys and filed seventeen charges of animal cruelty against Taub, under state law. The scientist was convicted on all the charges, but an appellate court decided that a federally funded researcher was

not required to comply with state laws. Eventually, Taub's lab lost its federal funding and discontinued animal research.

Many participants in the debate over animal rights view the 1981 seizure of the Silver Spring monkeys as a turning point for the animal rights movement in the United States, heading it in a more combative and less compromising direction.

Animal welfare has long been an issue in the United States. As early as the mid-1600s, the Puritans prohibited cruelty toward animals, and by the nineteenth century, groups such as the American Society for the Prevention of Cruelty to Animals and the American Anti-Vivisection Society had been organized. Animal experimentation has been controversial not only between the animal rights movement and the scientific and medical research communities but also between the activist groups themselves.

In the mid-1990s, U.S. researchers used over 20 million animals a year, three-quarters of them rats or mice. An ever increasing use of animals in biomedical research has fueled a concomitant growth in animal welfare organizations. Concerned that the activists would cause the dismantling of all animal research, the biomedical research community lobbied successfully for years against the passage of all legislation restricting such research. But in the early 1950s, Christine Stevens founded the Animal Welfare Institute and the Society for Animal Protective Legislation, which successfully worked against passage of state laws that would require pounds to turn their dogs and cats over to researchers. Stevens then began working for passage of federal legislation that would also protect laboratory animals. In 1966, Congress enacted the Animal Welfare Act (7 U.S.C.A. § 2131 et seq. [1994]), which regulates the treatment of animals in federally funded research. Congress charged the U.S. Department of Agri-

culture (USDA) with overseeing the inspection of laboratories for compliance.

In 1985, after Stevens documented continuing inhumane laboratory conditions, the Animal Welfare Act was amended to strengthen standards for the humane handling, treatment, and transportation of animals by dealers, research facilities, and exhibitors. In 1991, the secretary of agriculture issued regulations implementing the amended act.

During this period, the animal protection movement continued to expand. By the early 1990s, PETA had grown to more than four hundred thousand members and had an annual budget of nearly $10 million. Over four hundred animal rights groups had been organized in the United States, claiming a total membership of 10 million. Although each of these groups can be said to support the humane treatment of animals, their philosophies vary dramatically.

The most radical group is the Animal Liberation Front (ALF), an underground organization formed in 1982 with an estimated worldwide membership of several hundred as of the mid-1990s. ALF opposes the use of all animals in medical and scientific research, including psychological and surgical experimentation on living animals; ALF also opposes using animals for testing new drugs and cosmetics, for instructional purposes in biology and medical school classes, and for food, clothing, sports, circuses, and pets. ALF claimed responsibility for more than seventy-five attacks in the United States between 1979 and 1995, including stealing animals from labs in Arizona, California, Florida, Maryland, Oregon, Pennsylvania, and Washington, D.C.; burning and vandalizing the University of Arizona's veterinary lab and a new $3 million veterinary diagnostic center for farm animals at the University of California, Davis; vandalizing offices of researchers and stealing their research animals in Michigan and Texas; and starting small

IN FOCUS

WELCOME TO THE MONKEY LAB: THE BATTLE OVER ANIMAL RESEARCH
(CONTINUED)

fires in four of Chicago's largest department stores to protest the sale of furs. Although most of ALF's targets have been scientific research labs, the group claimed responsibility for bombing the cars of two research scientists in England in June 1990. ALF has also conducted raids in more than a dozen other countries.

By 1988, in response to raids by ALF and other groups, more than twenty states had enacted protective legislation prohibiting interference with animal research and agricultural facilities. In August 1992, citing the inability of state and local law enforcement agencies to conduct interstate or international investigations, Congress passed comparable federal legislation. The Animal Enterprise Protection Act of 1992 (18 U.S.C.A. § 43 [1994]) prohibits the disruption of "animal enterprises" such as research facilities and zoos by intentionally stealing or damaging property including animals or records.

Many scientists believe that ALF is a thinly disguised division of PETA. PETA denies any connection between the two groups, but has expressed its admiration for ALF's activities and often publicizes the group's raids. Both ALF and PETA share a common goal of ending all animal research, a philosophy that represents a fundamental split from other animal rights organizations such as Stevens's Animal Welfare Institute and the Humane Society of the United States, which accept animal experimentation but work for the humane treatment of animals in that and other contexts.

The biomedical research industry has responded vigorously to criticisms of animal research. The American Medical Association claims that medical advances such as heart bypass and cataract surgery, and treatments for cataracts, tuberculosis, smallpox, polio, mumps, cholera, and arthritis all are attributable to animal tests. A 1988 study by the National Research Council, the research arm of the National Academy of Sciences, acknowledged the controversy over animal testing, stating that although animal research has saved human lives, it has caused the animals involved suffering and death. Nevertheless, the study concluded that such experimentation has contributed significantly to the increase in human life expectancy since 1900 and that animals have been critical to research on most antibiotics and other drugs. Frankie Trull, executive director of the National Association for Biomedical Research, has argued that animal testing is necessary to sustain the human race.

Animal rights advocates respond that animal research is not necessarily useful in developing treatments for humans. They point out that the drug thalidomide, which caused massive birth defects in the 1960s, was first tested on animals and deemed to be safe, and that the most significant advances in AIDS and cancer research have not involved animals. They also claim that alternatives to animal research exist in the form of computer models and tissue cultures, but that the scientific community refuses to accept them.

In a nationwide survey conducted in

December 1993 by the *Los Angeles Times*, respondents were asked whether they agreed with the following statement by PETA's Newkirk: "Animals are like us in all important things—they feel pain, act with altruism, they talk and suffer fear. They value their lives, even if we don't understand those lives." Of the 1,612 adults polled, 47 percent agreed with Newkirk's statement and 51 percent disagreed. The survey also found that 54 percent opposed hunting for sport and 50 percent opposed the wearing of fur. Forty-six percent said the laws protecting animals from inhumane treatment were satisfactory, whereas 30 percent said the laws did not go far enough and 17 percent said the laws went too far. Animal rights leaders expressed surprise that so many Americans agreed with some of the principle tenets of the animal protection movement.

Animal protectionists have made dramatic gains during the twentieth century, including reducing the use of animals in product testing; forcing the tuna industry to protect dolphins; raising doubts about the treatment of animals in circuses, zoos, rodeos, and horse and dog racing; criticizing the use of fur, ivory, exotic leathers, and veal; and challenging the use of animals in scientific experiments. Movement leaders say they plan to broaden their struggle to encompass the fight to improve wild-animal habitat. Wayne Pacelle, of the Fund for Animals, said, "[W]e wholeheartedly accept the principle that wild animals need habitat, and the movement is shifting in that direction."

lina, North Dakota, Oregon, South Carolina, Tennessee, Virginia, Washington, and Wisconsin.

Several states also regulate the use of pound animals in research. Maine prohibits the use of pound animals for any research (Me. Rev. Stat. Ann. tit. 17, § 1025 [West 1994]). California requires that any pound or animal regulation department where animals are turned over to a research facility post a sign stating Animals Turned in to This Shelter May Be Used for Research Purposes, in a clearly visible place (Cal. Civ. Code § 1834.7 [West 1994]). In Oklahoma, pounds are required to supply unclaimed animals to research institutions, unless the owner of an animal bringing it to the pound specifies it is not to be used in research (Okla. Stat. Ann. tit. 4, § 394 [West 1994]).

At least three states regulate the sale of animals to research facilities. Minnesota law prohibits the transfer of a dog or cat by a person other than the owner to a research animal dealer, the possession of a dog or cat by a dealer without the owner's permission, or the transfer of a dog or cat by a dealer to an institution without the owner's permission (Minn. Stat. Ann. § 346.55 [West 1994]). California law provides that anyone who steals an animal for purposes of sale, medical research, or other commercial use, or who knowingly defrauds another person of any animal for purposes of medical research or slaughter, may be imprisoned for up to one year (Cal. Penal Code § 487g [West 1994]). New York law prohibits the selling or giving away of a dog to a research institution without the written permission of its owner (N.Y. Agric. & Mkts. Law § 366-a [McKinney 1994]).

On the federal level, the Animal Welfare Act was amended in 1990 to regulate the use of pound animals in research. A new section titled "Protection of pets" provides that dogs and cats acquired by a pound, humane society, or similar entity or research facility must be held for not less than five days before being sold to dealers, so as to allow their recovery by their owners or their adoption by other individuals (7 U.S.C.A. § 2158 [1994]).

The use of animals in scientific, medical, and commercial research promises to remain controversial. In her book *The Monkey Wars*, Deborah Blum advocated that animal rights activists and researchers share their viewpoints together in education programs to achieve a realistic understanding of the issues. According to Blum, such an understanding could end the two sides' long and bitter standoff. See also AGRICULTURE DEPARTMENT.

ANIMUS [*Latin, Mind, soul, or intention.*] A tendency or an inclination toward a definite, sometimes unavoidable, goal; an aim, objective, or purpose.

When *animus* is used in conjunction with other words of Latin origin, its most common meaning is "the INTENTION of." For example, *animus revocandi* is the intention of revoking; *animus possidendi* is the intention of possessing.

Animo, meaning "with intent," may be employed in a manner similar to *animus*. For example, *animo felonico* means with FELONIOUS intent.

ANNEXATION The act of attaching, uniting, or joining together in a physical sense; consolidating.

The term is generally used to signify the connection of a smaller or subordinate unit to a larger or principal unit. For example, a smaller piece of land may be annexed to a larger one.

Similarly, a smaller document may be annexed to a larger one, such as a CODICIL to a WILL.

Although physical joining is implied, actual contact is not always necessary. For example, an annexation occurs when a country acquires new territory even though the new territory is not immediately adjacent to the existing country.

In the law of REAL PROPERTY, annexation is used to describe the manner in which a CHATTEL is joined to property. See also FIXTURES.

ANNOTATION A note, summary, or commentary on some section of a book or a statute that is intended to explain or illustrate its meaning.

An annotation serves as a brief summary of the law and the facts of a case and demonstrates how a particular law enacted by Congress or a state legislature is interpreted and applied. Annotations usually follow the text of the statute they interpret in annotated statutes.

ANNUAL PERCENTAGE RATE The actual cost of borrowing money, expressed in the form of a yearly measure to allow consumers to compare the cost of borrowing money among several lenders.

The Federal Truth-in-Lending Act (15 U.S.C.A. § 1601 et seq. [1968]) mandates the complete disclosure of this rate in addition to other CREDIT terms. See also TRUTH-IN-LENDING ACT.

ANNUAL REPORT Annual reports measure a corporation's financial health. They focus on past and present financial performance, and make predictions about future prospects. By law, any CORPORATION that holds an annual meeting for stockholders or security holders is required to issue an annual report. Regulations set down by the SECURITIES AND EXCHANGE COMMISSION (SEC) specify in detail what information the report must include about the corporation's finances, markets, and management. The rules are strict: the SEC can levy stiff penalties if corporations fail to comply. Traditionally a rather dry and factual document, the annual report has acquired a larger audience in recent years as corporations increasingly treat it as not merely a legal obligation but also a public relations opportunity. Yet, even as annual reports take on the appearance of glossy magazines, promote corporate public relations, and make political arguments, they remain bound by legal concerns about completeness and accuracy, and sometimes expose corporations to lawsuits when they fall short.

Although federal law governing the financial industry is quite old, its application to annual reports grew in complexity from the mid-1970s to the mid-1990s. This authority derives from two laws: the Securities Act of 1933 (15 U.S.C.A. § 77a et seq.) and the Securities Exchange Act of 1934 (15 U.S.C.A. § 78a–78jj). The 1933 law requires issuers of SECURITIES to file financial information with the federal government; the 1934 law authorizes the SEC to act as a regulatory body over the financial industry. In 1974, the SEC tightened requirements on annual reports by specifying a broad range of information that must be provided, and it frequently amended them in subsequent years. Corporations have consequently made greater efforts to scrutinize their reports for compliance with the law, increasing the role of lawyers in producing what was once the work of accountants.

These requirements address financial and general information. An annual report must include a BALANCE SHEET reflecting changes in the corporation's financial worth, an income and cash flow statement, and other relevant documentation, all of which must be reviewed first by outside auditors. A statement by management must analyze past performance as well as discuss prospects for the following years; if circumstances change, corporations have a duty to issue corrected information. In addition, they must make public details about products and services, domestic and foreign markets, and the backgrounds of directors and executive officers.

Corporations that fail to comply with all the requirements can face enforcement proceedings. In such cases, the commission has the power to invalidate the election of DIRECTORS and decisions made at the shareholders' meeting, which can necessitate issuing a revised annual report. Administrative remedies also exist. Under the Securities Enforcement Remedies and Penny Stock Reform Act of 1990 (15 U.S.C.A. § 77g et seq.), the SEC can use violations of any securities laws to force corporations to make full disclosures in their reports. Corporations that are in the process of registering for the first time with the SEC are particularly scrutinized for overly optimistic projections.

Besides federal penalties, wishful thinking in annual reports can lead to lawsuits. Hoping to put the best spin possible on their achievements and prospects, corporations sometimes attract CLASS ACTION suits from shareholders who ALLEGE that the corporations have exaggerated or misled the public. One of many examples is a suit brought against Pizza Time Theatre (*In re Pizza Time Theatre*, 112 F.R.D. 15 [N.D. Cal. 1986]). Its 1982 annual report had cartoon characters bragging, "We're going full speed ahead!" And so they were: nine months later, Pizza Time Theatre declared BANKRUPTCY.

Shareholders brought a class action suit against the corporation and its directors, citing the report's overly optimistic tone.

Beyond requiring that annual reports meet financial and general information regulations, the law says nothing about the rest of their contents. Corporations are free to package their reports as they please, and the form itself is constantly evolving: current annual reports borrow from the flashy graphic styles of magazines, can be released on videodisc and computer disk, and sometimes even include gifts. Particularly interesting is a trend toward using these reports—usually in the president's letter—to address political issues. As powerful forces in the body politic, corporations rarely refuse an opportunity to make their influence felt on government, especially when pending legislation may affect their interests. In the early 1990s, for example, some annual reports from the medical industry targeted the ill-fated health care reform proposals of the Clinton administration.

CROSS-REFERENCES
Board of Directors; Financial Statement; Securities.

ANNUITY 📖 A right to receive periodic payments, usually fixed in size, for life or a term of years that is created by a contract or other legal document. 📖

The most common form of an annuity is akin to a savings account. The annuitant, the person who creates an annuity for his or her own benefit, deposits a sum of money, the PRINCIPAL, with an individual, business, or insurance company to be invested so that the principal will earn income at a certain percentage, usually specified by the terms of the annuity. This income is used by the company to pay the annuitant. Each payment received by the annuitant, sometimes called the primary beneficiary, represents a partial return of the principal and a portion of the income generated by its investment. Such annuities are employed frequently to provide a source of income to persons upon their retirement. A group annuity contract supplies periodic payments to a retired individual member of a group of employees covered by their employer's master contract. A retirement annuity is a policy paid to the annuitant after retirement. If the annuitant dies prior to the expiration of the annuity or wants to surrender the policy, an amount specified in the terms of the annuity is returned to the annuitant's ESTATE or designated beneficiary.

Classification Annuities are classified according to the nature of the payment and the duration of time for payment. A *fixed annuity* requires payment in a specified amount to be made for the term of the annuity regardless of economic changes due to inflation or the fluctuation of the ventures in which the principal is invested. A *variable annuity* provides for payments that fluctuate in size contingent upon the success of the investment of the principal. Such variation offsets the effect of inflation upon the annuitant. If, however, the investment has fared poorly, the size of the payments decreases.

A *straight annuity* is a contract by an insurance company to make variable payments at monthly or yearly intervals. A *life* or *straight life annuity* is payable to an annuitant only during the annuitant's lifetime and ceases upon his or her death. The size of the periodic payment is usually fixed based upon actuarial charts that project the expected life span of a person based upon age and physical condition. This type of annuity often contains provisions that promise payment to be made to a secondary beneficiary, named by the annuitant to receive benefits in case of the annuitant's death, or to the annuitant's heirs for a period of time even if the annuitant has died before the expiration of the designated period. A *deferred annuity* is one in which payments start at a stipulated future date only if the annuitant is alive at that time. Payment of the INCOME TAX due on the income generated is delayed until payments start. A deferred annuity is used primarily by a person who does not want to receive payments until he or she is in a lower tax bracket, such as upon retirement.

A *refund annuity*, sometimes called a *cash refund annuity*, is a policy that promises to pay a set amount annually during the annuitant's life. In case the annuitant dies before receiving payments for the full amount of the annuity, his or her estate will receive a sum that is the difference between the purchase price and the sum paid during the annuitant's lifetime.

A *joint annuity* is one that is payable to two named persons but upon the death of one, the annuity terminates. A *joint and survivorship annuity* is a policy payable to the named annuitants during their lives and continues for the benefit of the surviving annuitant upon the death of the other.

Tax Aspects When an annuity is paid to an annuitant, he or she receives a portion of the principal and part of the return it has earned. For federal and state income tax purposes, only the amount attributable to the income generated by the principal, not the principal itself, is considered taxable income. The Internal Revenue Code provides an exclusion ratio to determine the amount of taxable income paid to the annuitant. Special tax rules apply to annuities that are qualified employee retirement plans. See also PENSIONS.

The annuity payments made to the estate of a decedent might be subject to ESTATE AND GIFT TAX as an asset of the decedent's gross estate. Federal and state laws governing estate tax must be consulted to determine the liability for such taxes.

ANNULMENT 📖 A judgment by a court that retroactively invalidates a MARRIAGE to the date of its formation. 📖

An annulment differs from a DIVORCE, a court order that terminates a marriage, since it is a judicial statement that there was never a marriage. A divorce, which can only take place where there has been a VALID marriage, means that the two parties are no longer HUSBAND AND WIFE once the decree is issued. An annulment means that the individuals were never united in marriage as husband and wife.

Various religions have different methods for obtaining a church divorce, or annulment, but these procedures have no legal force or effect upon a marriage that complied with the requirements of law. Such a marriage must be legally annulled.

History English COMMON LAW did not provide for annulment. Prior to the mid-nineteenth century, the only courts in England with the power to annul an INVALID marriage, when fairness mandated it, were the ECCLESIASTICAL COURTS. There was no statute that provided relief of this kind.

Divorces or Annulments in U.S., 1970–1993

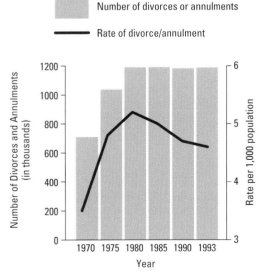

Number of divorces or annulments

Rate of divorce/annulment

Source: U.S. National Center for Health Statistics, *Vital Statistics of the United States*, annual.

A sample decision in an action to annul the marriage of a party under the age of consent

At a Special Term, Part _____ , of the Supreme Court of the State of New York, held in and for the County of _____ , at _____ , on the _____ day of _____ , _____ .

Present: Hon _____ , Justice.

_____
_____ , Plaintiff
-against-
_____ , Defendant
_____

DECISION
Index No. _____

    The above entitled action having been duly brought on by the plaintiff for a judgment of annulment in favor of the plaintiff and against the defendant on the ground of [*specify ground*], and the summons bearing the notation "Action To Annul A Marriage" having been duly personally served upon the defendant within [*without*] the State of New York, and the plaintiff having duly complied with the Conciliation Proceeding requirements specified in the Domestic Relations Law, and the defendant having appeared by _____ , Esq., and the verified complaint having been duly served upon said attorney for the defendant, within the statutory period prescribed therefor, and the defendant having served an answer [*containing a counterclaim, and the plaintiff having replied thereto*] and the above entitled action having regularly come on for trial before me, without a jury, at a Special Term of this Court on the _____ day of _____ , _____ , and the plaintiff having appeared by her attorney, _____ Esq., and the defendant having appeared by his attorney, _____ Esq., [*and the defendant having stipulated in open court to withdraw his answer*] and the issues raised by the pleadings having been tried by the Court and testimony having been given in open court satisfactorily proving the allegations of the complaint, and due deliberation having been had thereon, I decide and find as follows:

Findings of Fact

    1. That the plaintiff, _____ , married the defendant, _____ , in the _____ Church located at _____ , County of _____ , City of _____ , State of New York on the _____ day of _____ , _____ .

    2. That the plaintiff, _____ , was [*, and still is,*] a resident of the State of New York at the time of the commencement of the above entitled action.

    3. That the plaintiff, _____ , has been a resident of the State of New York for a continuous period of one year immediately preceding the commencement of the above entitled action, to wit: from on or about the _____ day of _____ , _____ to [*on or about the _____ day of _____ , _____*] date.

    4. That at the time of said marriage, the infant plaintiff, _____ , was under the age of legal consent being then _____ (_____) years of age, and that at the time of the commencement of this action, said infant plaintiff had not attained the age of eighteen (18) years.

    [*Specify facts to influence court to exercise its discretion to grant relief sought*]

    5. That the defendant, _____ , has failed and refused to provide a suitable home for the infant plaintiff herein, and has failed and refused to make adequate provision for her support and maintenance.

    6. That during the time the infant plaintiff cohabited with the defendant herein, said defendant treated the infant plaintiff in a cruel and inhuman manner and has repeatedly committed acts of cruelty and violence upon the infant plaintiff, rendering it dangerous for the infant plaintiff to continue to cohabit with the defendant.

(continued)

A sample decision
in an action to
annul the marriage
of a party under
the age of consent
(continued)

7. That the infant plaintiff has been living separate and apart from the defendant and continuously since the month of _____ , _____ , and has not voluntarily cohabited with the defendant since she reached the age of eighteen years.

8. That the defendant has refused to continue the marriage relationship with the infant plaintiff.

9. That there are no issue of said marriage.

Conclusions of Law

1. That the infant plaintiff, _____ , is entitled to judgment as of course in favor of the plaintiff, _____ , and against the defendant, _____ , annulling the marriage contract heretofore existing between the parties hereto, because of the nonage of the infant plaintiff herein, and the defendant's cruel and inhuman treatment of said plaintiff, and his failure and refusal to make adequate provision for her support and maintenance, as prayed for in the complaint.

I direct that judgment be entered accordingly.

Dated: _____ ,

_____

_____

Justice of the Supreme Court

Northeastern American colonies passed laws enabling courts or legislatures to grant annulments, while other colonies adhered more closely to English traditions. The American tradition of keeping church and state separate precluded the establishment of ecclesiastical courts in the United States. Following the American Revolution, the civil courts in a majority of states never assumed that they had the authority to hear annulment cases.

A number of states eventually enacted laws authorizing annulment in recognition of the belief that it is unfair to require people to fulfill marital duties when a marriage is invalid.

Currently, most states have annulment statutes. In states that do not, courts declare that no marriage exists if the laws regulating marriage have not been observed.

An annulment declares that a marriage, which appears to be valid, is actually invalid. Two kinds of invalid marriages exist: *void marriages* and *voidable marriages*. A VOID marriage is one that was invalid from its very beginning and, therefore, could never lawfully exist in any way. The major grounds for a void marriage are incest, bigamy, and lack of consent. Once these grounds are established, the court will grant a decree of annulment.

A VOIDABLE marriage is one that can be declared illegal but that continues as valid until an annulment is sought. The annulment takes effect only from the time a court renders its decision.

Grounds   State law governs the grounds for annulling a voidable marriage. Couples should not be obligated by the serious duties incident to marriage if both parties did not genuinely intend to be married.

FRAUD is the most prevalent ground for annulment. The misrepresentation, whether by lies or concealment of the truth, must encompass something directly pertinent to the marriage, such as religion, children, or sex, which society considers the foundation of a marital relationship.

Physical or emotional conditions may also be grounds for annulment, particularly when they interfere with sexual relations or procreation.

Other health conditions providing grounds for annulment include alcoholism, incurable insanity, and epilepsy. The mere existence of one of these conditions is a sufficient ground for an annulment in some states, whereas in others, an annulment may be obtained for fraud if such a condition was concealed.

Courts may also annul marriages that involved lack of consent, mistake, or duress. Lack of consent might arise if one party were senile, drunk, underage, or suffering from serious mental illness, or if there was no genuine intent to marry. A mistake as to some essential element of the marriage may also justify an annulment, for example, if the couple mistakenly believed that one party's insanity or impotence had been cured. Duress arises when one party compels the other to marry against his or her will.

Consequences State law governs the consequences of an annulment. Customarily, an annulment was a court declaration that no marriage had ever existed, but this created various problems. If a marriage was dissolved by divorce, the children of the marriage were legitimate and the parent awarded custody could be awarded alimony. No such provisions, however, were made in an annulment. A majority of states have rectified this situation by statutory provisions. In most states, children of voidable, and sometimes void, marriages are legitimate. In addition, some states provide for alimony and property settlements upon the granting of an annulment. Several other jurisdictions allow their courts to devise a fair allocation of property where necessary and equitable.

ANON. 🕮 An abbreviation for anonymous, nameless, or name unknown. 🕮

ANSWER 🕮 The first responsive PLEADING filed by the defendant in a CIVIL ACTION; a formal written statement that admits or denies the ALLEGATIONS in the COMPLAINT and sets forth any available AFFIRMATIVE DEFENSES. 🕮

The answer gives the plaintiff notice of the issues the defendant will raise as the case progresses and enables the plaintiff to adequately prepare a case. In most JURISDICTIONS, the answer must be filed within twenty days after receipt of the SUMMONS and complaint, although local rules and customs may dictate different filing times.

The answer begins with a CAPTION, which identifies the location of the ACTION, the court, the DOCKET or FILE number (assigned by the court), and the title of the case (comprising the names of the PARTIES, e.g., *Smith v. Jones*). Following the caption, the main body of the answer sets forth admissions or denials that respond to each allegation made in the complaint. In federal court and in jurisdictions that follow the Federal Rules of Civil Procedure, denials must be unambiguous and stated in concise language that clearly identifies the allegations being denied (Fed. R. Civ. P. 8(b)). For example, if the complaint alleges that the defendant was driving an automobile that struck the plaintiff on Addison Street in Chicago on March 11, an answer stating that the defendant was in Milwaukee on March 11 is unclear and ambiguous because it avoids the question of whether the defendant was also in Chicago at a different time on the same day.

The answer may plead any form of denial that is truthful and made in GOOD FAITH. Although general denials that deny the truth of every fact in the complaint or of every element of a charge are sometimes used, they are not considered a sufficient response. Courts discourage general denials because they fail to respond to specific allegations and do not give the plaintiff sufficient basis to prepare a case. If the defendant lacks the knowledge or information needed to respond to the truth or falsity of a charge, rule 8(b) and similar rules in other jurisdictions allow the defendant to state such in the answer. This has the effect of a denial (rule 8(b)). If the defendant fails to respond to an allegation by either denying it or by stating he or she does not have the information necessary to admit or deny it, it is considered admitted under rule 8(d).

Following the admissions and denials, the answer outlines any affirmative defenses available to the defendant. Affirmative defenses, which are grounded in SUBSTANTIVE LAW, state that an allegation may or may not be true, but that even if it is true, the law provides a legal defense that defeats the plaintiff's claim. The defendant must determine if the law allows an affirmative defense to a charge, and must allege sufficient facts to support the defense. For example, in a NEGLIGENCE action, the defendant might respond to an allegation that a duty of care was owed to the plaintiff by stating that, even if the allegation is true, the plaintiff assumed the risk of the activity that led to the injury. The defendant must then state the facts that support the defense. It is critical to the defendant's case that all applicable affirmative defenses are asserted. In most jurisdictions, affirmative defenses not raised in a timely manner in the defendant's responsive pleading are deemed to have been waived.

The answer, like the complaint, ends with a "wherefore" clause that summarizes the defendant's demands, such as demands for a jury trial and judgment in the defendant's favor. Only one wherefore clause is generally needed, although local practice may dictate that each denial and each affirmative defense have its own wherefore clause.

Counterclaims and cross-claims sometimes appear in the answer. A COUNTERCLAIM arises when the defendant's response includes a CLAIM against the plaintiff. A counterclaim may come from the same circumstances as the plaintiff's claim or from a different set of facts. A CROSS-CLAIM may be filed when one party to a suit charges another party with responsibility for the plaintiff's injuries or damages. Under Federal Rules of Civil Procedure rule 13(g), a cross-claim must arise out of "the transaction or occurrence that is the subject matter either of the original action or of a counterclaim therein or relating to any property that is the subject

A sample answer and counterclaim

UNITED STATES DISTRICT COURT FOR THE SOUTHERN
DISTRICT OF NEW YORK

Civil Action, File Number 000000

John Doe, Plaintiff)
)
v.)   ANSWER
)
Richard Roe Co., Inc., Defendant)

First Defense

The complaint fails to state a claim against defendant upon which relief can be granted.

Second Defense

If defendant is indebted to plaintiff for the goods mentioned in the complaint as having been sold and delivered by plaintiff to defendant, defendant owes plaintiff less than $10,000 (ten thousand dollars).

Third Defense

Defendant admits that it is a corporation incorporated under the laws of the State of New York; alleges that it is without knowledge or information sufficient to form a belief as to the truth of the allegation concerning the place of plaintiff's citizenship; and denies each and every other allegation contained in the complaint.

Fourth Defense

The right of action set forth in the complaint did not accrue within six years prior to the commencement of this action.

Counterclaim

After March 19, 1996, and continuously since that time, the plaintiff has been inducing suppliers not to sell ready-to-wear women's dresses to defendant and has otherwise been engaging in unfair trade practices and unfair competition against plaintiff to defendant's irreparable damage and has diverted business worth at least $100,000 away from defendant.

WHEREFORE, defendant demands judgment against plaintiff for the sum of $100,000 (one hundred thousand dollars), interest, and costs.

Signed: _____
                        Attorney for Defendant

Address: _____

matter of the original action." A cross-claim may also be filed separately from the answer. Because counterclaims and cross-claims raise new issues and initiate a separate cause of action, they must meet the procedural requirements of a complaint.

See also CIVIL PROCEDURE.

ANTARCTICA 📖 The polar land adjacent to the South Pole. 📖

According to the Antarctic Treaty of 1959, Antarctica is considered "international" territory, like that of the high seas; it is not under the jurisdiction of any single nation. Its legal status, therefore, is governed by INTERNATIONAL LAW.

ANTE 📖 [*Latin, Before.*] A reference to a previous portion of a report or textbook. 📖

Ante is synonymous with *supra*.

ANTECEDENT DEBT 📖 A legally enforceable obligation, which has been in existence prior to the time in question, to reimburse another with money or property. 📖

Principles of CONTRACT law vary from jurisdiction to jurisdiction regarding whether an antecedent debt constitutes good CONSIDERATION since the DEBTOR does not incur any new detriment at the time that he or she enters a contract with another party. COMMERCIAL PAPER that has been given in exchange for an antecedent debt is deemed by the UNIFORM COMMERCIAL CODE to be supported by adequate consideration.

Under statutes governing BANKRUPTCY, a transfer of property made by a debtor because of an antecedent debt might be considered a voidable PREFERENCE, depending upon the length of time between the creation of the debt and the filing of the petition for bankruptcy. A bankruptcy court may set aside a voidable preference since it gives one CREDITOR a better right to payment than other creditors who are similarly situated.

ANTHONY, SUSAN BROWNELL

People no longer are surprised when an American woman works outside the home, keeps her own bank account, maintains custody of her children after a divorce, or votes in a presidential election. Yet, not too long ago, these practices were uncommon, if not illegal, in the United States. Due in large part to the efforts of the remarkable Susan Brownell Anthony and other pioneers of feminism, women in the United States enjoy rights and opportunities that are simply taken for granted today.

Anthony was born in 1820, during an era when most women got married, produced children, and deferred completely to their husbands. Daniel Anthony, her father, belonged to the Society of Friends (better known as Quakers), a religious group that recognized the equality of men and women. Daniel encouraged his daughter to think independently and to speak her mind. He supported her educational pursuits and emphasized self-sufficiency.

Although Anthony's father was an admirable man and progressive for his time, her mother, Lucy Anthony, found little pleasure in her restricted, duty-bound life. She appeared overwhelmed by eight pregnancies and exhausted from running the household while keeping boarders and raising six surviving children. Historians believe that the withdrawn, careworn

BIOGRAPHY

Susan Brownell Anthony

Lucy became a symbol to Anthony of the unfair burdens of marriage. The institution seemed weighted against women, even those with kind and liberal-minded husbands. Anthony concluded that marriage was necessary only when a strong emotional bond existed between two people. This view put her at odds with most women of her generation, who considered matrimony a requirement for social and economic security. True to her principles, Anthony—who once referred to marriage as slavery and "a blot on civilization"—rejected several suitors' offers and remained single throughout her long life.

Anthony was an intelligent young girl who received the best education available at the time. Although she attended a well-regarded boarding school in Philadelphia, she did not enroll in college. In the 1830s, only one college in the United States, Ohio's Oberlin College, accepted women. Even with a college education, Anthony would have faced a limited number of employment opportunities. As a woman, her only options were to become a seamstress, a domestic, or a teacher. Anthony chose teaching and, in 1938, began the first of several teaching jobs. In 1846, she became headmistress at Canajoharie Academy in New York. There, she discovered that male teachers were paid $10.00 a week, whereas she received $2.50. Frustrated with the low pay and a lack of respect for her work, Anthony decided to devote her energies to social reform.

Although Anthony is best known for her fight for women's suffrage, she also crusaded for other causes. In 1852, Anthony became active in the temperance movement, a national campaign to ban the sale and consumption of alcohol. When it became clear that women were not allowed full leadership in the existing temperance organizations, Anthony helped form the Woman's State Temperance Society of New York.

Like her father, Anthony also was a fervent abolitionist. She became friends with Frederick Douglass and attended her father's antislavery meetings in the family home. Before and during

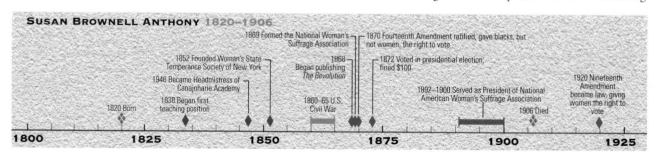

SUSAN BROWNELL ANTHONY 1820–1906

1869 Formed the National Woman's Suffrage Association

1870 Fourteenth Amendment ratified; gave blacks, but not women, the right to vote

1852 Founded Woman's State Temperance Society of New York

1868 Began publishing *The Revolution*

1872 Voted in presidential election; fined $100

1946 Became Headmistress of Canajoharie Academy

1892–1900 Served as President of National American Woman's Suffrage Association

1920 Nineteenth Amendment became law, giving women the right to vote

1838 Began first teaching position

1820 Born

1860–65 U.S. Civil War

1906 Died

1800   1825   1850   1875   1900   1925

the U.S. Civil War, Anthony devoted her organizational skills to the cause. As head of the Anti-Slavery Society of New York, she planned lecture schedules and spoke publicly against the evils of the Southern system and of the discriminatory practices in the North. During this time, she joined forces with another abolitionist, Elizabeth Cady Stanton, who was the acknowledged leader of the fledgling women's rights movement.

After the war, Anthony and Stanton continued to work together for social reform. They were bitterly disappointed when their fellow abolitionists refused to support their strategy for constitutionally mandating voting rights for women. A golden opportunity for female suffrage had arisen with the drafting of the Fifteenth Amendment to the U.S. Constitution. This amendment was necessary to grant voting rights to the former slaves who were liberated by President Abraham Lincoln's Emancipation Proclamation. However, the abolitionists supported the Fifteenth Amendment only to the extent that it gave African American males the right to vote. They were not concerned about the amendment's exclusion of women. With that defeat, Anthony focused her sights on a separate constitutional amendment to grant women the franchise.

In 1868, Anthony began publishing *The Revolution*, a weekly newsletter advocating suffrage and equal rights for women. In 1869, Anthony and Stanton formed the National Woman's Suffrage Association. An indefatigable worker, Anthony became a fixture on the lecture circuit and headed national petition drives to establish support for female voting rights.

In 1872, Anthony decided to test the legality of voting laws that allowed only white and African American males to go to the polls. She registered and voted in the 1872 presidential election in Rochester, New York. Anthony was prosecuted for the offense and fined $100, but she refused to pay. Her defiance rallied supporters of women's rights across the nation. In time, Anthony merged her suffrage organization with another one, to form the National American Woman Suffrage Association. She served as president of this association from 1892 to 1900.

Not surprisingly, Anthony fought hard for the liberalization of laws for married women. During most of the nineteenth century, a wife had very little protection under the law. Any income she produced automatically belonged to her husband, as did any inheritance she received. Her husband could apprentice their children without her permission and was desig-

nated sole guardian of their children, no matter how unfit he might be. A husband even had the right to pass on his guardianship of the children by will. In Anthony's home state of New York, her petition drives and lectures were instrumental in convincing the legislature to pass laws giving married women power over their incomes and guardianship of their children.

Anthony was not afraid to flout social conventions to achieve her goals. For a time, she wore bloomers, a controversial garment named after Amelia Jenks Bloomer, the woman who popularized it. Bloomers were loose-fitting trousers gathered at the ankle and worn underneath a knee-length skirt. The costume was intended as a protest against the tight-fitting corsets and unwieldy petticoats popularly worn by women at the time. Although she withstood ridicule to make her point, Anthony stopped wearing bloomers when she concluded that they were diverting attention from the more serious issues facing women.

Anthony's message of equality often met resistance, and not just from men. Many women in the nineteenth century were frightened by or skeptical of change. In 1870, Anthony lamented their wariness when she wrote, "The fact is, women are in chains, and their servitude is all the more debasing because they do not realize it." She urged women to recognize the inequities they faced and to speak and act for their own freedom.

When Anthony died in 1906, women did not yet have the right to vote in presidential elections. When the Nineteenth Amendment to the U.S. Constitution finally became law in 1920, it was called the Anthony amendment in recognition of her valiant efforts to gain suffrage.

Anthony was also honored in 1979 and 1980, when the U.S. Mint issued one dollar coins bearing her likeness. She became the first woman to be pictured on a U.S. coin in general circulation.

"MEN THEIR RIGHTS AND NOTHING MORE; WOMEN THEIR RIGHTS AND NOTHING LESS."

CROSS-REFERENCES

Fifteenth Amendment; Nineteenth Amendment; Stanton, Elizabeth Cady; Temperance Movement; Women's Rights.

ANTI-BALLISTIC-MISSILE TREATY OF 1972   The Anti-Ballistic-Missile Treaty of 1972 (ABM Treaty) limits the number of defensive antiballistic missile (ABM) systems that the United States and the former Soviet Union can use in preparation for nuclear war (23 UST 3435: TIAS 7503; 944 UNTS 13, U.S. Department of State, *Treaties in Force*, 1993). Restrictions on ballistic missile defenses (BMDs), military warning systems designed to alert and

protect a nation, compose the bulk of the treaty's articles. The treaty limited each country's supply of remote-controlled, long-range nuclear rockets, or intercontinental ballistic missiles (ICBMs). Although the ABM agreement still stood between the United States and Russia following the breakup of the Soviet Union, it was unclear which of the rest of the former Soviet republics would continue to adhere to it.

On May 26, 1972, at the U.S.-Soviet summit in Moscow, President Richard M. Nixon, of the United States, and President Leonid Brezhnev, of the Soviet Union, signed, in conjunction with the Strategic Arms Limitation Talks of 1969–72 (SALT I), the ABM Treaty. The treaty limited each party to two ABM sites, with no more than one hundred ABM launchers and interceptors at each site. One of these sites could protect an ICBM silo deployment area, and the second could protect the national capital. The treaty prohibited the development, testing, or deployment of sea-based, air-based, space-based, or mobile land-based ABM systems. Furthermore, it excluded the transfer or deployment of ABM systems to or in other nations. The fifteen articles of the treaty were of unlimited duration and would come up for renewal every five years.

The principles of the treaty explicitly reflected the policy of mutual assured destruction (MAD)—the belief that the best way to control nuclear arms is to allow both sides enough power to ensure the destruction of both nations in the event of war. As stated in article I of the treaty, each side agreed "not to deploy ABM systems for a defense of the territory of its country and not to provide a base for such a defense, and not to deploy ABM systems for defense of an individual region" (Durch 1988). Article II defines an ABM system as "a system to counter strategic ballistic missiles or their elements in flight trajectory, currently consisting of ABM interceptor missiles ... ABM launchers [and] ... ABM radars." Article III reiterates the ban on ABM deployment, excepting, for each side, one deployment area around the national capital and one around an ICBM launcher deployment area. This provision was later reduced, in 1974, to just one deployment area for each country, allowing "no more than 100 ABM interceptor missiles at launch sites." Articles IV to XV outline provisions for, among other issues, nuclear testing, radar deployment, amendments to the treaty, and the terms of treaty withdrawal.

After the ABM Treaty was ratified by the U.S. Congress, legislators refused to authorize funds for building an ABM site outside Washington, D.C. In early 1975, the United States deployed its single permitted system near the Minuteman Fields at Grand Forks Air Force Base in North Dakota. Within a year, however, the system was deactivated by Congress on the ground that it was not very cost-effective. The Soviets, meanwhile, used their ABM deployments to protect Moscow.

Despite attempts to follow the principles of SALT I, continued limitations on strategic arms fell apart with the SALT II Treaty of 1979. The U.S. Congress refused to ratify the treaty, which had been signed by Presidents Jimmy Carter and Leonid Brezhnev. SALT II went on to draw heavy fire in the 1980s from the newly empowered Reagan administration. Whereas the Soviets generally adhered to a strict interpretation of the ABM Treaty, President Ronald Reagan advocated "peace through strength" and pushed for new weapons programs and policies. Reagan reinterpreted the treaty liberally, putting it to its most serious test. His proposal to render nuclear ballistic missiles ineffective and obsolete, with the Strategic Defense Initiative (SDI), a space-based BMD system popularly known as Star Wars, caused great debate at home and considerable alarm in the Soviet Union.

Like Reagan, the opponents of the ABM Treaty believed that its limits were based on one-way accommodation, that is, allowing the Soviets to retain their numerical superiority, as seen in SALT II. The Soviets had previously established numerical superiority in ICBM de-

U.S. President Richard Nixon and Soviet President Leonid Brezhnev smile and shake hands after signing the Anti-Ballistic-Missile Treaty of 1972.

UPI/BETTMANN

ployment, and the ABM Treaty supposedly held back the development of further U.S. weapons technology. Especially troublesome to some was the Soviets' Krasnoyarsk radar system in western Siberia. According to article VI of the ABM Treaty, an early warning radar with this orientation should have been located on the Pacific coast or in the outer Arctic reaches of Siberia. Many believed that Moscow was cheating on its end of the deal, hence the treaty should go.

In the 1980s, tensions between the United States and the Soviet Union flared. In October 1985, the Reagan administration announced a new interpretation of the ABM Treaty, under which the development and testing of "exotic" ABM systems (those not spelled out in the treaty itself—e.g., Star Wars) would have no limit. In 1986, with the Strategic Arms Reduction Treaty (START) talks in full swing, the United States and the Soviet Union treated the ABM Treaty as a central bargaining chip. Moscow looked to maintain the treaty for at least another decade, with tight constraints on space testing. Washington, meanwhile, looked to abide by the treaty for at most another decade and expected lessened constraints on the space testing of exotic technologies.

The ensuing events of the late 1980s and early 1990s caught everyone by surprise. Although the United States' interest in the SDI continued into the Bush administration years and persisted through the eventual breakup of the Soviet Union, both the United States and the Soviet Union showed interest in pursuing at least the spirit of the ABM Treaty. True arms reductions talks developed with the Soviet demise. In 1991, Soviet nuclear forces were split up between four countries—Russia, Ukraine, Belarus, and Kazakhstan—and spokespersons on both sides saw revision of the ABM Treaty as necessary. The START agreements of 1992 shed new light on older concessions. As the chief U.S. architect of the original ABM Treaty, Henry Kissinger now joined others in declaring it obsolete in the new era of disarmament. As a gesture of good faith, the Soviets demolished their controversial Krasnoyarsk radar system (a shoe factory now occupies the site).

The United States and Russia worked together and strayed from the MAD doctrine. They turned their attention elsewhere, mainly to the developing world. New nations on the list of nuclear powers included Israel, India, Pakistan, Algeria, Egypt, Iran, Iraq, Libya, North Korea, and Syria, none of which had any formal attachment to the ABM Treaty. U.S. and former Soviet strategists went from analyzing BMD research provisions set forth in the ABM Treaty to setting up safeguards against attack from other powers.

CROSS-REFERENCES

Arms Control and Disarmament; Carter, James Earl; International Law; Nixon, Richard; Reagan, Ronald; Treaty.

ANTICIPATION The performance of an act or obligation before it is legally due. In PATENT law, the publication of the existence of an invention that has already been patented or has a patent pending, which are grounds for denying a patent to an invention that has substantially the same structure and function as the earlier invention.

In the law of NEGLIGENCE, anticipation refers to the knowledge that there is a reasonable probability that the consequences of particular conduct of one individual will result in injury to others.

The anticipation of an invention also occurs if the later invention is merely an adaptation of an earlier patent, which would be obvious to a skilled person who need only exercise some mechanical skill to develop the same adaptation.

ANTICIPATORY REPUDIATION The unjustifiable denial by a party to a CONTRACT of any intention to perform contractual duties, which occurs prior to the time PERFORMANCE is due.

This form of breach, also known as anticipatory breach of contract, occurs when one party positively states that he or she will not substantially perform a contract. The mere assertion that the party is encountering difficulties in preparing to perform, is dissatisfied with the bargain, or is otherwise uncertain whether performance will be rendered when due is insufficient to constitute a REPUDIATION. Another type of anticipatory breach consists of any voluntary act by a party that destroys, or seriously impairs, that party's ability to perform the contract.

The REMEDIES available to the nonrepudiating party upon an anticipatory repudiation entail certain obligations. If the nonrepudiating party chooses to ignore the repudiation and proceeds with his or her performance, the duty to MITIGATE DAMAGES—which imposes on the injured party an obligation to exercise reasonable effort to minimize losses—mandates that the nonrepudiating party not perform if the consequence of performance would be to increase the DAMAGES. In addition, this duty requires, where applicable, the procurement of a substitute performance.

If the nonrepudiating party implores or insists that the other party perform, this demand, in and of itself, does not divest the nonrepudiating party's right to damages. The presence or absence of a breach of contract depends solely upon the repudiating party's actions. The prevailing view is that the nonrepudiating party may pursue any remedy for breach of contract, even though he or she has informed the repudiating party that he would await the latter's performance.

The nonrepudiating party also possesses the option to do nothing and to commence an ACTION for breach after the time for performance. Under the majority view, such an action can be instituted without tendering the nonrepudiating party's performance or even alleging or proving that the party was ready, willing, and able to perform. The nonrepudiating party must demonstrate, however, that he or she would have been ready, willing, and able to perform but for the repudiation.

In regard to the law of SALES, the UNIFORM COMMERCIAL CODE (UCC), a body of law governing commercial transactions by the states, provides that anticipatory repudiation entails the right of one party to a contract to sue for breach before the performance date when the other party communicates the intention not to perform. The repudiation can, however, be retracted before the performance date if the nonrepudiating party has not acted on the basis of the repudiation. Some jurisdictions direct the injured party to await the performance date before instituting an action.

ANTILAWYER MOVEMENT Throughout early U.S. history, legal practitioners were the subject of ambivalence on the part of the general public. The attitude against lawyers reached its peak after the Revolutionary War and remained hostile until the beginning of the nineteenth century.

During the early days of the colonies, the system for the administration of justice was based on arbitration and religious principles, and lawyers specially educated and skilled in the law were presumably not needed and were often restricted or prohibited from practicing. Judges were ordinary men who used unpolished methods of questioning to determine the facts of each case; defendants were their own lawyers. This system remained successful as long as the population of each community remained small and manageable, and the people were clear about their rights and obligations to their neighbors and the community.

By the end of the seventeenth century, the colonies experienced a period of growth, and the original judicial system became unsatisfactory. Formal pleading and skilled lawyers began

to replace the primitive methods of earlier colonial times.

After the Revolutionary War, Americans sought a new form of jurisprudence to interact with their newly gained freedoms. Laws were less confining, due to the belief that moral fiber was more important to satisfactory conduct than legislation.

During this period, the antilawyer movement gained momentum. Historians speculate that it evolved as a result of former prejudices and conflicts toward the legal profession. Although lawyers in the past had not been viewed favorably, they achieved prominence and esteem as strong proponents of freedom from England during the Revolutionary War. After the war, lawyers were once again an important part of the legal system but were used primarily by the wealthy. As a result, they were often in conflict with those who were poor and could not pay their debts, which led to a resurrection of the old negative attitudes against them.

Lawyers were regarded with suspicion. They were accused of initiating unnecessary lawsuits, impeding the justice system, and prolonging

A wood engraving from an 1884 Harper's Monthly shows Daniel Shays and his comrades occupying a courthouse to prevent the court from directing legal action at debt-ridden farmers in 1786.

trials to secure additional fees from unsuspecting clients. They were also criticized for the use of legal jargon, causing simple matters to seem complicated.

Despite these attacks, lawyers managed to attain political power. They were regarded as conspirators, however, for people could not accept the idea that lawyers who served as politicians made the laws by which they secured a living as legal practitioners. It was also feared that lawyers, judges, and legislators would band together to control society, depriving the common people of some of their hard-won freedoms. Although the fears were exaggerated, they were true to some degree, for lawyers did earn a living from the ramifications that legislation had upon the general public.

Two remedies were recommended to reconcile the proponents of the antilawyer sentiment and lawyers. The first suggestion was an updated version of the early colonial justice system, which prohibited lawyers from practicing. A judge representing the interests of the community would preside over the court and instruct the jury. Judges were educated aristocrats who could be impeached if their conduct so warranted. If a legal representative was deemed necessary, a friend of the defendant could participate in the arbitration.

The second suggestion provided for a small group of professional lawyers to practice as public servants. Their salaries and actions would be controlled by the state, and their chief function would be to clarify legal principles of each case for the jury.

The conflicting feelings toward lawyers culminated in several incidents, the most noteworthy of which was known as Shays's Rebellion. The rebellion began in 1786 when Massachusetts voters elected a majority of nonlawyers to the General Court. This action led to a riot, and hostile agrarian mobs overran the courthouses, closing them down. The governor dispatched the state army, which successfully quelled the agitators.

Shays's Rebellion did not stop the people of Massachusetts from electing lawyers to political positions. The very tactics they feared in the courtroom were highly desirable in politics to control government officials; in spite of their conflicting feelings, voters were still attracted to legal skills.

The new methods of justice proved to be inefficient. Arbitration was fruitless, and laymen were fallible as lawyers. By 1790, most cases were again tried by lawyers, and the antilawyer movement began to wane.

See also SHAYS'S REBELLION.

ANTINOMY 📖 An expression in law and logic to indicate that two authorities, laws, or propositions are inconsistent with each other. 📖

ANTITRUST LAW 📖 Legislation enacted by the federal and various state governments to regulate trade and commerce by preventing unlawful restraints, price-fixing, and monopolies, to promote competition, and to encourage the production of quality goods and services at the lowest prices, with the primary goal of safeguarding public welfare by ensuring that consumer demands will be met by the manufacture and sale of goods at reasonable prices. 📖

Antitrust law seeks to make businesses compete fairly. It has had a serious effect on business practices and the organization of U.S. industry. Premised on the belief that free trade benefits the economy, businesses, and consumers alike, the law forbids several types of restraint of trade and monopolization. These fall into four main areas: agreements between competitors, contractual arrangements between sellers and buyers, the pursuit or maintenance of monopoly power, and mergers.

The Sherman Anti-Trust Act of 1890 (15 U.S.C.A. § 1 et seq.) is the basis for antitrust law, and many states have modeled their own statutes upon it. As weaknesses in the Sherman Act became evident, Congress added amendments to it at various times through 1950. The most important are the Clayton Act of 1914 (15 U.S.C.A. § 12 et seq.) and the Robinson-Patman Act of 1936 (15 U.S.C.A. § 13 et seq.). Congress also created a regulatory agency to administer and enforce the law, under the Federal Trade Commission Act of 1914 (15 U.S.C.A. §§ 41–58). In an ongoing analysis influenced by economic, intellectual, and political changes, the U.S. Supreme Court has had the leading role in shaping how these laws are applied.

Enforcement of antitrust law depends largely on two agencies, the Federal Trade Commission (FTC), which may issue cease and desist orders to violators, and the U.S. Department of Justice's Antitrust Division, which can litigate. Private parties may also bring civil suits. Violations of the Sherman Act are FELONIES carrying fines of up to $10 million for corporations, and fines of up to $350,000 and prison sentences of up to three years for persons. The federal government, states, and individuals can collect triple the amount of DAMAGES they have suffered as a result of injuries.

Origins Antitrust law originated in reaction to a public outcry over *trusts*, which were late-nineteenth-century corporate monopolies that dominated U.S. manufacturing and mining. Trusts took their name from the quite legal device of business incorporation called trusteeship, which consolidated control of industries by transferring stock in exchange for trust certificates. The practice grew out of necessity. Twenty-five years after the Civil War, rapid industrialization had blessed and cursed business. Markets expanded and productivity grew, but output exceeded demand and competition sharpened. Rivals sought greater security and profits in CARTELS (mutual agreements to fix prices and control output). Out of these arrangements sprang the trusts. From sugar to whiskey to beef to tobacco, the process of merger and consolidation brought entire industries under the control of a few powerful people. Oil and steel, the backbone of the nation's heavy industries, lay in the hands of the corporate giants John D. Rockefeller and J. P. Morgan. The trusts could fix prices at any level. If a competitor entered the market, the trusts would sell their goods at a loss until the competitor went out of business and then raise prices again. By the 1880s, abuses by the trusts brought demands for reform.

History gave only contradictory direction to the reformers. Before the eighteenth century, COMMON LAW concerned itself with CONTRACTS, combinations, and conspiracies that resulted in restraint of free trade, but it did little about them. English courts generally let restrictive contracts stand because they did not consider themselves suited to judging adequacy or fairness. Over time, courts looked more closely into both the purpose and the effect of any

restraint of trade. The turning point came in 1711 with the establishment of the basic standard for judging close cases, "the rule of reason." Courts asked whether the goal of a contract was a general restraint of competition (*naked restraint*) or particularly limited in time and geography (*ancillary restraint*). Naked restraints were unreasonable, but ancillary restraints were often acceptable. Exceptions to the rule grew as the economic philosophy of *laissez-faire* (meaning "let the people do what they please") spread its doctrine of noninterference in business. As rival businesses formed cartels to fix prices and control output, the late-eighteenth-century English courts often nodded in approval.

By the time the U.S. public was complaining about the trusts, common law in U.S. courts was somewhat tougher on restraint of trade. Yet it was still contradictory. The courts took two basic views of cartels: tolerant and condemning. The first view accepted cartels as long as they did not stop other merchants from entering the market. It used the rule of reason to determine this, and put a high premium on the freedom to enter contracts. Businesses and contracts mattered. Consumers, who suffered from PRICE-FIXING, were irrelevant; the wisdom of the market would protect them from exploitation. The second view saw cartels as thoroughly bad. It reserved the rule of reason only for judging more limited ancillary restrictions. Given these competing views, which varied from state to state, no comprehensive common law could be said to exist. But one approach was destined to win out.

John D. Rockefeller (left) and J. P. Morgan (right) controlled trusts in the areas of oil and steel, essential to the operation of U.S. heavy industry during the 1880s.

The Sherman Act and Early Enforcement In 1890, Congress took aim at the trusts with passage of the Sherman Anti-Trust Act, named for Senator John Sherman (R-Ohio). It went far beyond the common law's refusal to enforce certain offensive contracts. Clearly persuaded by the more restrictive view that saw great harm in restraint of trade, the Sherman Act outlawed trusts altogether. The landmark law had two sections. Section 1 broadly banned group action in agreements, forbidding "[e]very contract, combination in the form of trust or otherwise, or conspiracy," that restrained interstate or foreign trade. Section 2 banned individuals from monopolizing or trying to monopolize. Violations of either section were punishable by a maximum fine of $50,000 and up to one year in jail. The Sherman Act passed by nearly unanimous votes in both houses of Congress.

Although sweeping in its language, the Sherman Act soon revealed its limitations. Congress had wanted action even though it did not know what steps to take. Historians would later dispute what its precise aims had been, but clearly the lawmakers intended courts to play the leading role in promoting competition and attacking monopolization: judges would make decisions as cases arose, slowly developing a body of opinions that would replace the confusing precedents of state courts. For a public expecting overnight change, the process worked all too slowly. President Grover Cleveland's Justice Department, which disliked the Sherman Act, made little effort to enforce it.

Initial setbacks also came from the Supreme Court's first consideration of the statute, in *United States v. E. C. Knight Co.*, 156 U.S. 1, 15 S. Ct. 249, 39 L. Ed. 325 (1895). Rejecting a challenge to a sugar trust that controlled over 98 percent of the nation's sugar refining capacity, the Court held that manufacturing was not interstate commerce. This was good news for trusts. If manufacturing was exempt from the Sherman Act, then they had little to worry about. The Court only began strongly supporting use of the law in the late 1890s, starting with cases against railroad cartels. By 1904, some three hundred large companies still controlled nearly 40 percent of the nation's manufacturing assets and influenced at least 80 percent of its vital industries.

After the turn of the twentieth century, federal enforcement picked up speed. President Theodore Roosevelt's announcement that he was a "trustbuster" predicted one important aspect of the future of antitrust enforcement: it would depend largely on political will from the executive branch of government. Roosevelt and his successor, President William Howard Taft, responded to public criticism over the rapid merger of even more industries by pursuing more vigorous legal action, and steady prosecution in the first decade of the twentieth century brought the downfall of trusts.

In 1911, the Supreme Court ordered the dissolution of the Standard Oil Company and the American Tobacco Company in landmark rulings that brought down two of the most powerful industrial trusts. But these were ambiguous victories. In *Standard Oil Co. of New Jersey v. United States*, 221 U.S. 1, 31 S. Ct. 502, 55 L. Ed. 619, for example, the Court dissolved the trust into thirty-three companies, but held that the Sherman Act outlawed only restraints that were anticompetitive—subject, furthermore, to a rule of reason. Critics of all stripes jumped on this decision. Some feared that conservative judges would now gut the Sherman Act; others predicted a return to lax enforcement; and businesses worried that in the absence of specific unlawful restraints, the rule of reason gave courts too much freedom to read the law subjectively.

Congressional Reform up to 1950 Dissatisfaction brought new federal laws in 1914. The first of these was the Clayton Act, which answered the criticism that the Sherman Act was too general. It declared four practices illegal but not criminal: (1) price discrimination—selling a product at different prices to similarly situated buyers; (2) tying and exclusive-dealing contracts—sales on condition that the buyer stop dealing with the seller's competitors; (3) corporate mergers—acquisitions of competing companies; and (4) INTERLOCKING DIRECTORATES—boards of competing companies, with common members.

Quick to hedge its bets, the Clayton Act qualified each of these prohibited activities. They were only illegal where the effect "may be substantially to lessen competition" or "tend to create a monopoly." This language was intentionally vague. Despite specifying different tests for violations, Congress still wanted the courts to make the difficult decisions. One important limitation was added: the Clayton Act exempted unions from the scope of antitrust law, refusing to treat human labor as a commodity.

The second piece of federal legislation in 1914 was the Federal Trade Commission Act. Without attaching criminal penalties, the law provided that "unfair methods of competition in or affecting commerce, and unfair or deceptive acts or practices in or affecting commerce are hereby declared illegal." This was more than a symbolic attempt to buttress the Sherman Act. The law also created a regulatory agency, the FTC, to interpret and enforce it. Lawmakers fearing judicial hostility to the Sherman Act saw the FTC as a body that would more closely follow their preferences. Originally, the commission was designed to issue prospective decrees and share responsibilities with the Antitrust Division of the Justice Department. Later court rulings would allow it greater latitude in attacking Sherman Act violations.

These laws helped satisfy the short-term demand for tougher, more explicit action from Congress. Before long, antitrust enforcement would shift with the mood of the country. As World War I and the 1920s reversed the outlook of previous years, antitrust policy was characterized by the hands-off policies of President Calvin Coolidge, who declared, "The business of America is business." Economic trends created and supported this attitude; prosperity seemed a worthwhile reward. In this era, the Justice Department gave more attention to promoting fairness than it did to attacking restrictive practices and monopoly power. Although activities such as price-fixing still came under attack, other kinds of business cooperation flourished and even received official encouragement in the early years of the New Deal. This flirtation lasted a good fifteen years, intensifying after the stock market crash of 1929.

Following what historians called the era of neglect, antitrust made a resurgence. In 1935, the Supreme Court struck down President Franklin D. Roosevelt's National Industrial Recovery Act, which coordinated industrywide output and pricing, in *ALA Schechter Poultry Corp. v. United States*, 295 U.S. 495, 55 S. Ct. 837, 79 L. Ed. 1570. The decision radically affected New Deal–era policy. The following year, Congress passed the Robinson-Patman Act, an attempt to make sense of the Clayton Act's bans on price discrimination. The Robinson-Patman Act explicitly forbade forms of price discrimination, in order to protect small producers from extinction at the hands of larger competitors. By 1937, economic decline brought federal antitrust enforcement back with a vengeance, as Roosevelt's administration began an extensive investigation into monopolies. The effort resulted in more than eighty antitrust suits in 1940.

One federal court case in this period, *United States v. Aluminum Co. of America*, 148 F.2d 416 (2d Cir. 1945) (hereinafter *Alcoa*), changed antimonopoly law for years to come. Since the 1920s, the Supreme Court had looked skeptically on the role of a business's size in judging monopoly cases. In *United States v. United States Steel Corp.*, 251 U.S. 417, 40 S. Ct. 293, 64 L. Ed. 343 (1920), it said, "[T]he law does not make mere size an offense, or the existence of unexerted power an offense. It, we repeat, requires overt acts." The decision weakened the monopoly ban of the Sherman Act. Rather than focus on abusive business conduct, *Alcoa* emphasized the role of market power. Judge Learned Hand wrote for the court, "Many people believe that possession of unchallenged economic power deadens initiative, discourages thrift and depresses energy; that immunity from competition is a narcotic, and rivalry is a stimulant, to industrial progress; that the spur of constant stress is necessary to counteract an inevitable disposition to let well enough alone." The standard that emerged from this decision applied a two-part test for determining illegal monopolization: the defendant (1) must possess monopoly power in a relevant market and (2) must have improperly used exclusionary acts to gain or protect that power.

Congress added its last piece of important legislation in 1950 with the Celler-Kefauver Antimerger Act, addressing a weakness in the Clayton Act. Because only anticompetitive stock purchases had been forbidden, businesses would circumvent the Clayton Act by targeting the assets of their rivals. Supreme Court decisions had also undermined the law by allowing businesses to transfer stock purchases into assets before the government filed a complaint. The Celler-Kefauver amendment closed these loopholes.

The Supreme Court and Evolving Doctrine Vigorous enforcement of antitrust legislation created an immense body of case law. After 1950, Supreme Court decisions did more than anything else to shape antitrust doctrine. Two competing outlooks emerged. One regarded markets as fragile, easily distorted by private firms, and readily correctable through public intervention. Economic efficiency mattered less, in this view, than the belief in the antitrust doctrine's ability to meet social and political goals. The opposing view saw business rivalry as generally healthy, doubted that public intervention could cure defects, and emphasized the self-correcting ability of markets to erode private restraints and private power. This outlook opposed the use of antitrust measures except to stop behavior that clearly harms the efficiency of business.

The most aggressive doctrine was developed under Chief Justice Earl Warren. The Warren Court often saw the need for decentralized social, political, and economic power, a goal it put ahead of the ideal of economic efficiency. In 1962, its first ruling on the Celler-Kefauver Act, *Brown Shoe Co. v. United States*, 370 U.S. 294, 82 S. Ct. 1502, 8 L. Ed. 2d 510, held that a merger between two firms accounting for only five percent of total industry output violated the principal antimerger provision of the antitrust laws. *Brown Shoe* also reflected the Court's hostility toward *vertical restraints* (restrictions imposed in contracts by the seller on the buyer, or vice versa).

This aggressive trend peaked in 1967 in *United States v. Arnold, Schwinn & Co.*, 388 U.S. 365, 87 S. Ct. 1856, 18 L. Ed. 2d 1249. *Arnold* concerned *nonprice vertical restraints* (territorial or customer restrictions on the resale of goods). The majority ruled that such restraints were per se illegal—in other words, so harmful to competition that they need not be evaluated. In ensuing years, critics condemned the Court's use of "per se" tests to invalidate agreements between competitors or between sellers and buyers. The so-called Chicago school, led by scholars Robert H. Bork and Richard A. Posner, argued that some nonprice vertical restraints actually led to gains in economic efficiency. These ideas would soon take hold.

By the mid-1970s, the Court backed off its robust interventionism. Two pivotal decisions came in 1977, including the most important since World War II, *Continental TV v. GTE Sylvania*, 433 U.S. 36, 97 S. Ct. 2549, 53 L. Ed. 2d 568. In a decisive departure from the previous decade's rulings, the Court abandoned its hostility toward efficiency. Now, for evaluating nonprice vertical restraints, it returned to the use of a rule of reason. Per se rules would remain influential, but economic analysis would be the primary tool in formulating and applying antitrust rules. The second powerful change in doctrine was *Brunswick Corp. v. Pueblo Bowl-O-Mat*, 429 U.S. 477, 97 S. Ct. 690, 50 L. Ed. 2d 701. *Brunswick* said antitrust laws "were enacted for the 'protection of competition, not competitors.' " The irony was addressed to private antitrust litigants. If they wanted to sue, the Court said, they would have to prove "antitrust injury." This decision threw out the old view that the demise of individual firms was plainly bad for competition. Replacing it was the view that adverse effects to businesses are sometimes offset by gains in reduced costs and increased output. Increasingly, after *Brunswick*, the Supreme Court and lower courts would accept

economic efficiency as a justification for dominant firms to defend their market position. By 1986, efficiency-based analysis was widely accepted in federal courts.

Even against this restrictive background, explosive change occurred. The early 1980s saw the dramatic conclusion of a historic monopoly case against the telephone giant American Telephone and Telegraph (AT&T) (*United States v. American Telephone & Telegraph Co.*, 552 F. Supp. 131 [D.D.C. 1982], *aff'd in Maryland v. United States*, 460 U.S. 1001, 103 S. Ct. 1240, 75 L. Ed. 2d 472 [1983]). The Justice Department settled claims that AT&T had impeded competition in long-distance telephone service and telecommunications equipment. The result was the largest divestiture in history: a federal court severed the Bell System's operating companies and manufacturing arm (Western Electric) from AT&T, transforming the nation's telephone services. But the historic settlement was an exception to the political philosophy and level of enforcement that characterized the decade. As the 1980s were ending, the Justice Department dropped its thirteen-year suit against International Business Machines (IBM). This lengthy battle had sought to end IBM's dominance by breaking it up into four computer companies. Convinced that market forces had done the work for them, prosecutors gave up.

Throughout the 1980s, political conservatism in federal enforcement complemented the Supreme Court's doctrine of nonintervention. The administration of President Ronald Reagan reduced the budgets of the FTC and the Department of Justice, leaving them with limited resources for enforcement. Enforcement efforts followed a restrictive agenda of prosecuting cases of output restrictions and large mergers of a *horizontal* nature (involving firms within the same industry and at the same level of production). Mergers of companies into conglomerates, on the other hand, were looked on favorably, and the years 1984 and 1985 produced the greatest increase in corporate acquisitions in the nation's history.

As the Supreme Court strengthened requirements for evidence, injury, and the right to bring suit, antitrust cases became harder for plaintiffs to win. Most decisions in this period narrowed the reach of antitrust. A few rare exceptions, such as *Aspen Skiing Co. v. Aspen Highlands Skiing Corp.*, 472 U.S. 585, 105 S. Ct. 2847, 86 L. Ed. 2d 467 (1985), which condemned a monopolist's unjustified refusal to deal with a rival, faintly recalled the tough outlook of the Warren Court. Nonintervention, however, took precedence. In the strongest example, *Matsushita Electrical Industrial Co. v. Zenith Radio Corp.*, 475 U.S. 574, 106 S. Ct. 1348, 89 L. Ed. 2d 538 (1986), the majority dismissed allegations that Japanese television manufacturers had engaged in a twenty-year pricing conspiracy designed to drive U.S. electronics equipment manufacturers out of business. The Court discouraged claims that rested on ambiguous CIRCUMSTANTIAL EVIDENCE or lacked "economic rationality," suggesting that lower courts settle these by SUMMARY JUDGMENT (judicial decision without a trial).

The 1990s Once again proving that antitrust law never remains static, the late 1980s and early 1990s brought more changes in enforcement, economic analysis, and court doctrine. At the state level in the late 1980s, governments attacked mergers and restraints. The Supreme Court gave these efforts support in *California v. American Stores Co.*, 495 U.S. 271, 110 S. Ct. 1853, 109 L. Ed. 2d 240 (1990), upholding the ability of state governments to break up illegal mergers. Another trend came again from academia, where, for years, critics of the Chicago school had been reevaluating its highly influential efficiency model. They concluded that a proper analysis of efficiency goals showed that efficiency demanded tighter antitrust controls, not stubborn nonintervention.

An important 1992 Supreme Court case seemed to support this view. *Eastman Kodak Co. v. Image Technical Services*, 504 U.S. 451, 112 S. Ct. 2072, 119 L. Ed. 2d 265 (hereinafter *Kodak*), concerned *tying arrangements* (contracts between buyer and seller that restrict competition) in the sale and service of photocopiers. Kodak sold replacement parts only to buyers who agreed to have Kodak exclusively service the machines, and the restriction prompted a lawsuit from eighteen independent service organizations (ISOs). The company defended itself by arguing that even if it did monopolize the market, it lacked the necessary market power for a Sherman Act violation. The Court rejected the idea that this was enough to create a legal rule that equipment competition precluded any finding of monopoly power in the parts and services industry. In declaring Kodak's arrangement illegal, Justice Harry A. Blackmun warned about the dangers of relying on economic theory as a substitute for "actual market realities"—in this case, the harm done to ISOs who were shut out of the service market.

After the Reagan years, antitrust attitudes sharpened in Washington, D.C. The administration of President George Bush adopted a slightly more activist approach, reflected in joint guidelines on mergers issued in 1992 by the FTC and the Justice Department. In following the trend away from strict Chicago school efficiency standards, the guidelines looked more closely at competitive effects and tightened requirements. But understaffed government attorneys generally lost court cases. President Bill Clinton took this activism further. Anne K. Bingaman, his appointee to head the Department of Justice's Antitrust Division, beefed up the division's staff with sixty-one new attorneys, declaring her organization the competition agency. The Antitrust Division filed thirty-three civil suits in 1994, roughly three times the annual number brought under Reagan and Bush. It won some victories without going to court, in one instance compelling AT&T to keep a subsidiary private, but it lost a major lawsuit claiming that General Electric had conspired with the South African firm of DeBeers to fix industrial diamond prices.

Under President Clinton, the most important antitrust action involved a federal probe of the computer software giant Microsoft Corporation. In its potential for far-reaching action, this was the biggest antitrust case since those involving AT&T and IBM. Competitors complained that Microsoft used illegal arrangements with buyers to ensure that its disk operating system would be installed in nearly 80 percent of the world's computers. In-depth investigations by the FTC and the Department of Justice followed. In mid-1994, under threat of a federal lawsuit, Microsoft entered a consent decree designed to increase competitors' access to the market. All the parties involved—the original complainants, Microsoft, and the government—expressed relative satisfaction. But in early 1995, a federal judge rejected the agreement, citing evidence of other monopolistic practices by Microsoft. In a highly unusual move, the Justice Department and Microsoft together appealed the decision. The uncertain future of the case carried the threat of further action against the nation's fifth-largest industry.

CROSS-REFERENCES

Bork, Robert; Chicago School; Clayton Act; Corporation; Justice Department; Mergers and Acquisitions; Monopoly; Posner, Richard; Restraint of Trade; Robinson-Patman Act; Sherman Anti-Trust Act; Unfair Competition.

A POSTERIORI [*Latin, From the effect to the cause.*]

A posteriori describes a method of reasoning from given, express observations or experiments to reach and formulate general principles from them. This is also called inductive reasoning.

APPARENT 📖 That which is clear, plain, and evident. 📖

In the law of AGENCY, an AGENT has *apparent authority* to represent the person, or principal, for whom he or she acts, when the principal acts in such a manner toward the agent that a reasonable person would plainly assume that the agent was acting for the principal.

APPEAL 📖 Timely resort by an unsuccessful party in a lawsuit or administrative proceeding to an appropriate superior court empowered to review a FINAL DECISION on the ground that it was based upon an erroneous application of law. 📖

A person who initiates an appeal—the APPELLANT, sometimes called the PLAINTIFF IN ERROR—must file a NOTICE of appeal, along with the necessary documents, to commence appellate REVIEW. The person against whom the appeal is brought, the APPELLEE, then files a BRIEF in response to the appellant's ALLEGATIONS.

There are usually two stages of review in the federal court and in many state court systems: an appeal from a trial court to an intermediate appellate court and thereafter to the highest appellate court in the jurisdiction. Within the appellate rules of administrative procedure, there might be several levels of appeals from a determination made by an ADMINISTRATIVE AGENCY. For example, an appeal of the decision of an administrative law judge may be heard by a reviewing body within the agency, and from that body, the appeal may go to a trial court, such as a federal district court. Thereafter, the appeal might travel the same route as an appeal taken from a judicial decision, going from an intermediate to a superior appellate court, or it might go directly to a superior appellate court for review, bypassing the intermediate stage. The rules of appellate procedure applicable to a particular court govern its review of cases.

Right to Appeal There is no absolute right of appeal for all decisions rendered by a lower court or administrative agency. Federal and state constitutions and statutory provisions create appellate courts and prescribe the types of cases that are within their JURISDICTION. An appeal may be granted as a matter of right, such as from a trial court to an intermediate appellate court, or only at the discretion of a superior appellate court, for example, by a grant of CERTIORARI by the Supreme Court. If the decision presented does not meet the statutory requirements for review, the appellate court is powerless to hear the appeal and review is denied.

The right to appeal a decision is limited to those PARTIES to the proceeding who are ag-grieved by the decision because it has a direct and adverse effect upon their persons or property. In addition, an actual case or controversy must exist at the time of review. Issues that have become MOOT while the appeal is pending and cases that have been settled during that time are not reviewable.

Final Decision A final JUDGMENT or ORDER must have been reached by the trial court in order for a case to be appealable. A judgment is considered final for purposes of appeal when it ends the action in the court in which it was brought and nothing more is to be decided. This rule is intended to prevent the piecemeal litigation of a lawsuit, to avoid delay resulting from INTERLOCUTORY appeals, and to give the trial court the opportunity to render a decision in the case to the satisfaction of both parties, thereby obviating the need for appeal. The consideration of incidental matters, such as the computation of interest, attorneys' fees, or court costs, does not prevent a judgment or order from being appealed.

Grounds ERROR is the basis for review of a final decision rendered by a court or administrative agency. Error is called to the attention of a court through the use of OBJECTIONS, protests made during the course of a proceeding that an

Criminal Appeals from U.S. District Courts Filed in U.S. Court of Appeals

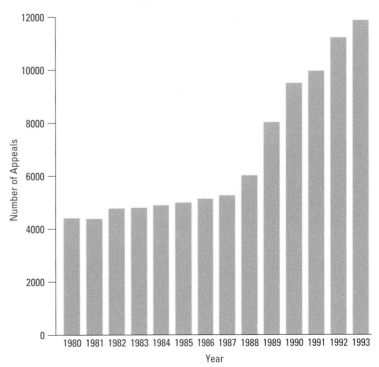

Source: Administrative Office of the United States Courts, *Annual Report of the Director,* annually, 1980 to 1993 editions.

action taken by the opposing side in a controversy is unfair or illegal. Decisions rendered in favor of one party at trial level are presumed by an appellate court to be correct unless objections have been made to the issues in question during the trial. Failure to do so will preclude their review on appeal. An objection must be made as promptly and specifically as possible for each act to which it is directed so that the court may make an intelligent decision regarding its merits. The trial judge rules on the objection, and the decision is included in the trial record. If the attorney for either party disagrees with the ruling, he or she may take an EXCEPTION, an objection taken to a decision of a court on a MATTER OF LAW, which is noted in the trial record to be preserved for purposes of appeal. Appellate jurisdiction is limited only to a review of actions taken by an inferior court. No new objections can be raised before an appellate court for its consideration unless exceptional circumstances exist to justify the appellate court raising the issues SUA SPONTE, on its own motion. Exceptional circumstances mean the presence at trial of plain error, a mistake in the proceedings that substantially affects the rights of the party against whom the decision has been made and undermines the fairness and integrity of the judicial system, causing a MISCARRIAGE OF JUSTICE.

Time of Appeal Appeals must be made within the time prescribed by statute or by the governing rules of the appellate court. Such statutes begin to run only after a final decision has been made. The timely filing of the notice of appeal with the CLERK of the appellate court and the appellee completes, or PERFECTS, the procedure. If the appeal is not taken and perfected within the time set by statute, the right to appeal is foreclosed. Extensions of time for the filing of an appeal may be granted, however, if extenuating circumstances exist, such as if either party is adjudicated incompetent or dies.

Notice of Appeal A notice of appeal—a written document filed by the appellant with the court and a copy of which is sent to the appellee—is the initial step in the appeals process. It informs the court and the party in whose favor a judgment or order has been made that the unsuccessful party seeks a review of the case. Failure to file a notice of appeal according to the statutory requirements will preclude appeal.

Bonds An appeal BOND, a promise to pay a sum of money, must often be posted by an appellant to secure the appellee against the costs of the appeal, if the appellee is successful and the appellant fails to pay. Its amount is determined by the court itself or by statute. The imposition of such a bond discourages frivolous appeals. If successive appeals are taken from an intermediate appellate court to a superior one, a new bond is usually required.

Record on Appeal The function of the appellate court is limited to a review of the trial record sent up from the lower court and the briefs filed by the appellant and appellee. AMICUS CURIAE briefs, if permitted by the appellate court, also become part of the record on appeal. The trial record, sometimes called the record proper, must show the PLEADINGS that initiated the case, the complete TRANSCRIPT (in cases of jury trial) of lower court proceedings, the VERDICT, and the ENTRY OF the final JUDGMENT or order. The appellant must clearly demonstrate that the grounds for review had been raised and unsuccessfully decided upon at the trial level and, therefore, prejudicial error exists to warrant the reversal of the decision of the lower court.

In some jurisdictions, a bill of exceptions—a written statement of the objections made by a party to the ruling, decision, charge, or opinion of the trial judge—must be submitted to the appellate court to provide a history of the trial proceedings. It should not include matters that belong in the record proper but, instead, should state those points concerning questions of law raised by the exceptions taken during the trial. The appellant's attorney prepares the bill and presents it to the trial judge for settlement, an agreement between the trial judge and the appellant that the bill contains a truthful account of the events of the trial. If there is disagreement, the judge returns the bill to the appellant with an explanation. The appellee must be given notice of the time and place of the settlement of the bill of exceptions in order to object to or approve its contents. The settled bill of exceptions becomes part of the trial transcript, which is part of the record on appeal. The appellant must submit a complete unabridged transcript of the trial that is prepared by the clerk of the trial court.

The entire trial record is printed and filed with the appellate court, and a copy is also sent to the appellee.

Assignment of Errors A statement by the appellant of the errors alleged to have been committed in the lower court is an assignment of errors, a type of appellate pleading used to point out to the appellate court the grounds for review. It controls the scope of an appeal because if a ground for review is not contained in it, it will not ordinarily be considered by the court. The assignment of errors is usually part of the notice of appeal, the bill of exceptions, the transcript of the record, or the brief, although in some jurisdictions, it is a separate document.

Appellate Brief The appellant and appellee must file individual briefs to aid the appellate court in its consideration of the issues presented. Failure to do so results in a dismissal of the appeal. The facts of the case, the grounds for review, and the arguments relating to those questions must be concisely stated. Any statements referring to the trial record must be supported by an appropriate reference to it.

The appellant's brief must specifically discuss the alleged errors that entitle the appellant to a reversal and discuss why each ruling of the lower court was wrong, citing authority, such as a case in which a similar point of law has been decided or a statute that applies to the particular point in issue. Disrespectful or abusive language directed against the lower court, the appellate court, the parties, witnesses, or opposing counsel cannot be used. If it is, it will be stricken from the brief, and the costs of the brief that might have been awarded are disallowed.

Review Appellate courts have jurisdiction to decide only issues actually before them on appeal and nothing else. They cannot render opinions on controversies or declare principles of law that have no practical effect in settling the rights of the litigants.

Only CONCLUSIONS OF LAW, not findings of FACT made by a lower court, are reviewable.

Harmless Error The appellate court must decide whether the errors alleged to have been made by the trial court are harmless or prejudicial. If the error substantially injures the rights of one party, it is called a prejudicial or reversible error and warrants the reversal of the final judgment or order. However, when the error is technical or minimally affects the rights of the parties or the outcome of the lawsuit, it is considered a HARMLESS ERROR, insufficient to require a reversal or modification of the decision of the lower court.

Hearing The clerk of the appellate court schedules on the court CALENDAR the date of the HEARING on which each side may present an oral argument. Oral arguments, usually ten to fifteen minutes for each side, help the court understand the issues argued in the brief and persuade the court to rule in favor of the arguing party. During the arguments of appellant and appellee, it is not unusual for the appellate judge to interrupt with questions on particular issues or points of law.

The appellant's argument briefly discusses the facts on which the cause of action is based and traces the history of the case through the lower courts. It includes the legal issues raised by the exceptions taken to the allegedly erroneous rulings of the trial judge. Thereafter, the appellee's counsel presents arguments in favor of affirming the original decision.

Determination An appellate court has broad powers over the scope of its decision and the relief to be granted. After reviewing the controlling issues in an action, it may AFFIRM the decision of the inferior tribunal, modify it, REVERSE it, or REMAND the case for a new trial in the lower court pursuant to its order.

When a decision is affirmed, the appellate court accepts the decision of the lower court and rejects the appellant's contention that it was erroneously made. The MODIFICATION of a decision by an appellate court means that, while it accepts part of the trial court's decision, the appellant was correct that the decision was partly erroneous. The trial court's decision is then modified accordingly.

A reversal of a decision means that the appellate court agrees with the appellant that the decision was erroneously made. The party who lost the case at the trial level becomes the winning party in appellate court.

In some cases, a decision might be reversed but the lawsuit is still unresolved. The appellate court then orders the reversal with the direction that the case be remanded to a lower court for the determination of the issues that remain unsettled.

If a judgment or order is reversed in an intermediate appellate court, the losing party may file an appeal with a superior appellate court for relief, and the appellate process begins again. The decision rendered by a superior appellate court cannot ordinarily be reviewed. In state cases involving issues based on federal statutes or the Constitution, however, an appeal may be brought in the federal court system on those questions that are within its jurisdiction.

CROSS-REFERENCES

Appellate Advocacy; Appellate Court; Courts; Federal Courts.

APPEAR 📖 To come before a court as a party or a witness in a lawsuit. 📖

APPEARANCE 📖 A coming into court by a PARTY to a suit, either in person or through an ATTORNEY, whether as PLAINTIFF or DEFENDANT. The formal proceeding by which a defendant submits to the JURISDICTION of the court. The voluntary submission to a court's jurisdiction. 📖

In a criminal prosecution, an appearance is the initial court proceeding in which a defendant is first brought before a judge. The conduct of an appearance is governed by state and federal rules of CRIMINAL PROCEDURE. The rules vary from state to state, but they are generally consistent. During an appearance, the judge advises the defendant of the CHARGES and of the defendant's rights, considers BAIL or other conditions of release, and schedules a PRELIMINARY HEARING. If the crime charged is a MISDEMEANOR, the defendant may sometimes, depending on the local rules of court, enter a PLEA of guilty or not guilty at the initial appearance; if the crime is a FELONY, the defendant usually enters the plea at a later court proceeding. A criminal defendant may have an attorney present and may confer with the attorney during the appearance.

In some situations, a defendant may not need to appear in court in person and may even make an appearance by mail. A common example of this is when a person receives a traffic ticket and simply sends in a check for the amount of the fine.

Many state statutes permit appearances to be made by two-way, closed-circuit television. For instance, North Carolina's rule on video appearances reads,

> A first appearance in a noncapital case may be conducted by an audio and video transmission between the judge and defendant in which the parties can see and hear each other. If the defendant has counsel, the defendant shall be allowed to communicate fully and confidentially with his attorney during the proceeding (N.C. Gen. Stat. § 15A-601(a1) [1994]).

An appearance is also a coming into court as a party to a civil lawsuit. Although an appearance can be made by either the *plaintiff* (the one who has sued) or the *defendant* (the one being sued), the term most often refers to the action of the defendant.

The subject of appearance is closely related to the subject of PERSONAL JURISDICTION, which is the court's authority over an individual party. An appearance is some overt act by which the defendant comes before the court to either submit to or challenge the court's jurisdiction.

Any party can appear either in person or through an attorney or a duly authorized representative; the party need not be physically present. In most instances, an attorney makes the appearance. An appearance can also be made by filing a NOTICE of appearance with the CLERK of the court and the plaintiff, which states that the defendant will either submit to the authority of the court or challenge its jurisdiction. In a lawsuit involving multiple defendants, an appearance by one is not an ap-

pearance for the others. Valid SERVICE OF PROCESS is not required before an appearance can be made.

Historically, appearances have been classified with a variety of names indicating their manner or significance. A *compulsory* appearance is compelled by process served on the party. A *conditional* appearance is coupled with conditions as to its becoming or being taken as a general appearance (defined later in this article). A *corporal* appearance indicates that the person is physically present in court. A *de bene esse* (Latin, "of well being," sufficient for the present) appearance is provisional and will remain good only upon a future contingency. A *gratis* (Latin, "free" or "freely") appearance is made by a party to the action before the service of any process or legal notice to appear. An *optional* appearance is entered by a person who is intervening in the action to protect his or her own interests, though not joined as a party. A *subsequent* appearance is made by a defendant after an appearance has already been entered for him or her by the plaintiff. Finally, a *voluntary* appearance is entered by a party's own will or consent, without service of process, although process might be outstanding.

The two most common categories of appearances are general and special.

General Appearance   Any action by which the defendant recognizes the jurisdiction of the court constitutes a GENERAL APPEARANCE. This is an unqualified submission to the court's personal jurisdiction over the defendant, and is treated as the equivalent of a valid service of process.

By making a general appearance, the defendant agrees that the court has the power to bind her or him by its actions, and waives the right to raise any jurisdictional defects (e.g., by claiming that the service of process was improper). The defendant also waives the objection that the case is brought in the wrong VENUE. The defendant does not, however, waive any substantive rights or defenses, such as the claim that the court lacks jurisdiction over the subject matter of the case, or authority to hear the particular type of case (e.g., a bankruptcy court will not hear personal injury cases).

Special Appearance   A SPECIAL APPEARANCE is one made for a limited purpose. It can be made, for example, to challenge the sufficiency of the service of process. But most often, a special appearance is made to challenge the court's personal jurisdiction over the defendant. It prevents a DEFAULT JUDGMENT from being rendered against the defendant for failing to file a PLEADING. (A default judgment is an automatic

RICHARD HUTCHINGS/PHOTOEDIT

loss for failing to answer the complaint properly.)

When a defendant makes a special appearance, no other issues may be raised without that appearance's becoming a general appearance. If a party takes any action dealing with the MERITS of the case, the party is deemed to have made a general appearance and submitted to the jurisdiction of the court.

If a challenge is successful and the court agrees that it does not have personal jurisdiction over the defendant, it will dismiss the action. If the court finds against the defendant on that issue, that decision can later be appealed.

The right to make a special appearance is almost universally recognized, except where abolished by statute. As a rule, leave of court (permission) must be obtained before a special appearance can be made, but this is not always the case.

Federal Rules FEDERAL COURTS and states that have adopted the Federal Rules of Civil Procedure have eliminated the distinction between a general and a special appearance. Instead of challenging the court's personal juris-

This teenaged boy is accompanied by his parents as he makes an appearance in court.

diction in a special appearance, a defendant can do so by use of a pretrial motion to dismiss the CAUSE OF ACTION, or in an answer to the COMPLAINT. A REMOVAL proceeding, in which a defendant asks to have the case moved from state court to federal court, is regarded as a special appearance.

Limited Appearance In a number of states, a defendant in a lawsuit based on QUASI IN REM JURISDICTION may make a *limited* appearance. *Quasi in rem* is a Latin phrase for a type of jurisdiction in which the court has power over the defendant's property because it lies within the geographic boundaries of the court's jurisdiction. The presence of the property gives the court jurisdiction over the person of the defendant. To invoke *quasi in rem* jurisdiction, the court must find some connection between the property and the subject matter of the lawsuit.

A limited appearance enables a defendant to defend the action on the merits, but should the defendant lose, he or she will be held liable only up to the value of the identified property and not for all possible DAMAGES. A defendant who makes a limited appearance and wins the case can be sued again by the same plaintiff in a different court.

In states that have no provision for a limited appearance, a defendant can avoid being subject to the personal jurisdiction of the court by refusing to appear, thereby causing a default and a consequent FORFEITURE of the property. Or the defendant can submit to the court's personal jurisdiction, defend the case on its merits, and face the possibility of full LIABILITY. The defendant must decide which course of action is best, after comparing the value of the seized property with the damages being sought by the plaintiff and considering the likelihood of winning the case at trial.

The Federal Rules of Civil Procedure do not provide for limited appearances in federal court but instead defer to state law on that issue. A slightly greater number of courts permit limited appearances than do not. The law of the jurisdiction in which the action is brought must be consulted to determine whether limited appearances are permitted.

Withdrawal If an appearance has been entered through FRAUD or MISTAKE or after the plaintiff's complaint has been materially amended, the discretion of the court may permit the appearance to be withdrawn. A proper withdrawal is treated as if no appearance at all had been entered in the case. A defendant who has withdrawn a general appearance may ask the court for leave to file a special appearance to challenge the court's jurisdiction.

If someone makes an unauthorized appearance on behalf of the defendant, it may be stricken or set aside by a motion of any party with an interest in the proceeding.

Delay or Failure to Appear A defendant who fails to appear in court pursuant to a service of process might have a default judgment entered against her or him and be held in CONTEMPT of court. A failure to appear does not, however, result in a waiver of objections to the court's jurisdiction.

If a defendant fails to make an appearance in the time allotted by statute or court rules, he or she may lose certain rights. But if the circumstances warrant it, a court may extend the time of appearance.

See also CIVIL PROCEDURE.

APPELLANT 📖 A person who, dissatisfied with the judgment rendered in a lawsuit decided in a lower court or the findings from a proceeding before an administrative agency, asks a superior court to review the decision. 📖

An appellant, sometimes called the PETITIONER, must demonstrate sufficient grounds for APPEAL, which are usually specified by statute, in order to challenge the judgment or findings.

Whether a party was a plaintiff or defendant in the lower court has no bearing on his or her status as an appellant.

APPELLATE 📖 Relating to APPEALS; reviews by superior courts of decisions of inferior courts or administrative agencies and other proceedings. 📖

APPELLATE ADVOCACY The U.S. Constitution provides that "[t]he judicial Power of the United States, shall be vested in one [S]upreme Court, and in such inferior Courts as the Congress may from time to time ordain and establish" (art. III, § 1). The federal court system is thus three tiered, with the Supreme Court at the top, the district trial courts at the base, and the circuit courts of appeals in the middle. States, likewise, have trial courts (district courts), courts of appeals, and supreme courts.

The U.S. courts of appeals were created by the Evarts Act of 1891 (28 U.S.C.A. § 43) and are divided into thirteen judicial circuits (see the accompanying table). The central location of each court is determined by statute (28 U.S.C.A. § 41 [1995]). In addition, a court may sit any place within its circuit, and is required by statute to sit in certain locations other than its central location (28 U.S.C.A. § 44 [1995]). Appeals are heard and decided by panels of three judges that are selected randomly, by the circuit court EN BANC (in its entirety), or by a division established to perform the court's *en banc* function in larger circuits.

The circuit courts' ORIGINAL JURISDICTION included all matters not exclusively reserved for the district trial courts. The circuit courts also had appellate JURISDICTION to review district trial court decisions in civil cases in which the amount in controversy exceeded $50 and in ADMIRALTY cases in which the amount in controversy exceeded $300. They have jurisdiction to review final decisions of the federal district trial courts, both civil and criminal. Their jurisdiction extends only to matters authorized by Congress. An appellate court has no discretion in deciding whether to consider the MERITS of an appeal over which it has no jurisdiction. The most common basis for appellate jurisdiction is an appeal from a final district court judgment (324 U.S. 229, 28 U.S.C.A. § 1291 [1995]). When a judgment is entered that "ends the litigation on the merits and leaves nothing for the court to do but execute the judgment," a case is completed (*Catlin v. United States*, 65 S. Ct. 631 [1945]).

Congress has progressively limited the Supreme Court's power to directly review trial court decisions without a HEARING in the courts of appeals. Because Supreme Court review is usually discretionary in the overwhelming majority of cases, a court of appeals is the highest federal tribunal where a litigant or defendant can receive a hearing on the merits.

The Appeals Process An unsuccessful party in a lawsuit or administrative proceeding may file a timely appeal to an appropriate superior court empowered to review a final decision on the ground that it was based upon an erroneous application of law. The person who initiates the appeal, called the APPELLANT, must file a NOTICE of appeal, along with other necessary documents, to commence appellate REVIEW. The person against whom the appeal is brought, the APPELLEE, then files a BRIEF in response to the appellant's ALLEGATIONS.

Usually, review in the federal and state courts goes through two stages: an appeal from a trial court to an intermediate appellate court, and then to the highest appellate court in the jurisdiction. An appeal may be granted as a matter of right or as a matter of CERTIORARI (at the discretion of a superior appellate court). For example, a party may appeal from a federal district trial court to a U.S. court of appeals as a matter of right, but may appeal to the U.S. Supreme Court only by a grant of *certiorari*. An appellate court may hear an appeal only if the decision presented meets the statutory requirements for review.

The right to appeal is limited to the PARTIES to the proceedings who are aggrieved by the decision because it has a direct and adverse effect upon them or their property. Also, an actual case or controversy must exist at the time of review. Issues that have become MOOT while the appeal is pending and cases that have been settled are not reviewable.

For a case to be appealable, a final JUDGMENT or ORDER must have been reached by a trial court. A judgment is considered final for purposes of appeal when the action is ended in the court where it was brought and nothing more is to be decided.

An appeal must be made within the time prescribed by statute or by the rules governing the appellate court. The time for filing an appeal begins to run once a final decision has been made by the trial court. The appellant must file a notice of appeal with the CLERK of the appellate court in order to begin the appeal, and send a copy to the appellee. If the appeal process is not begun within the time set by statute, any right to appeal is lost. If extenuating circumstances exist, an extension of time for filing the appeal may be granted.

The appellate court can review only the trial court record and the briefs filed by the appellant and appellee. If permitted by the appellate court, AMICUS CURIAE briefs may also become part of the record on appeal. (Amicus curiae means "friend of the court." A person who is not a party to the action may petition the court for permission to file such a brief.) The briefs must contain the facts of the case, the grounds for review, and arguments relating to the issues raised.

The appellant's brief must specifically discuss the alleged ERRORS that entitle the appellant to a reversal of the trial court's decision and discuss why each ruling was wrong, citing authority such as a case or statute that applies to the particular point at issue. The appellee may file a brief containing arguments against reversal, discussing why the trial court's ruling was correct. Only CONCLUSIONS OF LAW, not findings of fact, made by a lower court are reviewable. Appellate courts can decide only issues actually before them on appeal.

The appellate court must decide whether the errors alleged to have been made by the trial court are harmless or prejudicial. If an error substantially injures the rights of the appellant, it is called a *prejudicial error*, or reversible error, and warrants the reversal of the final judgment or order. If the appeals court determines that the error is technical or minimally affects the rights of the parties or the outcome of the

Federal Judicial Circuits

Circuit	Area
District of Columbia	District of Columbia
First	Maine, Massachusetts, New Hampshire, Puerto Rico, Rhode Island
Second	Connecticut, New York, Vermont
Third	Delaware, New Jersey, Pennsylvania, Virgin Islands
Fourth	Maryland, North Carolina, South Carolina, Virginia, West Virginia
Fifth	Canal Zone, Louisiana, Mississippi, Texas
Sixth	Kentucky, Michigan, Ohio, Tennessee
Seventh	Illinois, Indiana, Wisconsin
Eighth	Arkansas, Iowa, Minnesota, Missouri, Nebraska, North Dakota, South Dakota
Ninth	Alaska, Arizona, California, Hawaii, Idaho, Montana, Nevada, Oregon, Washington, Guam, Northern Mariana Islands
Tenth	Colorado, Kansas, New Mexico, Oklahoma, Utah, Wyoming
Eleventh	Alabama, Florida, Georgia
Federal	All federal judicial districts

lawsuit, it is considered a HARMLESS ERROR and insufficient to require a reversal or modification of the decision of the trial court.

The appellate court may hear oral arguments from each side. These arguments, which usually last ten to fifteen minutes for each side, are intended to help the court understand the issues and to persuade the court to rule in favor of the arguing party. During the arguments, the appellate judge or judges may interrupt with questions on particular issues or points of law.

After reviewing the appeal, the appellate court may AFFIRM the decision of the lower court, modify it, REVERSE it, or REMAND the case for a new trial in the lower court. When a decision is *affirmed*, the appellate court accepts the decision of the lower court and rejects the appellant's contention that the decision was erroneous. When the appellate court *modifies* the lower court's decision, it accepts part of the trial court's decision and determines that the appellant was partly correct in saying that the decision was erroneous. The trial court's decision is then modified accordingly. In *reversing* a decision, the appellate court indicates that it agrees with the appellant that the lower court's decision was erroneous. The party who lost the case at the trial court level then becomes the winning party in appellate court. Occasionally, a decision will be reversed but the lawsuit is still unresolved. Then, the appellate court orders that the case be *remanded* (returned) to the lower court for the determination of issues that remain unresolved.

Federal Criminal Appellate Advocacy The Sixth Amendment to the U.S. Constitution guarantees a criminal defendant the right to a jury trial and the right to an attorney. The FOURTEENTH AMENDMENT says states must provide criminal defendants with these same guarantees. The U.S. Supreme Court has re-

The U.S. Supreme Court is the forum for appeals of lower court decisions.

peatedly held that a person found guilty in a criminal proceeding has no constitutional right to appeal. A federal criminal defendant's right to appeal, therefore, is based on an act of Congress.

Prior to the nation's founding, many colonial legislatures allowed, by special act, new trials of criminal defendants. But generally, criminal appeals did not exist when the U.S. Constitution was drafted, and the Judiciary Act of 1789 (ch. 20, 1 Stat. 73) did not provide for appellate review of criminal cases. Thus, history does not support a constitutional right to criminal appeal. The issue was left to Congress.

Between 1855 and 1860, Congress refused to provide for federal criminal appellate jurisdiction, although several bills were introduced. Finally, in 1879, Congress authorized the federal circuit courts to issue WRITS of ERROR in criminal cases on a discretionary basis. In 1889, Congress gave defendants sentenced to death the right of direct appeal to the U.S. Supreme Court. In 1891, it extended the Supreme Court's jurisdiction for review to all "cases of conviction of a capital or otherwise infamous crime" (26 Stat. 827, quoted in 775 S. Ct. 1332 [1957]). Because of the burden on the Supreme Court of hearing a large number of criminal appeals, in 1897, Congress transferred jurisdiction over noncapital appeals to the circuit courts of appeals. In 1911, Congress abolished the right of direct appeal to the Supreme Court in capital cases, and the circuit courts became the appellate courts for all criminal cases.

In 1894, in *McKane v. Durston*, 153 U.S. 684, 14 S. Ct. 913, 38 L. Ed. 867, a unanimous Supreme Court determined that no matter how serious the offense, a criminal defendant had no constitutional right to appeal her or his conviction.

The Criminal Justice Act (18 U.S.C.A. § 3006A [1995]) is an outgrowth of the Sixth Amendment right to counsel. The act requires courts to develop and implement plans to furnish representation for defendants charged with FELONIES or MISDEMEANORS, other than petty offenses, who are financially unable to obtain an attorney. Although the act is directed primarily to proceedings at the trial court level, it provides that any person for whom counsel is appointed shall be represented at every stage of the criminal proceedings, from the defendant's initial appearance through the appeal process.

State Criminal Appellate Advocacy

All fifty states provide defendants some form of appeal from a criminal conviction. Appeals were well-established elements of state criminal proceedings throughout the nineteenth century. They probably developed earlier in state court systems because state governments had primary responsibility for enforcing criminal laws from the founding of the nation through the 1800s, since very few federal statutory offenses existed during this period.

Because states decided that criminal appeals were necessary to protect the innocent, the Supreme Court determined that appellate procedures must comply with the federal constitutional guarantees of DUE PROCESS and EQUAL PROTECTION (*Griffin v. Illinois*, 351 U.S. 12, 76 S. Ct. 585, 100 L. Ed. 891 [1956]). In *Douglas v. California*, 372 U.S. 353, 83 S. Ct. 814, 9 L. Ed. 2d 811 (1963), the Supreme Court held that a state violates a defendant's constitutional protections when it forces an indigent, who has a statutory right to appeal, to attempt the appeal without the assistance of an attorney. The Supreme Court reasoned that without an attorney, an appeal constituted nothing more than a "meaningless ritual." Therefore, a state must provide counsel to a defendant who wants to exercise the right to appeal but cannot afford to hire a lawyer.

In 1985, the Supreme Court held that a defendant has the right to the effective assistance of appellate counsel. The Court concluded that a defendant whose counsel does not provide effective representation is "in no better position than one who has no counsel at all" (*Evitts v. Lucey*, 469 U.S. 387, 105 S. Ct. 830, 83 L. Ed. 2d 821 [1985]). However, in *Ross v. Moffitt*, 417 U.S. 600, 94 S. Ct. 2437, 41 L. Ed. 2d 341 (1974), the Supreme Court held that a criminal defendant does not have a constitutional right to appointed counsel on a discretionary review.

CROSS-REFERENCES

Appeal; Appellate Court; Criminal Law; Federal Courts; Right to Counsel; Sixth Amendment; Supreme Court of the United States.

APPELLATE COURT ▯ A court having JURISDICTION to REVIEW decisions of a trial-level or other lower court. ▯

An unsuccessful party in a lawsuit must file an appeal with an appellate court in order to have the DECISION reviewed. In the United States, appellate courts exist at both the federal and the state levels. On the federal level, decisions of the U.S. district courts, where civil and criminal matters are tried, can be appealed to the U.S. court of appeals for the circuit covering the district court. Eleven numbered federal judicial circuits have been established. Each circuit comprises a number of states that are usually, though not always, in close geographic proximity. For example, the Eighth Circuit includes Arkansas, Iowa, Minnesota, Missouri, Nebraska, and North and South Dakota, and the Sixth Circuit is made up of Kentucky, Michigan, Ohio, and Tennessee. Washington, D.C., has two U.S. courts of appeals: the District of Columbia Circuit Court of Appeals, which hears appeals arising out of decisions of the Federal District Court for the District of Columbia, and the U.S. Court of Appeals for the Federal Circuit, which has exclusive and nationwide jurisdiction in appeals from U.S. District Court decisions in patent, copyright, trademark, and other specialized areas.

A decision of a U.S. court of appeals may be appealed to yet another appellate court, the Supreme Court of the United States. An appeal to the Supreme Court is made by filing a *petition for certiorari* (a document requesting a review of court records). The Supreme Court has broad discretion in determining whether to review decisions. The Court receives thousands of petitions a year, but can only review about one hundred cases in that span of time. It most often denies CERTIORARI and hears only cases that raise important and unsettled constitutional questions or in which the federal appellate courts have reached conflicting decisions on the same issue.

On the state level, a decision of a state trial court—usually a district or other local court—can be appealed to a state appellate court for review. In most states, a case must first be appealed to an intermediate appellate court. If it receives an unfavorable ruling at the intermediate level, the case can then be appealed to the highest appellate court in the state, usually the state supreme court. Like the Supreme Court of the United States, a state's highest court usually has the discretion to decide whether to review a decision reached by the intermediate court. Some cases decided by the highest court in a state also can be appealed to the Supreme Court, though again the U.S. Supreme Court will hear only appeals of major significance.

In both state and federal matters, in general, an appeal can be brought only after a FINAL DECISION, or final judgment, in the action has been entered. A JUDGMENT is final for the purposes of an appeal when nothing more is to be decided in the action, and it concludes all rights that were subject to litigation. This rule is based in part on the desire for judicial economy: it is more efficient for all matters to be heard in one appeal than for a case to be conducted "piecemeal" (in several appeals) before it is finally resolved. However, both state and federal courts will in some instances hear an INTERLOCUTORY appeal, which is an appeal of a matter that does not decide the entire case but must be addressed before the case can be decided on its merits. In other instances, whether an interlocutory appeal will be granted depends on the issue at hand. If the issue concerns whether the lawsuit should go forward at the trial level, it is more likely to be heard, since it may avoid an unnecessary trial. For example, an interlocutory appeal may be permitted from an order granting or denying an INJUNCTION even though the main issues in the case have yet to be tried.

On the federal level, decisions of the U.S. district courts can be appealed to the U.S. court of appeals for the circuit covering the district court.

Both the APPELLANT (the party appealing the lower-court ruling) and the APPELLEE (the party against whom the appeal has been brought) file written briefs with the appellate court. The *briefs*—which recite the facts of the case, the arguments being raised on appeal, and the applicable law—help the court decide whether the trial court erred in its decision.

The appellate court may also hear *oral arguments* in the case. During oral argument, each party has ten to fifteen minutes to persuade the appellate court to rule in its favor. If numerous issues have been raised, a party may choose to use most of this time to cover the issues that are most crucial to the decision to be made. The court is free to interrupt an oral argument with questions concerning the facts of the case or the particular areas of law involved. The appellate court, at its discretion, may determine that oral argument is not necessary and may decide the case based only on the trial court record and the written briefs.

In making its decision, the appellate court may *affirm* the trial court, meaning that it accepts the decision of the lower court, or may *reverse* it, thus agreeing with the appellant's contention that the trial court's decision was erroneous. It may also *modify* the decision; in this instance, the court may accept part of the trial court's decision while ruling that other issues were erroneously decided.

The appellate court usually issues its decision in the form of a written OPINION stating its reasons for the decision. The opinion will discuss the relevant facts, and apply the law to those facts. Appellate court opinions are usually published, thus forming a body of law, known as PRECEDENT, that attorneys and judges can consult for guidance in resolving similar legal questions.

CROSS-REFERENCES

Appeal; Appellate Advocacy; Courts; Federal Courts.

APPELLEE A party who has won a judgment in a lawsuit or favorable findings in an administrative proceeding, which judgment or findings the losing party, the APPELLANT, seeks to have a higher court reverse or set aside.

The designation as appellee is not related to a person's status as PLAINTIFF or DEFENDANT in the lower court.

Another name for *appellee* is RESPONDENT. See also APPEAL.

APPOINT To designate, select, or assign authority to a position or an office.

Although sometimes used interchangeably, elect and appoint do not have the same meaning. ELECTION refers to the selection of a public

The proceedings in the federal and state appellate courts are quite different from those that take place in a trial court. At the TRIAL level, witnesses are called to testify and a jury is often present to hear evidence and reach a verdict. At the appellate level, the trial court record and BRIEFS prepared by both parties are reviewed, and oral arguments may be heard; witnesses are not called and no jury is convened. The *trial court record* usually contains the PLEADINGS that first initiated the case, a complete TRANSCRIPT of the court proceedings, materials admitted into evidence, and documents indicating the final judgment.

An appellate court differs from a trial court in another important respect: only the trial court determines the factual issues in a case. In its review, the appellate court does not try factual issues. Instead, it determines only whether there is sufficient evidence to support the findings of the trial court and whether the trial court correctly applied the law.

officer by the qualified voters of the community, and *appointment* refers to the selection of a public officer by one authorized by law to do so.

APPORTIONMENT ▢ The process by which legislative seats are distributed among units entitled to representation. Determination of the number of representatives that a state, county, or other subdivision may send to a legislative body. The U.S. Constitution provides for a CENSUS every ten years, on the basis of which Congress apportions representatives according to population; but each state must have at least one representative. "Districting" is the establishment of the precise geographical boundaries of each such unit or constituency. Apportionment by state statute that denies the rule of ONE-PERSON, ONE-VOTE is violative of equal protection of laws.

Also, the allocation of a charge or cost such as real estate taxes between two parties, often in the same ratio as the respective times that the parties are in possession or ownership of property during the fiscal period for which the charge is made or assessed. ▢

> Who are to be the electors of the Federal Representatives? Not the rich more than the poor; not the learned more than the ignorant; not the haughty heirs of distinguished names, more than the humble sons of obscurity and unpropitious fortune. The electors are to be the great body of the people of the United States (James Madison, *The Federalist No. 57*)
>
> The difference most relied upon, between American and other republics, consists in the principle of representation (James Madison, *The Federalist No. 63*)

James Madison and his fellow founders of the United States of America sought many objectives as they framed the U.S. Constitution. Among the goals these champions of democracy fought for was the notion of equal representation in government, by congresspeople, for citizens of the United States. To ensure that equal representation occurred, the founders proposed that the U.S. population be counted at regular intervals with a census. They later agreed, in the Great Compromise of 1787, that congressional representation should be assigned—in other words, *apportioned*—to various regions of the country based on a total population standard. Both article 1, section 2, clause 3, and amendment 14, section 2, of the Constitution provide that representatives shall be apportioned among the states according to their respective numbers and that a population count will be taken by census every ten years. Apportionment requires that each state's total popu-

lation be divided by the population of "the ideal district" to determine the appropriate number of representatives. The population of an ideal district, for purposes of federal apportionment, is defined as the total population of the state (as determined by census) divided by one hundred (for the House of Representatives), or by fifty (for the Senate).

In the centuries that have followed the United States' adoption of the Constitution, apportionment for the federal Congress has been based on total population—with the exception that a slave, until the Civil War, was considered property and thus counted only as three-fifths of a white person. Efforts to limit federal congressional apportionment to only people who are citizens or voters have been defeated, because the exclusion of groups such as illegal aliens, nonvoters, and children could significantly affect some areas of the country, since some states have large populations of these groups. Shifting political power away from an area means fewer legislators to demand a fair share of government resources for that area. One such effort to exclude these groups, which occurred during the 1866 debates over the passage of the Fourteenth Amendment, ultimately led to Congress's voting to continue basing apportionment on total population and to count the "whole number of persons in each state." In contrast, state legislatures have only been required to be based substantially on population since 1964 (*Reynolds v. Sims*, 377 U.S. 533, 84 S. Ct. 1362, 12 L. Ed. 2d 506). In 1968, the U.S. Supreme Court extended this requirement to municipal governments as well (*Avery v. Midland County*, 390 U.S. 474, 88 S. Ct. 1114, 20 L. Ed. 2d 45).

Apportionment is related to, but is not the same as, the electoral system and the districting process: *apportionment* is the manner in which representation is distributed; the *electoral system* is the way an individual representative is elected; and the *districting process* establishes the precise electoral boundaries of a representative's district. Apportionment for the U.S. Congress, which consists of the Senate and the House of Representatives, has always been determined by the Constitution. Each state is assigned two senators, who were originally elected by state legislatures but have since the adoption of the Seventeenth Amendment in 1913 been chosen by direct voter election.

Membership in the House of Representatives is also assigned to the states and is apportioned according to population, with each state being constitutionally guaranteed at least one representative. The House of Representatives grew proportionally with the population of the

United States until 1912, when the House froze its size at 435 members. Since 1941, the Bureau of the Census has used the system of *equal proportions* to determine how many of the 435 representatives each state is entitled to have. This method, developed in 1920 by Professor Edward V. Huntington, of Harvard University, establishes the smallest possible difference between the representation of any two states, since a state's fair share of representatives will rarely be a whole number. The 1941 federal statute 2 U.S.C.A. §§ 2a and 2b provides that

> under the "equal proportions" method, the priority list of states or counties among which Representatives in excess of one per state or county are to be allocated is obtained by dividing the population of each state or county by the geometric mean of successive numbers of Representatives.

Congress must decide how to treat the fractional components whenever it reapportions congressional seats based on new census data. This decision affects the distribution of only a

few seats in Congress and the electoral college, but in closely contested matters, such as the presidential election of 1876, those seats could mean the difference between victory and defeat. (The electoral college is the body of electors of each state chosen to elect the president and vice president. Apportionment affects the electoral college because it influences the number of electoral votes coming from various areas of the country.) Each state legislature is responsible for establishing the district boundaries of the congressional seats apportioned to the state by the federal government.

From 1842 to 1911, Congress required that all congressional districts be of compact and connecting territory. That stipulation was not continued after 1912, and by the 1960s, the districts within some states differed greatly in size. These disparities were caused in some cases by *gerrymandering*, which is the process of drawing boundaries for election districts so as to give one party a greater political advantage. Large disparities led a group of urban Tennessee voters to bring suit against their state's

U.S. House of Representatives Membership

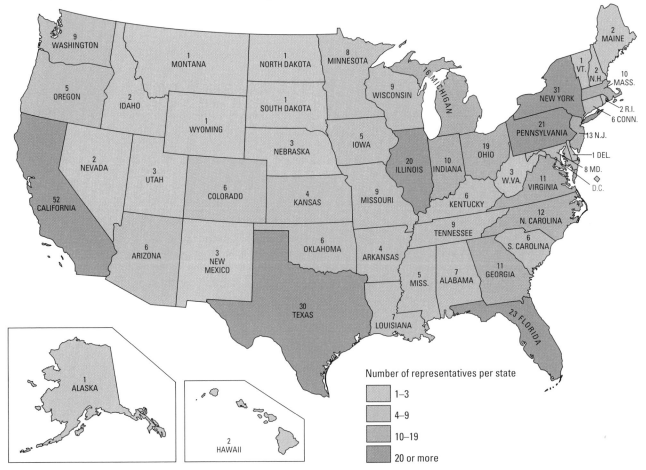

electoral commission on the ground that the apportionment of the legislature was unfair. The Supreme Court's March 1962 decision in favor of the voters in *Baker v. Carr*, 369 U.S. 186, 82 S. Ct. 691, 7 L. Ed. 2d 663, established the rule that a citizen may bring suit against legislative malapportionment when it deprives that citizen of equal protection under the law as guaranteed by the Fourteenth Amendment. Previously, in *Colegrove v. Green*, 328 U.S. 549, 66 S. Ct. 1198, 90 L. Ed. 1432 (1946), the Court had refused to accept JURISDICTION in apportionment cases.

Although the Supreme Court's decision in *Baker* was limited, it did rule that if a system other than one based on population is used for apportionment, the resulting districts must not be arbitrary or irrational in nature. In 1964, the Supreme Court extended *Baker* by ruling in *Wesberry v. Sanders*, 376 U.S. 1, 84 S. Ct. 526, 11 L. Ed. 2d 481, that legislative districts for the House of Representatives must be drawn so as to provide "equal representation for equal numbers of people," a concept often referred to as the "one-person, one-vote" standard. Later that same year, in lawsuits directly involving fifteen states, the Supreme Court ruled in *Reynolds v. Sims*, 377 U.S. 533, 84 S. Ct. 1362, 12 L. Ed. 2d 506, that districts for state legislatures must also be substantially equal in population. Further extending the principle, the Court ruled in *Avery v. Midland County*, 390 U.S. 474, 88 S. Ct. 1114, 20 L. Ed. 2d 45 (1968), that if county, city, and town governments elect their representatives from individual districts, the districts must be substantially equal in population.

Other individuals and states have subsequently challenged the method of apportionment used in the United States when that method has proved unfavorable for them. For example, in *Franklin v. Massachusetts*, 505 U.S. 788, 112 S. Ct. 2767, 120 L. Ed. 2d 636 (1992), Massachusetts and two of its registered voters filed an action against U.S. Secretary of Commerce Barbara B. Franklin, alleging, among other things, that the decision to allocate overseas employees was inconsistent with the Constitution. In June 1992, the Court reversed a federal district court decision in favor of Massachusetts, ruling that the allocation of overseas federal employees to their designated home states was consistent with the "usual-residence" standard used in early censuses and served the purpose of making representation in Congress more equal.

The state of Montana also sued the U.S. Department of Commerce, following the 1990 census, when it and eleven other states each lost one House seat. In seeking to keep the two seats it had held since 1910, Montana argued that the method of equal proportions was unconstitutional because it left the state with a single congressional district of 803,655 people—a number almost 40 percent larger than "ideal district size," which is a national average of 572,466 people. Montana also alleged that the variance between the single district's population and that of an ideal district could not be justified under the one-person, one-vote standard developed in *Wesberry*. The Montana case was appealed to the U.S. Supreme Court, which in March 1992 unanimously upheld the method Congress uses to reallocate congressional seats among the states after a census (*United States Department of Commerce v. Montana*, 503 U.S. 442, 112 S. Ct. 1415, 118 L. Ed. 2d 87).

CROSS-REFERENCES

Baker v. Carr; Congress of the United States; Electoral College; Equal Protection; Fourteenth Amendment; Gerrymander; *Reynolds v. Sims*; Voting Rights.

APPRAISAL ▨ A valuation or an approximation of VALUE by impartial, properly qualified persons; the process of determining the value of an ASSET or LIABILITY, which entails expert opinion rather than express commercial transactions. ▨

Before putting it up for sale, the owners of this house probably received an appraisal of its market value.

APPRAISER ▨ A person selected or appointed by a competent authority or an interested party to evaluate the financial worth of property. ▨

Appraisers are frequently appointed in PROBATE and CONDEMNATION proceedings and are also used by banks and real estate concerns to determine the MARKET VALUE of REAL PROPERTY.

APPRECIATION ▣ The fair and reasonable estimation of the VALUE of an item. The increase in the financial worth of an ASSET as compared to its value at a particular earlier date as a result of inflation or greater market demand. ▣

APPREHENSION ▣ The seizure and arrest of a person who is suspected of having committed a crime.

A reasonable belief of the possibility of imminent injury or death at the hands of another that justifies a person acting in SELF-DEFENSE against the potential attack. ▣

An apprehension of attack is an element of the defense of self-defense that can be used in a criminal prosecution for ASSAULT AND BATTERY, MANSLAUGHTER, or MURDER. An individual who acts under apprehension of attack does not have to fear injury. It is sufficient that there is a likelihood of actual injury to justify the person's taking steps to protect himself or herself.

APPRENTICE ▣ A person who agrees to work for a specified time in order to learn a trade, craft, or profession in which the employer, traditionally called the MASTER, assents to instruct him or her. ▣

Both MINORS and adults can be legally obligated under the terms of an apprenticeship CONTRACT, and any person who has the capacity to manage his or her own affairs may engage an apprentice. In some states, a minor may VOID a contract of apprenticeship, but in cases where the contract is beneficial to the minor, other jurisdictions do not permit the minor to void it. There must be strict compliance with statutes that govern a minor's actions concerning an apprenticeship.

An apprenticeship must arise from an agreement, sometimes labeled an INDENTURE, which possesses all the requisites of a valid contract. If the contract cannot be performed within a year, it must be in writing, in order to satisfy the STATUTE OF FRAUDS, an old English law adopted in the United States, which requires certain agreements to be in writing. The apprentice, the employer, and, if the apprentice is a minor, his or her parents or guardians must sign the apprenticeship agreement. Some jurisdictions require explicit consensual language in addition to the signature or signatures of one or both parents, depending upon the applicable statute. The contract must include the provisions required by law and drafted for the benefit of the minor such as those relating to his or her education and training. A breach of apprenticeship contract might justify an award of DAMAGES, and, unless authorized by statute, there can be no ASSIGNMENT, or transfer, of the contract of apprenticeship to another that would bind the apprentice to a new service.

A person who lures an apprentice from his or her employer may be sued by the employer, but the employer cannot recover unless the defendant knew of the apprentice relationship.

The apprenticeship may be concluded by either party for good cause, where no definite term of service is specified, by mutual consent, or by a dismissal of the apprentice. Automatic termination ensues from the expiration of the term of service, involuntary removal of the apprentice from the jurisdiction where he or she was bound, or service in the armed forces even though voluntary and without the consent of the employer. The death of either party terminates the relationship, as does the attainment of the AGE OF MAJORITY by the apprentice, in most instances. Courts may terminate such contracts when they violate statutes. The master's cruelty, immorality, interference with the apprentice's religious beliefs or duties, or other misconduct and the misbehavior of the apprentice also constitute grounds for termination.

APPROPRIATION ▣ The designation by the government or an individual of the use to which a fund of money is to be applied. The selection and setting apart of privately owned land by the government for public use, such as a military reservation or public building. The diversion of water flowing on PUBLIC DOMAIN from its natural course by means of a canal or ditch for a private beneficial use of the appropriator. ▣

An *appropriation bill* is a proposal placed before the legislative branch of the government by one or a group of its members to earmark a particular portion of general revenue or treasury funds for use for a governmental objective. Federal appropriation bills can originate only in the House of Representatives as mandated by Article I, Section 7 of the Constitution. Once an appropriation law is enacted, a definite amount of money is set aside so that public officials can pay incurred or anticipated expenditures. When a law authorizes funds to be used for a particular purpose, it is known as a *specific appropriation*. See also FEDERAL BUDGET.

The appropriation of money by an individual occurs within the context of a debtor-creditor relationship. If a CREDITOR is owed two separate debts by the same DEBTOR who makes a payment without specifying the debt to which it is to be applied, the creditor can appropriate the payment to either debt.

Appropriation also refers to the physical taking and occupation of property by the government or its actual, substantial interference with the owner's right to use the land according to personal wishes by virtue of the government's power of EMINENT DOMAIN.

This right of an individual to use water that belongs to the public is embodied in the *prior appropriation doctrine* applied in arid western states where water supplies are not available in sufficient quantity to all who might need them. An individual landowner who first diverts water for personal benefit is entitled to its continued use as long as there is a reasonable need and the water is actually used. See also WATER RIGHTS.

APPROVAL 📖 The present confirmation, ratification, or assent to some action or thing done by another, which is submitted to an individual, group, or governmental body for judgment. The acceptance by a judge of a bond, security, or other document that is required by law to meet with the judge's satisfaction before it becomes legally effective. 📖

APPURTENANCE 📖 An accessory or adjunct that is attached and incidental to something that has greater importance or value. As applied to REAL PROPERTY, an object attached to or a right to be used with land as an incidental benefit but which is necessary to the complete use and enjoyment of the property. 📖

When a landowner has been given an EASEMENT for the passage of light and air over an adjoining lot, the easement is an appurtenance to the land. Other common appurtenances to land include barns, outhouses, fences, drainage and irrigation ditches, and rights of way.

A PRIORI 📖 [Latin, *From the cause to the effect.*] 📖

This phrase refers to a type of reasoning that examines given general principles to discover what particular facts or real-life observations can be derived from them. Another name for this method is deductive reasoning.

ARBITER 📖 [Latin, *One who attends something to view it as a spectator or witness.*] Any person who is given an absolute power to judge and rule on a matter in dispute. 📖

An arbiter is usually chosen or appointed by parties or by a court on their behalf. The decision of an arbiter is made according to the rules of law and equity. The arbiter is distinguished from the arbitrator, who proceeds at his or her own discretion, so that the decision is made according to the judgment of a reasonable person.

An arbiter may perform the same function as an UMPIRE, a person who decides a controversy when arbitrators cannot agree.

See also ALTERNATIVE DISPUTE RESOLUTION; ARBITRATION.

ARBITRAGE 📖 The simultaneous purchase in one market and sale in another of a security or COMMODITY in hope of making a profit on price differences in the different markets. 📖

In its simplest form, arbitrage is "buying low and selling high." In this sense, any trader who buys something in one market—whether it is a commodity like grain, financial securities such as STOCK in a company, or a currency such as the Japanese yen—and sells it in another market at a higher price is engaged in arbitrage. That trader is called an arbitrageur. In economic theory, arbitrage is a necessary activity in any market, helping to reduce price disparities between different markets and to increase a market's liquidity (ability to buy and sell).

Arbitrage can be divided into the categories of riskless and risk. As an example of riskless arbitrage, imagine that the price of Microsoft Corporation common stock on the Pacific Coast Stock Exchange is less than the price of the same stock on the New York Stock Exchange. A trader who buys Microsoft stock at the lower price on the Pacific Coast exchange and *simultaneously* sells it for a higher price on the New York exchange is engaging in an essentially riskless transaction. Aided by the speed of modern communications, the buying and selling occur at virtually the same time. This type of exchange occurs daily in the currency market, where a trader may buy French francs at a lower price in London and sell them at a higher price in Singapore.

Much arbitrage falls into the risk category. This type of arbitrage is not always completed with a sale at a higher price; it involves a risk that the price of the item being traded will fall before the trader can sell it. RISK ARBITRAGE came into prominence during the 1980s, when investors began to take advantage of a business atmosphere encompassing a large number of company MERGERS AND ACQUISITIONS. In a merger or acquisition, one company buys or takes over another company. When the management of the targeted company does not want to be acquired by a particular investor or group of investors, the merger is called a hostile TAKEOVER. Quite often, the aggressors in such takeovers are smaller in terms of assets than their targets. A hostile takeover is usually initiated when someone believes that the stock of a particular company is lower than its potential value, whether because of poor management or because of a lack of information about the true value of that company.

One way that hostile takeovers are initiated is through a device called the cash TENDER OFFER. The party attempting to initiate the takeover announces that it will pay cash for the target company's stock at a price well above the current MARKET VALUE. At this point, risk arbitrageurs become involved in the game. They buy stock from shareholders in the target company, then attempt to sell that stock at the higher price to the party attempting the take-over. If the takeover succeeds and the arbi-trageurs receive a higher price for their stock, they profit; if the takeover fails or the arbi-trageurs receive a lower price for their stock, they lose. Gauging the risk of a takeover's failure is therefore crucial to an arbitrageur's success.

An arbitrageur who purchases securities on the basis of inside information—that is, infor-mation about a pending takeover that is not available to the general public—violates the Securities Exchange Act of 1934 (§ 10[b], as amended, 15 U.S.C.A. § 78j[b]). However, pur-chasing securities on the basis of rumors about an imminent takeover is not illegal.

Ivan F. Boesky was one example of a risk arbitrageur who was found guilty of engaging in INSIDER trading. Boesky profited enormously from the many corporate takeovers of the mid-1980s. By 1985, he had become famous in financial circles and had published a book, *Merger Mania: Arbitrage: Wall Street's Best Kept Money-Making Secret*, that extolled the opportu-nities in risk arbitrage and the benefits the practice gave to the market. In 1986, only one year later, Boesky admitted that he had illegally traded on insider information obtained from Drexel Burnham Lambert, the securities firm that arranged the financing of many of the takeovers of the era. In return for a reduced sentence of three years in prison, Boesky agreed to pay a $100 million penalty and to cooperate with the government's continuing investigation. Boesky named Drexel employee Michael R. Milken as a member of the insider trading network. In 1990, Boesky was released from prison after serving two years.

CROSS-REFERENCES

Corporations; Securities; Securities Regulation.

ARBITRARY ▥ Irrational; capricious. ▥

The term *arbitrary* describes a course of action or a decision that is not based on reason or judgment but on personal will or discretion without regard to rules or standards.

An arbitrary decision is one made without regard for the facts and circumstances pre-sented, and it connotes a disregard of the evi-dence.

In many instances, the term implies an ele-ment of BAD FAITH, and it may be used synony-mously with tyrannical or despotic.

ARBITRATION ▥ The submission of a dis-pute to an unbiased third person designated by the parties to the controversy, who agree in advance to comply with the AWARD—a decision to be issued after a hearing at which both parties have an opportunity to be heard. ▥

Arbitration is a well-established and widely used means to end disputes. It is one of several kinds of ALTERNATIVE DISPUTE RESOLUTION, which provide parties to a controversy with a choice other than LITIGATION. Unlike litigation, arbitra-tion takes place out of court: the two sides select an impartial third party, known as an arbitrator; agree in advance to comply with the arbitrator's award; and then participate in a HEARING at which both sides can present EVI-DENCE and TESTIMONY. The arbitrator's decision is usually final, and courts rarely reexamine it. Traditionally, labor and commerce were the two largest areas of arbitration. However, since the mid-1970s, the technique has seen great expan-sion. Some states have mandated arbitration for certain disputes such as auto insurance claims, and court decisions have broadened its scope into areas such as securities, antitrust, and even employment discrimination. International busi-ness issues are also frequently resolved using arbitration.

Arbitration in the United States dates to the eighteenth century. Courts frowned on it, though, until attitudes started to change in 1920 with the passage of the first state arbitra-tion law, in New York. This statute served as a model for other state and federal laws, includ-ing, in 1925, the U.S. Arbitration Act, later known as the Federal Arbitration Act (FAA) (9 U.S.C.A. § 1 et seq.). The FAA was intended to give arbitration equal status with litigation, and, in effect, created a body of federal law. After World War II, arbitration grew increasingly important to labor-management relations. Con-gress helped this growth with passage of the Taft-Hartley Act (29 U.S.C.A. § 141 et seq.) in 1947, and over the next decade, the U.S. Su-preme Court firmly cemented arbitration as the favored means for resolving labor issues, by limiting the judiciary's role. In the 1970s, arbi-tration began expanding into a wide range of issues that eventually included prisoners' rights, medical malpractice, consumer rights, and many others. In 1995, at least forty-four states had modern arbitration statutes.

Arbitration can be voluntary or required. The traditional model is voluntary, and closely linked to contract law: parties often stipulate in contracts that they will arbitrate, rather than litigate, when disputes arise. For example, unions and employers almost always put an arbitration clause in their formal negotiations, known as COLLECTIVE BARGAINING AGREEMENTS. By doing so, they agree to arbitrate any future employee grievances over wages, hours, working conditions, or job security—in essence, they agree not to sue if disagreements occur. Similarly, a purchaser and a provider of services who disagree over the result of a business deal may submit the problem to an arbitrator instead of a court. Mandatory arbitration is a more recent phenomenon. States such as Minnesota, New York, and New Jersey have enacted statutes that force disputes over automobile insurance claims into this forum. In addition, courts sometimes order disputants into arbitration.

In theory, arbitration has many advantages over litigation. Efficiency is perhaps the greatest. Proponents say arbitration is easier, cheaper, and faster. Proponents also point to the greater flexibility with which parties in arbitration can fashion the terms and rules of the process. Furthermore, although arbitrators can be lawyers, they do not need to be. They are often selected for their expertise in a particular area of business, and may be drawn from private practice or from organizations such as the American Arbitration Association (AAA), a national nonprofit group founded in 1926. Significantly, arbitrators are freer than judges to make decisions, because they do not have to abide by the principle of *stare decisis* (the policy of courts to follow principles established by legal precedent) and do not have to give reasons to support their awards (although they are expected to adhere to the Code of Ethics for Arbitrators in Commercial Disputes, established in 1977 by the AAA and the American Bar Association).

These theoretical advantages do not always hold up in practice. Even when efficiency is achieved, some critics argue, the price is a lower quality of justice, and it can be made worse by the difficulty of appealing an award. The charge is frequently made that arbitration only results in "splitting the baby"—dividing awards evenly among the parties. The AAA rebuts this claim: its 1993 statistics for construction cases show that only 11 percent of the awards were divided equally. Yet even arbitrators agree that as arbitration has become increasingly formal, it sometimes resembles litigation in its complexity. This may not be an inherent problem with

the process as much as a result of flawed use of it. Parties may undermine arbitration by acting as lawyers do in a lawsuit: excessively demanding DISCOVERY (evidence from the other side), calling witnesses, and filing motions.

Ultimately, the decision to use arbitration cannot be made lightly. Most arbitration is considered *binding*: parties who agree to arbitration are bound to that agreement and also bound to satisfy any award determined by the arbitrator. Courts in most jurisdictions enforce awards. Moreover, they allow little or no option for APPEAL, expecting parties who arbitrate to assume the risks of the process. In addition, arbitration is subject to the legal doctrines of RES JUDICATA and COLLATERAL ESTOPPEL, which together strictly curtail the option of bringing suits based on issues that were or could have been raised initially. (*Res judicata* means that a final judgment on the merits is conclusive as to the rights of the parties and their privies, and, as to them, operates as an absolute bar to a subsequent action involving the same CLAIM, DEMAND, or CAUSE OF ACTION. *Collateral estoppel* means that when an issue of ULTIMATE FACT has been determined by a valid judgment, that issue cannot be relitigated between the same parties in future litigation.) Thus, often the end is truly in sight at the conclusion of an arbitration hearing and the granting of an award.

The FAA gives only four grounds on which a court may VACATE, or overturn, an award: (1) where the award is the result of corruption, FRAUD, or undue means; (2) where the arbitrators were evidently partial or corrupt; (3) where the arbitrators were guilty of misconduct in refusing to postpone the hearing or hear pertinent evidence, or where their misbehavior prejudiced the rights of any party; and (4) where the arbitrators exceeded their powers or imperfectly executed them so that a mutual, final, and definite award was not made. In the 1953 case *Wilko v. Swan*, 346 U.S. 427, 74 S. Ct. 182, 98 L. Ed. 168, the U.S. Supreme Court suggested, in passing, that an award may be set aside if it is in "manifest disregard of the law," and federal courts have sometimes followed this principle. PUBLIC POLICY can also be grounds for vacating,

Any controversy or claim arising out of or relating to this contract, or the breach thereof, shall be settled by arbitration administered by the American Arbitration Association under its Commercial Arbitration Rules, and judgment on the award rendered by the arbitrator(s) may be entered in any court having jurisdiction thereof.

An example of an arbitration clause that is recommended by the American Arbitration Association

but this recourse is severely limited to well-defined policy based on legal PRECEDENT, a rule emphasized by the Supreme Court in the 1987 case *United Paperworkers International Union v. Misco*, 484 U.S. 29, 108 S. Ct. 364, 98 L. Ed. 2d 286.

The growth of arbitration is taken as a healthy sign by many legal commentators. It eases the load on a constantly overworked judicial system, while providing disputants with a relatively informal, inexpensive means to solve their problems. The greatest recent boost to arbitration came from the U.S. Supreme Court, which held in 1991 that age discrimination claims in employment are arbitrable (*Gilmer v. Interstate/Johnson Lane Corp.*, 500 U.S. 20, 111 S. Ct. 1647, 114 L. Ed. 2d 26). Writing for the majority, Justice Byron R. White concluded that arbitration is as effective as a trial for resolving employment disputes. *Gilmer* has led several major employers to treat all employment claims through binding arbitration, sometimes as a condition of employment.

ARCHITECT 📖 A person who prepares the plan and design of a building or other structure and sometimes supervises its construction. 📖

A landscape architect is responsible for the arrangement of scenery over a tract of land for natural or aesthetic purposes in order to enhance or preserve the property.

Regulation The practice of planning and designing a building requires the application of specialized skill and knowledge. Because the product of an architect's work is used by members of the general public, the legislature of a state may regulate the practice of those engaged in the profession. Regulatory statutes designed to protect public health and safety are created under the inherent authority of a state to protect the welfare of its citizens. As a general rule, regulatory statutes are valid, provided they are not unreasonable.

Statutes requiring that architects must be registered and licensed are based on public policy aimed at protecting citizens from unqualified practitioners. In many states, statutes call for the revocation of a LICENSE for such conduct as FRAUD, dishonesty, recklessness, incompetence, or MISREPRESENTATION when an architect acts in his or her professional capacity.

The power to revoke a license is commonly given by the legislature to a state board of architects who must act in a manner prescribed by statute. Generally, an architect is entitled to NOTICE and a HEARING when the board seeks to revoke his or her license. The architect can appeal a revocation.

Qualifications Statutes setting forth the requirements for obtaining a license or registration generally require that the applicants be of legal age and of good moral character, have completed a certain course of study, and have a certain amount of practical experience. Many states have an additional requirement that applicants must pass an examination. A legislature may provide that certain persons who have practiced architecture for a period of time prior to legislation requiring an examination may register as architects without an examination. Such a statutory provision is called a GRANDFATHER CLAUSE.

Persons who present themselves to the public as architects must comply with the statutory registration and licensing requirements. The failure to do so is unlawful. In most states, persons who falsely hold themselves out as licensed architects are guilty of a MISDEMEANOR, and contracts rendered by them with others are VOID and unenforceable.

Architect Frank Lloyd Wright, best known for his houses and buildings, designed this chair for the Imperial Hotel in Tokyo.

THE BETTMANN ARCHIVE

Employment The terms and conditions of an architect's employment are designated in a contract and are governed by general rules of CONTRACT law. Ordinarily, the person who employs the architect becomes the owner of the plans, unless the employment contract states otherwise. Customarily, the architect retains the plans after they have been paid for and the builder may possess and use them while constructing the building.

Authority and Powers The power and authority of architects are determined by general rules of AGENCY law. In most cases, unless the employment contract states otherwise, architects are held to be AGENTS with limited authority. An employer is liable for acts of an architect when they are within the scope of the architect's agency, although the contracting parties may further restrict the powers if they so desire.

Architects have a duty to exercise their personal skill and judgment in the performance of their work, and they may not delegate this duty

A model of Christ the Savior Cathedral in Moscow helps the architects plan for the full-scale structure.

AFP/BETTMANN

without express authority to do so. They may, however, delegate responsibility to subordinates while performing their duties as agents.

A supervising architect does not have implied authority to perform work that has been assigned to a contractor or to employ or discharge workers. The supervising architect does, however, have authority to make decisions concerning proper workmanship, fitness of materials, and the manner of work.

Duties and Liabilities Although the duties of architects generally depend on what is designated in the employment contract, some duties are carried out as a matter of custom, such as the duty to supervise construction.

Architects are in a FIDUCIARY relationship with their employers, and as such they must exercise good faith and loyalty toward them. As professionals, they are held to a standard of reasonable and ordinary care and skill in applying their knowledge and must conform to accepted architectural practices. The failure to exercise reasonable care and skill can result in LIABILITY for DAMAGES and the loss of the right to recover compensation for their services.

Compensation Architects have a right to compensation for their services unless there is an agreement that they shall work gratuitously. To be entitled to compensation, they must carry out their contract with reasonable skill and care and without any substantial omissions or imperfections in performance. The employment contract usually fixes the amount of compensation. A standard payment scale created by the American Institute of Architects is customarily used to determine the amount of compensation.

In the event that an architect is refused payment for services, he or she may sue for the amount of compensation agreed upon in the employment contract or, in the absence of an agreement, for the reasonable value of the services under the theory of QUANTUM MERUIT.

ARCHITECT OF THE CAPITOL Established as a permanent office in 1876 (40 U.S.C.A. §§ 162, 163), the architect of the capitol oversees the mechanical and structural maintenance of the Capitol, the conservation and care of works of art in the building, the upkeep and improvement of the Capitol grounds, and the arrangement of inaugural and other ceremonies held in the building or on the grounds. In addition, the architect is responsible for the upkeep of all the congressional office buildings, the Library of Congress buildings, the U.S. Supreme Court building, the Federal Judiciary Building, the Capitol Power Plant, the Capitol Police headquarters, and the

Robert A. Taft Memorial. The architect also serves as the acting director of the U.S. Botanic Garden.

The functions of the architect have become increasingly administrative, and the architectural or engineering dimensions less important. Special projects carried out by the architect include building renovation and restoration, including installation of broadcasting and security equipment in the Capitol.

Before 1989, the position of architect of the capitol was filled for an indefinite term by presidential appointment. Legislation enacted in 1989 (Pub. L. No. 101-163, 103 Stat. 1068 [codified at 40 U.S.C.A. § 162–1]) provided that the architect be appointed for a ten-year term by the president, with the advice and consent of the Senate, from a list of three candidates recommended by a congressional commission. Upon confirmation by the Senate, the architect becomes an official of the legislative branch as an officer and agent of Congress and is eligible for reappointment after completion of a term.

ARCTIC, LEGAL STATUS OF Establishment of territorial SOVEREIGNTY over portions of the Arctic and its seabed has become increasingly attractive to many nations for military purposes or as a source of minerals. Under INTERNATIONAL LAW, national claims of sovereignty over the Arctic traditionally were recognized only if accompanied by physical occupation. Consequently, two competing theories developed: (1) that no nation could achieve sovereignty over the Arctic (*res nullius*), and (2) that every nation shared in undivided sovereignty over the area (*res communes*). According to international law today, sovereignty is considered to be a derivative of the exercise of government functions and of notoriety over new territory. Therefore, national claims of sovereignty over portions of the Arctic that are supported by such governmental activity have become more plausible. Many such claims have rested on the sector principle, a version of the doctrine of contiguity, to define the area included in the claim. The sector principle traces longitudinal parallels from borders of countries adjacent to the Arctic Circle to the North Pole, assigning the sectors so formed to the neighboring nations. Claims resting solely on the sector principle have been denied legal force by many nations, including the United States, and it appears that only those claims of sovereignty accompanied by government control may be eventually accepted under international law. See also BOUNDARIES; TERRITORY.

ARGUENDO In the course of the argument.

When the phrase *in arguendo* is used by a judge during the course of a trial, it indicates that his or her comment is made as a matter of argument or illustration only. The statement does not bear directly upon the remainder of the discussion.

ARGUMENT A form of expression consisting of a coherent set of reasons presenting or supporting a point of view; a series of reasons given for or against a matter under discussion that is intended to convince or persuade the listener.

For example, an argument by counsel consists of a presentation of the facts or evidence and the inferences that may be drawn therefrom, which are aimed at persuading a judge or jury to render a verdict in favor of the attorney's client.

An attorney may begin to develop an argument in the OPENING STATEMENT, the initial discussion of the case in which the facts and the pertinent law are stated. In most cases, however, an attorney sets forth the main points of an argument in the CLOSING ARGUMENT, which is the attorney's final opportunity to comment on the case before a judge or jury retires to begin deliberation on a verdict.

ARGUMENTATIVE Controversial; subject to argument.

PLEADING in which a point relied upon is not set out, but merely implied, is often labeled argumentative. Pleading that contains arguments that should be saved for trial, in addition to ALLEGATIONS establishing a CAUSE OF ACTION or DEFENSE, is also called argumentative.

BIOGRAPHY

THE BETTMANN ARCHIVE

Aristotle

ARISTOTLE Aristotle was born in 384 B.C., in Stagira, Greece. He achieved prominence as an eminent philosopher who greatly influenced the basic principles of philosophy and whose ideologies are still practiced today.

Aristotle was a student of the renowned philosopher Plato and tutored Alexander the Great, who became King of Macedonia in 336 B.C.

Aristotle established his own school in the Lyceum, near Athens, in 335 B.C. He often lectured his students in the portico, or walking place, of the Lyceum. The school was subsequently called Peripatetic, after the Greek word *peripatos* for "walking place."

In 323 B.C. the reign of Alexander ended with his death, and Aristotle sought refuge at Chalcis.

Aristotle formulated numerous beliefs about the reasoning power of humans and the essence of being. He stressed the importance of nature

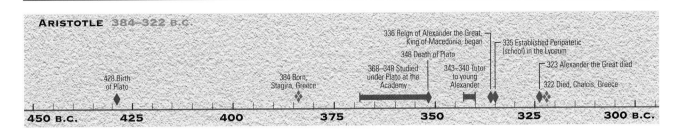

ARISTOTLE 384–322 B.C.

336 Reign of Alexander the Great,
King of Macedonia, began

335 Established Peripatetic
(school) in the Lyceum

348 Death of Plato

428 Birth
of Plato

384 Born,
Stagira, Greece

368–348 Studied
under Plato at the
Academy

343–340 Tutor
to young
Alexander

323 Alexander the Great died

322 Died, Chalcis, Greece

450 B.C.   425   400   375   350   325   300 B.C.

and instructed his pupils to closely study natural phenomena. When teaching science, he believed that all ideas must be supported by explanations based upon facts.

Concerning the realm of politics, Aristotle propounded that humans are inherently political and demonstrate an essential part of their humanity when participating in civic affairs.

Philosophy was a subject of great interest to Aristotle, and he theorized that philosophy was the foundation of the ability to understand the basic axioms that comprise knowledge. In order to study and question completely, Aristotle viewed logic as the basic means of reasoning. To think logically, one had to apply the syllogism, which was a form of thought comprised of two premises that led to a conclusion; Aristotle taught that this form can be applied to all logical reasoning.

To understand reality, Aristotle theorized that it must be categorized as substance, quality, quantity, relation, determination in time and space, action, passion or passivity, position, and condition. To know and understand the reality of an object required an explanation of its material cause, which is why it exists or its composition; its formal cause, or its design; its efficient cause, or its creator; and its final cause, or its reason for being.

Aristotle agreed with his mentor, Plato, concerning the field of ethics. The goodness of a being depended upon the extent to which that being achieved its highest potential. For humans, the ultimate good is the continual use and development of their reasoning powers to fullest capacity. To effect fulfillment and contentment, humans must follow a life of contemplation, rather than pleasure.

The fundamental source of Aristotle's theories were his lectures to his students, which were compiled into several volumes. They include *Organum*, which discusses logic; *Physics*; *Metaphysics*; *De Anima*, concerning the soul; *Rhetoric*; *Politics*; *Nichomachean Ethics and Eudemian Ethics*, involving principles of conduct; and *De Poetica*, or poetics.

He also wrote *Constitution of Athens*, a de-

"MAN IS BY NATURE A

POLITICAL ANIMAL."

scription of the foundations of the government of Athens. The work was discovered in the late nineteenth century.

Aristotle died in 322 B.C., in Chalcis, Greece.

ARMED SERVICES The Constitution authorizes Congress to raise, support, and regulate armed services for the national defense. The president is commander in chief of all the branches of the service and has ultimate control over most military matters.

The United States has always been wary of maintaining a strong military force. This care was shown by the Framers of the Constitution when they finally allowed the creation of a standing army but at the same time limited the process by which money could be raised to support the military, by requiring that Congress review the appropriations every two years. In this way, they ensured that each new Congress would address their lingering concerns about domestic tyranny with a fresh perspective. Furthermore, they ensured that the states could maintain their own MILITIAS and protect themselves from federal military domination, by recognizing "the right of the people to keep and bear Arms" (U.S. Const. amend. 2).

The various branches of the armed services were created at different times to serve different purposes. The earliest branch was the Army, instituted on July 14, 1775, followed closely by the Navy and the Marine Corps in the same year. All three were established to respond to the needs of the revolutionary forces fighting the British. The Navy and the Marine Corps were disbanded after the Revolutionary War but were reestablished in 1798. The Coast Guard traces its origins to 1790 but was officially created in 1915. Finally, the Air Force had its genesis in the Signal Corps of the Army and was formally established as the Army Air Service in 1920.

Military personnel are governed by a set of laws that is separate from and independent of civil law. The Uniform Code of Military Justice (10 U.S.C.A. § 801 et seq.) outlines the basic laws and procedures governing members of the armed services. Military law is mainly con-

The Branches of the Armed Services

The five branches of the armed services are staffed by volunteer enlisted men and women who hold various ranks. Military personnel are no longer conscripted, or drafted, into service.

Army

The Army was the first branch of the armed services established by Congress. The U.S. Army evolved from the Continental Army, created on July 14, 1775, by the Continental Congress to fight the Revolutionary War against the British.

The three segments of the Army are the Army Reserve, the Army National Guard, and the Active Army. The Army Reserve provides training and combat support to the Active Army in times of emergency. The Army National Guard, the oldest military force in the United States, began in the Massachusetts Bay Colony in 1636. During peacetime, the National Guard unit in each state is commanded by the state governor. The National Guard often assists in natural disasters, such as earthquakes or floods, or in civil unrest, such as riots. The president has the authority to call the Guard to federal duty when necessary. For example, President Dwight D. Eisenhower federalized the Arkansas National Guard in 1957, and assigned them to control angry mobs protesting the enrollment of African American students in a previously segregated Little Rock high school. Similarly, President George Bush assigned Guard units to duty with the Active Army during the Persian Gulf War of 1992.

The Army's many responsibilities are carried out by combat, combat support, and combat service support arms. The combat arms, including the infantry, armored divisions, air defense artillery, field artillery, and aviation, are directly involved in fighting. The combat support arms include the Corps of Engineers, the Signal Corps, the Military Police Corps, the Chemical Corps, and military intelligence. The combat service support arms provide logistical and administrative assistance to the other arms.

Women were originally restricted to the Women's Army Corps (WAC) but now serve alongside men in almost all capacities. Their roles have been gradually expanded, and they now serve in combat units, which gives them equal opportunities with men for higher pay and advancement in rank.

The U.S. Military Academy, the oldest of the service academies, was established at West Point, New York, in 1802. It was originally charged with training army engineers, but evolved into the training ground for those wishing to become officers in the Army. West Point has been coeducational since 1976.

Navy

The Navy traces its origins to 1775 and the American Revolution. A fleet established to fight the British was disbanded after the war, but the need for a naval force was again recognized in 1798, when Congress established the Navy Department. The Navy was a separate branch of the government until the National Security Act of 1947 (5 U.S.C.A. § 101 et seq., 10 U.S.C.A. § 101 et seq., 50 U.S.C.A. § 401 et seq.) created the Department of Defense with a cabinet-level secretary to oversee all the branches of the military.

The Navy's forces are grouped into various fleets that serve in different areas of the world. Tradition-

cerned with maintaining order and discipline within the ranks. It is unrelated to MARTIAL LAW, which is the temporary imposition of military rule during a national or regional crisis. Offenses committed by members of the armed services are tried by a court-martial, a special tribunal created specifically to hear a military case and then disbanded once judgment and punishment are pronounced.

The constitutionality of the military legal system has been challenged several times, without success. In 1994, the Supreme Court reaffirmed the constitutionality of the system with a unanimous decision in *Weiss v. United States,* 510 U.S. 163, 114 S. Ct. 752, 127 L. Ed. 2d 1. At issue were the selection process and tenure of military judges, who are chosen by their branch's JUDGE ADVOCATE general. The plaintiffs claimed that because the judges could be removed at any time by the judge advocate general, they were biased toward the prosecution and could not be impartial. The Court held that sufficient safeguards were in place to protect against improper influence by the judge advocate general and that the defendants' Fifth Amendment DUE PROCESS rights had not been violated.

Military Ban on Homosexuality One controversial and divisive issue facing the military is the inclusion of homosexuals. For more than fifty years, the U.S. armed services prohibited gay men and lesbians from serving in the military. In the past, members who disclosed that they were homosexual were subject to

ally, odd-numbered fleets, such as the Third and Seventh Fleets, have served in the Pacific Ocean. Even-numbered fleets, like the Second and Sixth Fleets, have served in the Atlantic Ocean. Over the years, U.S. Navy fleets have been disestablished (removed from service) and reconstituted (restored to service) as the distribution of military power throughout the world has changed.

A naval reserve force is made up of civilians who train regularly and stand ready to be called in times of need.

Although women originally could only join the Women Accepted for Voluntary Emergency Service (WAVES), they now serve alongside men, drawing equal pay and attaining equivalent rank.

The Naval Academy, at Annapolis, Maryland, was established in 1845 to train young men to be officers in the Navy and the Marine Corps. Women have been admitted since 1976.

Air Force

The Aeronautical Division of the Army Signal Corps, the precursor to the U.S. Air Force, was established on August 1, 1907. The First Aero Squadron was organized in 1914 and served with the Mexican Border Expedition in 1916. The Air Force remained a division of the Army until 1947.

The Air Force is responsible for domestic security in such areas as the Strategic Air Command (SAC), which plays a major role in deterring air and missile attacks as well as conducting space surveillance. Other responsibilities of the Air Force include maintaining a combat-ready mobile strike force and operating air bases in key areas around the world.

The Air Force's chief of staff, along with the chiefs of staff of the Army and the Navy, is a member of the Joint Chiefs of Staff, which advises the president and the secretary of defense.

The Air Force Academy, authorized in 1954 and located in Colorado Springs, Colorado, prepares college students to become officers in the Air Force. Women were admitted beginning in 1976.

Marine Corps

Steeped in history, tradition, and folklore, the Marine Corps, a self-contained amphibious combat force within the Department of the Navy, traces its roots to the Revolutionary War. During its two hundred–year history, the U.S. Marines has fulfilled its obligation to provide air, land, and sea support for naval forces, establish beachheads during war, and protect U.S. lives and interests at foreign embassies and legations.

The Marines maintains a large reserve unit, which, when mobilized in times of crisis, can increase its strength by 25 percent within weeks.

The Marine Corps Women's Reserve, established in 1942, provides support in the mainland United States and in Hawaii so that men are available for combat.

Marine Corps officers are trained mainly at the U.S. Naval Academy, at Annapolis.

Coast Guard

The U.S. Coast Guard, first established in 1790, operates under the Department of Transportation. It is charged with guarding the country's coasts against smuggling, enforcing customs laws, and responding to emergencies along the coasts.

The Coast Guard provides officer training for college students at the Coast Guard Academy, at New London, Connecticut, which began admitting women in 1976.

---

immediate discharge. That policy was challenged in several prominent cases during the late 1980s and early 1990s, and the Clinton administration addressed the issue with a new approach that ultimately led to more confusion and controversy.

The federal courts tackled the question of whether the military's automatic ouster of homosexual personnel is constitutional, in *Meinhold v. United States Department of Defense*, 34 F.3d 1469 (9th Cir. 1994). The plaintiff, Petty Officer Keith Meinhold, of the Navy, announced on a national television broadcast in May 1992 that he is gay. As a result, discharge proceedings were begun against him. Meinhold was dismissed solely on the basis of his televised statement. He sued the Navy and the Department of Defense, claiming that their policy was unconstitutional. The district court agreed, holding that the Navy's actions denied gay men and lesbians EQUAL PROTECTION under the law. In August 1994, the Court of Appeals for the Ninth Circuit agreed that Meinhold could not be discharged merely for stating that he was gay. However, the appeals court disagreed with the district court's finding that the military's policy was unconstitutional and instead found that by discharging Meinhold because of his status as a homosexual and not because of any actions on his part, the Navy was equating status with prohibited conduct. The court conceded that the Navy could legally discharge someone who manifested a "fixed or expressed desire to commit a prohibited act," such as engaging in homosexual sex, but found that Meinhold had not manifested any such desire and therefore must be reinstated. In November 1994, the Clinton administration announced it was dropping its efforts to bar Meinhold from serving and would not appeal the Ninth Circuit's ruling.

Another challenge to the military ban on homosexuals came in *Steffan v. Aspin*, 8 F.3d 57 (D.C. Cir. 1993). The plaintiff, Joseph Steffan, admitted to being a homosexual just six weeks before his expected graduation from the U.S. Naval Academy, at Annapolis, Maryland, in 1987. Steffan was one of the top ten students in his class. He had consistently received outstanding marks for leadership and military performance. In his junior year, he was named a battalion commander in charge of one-sixth of the academy's forty-five hundred students. After Steffan acknowledged his homosexuality to a classmate and a chaplain, he was brought before a disciplinary board, which recommended that he be discharged. Rather than face dismissal, he resigned. Sometime later, he asked to be reinstated. His request was denied, and he then sued for reinstatement to his commission, claiming that he was forced to resign because of his status as a homosexual, not because of any conduct—in violation of the Constitution's equal protection guarantee.

The district court granted summary judgment for the government (*Steffan v. Cheney*, 780 F. Supp. 1 [D.D.C. 1991]). A three-judge panel for the court of appeals reversed, stating that the dismissal policy had no rational basis and that it violated the Equal Protection Clause of the Fifth Amendment. The appeals court ordered the academy to award Steffan his diploma and reinstate him to his commission.

The government petitioned the court for a rehearing on whether the three-judge panel had exceeded its authority. The full court of appeals vacated the decision of the panel and ordered a rehearing before the full court on the constitutionality question. In November 1994, the full court reversed the decision of the three-judge panel and held that Steffan's dismissal did not violate the Constitution. The court said that the Navy's ban on homosexuals, like its height or eyesight requirements, did have a rational basis. The court also dismissed Steffan's argument that the ban punished status rather than conduct. Judge Laurence H. Silberman, writing for the majority, said, "Steffan's claim that the Government cannot rationally infer that one who states he or she is a homosexual is a practicing homosexual, or is at least likely to engage in homosexual acts, is so strained a constitutional argument as to amount to a basic attack on the policy itself" (*Steffan v. Perry*, 41 F.3d 677, 693 [D.C. Cir. 1994]). In an impassioned dissent, Judge Patricia M. Wald wrote, "In years to come, we will look back with dismay at these unconstitutional attempts to enforce silence upon individuals of homosexual orientation, in the military and out. Pragmatism should not be allowed to trump principle, or the soul of a nation will wither" (41 F.3d 677, 721).

In January 1995, Steffan announced that for tactical reasons, he would not appeal the decision to the Supreme Court. Steffan's case was brought under the old policy, and he and his attorneys felt that the best case to have the Supreme Court address was one involving the new policy, which they believed was more vulnerable to constitutional attack. After his discharge from the naval academy, Steffan became a lawyer.

The case of Colonel Margarethe Cammermeyer further clouded official policy on homosexuals in the military (*Cammermeyer v. Aspin*, 850 F. Supp. 910 [W.D. Wash. 1994]). Cammermeyer was dismissed from the Washington State National Guard in June 1992 when she acknowledged in a security-clearance interview that she is a lesbian. Under the rules in effect at the time, her statement was grounds for dismissal, and Cammermeyer was given an honorable discharge. She was the highest-ranking officer to be discharged solely because of homosexual orientation.

Cammermeyer, a highly respected nurse who was awarded the Bronze Star for her service with the Army in Vietnam, appealed the dismissal. In June 1994, Judge Thomas Zilly, of the Federal District Court for the District of Washington, ordered the military to reinstate Cammermeyer, holding that the policy in effect at the time of her dismissal violated the Equal Protection Clause. Zilly's decision dismantled the assumptions that form the basis for both the old and the new government policies regarding homosexuals in the military. Zilly held that "there is no rational basis for the Government's underlying contention that homosexual orientation equals 'desire or propensity to engage' in homosexual conduct" (850 F. Supp. at 920). The judge was direct and harsh in his criticism of the government's policy. He wrote, "The Government has discriminated against Colonel Cammermeyer solely on the basis of her status as a homosexual and has failed to demonstrate a rational basis for doing so" (850 F. Supp. at 926). Noting that military experts "conceded that their justifications for the policy are based

JIM LEVIT/IMPACT VISUALS

Margarethe Cammermeyer was discharged from the Washington State National Guard in June 1992 under a policy that made her status as a lesbian grounds for dismissal. She appealed the action.

on heterosexual members' fear and dislike of homosexuals," Zilly went on to say, "[m]ere negative attitudes, or fear, are constitutionally impermissible bases for discriminatory governmental policies" (850 F. Supp at 925).

The Justice Department moved to delay Cammermeyer's reinstatement, but the U.S. Court of Appeals for the Ninth Circuit refused the request. Cammermeyer returned to her position as chief of nursing services for the 164th Mobile Army Surgical Hospital in July 1994.

At the same time that *Meinhold, Steffan,* and *Cammermeyer* were being decided, the Clinton administration was formulating and implementing a new policy that it hoped would deal with the issue of homosexuals in the military and put the controversies surrounding the old policy to rest. Before he was elected, Bill Clinton had promised that as president, he would lift the ban on gay men and lesbians in the armed services. However, after taking office, Clinton faced strenuous opposition from the Joint Chiefs of Staff and the heads of the service branches, who argued that summarily eliminating the ban on homosexuals would lead to dissension among the troops and diminished military readiness. In December 1993, the Pentagon announced a compromise plan, which came to be known as the "don't ask, don't tell, don't pursue" policy (Policy Concerning Homosexuality in the Armed Forces, Pub. L. No. 103-160, 1993 H. R. 2401 § 571(a) [amending 10 U.S.C.A. § 654]). Under the new rules, gay

men and lesbians could serve in the military as long as they kept their sexual orientation private and did not engage in homosexual activity. The policy stated that sexual orientation is a "personal and private matter" about which recruits and members of the armed forces would no longer be required to answer questions. Criminal investigations and security checks conducted solely to determine sexual orientation would be eliminated. Homosexual orientation alone would not be a bar to service. However, homosexual conduct, which could take the form of "a homosexual act, a statement by the member that demonstrates a propensity or intent to engage in homosexual acts, or a homosexual marriage or attempted marriage" would subject the individual to dismissal. An acknowledgement of homosexual orientation would not be sufficient grounds for expulsion but could be the basis for an investigation into whether the individual engaged in homosexual acts.

Gay rights advocates immediately and vigorously criticized the new policy, saying it infringed on the free speech rights of gay service members and vowing to challenge it in court. In the months following implementation of the new rules, it became clear that, far from easing the plight of homosexual service members, "don't ask, don't tell, don't pursue" was actually making life worse for many of them. Some commanding officers were overly aggressive in implementing the new rules, and many critics felt that the policy further polarized attitudes among service members. Furthermore, the policy shifted the burden of proof to the individual to show that she or he had not engaged in homosexual acts.

The first legal challenge to the "don't ask, don't tell, don't pursue" policy was filed in March 1994 by the American Civil Liberties Union and the Lambda Legal Defense and Education Fund. Six service members who had declared their homosexuality filed suit in the U.S. District Court for the Eastern District of New York, asking for injunctive relief and a declaration that the policy was unconstitutional. The case was heard by Judge Eugene H. Nickerson who issued orders on April 4, 1994, and June 3, 1994, enjoining the Army from pursuing discharge proceedings against the plaintiffs. Nickerson based his decision on the plaintiffs' showing that they would suffer irreparable harm if the INJUNCTION were not granted and that the case involved "sufficiently serious questions" that would warrant its going forward for a decision on its merits.

The U.S. Court of Appeals for the Second Circuit found that Nickerson had used an incorrect standard in determining whether the injunction should be granted. It held that in a case such as this, where an injunction is sought against a "government action taken in the public interest pursuant to a statutory or regulatory scheme," a more rigorous showing that the case has a "likelihood of success" must be made (*Able v. United States*, 44 F.3d 128 [1995] [per curiam]). The court allowed the injunctions to stand but remanded the case to the district court for a decision on the plaintiffs' constitutional claims within three months.

On March 30, 1995, Judge Nickerson delivered the decision the plaintiffs had hoped for. He held that the "don't ask, don't tell, don't pursue" policy violated the First and Fifth Amendments, and enjoined the government from enforcing the policy against the plaintiffs (*Able*, 880 F. Supp. 968 [E.D.N.Y.]). The court found that the FIRST AMENDMENT prohibits a restraint on the right of a serviceperson to declare his or her homosexuality. According to the court, "Plaintiffs have done no more than acknowledge who they are, that is, their status. The speech at issue in this case implicates the First Amendment value of promoting individual dignity and integrity, and thus is protected by the First Amendment from efforts to prohibit it because of its content." The court further found that to regulate speech content, even in the military context, the government must show a "compelling interest" and prove that it has chosen the "least restrictive means" to further that interest. Nickerson criticized the legal hairsplitting in the policy directives, which purported to differentiate between a homosexual "orientation" and a homosexual "propensity." Once a member has admitted or acknowledged being a homosexual, he or she has only a "hypothetical" chance of escaping discharge. "Thus, the policy treats a statement of homosexual orientation as proof of the case," said Nickerson. "Once such a statement is made, the speaker is judged guilty until proven innocent of committing misconduct the government considers so threatening to the military mission that a member may be discharged for it. This seems to the court a rather draconian consequence of merely admitting to an orientation that Congress has determined to be innocuous."

Turning to the government's argument that the presence of openly homosexual members would be detrimental to morale and troop cohesion, the court found that sufficient sanctions were available for dealing with "inappropriate behavior by a homosexual, whether in the closet or not." Nickerson further stated his belief that the policy may actually be detrimental to the military because "secrecy and deception invite suspicion, which in turn erodes trust, the rock on which cohesion is built." He noted that a 1993 study conducted by the RAND Corporation found that in countries that have nondiscrimination policies, "no serious problems were reported concerning the presence of homosexuals in the force."

Finally, on the Fifth Amendment equal protection question, the court found that the government had failed to show that the policy, which denied to homosexuals the same free speech rights guaranteed to heterosexuals, was "tailored to serve a substantial governmental interest." The policy therefore violated the Fifth Amendment as well as the First, and the court enjoined the government from enforcing it.

Sexual Harassment in the Armed Services The inclusion of women in virtually all aspects of military life has changed the service from a male-dominated enterprise, strictly segregated by gender, into a microcosm of modern society. Although most men and women serve side by side without incident, charges of sexual harassment in the military became increasingly numerous in the 1980s and early 1990s.

Perhaps the most explosive and far-reaching incidence of this problem took place at the Tailhook Association convention in Las Vegas in September 1991. The Tailhook Association—named for the hook on a Navy jet that catches on the cables that stop it as it lands on an aircraft carrier—is a private group of active and retired Navy and Marine Corps pilots. After its 1991 meeting, Navy lieutenant Paula A. Coughlin charged that she and other women who unwittingly stumbled upon the Tailhook hospitality suites at the Las Vegas Hilton were forced to go through a "gauntlet" of drunken Navy and Marine officers who assaulted them, tore at their clothing, and grabbed at their bodies as they were propelled down the hallway. Coughlin's allegations launched an investigation that revealed drunken, lewd, and out-of-control behavior by the officers. In the ensuing months, the Navy severed its ties to the Tailhook Association and submitted the names of more than sixty officers for possible disciplinary action. Nevertheless, a conspiracy of silence among the aviators hampered the investigation. In September 1992, the Pentagon's inspector general issued a report criticizing the Navy's inquiry into the incident and suggesting that top Navy officials deliberately undermined the investigation to avoid negative publicity. The commander of the Naval Investigative Service and the Navy's judge advocate general were relieved of their commands. The following April, the inspector general accused 140 aviators of indecent exposure, assault, and lying under oath in the incident. However, no one was ever court-martialed as a result of the charges, and those who were disciplined received only small fines or reprimands.

The Tailhook scandal set off a tidal wave within the upper echelons of the Navy. Navy Secretary H. Lawrence Garrett III resigned in June 1992, accepting full responsibility for the failure of leadership that allowed the incident to occur. In October 1993, his replacement, John H. Dalton, asked for the removal of Admiral Frank B. Kelso II, chief of naval operations, who was present at the convention but denied any knowledge of the debauchery. Dalton's request was overruled by Secretary of Defense Les Aspin. In February 1994, a military judge cited Kelso for using "unlawful command influence" to "manipulate the initial investigative process" and the Navy's disciplinary procedures "to shield his personal involvement" in Tailhook. Kelso, who was to retire on June 30, 1994, angrily denied any wrongdoing and declared that he would not resign early. In the end, however, he was persuaded to step down two months ahead of schedule in exchange for a tribute from Defense Secretary William J. Perry that would clear his name. After a bitter debate, the U.S. Senate voted 54–43 to allow Kelso, the Navy's top admiral and a thirty-eight-year veteran, to retire at his full four-star rank and with a full pension. The women in the Senate, along with many of their male colleagues, vehemently opposed the arrangement, but they were ultimately overruled.

Coughlin resigned from the Navy in February 1994, stating that the assault and "the covert attacks on me that followed have stripped me of my ability to serve." Coughlin was successful in a civil suit against the Tailhook Association, with whom she settled for an undisclosed amount. She also won a civil suit against the Hilton Hotels Corporation, parent company of the Las Vegas Hilton, which she accused of lax security; in October 1994, a jury awarded her $1.7 million in COMPENSATORY DAMAGES and an additional $5 million in PUNITIVE DAMAGES. Still suffering depression and post-traumatic stress from the incident, Coughlin expressed satisfaction with the award but uncertainty about her future, saying, "I'm hoping to slip into obscu-

rity. I want to paint my house. I just want to go home."

Anxious to restore the Navy's tarnished image after the sordid series of events, top officials vowed to handle sexual harassment charges swiftly and sensitively. The Navy's new "zero-tolerance" policy on sexual harassment requires automatic dismissal for aggravated sexual harassment or repeat offenses. Under the policy, about ninety officers and sailors had been dismissed by the end of 1994.

In spite of the publicity generated by Tailhook and other scandals, and the efforts of the military to clamp down on sexual harassment, charges continue to come to light. In one 1994 case that tested the resolve of Admiral Jeremy M. Boorda, Admiral Kelso's successor as chief of naval operations, two officers were reprimanded for failing to act properly on complaints by Lieutenant Darlene Simmons. Simmons charged that her commanding officer, Lieutenant Commander Arthur Catullo, had offered to advance her career in exchange for sexual favors. Catullo was censured. Simmons, who had an impeccable record before she brought the charges but received an "adverse" evaluation afterward, received an apology from Navy Secretary Dalton. Dalton also cleared her record and offered to extend her active-duty Navy service by two years.

Another egregious incident, again involving the Navy, occurred in 1994 when four male instructors were court-martialed and six others punished for sexually harassing sixteen women students at the Naval Training Center in San Diego. The women, who were learning to operate the Navy's computer and telephone networks, claimed that the male instructors made unwanted verbal and physical advances. After a seven-month investigation, the Navy found all but one of the instructors guilty of the charges and imposed various sanctions, from a criminal conviction and $1,000 fine, to a loss in pay, counseling, and punitive letters placed in their files.

Sexual harassment was also found among the ranks at the U.S. Military Academy, at West Point, New York. In October 1994, female cadets complained that they had been groped at a pep rally by members of the West Point football team as the players ran past them in a regimental "spirit run." Lieutenant General Howard D. Graves, superintendent of West Point, launched an immediate investigation that resulted in three players being suspended from the team for the rest of the season, restricted to academy grounds for ninety days, and given eighty hours of marching discipline. Representative Patricia Schroeder (D-Colo.), a member of the House Armed Services Committee, criticized the punishment as too lenient, saying, "[I]t looks like [the incident] was treated as a prank and not as a serious violation of the code of conduct."

Base Closures and Troop Reductions

With the breakup of the Soviet Union and the end of the cold war, the U.S. government began the politically charged task of reducing military budgets and closing or shrinking unnecessary military installations. The Defense Base Closure and Realignment Act (10 U.S.C.A. § 2687), passed by Congress in 1990, set off a firestorm of controversy over which bases should be closed and whether the country's military readiness was being irrevocably compromised. The act created a presidential commission to decide which bases to close based on Pentagon recommendations. The commission's decisions are sent to the president, who accepts or rejects them in their entirety. If accepted, the recommendations are sent to Congress, which can only block the closings if both houses pass a resolution of disapproval within forty-five days. Commissions meeting in 1988, 1991, and 1993 decided to close a total of seventy major installations.

The base closures came under immediate fire as senators and representatives tried to prevent bases in their home states or districts from being shut down. One group of elected officials, including the four senators from Pennsylvania and New Jersey, brought suit in federal court to challenge the procedures under the Defense Base Closure and Realignment Act and to block the closing of the Philadelphia Naval Shipyard, one of the region's biggest employers. The case never went to trial. Instead, the Supreme Court agreed to hear the Clinton administration's appeal on the question of whether the suit could be brought at all. The Court held that the government's choice of which bases to close under the act could not be challenged in federal court (*Dalton v. Specter*, 511 U.S. 462, 114 S. Ct. 1719, 128 L. Ed. 2d 497 [1994]).

At about the same time as the *Dalton* decision was announced, the Defense Department, concerned about the effect of base closings on surrounding communities, began planning to postpone the final round of shutdowns scheduled to follow the commission's 1995 meeting. A senior Pentagon official defended the delays, saying, "As the defense budget goes down and we close bases, the issue now is the pace of closures so people and communities can adjust." Some critics claimed that the delays were a political move designed to take pressure off the president and Congress until after the 1996 election.

The issue of cost and the shrinking military budget loomed large in the debate. The purpose of closing the bases is to eliminate unnecessary costs, but the process of preparing a base for nonmilitary use is itself expensive. Military bases are exempt from federal environmental regulations, but when they are converted to private use, all the stockpiled weaponry and toxic waste must be disposed of in order to avoid liability. The government has set aside $3 billion a year to cover environmental cleanup plus construction and repair of buildings and roads. Still, the projected savings by the end of the 1990s is $4.6 billion a year.

The Joint Chiefs of Staff were adamant that the base closings continue apace. "We really need this," said Admiral Boorda. "There's not enough money to maintain infrastructure we no longer need." But the base shutdowns have exacted a heavy human toll. Communities surrounding the closed bases suffered dire economic consequences. In 1993, for example, the states where base closings were concentrated—Florida, Virginia, California, and South Carolina—lost a total of over fifty thousand civilian jobs. In addition, many industries that depended on military contracts cut their workforces in response to reduced orders. For

Military Personnel on Active Duty, 1970 to 1994

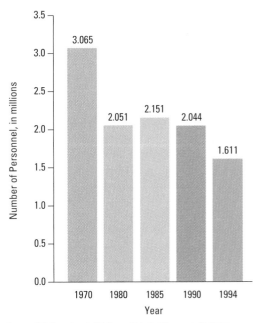

Source: U.S. Department of Defense, *Selected Manpower Statistics*, annual; U.S. Office of Management and Budget, *Budget*, annual.

As military budgets shrink and bases are closed, members of Congress and others worry about the services' combat readiness.

example, in September 1994, Northrop Grumman Corporation, which built B-2 and FA-18 fighter jets, announced it would cut its staff by 18 percent by the end of 1995. McDonnell Douglas Corporation shaved its workforce from 132,900 to 80,000 between 1990 and 1994. The layoffs left many educated, formerly well paid professionals without work in a stubbornly sluggish economy. Many were forced to take temporary or part-time jobs at salaries far below what they had previously been paid.

Shrinking military budgets and closing bases inevitably led to questions about the services' combat readiness. Conservative members of Congress, traditional supporters of military spending, disputed the Pentagon's assurances that equipment and troop levels remained at the optimal "two-war" level, that is, at a level where the country could fight two regional wars nearly simultaneously. Liberals, on the other hand, argued that the military exaggerated its needs. Sweeping Republican victories in both the House and the Senate in 1994 seemed to embolden the branches of the service in their long-standing rivalry for funds. Critics claimed that the Army created an unduly bleak picture of its combat readiness. Admiral Boorda, who had previously supported spending reductions, changed his position and began lobbying for increases in the Navy's fleet. For his part, President Clinton responded to criticisms that the military was underfunded with a request for a $25 billion increase in the Pentagon's

budget between 1995 and 2001. Not surprisingly, the move was criticized both by liberals who felt it was an unnecessary political maneuver and by conservatives who felt that it hardly went far enough.

CROSS-REFERENCES

Court-Martial; Defense Department; Gay and Lesbian Rights; Military Law; National Guard; Sexual Harassment; Veterans Affairs Department; War.

ARMISTICE ⬛ A suspending or cessation of hostilities between belligerent nations or forces for a considerable time. An armistice differs from a mere "suspension of arms" in that the latter is concluded for very brief periods and for local military purposes only, whereas an armistice not only covers a longer period, but is agreed upon for political purposes. It is said to be *general* if it relates to the whole area of the war, and *partial* if it relates to only a portion of that area. Partial armistices are sometimes called truces but there is no hard and fast distinction. ⬛

Armistice Day originated as a day set aside by the United States, Great Britain, and France to commemorate the signing of the armistice on November 11, 1918, that brought an end to World War I. After World War II, it became a day for tribute to those who lost their lives in that conflict as well. In Canada, it became known as Remembrance Day, and in Britain the Sunday closest to November 11 was declared

General Douglas MacArthur (top) signs the Japanese surrender documents on board the USS Missouri *in Tokyo Bay on September 1, 1945. The Japanese delegation boarded the ship in order to sign the documents. Although this armistice effectively ended the war in the Pacific, the formal peace treaty concluding the war was not signed until September 8, 1951.*

Remembrance Sunday to honor the dead of both world wars. In 1938, the day was made a federal holiday in the United States.

In 1954, after the Korean War, President Dwight D. Eisenhower signed an act of Congress (5 U.S.C.A. § 6103 (a) [1995]) to change the name of the holiday to Veterans Day "to honor veterans on the eleventh day of November of each year . . . a day dedicated to world peace." Thus, Veterans Day now honors all U.S. veterans of all wars. From 1971 to 1977, the holiday was celebrated on the fourth Monday in October, but in 1978, the traditional date of November 11 was restored.

Veterans Day celebrations in towns and cities in the United States usually include parades, speeches, and floral tributes placed on soldiers' graves or memorials, with special services held at the Tomb of the Unknown Soldier in Arlington National Cemetery, in Arlington, Virginia, outside Washington, D.C. Group naturalization ceremonies, in which individuals are made

citizens of the United States, have also become part of Veterans Day celebrations.

ARMS CONTROL AND DISARMAMENT

One of the major efforts to preserve international peace and security in the twentieth century has been to control or limit the number of weapons and the ways in which weapons can be used. Two different means to achieve this goal have been disarmament and arms control. *Disarmament* is the reduction of the number of weapons and troops maintained by a state. *Arms control* refers to treaties made between potential adversaries that reduce the likelihood and scope of war, usually imposing limitations on military capability. Although disarmament always involves the reduction of military forces or weapons, arms control does not. In fact, arms control agreements sometimes allow for the increase of weapons by one or more parties to a treaty.

History Arms control developed both in theory and in practice during the cold war, a period between the late 1940s and 1991 when the two military superpowers, the United States and the Union of Soviet Socialist Republics (U.S.S.R.), dealt with one another from a position of mutual mistrust. Arms control was devised consciously during the postwar period as an alternative to disarmament, which for many had fallen into discredit as a means of reducing the likelihood of war. Germany had been forced to disarm following World War I, but soon became belligerent again during the 1930s, resulting in World War II. Although Germany's weapons had been largely eliminated, the underlying causes of conflict had not. Germany's experience thus illustrated that no simple cause-and-effect relationship existed between the possession of weapons and a tendency to create war.

Following World War II, advocates of arms control as a new approach to limiting hostility between nations emphasized that military weapons and power would continue to remain a part of modern life. It was unrealistic and even dangerous, they felt, for a country to seek complete elimination of weapons, nor would it necessarily reduce the likelihood of war. Whereas disarmament had formerly been seen as an alternative to military strength, arms control was now viewed as an integral part of it. Arms control proponents sought to create a stable balance of power in which the forces that cause states to go to war could be controlled and regulated. The emphasis in arms control is thus upon overall stability rather than elimination of arms, and proponents recognize that an increase in weaponry is sometimes required to preserve a balance of power.

The development of arms control owes a great deal to the existence of nuclear weapons as well. By the 1950s, when both the United States and the Soviet Union possessed nuclear weapons, the superpowers became convinced that they could not safely disarm themselves of those weapons. In the absence of guaranteed verification—the process whereby participants in a treaty monitor each other's adherence to the agreement—neither side could disarm without making itself vulnerable to cheating by the other side. The goal of the superpowers and other nations possessing nuclear weapons therefore became not total elimination of those weapons, but control of them so that a stable nuclear deterrent might be maintained. According to the idea of *nuclear deterrence*, a state possessing nuclear weapons is deterred, or prevented, from using them against another nuclear power because of the threat of retaliation. No state is willing to attempt a first strike, because it cannot prevent the other side from striking back. Nuclear deterrence is therefore predicated upon a mutual abhorrence of the destructive power of nuclear weapons. This idea has come to be called mutual assured destruction (MAD). Many experts see deterrence as the ultimate goal of nuclear arms control.

Because many civilians generally assume that arms control and disarmament are the same thing, there has often been public disappointment when treaties have resulted in an increase in the number or power of weapons. An advantage of arms control over disarmament, however, is that even states with a high degree of suspicion or hostility toward each other can still negotiate agreements. Disarmament agreements, on the other hand, require a high degree of trust, and their formation is unlikely between hostile nations.

Arms control is often used as a means to avoid an *arms race*—a competitive buildup of weapons between two or more powers. Such a race can be costly for both sides, and arms control treaties serve the useful purpose of limiting weapons stockpiles to a level that preserves deterrence while conserving the economic and social resources of a state for other uses.

Modern Arms Control Although disarmament and arms control agreements were forged prior to World War II (1939–45), the modern arms control effort began in earnest after the Cuban Missile Crisis of 1962. That situation erupted when the United States discovered that the Soviet Union was constructing launch sites for nuclear missiles on the island of Cuba, thereby threatening to put nuclear weapons very close to U.S. soil. President John F. Kennedy declared a naval BLOCKADE of the island, and for two weeks, the United States and the U.S.S.R. existed in a state of heightened tension. Finally, the U.S.S.R. and its leader, Nikita Khrushchev, gave in. With the United States' promise not to overthrow Fidel Castro's government in Cuba, the Soviets canceled plans to install the missiles. After the crisis, Kennedy wrote to Khrushchev, "I agree with you that we must devote urgent attention to the problem of disarmament. . . . Perhaps . . . we can together make real progress in this vital field."

Among the earliest arms control treaties were the Limited Test Ban Treaty (LTBT), an agreement that prohibited nuclear test explosions in the atmosphere, under water, or in space, which was signed in 1963 by the United States, Britain, and the U.S.S.R., and the 1972 Biological Weapons Convention, a superpower treaty that banned biological weapons and provided for the destruction of existing stockpiles. The 1972 convention was the first and only example, since 1945, of true disarmament of an entire weapons category. Although negotiation on a comprehensive test ban—an agreement that would prohibit all nuclear testing—continued, this solution remained elusive. Nevertheless, in 1974, the superpowers signed the Threshold Test Ban Treaty (TTBT), which limits nuclear tests to explosive yields of less than 150 kilotons. (A kiloton represents the explosive force of one thousand tons of TNT). But the TTBT did not prevent the superpowers from developing nuclear warheads (the bomb-carrying segments of a nuclear missile) with power exceeding 150 kilotons; warheads on the Soviet SS-17 missile possess as much as a 3.6-megaton capacity. (A megaton equals 1 million tons of TNT.) In 1976, the superpowers signed the Peaceful Nuclear Explosions Treaty (PNET), which banned so-called peaceful nuclear testing.

Numerous arms control agreements have been designed to improve communications between the superpowers. The first of these, coming just after the Cuban Missile Crisis, was the 1963 Hot Line Agreement, setting up a special telegraph line between Moscow and Washington. In 1978, the hot line was updated by a satellite link between the two superpowers. The United States and the U.S.S.R. also sought to create protocols designed to prevent an accidental nuclear war. This led to the 1971 agreement, Measures to Reduce the Risk of Outbreak of Nuclear War, which required advance warning for any missile tests and immediate

MISSILE EQUIPMENT
MARIEL PORT FACILITY

4 MISSILE TRANSPORTERS

OXIDIZER TRAILERS

FUEL TRAILERS

LAUNCH STANDS

17 MISSILE ERECTORS

2

(APPROX 3.5 NM NORTH OF MAIN PORT FACILITY)

The Soviet Union constructed missile erectors and launch stands in Cuba in the early 1960s. After the Cuban Missile Crisis, a standoff between the United States and the U.S.S.R., the U.S.S.R. backed down and dismantled the equipment in exchange for a U.S. promise not to overthrow the Cuban government.

notification of any accidents or missile warning alerts.

One highly celebrated arms control agreement is the 1968 Treaty on the Non-Proliferation of Nuclear Weapons, or Non-Proliferation Treaty, designed to prevent the spread of nuclear weapons to other countries. The agreement involves well over one hundred states. Under it, countries not possessing nuclear weapons give up their right to acquire such weapons, and countries with nuclear weapons waive their rights to export nuclear weapons technology to countries lacking that technology.

Another class of arms control treaties seeks to ban weapons from as-yet-unmilitarized areas. These include the 1959 Antarctic Treaty, which prohibits military bases, maneuvers, and tests on the Antarctic Continent; the 1967 Outer Space Treaty, a ban on the testing or deployment of "weapons of mass destruction" in earth's orbit or on other bodies in the solar system; the 1967 Tlatelolco Treaty, prohibiting nuclear weapons in Latin America; and the 1971 Seabed Treaty, banning the placement of

weapons of mass destruction on or below the seabed.

SALT I and After The Strategic Arms Limitation Talks (SALT I and SALT II) were first undertaken in the era of détente in the early 1970s, when relations between the United States and the U.S.S.R. became more amicable. SALT I led to two agreements: the Anti-Ballistic-Missile Treaty of 1972 (ABM Treaty), which eventually limited each superpower to one site for antiballistic missiles (ABMs), the missiles designed to intercept and destroy incoming missiles; and an "interim" arms agreement limiting the number of intercontinental ballistic missile (ICBM) launchers and submarine-launched ballistic missiles (SLBMs) to those already deployed by specific dates in 1972. It also required that any modernization and replacement of ICBMs and SLBMs be on a one-for-one basis and prohibited any development of new, more powerful ICBMs. The agreement was meant to set limits before a more definitive SALT II treaty could be negotiated. When the SALT II Treaty was signed in 1979, it set a limit of twenty-four hundred strategic missiles and bombers for each side. Although the U.S. Senate did not ratify this treaty, the United States abided by it for several years.

The ABM Treaty of SALT I was much more successful than the interim ICBM-SLBM agreement. Because the SALT agreements limited only the number of ICBM launchers, or missiles, both superpowers went on in the 1970s to develop missiles with multiple warheads, called multiple independently targetable reentry vehicles (MIRVs). Launcher totals thus remained constant, but the number of warheads increased dramatically. Adding warheads to missiles also made nuclear deterrence more shaky; a superpower with MIRVs could have enough warheads to destroy the opponent's retaliatory capability, thereby making MAD ineffective. Both superpowers felt that their land-based missile forces had become vulnerable to a first strike from the other side.

Compliance with the SALT treaties became a contentious issue in the 1980s when the United States accused the U.S.S.R. of violating treaty provisions on the development of new missiles. The administration of President Ronald Reagan decided that alleged Soviet violations made it necessary to end U.S. compliance with the agreements. In 1986, the United States exceeded limits set by SALT II when a

B-52 bomber equipped with cruise missiles (nuclear missiles that fly at a low altitude) entered active service. Another U.S. military proposal, the Strategic Defense Initiative (SDI), also complicated the ABM Treaty. In 1983, Reagan made a televised speech in which he announced plans to develop a space-based missile defense system. He presented SDI as an alternative to MAD. SDI would, he claimed, effectively shield the United States from a Soviet missile launch, including an accidental or third-party attack. SDI would also protect the land-based leg of the United States' nuclear triad, the other two legs of which are aircraft bombers and submarine-launched missiles. Many doubted whether such a missile defense system could actually be created, and others criticized SDI as a dangerous upsetting of the nuclear balance. A debate also arose as to whether SDI was in violation of the ABM Treaty.

Relations between the superpowers eventually warmed when Mikhail Gorbachev emerged as leader of the Soviet Union in the mid-1980s. Relatively young and dynamic compared with his predecessors, Gorbachev initiated reforms of openness in the Soviet Union that facilitated arms control agreements. In 1987, President Reagan and Soviet General Secretary Gorbachev signed the Intermediate-Range Nuclear

U.S. president Jimmy Carter and Soviet president Leonid Brezhnev shake hands after signing the SALT II Treaty in June 1979.

Forces Treaty (INF Treaty), another major step in arms control. The INF Treaty called for the elimination of an entire class of short- and intermediate-range (300- to 3,400-mile) nuclear missiles. These included 1,752 Soviet and 859 U.S. missiles. It was the first treaty to result in a reduction in the number of nuclear weapons. The agreement also involved the most complete verification procedures ever for an arms control treaty. These included data exchanges, on-site inspections, and monitoring by surveillance satellites.

After the INF Treaty, the superpowers continued to try to work out a strategic arms reduction treaty that would cut the number of long-range missiles by 50 percent. By that time the superpowers each had nuclear arsenals that could destroy the other many times over, and a 50 percent reduction would still leave nuclear deterrence well intact.

A New World Order Between 1989 and 1991, a number of significant events brought about the end of the cold war. In 1989, Gorbachev surprised the world when he led the Soviet Union in its decision to give up its control over Eastern Europe. By the summer of 1991, not only had the Warsaw Pact—a unified group consisting of the Soviet Union and its allies in Eastern Europe—dissolved, but so had the Soviet Union itself. Soviet Communism, one-half of the superpower equation for over forty years, had imploded.

During this time of increasingly warm relations between the superpowers, a number of major arms control treaties were created. On November 19, 1990, the United States, the U.S.S.R., and twenty other countries signed the Conventional Forces in Europe Treaty (CFE Treaty), which President George Bush called "the farthest-reaching arms agreement in history," an accord that "signals the new world order that is emerging." The treaty grew out of a 1989 proposal by Bush that the superpowers each be limited to 275,000 troops in Europe. As events unfolded in Eastern Europe, however, and the countries of the former Eastern Bloc became independent from the U.S.S.R., that number of troops began to seem high. Under the CFE Treaty, each side was allowed to deploy, in the area between the Atlantic Ocean and the Ural Mountains, no more than 20,000 tanks, 30,000 armored troop carriers, 20,000 artillery pieces, 6,800 combat airplanes, and 2,000 attack helicopters. The treaty required the Soviet Union to disarm or destroy nearly 20,000 tanks, artillery pieces, and other weapons, to give a 27 percent reduction in Soviet armaments west of the Urals. That decrease was small, however, compared with the 59,000 weapons the U.S.S.R. shipped east of the Urals to central Asia between 1989 and 1990 as it sought to realign its forces in response to world events. On the other side, the North Atlantic Treaty Organization (NATO) forces—the postwar alliance of Western European and North American states, including the United States—were required to destroy fewer than 3,000 pieces of military equipment. In May 1991,

Soviet president Mikhail Gorbachev and U.S. president Ronald Reagan shake hands after signing the INF Treaty in December 1987.

NATO decided to reduce its forces even further. The United States, for its part, cut the 320,000 troops it had in Europe by at least 50 percent.

Arms agreements on nuclear weapons were also reached during this period. On July 31, 1991, Presidents Bush and Gorbachev signed the first Strategic Arms Reduction Treaty (START I). Negotiations on the technically complex accord had begun as early as 1982. The agreement requires the U.S.S.R. to reduce its nuclear arsenal by roughly 25 percent and the United States to reduce its arsenal by 15 percent, within seven years after ratification by both nations. Numerically speaking, the U.S.S.R. will reduce its nuclear warheads from 10,841 to 8,040, and the United States will reduce its warheads from 12,081 to 10,395. These amounts will bring the nuclear arsenals of each nation roughly back to levels that existed in 1982, when START negotiations began. The agreement also limits the development of new missiles and requires a number of verification procedures, including on-site inspections with spot checks, monitoring of missile production plants, and exchange of data tapes from missile tests.

Arms Control in the Post–Cold War Era In June 1992, U.S. president George Bush met with Russian president Boris Yeltsin. In a "joint understanding," the two sides agreed to reductions of nuclear weapons beyond the levels provided for in the 1991 START agreement, with the ultimate goal of decreasing the total number of warheads on each side to between three thousand and thirty-five hundred by the year 2003. The two presidents also agreed to eliminate MIRVs by 2003. This agreement was signed, as START II, in early 1993.

The administration of President Bill Clinton, who became president of the United States in 1993, revived the debate surrounding missile defense systems—and created fears that a new arms race might begin—when it developed proposals for the Theater High-Altitude Area-Defense System (THAAD). THAAD would be an elaborate missile defense system aimed at protecting allied nations from short-range missile attacks launched by countries such as North Korea. Critics maintain that THAAD would violate the ABM provisions of SALT I, widely believed to be the most successful arms control provisions ever; upset the nuclear balance; and possibly lead to an arms race. Proponents of THAAD maintain that the ABM Treaty is a relic of the cold war and that missile defenses can protect against accidental nuclear launches.

As for Europe, the new structure of power there will also create new challenges for arms control. Agreements such as the CFE were made when the Soviet Union still existed, and do not necessarily conform to new realities. As the war in the former Yugoslavia demonstrated during the early 1990s, a new political situation poses new risks. Will certain states become regional powers and upset the balance of power? Will agreements that were stabilizing for the Soviet Union turn out to be destabilizing for Russia and other states of the former U.S.S.R.? Will nationalism rise as a destructive force, as it has in previous wars?

Some experts are proposing that the Conference on Security and Cooperation in Europe (CSCE) develop conventional arms control agreements to replace the CFE Treaty. The CSCE was formed in 1973 in an attempt to promote détente between the United States and the U.S.S.R. It includes fifty-two countries—fifty European nations and the United States and Canada. European leaders hope the CSCE will play a greater role in determining a peaceful, stable future for Europe, with efforts in arms control being one of its major goals. Formally declaring this goal, European leaders signed the Pact of Paris in November 1990. Some leaders are proposing that the CSCE replace NATO as the chief military and political organization in Europe.

What should be the priorities of arms control in the post–cold war era? Advocates say arms control will be more important than ever, and that it must broaden its range to deal with new problems, many of them beyond the old sphere of U.S.-Soviet relations. In this new era, arms control will have a number of different goals, including nuclear nonproliferation; control of regional conflicts—particularly in the Middle East, the Korea Peninsula, and the India subcontinent; lessening the economic burden of defense preparations; and naval arms control.

CROSS-REFERENCES

Anti-Ballistic-Missile Treaty of 1972; Bush, George; Clinton, Bill; Hot Line Agreement; Intermediate-Range Nuclear Forces Treaty; International Law; Kennedy, John F.; Nixon, Richard; Nuclear Nonproliferation Treaty; Reagan, Ronald; War.

ARRAY ▥ The entire group of jurors selected for a trial from which a smaller group is subsequently chosen to form a PETIT JURY or a GRAND JURY; the list of potential jurors. ▥

Virtually all states have enacted statutes delineating requirements for JURY service. In most states, convicted felons and insane persons cannot be jurors. Professional persons such as judicial and government officials, lawyers, ministers, and medical personnel may be exempted by statute from jury service.

As a general rule, a group of local officials acting within the statutory framework select the persons who will make up the array.

ARREARS 📖 A sum of money that has not been paid or has only been paid in part at the time it is due. 📖

A person who is "in arrears" is behind in payments due and thus has outstanding DEBTS or liabilities. For example, a tenant who has not paid rent on the day it is due is in arrears.

Arrears may also refer to the late distribution of the DIVIDENDS of cumulative PREFERRED STOCK.

ARREST OF JUDGMENT 📖 The postponement or stay of an official decision of a court, or the refusal to render such a determination, after a VERDICT has been reached in an ACTION at law or a criminal prosecution, because some defect appears on the face of the record that, if a decision is made, would make it erroneous or reversible. 📖

Although the Federal Rules of Civil Procedure make no such provision, state codes of CIVIL PROCEDURE should be consulted concerning the issuance of an arrest of judgment in actions at law.

In criminal proceedings, a defendant must make a motion for an arrest of judgment when the INDICTMENT or INFORMATION fails to charge the accused with an offense or if the court lacks JURISDICTION over the offense charged. State and federal rules of CRIMINAL PROCEDURE govern an arrest of judgment in criminal prosecutions.

ARREST WARRANT 📖 A written order issued by authority of the state and commanding the seizure of the person named. 📖

An arrest WARRANT must be based on a COMPLAINT that alleges PROBABLE CAUSE that the person named has committed a specific offense, and it must be issued according to the formalities required by the rules of the court. The Federal Rules of Criminal Procedure specify that the warrant must be signed by the magistrate and must describe the offense charged. The defendant must be named or described in such a way that he or she can be identified with reasonable certainty. The warrant must also command that the defendant be arrested and brought before the nearest available magistrate.

ARROGATION 📖 Claiming or seizing something without justification; claiming something on behalf of another. In CIVIL LAW, the adoption of an adult who was legally capable of acting for himself or herself. 📖

Arrears: Delinquency Rates on Bank Installment Loans, 1985 to 1994
Numbers shown are percentages

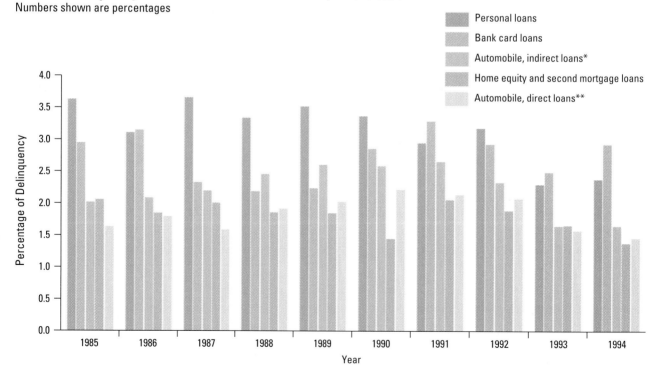

*Made directly by bank's lending function.
**Made by automobile dealerships; loan in bank's portfolio.

Source: American Bankers Association, Washington, D.C., *Consumer Credit Delinquency Bulletin,* quarterly.

A sample federal
arrest warrant

United States District Court

_____ DISTRICT OF _____

United States of America
V.

WARRANT FOR ARREST
CASE NUMBER:

To: The United States Marshal
    and any Authorized United States Officer
    YOU ARE HEREBY COMMANDED to arrest _____
                                                    Name
and bring him or her forthwith to the nearest magistrate to answer a(n)
☐ Indictment ☐ Information ☐ Complaint ☐ Order of Court ☐ Violation Notice
☐ Probation Violation Petition
charging him or her with (brief description of offense)
in violation of Title _____ United States Code, Section(s) _____

_____   _____
Name of Issuing Officer   Title of Issuing Officer

_____   _____
Signature of Issuing Officer   Date and Location

Bail fixed at $ _____ by _____
                                        Name of Judicial Officer

RETURN
This warrant was received and executed with the arrest of the above-named defendant at _____

DATE RECEIVED	NAME AND TITLE OF ARRESTING OFFICER	SIGNATURE OF ARRESTING OFFICER
DATE OF ARREST		

A sample federal
arrest warrant
(back page)

THE FOLLOWING IS FURNISHED FOR INFORMATION ONLY:

DEFENDANT'S NAME: _____
ALIAS: _____
LAST KNOWN RESIDENCE: _____
LAST KNOWN EMPLOYMENT: _____
PLACE OF BIRTH: _____
DATE OF BIRTH: _____
SOCIAL SECURITY NUMBER: _____
HEIGHT: _____ WEIGHT: _____
SEX: _____ RACE: _____
HAIR: _____ EYES: _____
SCARS, TATTOOS, OTHER DISTINGUISHING MARKS: _____

FBI NUMBER: _____
COMPLETE DESCRIPTION OF AUTO: _____

INVESTIGATIVE AGENCY AND ADDRESS: _____

ARSON 📖 At COMMON LAW, the malicious burning or exploding of the dwelling house of another, or the burning of a building within the CURTILAGE, the immediate surrounding space, of the dwelling of another. 📖

Modern legislation has extended the definition of arson to include the burning or explod-ing of commercial and public buildings—such as restaurants and schools—and structures—such as bridges. In many states, the act of burning any insured dwelling, regardless of whether it belongs to another, constitutes arson if it is done with an intent to DEFRAUD the insurer. Finally, the common-law rule that the property burned must belong to another person has been completely eliminated by statute in some states.

Elements The main elements necessary to prove arson are evidence of a burning and evidence that a criminal act caused the fire. The accused must intend to burn a building or other structure. Absent a statutory description of the conduct required for arson, the conduct must be malicious, and not accidental. MALICE, however, does not mean ill will. Intentional or outrageously reckless conduct is sufficient to constitute malice. MOTIVE, on the other hand, is not an essential element of arson.

Unless a statute extends the crime to other property, only a house used as a residence, or buildings immediately surrounding it, can be the subject of arson. If a house is vacated, is closed up, or becomes unfit for human habitation, its burning will not constitute arson. A temporary absence from a dwelling will not negate its character as a residence.

Generally, the actual presence of a person within a dwelling at the moment it is burned is not necessary. It may, however, be required for a particular degree of the crime. The fact, and not the knowledge, of human occupancy is what is essential. If a dwelling is burned under the impression that it is uninhabited when people actually live in it, the crime is committed.

Absent a statute to the contrary, a person is innocent of arson if that individual burns his or her own property while living there. The common exception to this rule is the burning of one's own property with an intent to defraud or prejudice the property insurer. In addition, under statutes that punish the burning of a dwelling house without expressly requiring it to be the property of another, a person who burns his or her own property might be guilty of arson. An owner, for purposes of arson, is the person who possesses the house and has the care, control, and management of it. In those states that have maintained the common-law rule that the property burned must belong to another person, an owner who burns his or her house while it is in the possession of a lawful tenant is guilty of arson.

Degrees In many states arson is divided into degrees, depending sometimes on the value of the property but more commonly on its use and whether the crime was committed in the day or night. A typical statute might make the

Number of Incendiary or Suspicious Fires, 1989 to 1992

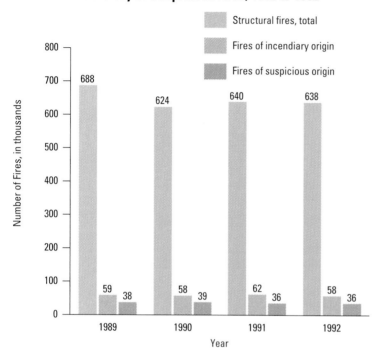

Property Loss in Incendiary or Suspicious Fires, 1989 to 1992

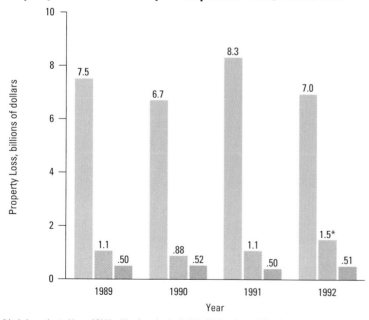

* Includes estimated loss of $567 million from the April 1992 civil disturbance in Los Angeles, CA.
** Direct property loss only.

Source: National Fire Protection Association, Quincy, MA, "NFPA Reports on U.S. Fire Loss–1992," NFPA JOURNAL, September 1993, and prior issues (copyright 1993).

burning of an inhabited dwelling house at night first-degree arson, the burning of a building close enough to a dwelling so as to endanger it second-degree arson, and the burning of any structure with an intent to defraud an insurer thereof, third-degree arson. Many statutes vary the degree of the crime according to the criminal intent of the accused.

Punishment Arson is a serious crime that was punishable by death under the common law. Presently, it is classified as a FELONY under most statutes, punishable by either imprisonment or death. Many jurisdictions impose prison sentences commensurate with the seriousness of the criminal intent of the accused. A finding, therefore, that the offense was committed intentionally will result in a longer prison sentence than a finding that it was done recklessly. When a human life is endangered, the penalty is most severe.

ARTHUR, CHESTER ALAN Chester Alan Arthur was born October 5, 1830, in Fairfield, Vermont. He achieved prominence as a politician and as president of the United States.

An 1848 graduate of Union College, Arthur was admitted to the New York City bar in 1851, and he established a legal practice in New York City that same year.

With the onset of the Civil War, Arthur served as quartermaster general and inspector general of New York. After the war, from 1871 to 1878, he performed the duties of collector for the Port of New York. Although Arthur was a believer in the spoils system, a practice that rewards loyal political party members with jobs that require official appointment, he served his office as an honest administrator. President Rutherford B. Hayes was, however, an advocate of the CIVIL SERVICE system, which provided that qualified people receive employment fairly based upon their qualifications, and removed Arthur from the office of collector.

Arthur returned to politics with his election as vice president of the United States in March of 1880. In September 1881, he assumed the duties of president, after the assassination of President James Garfield.

As president, Arthur advocated the passage of the Pendleton Civil Service Reform Bill in 1883, adopting a view that was contrary to his previous support of the spoils system. He also signed laws allowing for the modernization of the United States Navy and supported the prosecution of the Star Route Trials, which exposed fraudulent activities in the United States Post Office Department. He also vetoed a Congressional bill, the Rivers and Harbours Bill of 1882, charging that the allotment of funds was too extravagant.

Arthur's presidential term ended in 1885; due to ill health, he did not seek renomination. He died November 18, 1886, in New York, New York.

ARTICLES Series or subdivisions of individual and distinct sections of a document, statute, or other writing, such as the Articles of Confederation. Codes or systems of rules created by written agreements of parties or by statute that establish standards of legally acceptable behavior in a business relationship, such as articles of incorporation or articles of partnership. Writings that embody contractual terms of agreements between parties.

ARTICLES OF CONFEDERATION The document that set forth the terms under which the original thirteen states agreed to participate in a centralized form of government, in addition to their self-rule, and that was in effect from March 1, 1781, to March 4, 1789, prior to the adoption of the Constitution.

The Articles of Confederation served as the first constitution of the newly formed United States. As it was originally drafted in 1776, the document provided for a strong central government. However, by the time it was ratified in 1781, advocates of states' rights had greatly weakened its provisions. Many of these advocates feared a centralization of power and wished to preserve a great degree of independence and sovereignty for each state. Accordingly, the Articles as they were ratified provided only for a "firm league of friendship," in which, according to article II of the document, "[e]ach State retains its sovereignty, freedom and independence."

The Articles included provisions for military cooperation between the states, freedom of travel, extradition of criminal suspects, and

BIOGRAPHY

Chester Alan Arthur

"MEN MAY DIE, BUT THE FABRIC OF FREE INSTITUTIONS REMAINS UNSHAKEN."

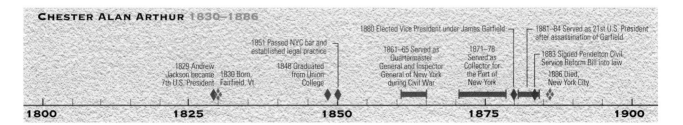

CHESTER ALAN ARTHUR 1830–1886

1829 Andrew Jackson became 7th U.S. President

1830 Born, Fairfield, Vt.

1848 Graduated from Union College

1851 Passed NYC bar and established legal practice

1861–65 Served as Quartermaster General and Inspector General of New York during Civil War

1871–78 Served as Collector for the Port of New York

1880 Elected Vice President under James Garfield

1881–84 Served as 21st U.S. President after assassination of Garfield

1883 Signed Pendelton Civil Service Reform Bill into law

1886 Died, New York City

1800   1825   1850   1875   1900

ARTICLES OF CONFEDERATION
(1777)

To all to whom these Presents shall come, we the undersigned Delegates of the States affixed to our Names send greeting

Whereas the Delegates of the United States of America in Congress assembled did on the fifteenth day of November in the Year of our Lord One Thousand Seven Hundred and Seventy-seven, and in the Second Year of the Independence of America agree to certain articles of Confederation and perpetual Union between the States of Newhampshire, Massachusetts-bay, Rhode-island, and Providence Plantations, Connecticut, New York, New Jersey, Pennsylvania, Delaware, Maryland, Virginia, North-Carolina, South-Carolina and Georgia in the Words following, viz.

Articles of Confederation and perpetual Union between the States of New-hampshire, Massachusetts-bay, Rhodeisland and Providence Plantations, Connecticut, New-York, New-Jersey, Pennsylvania, Delaware, Maryland, Virginia, North-Carolina, South-Carolina and Georgia

Article I.   The stile of this confederacy shall be "The United States of America."

Article II.   Each State retains its sovereignty, freedom and independence, and every power, jurisdiction and right, which is not by this confederation expressly delegated to the United States, in Congress assembled.

Article III.   The said States hereby severally enter into a firm league of friendship with each other, for their common defence, the security of their liberties, and their mutual and general welfare, binding themselves to assist each other, against all force offered to, or attacks made upon them, or any of them, on account of religion, sovereignty trade or any other pretence whatever.

Article IV.   The better to secure and perpetuate mutual friendship and intercourse among the people of the different States in this Union, the free inhabitants of each of these States, paupers, vagabonds and fugitives from justice excepted, shall be entitled to all privileges and immunities of free citizens in the several States; and the people of each State shall have free ingress and regress to and from any other State, and shall enjoy therein all the privileges of trade and commerce, subject to the same duties, impositions and restrictions as the inhabitants thereof respectively, provided that such restrictions shall not extend so far as to prevent the removal of property imported into any State, to any other State of which the owner is an inhabitant; provided also that no imposition, duties or restriction shall be laid by any State, on the property of the United States, or either of them.

If any person guilty of, or charged with treason, felony, or other high misdemeanor in any State, shall flee from justice, and be found in any of the United States, he shall upon demand of the Governor or Executive power, of the State from which he fled, be delivered up and removed to the State having jurisdiction of his offense.

Full faith and credit shall be given in each of these States to the records, acts and judicial proceedings of the courts and magistrates of every other State.

Article V.   For the more convenient management of the general interests of the United States, delegates shall be annually appointed in such manner as the legislature of each State shall direct, to meet in Congress on the first Monday in November, in every year, with a power reserved to each State, to recall its delegates, or any of them, at any time within the year, and to send others in their stead, for the remainder of the year.

No State shall be represented in Congress by less than two, nor by more than seven members; and no person shall be capable of being a delegate for more than three years in any term of six years; nor shall any person, being a delegate, be capable of holding any office under the United States, for which he, or another for his benefit receives any salary, fees or emolument of any kind.

Each State shall maintain its own delegates in a meeting of the States, and while they act as members of the committee of the States.

In determining questions in the United States, in Congress assembled, each State shall have one vote.

Freedom of speech and debate in Congress shall not be impeached or questioned in any court, or place out of Congress, and the members of Congress shall be protected in their persons from arrests and imprisonments, during the time of their going to and from, and attendance on Congress, except for treason, felony, or breach of the peace.

Article VI.   No State without the consent of the United States in Congress assembled, shall send any embassy to, or receive any embassy from, or enter into any conference, agreement, alliance or treaty with any king, prince or state; nor shall any person holding any office of profit or trust under the United States, or any of them, accept of any present, emolument, office or title of any kind whatever from any king, prince or foreign state; nor shall the United States in Congress assembled, or any of them, grant any title of nobility.

No two or more States shall enter into any treaty, confederation or alliance whatever between them, without the consent of the United States in Congress assembled, specifying accurately the purposes for which the same is to be entered into, and how long it shall continue.

No State shall lay any imposts or duties, which may interfere with any stipulations in treaties, entered into by the United States in Congress assembled, with any king, prince or state, in pursuance of any treaties already proposed by Congress, to the courts of France and Spain.

No vessels of war shall be kept up in time of peace by any State, except such number only, as shall be deemed necessary by the United States in Congress assembled, for the defence of such State, or its trade; nor shall any body of forces be kept up by any State, in time of peace, except such number only, as in the judgment of the United States, in Congress assembled, shall be deemed requisite to garrison the forts necessary for the defence of such State; but every State shall always keep up a well regulated and disciplined militia, sufficiently armed and accoutered, and shall provide and constantly have ready for use, in public stores, a due number of field pieces and tents, and a proper quantity of arms, ammunition and camp equipage.

No State shall engage in any war without the consent of the United States in Congress assembled, unless such State be actually invaded by enemies, or shall have received certain advice of a resolution being formed by some nation of Indians to invade such State, and the danger is so imminent as not to admit of a delay, till the United States in Congress assembled can be consulted: nor shall any State grant commissions to any ships or vessels of war, nor letters of marque or reprisal, except it be after a declaration of war by the United States in Congress assembled, and then only against the kingdom or state and the subjects thereof, against which war has been so declared and under such regulations as shall be established by the United States in Congress assembled, unless such State be infested by pirates, in which case vessels of war may be fitted out for that occasion, and kept so long as the danger shall continue, or until the United States in Congress assembled shall determine otherwise.

Article VII.   When land-forces are raised by any State for the common defence, all officers of or under the rank of colonel, shall be appointed by the Legislature of each State respectively by whom such forces shall be raised, or in such manner as such State shall direct, and all vacancies shall be filled up by the State which first made the appointment.

Article VIII.   All charges of war, and all other expenses that shall be incurred for the common defence or general welfare, and allowed by the United States in Congress assembled, shall be defrayed out of a common treasury, which shall be supplied by the several States, in proportion to the value of all land within each State, granted to or surveyed for any person, as such land and the buildings and improvements thereon shall be estimated according to such mode as the United States in Congress assembled, shall from time to time direct and appoint.

The taxes for paying that proportion shall be laid and levied by the authority and direction of the Legislatures of the several States within the time agreed upon by the United States in Congress Assembled.

Article IX.   The United States in Congress assembled, shall have the sole and exclusive right and power of determining on peace and war, except in the cases mentioned in the sixth article—of sending and receiving ambassadors—entering into treaties and alliances, provided that no treaty of commerce shall be made whereby the legislative power of the respective States shall be restrained from imposing such imposts and duties on foreigners, as their own people are subjected to, or from prohibiting the exportation or importation of any species of goods or commodities whatsoever—of establishing rules for deciding in all cases, what captures on land or water shall be legal, and in what manner prizes taken by land or naval forces in the service of the United States shall be divided or appropriated—of granting letters of marque and reprisal in times of peace—appointing courts for the trial of piracies and felonies committed on the high seas and establishing courts for receiving and determining finally appeals in all cases of captures, provided that no member of Congress shall be appointed a judge of any of the said courts.

The United States in Congress assembled shall also be the last resort on appeal in all disputes and differences now subsisting or that hereafter may arise between two or more States concerning boundary, jurisdiction or any other cause whatever; which authority shall always be exercised in the manner following. Whenever the legislative or executive authority or lawful agent of any State in controversy with another shall present a petition to Congress, stating the matter in question and praying for a hearing, notice thereof shall be given by order of Congress to the legislative or executive authority of the other State in controversy, and a day assigned for the appearance of the parties by their lawful agents, who shall then be directed to appoint by joint consent, commissioners or judges to constitute a court for hearing and determining the matter in question: but if they cannot agree, Congress shall name three persons out of each of the United States, and from the list of such persons each party shall alternately strike out one, the petitioners beginning, until the number shall be reduced to thirteen; and from that number not less than seven, nor more than nine names as Congress shall direct, shall, in the presence of Congress be drawn out by lot, and the persons whose names shall be so drawn or any five of them, shall be commissioners or judges, to hear and finally determine the controversy, so always as a major part of the judges who shall hear the cause shall agree in the determination: and if either party shall neglect to attend at the day appointed, without showing reasons, which Congress shall judge sufficient, or being present shall refuse to strike, the Congress shall proceed to nominate three persons out of each State, and the Secretary of Congress shall strike in behalf of such party absent or refusing; and the judgment and sentence of the court to be appointed, in the manner before prescribed, shall be final and conclusive; and if any of the parties shall refuse to submit to the authority of such court, or to appear or defend their claim or cause, the court shall nevertheless proceed to pronounce sentence, or judgment, which shall in like manner be final and decisive, the judgment or sentence and other proceedings being in either case transmitted to Congress, and lodged among the acts of Congress for the security of the parties concerned: provided that every commissioner, before he sits in judgment, shall take an oath to be administered by one of the judges of the supreme or superior court of the State where the cause shall be tried, "well and truly to hear and determine the matter in question, according to the best of his judgment, without favour, affection or hope of reward:" provided also that no State shall be deprived of territory for the benefit of the United States.

All controversies concerning the private right of soil claimed under different grants of two or more States, whose jurisdiction as they may respect such lands, and the States which passed such grants are adjusted, the said grants or either of them being at the same time claimed to have originated antecedent to such settlement of jurisdiction, shall on the petition of either party to the Congress of the United States, be finally determined as near as may be in the same manner as is before prescribed for deciding disputes respecting territorial jurisdiction between different States.

The United States in Congress assembled shall also have the sole and exclusive right and power of regulating the alloy and value of coin struck by their own authority, or by that of the respective States.—fixing the standard of weights and measures throughout the United

States.—regulating the trade and managing all affairs with the Indians, not members of any of the States, provided that the legislative right of any State within its own limits be not infringed or violated—establishing and regulating post-offices from one State to another, throughout all the United States, and exacting such postage on the papers passing thro' the same as may be requisite to defray the expenses of the said office—appointing all officers of the land forces, in the service of the United States, excepting regimental officers—appointing all the officers of the naval forces, and commissioning all officers whatever in the service of the United States—making rules for the government and regulation of the said land and naval forces, and directing their operations.

The United States in Congress assembled shall have authority to appoint a committee, to sit in the recess of Congress, to be denominated "a Committee of the States," and to consist of one delegate from each State; and to appoint such other committees and civil officers as may be necessary for managing the general affairs of the United States under their direction—to appoint one of their number to preside, provided that no person be allowed to serve in the office of president more than one year in any term of three years; to ascertain the necessary sums of money to be raised for the service of the United States, and to appropriate and apply the same for defraying the public expenses—to borrow money or emit bills on the credit of the United States transmitting every half year to the respective States an account of the sums of money so borrowed or emitted,—to build and equip a navy—to agree upon the number of land forces, and to make requisitions from each State for its quota, in proportion to the number of white inhabitants in such State; which requisition shall be binding, and thereupon the Legislature of each State shall appoint the regimental officers, raise the men and cloath, arm and equip them in a soldier like manner, at the expense of the United States; and the officers and men so cloathed, armed and equipped shall march to the place appointed, and within the time agreed on by the United States in Congress assembled: but if the United States in Congress assembled shall, on consideration of circumstances judge proper that any State should not raise men, or should raise a smaller number than its quota, and that any other State should raise a greater number of men than the quota thereof, such extra number shall be raised, officered, cloathed, armed and equipped in the same manner as the quota of such State, unless the legislature of such State shall judge that such extra number cannot be safely spared out of the same, in which case they shall raise officer, cloath, arm and equip as many of such extra number as they judge can be safely spared. And the officers and men so cloathed, armed and equipped, shall march to the place appointed, and within the time agreed on by the United States in Congress assembled.

The United States in Congress assembled shall never engage in a war, nor grant letters of marque and reprisal in time of peace, nor enter into any treaties or alliances, nor coin money, nor regulate the value thereof, nor ascertain the sums and expenses necessary for the defence and welfare of the United States, or any of them, nor emit bills, nor borrow money on the credit of the United States, nor appropriate money, nor agree upon the number of vessels of war, to be built or purchased, or the number of land or sea forces to be raised, nor appoint a commander in chief of the army or navy, unless nine States assent to the same: nor shall a question on any other point, except for adjourning from day to day be determined, unless by the votes of a majority of the United States in Congress assembled.

The Congress of the United States shall have power to adjourn to any time within the year, and to any place within the United States, so that no period of adjournment be for a longer duration than the space of six months, and shall publish the journal of their proceedings monthly, except such parts thereof relating to treaties, alliances or military operations, as in their judgment require secresy; and the yeas and nays of the delegates of each State on any question shall be entered on the journal, when it is desired by any delegate; and the delegates of a State, or any of them, at his or her request shall be furnished with a transcript of the said journal, except such parts as are above excepted, to lay before the Legislatures of the several States.

Article X.   The committee of the States, or any nine of them, shall be authorized to execute in the recess of Congress, such of the powers of Congress as the United States in Congress assembled, by the consent of nine States, shall from time to time think expedient to vest them with; provided that no power be delegated to the said committee, for the exercise of which, by the articles of confederation, the voice of nine States in the Congress of the United States assembled is requisite.

Article XI.   Canada acceding to this confederation, and joining in the measures of the United States, shall be admitted into, and entitled to all the advantages of this Union: but no other colony shall be admitted into the same, unless such admission be agreed to by nine States.

Article XII.   All bills of credit emitted, monies borrowed and debts contracted by, or under the authority of Congress, before the assembling of the United States, in pursuance of the present confederation, shall be deemed and considered as a charge against the United States, for payment and satisfaction whereof the said United States, and the public faith are hereby solemnly pledged.

Article XIII.   Every State shall abide by the determinations of the United States in Congress assembled, on all questions which by this confederation are submitted to them. And the articles of this confederation shall be inviolably observed by every State, and the Union shall be perpetual; nor shall any alteration at any time hereafter be made in any of them; unless such alteration be agreed to in a Congress of the United States, and be afterwards confirmed by the Legislatures of every State.

And whereas it has pleased the Great Governor of the world to incline the hearts of the Legislatures we respectively represent in Congress, to approve of, and to authorize us to ratify the said articles of confederation and perpetual union. Know ye that we the undersigned delegates, by virtue of the power and authority to us given for that purpose, do by these presents, in the name and in behalf of our respective constituents, fully and entirely ratify and confirm each and every of the said articles of confederation and perpetual union, and all and singular the matters and things therein contained: and we do further solemnly plight and engage the faith of our respective constituents, that they shall abide by the determinations of the United States in Congress assembled, on all questions, which by the said confederation are submitted to them. And that the articles thereof shall be inviolably observed by the States we re[s]pectively represent, and that the Union shall be perpetual.

In witness whereof we have hereunto set our hands in Congress.

Done at Philadelphia in the State of Pennsylvania the ninth day of July in the year of our Lord one thousand seven hundred and seventy-eight, and in the third year of the independence of America.

On the part and behalf of the State of New Hampshire

JOSIAH BARTLETT,   JOHN WENTWORTH, Junr.,
                                                             August 8th, 1778.

On the part and behalf of the State of Massachusetts Bay

JOHN HANCOCK,   FRANCIS DANA,
SAMUEL ADAMS,   JAMES LOVELL,
ELBRIDGE GERRY,   SAMUEL HOLTEN.

On the part and behalf of the State of Rhode Island
and Providence Plantations

WILLIAM ELLERY,   JOHN COLLINS.
HENRY MARCHANT,

On the part and behalf of the State of Connecticut

ROGER SHERMAN,   TITUS HOSMER,
SAMUEL HUNTINGTON,   ANDREW ADAMS.
OLIVER WOLCOTT,

On the part and behalf of the State of New York

JAS. DUANE,   WM. DUER,
FRA. LEWIS,   GOUV. MORRIS.

On the part and in behalf of the State of New Jersey, Novr. 26, 1778

JNO. WITHERSPOON,   NATHL. SCUDDER.

On the part and behalf of the State of Pennsylvania

ROBT. MORRIS,   WILLIAM CLINGAN,
DANIEL ROBERDEAU,   JOSEPH REED,
JONA. BAYARD SMITH,   22d July, 1778.

On the part & behalf of the State of Delaware

THO. M'KEAN, Feby. 12, 1779.   NICHOLAS VAN DYKE.
JOHN DICKINSON, May 5th, 1779

On the part and behalf of the State of Maryland

JOHN HANSON,   DANIEL CARROLL,
    March 1, 1781.   Mar. 1, 1781.

On the part and behalf of the State of Virginia

RICHARD HENRY LEE,   JNO. HARVIE,
JOHN BANISTER,   FRANCIS LIGHTFOOT LEE.
THOMAS ADAMS,

On the part and behalf of the State of No. Carolina

JOHN PENN, July 21st, 1778.   JNO. WILLIAMS.
CORNS. HARNETT,

On the part & behalf of the State of South Carolina

HENRY LAURENS,   RICHD. HUTSON,
WILLIAM HENRY DRAYTON,   THOS. HEYWARD, Junr.
JNO. MATHEWS,

On the part & behalf of the State of Georgia

JNO. WALTON, 24th July, 1778.   EDWD. LANGWORTHY.
EDWD. TELFAIR,

equal privileges and immunities for citizens. They also created a national legislature called the Congress. Each state had one vote in this body, that vote to be determined by a delegation of from two to seven representatives. The Articles called for Congress to conduct foreign relations, maintain a national army and navy, establish and maintain a postal service, and perform a number of other duties. The Articles did not create, as the Constitution later did, executive and judicial branches of government.

The Congress created by the Articles was successful on a number of fronts. In 1783, it negotiated with Great Britain a peace treaty that officially ended the Revolutionary War; it arranged to pay war debts; and it passed the NORTHWEST ORDINANCE, which allowed for settlement and statehood in new regions in the western part of the United States. However, with time, it became apparent that the Articles had created an unsatisfactory union of the states, chiefly because they established a weak central government. For example, under the Articles of Confederation, Congress did not have the power to tax or to effectively regulate commerce. The resulting national government did not prove competent at such tasks as raising a military or creating a stable currency. In addition, because amendments to the Articles required a unanimous vote of all thirteen states, the Articles proved to be too inflexible to last.

A series of incidents in the 1780s made it clear to many early U.S. leaders that the Articles of Confederation would not serve as an effective constitution. Among these incidents was Shays's Rebellion, in 1786–87, an insurrection in which economically depressed farmers demanded debt relief and closed courts of law in western Massachusetts. The Congress of the Confederation was not able to raise a force to respond to this civil unrest, which was later put down by a state militia. George Washington and other leaders perceived this as a grievous failure. Therefore, when a constitutional convention assembled in 1787 to amend the Articles, it quickly decided to abandon them altogether in favor of a new constitution. By June 21, 1788, nine states had ratified the new U.S. Constitution and made it effective. It has survived as the basis of U.S. government for over two hundred years.

CROSS-REFERENCES

Constitution; Constitution of the United States; Federalism; Shays's Rebellion; Washington, George.

ARTICLES OF IMPEACHMENT ▦ Formal written allegations of the causes that warrant the criminal trial of a public official before a quasi-political court. ▦

In cases of IMPEACHMENT, involving the president, vice president, or other federal officers, the House of Representatives prepares the articles of impeachment, since it is endowed with the " . . . sole Power of Impeachment," under Article I, Section 2, Clause 5 of the Constitution. The articles are sent to the Senate, which has the exclusive power to " . . . try all Impeachments" by virtue of Article I, Section 3, Clause 6.

The use of articles of impeachment against state officials is governed by state constitutions and statutes.

Articles of impeachment are analogous to INDICTMENTS that initiate criminal prosecutions of private persons.

ARTICLES OF INCORPORATION ▦ The document that must be filed with an appropriate government agency, commonly the office of the secretary of state, if the owners of a business want it to be given legal recognition as a CORPORATION. ▦

Articles of incorporation, sometimes called a certificate of incorporation, must set forth certain information as mandated by statute. Although laws vary from state to state, the purposes of the corporation and the rights and liabilities of shareholders and directors are typical provisions required in the document. Official forms are prescribed in many states.

Once the articles of incorporation are filed with the secretary of state, corporate existence begins. In some jurisdictions, a formal certificate of incorporation attached to a duplicate of the articles must be issued to the applicant before the business will be given legal status as a corporation.

ARTICLES OF PARTNERSHIP ▦ A written compact by which parties agree to pool their money, labor, and/or skill to carry on a business for profit. The parties sign the compact with the understanding that they will share proportionally the losses and profits according to the provisions and conditions that they have mutually assented would govern their business relationship. ▦

See also PARTNERSHIP.

ARTICLES OF WAR ▦ Codes created to prescribe the manner in which the ARMED SERVICES of a nation are to be governed. ▦

For example, the Uniform Code of Military Justice is an article of war applied to the Army, the Navy, the Coast Guard, and the Air Force of the United States. See also MILITARY LAW.

ARTIFICIAL INSEMINATION ▦ The process by which a woman is medically impregnated using semen from her husband or from a third-party donor. ▦

Artificial insemination is employed in cases of infertility or impotence, or as a means by which an unmarried woman may become pregnant. The procedure, which has been used since the 1940s, involves injecting collected semen into the woman's uterus and is performed under a physician's supervision.

Artificial insemination raises a number of legal concerns. Most states' laws provide that a child born as a result of artificial insemination using the husband's sperm, referred to as AIH, is presumed to be the husband's legal child. When a child is born after artificial insemination using the sperm of a third-party donor, referred to as AID, the law is less clear. Some states stipulate that the child is presumed to be the legal child of the mother and her husband, whereas others leave open the possibility that the child could be declared illegitimate.

Artificial insemination has grown in popularity as infertility becomes more prevalent and as more women opt to become single mothers. Eighty thousand such procedures using donor sperm are performed each year, resulting in the births of thirty thousand babies. By 1990 artificial insemination was a $164 million industry involving eleven thousand private physicians, four hundred sperm banks, and more than two hundred fertility centers.

The practice of artificial insemination is largely unregulated, and secrecy surrounding the identity of donors and recipients is the

_____ [ARTICLES *or* CERTIFICATE] of INCORPORATION
OF
_____ [Name of corporation]

ARTICLE ONE. *Name.* The name of this corporation is _____ .

ARTICLE TWO. *Purposes.* The purpose for which this corporation is formed
is _____ .

ARTICLE THREE. *Registered Office; Registered Agent.* The address of the initial registered office of the corporation is _____ [*street address*], _____ [*city*],
_____ County, _____ [*state*], _____ [*ZIP code*], and the name of its initial registered agent at such address is _____ [*agent*].

ARTICLE FOUR. *Principal Office.* The business address of the corporation's principal
office is _____ [*use street number and address or other particular description*],
_____ [*city*], _____ County, _____ [*state*].

ARTICLE FIVE. *Duration.* The period of this corporation's duration is _____ .

ARTICLE SIX. *Directors.* (a) The number of directors constituting the initial board of
directors is _____ , and the names and addresses of the persons who are to serve as directors until the first annual meeting of the shareholders or until their successors are elected
and qualified are:

Name   Address
_____   _____
_____   _____
_____   _____

(b) The number of directors of the corporation set forth in Clause (a) of this Article shall
constitute the authorized number of directors until changed by an amendment of
_____ [these articles *or* this certificate] of incorporation or by a bylaw duly adopted by
the vote or written consent of the holders of a majority of the then outstanding shares of
stock in the corporation.

ARTICLE SEVEN. *Incorporators.* The names and addresses of the incorporators are:

Name   Address
_____   _____
_____   _____
_____   _____

ARTICLE EIGHT. *Capitalization.* The total number of shares of all classes of stock
which the corporation shall have authority to issue is _____ , divided into _____
[*number*] shares of common stock at _____ Dollars ($ _____) par value each and
_____ [*number*] shares of preferred stock, at _____ Dollars ($ _____) par value
each. _____ [*State designations and powers, preferences, and rights, and the qualifications,
limitations, or restrictions of the classes of stock.*]

This corporation will not commence business until it has received for the issuance of its
shares consideration of the value of _____ Dollars ($ _____), consisting of money, la-
bor done, or property actually received, which sum is not less than _____ Dollars
($ _____).

This Article can be amended only by the vote or written consent of the holders of
_____ percent (_____ %) of the outstanding shares.

For the purpose of forming a corporation under the laws of _____ [*state*], we, the
undersigned, have personally executed _____ [these articles *or* this certificate] of incorporation on _____ [*date*].

[*Signatures*]

[*Acknowledgments*]

norm. Surveys of parents indicate that most do not plan to tell their children the circumstances of their births. This raises ethical questions about the right of an individual to be informed about his or her heritage. People who inadvertently discover they were conceived through artificial insemination often experience distress and feelings of confused identity. Many doctors compound the problem by failing to keep records on the identities and medical histories of donors.

The legal minefield created by artificial insemination continues to erupt with new and unprecedented issues. In 1990, Julia Skolnick sued a fertility clinic and a sperm bank for NEGLIGENCE and medical MALPRACTICE, charging that they mistakenly substituted another man's sperm for that of her late husband. The woman, who is white, gave birth to a child with African American features, and DNA analysis confirmed that her husband, who was also white, could not have been the child's father. In another case, Junior Lewis Davis sued to prevent his ex-wife, Mary Sue Davis Stowe, from using or donating fertilized embryos the couple had frozen for later use. The Tennessee Supreme Court held that individuals have "procreational autonomy" and have the right to choose whether to have a child (*Davis v. Davis*, 842 S.W.2d 588 (Tenn. June 1992). Arthur L. Caplan, former director of the Center for Biomedical Ethics at the University of Minnesota, commented, "In this case, the court said that a man cannot be made to become a parent against his will." The *Davis* case raises the question of the right of a sperm donor to prevent the use of his sperm by specific individuals.

Serious health questions also surround the issue of artificial insemination. AIDS, hepatitis, and other infectious diseases pose risks to women undergoing the procedure and their potential children. Although the American Fertility Society recommends that donors be tested for infectious diseases, the guidelines are not binding. In fact, some doctors merely request that donors answer questions about their health history and sex life, and only a handful of states require testing. This casual approach to donor screening can lead to disaster. In 1994, Mary Orsak, of Downey, California, sued the Tyler Medical Clinic, in Westwood, California, for negligence when she discovered she was HIV-positive as a result of artificial insemination with donor sperm. In at least six other cases, HIV transmission through artificial insemination has been confirmed.

Other legal pitfalls open up as technology makes artificial insemination more sophisti-cated and more available. Now that sperm can be frozen for future use, a woman can be impregnated at any time, even after her husband's death. In 1990, Nancy Hart and Edward Hart, of Covington, Louisiana, anticipating that Edward might not survive his bout with cancer and knowing that chemotherapy might leave him sterile, decided to place a sample of his sperm in a New Orleans sperm bank. Edward died in June 1990. Three months later, Nancy underwent artificial insemination using his sperm, and on June 4, 1991, their daughter Judith was born. Under Louisiana law (L.S.A.-C.C. Art. 185), the state would not acknowledge Edward as the child's father because she had been born more than three hundred days after his death. As a result, Nancy was unable to receive Social Security survivors benefits for her daughter. She sued both the state of Louisiana and the federal government. In June 1995 Administrative Law Judge Elving Torres ruled that the Social Security Administration (SSA) must pay Judith a $10,000 lump sum and $700 per month in survivor's benefits. According to Torres, the DNA evidence presented to him proved that Judith is Nancy and Edward Hart's child.

Medical technology now allows recipients of artificial insemination to select the sex of their offspring, which raises still more ethical questions. Some religions condemn this practice as unnatural, although other theologians disagree. Some commentators have even suggested that it is unethical and exploitative to offer expensive, difficult, painful, and frustrating fertility procedures to desperate people when there may be little chance that a successful pregnancy will result.

The legal, ethical, and medical quagmires created by artificial insemination have not deterred thousands of couples and single women from seeking the procedure. Artificial insemination is sometimes the best, if not the only, solution for a person determined to achieve pregnancy.

CROSS-REFERENCES

Family Law; Illegitimacy; Parent and Child; Reproduction.

ARTIFICIAL PERSON ▥ A legal entity that is not a human being but for certain purposes is considered by virtue of statute to be a natural person. ▥

A CORPORATION is considered an artificial person for SERVICE OF PROCESS.

ART LAW The Framers of the Constitution acknowledged the importance of the arts when

The WPA Federal Theater Project sponsored productions of plays and musicals such as Brother Mose *in Newark, New Jersey, in 1936.*

they wrote that Congress shall have the power "[t]o promote the Progress of Science and useful Arts, by securing for limited Times to Authors and Inventors the exclusive Right to their respective Writings and Discoveries" (Art. I, § 8). Despite this provision, or perhaps because of its very limited nature, the federal government offered little assistance to artists until the 1930s. Early unsuccessful attempts to aid the arts included an effort by President James Buchanan to establish the National Commission of Fine Arts, a project that failed within a year when Congress did not appropriate funds. President Theodore Roosevelt also encountered a reluctant Congress in 1909 when he proposed the Council of Fine Arts, but success came the next year when a new president, William Howard Taft, persuaded Congress to create the National Commission of Fine Arts.

Even after the National Commission of Fine Arts was established, the federal government continued to play a minor role in funding for the arts, but several municipal programs attempted to fill the void. In New York City, the Civil Works Administration (CWA) sponsored paintings, murals, and art education. The CWA's primary goal was to create employment for artists receiving government relief. With the only requirement for employment being an assertion that the applicant was an artist, the art produced under the CWA was often the work of unskilled amateurs.

Federal funding for the arts took off during the Great Depression with the creation of the Federal Art Project, a branch of the Works Progress Administration (WPA). The Federal Art Project was modeled on some of the earlier municipal attempts but avoided their problems by emphasizing the production of works of high technical competence, utilizing defined hiring guidelines, and encouraging creativity and experimentation. The Federal Art Project paid a *security wage*, an amount that was calculated to fall between the prevailing wage and the relief grants of the region involved and was graduated according to skill level. The WPA spent $35 million on the Federal Art Project and supported the production of approximately 1,500 murals, 18,800 sculptures, and 108,000 paintings as well as other works of art. The onset of World War II effectively ended the WPA.

In the cold war era following World War II, the federal government funded cultural exchanges to promote diplomatic ends. The major cultural institutions were located primarily in large cities, such as New York, Los Angeles, Chicago, and Boston. In 1965, only five state arts agencies existed. The quality of performances and exhibitions was inconsistent, and support for the best art depended on the discretion and charity of a few patrons. As a result, opportunities for artists were limited, and rural audiences had few chances to see the best productions or visit outstanding exhibitions.

In the mid-1990s, federal financial support for the arts and humanities was provided through several distinct agencies: the National Commission of Fine Arts, the National Endowment for the Arts (NEA), and the National Endowment for the Humanities (NEH). The Commission of Fine Arts, established in 1910, advises the president, Congress, and government department heads on matters of architecture, sculpture, painting, and other fine arts. The commission's primary function is to preserve and enhance the appearance of the nation's capital, Washington, D.C. (40 U.S.C.A. § 104 [1986]).

The National Foundation for the Arts and Humanities Act of 1965 (20 U.S.C.A. §§ 951–968 [West Supp. 1990]) established the NEA and the NEH. The NEA provides grants to, or contracts with, groups and individuals of exceptional talent, and state or regional organizations engaged in or concerned with the arts. NEA programs encourage individual and institutional development of the arts, preservation of the American artistic heritage, wider availability of the arts, leadership in the arts, and the stimulation of nonfederal sources of support for the nation's artistic activities. The goal of the NEA is not to provide employment, as the WPA did, but rather to make the arts more widely available to U.S. citizens, to preserve the nation's rich cultural heritage, and to encourage the creative development of the nation's finest artistic talent. By the mid-1990s, the NEA had made approximately eighty-five thousand grants for theater, dance, symphonic music, painting, and poetry. As a major financier of the arts, the NEA has been a significant influence on much of the publicly exhibited art in the United States. For many years, it led a quiet administrative existence, and, although it was a force in the artistic community, the general public knew little about it. In late 1989, however, the organization became the center of controversy when some members of Congress questioned whether some works of art and performances funded by the NEA were obscene.

Lucile Lloyd puts the finishing touches on a new mural in the California State Building at Los Angeles. The painting was completed under the auspices of the Federal Art Project in 1936.

The NEH funds activities designed to improve the quality of education and teaching in the humanities, strengthen the scholarly foundation for humanities study and research, and advance understanding of the humanities among general audiences. The NEH provides support through outright grants, matching grants, and a combination of the two. Schools, higher education institutions, libraries, museums, historical organizations, professional associations, other cultural institutions, and individuals are eligible to apply for NEH grants.

From January, 1981, to January, 1995, Congress actively supported the arts through the Congressional Arts Caucus. This legislative service organization, composed of nearly 250 members of Congress who recognized and supported the arts, acted as an information clearinghouse on arts issues. The caucus reported on legislation affecting artists and arts institutions, both commercial and nonprofit. It helped members of Congress prepare testimony and speeches on the arts. The caucus offerred members of Congress access to performances, cultural fact-finding trips, specially arranged tours of art exhibits, and meetings with nationally known arts leaders. Each year, the caucus honored exceptional artists and organizations that have made major contributions to the arts in the United States.

The government also provides indirect aid designed to create a heightened public awareness of art and to provide artists with new outlets for their work. One effective means of indirect aid is the regulations adopted by many state and municipal governments, which require a percentage of the cost of building new government structures to be spent on art.

Federal, state, and local governments indirectly promote a heightened public awareness of the arts in the community through zoning. Zoning laws divide a city into districts and set forth the types of structural and architectural designs of buildings in those districts, and the uses to which buildings may be put. Some zoning regulations and laws are designed to preserve the aesthetic features or values of an area. Most state courts now allow the use of zoning laws for solely aesthetic purposes. These laws may, for example, restrict the placement of billboards or television satellite dishes, or require that junkyards be screened or fenced.

State and local governments have become involved in improving the appearance of publicly funded buildings, or any building built on public land, by requiring that new building designs and locations be approved by the local government. Local control over design was held

Money and the Arts

Federal arts aid available and granted through the National Endowment for the Arts and National Endowment for the Humanities, 1985 to 1993

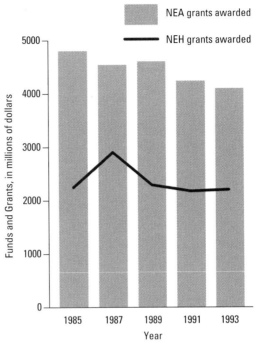

Source: U.S. National Endowment for the Arts, *Annual Report*; U.S. National Endowment for the Humanities, *Annual Report*.

constitutional in *Walnut & Quince Streets Corp. v. Mills*, 303 Pa. 25, 154 A. 29, *appeal dismissed*, 284 U.S. 573, 52 S. Ct. 16, 76 L. Ed 498 (1931). In *Walnut & Quince Streets*, a municipal arts panel refused to permit a theater owner to construct a large marquee extending over the sidewalk. The owner unsuccessfully argued that a local statute permitted the jury to act in an arbitrary fashion that deprived him of due process of law, and, furthermore, that the legislature did not have the authority to regulate aesthetics and thus could not delegate such authority to an arts jury. The court upheld the statute as a legitimate legislative regulation of public property.

Many governments have enacted statutes and regulations prohibiting the destruction and alteration of historic landmarks. Landmark preservation laws indirectly aid the arts by increasing the public's awareness of the need for beautification and for preserving the work of past generations of artists. The earliest efforts to preserve the nation's heritage focused on particular buildings, or national monuments. The application of historic preservation laws to limit a property owner's right to her or his property was declared constitutional in *Penn Central Transportation Co. v. New York City*, 438

U.S. 104, 98 S. Ct. 2646, 57 L. Ed. 2d 631 (1978). In *Penn Central*, the U.S. Supreme Court held that the New City Landmarks Preservation Commission's failure to approve plans for construction of a fifty-story office building over Grand Central Terminal, a designated landmark, was not an unconstitutional taking of property.

Historic preservation law is an active and expansive area of zoning and planning law. According to the National Trust for Historic Preservation, over seventeen hundred communities have enacted preservation laws. Federal efforts to encourage preservation include the enactment of laws providing some tax credits for the protection and restoration of old buildings (26 U.S.C.A. § 48 (g)(3)(A) [1986]), and for the protection of archaeological sites (16 U.S.C.A. § 461 [1986]).

CROSS-REFERENCES

Helms, Jesse; Land Use Control; National Foundation on the Arts and the Humanities; Zoning.

AS IS A term used to describe a sales transaction in which the seller offers goods in their present, existing condition to prospective buyers.

The term *as is* gives notice to buyers that they are taking a risk on the quality of the goods. The buyer is free to inspect the goods before purchase; but if any hidden defects are discovered after purchase, the buyer has no recourse against the seller. Any implied or express WARRANTIES that usually accompany goods for sale are excluded in an "as is" sale.

Contract law and the UNIFORM COMMERCIAL CODE regulate "as is" sales.

AS PER A phrase commonly recognized to mean "in accordance with the terms of" a particular document—such as a contract, deed, or affidavit—or "as authorized by the contract."

ASPORTATION The removal of items from one place to another, such as carrying things away illegally.

Asportation is one of the elements required to establish the crime of LARCENY. In order to prove that asportation has occurred, it is not necessary to show that the goods were moved a substantial distance, but only that they were moved.

Asportation was one of the elements necessary to establish common-law KIDNAPPING, and in many states it remains as an element of statutory kidnapping.

ASSASSINATION Murder committed by a perpetrator without the personal provocation of the victim, who is usually a government official.

First used in medieval times to describe the murders of prominent Christians by the Hashshashin, a secret Islamic sect, the word *assassination* is now used to describe murders committed for political reasons, especially against government officials. Assassination may be used as a political weapon by a state as well as by an individual; it may be directed at the establishment or used by it.

The term *assassination* is generally applied only to political murders—in the United States, most commonly to attempts on the life of the president. However, the classification of any one incident as an assassination may be in part a matter of perception. The "assassination" of the outlaw Jesse James, in 1882, provides an example of the difficulties. Thomas T. Crittenden, governor of Missouri, assumed that being seen as responsible for the death of the notorious outlaw would be good for his political career. For this reason, Crittenden granted the killers PARDONS in addition to a $10,000 reward. But the American public spoke vehemently against James's killers, dubbing them assassins and his death an assassination. Crittenden was vilified by the American people, and his political career was destroyed.

It is not always easy to guess the motivations of those who attempt assassinations, or to understand the historical and legal implications of their actions. The anticonstitutional nature of assassination has made it a focal point for conspiracies and conspiracy theories from the beginning. The first attempt at the assassination of a U.S. president was Richard Lawrence's attack on Andrew Jackson, in 1835. Although a jury acquitted Lawrence on the ground of insanity, Jackson was convinced that the attack was part of a Whig conspiracy.

The 1865 assassination of President Abraham Lincoln by John Wilkes Booth prompted its own set of theories. In a controversial decision, a military tribunal convicted nine people of conspiring in Lincoln's assassination. In the case of one of those hanged for the crime, Mary E. Surratt, all that could be proved was that she owned the rooming house in which the conspirators plotted. Nonetheless, high emotions at the end of the Civil War guaranteed her death. After sentiments cooled and talk of conspiracies calmed, the two surviving conspirators imprisoned for Lincoln's death gained pardons from President Andrew Johnson.

Even greater controversy was caused when

the public was deprived of the opportunity to see Lee Harvey Oswald tried for the assassination, in 1963, of President John F. Kennedy. Oswald's death at the hands of Jack Ruby sparked theories of conspiracy that ranged from Communist plots to Mafia hits to cover-ups by U.S. officials. President Lyndon B. Johnson appointed a group of national figures, led by Chief Justice Earl Warren, of the Supreme Court, to investigate the assassination and issue a report. The Warren Commission concluded that Oswald had acted alone.

Despite this, conspiracy theories remained widespread in books and in films like Oliver Stone's *JFK* (released in 1991). In an attempt to calm public suspicions surrounding the Kennedy assassination, the President John F. Kennedy Assassination Records Collection Act of 1992 (44 U.S.C.A. § 2107) was passed by Congress. The act released much of the Kennedy assassination material in government files. Its effectiveness at stilling concern over a possible conspiracy remains to be seen.

It has become clear that the public demands a thorough investigation of any attempt on a president's life. Because it is a crime to advocate the assassination of any U.S. president, even threats are carefully investigated. In U.S. history, four presidents have lost their lives to assassins: Abraham Lincoln, James Garfield, William McKinley, and John F. Kennedy.

CROSS-REFERENCES

Garfield, James; Kennedy, John F.; Lincoln, Abraham; Lincoln, Abraham *In Focus: Lincoln Assassination Conspiracy*; McKinley, William; Warren Commission.

ASSAULT 📖 At common law, an intentional act by one person that creates an apprehension in another of an imminent harmful or offensive contact. 📖

An assault is carried out by a threat of bodily harm coupled with an apparent, present ability to cause the harm. It is both a CRIME and a TORT and, therefore, may result in either criminal or civil LIABILITY. Generally, the COMMON LAW defi-

John Wilkes Booth assassinated President Abraham Lincoln in 1865 when Lincoln and his wife were at the theater.

nition is the same in criminal and tort law. There is, however, an additional criminal law category of assault consisting of an attempted but unsuccessful battery.

Statutory definitions of assault in the various jurisdictions throughout the United States are not substantially different from the common-law definition.

Elements Generally, the essential elements of assault consist of an act intended to cause an apprehension of harmful or offensive contact that causes apprehension of such contact in the victim.

The act required for an assault must be overt. Although words alone are insufficient, they might create an assault when coupled with some action that indicates the ability to carry out the threat. A mere threat to harm is not an assault; however, a threat combined with a raised fist might be sufficient if it causes a reasonable apprehension of harm in the victim.

INTENT is an essential element of assault. In tort law, it can be SPECIFIC INTENT—if the assailant intends to cause the apprehension of harmful or offensive contact in the victim—or GENERAL INTENT—if he or she intends to do the act that causes such apprehension. In addition, the intent element is satisfied if it is substantially certain, to a REASONABLE PERSON, that the act will cause the result. A defendant who holds a gun to a victim's head possesses the requisite intent, since it is substantially certain that this act will produce an apprehension in the victim. In all cases, intent to kill or harm is irrelevant.

In criminal law, the attempted BATTERY type of assault requires a specific intent to commit battery. An intent to frighten will not suffice for this form of assault.

There can be no assault if the act does not produce a true apprehension of harm in the victim. There must be a reasonable fear of injury. The usual test applied is whether the act would induce such apprehension in the mind of a reasonable person. The status of the victim is taken into account. A threat made to a child might be sufficient to constitute an assault, while an identical threat made to an adult might not.

Virtually all jurisdictions agree that the victim must be aware of the danger. This element is not required, however, for the attempted battery type of assault. A defendant who throws a rock at a sleeping victim can only be guilty of the attempted battery assault, since the victim would not be aware of the possible harm.

Aggravated Assault An AGGRAVATED ASSAULT, punishable in all states as a FELONY, is committed when a defendant intends to do more than merely frighten the victim. Common types of aggravated assaults are those accompanied by an intent to kill, rob, or rape. An assault with a dangerous weapon is aggravated if there is an intent to cause serious harm. Pointing an unloaded gun at a victim to frighten the individual is not considered an aggravated assault.

Punishment A defendant adjudged to have committed civil assault is liable for DAMAGES. The question of the amount that should be awarded to the victim is determined by a jury. COMPENSATORY DAMAGES, which are aimed at compensating the victim for the injury, are common. NOMINAL DAMAGES, a small sum awarded for the invasion of a right even though there has been no substantial injury, may be awarded. In some cases, courts allow PUNITIVE DAMAGES, which are designed to punish the defendant for the wrongful conduct.

The punishment for criminal assault is a fine, imprisonment, or both. Penalties are more severe when the assault is aggravated. Many states have statutes dividing criminal assault into various degrees. As in aggravated assault, the severity of the crime, the extent of violence and harm, and the criminal intent of the defendant are all factors considered in determining the sentence imposed.

ASSAULT AND BATTERY ▣ Two separate offenses against the person that when used in one expression may be defined as any unlawful and unpermitted touching of another. ASSAULT is an act that creates an apprehension in another of an imminent, harmful, or offensive contact. The act consists of a threat of harm accompanied by an apparent, present ability to carry out the threat. BATTERY is a harmful or offensive touching of another ▣

The main distinction between the two offenses is the existence or nonexistence of a touching or contact. While contact is an essential element of battery, there must be an absence of contact for assault. Sometimes assault is defined loosely to include battery.

Assault and battery are offenses in both criminal and TORT law and, therefore, they can give rise to criminal or civil LIABILITY. In CRIMINAL LAW, an assault may additionally be defined as any attempt to commit a battery.

At COMMON LAW, both offenses were MISDEMEANORS. Today, under virtually all criminal codes, they are either misdemeanors or FELONIES. They are characterized as felonious when accompanied by a criminal intent, such as an intent to kill, rob, or rape, or when they are committed with a dangerous weapon.

Intent INTENT is an essential element of both offenses. Generally, it is only necessary for the defendant to have an intent to do the act that causes the harm. In other words, the act must be done voluntarily. Although an intent to harm the victim is likely to exist, it is not a required element of either offense. There is an exception to this rule for the attempted battery type of criminal assault. If a defendant who commits this crime does not have an intent to harm the victim, the individual cannot be guilty of the offense.

Defenses

Consent In almost all states, CONSENT is a defense to civil assault and battery. Some jurisdictions hold that in the case of mutual combat, consent will not suffice and either party may sue the other. Jurisdictions also differ on the question of whether consent is a defense to criminal assault and battery.

Consent must be given voluntarily in order to constitute a defense. If it is obtained by FRAUD or DURESS, or is otherwise unlawful, it will not suffice. When an act exceeds the scope of the given consent, the defense is not available. A person who participates in a football game implies consent to a certain amount of physical contact; however, the individual is not deemed to consent to contact beyond what is commonly permitted in the sport.

Self-Defense Generally, a person may use whatever degree of force is reasonably necessary for protection from bodily harm. The question of whether or not this defense is valid is usually determined by a jury. A person who initiates a fight cannot claim SELF-DEFENSE unless the opponent responded with a greater and unforeseeable degree of force. When an aggressor retreats and is later attacked by the same opponent, the defense may be asserted.

DEADLY FORCE may be justified if initially used by the aggressor. The situation must be such that a reasonable person would be likely to fear for his or her life. In some states, a person must retreat prior to using deadly force if the individual can do so in complete safety. A majority of states, however, allow a person to stand his or her ground even though there is a means of safe escape.

Whether the degree of force used is reasonable depends upon the circumstances. The usual test applied involves determining whether a REASONABLE PERSON in a similar circumstance would respond with a similar amount of force. Factors such as age, size, and strength of the parties are also considered.

Defense of Others Going to the aid of a person in distress is a valid defense, provided the defender is free from fault. In some states, the defender is treated as though he or she

Assault

Victimization rates for assaults by crime and characteristic, 1992

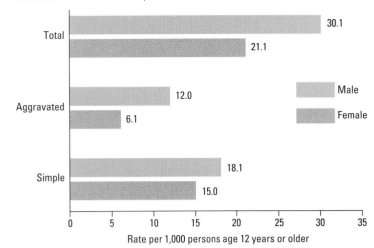

Source: U.S. Bureau of Justice Statistics, *Criminal Victimization in the United States*, annual.

stands in the shoes of the person protected. The defender's right to claim defense of others depends upon whether the person protected had a justified claim of self-defense. In a minority of jurisdictions, the defense may be asserted if the defender reasonably believed the third party was in need of aid.

Defense of Property Individuals may use a reasonable amount of force to protect their PROPERTY. The privilege to defend one's property is more limited than that of self-defense because society places a lesser value on property than on the integrity of human beings. Deadly force is usually not permitted. In most states, however, deadly force might be justified if it is used to prevent or stop a felony. An owner of REAL PROPERTY or a person who rightfully possesses it, such as a tenant, may use force against a trespasser. Generally, a request to leave the property must be made before the application of force, unless the request would be futile. The amount of force used must be reasonable, and, unless it is necessary for self-defense, the infliction of bodily harm upon an intruder is improper. Courts have traditionally been more liberal in allowing the use of force to protect one's dwelling. Recent cases, however, have indicated that there must be a threat to the personal safety of the occupants.

The states are divided on the question of whether a person who is legally entitled to property may use force to recover possession of it. In most jurisdictions, a landowner is not liable for assault and battery if the owner forcibly expels someone who is wrongfully on the property. The owner must not, however, use excessive force; and the fact that the person may not be held civilly liable does not relieve the owner of criminal liability. In some states, the use of force against a person wrongfully in possession of land is not permitted unless such person has tortiously dispossessed the actor or the actor's predecessor in TITLE.

If possession of real or PERSONAL PROPERTY is in dispute, the universal rule is that force cannot be used. The dispute must be settled by a court.

With respect to personal property, the general view is that an owner may not commit an assault or battery upon the wrongdoer in order to recover property. A majority of jurisdictions recognize the right of an owner in HOT PURSUIT of stolen property to use a reasonable amount of force to retrieve it. In some states, stolen property may be taken back peaceably wherever it is found, even if it is necessary to enter another's premises. In all cases, the infliction of an unreasonable amount of harm will vitiate the defense.

Performance of Duty and Authority A person may use reasonable force when it becomes necessary in the course of performing a duty. A police officer, for example, may use force when apprehending a criminal. Private citizens may also use reasonable force to stop a crime committed in their presence. Certain businesses, such as restaurants or nightclubs, are authorized to hire employees who may use reasonable force to remove persons who disturb other patrons. Court officers, such as judges, may order the removal of disruptive persons who interfere with their duties.

Persons with authority in certain relationships, such as parents or teachers, may use force as a disciplinary measure, provided they do not exceed the scope of their authority. Punishment may not be cruel or excessive.

Punishment The law considers an assault and battery to be an invasion of the personal security of the victim for which the wrongdoer is required to pay for DAMAGES. The determination of the amount of damages to which a victim might be entitled if a defendant is found civilly liable is usually made by a jury. Generally, a plaintiff is entitled to COMPENSATORY DAMAGES that compensate for injuries that are both directly and indirectly related to the wrong. Examples of compensatory damages include damages for pain and suffering, damages for medical expenses, and damages for lost earnings resulting from the victim's inability to work. NOMINAL DAMAGES, given although there is no harm at all, or merely a slight one, may also be awarded in an assault and battery action. Some jurisdictions allow the award of PUNITIVE DAM-

AGES. They are often given when the offense was committed wantonly or maliciously to punish the defendant for the wrongful act, and to deter others from engaging in similar acts in the future. The defendant might additionally be subject to criminal liability.

If a defendant is found criminally liable, the punishment is imprisonment, a fine, or both. The amount of time a defendant must serve in prison depends upon the statute in the particular jurisdiction. When the offense is committed with an intent to murder or do serious harm, it is called AGGRAVATED ASSAULT and battery. An aggravated assault and battery is often committed with a dangerous weapon, and it is punishable as a felony in all states.

ASSEMBLY 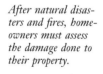 The congregation of a number of persons at the same location.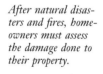

Political assemblies are those mandated by the Constitution and laws, such as the general assembly.

The lower, or more populous, arm of the legislature in several states is also known as the "House of Assembly" or the "Assembly."

ASSENT An intentional approval of known facts that are offered by another for acceptance; agreement; consent.

Express assent is manifest confirmation of a position for approval. *Implied assent* is that which the law presumes to exist because the conduct of the parties demonstrates their intentions. *Mutual assent*, sometimes called the MEETING OF THE MINDS of the parties, is the reciprocal agreement of each party to accept all the terms and conditions in a contract.

ASSESS To determine financial worth. To ascertain the amount of damages. To fix and adjust the individual shares to be contributed by several persons toward a common beneficial objective in proportion to the benefit each

After natural disasters and fires, homeowners must assess the damage done to their property.

© 1991 DAVID MAUNG/IMPACT VISUALS

person will receive. To tax by having qualified experts estimate the value of property by considering the nature of the property, its size, the value of other comparable property, and the proportionate share of services that is used by that property. To levy a charge on the owner of property that has been improved at the expense of the local government unit, such as when sewers or sidewalks are installed. ▥

ASSESSED VALUATION ▥ The financial worth assigned to property by taxing authorities that is used as a basis or factor against which the TAX RATE is applied. ▥

A prescribed amount of the value of each unit must be paid as taxes in the future. In most cases, the assessed value is not representative of the FAIR MARKET VALUE of the property.

ASSESSMENT ▥ The process by which the financial worth of property is determined. The amount at which an item is valued. A demand by the BOARD OF DIRECTORS of a CORPORATION for the payment of any money that is still owed on the purchase of CAPITAL STOCK. The determination of the amount of damages to be awarded to a plaintiff who has been successful in a lawsuit. The ascertainment of the pro rata share of taxes to be paid by members of a group of taxpayers who have directly benefited from a particular common goal or project according to the benefit conferred upon the individual or his or her property. This is known as a SPECIAL ASSESSMENT. The listing and valuation of property for purposes of fixing a tax upon it for which its owner will be liable. The procedure by which the Internal Revenue Service, or other government department of taxation, declares that a taxpayer owes additional tax because, for example, the individual has understated personal gross income or has taken deductions to which he or she is not entitled. This process is also known as a *deficiency assessment.* ▥

ASSET ▥ REAL or PERSONAL PROPERTY, whether TANGIBLE or intangible, that has financial value and can be used for the payment of its owner's debts. ▥

An *accrued asset* is one that arises from revenue earned but not yet due. For example, an accrued dividend is a share of the net earnings of a corporation that has been declared but has not yet been paid out to its shareholder(s).

In BANKRUPTCY, an asset is any form of property owned by a debtor who is insolvent that is not exempt from being used to repay debts.

For income tax purposes, a *capital asset* is property held by a taxpayer for personal enjoyment or investment, such as a home, furniture, stocks and bonds, or an automobile, but does not include inventory, commercial accounts, and notes receivable, depreciable property, commercial property, copyrights, and short-term government obligations. When a capital asset is sold, any gain received is given preferential tax treatment.

A *current, liquid,* or *quick asset* is an item that can be readily converted to cash, such as stocks and bonds.

A *fixed asset* is one of a permanent or long-term nature used in the operation of a business and not intended for sale.

A *frozen asset* is one that cannot be easily converted into cash, such as real estate when there is no market, or that cannot be used because of a legal restriction, such as a SPEND-THRIFT TRUST.

An INTANGIBLE ASSET is one to which an arbitrary dollar value is attached because it has no intrinsic market value but represents financial value, such as the GOOD WILL of a business, TRADEMARKS, or PATENTS.

See also CAPITAL ASSET; FIXED ASSET; LIQUID ASSET.

ASSIGN ▥ To transfer to another, as to assign one's right to receive rental income from property to another. To designate for a particular function, as to assign an attorney to defend an indigent in a criminal prosecution. To specify or point out, as to assign errors in a lower court proceeding on a WRIT of ERROR that is submitted to request a court to reverse the judgment of the lower court. ▥

ASSIGNED ACCOUNT ▥ A type of secured transaction whereby an ACCOUNT RECEIVABLE is pledged to a bank, FACTOR, or other lender to secure the repayment of a loan. ▥

It is common commercial practice for a manufacturer or wholesaler to sell inventory on OPEN ACCOUNT, a debt owed to the seller of inventory that is to be repaid by its buyer as the merchandise is sold. This arrangement creates an account receivable that the seller uses as COLLATERAL for a loan.

ASSIGNED RISK ▥ A danger or hazard of loss or injury that an insurer will not normally accept for coverage under a policy issued by the insurer, but that the INSURANCE company is required by state law to offer protection against by participating in a pool of insurers who are also compelled to provide coverage. ▥

ASSIGNED RISK PLAN ▥ An INSURANCE plan created and imposed by state statute under which persons who normally would be denied insurance coverage as bad risks are permitted to purchase insurance from a pool of insurers who must offer coverage to such individuals. ▥

ASSIGNMENT ▥ A transfer of rights in real property or personal property to another that gives the recipient—the transferee—the rights that the owner or holder of the property—the transferor—had prior to the transfer.

An *assignment of wages* is the transfer of the right to collect wages from the wage earner to his or her CREDITOR. Statutes regulate the extent to which an assignment may be made.

ASSIGNMENT FOR BENEFIT OF CREDITORS

The voluntary transfer of all or most of a debtor's property to another person in TRUST so that he or she will collect any money that is owed to the DEBTOR, sell the debtor's property, and apply the money received to the payment of the DEBTS, returning any surplus to the debtor.

The debtor is the *assignor*, the transferor; and the person who takes LEGAL TITLE to the property is the *assignee*.

Types There are three types of assignments that are categorized according to the limitations imposed upon the arrangement. A general assignment is one involving the transfer of all the debtor's property for the benefit of all his or her CREDITORS. A partial assignment is one in which only part of a debtor's property is transferred to benefit all the creditors. When property is assigned to benefit only designated creditors, it is a special assignment.

The assignment results in the property being beyond the control of the debtor. It is different from agency arrangements, pledges, or mortgages.

Trust Law Unless otherwise expressly provided, trust law governs assignments for the benefit of creditors. The assignee is considered a trustee and his or her duties and responsibilities to the debtor's creditors are the same as a trustee's to the beneficiaries of a trust. The document that embodies the terms of the assignment authorizes the assignee to liquidate the debtor's property in satisfaction of the creditors' claims against the debtor as quickly as possible. Under COMMON LAW, this was the assignee's chief function. Even if the assignment instrument does not expressly empower an assignee to sell the property, the assignee still has the power to do so in order to pay the creditors.

Creation It is not necessary for a debtor to obtain the consent of creditors before making an assignment for their benefit. An owner of property has a right to transfer legal title to it by virtue of ownership. The limitation derived from common law that is placed upon its creation is that it cannot be done to dishonestly deprive a debtor's creditors of their rights to have property sold to repay debts. When an assignment for the benefit of creditors is intended by the debtor to place his or her property beyond the legal reach of creditors, it is

called a FRAUDULENT CONVEYANCE. This type of assignment is VOID, or legally ineffective, under statutes that prohibit such arrangements. An assignment by which the assignor-debtor retains any interest, benefit, or advantage from the conveyance, such as keeping the right to revoke the assignment, made to defraud creditors is also a fraudulent conveyance, as is an assignment by which the assignee is required to delay LIQUIDATION of the assets.

In some jurisdictions, a partial assignment is considered a fraudulent conveyance because the creditors are hindered and delayed in receiving payment if they must seek payment from the debtor after first being referred to the assignee. Other jurisdictions treat any assignment by a solvent debtor as fraudulent on the theory that such an arrangement prevents the immediate sale of the property so that creditors are delayed and hindered.

Deficiency A debtor is still liable to pay his or her creditors if the proceeds from the sale of personal and real property pursuant to an assignment for the benefit of creditors are not sufficient to completely repay the debts. When, however, creditors agree to accept the proceeds in satisfaction of the debtor's obligations, such an agreement is called a COMPOSITION WITH CREDITORS. For this reason, assignments for the benefit of creditors are used by corporate, rather than individual, debtors.

Since PREFERENCES are permissible under common law, a common-law assignment for the benefit of creditors that provides for preferential payments to designated creditors is not a fraudulent conveyance. Most courts have held that debtors cannot use preferences to obtain discharges from creditors by conditioning preferences on their release from unpaid portions of their debts. To do so is considered a fraudulent conveyance, since a creditor would have to accept virtually any condition that the debtor decided upon if the creditor were to receive any money from the assignee.

Legality of Assignments Most states have enacted statutes that regulate assignments for the benefit of creditors. Some states require that an assignment must comply with statutory requirements or be invalid, while in others the debtor may make a common-law assignment, which is regulated by common law, or a statutory assignment, which is controlled by applicable statutes.

The state statutes require that the assignment be recorded, schedules of assets and liabilities be filed, notice be given to the creditors, the assignee be bonded, and the assignor be supervised by the court. Almost every juris-

A sample
assignment for the
benefit of creditors

Whereas I _____ , of _____ , am indebted to several persons in amounts which I am unable to pay, and it is my desire to assign all of my property for the benefit of all such persons to whom I am indebted in proportion to the amount of their respective claims in order that after payment of costs and disbursements thereof, including attorney's fees allowed by law in case of judgment, out of my estate, such claims presented shall share pro rata in my estate in the manner provided by statute.

Now therefore for valuable consideration the receipt of which is hereby acknowledged, I, the said _____ , do hereby grant, bargain, sell, assign, transfer, and set over unto _____ of _____ , _____ , all my lands, tenements, hereditaments, goods, chattels, property, and rights of action of every nature and description, wheresoever located, excepting such property as may be exempt from execution by statute, in trust, however, for the following uses and purposes:

1. To pay all costs and charges which may be lawfully made against _____ in the course of the execution of the trust hereby created.

2. To pay all debts and liabilities owed by me; provided, that if there shall be insufficient funds to pay all debts and liabilities, then such are to be paid pro ratably and in proportion.

3. To repay to me any surplus which may be left after the discharge of all debts and liabilities owed by me.

Signed this _____ day of _____ , _____ .

_____

[Add acknowledgment]

---

diction prohibits the granting of a preference. All creditors except those with LIENS or statutorily created priorities are treated equally. Some statutes empower an assignee to set aside prior fraudulent conveyances, and others authorize the assignee to set aside preferences made before the assignment.

If a debtor has made substantial preferences, fraudulent conveyances, or allowed liens voidable in BANKRUPTCY to attach to his or her property, then creditors might be able to force the debtor into bankruptcy if they decide that the assignment does not adequately protect their rights. An efficiently handled assignment for benefit of creditors is frequently more advantageous to creditors than bankruptcy because it usually brings about better liquidation prices and its less rigid and formal structure saves time and money.

ASSIGNS Individuals to whom property is, will, or may be transferred by conveyance, will, descent and distribution, or statute; assignees.

The term *assigns* is often found in DEEDS; for example, "heirs, administrators, and assigns to denote the assignable nature of the interest or right created."

ASSISTANCE, WRIT OF A court order issued to enforce an existing judgment.

ASSIZE, OR ASSISE A judicial procedure in early England whereby a certain number of men in a community were called together to hear and decide a dispute; a type of court. A type of WRIT, commanding the convening of such a tribunal in order to determine disputed rights to possess land. An edict or statute issued by an ancient assembly.

For example, the Assize of Clarendon was a statute, or ordinance, passed in the tenth year of the reign of King Henry II (1164). It proclaimed that those who were accused of a heinous crime and were unable to exonerate themselves had forty days to gather provisions from friends to provide for their sustenance before they were sent into exile.

The word *assize* comes from the Latin *assideo*, which describes the fact that the men taking action sat together. An assize could be a number of citizens, eventually settled at the number twelve, called to hear cases. They decided on the basis of information they had or could gather in the community. This group of neighbors was presumed to know the facts well enough to determine who was entitled to possession of disputed lands. A writ of assize could be issued on behalf of the king to commission this body of twelve to hear a dispute.

Eventually, the writs gave birth to forms of action for lawsuits concerning real property. For example, the assize of novel disseisin was a form of action for the recovery of lands after the claimant had been wrongfully dispossessed (disseised). The assize of nuisance was proper to secure the abatement of a nuisance or for monetary damages to compensate for the harm done by the nuisance.

See also CLARENDON, CONSTITUTIONS OF; HENRY II OF ENGLAND.

ASSOCIATE JUSTICE 📖 The designation given to a judge who is not the chief or presiding justice of the court on which he or she sits. 📖

An associate judge is usually a member of an APPELLATE COURT.

ASSOCIATION, FREEDOM OF See FREEDOM OF ASSOCIATION.

ASSUMPSIT 📖 [*Latin, He undertook or he promised.*] A promise by which someone assumes or undertakes an obligation to another person. The promise may be oral or in writing, but it is not under SEAL. It is EXPRESS when the person making the promise puts it into distinct and specific language, but it may also be IMPLIED because the law sometimes imposes obligations based on the conduct of the parties or the circumstances of their dealings. 📖

Assumpsit was one of the common-law FORMS OF ACTION. It determined the right to sue and the relief available for someone who claimed that a contract had been breached.

When the COMMON LAW was developing in England, there was no legal remedy for the breach of a contract. RANULF GLANVILL, a famous legal scholar, wrote just before the year 1200 that "[i]t is not the custom of the court of the lord king to protect private agreements, nor does it concern itself with such contracts as can be considered private agreements." Ordinary lawsuits could be heard in local courts, but the king was primarily interested in royal rights and the disputes of his noblemen. As commerce began to develop, the king's courts did allow two forms of action for breach of contract—the actions of covenant and debt. Covenant could be maintained only if the agreement had been made in writing and under seal and only if the action of debt was not available. One could sue on the debt only if the obligations in the contract had been fully performed and the breach was no more than a failure to pay a specific sum of money.

Finally, in 1370, a plaintiff sought to sue a defendant who had undertaken to cure the plaintiff's horse but treated it so negligently that the horse died, and the action was allowed. In 1375, another man was permitted to sue a surgeon who had maimed him while trying to cure him. These cases showed a new willingness to permit a lawsuit for monetary damages arising directly from the failure to live up to an agreement. For the next hundred years the courts began to allow lawsuits for badly performed obligations but not for a complete fail-

ure to perform what was required by contract. Unexpectedly, this restriction was abandoned also, and a new form of action was recognized by the courts, an action in *special assumpsit* for breach of an express agreement.

Special assumpsit gave a new legal right to parties who could not sue on a debt. Gradually, it became possible to sue in *assumpsit* if the defendant owed a debt and then violated a fresh promise to pay it. This action came to be known as *indebitatus assumpsit*, which means "being indebted, he promised."

As time passed, courts were willing to assume that the fresh promise had been made and to impose obligations as if it had. This allowed lawsuits for a whole range of contract breaches, not just those recognized by an action on the debt or in *special assumpsit*. If the plaintiff could claim that services had been performed or goods had been delivered to the defendant, then the law would assume that the defendant had promised to pay for them. Any failure to do so gave the plaintiff the right to sue in *assumpsit*. This development allowed such a wide range of lawsuits based on promises to private parties that it came to be known as *general assumpsit*.

Eventually, the right to sue was extended even to situations where the defendant had no intention to pay but it was only fair that he or she be made to do so. This form was called *assumpsit on quantum meruit*. *Special assumpsit*, *general assumpsit* (or *indebitatus assumpsit*), and *quantum meruit* are all *ex contractu*, arising out of a contract. Their development is the foundation of our modern law of CONTRACTS. See also QUANTUM MERUIT.

ASSUMPTION 📖 The undertaking of the repayment of a DEBT or the performance of an obligation owed by another. 📖

When a purchaser of REAL PROPERTY assumes the MORTGAGE of the seller, he or she agrees to adopt the mortgage debt, becoming personally liable for its full repayment in case of DEFAULT. If a FORECLOSURE sale of the mortgaged property does not satisfy the debt, the purchaser remains financially responsible for the outstanding balance.

In contrast, a purchaser who takes subject to the seller's mortgage agrees to repay the mortgage debt, but that person's liability is limited only to the amount that the mortgaged property is sold for in the case of foreclosure. If the property is sold for less than the mortgage debt, the mortgagee must seek the remaining balance due from the seller, the original mortgagor.

ASSUMPTION OF RISK 📖 A DEFENSE, facts offered by a party against whom proceedings have been instituted to diminish a plaintiff's

CAUSE OF ACTION or defeat RECOVERY to an action in NEGLIGENCE, which entails proving that the plaintiff knew of a dangerous condition and voluntarily exposed himself or herself to it. 📖

Under the federal rules of CIVIL PROCEDURE, assumption of the risk is an affirmative defense that the defendant in a negligence action must plead and prove. The doctrine of assumption of risk is also known as *volenti non fit injuria*.

Situations that encompass assumption of the risk have been classified into three broad categories. In its principal sense, assumption of the risk signifies that the plaintiff, in advance, has consented to relieve the defendant of an obligation of conduct toward him or her, and to take a chance of injury from a known risk ensuing from what the defendant is to do or leave undone. The consequence is that the defendant is unburdened of all legal duty to the plaintiff, and, therefore, cannot be held liable in negligence.

A second situation occurs when the plaintiff voluntarily enters into some relation with the defendant, knowing that the defendant will not safeguard the plaintiff against the risk. The plaintiff can then be viewed as tacitly or implicitly consenting to the negligence, as in the case of riding in a car with knowledge that the steering apparatus is defective, which relieves the defendant of the duty that would ordinarily exist.

In the third type of situation, the plaintiff, cognizant of a risk previously created by the negligence of the defendant, proceeds voluntarily to confront it, as where he or she has been provided with an article that the plaintiff knows to be hazardous, and continues to use it after the danger has been detected. If this is a voluntary choice, the plaintiff is deemed to have accepted the situation and assented to free the defendant of all obligations.

In all three situations, the plaintiff might be acting in a reasonable manner, and not be negligent in the venture, because the advantages of his or her conduct outweigh the peril. The plaintiff's decision might be correct, and he or she might even act with unusual circumspection because he or she is cognizant of the danger that will be encountered. If that is the case, the defense operates to refute the defendant's negligence by denying the duty of CARE that would invoke this LIABILITY, and the plaintiff does not recover because the defendant's conduct was not wrongful toward the plaintiff.

With respect to the second and third situations, however, the plaintiff's conduct in confronting a known risk might be in itself unreasonable, because the danger is disproportionate

to the advantage the plaintiff is pursuing, as where, with other transportation available, the individual chooses to ride with an intoxicated driver. If this occurs, the plaintiff's conduct is a type of contributory negligence, an act or omission by the plaintiff that constitutes a deficiency in ordinary care, which concurs with the defendant's negligence to comprise the direct or proximate cause of injury. In such cases, the defenses of assumption of risk and contributory negligence overlap.

In this area of intersection, the courts have held that the defendant can employ either defense, or both. Since ordinarily either is sufficient to bar the action, the defenses have been distinguished on the theory that assumption of risk consists of awareness of the peril and intelligent submission to it, while contributory negligence entails some deviation from the standard of conduct of the REASONABLE PERSON, irrespective of any remonstration or unawareness displayed by the plaintiff. The two concepts can coexist when the plaintiff unreasonably decides to incur the risk, or can exist independently of each other. The distinction, when one exists, is likely to be one between risks that were in fact known to the plaintiff, and risks that the individual merely might have discovered by the exercise of ordinary care.

Express Agreement   The parties can enter into a written agreement absolving the defendant from any obligation of care for the benefit of the plaintiff, and liability for the consequence of conduct that would otherwise constitute negligence. In the ordinary case, PUBLIC POLICY does not prevent the parties from contracting in regard to whether the plaintiff will be responsible for the maintenance of personal safety. A person who enters into a lease, or rents an animal, or enters into a variety of similar relations entailing free and open bargaining between the parties, can assent to relieving the defendant of the obligation to take precautions, and thereby render the defendant free from liability for negligence.

The courts have refused to uphold such agreements, however, if one party possesses a patent disadvantage in bargaining power. For example, a CONTRACT exempting an employer from all liability for negligence toward employees is VOID as against public policy. A CARRIER transporting cargo or passengers for hire cannot evade its public responsibility in this manner, even though the agreement limits recovery to an amount less than the probable DAMAGES. The contract has been upheld, however, where it represents a realistic attempt to assess a value as liquidated or ascertained damages in advance,

UPI/CORBIS-BETTMANN

Visitors to professional sporting events assume the risk that they may be struck by a baseball or other piece of sports equipment.

and the carrier graduates its rates in accordance with such value, so that complete protection would be available to the plaintiff upon paying a higher rate. The same principles apply to innkeepers, public warehousemen, and other professional BAILEES—such as garage, parking lot, and checkroom attendants—on the basis that the indispensable necessity for their services deprives the customer of all meaningful equal bargaining power.

An EXPRESS agreement can relieve the defendant from liability for negligence only if the plaintiff comprehends its terms. If the plaintiff is not cognizant of the provision in his or her contract, and a reasonable person in the same position would not have known of it, it is not binding upon the individual, and the AGREEMENT fails for lack of mutual assent. The expressed terms of the agreement must apply to the particular misconduct of the defendant. Such contracts generally do not encompass gross, willful, wanton, or reckless negligence or any conduct that constitutes an intentional TORT.

Implied Acceptance of Risk In a majority of cases, the CONSENT to assume the risk is IMPLIED from the conduct of the plaintiff under the circumstances. The basis of the defense is not contract, but consent, and it is available in many cases where no express agreement exists.

By entering voluntarily into any relationship or transaction where the negligence of the defendant is evident, the plaintiff is deemed to accept and consent to it, to assume responsibility for personal safety, and to unburden the defendant of the obligation. Spectators at certain sports events assume all the known risks of injury from flying objects. Plaintiffs who enter business premises as invitees and detect dangerous conditions can be deemed to assume the risks when they continue voluntarily to encounter them.

Knowledge of Risk The plaintiff will not normally be regarded as assuming any risk of either conditions or activities of which he or she has no knowledge. The plaintiff must not merely create the danger but must comprehend and appreciate the danger itself.

The applicable standard is basically subjective in nature, tailored to the particular plaintiff and his or her situation, as opposed to the objective standard of the reasonable person of ordinary prudence, which is employed in contributary negligence. If, because of age, lack of information, or experience, the plaintiff does not comprehend the risk entailed in a known situation, the individual will not be regarded as consenting to assume it. Failure to exercise ordinary care to discover the danger is not encompassed within assumption of risk, but in the defense of contributory negligence.

An entirely subjective standard, however, allows the plaintiff considerable latitude in testifying that he or she did not know or comprehend the risk. To counteract the adverse effects of the application of this liberal standard, courts have interjected an objective element by holding that a plaintiff cannot evade responsibility by alleging that he or she did not comprehend a risk that must have been obvious.

A denial of COGNIZANCE of certain matters that are common knowledge in the community is not credible, unless a satisfactory explanation exists. As in the case of negligence itself, there are particular risks that any adult must appreciate, such as falling on ice, lifting heavy objects, and driving a defective vehicle. In addition, a plaintiff situated for a considerable length of time in the immediate vicinity of a hazardous condition is deemed to have detected and to comprehend the ordinary risks entailed in that situation. If the person completely understands the risk, the fact that he or she has temporarily forgotten it does not provide protection.

Even where there is knowledge and appreciation of a risk, the plaintiff might not be prohibited from recovery where the circumstances introduce a new factor. The fact that the plaintiff is totally cognizant of one risk, such as the speed of a vehicle, does not signify that he or she assumes another of which he or she is unaware, such as the intoxication of the driver.

Although knowledge and understanding of the risk incurred are encompassed within the concept of assumption of the risk, it is possible for the plaintiff to assume risks of whose specific existence he or she is unaware—to consent to venture into unknown conditions. In a majority of instances, the undertaking is express, although it can arise by implication in a few cases. A guest who accepts a gratuitous ride in an automobile has been regarded as assuming the risk of defects in the vehicle, unknown to the driver.

Voluntary Assumption The doctrine of assumption of risk does not bar the plaintiff from recovery unless the individual's decision is free and voluntary. There must be some manifestation of consent to relieve the defendant of the obligation of reasonable conduct. A risk is not viewed as assumed if it appears from the plaintiff's words, or from the circumstances, that he or she does not actually consent. If the plaintiff relinquishes his or her better judgment upon assurances that the situation is safe, or that it will be remedied, or upon a promise of protection, the plaintiff does not assume the risk, unless the danger is so patent and so extreme that there can be no reasonable reliance upon the assurance.

Even where the plaintiff does not protest, the risk is not assumed where the conduct of the defendant has provided the individual with no reasonable alternative, causing him or her to act under DURESS. Where the defendant creates a peril, such as a burning building, those who dash into it to save their own property or the lives or property of others do not assume the risk where the alternative is to permit the threatened injury to occur. If, however, the danger is disproportionate to the value of the interest to be protected, the plaintiff might be charged with contributory negligence in regard to his or her own unreasonable conduct. Where a reasonably safe alternative exists, the plaintiff's selection of the hazardous route is free and can constitute both contributory negligence and assumption of risk.

The defendant has a legal duty, which he or she is not at liberty to refuse to perform, to exercise reasonable care for the plaintiff's safety, so that the plaintiff has a parallel legal right to demand that care. The plaintiff does not assume the risk while using the defendant's services or facilities, notwithstanding knowledge of the peril, where he or she acts reasonably, and the defendant has provided no reasonable alternative other than to refrain completely from exercising the right. A COMMON CARRIER, or other PUBLIC UTILITY, which has negligently furnished a dangerously defective set of steps, cannot assert assumption of risk against a patron who uses the steps as the sole convenient means of access to the company's premises. The same principle applies to a city maintaining a public roadway or sidewalk, or other public area that the plaintiff has a right to use, and premises onto which the plaintiff has a contractual right to enter. Where a reasonable alternative is available, the plaintiff's recalcitrance in unreasonably encountering danger constitutes contributory negligence, as well as assumption of risk.

Violation of Statute The plaintiff still assumes the risk where the defendant's negligence consists of the violation of a statute. A guest who accepts a nighttime ride in a vehicle with inoperative lights has been regarded as consenting to relieve the defendant of the duty of complying with the standard established by the statute for protection, and cannot recover for injuries. Particular statutes, however, such as child labor acts and safety statutes for the benefit of employees, safeguard the plaintiff against personal inability to protect himself or herself due to improvident judgment or incapability to resist certain pressures. Since the basic objective of such states would be frustrated if the plaintiff were allowed to assume the risk, it is generally held that the plaintiff cannot do so, either expressly or impliedly.

Abolition of the Defense Numerous states have abrogated the defense of assumption of risk in AUTOMOBILE cases through the enactment of no-fault INSURANCE legislation or comparative negligence acts. The theories underlying its abolition are that it serves no purpose that is not completely disposed of by the other doctrines, it increases the likelihood of confusion, and it bars recovery in meritorious cases.

Assumption of risk is not a defense under state WORKERS' COMPENSATION laws or in Federal Employer's Liability Act actions. The worker's compensation laws abolished the defense in recognition of the severe economic pressure a threatened loss of employment exerted upon workers. A worker was deemed to have assumed the risk even when acting under a direct order that conveyed an explicit or implicit threat of discharge for insubordination.

The Federal Employers' Liability Act (45 U.S.C.A. § 51 et seq. [1908]) was intended to furnish an equitable method of compensation for railroad workers injured within the scope of their employment. The act provides that an employee is not deemed to have assumed the risks of employment where injury or death ensued totally or partially from the negligence of the carrier's officers, agents, or employees, or from the carrier's violation of any statute enacted for the safety of employees, where the infraction contributed to the employee's injury or death. This doctrine was abolished because of the extreme hardship it imposed on workers in this dangerous line of employment.

ASSURED 📖 A person protected by INSURANCE coverage against loss or damage stipulated by the provisions of a policy purchased from an insurance company or an underwriter. 📖

Assured is synonymous with insured.

ASYLUM See ALIENS.

ASYLUMS 📖 Establishments that exist for the aid and protection of individuals in need of assistance due to disability, such as insane persons, those who are physically handicapped, or persons who are unable to properly care for themselves, such as orphans. 📖

The term *asylum* has been used, in constitutional and legislative provisions, to encompass all institutions that are established and supported by the general public.

An *insane asylum* is one in which custody and care is provided for people with mental problems. An orphanage is an asylum set up as a shelter or refuge for infants and children who do not have parents or guardians.

Establishment and Maintenance In the absence of constitutional restrictions, the state is permitted to fulfill its obligation to aid or support individuals in need of care by contributions to care facilities established or maintained by political subdivisions and private charity. In addition, the state may inaugurate a state asylum, delegating the management responsibility thereof to a private corporation. Some authorities view contributions to asylums of religious organizations or private enterprises as violative of constitutional prohibitions of government aid to parochial institutions or individuals. Express exceptions can be made by state statute or constitution for the payment of funds for designated purposes to specific types of asylums. In situations that are embraced by such exceptions, the contribution that the state makes to the maintenance of the asylum is not regarded as a charity but as part of the state's duty to aid its citizens who cannot do so themselves. See also ESTABLISHMENT CLAUSE.

Public Asylums

Ownership and Status An asylum founded and supported by the state has the status of a public institution. The state has the true ownership of the property that a state asylum occupies, and the character of the state's interest in such property is dependent upon the terms of the deed or contract under which it is held for the institution.

When a county conveys property to a board of directors of an insane asylum acting as TRUSTEES, TITLE is not vested in the state to the extent that the power to reconvey the land to the county is restricted. In a situation where property has been conveyed for a particular purpose connected to the operation of the asylum, it has been held that the trustees are permitted to reconvey the property to the county for the establishment of a general hospital.

Location and Support Where no constitutional provision prescribing the location of public institutions exists, the state may designate a location or arrange for a place to be found by a specially appointed committee or commission.

A state asylum may be funded either by general state taxation or through an allocation of a portion or all of the costs among political subdivisions or to the inmates of the asylum.

Regulation Under the POLICE POWER of the state, the establishment and regulation of private asylums are subject to the state legislative authority. Such powers may be delegated to political subdivisions and ADMINISTRATIVE AGENCIES. If legislative authority is delegated in such situations, guidelines and standards for regulatory enforcement must be present.

In order for a regulation to be valid, it must be reasonable, applied uniformly, and it must not infringe upon constitutional rights. A state or political subdivision cannot proscribe the lawful operation of an asylum or care facility, or create or enforce unreasonable or arbitrary requirements regarding its construction or physical location. Similarly, it cannot make capricious requirements relating to the classification and nature of individuals to be admitted. Regulations and practices must comply with constitutional and statutory provisions.

The governing board of an asylum or institutional care facility is empowered to create all necessary rules and bylaws and is responsible for its policies and general administration. The courts will neither prescribe rules nor alter those created by the authorities, unless they are unreasonable or inappropriate.

Investigation and Inspection The legislature has the exclusive power to order an investigation of the management of an asylum or care facility. Private individuals may not conduct an investigation. When an investigation is initiated, the institution's governing board has the power to set forth regulations regarding relations with employees and patients and access to the records. A nursing home operator must make records kept pursuant to a public health statute available for inspection by authorized public officials. In addition, a private facility can be required to turn over annual fiscal reports to a regulatory agency.

Statutory requirements for the safety of individuals in institutions are imposed and must be observed. Similarly, standards concerning the type of personnel needed to care for the patients are usually set forth, but they must not be unreasonable.

Licenses Ordinarily, a LICENSE is required to operate an asylum or institutional care facility to ensure that minimal health and safety requirements imposed by law are observed. When a license is necessary, operation of a facility without one may be enjoined and, under certain statutes, a CONTRACT made by an unlicensed person is VOID, which would bar recovery for NECESSARIES provided for individuals. The procedure for procuring a license is governed by statute, and the state licensing authorities have the discretion concerning whether or not it should be granted. Where there is a final decision, determinations in licensing proceedings may be subject to judicial review. The proceed-

The Bethesda Retirement and Nursing Center, visited by First Lady Barbara Bush, is considered an asylum.

ings on judicial review are generally regulated by statutory provisions that limit the proceedings to those initiated by aggrieved individuals.

Under some statutes, before an institutional care facility can be built, a certificate of need, which establishes approval of its construction by a public agency, is required.

Officers and Employees The rules that generally apply to public service employees govern the status of officers and employees of institutions. Statutory provisions may provide for the termination of such officers and employees.

Inmates, Patients, and Residents Statutory provisions, administrative regulations, and discretion of its administrator govern the admission of inmates or patients to a public institution. When a public asylum is founded for the reception of a specific class of individuals, anyone in the designated class may be admitted.

A constitutional provision that requires the advancement and support of certain specified institutions does not mandate that the state incur the total cost of maintaining institutionalized individuals. The expedience of soliciting repayment from responsible people for the expense of care, support, and maintenance of a patient cannot be based exclusively upon whether the commitment is voluntary or involuntary. In addition, recovery might be permitted for services actually rendered.

The individual in charge of an asylum that stands IN LOCO PARENTIS to infants upon their admission has CUSTODY of the children who are committed to its care. Unless otherwise prohibited by statute, qualified people may examine the records of children in private institutions when so authorized by its administrators. Where a statute exists that guarantees the adult residents of proprietary adult homes the right to manage their own financial affairs, their handling of such matters cannot be subject to judicial challenge. An institution may be mandated to meet the individual needs of its patients under rules that monitor the operation of private care facilities for the purpose of the Medicaid program.

Appropriate regulations may govern the visitation rights of individuals in an asylum.

An individual may be dismissed from the institution for conduct proscribed by the bylaws under penalty of expulsion, provided the person is first afforded notice and an opportunity to be heard.

Contracts for Care and Occupancy The admission of an individual to a public institution for care can be the subject of a contract between the patient and the institution concerning the transfer of property to the institution. Even without an express agreement, however, the circumstances may bring about a QUASI CONTRACT to provide for services rendered.

An individual may not rescind an occupancy agreement and regain an admission fee without proof of a breach of contract by the institution.

Management The management of public institutions is usually entrusted to specific governing bodies or officers. The appropriate body can hire employees to operate the asylum but cannot relinquish its management responsibilities. Physicians who wish to visit patients in private nursing homes can be excluded. If an institution does not provide reasons at the time of the exclusion, it does not preclude the institution from excluding the physician, provided that valid reasons exist and are communicated upon request.

Generally, the governing body of an asylum has the power to decide how funds appropriated for its support shall be spent, in the absence of contrary legislative provision. Funds appropriated by a legislature for specific purposes cannot, however, be diverted, and the governing body of the asylum does not have the power to compel the state to provide funding for services other than those for which the money was appropriated. Similarly, they are not empowered to borrow money or incur debts beyond allotments made for the support of institutions.

It is proper procedure to make a provision that an asylum may only accept as many inmates for admission as the facilities can adequately accommodate.

An institution may not initiate a visitation plan that limits a patient's right to allocate his or her visiting time among particular people, unless such limitation bears a rational relationship to the patient's treatment or security.

Liabilities An asylum or institutional care facility has the obligation to exercise reasonable care toward patients, and can be held liable for a breach of this duty of care. The care taken toward inmates should be in the light of their mental and physical condition.

Recovery for injuries precipitated by an institution's NEGLIGENCE can be barred or limited by the contributory negligence of the injured party. The defense of contributory negligence cannot, however, be used when an individual is physically or mentally incapable of self-care.

CROSS-REFERENCES

Disabled Persons; Health Care; Insanity; Patients' Rights.

AT ISSUE ▥ A phrase that describes the status of PARTIES in a lawsuit when they make contradictory statements about a point specified in their PLEADINGS. ▥

AT LARGE ▥ Not limited to any place, person, or topic; for example, a representative at large is elected by the voters of the state as a whole rather than voters of a particular district. Free from control or restraint, such as a criminal at large. ▥

AT LAW ▥ According to law; by, for, or in the law, as in the professional title *attorney at law*. Within or arising from the traditions of the COMMON LAW as opposed to EQUITY, the system of law that developed alongside the common law and emphasized fairness and justice rather than enforcement of technical rules. ▥

ATTACHMENT ▥ The legal process of seizing property to ensure SATISFACTION of a JUDGMENT. ▥

The document by which a court orders such a SEIZURE may be called a WRIT of ATTACHMENT or an ORDER of attachment.

Originally, the main purpose of attachment was to coerce a defendant into appearing in court and answering the plaintiff's claim. The court's order pressured the SHERIFF to take the defendant's property into CUSTODY, depriving the individual of the right to use or sell it. If the defendant obstinately refused to appear, the property could be sold by the court to pay off any monetary judgment entered against him or her. Today, the process of attachment has two functions, as a jurisdictional predicate and as a provisional remedy.

Attachment of property within reach of the court's JURISDICTION gives the court authority over the defendant to the extent of that property's value even if the court cannot reach the defendant personally. For example, a court must have some connection with the defendant in order to require that person to appear and defend himself or herself in an action before that court.

A variety of different facts are sufficient to give the court jurisdiction over the defendant's person; for example, the defendant's residence within the state, the defendant's commission of a wrongful act within the state, or the defendant's doing business within the state.

If none of these kinds of facts exist to give the court jurisdiction over the defendant's person, the court may nevertheless assert its authority over property that the defendant owns within the state. In such a case, the plaintiff cannot recover a monetary judgment for an amount larger than the value of the property nor can the individual reach the defendant's property outside the state, but this sort of jurisdiction, called jurisdiction IN REM or QUASI IN REM, may be the best the plaintiff can get. Before the court can exercise jurisdiction over the property, the plaintiff must obtain a writ of attachment to bring it into custody of the court.

Attachment may also be a PROVISIONAL remedy, that is, relief that temporarily offers the plaintiff some security while pursuing a final judgment in the lawsuit. For example, a plaintiff who has good reason to believe that the person he or she is suing is about to pack up and leave the state will want the court to prevent this until the plaintiff has a chance to win the action and collect on the judgment. The plaintiff can apply for an order of attachment that brings the property into the custody of the court and takes away the defendant's right to remove it or dispose of it.

Attachment is considered a very harsh REMEDY because it substantially interferes with the defendant's property rights before final resolution of the overall dispute. For this reason, there have been a number of challenges to the attachment procedures in different states, and the Supreme Court has established standards that are the least that DUE PROCESS requires. For example, for centuries attachment of a defendant's property was granted EX PARTE, that is, without first allowing the defendant to argue against it. The theory was that any defendant was likely to leave the state if he or she knew beforehand that his or her property was about to be attached. This collides with the individual's right to be free of interference with his or her rights unless the individual is given NOTICE and an opportunity to be heard in the matter. States, therefore, now generally provide that notice must be given to the defendant before the seizure of property whenever practical, and the defendant must be given a HEARING promptly after the seizure. Furthermore, a court cannot sanction a seizure that is made without a court order of attachment. To obtain the order, the plaintiff must swear to a set of facts that justify such a drastic interference with the defendant's property.

The process of attachment varies in detail from state to state, but it is not overly complicated. The plaintiff submits an application to the court describing the CAUSE OF ACTION against the defendant and the grounds for seeking an attachment. The plaintiff may have to include documents or other evidence to support the claim that he or she will probably win the lawsuit, and the individual usually is required to make the application under oath. States generally require that the plaintiff post a BOND or

A sample order of attachment from the state of New York

At a Special Term, Part _____ of the Supreme Court of the State of New York, County of _____, held at the Courthouse, No. _____ _____ Avenue, _____, New York, on the _____ day of _____, _____.

Present: Hon. _____, Justice.

_____

_____ and _____, Plaintiffs,
-against-
_____ and _____, Defendants.

_____

ORDER OF ATTACHMENT

Index No. _____

TO THE SHERIFF OF ANY COUNTY OF THE STATE OF NEW YORK OR OF THE CITY OF NEW YORK:

Whereas an application has been made to the undersigned by _____ and _____, plaintiffs, for an Order of Attachment against the property of one of the defendants, _____, in an action in the Supreme Court, now, upon reading and filing the affidavit of _____, duly sworn to on the _____ day of _____, _____, and the affidavit of _____, Esq., duly sworn to on the _____ day of _____, _____, and it satisfactorily appearing to the Court from said affidavits that one of the grounds for attachment set down in CPLR 6201 exists in favor of the plaintiffs and against the defendant, _____, to recover a sum of money, to wit, the sum of _____ ($ _____) Dollars in behalf of _____ to recover damages for personal injuries, the sum of _____ ($ _____) Dollars in behalf of _____ to recover damages for personal injuries and the sum of _____ ($ _____) Dollars in behalf of _____ to recover damages for loss of services, that the plaintiffs are entitled to recover said sums over and above all counter claims known to them, and that the defendant _____ is not a resident or domiciliary of the State of New York but resides at _____, and the plaintiffs having given an undertaking with corporate surety in the amount of _____ ($ _____) Dollars, it is, therefore,

On motion of _____ & _____, attorneys for the plaintiffs,

ORDERED that an Order of Attachment be and the same hereby is granted, and it is further

ORDERED, that the amount to be secured by this order of attachment, including any interest, costs and sheriff's fees and expenses shall be _____ ($ _____) Dollars.

Now, you are commanded to levy within your jurisdiction at any time before final judgment, upon the contractual obligation of _____ Accident and Indemnity Company to defend and indemnify defendant, _____, under a policy of automobile liability insurance issued to said _____, for the purpose of securing and satisfying the aforesaid sum of _____ ($ _____) Dollars, and that you proceed hereon in the manner and make your return within the time prescribed by law. (Note that where an order of attachment is granted ex parte, it may also provide as follows: You will refrain from taking any property levied upon into your actual custody, pending further order of this court. See Comment below.)

(Where an order of attachment is granted ex parte, it must also provide substantially as follows:) It is further Ordered that the plaintiff shall move within _____ days after levy hereunder [5 days or within a shorter period set by the court] on (specify such notice as the court directs to be made to the defendant, the garnishee, if any, and the sheriff) for an order confirming this order of attachment.

Enter,

_____
J. S. C.

_____ & _____
Attorneys for Plaintiff
P. O. Address
Tel. No.

undertaking in an amount sufficient to secure payment of damages to the defendant if it turns out that the plaintiff was not in fact entitled to the attachment.

The court issues a writ of attachment directing the sheriff or other law enforcement officer to serve a copy of the order on the defendant and to seize property equal in value to the sum specified in the writ. This is called a LEVY of attachment. The defendant then has a right to challenge the seizure or to post bond for the release of the property, in effect substituting the bond for the property in the court's custody. The order of attachment is effective only for a limited period, the time necessary to wind up the lawsuit between plaintiff and defendant or a specified period intended to permit resolution of the controversy. Provisions are usually made for special circumstances or extreme hardship.

Not every kind of property owned by the defendant is subject to attachment. The laws of a state may provide exemptions for certain household items, clothing, tools, and other essentials. The defendant's salary may be subject to attachment, but a certain amount is exempt in order to allow for personal support or for family support. Property belonging to the defendant but in the hands of someone else, such as salary owed or a debt not yet paid, may also be seized, but this procedure is usually called GARNISHMENT rather than attachment.

Courts always have the discretion to exempt more property than that specified in a statute or to deny the attachment altogether under the proper circumstances. This may be done, for example, when the court believes that the property sought to be attached is worth much more than any judgment the plaintiff could hope to win, or where the property is an ongoing business that would be destroyed by attachment.

See also SEARCHES AND SEIZURES.

ATTAINDER 📖 At common law, that extinction of civil rights and capacities that took place whenever a person who had committed treason or a felony received a sentence of death for the crime.

The effect of *attainder* upon a felon was, in general terms, that all estate, real and personal, was forfeited. In common law, attainder resulted in three ways: *by confession, by verdict,* and *by process* or *outlawry.* The first case was where the prisoner pleaded guilty at the bar, or having fled, confessed guilt and abjured the realm to save his or her life. The second was where the prisoner pleaded not guilty at the bar, and the jury brought in a verdict against him or her. The third, when the person accused made his or her escape and was outlawed.

In England, by statute 33 & 34 Vict. c. 23, attainder upon conviction, with consequent corruption of blood, forfeiture, or escheat, was abolished. In the United States, the doctrine of attainder is now scarcely known, although during and shortly after the Revolution acts of attainder were passed by several of the states. The passage of such bills is expressly forbidden by the Constitution (Art. I, Sec. 9).

Bills of attainder are special acts of the legislature that inflict capital punishments upon persons supposed to be guilty of high offenses, such as treason and felony, without any conviction in the ordinary course of judicial proceedings. If an act inflicts a milder degree of punishment than death, it is called a *bill of pains and penalties,* but both are included in the prohibition in the Constitution (Art. I, Sec. 9). 📖

The term *attainder* is derived from *attincta,* Latin for stained or blackened. When attainder occurred, the condemned person was considered to bear a mark of infamy that corrupted his or her blood. Attainder was eventually abolished in England by statute.

In the United States, attainder is scarcely known today, although several states enacted acts of attainder during the Revolutionary War period. A few states consider the disqualification of a person IMPEACHED and convicted to hold any government office to be a type of attainder. Attainder is akin to the concept of CIVIL DEATH, the forefeiture of certain rights and privileges upon conviction of a serious crime.

ATTEMPT 📖 An undertaking to do an act that entails more than mere preparation but does not result in the successful completion of the act. 📖

In CRIMINAL LAW, an attempt to commit a crime is an offense when an accused makes a substantial but unsuccessful effort to commit a crime. The elements of attempt vary, although generally, there must be an intent to commit the crime, an OVERT ACT beyond mere preparation, and an apparent ability to complete the crime.

Generally, attempts are punishable by imprisonment, with sentence lengths that vary in time, depending upon the severity of the offense attempted.

ATTENUATE 📖 To reduce the force or severity; to lessen a relationship or connection between two objects. 📖

In CRIMINAL PROCEDURE, the relationship between an illegal search and a CONFESSION may be sufficiently attenuated as to remove the confession from the protection afforded by the FRUIT OF THE POISONOUS TREE doctrine, thereby making it admissible as evidence in a criminal prosecution depending upon the facts of the case.

ATTEST ▣ To solemnly declare verbally or in writing that a particular document or testimony about an event is a true and accurate representation of the facts; to bear WITNESS to. To formally certify by a SIGNATURE that the signer has been present at the execution of a particular writing so as to rebut any potential challenges to its authenticity. ▣

ATTESTATION ▣ The act of attending the execution of a document and bearing WITNESS to its authenticity, by signing one's name to it to affirm that it is genuine. The certification by a custodian of records that a copy of an original document is a true copy that is demonstrated by his or her signature on a certificate. ▣

An attestation is a declaration by a witness that an instrument has been executed in his or her presence according to the formalities required by law. It is not the same as an ACKNOWL-EDGMENT, a statement by the maker of a document that verifies its authenticity.

An attestation clause is frequently found in legal documents that must be witnessed if they are to be valid, for example, a WILL or a DEED. It states that the instrument has been completed in the manner required by law in the presence of the witness who places his or her SIGNATURE in the designated space.

ATTORN ▣ To turn over money, rent, or goods to another. To assign to a specific function or service. ▣

ATTORNEY ▣ A person admitted to practice law in at least one jurisdiction and authorized to perform criminal and civil legal functions on behalf of clients. These functions include providing legal counsel, drafting legal documents, and representing clients before courts, administrative agencies, and other tribunals. ▣

Unless a contrary meaning is plainly indicated this term is synonymous with "attorney at law," "lawyer," or "counselor at law."

In order to become an attorney, a person must obtain a Juris Doctor degree from an accredited law school, although this requirement may vary in some states. Attendance at law school usually entails three years of full-time study, or four years of study in evening classes, where available. A bachelor's degree is generally a prerequisite to admission to law school.

With few exceptions, a person must pass the BAR EXAMINATION of that state in order to be admitted to practice law there. After passing a bar examination and practicing law for a specified period, a person may be admitted to the bars of other states, pursuant to their own court rules.

Status in Practice, 1991

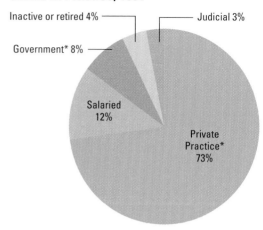

*Lawyers who were in both private practice and government service are coded in private practice.

Source: *1991 Lawyer Statistical Report: The U.S. Legal Profession in the 1990s,* copyright 1994.

Although an attorney might be required by law to render some services pro bono (free of charge), the individual is ordinarily entitled to compensation for the reasonable value of services performed. He or she has a right, called an ATTORNEY'S LIEN, to retain the property or money of a client until payment has been received for all services. An attorney must generally obtain court permission to discontinue representation of a client during the course of a trial or criminal proceedings.

Certain discourse between attorney and client is protected by the attorney-client privilege. In the law of EVIDENCE, the client can refuse to divulge and prohibit anyone else from disclosing confidential communications transmitted to and from the attorney.

CROSS-REFERENCES

Attorney-Client Privilege; Attorney Misconduct; Legal Education; Legal Representation; Pro Bono; Right to Counsel.

ATTORNEY-CLIENT PRIVILEGE ▣ In law of EVIDENCE, client's privilege to refuse to disclose and to prevent any other person from disclosing confidential communications between the client and his or her attorney. Such privilege protects communications between attorney and client made for the purpose of furnishing or obtaining professional legal advice or assistance. That privilege that permits an attorney to refuse to testify as to communications from the client though it belongs to the client, not the attorney, and hence the client may waive it. In federal courts, state law is applied with respect to such privilege. ▣

The attorney-client privilege encourages clients to disclose to their attorneys all pertinent information in legal matters by protecting such disclosures from discovery at trial. The privileged information, held strictly between the attorney and the client, may remain private as long as a court does not force disclosure. The privilege does not apply to communications between an attorney and a client made to further a fraud or crime. The responsibility for designating which information should remain confidential rests with the client. In its most common use, however, the attorney claims the privilege on behalf of the client in refusing to disclose to the court or any other party requested information about the client's case.

As a basic construction in the judicial system, the privilege is an ancient device. It can be found even in ROMAN LAW—for example, Marcus Tullius Cicero, while prosecuting the governor of Sicily, could not call the governor's advocate as a witness, because if he were to have done so, the governor would have lost confidence in his own defender. Over the years, the close tie between attorney and client developed further with reforms in English COMMON LAW.

Because attorney-client privilege often balances competing interests, it defies a rigid definition. However, one often-cited characterization was articulated in *United States v. United Shoe Machinery Corp.*, 89 F. Supp. 357 (D. Mass. 1950). The court articulated five requirements: first, the person asserting the privilege must be a client, or must have sought to become a client at the time of disclosure; second, the person connected to the communication must be acting as a lawyer; third, the communication must be between the lawyer and the client exclusively—no non-clients may be included in the communication; fourth, the communication must be for the purpose of securing a legal opinion, legal services, or assistance in some legal proceeding, and not for the purpose of committing a crime; fifth, the privilege may be claimed or waived by the client only (usually, as mentioned, through counsel).

Sometimes, even when all five of the *United Shoe* requirements have been met, courts will still compel disclosure of the information sought. The courts base exceptions to the privilege on rule 501 of the Federal Rules of Evidence, which states that "the recognition of a privilege based on a confidential relationship ... should be determined on a case-by-case basis." In examining the privilege on a case-by-case basis, courts weigh the benefits to be gained by upholding the privilege (preserving the confidence between attorney and client) against the harms that may be caused if they deny it (the loss of information valuable to the opposing party).

The courts have declared that the fact of an attorney-client relationship itself need not always remain privileged information (*National Union Fire Insurance Co. of Pittsburgh v. Aetna Casualty & Surety Co.*, 384 F.2d 316 [5th Cir. 1967]); the privilege may be upheld, however, if the very existence of an attorney-client relationship could prove incriminating to the client (*In re Michaelson*, 511 F.2d 882 [9th Cir. 1975], *cert. denied*, 421 U.S. 978, 95 S. Ct. 1979, 44 L. Ed. 2d 469 [1975]). Also, the attorney-client privilege does not always protect the client's name or the amount paid to an attorney (*Wirtz v. Fowler*, 372 F.2d 315 [5th Cir. 1966]). Further, the attorney's perception of the client's mental competency will not always be protected (*United States v. Kendrick*, 331 F.2d 110 [4th Cir. 1964] [holding that attorney's testimony that client was responsive, logical in conversation and reasoning, and understood the proceedings did not address confidential matters]).

In general, exceptions to the attorney-client privilege can prove problematic to defense attorneys, who try to keep a client's potentially incriminating disclosures confidential. One exception, however, is intended to protect attorneys: *Meyerhofer v. Empire Fire & Marine Insurance Co.*, 497 F.2d 1190 (2d Cir. 1974), *cert. denied*, 419 U.S. 998, 95 S. Ct. 314, 42 L. Ed. 2d 272 (1974), held that an attorney may circumvent the privilege if revealing information would relieve her or him of accusations of wrongdoing.

A client is not always a person; a CORPORATION can be a client and may have a right to the attorney-client privilege. The Supreme Court's decision in *Upjohn Co. v. United States*, 449 U.S. 383, 101 S. Ct. 677, 66 L. Ed. 2d 584 (1981), ensured greater protection for confidential information between a corporation and its lawyers. In the mid-1970s, Upjohn Company faced accusations of making questionable payments to officials of foreign governments in order to secure business from those governments. In response to those accusations, Upjohn authorized its corporate attorneys to conduct investigations of foreign payments. When the Internal Revenue Service (IRS) issued a summons for the investigative documents that Upjohn had left to its lawyers, Upjohn refused to comply with the request. Upjohn argued that the documents were privileged. The Supreme Court ruled in favor of Upjohn, and this decision became the standard for determining the nature of services—either legal or business—provided by the corporate attorney.

By the early 1990s, the attorney-client privilege was narrowed by federal guidelines intended to combat money laundering. The federal government, in conjunction with President George Bush's crackdown on drug trafficking (called the war on drugs), pressed an IRS policy that would hinder drug dealers and other criminals from disguising profits. The law required attorneys to disclose to the government any cash payment in excess of $10,000, and the name of the client making the payment (26 U.S.C.A. § 6050 I).

In *United States v. Leventhal,* 961 F.2d 936 (11th Cir. 1992), Robert Leventhal, an attorney in Florida, refused to disclose to the IRS the names of clients who had paid him over $10,000 in cash. Leventhal's clients wished to remain anonymous, and Leventhal argued that the attorney-client privilege gave them that right. Leventhal cited the Florida Rules of Professional Conduct, which require disclosure of confidential client information only in rare circumstances. The federal government sued Leventhal. The court ruled that disclosing the clients' identities revealed only the existence of an attorney-client relationship, a simple factual matter not within the scope of the privilege. Therefore, Leventhal had to reveal the sources of the payments.

The Sixth Circuit Court of Appeals followed *Leventhal* in *United States v. Ritchie,* 15 F.3d 592 (1994), *cert. denied,* __ U.S. __, 115 S. Ct. 188, 130 L. Ed. 2d 121 (1994). Attorney Robert Ritchie had challenged the same IRS policy, but the court noted that Congress gave the IRS broad powers to ensure compliance with the tax code. Appeals court judge Alice M. Batchelder held that there was no "constitutionally protected liberty interest in spending large amounts of cash without having to account for it."

Attorneys have decried the federal government's position in such cases. But the attorney-client privilege remains useful as a defensive measure in more general circumstances. The privilege remains an exception to the general rule that individuals must testify to all facts within their knowledge. Rooted in ancient principles, it fosters trust within this important relationship and helps attorneys fully develop their clients' cases by encouraging complete disclosure of relevant information.

CROSS-REFERENCES

Attorney Misconduct; Drugs and Narcotics; Ethics; Legal Representation; Model Rules of Professional Conduct.

ATTORNEY GENERAL The attorney general is head of the U.S. Department of JUSTICE and chief law officer of the federal government. He or she represents the United States in legal matters generally, and gives advice and opinions to the president and to other heads of executive departments as requested. In cases of excep-

tional gravity or special importance, the attorney general may appear in person before the U.S. Supreme Court to represent the interests of the government.

As head of the Department of Justice, the attorney general is charged with enforcing federal laws, furnishing legal counsel in federal cases, construing the laws under which other executive departments act, supervising federal penal institutions, and investigating violations of federal laws. The attorney general also supervises and directs the activities of the U.S. attorneys and U.S. MARSHALS in the various judicial districts. (U.S. attorneys prosecute all offenses against the United States, and prosecute or defend, for the government, all CIVIL ACTIONS, suits, or proceedings in which the United States is concerned; U.S. marshals execute all lawful WRITS, PROCESSES, and ORDERS issued under authority of the United States.)

The office of the attorney general was created by the First Congress in the JUDICIARY ACT OF 1789 (An Act to Establish the Judicial Courts of the United States, ch. 20, § 35, 1 Stat. 73, 92–93). The First Congress did not expect the attorney general—a part-time employee with scant pay, no staff, and little power—to play a major role in the emerging federal government. As the members of the First Congress established a system for the enforcement of federal laws, their primary concern was to protect state and individual freedoms and to avoid the creation of a central legal system that would allow the tyrannies they had experienced as American colonists under George III. Therefore, the Judiciary Act gave the attorney general just two principal duties: (1) to prosecute and conduct all suits in the SUPREME COURT OF THE UNITED STATES that concerned the United States and (2) to give an opinion on QUESTIONS OF LAW when asked to do so by the president or heads of other executive departments.

The early attorneys general spent little time arguing before the Supreme Court, because few cases had traveled through the nation's developing court system and even fewer warranted Supreme Court review. Together, the first three attorneys general—EDMUND RANDOLPH, WILLIAM BRADFORD, and Charles Lee—represented the United States in the Supreme Court only six times in their collective years in office.

Furthermore, early attorneys general were specifically restricted by the Judiciary Act from participating in lower-court actions. District attorneys (known today as U.S. attorneys) held the authority to represent the United States in district and circuit courts. Each district attorney could independently decide which cases to pursue and on what grounds—a situation that soon resulted in a number of contradictory legal positions for the federal government. Because the attorney general had no power to direct district attorneys in their lower-court litigation, the officeholder was often unaware of litigation that concerned the interests of the United States.

In a letter to President GEORGE WASHINGTON dated December 26, 1791, Attorney General Randolph expressed concern about the limitations of his office and complained specifically about the lack of a defined relationship with the district attorneys. Randolph was the first of many attorneys general to point out that their prescribed duties did not allow them to fully look after the interests of the United States, and he was the first to propose an expansion of the office's duties and jurisdiction.

Ignoring complaints and proposals, Congress remained reluctant to expand the duties of the attorney general and often passed legislation that assigned special legal functions to officials in other government departments. For example, in the early 1800s, Congress created a solicitor of the treasury to handle all suits for the recovery of money or property in the United States—a move that further complicated the attorney general's efforts to fully look after the interests of the government.

With court appearances limited by the lack of both cases before the Supreme Court and jurisdiction to oversee lower-court cases, opinion writing consumed most of the time of early attorneys general. Together, Attorneys General Randolph, Bradford, and Lee wrote more than forty formal opinions on such diverse issues as immunity for diplomats, applications for patents, and the choice of directors for the nation's first federal bank. However, early attorneys general were not required to provide the government with written records of their opinions. When WILLIAM WIRT, the eleventh attorney general, took office in 1817, he found that his predecessors had provided no record of their past opinions to guide his deliberations. Understandably, early attorneys general, who received only a small stipend for their services and relied on the private practice of law for their personal income, spent little money to hire clerks to transcribe and preserve their work. They simply relied on the recipients of their opinions to retain them for future reference. Still, legislative attempts to provide the attorney general with an office, a clerk, and supplies continually failed to win support.

The limited duties outlined for the attorney general by the First Congress, along with the lack of perquisites for the office, made it hard for presidents to attract qualified appointees

U.S. Attorneys General

Name	Term	President
Edmund Randolph (Va.)	1789–94	George Washington
William Bradford (Pa.)	1794–95	George Washington
Charles Lee (Va.)	1795–97	George Washington
	1797–1801	John Adams
Theophilus Parsons (Mass.)	1801	John Adams
Levi Lincoln (Mass.)	1801–5	Thomas Jefferson
Robert Smith (Md.)	1805	Thomas Jefferson
John Breckenridge (Ky.)	1805–7	Thomas Jefferson
Caesar A. Rodney (Del.)	1807	Thomas Jefferson
	1807–11	James Madison
William Pinkney (Md.)	1811–14	James Madison
Richard Rush (Pa.)	1814–17	James Madison
	1817	James Monroe
William Wirt (Va.)	1817–25	James Monroe
	1825–29	John Quincy Adams
John M. Berrien (Ga.)	1829–31	Andrew Jackson
Roger B. Taney (Md.)	1831–33	Andrew Jackson
Benjamin F. Butler (N.Y.)	1833–37	Andrew Jackson
	1837–38	Martin Van Buren
Felix Grundy (Tenn.)	1838–40	Martin Van Buren
Henry D. Gilpin (Pa.)	1840–41	Martin Van Buren
John J. Crittenden (Ky.)	1841	William H. Harrison
	1841	John Tyler
Hugh S. Legare (S.C.)	1841–43	John Tyler
John Nelson (Md.)	1843–45	John Tyler
John Y. Mason (Va.)	1845–46	James Polk
Nathan Clifford (Maine)	1846–48	James Polk
Isaac Toucey (Conn.)	1848–49	James Polk
Reverdy Johnson (Md.)	1849–50	Zachary Taylor
John J. Crittenden (Ky.)	1850–53	Millard Fillmore
Caleb Cushing (Mass.)	1853–57	Franklin Pierce
Jeremiah S. Black (Pa.)	1857–60	James Buchanan
Edwin M. Stanton (Pa.)	1860–61	James Buchanan
Edward Bates (Mo.)	1861–64	Abraham Lincoln
James Speed (Ky.)	1864–65	Abraham Lincoln
	1865–66	Andrew Johnson
Henry Stanbery (Ohio)	1866–68	Andrew Johnson
William M. Evarts (N.Y.)	1868–69	Andrew Johnson
Ebenezer R. Hoar (Mass.)	1869–70	Ulysses S. Grant
Amos T. Akerman (Ga.)	1870–71	Ulysses S. Grant
George H. Williams (Oreg.)	1871–75	Ulysses S. Grant
Edwards Pierrepont (N.Y.)	1875–76	Ulysses S. Grant
Alphonso Taft (Ohio)	1876–77	Ulysses S. Grant
Charles Devens (Mass.)	1877–81	Rutherford B. Hayes
Wayne MacVeagh (Pa.)	1881–82	James Garfield
Benjamin H. Brewster (Pa.)	1882–85	Chester A. Arthur
Augustus Garland (Ark.)	1885–89	Grover Cleveland
William H. H. Miller (Ind.)	1889–93	Benjamin Harrison
Richard Olney (Mass.)	1893–95	Grover Cleveland
Judson Harmon (Ohio)	1895–97	Grover Cleveland
Joseph McKenna (Calif.)	1897–98	William McKinley
John W. Griggs (N.J.)	1898–1901	William McKinley
Philander C. Knox (Pa.)	1901	William McKinley
	1901–4	Theodore Roosevelt
William H. Moody (Mass.)	1904–6	Theodore Roosevelt
Charles J. Bonaparte (Md.)	1906–9	Theodore Roosevelt
George W. Wickersham (N.Y.)	1909–13	William Howard Taft
J. C. McReynolds (Tenn.)	1913–14	Woodrow Wilson
Thomas W. Gregory (Tex.)	1914–19	Woodrow Wilson
A. Mitchell Palmer (Pa.)	1919–21	Woodrow Wilson
Harry M. Daugherty (Ohio)	1921–23	Warren G. Harding
	1923–24	Calvin Coolidge
Harlan F. Stone (N.Y.)	1924–25	Calvin Coolidge
John G. Sargent (Vt.)	1925–29	Calvin Coolidge
William D. Mitchell (Minn.)	1929–33	Herbert Hoover
Homer S. Cummings (Conn.)	1933–39	Franklin D. Roosevelt
Frank Murphy (Mich.)	1939–40	Franklin D. Roosevelt
Robert H. Jackson (N.Y.)	1940–41	Franklin D. Roosevelt
Francis Biddle (Pa.)	1941–45	Franklin D. Roosevelt
Thomas C. Clark (Tex.)	1945–49	Harry S. Truman
J. Howard McGrath (R.I.)	1949–52	Harry S. Truman
J. P. McGranery (Pa.)	1952–53	Harry S. Truman
Herbert Brownell, Jr. (N.Y.)	1953–57	Dwight D. Eisenhower
William P. Rogers (Md.)	1957–61	Dwight D. Eisenhower
Robert F. Kennedy (Mass.)	1961–63	John F. Kennedy
	1963–64	Lyndon B. Johnson

(table continued on next page)

U.S. Attorneys General—Continued

Name	Term	President
Nicholas de B. Katzenbach (Ill.)	1964–67	Lyndon B. Johnson
Ramsey Clark (Tex.)	1967–69	Lyndon B. Johnson
John N. Mitchell (N.Y.)	1969–72	Richard M. Nixon
Richard G. Kleindienst (Ariz.)	1972–73	Richard M. Nixon
Elliot L. Richardson (Mass.)	1973–74	Richard M. Nixon
William B. Saxbe (Ohio)	1974	Richard M. Nixon
	1974–75	Gerald R. Ford
Edward H. Levi (Ill.)	1975–77	Gerald R. Ford
Griffin B. Bell (Ga.)	1977–79	Jimmy Carter
Benjamin R. Civiletti (Md.)	1979–81	Jimmy Carter
William French Smith (Calif.)	1981–85	Ronald Reagan
Edwin Meese III (Calif.)	1985–88	Ronald Reagan
Richard Thornburgh (Pa.)	1988–89	Ronald Reagan
	1989–91	George Bush
William P. Barr (N.Y.)	1991–93	George Bush
Janet Reno (Fla.)	1993–	Bill Clinton

and keep them in office. Even President Washington had difficulty convincing his personal attorney and long-time friend, Randolph, to take the job. Washington finally won Randolph over by pointing out that service as attorney general might enhance his earning opportunities in private practice. In fact, Randolph did not profit much from the prestige of the office during or after his tenure. Subsequent attorneys general did profit handsomely from the experience, but early officeholders often had difficulty balancing the dual commitments to private practice and public service.

The commitment to public service for early attorneys general was further complicated by institutional tensions between the executive, legislative, and judicial branches of government, which all claimed the officeholder's time, services, and allegiance. It has been said that the attorney general serves "three masters": the president, the Congress, and the courts (American Enterprise Institute for Public Policy Research 1968). Although the attorney general advises the president, the basic authority of the office is derived from Congress and the functions of the office are subject to congressional control. In addition, the attorney general is a member of the bar and therefore an OFFICER OF THE COURT subject to the directives of the judicial branch.

Although the First Congress defined the relationship between the attorney general and the president, it did not define the relationship between the attorney general and Congress. And it was notably silent regarding who was ultimately to decide when and whether the interests of the United States were "concerned": nothing in the Judiciary Act of 1789 specified who should control the attorney general or to whom she or he should report. Early attorneys general took orders from the Congress as well as from the president and the heads of other executive departments. Attorneys general were often asked to deliver opinions to Congress on legislative proposals, and they came to be viewed as authorities on constitutional issues—much to the chagrin of both legislators, who frequently disagreed with their interpretations, and members of the judiciary, who assumed that they themselves were the final arbiters in constitutional matters.

The attorney general has also been said to straddle the legal and political worlds. When Congress created the executive departments, it did not specify who should or should not be members of the president's CABINET—and it could not predict the level of influence held by any one individual. In the early years, the attorney general did not have cabinet rank but served as counsel to those who did. However, as Washington's personal legal adviser, Randolph participated in cabinet meetings as early as 1792, establishing the precedent for attorneys general to have a hand in making policy as well as in interpreting and enforcing the laws. The attorney general's role in policy making soon brought into question the extent to which party lines and presidential preferences influenced his or her legal advice. Over time, some attorneys general have handled the dichotomy with more integrity, and less partisanship, than others.

The lack of centralized authority and the lack of basic institutional support for the office of the attorney general began to be remedied by Congress in the early nineteenth century. Subsequently, many of the issues caused or influenced by conflicting allegiances were dissolved or clarified through administrative policy and legislation.

In 1814, during Attorney General RICHARD RUSH's term, President JAMES MADISON made the first move to expand formally the presence (if not the duties) of the attorney general, by proposing a requirement that the attorney general reside in or near Washington, D.C., while Congress was in session. The residency requirement had previously been resisted by some attorneys general. Although it made the officeholder available to the president and Congress when the attorney general was most needed, it also made the private practice of law more inconvenient to an attorney general who lived far from the Capitol.

Attorney General Wirt (1817–29), under Presidents JAMES MONROE and JOHN QUINCY ADAMS, was the first to comprehend fully the officeholder's need for administrative structure. During his tenure, the attorney general was finally given government office space, a transcribing clerk, and a small fund for office supplies. The practice of providing opinions to Congress was also curtailed during this period, when Wirt presented a paper to President Monroe outlining the extent of his congressional workload and his objections. Wirt told the president that opinions had been provided to Congress in the past as a courtesy—not as a matter of law. Wirt told the president the practice would not continue unless Congress revised the law and made it mandatory.

By 1853, when CALEB CUSHING became attorney general under President FRANKLIN PIERCE, the officeholder had four clerks and—for the first time—a salary comparable to those of other cabinet officers. Also in 1853, Cushing decided it was no longer appropriate to continue the private practice of law while in office. He was the nation's first full-time attorney general.

Recommendations that a department of law be created by Congress were discussed as early as 1830 and were championed by numerous presidents and attorneys general. A department of justice was first suggested in 1851 by Alex H. H. Stuart, secretary of the newly established Department of the Interior.

No action was taken by Congress until February 25, 1870, when the Joint Committee on Retrenchments (appointed to find ways of reducing government expenditures) drafted a bill to consolidate legal functions and create a department of justice. The bill was made into law four months later, and the Department of Justice officially came into existence on July 1, 1870 (An Act to Establish the Department of Justice, §17, 16 Stat. 162 [June 22, 1870]).

The June 22, 1870, law created a new position, that of SOLICITOR GENERAL, whose holder is in charge of representing the government in suits and appeals in the Supreme Court and in lower federal trial and appellate courts, in cases involving the interests of the United States. The law also provided for two assistant attorneys general. It gave the attorney general complete direction and control of the U.S. attorneys and all other counsel employed on behalf of the United States. And it finally gave the attorney general supervisory powers over the accounts of district attorneys, marshals, clerks, and other officers of the court involved in federal matters.

The first attorney general to head the new department was AMOS T. AKERMAN, of Georgia, appointed by President ULYSSES S. GRANT in 1870. So, eighty-one years after the creation of the office of the attorney general, the nation finally had a full-fledged organization to administer and enforce its laws. According to one author, the creation of the Department of Justice was "the culmination of the evolutionary process through which the Attorney Generalship developed its essential nature" (Baker 1985).

The growth of the office of the attorney general from a part-time, one-person operation into a vast and complex law enforcement organization is an inseparable part of the story of the United States and the development of its institutions. As the role of government has expanded, so too has the role of the nation's attorney general. And, though the attorney general's role continues to grow and evolve, the basic duties of the office and the structure of its supporting organization have been in place since the Civil War.

The men and women who have served as attorney general have played an integral part in U.S. history. Every attorney general from Randolph's time to the present has participated in great events and crises of her or his day. Many have served in other capacities following their term in office. Former attorneys general can be found on the U.S. Supreme Court, in cabinet-level positions, and at diplomatic posts around the world. Attorneys general have also gone on to serve in the U.S. Senate and House of Representatives and as governors of various states.

ATTORNEY MISCONDUCT ▣ Behavior by an attorney that conflicts with established rules of professional conduct and is punishable by disciplinary measures. ▣

More than any other profession, the legal profession is self-governing. That is, it is largely regulated by lawyers and judges themselves rather than by the government or outside agencies. In particular, the American Bar Association (ABA), the largest professional association for attorneys, governs the practice of law through its establishment of rules of conduct. These rules are then adopted, sometimes in a modified form, by state courts and enforced by court-appointed disciplinary committees or bar associations. Attorneys found to be in violation of professional standards are guilty of misconduct and subject to disciplinary procedures. Disciplinary action by a state bar association or other authority may include private reprimands; public censure; suspension of the ability to practice law; and, most severe of all, disbarment—permanent denial of the ability to practice law in that jurisdiction. The state supreme court is the final arbiter in questions of professional conduct in most jurisdictions.

Since 1908, the ABA has been responsible for defining the standards of proper conduct for the legal profession. These standards, many of them established by the ABA's Standing Committee on Ethics and Professional Responsibility, are continuously evolving as society and the practice of law change over time. In 1969, the ABA passed its Model Code of Professional Responsibility, guidelines for proper legal conduct that were eventually adopted by all jurisdictions. The ABA modified the code by adopting the Model Rules of Professional Conduct in 1983. The model rules have been used by forty states to create official guidelines for professional conduct; eleven states or jurisdictions, including Washington, D.C., and the Virgin Islands, have continued to base their ethical codes on the earlier model code. California has developed its own rules of professional conduct. Whatever their basis, these codes or rules define the lawyer's proper role and relationship to the client. It is essential that lawyers understand the ethical codes under which they must operate. Failure to do so may result in not only disciplinary action by the relevant professional authorities but also malpractice suits against the lawyer. A malpractice suit may result in loss of money or of the ability to work with specific clients.

Rule 8.4 of the Model Rules of Professional Conduct contains the following statements on attorney misconduct:

> It is professional misconduct for a lawyer to:
> (a) Violate or attempt to violate the Rules of Professional Conduct, knowingly assist or induce another to do so, or do so through the acts of another;
> (b) Commit a criminal act that reflects adversely on the lawyer's honesty, trustworthiness or fitness as a lawyer in other respects;
> (c) Engage in conduct involving dishonesty, fraud, deceit or misrepresentation;
> (d) Engage in conduct that is prejudicial to the administration of justice;
> (e) State or imply an ability to influence improperly a government agency or official;
> (f) Knowingly assist a judge or judicial officer in conduct that is a violation of applicable rules of judicial conduct or other law.

Besides issuing these general statements, the model rules set down many specific requirements for attorney conduct in different situations.

Because of an attorney's special relationship to the law, he or she is held to a special standard of conduct before the law, as the ABA asserts in its *Lawyers' Manual on Professional Conduct:*

> As members of the bar and officers of the court, lawyers are beneficiaries of the privilege of the practice of law and also are subject to higher duties and responsibilities than are non-lawyers. A lawyer's fiduciary duties arise from his status as a member of the legal profession and are expressed, at least in part, by the applicable rules of professional conduct

The word *fiduciary* in this quote comes from the Latin word *fiducia*, meaning "trust"; as a FIDUCIARY, then, the attorney acts as the trusted representative of the client. Trust is thus a defining element of the legal profession, and without it, the practice of law could not exist. For that reason, the legal profession has created strict rules of conduct regarding the attorney's relationship with the client.

Attorney-Client Relationship   The model rules set forth specific guidelines defining the attorney-client relationship. An attorney will be guilty of misconduct, for example, if she or he fails to provide competent representation to a client, to act with DILIGENCE and promptness regarding a client's legal concerns, or to keep a client informed of legal proceedings. Charging exorbitant fees or overbilling is also considered misconduct, as is counseling a client to commit a crime. For example, trial lawyer Harvey Myerson was suspended in 1992 from the practice of law by the New York Supreme Court after he was convicted of overbilling by millions of dollars (*In re Myerson*, 182 A.D.2d 242, 588 N.Y.S.2d 142 [N.Y. App. Div. 1992]).

Many types of attorney misconduct involve a CONFLICT OF INTEREST on the part of the attorney. A conflict of interest arises when an attorney puts personal interests ahead of professional responsibilities to the client. The model rules specify the potential for conflict of interest in many different situations. Thus, for example, an attorney who by representing one client adversely affects another client has a conflict of interest and is guilty of misconduct. Conflict of interest rules also forbid an attorney to enter into a business transaction with a client unless the client is fully aware of how the transaction will affect his or her legal representation and agrees to the transaction in writing. Similarly, an attorney is guilty of misconduct if he or she makes a deal with the client for acquisition of the book, film, or media rights to the client's story. Providing a client with financial assistance also introduces a conflict of interest into the attorney-client relationship.

If an attorney is related to another attorney as parent, child, sibling, or spouse, that attorney may not represent a client in opposition to the related attorney except when given consent to do so by the client. This type of conflict of interest has become increasingly common as more women enter the legal profession and the number of marriages between attorneys grows. State bar associations, such as that of Michigan, have held that these guidelines also apply to lawyers who are living together or dating but are not married. The potential for conflict of interest when the opposing attorneys are married or romantically involved is clear. Imagine a woman representing a client in a personal injury lawsuit seeking millions of dollars worth of damages from a manufacturer, with her husband representing the manufacturer. As a couple, they have a monetary interest in gaining a large settlement from the manufacturer, thereby giving the husband an incentive to lose his case. Given this conflict of interest, the couple is obligated to reveal to their clients the fact that they are married. If the clients agree to go ahead with the case regardless of the conflict of interest, then the attorneys may decide to continue their representation.

Special examples of conflict of interest have arisen in cases involving indigent defendants who must use publicly provided defense attorneys. In many jurisdictions, it is considered misconduct for an attorney to refuse court appointment as a public service defender for a poor client, even when a spouse's legal associate or firm is involved on the opposing side of the case. Normally, for example, state bar associations allow a district attorney to prosecute persons defended by partners or associates of the district attorney's spouse as long as the client is notified of the situation; similarly, they will allow a district attorney's spouse to defend persons prosecuted by other members of the district attorney's staff. Nevertheless, in a 1992 case, *Haley v. Boles*, 824 S.W.2d 796, the Texas Court of Appeals found that a conflict of interest gave a court-appointed attorney grounds to refuse appointment as a public defender for a poor client. The prosecutor was married to the court-appointed counsel's law partner, creating a potential conflict of interest. According to the court's decision, a poor defendant who must rely on a public defender has fewer choices for legal representation than a defendant who can afford to employ her or his own attorney. Therefore, an attorney who has a conflict of interest must be able to refuse to represent a client as a public defender without being charged with misconduct, thereby ensuring that the client receives legal representation free of a conflict of interest.

Any breach of the trust that underlies the relationship between an attorney and a client by the attorney can be considered misconduct. For example, an attorney is often called upon to hold or transfer money for a client, and in this situation, the client places an extraordinary amount of trust in the lawyer. Any misuse of the client's money by the attorney—called misappropriation of client funds—constitutes a serious breach of trust and a gross example of misconduct. This offense includes stealing from the client, mingling the attorney's money with that of the client, and controlling client funds without authorization. The model rules require that funds given to a lawyer by a client be kept in an account separate from the lawyer's own account.

To encourage clients to inform their attorneys of all details relevant to a case, ethical codes also entrust attorneys with preserving the confidentiality of the information their clients give them; any failure to do so constitutes misconduct on the part of the attorney. The law protects attorney-client confidentiality with the principle of attorney-client privilege, and under very few circumstances is it lawful to breach this privilege of confidentiality. The privilege may be revoked to prevent the client from "committing a criminal act that . . . is likely to result in imminent death or substantial bodily harm" (*Model Rules of Professional Conduct*, Rule 1.6 1983), or to respond to civil or criminal proceedings made by the client against the attorney. Except for these rare cases, only the client may waive the attorney-client privilege of confidentiality.

Sexual contact between an attorney and a client is almost always considered a breach of conduct. Sexual contact represents a clear breach of attorney-client trust. It is also a clear conflict of interest because it can easily result in the attorney's placing his or her own needs above those of the client, and it makes it difficult for the attorney to argue the client's case dispassionately. See also box on attorney-client sexual relations.

Other Types of Misconduct As the model rules indicate, an attorney may be charged with misconduct if she or he commits a criminal act. However, not all violations of the law may result in professional censure. According to the ABA, a lawyer is professionally responsible "only for offenses that indicate lack of those characteristics relevant to law practice."

Attorney-Client Sexual Relations

The American Bar Association (ABA) has recognized sexual relations between attorneys and their clients as a significant ethical problem for the legal profession. The ABA's Standing Committee on Ethics and Professional Responsibility addressed this issue in 1992 by issuing a formal opinion (no. 92-364). Although the opinion acknowledged that the Model Rules of Professional Conduct do not specifically address the issue of attorney-client sex, it argued that an attorney's sexual relationship with a current client "may involve unfair exploitation of the lawyer's fiduciary position and presents a significant danger that the lawyer's ability to represent the client adequately may be impaired, and that as a consequence the lawyer may violate both the Model Rules and the Model Code." Becoming sexually intimate with a client, the opinion adds, undermines the "objective detachment" necessary for legal representation because "[t]he roles of lover and lawyer are potentially conflicting ones." In addition, the opinion argued, attorney-client sex introduces a clear conflict of interest into a case, and it may also compromise attorney-client privilege, the principle that ensures the confidentiality of lawyer-client communication. Any secrets revealed to an attorney by a client outside of their legal relationship may not be protected by attorney-client privilege.

Proponents of professional rules against attorney-client sexual contact argue that the legal profession should follow the example of other professions such as psychology and psychiatry, and create strict sanctions against sex with clients. Legal clients, these proponents say, are often vulnerable when dealing with attorneys, particularly in such areas of legal practice as family law. A lawyer who becomes sexually involved with a client in a divorce proceeding can take advantage of the client under-going emotional trauma. That lawyer may hinder any attempts at reconciliation between a couple and complicate matters for any children involved. Sexual relationships between lawyer and client may also affect custody and child visitation decisions in the case. The American Academy of Matrimonial Lawyers, in its Standards of Conduct in Family Law Litigation, specifically prohibits attorney-client sex: "An attorney should never have a sexual relationship with a client or opposing counsel during the time of the representation" (§ 2.16 [1991]).

Some attorneys object to such rules, arguing that they interfere with their First Amendment rights to freedom of association. They bristle at the notion of state bar associations regulating the private affairs of consenting adults. Nevertheless, attorneys are increasingly being disciplined for becoming sexually involved with clients, and state bar associations are drafting clearer and more stringent rules against attorney-client sexual contact. Wisconsin's Supreme Court, for example, in 1987, revoked the license of an attorney in part because he had sex with a client (*In re Hallows*, 136 Wis. 2d 72, 401 N.W.2d 557). The attorney, the court argued, was "placing his interests above" those of his client. In 1990, the same court for the first time suspended the license of a criminal lawyer who had sex with a client (*In re Ridgeway*, 158 Wis. 2d 452, 462 N.W.2d 671). Oregon and Minnesota have adopted outright bans on attorney-client sexual contact. Rule 1.8(k) of the Minnesota Rules of Professional Conduct, which became effective July 1, 1994, forbids attorney-client sexual contact during the conduct of a professional legal relationship. It allows exceptions to the rule only for relationships beginning before legal representation has commenced or after it has ended. In the case of clients that are organizations rather than individuals, an attorney may not have sexual contact with any member of the client organization directly overseeing the case.

These include violations involving "violence, dishonesty, breach of trust, or interference with the administration of justice" (*Model Rules of Professional Conduct*, Rule 3). Nevertheless, violations of the law may seriously impair an attorney's professional standing.

Ethical rules also govern the conduct of attorneys before courts. Thus, an attorney is guilty of misconduct toward the court if he or she brings a frivolous, or unnecessary, proceeding to court; makes false statements to the court; offers false evidence; or unlawfully obstructs another party's access to evidence. It is also considered misconduct if an attorney at-tempts to influence a judge or juror by illegal means, such as BRIBERY or intimidation, or states personal opinions regarding the justness of a cause or the credibility of a witness. Special rules govern trial publicity as well. These forbid an attorney to make statements outside of court that will influence a court proceeding. For example, an attorney may not make statements related to the character, credibility, guilt, or innocence of a suspect or witness in a court proceeding. Attorneys are forbidden to communicate directly or indirectly with a party represented by another lawyer in the same matter, unless they receive permission from the other attorney. This law is designed to protect laypersons involved in legal proceedings from possibly hurting their cases by speaking with the opposing lawyer.

Federal and state laws also define attorney misconduct and empower judges to discipline wayward attorneys. Rule 11 of the Federal Rules of Civil Procedure (28 U.S.C.A.), for example, requires sanctions for lawyers and clients who file frivolous or abusive claims in court. In a 1989 case, *Nasco, Inc. v. Calcasieu Television & Radio*, 124 F.R.D. 120 (W.D. La.), a federal district judge suspended two lawyers and disbarred another for "illegal and fraudulent schemes and conspiracies" designed to slow a case in court for the benefit of their client.

Beginning in the late 1980s, attorneys have been required to report the misconduct of other lawyers, with failure to do so considered to be misconduct in itself and resulting in serious disciplinary measures. A 1989 Illinois Supreme Court ruling, *In re Himmel*, 125 Ill. 2d 531, 533 N.E.2d 790, found that attorneys have a duty to report other lawyers' misconduct even when a client has instructed them not to do so. The Illinois Supreme Court suspended James H. Himmel from the practice of law for one year after he failed to report a misappropriation of client funds by another lawyer, a violation of rule 1-103(a) of the Illinois Code of Professional Responsibility. Himmel's failure to report, the court found, had allowed the offending attorney to bilk other clients as well. The attorney guilty of misappropriating funds was disbarred.

Lawyers have also been found guilty of misconduct with regard to advertising of their services. It is legal and ethical for attorneys to advertise, but if that advertising is false, deceptive, or misleading, makes unsubstantiated comparisons to another lawyer's services, or proposes means contrary to rules of professional conduct, the attorney can be charged with misconduct. For example, an attorney was disbarred in Maryland for publishing misleading advertisements soliciting customers for "quickie" foreign divorces and misrepresenting his competence and knowledge of the law (*Attorney Grievance Committee v. McCloskey*, 306 Md. 677, 511 A.2d 56 [1986]).

CROSS-REFERENCES

American Bar Association; Attorney-Client Privilege; Civil Procedure; Ethics; Legal Advertising; Legal Representation; Malpractice; Model Rules of Professional Conduct; Public Defender; Trial.

ATTORNEY'S LIEN The right of a lawyer to hold a client's property or money until payment has been made for legal aid and advice given.

In general, a LIEN is a security interest used by a creditor to ensure payment by a debtor for money owed. Since an attorney is entitled to payment for services performed, the attorney has a claim on a client's property until compensation is duly made.

A *charging lien* is an attorney's right to a portion of the JUDGMENT that was won for the client through professional services. It is a specific lien and only covers a lawyer's claim on money obtained in a particular ACTION.

A *retaining lien* is more general in its scope. It extends to all of a client's property that an attorney might come into possession of during the course of a lawsuit. Until an attorney is compensated for services, he or she has a claim or interest in such property.

AUCTIONS A sale open to the general public and conducted by an auctioneer, a person empowered to conduct such a sale, at which property is sold to the highest bidder.

A *bid* is an offer by a *bidder*, a prospective purchaser, to pay a designated amount for the property on sale.

A Dutch auction is a method of sale that entails the public offer of the property at a price in excess of its value, accompanied by a gradual reduction in price until the item is purchased.

According to the Uniform Commercial Code (UCC), a body of law governing commercial transactions that has been adopted by the states, the auction sale of any item concludes with the fall of the hammer or in any other customary manner. Such a sale is "with reserve," which denotes that the goods can be withdrawn at any time, until the auctioneer announces the completion of the sale, unless the goods are explicitly put up "without reserve," which signifies that the article cannot be withdrawn after the call for bids unless no bid is made within a reasonable time. In both types of auctions, the bidder can withdraw a bid prior to the auctioneer's announcement that the sale has been completed.

Regulation As a legitimate business enterprise, auctions cannot be proscribed. They are not above reasonable regulation by both state and local authorities. Some states subject auction sales to taxation.

In the absence of statutes, any person can act as an auctioneer, but a LICENSE, which usually restricts his or her authority to a certain region, is often required. Licensing officers can refuse to issue a license, but only if done reasonably, impartially, and to promote the interest of the community.

PHOTOREPORTERS

Sotheby's auctions are well known and are the setting for the sale of many valuable art pieces and artifacts.

Agency of Auctioneer   An auctioneer serves as the AGENT of the seller who employs him or her, and the auctioneer must act in GOOD FAITH, advance the interest of the seller, and conduct the sale in accordance with the seller's instructions. If REAL PROPERTY or goods priced at $500 or more are sold at auction, a written agreement is necessary to satisfy the STATUTE OF FRAUDS, an old English law adopted in the United States that requires certain CONTRACTS to be in writing. The auctioneer is authorized to sign a memorandum of sale on behalf of both parties, but this authority is limited and expires shortly after the sale has been concluded. Both the buyer and the seller are bound by the announcement of the auctioneer concerning the identity of the property and the terms and conditions of the sale.

In the absence of a statutory provision requiring authority to be in writing, an agent, pursuant to oral authorization, can execute any contract required to be in writing. The statutory provisions vary, however, in regard to the execution of contracts to purchase real property.

Because of the trust and confidence the seller reposes in an auctioneer, the individual cannot delegate the power to sell without special authority from the seller. The delegation of insignificant duties, such as the striking of the hammer and the announcement of the sale, is allowable if conducted pursuant to the auctioneer's immediate supervision and direction.

An auctioneer's authority normally terminates upon the completion of the sale and the collection of the purchase price, but the seller can revoke the authority at any time prior to the sale. According to some authorities, the buyer or seller can end the auctioneer's authority to sign a memorandum on his or her behalf be-tween the time of the fall of the hammer and the signing of the memorandum, but the prevailing view deems the auctioneer's authority to be irrevocable. Private sales by an auctioneer are generally impermissible.

Conduct and Validity of Sale   The owner of the property has the right to control the sale until its conclusion. Unless conditions are imposed by the seller, the auctioneer is free to conduct the sale in any manner chosen, in order to bar fraudulent bidders and to earn the confidence of honest purchasers. The auctioneer cannot amend the printed terms and conditions of the auction, but he or she is empowered to postpone the sale, if that is the desire. The auctioneer can modify the sale terms of goods advertised in a catalog at any time during the sale, if announced publicly and all of the bidders present are cognizant of it. The auctioneer may also retain the right to resell should there be an error or a dispute concerning the sale property. The description of the property in the catalog must be unambiguous. A significant error in a description might cause the cancellation of the sale, although trivial discrepancies between the property and the description are not problematic. The seller can withdraw property until the acceptance of a bid by an auctioneer.

A bid is an offer to purchase, and no obligations are imposed upon the seller until the bid is accepted. It can be made in any manner that demonstrates the bidder's willingness to pay a particular price for the auctioned property, whether orally, or in writing, or through bodily movements, such as a wave of the hand. Secret signals between the bidder and the auctioneer militate against equality in bidding and are thereby prohibited. The auctioneer accepts a bid by the fall of the hammer or by any other perceptible method that advises the bidder that the property is his or hers upon tendering the amount of the bid in accordance with the terms of the sale. An auctioneer can reject a bid on various grounds, such as where it is combined with terms or conditions other than those of the sale, or is below the minimum price acceptable to the owner.

As a general rule, any act of the auctioneer, seller, or buyer that prevents an impartial, free, and open sale or that reduces competition in the bidding is contrary to public policy. An agreement among prospective buyers not to bid has been held to VOID the sale to any buyer within this group. A purchase by a person who has not participated in the illegal agreement remains in effect. A *puffer* is a person who has no intention of buying but is hired by the seller to place fictitious bids in order to raise the bidding of genuine purchasers. In general, if a purchaser at an auction can prove that a puffer was employed, he or she can void the sale. Some jurisdictions require the buyer to have been financially hurt by the puffer, but others permit an individual to void a sale even if no harm occurred. Puffing and *by-bidding* are synonymous.

A deposit is not a PLEDGE but a partial payment of the purchase price, usually made payable to the auctioneer who retains it until the completion of the sale.

The property of one person should not be commingled and sold with the property of another by the auctioneer unless notice is furnished to all interested parties, or it might constitute FRAUD.

An auctioneer is not entitled to bid on property that he or she has been hired to sell, but the auctioneer can, however, bid a particular sum for a purchaser without violating any duties to the seller or even to other prospective bidders.

An auctioneer who does not have the required license but who executes a sale can be penalized, but the sale remains valid; an auction is void, however, when it is conducted without the owner's consent.

Rights and Liabilities of Buyer and Seller

In an unconditional sale, title passes to the bidder when the auctioneer's hammer falls. If conditions exist, title passes upon their fulfillment or through their WAIVER, the intentional relinquishment of a known right. The bidder is ordinarily entitled to possession when he or she pays the amount bid.

A person who bids on behalf of another is personally liable for the bid unless the person discloses this relationship to the auctioneer.

Fraud, or a misrepresentation of a material fact on which the buyer detrimentally relied, or the seller's failure to provide good TITLE furnishes a basis for setting aside the sale.

The seller has a LIEN, a security interest, on the property until the price is paid. If the purchaser fails to comply with the conditions of a sale, the seller can regard the sale as abandoned and sue for DAMAGES. Where a resale occurs, and the price is lower than the contract price, the defaulting buyer in some jurisdictions is liable to the seller for the difference between what he or she had agreed to pay and what the seller receives on the resale. In general, whether a deposit or a partial payment must be repaid depends upon which party was responsible for the incompleted sale. If the buyer is responsible, he or she cannot recover either the deposit or partial payment.

Compensation

The party employing the auctioneer pays a commission regardless of whether he or she procures a sale, unless the auctioneer is responsible for the failure of the sale. The auctioneer is entitled to a reasonable sum unless a statute or contract provision determines the amount.

Liabilities of Auctioneer

An auctioneer is usually liable to the seller for monetary losses attributable to his or her NEGLIGENCE in failing to follow the seller's instructions. The auctioneer can also be responsible to the buyer for fraud, conduct in excess of authority, and failure to deliver the goods. Since the auctioneer is a stakeholder, a third party designated by two or more persons to retain on deposit money or property that is the subject of a dispute, the auctioneer is liable to the buyer in those instances where the buyer is entitled to the return of the deposit. An auctioneer who sells property on behalf of one who does not own it, and delivers the proceeds to that person, is personally liable to the rightful owner even though the auctioneer acted in good faith and without knowledge of the absence of title. He or she can recover his or her losses from the person who received the proceeds in the form of damages that he or she was ordered to pay to the actual owner.

See also SALES; UNIFORM COMMERCIAL CODE.

AUDIT A systematic examination of financial or accounting records by a specialized inspector, called an auditor, to verify their accuracy and truthfulness. A HEARING during which financial data are investigated for purposes of AUTHENTICATION.

BIOGRAPHY

AUGUSTUS, JOHN During the nineteenth century criminal law, in particular, was slowly evolving toward a more humanistic and equitable approach than had previously been taken. One man in Massachusetts, through an act of compassion, initiated a procedure that was the forerunner of the PROBATION system.

John Augustus, born 1785, was a cobbler in Boston during the 1840s. He was interested in the legal process and often visited the criminal courts in Boston. In 1841, he was especially touched by the plight of a person convicted of public intoxication who begged the court not to incarcerate him and promised to give up alcohol in return for his freedom. Augustus, sensing hope for the man's rehabilitation, paid the man's bail; three weeks later, Augustus returned to court with his sober charge. The judge was favorably moved, and the man was allowed to go free.

After his initial success, John Augustus continued to take custody of convicted criminals.

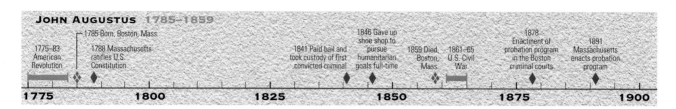

JOHN AUGUSTUS 1785–1859

1775–83 American Revolution

1785 Born, Boston, Mass.

1788 Massachusetts ratifies U.S. Constitution

1841 Paid bail and took custody of first convicted criminal

1846 Gave up shoe shop to pursue humanitarian goals full-time

1859 Died, Boston, Mass.

1861–65 U.S. Civil War

1878 Enactment of probation program in the Boston criminal courts

1891 Massachusetts enacts probation program

1775   1800   1825   1850   1875   1900

By the time he died in 1859, he had helped nearly 2,000 prisoners. He used his own money for bail or received financial aid from other residents of Boston who believed in his cause; several of these followers continued the program after his death.

Augustus's benevolence was made an official practice in 1878 when a law was enacted assigning a regular probation officer to the Boston criminal courts. In 1891, the commonwealth of Massachusetts adopted a similar program, and during the next nine years, other states began to provide for probationary programs based on the humanitarian actions of John Augustus.

Augustus died June 21, 1859, in Boston, Massachusetts.

AUSTIN, JOHN John Austin was a nineteenth-century legal theorist and reformer who achieved fame posthumously for his published work on *analytical jurisprudence*, the legal philosophy that separates positive law from moral principles.

According to Austin, positive law is a series of both explicit and implicit commands from a higher authority. The law reflects the sovereign's wishes and is based on the sovereign's power. Backed by sanctions and punishment, it is not the same as divine law or human-inspired moral precepts. Viewing the law in this way, Austin did not so much question what it ought to be but revealed it for what he thought it was. Analytical jurisprudence sought to consider law in the abstract, outside of its ethical or daily applications. In Austin's view, religious or moral principles should not affect the operation of law.

Austin was not as influential in his lifetime as his fellow Utilitarians Jeremy Bentham, James Mill, and John Stuart Mill. His intellectual

BIOGRAPHY

"A LAW . . . IN ITS LITERAL MEANING . . . MAY BE SAID TO BE A RULE LAID DOWN FOR THE GUIDANCE OF AN INTELLIGENT BEING BY AN INTELLIGENT BEING HAVING POWER OVER HIM."

output did not match his potential, owing in part to poor health and a self-defeating attitude. Yet Austin is regarded by legal historians as a significant figure in the development of modern English jurisprudence.

Austin was born in England in 1790, the son of a prosperous miller. After a stint in the army, he studied law but was not an enthusiastic or especially capable practitioner. Reflecting a keen, analytical mind, Austin's skills lay in writing and theory rather than in equity pleadings. Austin gave up his law practice in 1825 and, in 1826, was named the first professor of jurisprudence at the University of London. To strengthen his academic credentials, Austin studied Roman law and German civil law in Heidelberg and Bonn from 1827 to 1828.

Austin's professional pursuits were undermined by his ill health and self-doubt. In 1832, he resigned from teaching because his lectures were poorly attended. During the same year, Austin published the barely noticed *The Province of Jurisprudence Determined*, a collection of his university lectures. Shortly thereafter, he accepted a post on the Criminal Law Commission, but he resigned from that when his suggestions were not followed. Austin's attempt, in 1834, to resume his legal lectures for the Society of the Inner Temple failed.

In 1838 Austin served on a commission investigating complaints about the management of Malta, a British colony. This time, his efforts were successful, as his work led to tariff reform and improvements in the Maltese government.

The following decade, Austin lived abroad with his wife, Sarah Taylor Austin. In 1848, the couple returned to England, where Austin died on December 1, 1859. In 1863, his widow republished *The Province of Jurisprudence Deter-*

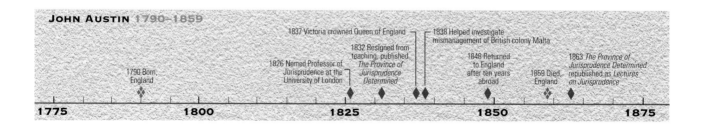

JOHN AUSTIN 1790–1859

1790 Born, England

1826 Named Professor of Jurisprudence at the University of London

1837 Victoria crowned Queen of England

1832 Resigned from teaching; published *The Province of Jurisprudence Determined*

1838 Helped investigate mismanagement of British colony Malta

1848 Returned to England after ten years abroad

1859 Died, England

1863 *The Province of Jurisprudence Determined* republished as *Lectures on Jurisprudence*

1775   1800   1825   1850   1875

mined under the new title *Lectures on Jurisprudence*. This single volume received the widespread acclaim that had eluded Austin during his lifetime.

Although critics of analytical jurisprudence do not accept Austin's separation of social and moral considerations from the law, they value his contributions to the discussion. Austin's writings influenced other prominent legal theorists, including U.S. Supreme Court justice Oliver Wendell Holmes, Jr.

CROSS-REFERENCES

Bentham, Jeremy; Holmes, Oliver Wendell; Jurisprudence; Mill, John Stuart; Utilitarianism.

AUTHENTICATION

The confirmation rendered by an OFFICER OF A COURT that a CERTIFIED COPY of a JUDGMENT is what it purports to be, an accurate duplicate of the original judgment. In the law of EVIDENCE, the act of establishing a statute, record, or other document, or a certified copy of such an instrument as genuine and official so that it can be used in a lawsuit to prove an issue in dispute.

Self-authentication of particular categories of documents is provided by federal and state rules of evidence. A deed or conveyance that has been acknowledged by its signers before a NOTARY PUBLIC, a certified copy of a public record, or an official publication of the government are examples of self-authenticating documents.

AUTHORITIES

Legal powers. Governmental agencies created by statute for specific public purposes, such as a county highway authority. References to statutes, precedents, judicial decision, and legal textbooks that support the position of a party to a lawsuit made in the BRIEFS submitted by the attorneys for the parties to the court that is to hear the case or during the trial in the oral arguments.

PRIMARY AUTHORITIES are citations to statutes, court decisions, and government regulations that, if having the force of law, must be applied by the court to dispose of the issue in dispute if they are relevant to the matter. SECONDARY AUTHORITIES are references to TREATISES, textbooks, or RESTATEMENTS that explain and review general principles of law that buttress a party's position in a lawsuit. Such authorities have no legal effect and can be disregarded by the court.

Authorities are also cited by scholars in legal treatises, HORNBOOKS, and restatements to establish the bases of the statements and conclusions contained in the works.

AUTHORIZE

To empower another with the legal right to perform an action.

The Constitution authorizes Congress to regulate interstate commerce.

AUTOMOBILES

No invention has so transformed the landscape of the United States of America as the automobile, and no other country has so thoroughly adopted the automobile as its favored means of transportation. Automobiles are used both for pleasure and for commerce and are typically the most valuable type of PERSONAL PROPERTY owned by U.S. citizens. Because autos are expensive to acquire and maintain, heavily taxed, favorite targets of thieves, a major cause of air and noise pollution, and capable of causing tremendous personal injuries and property damage, the body of law surrounding them is quite large. Automobile law covers the four general phases in the life cycle of an automobile: its manufacture, sale, operation, and disposal.

Brief History of the Automobile The first automobile powered by an internal combustion engine was invented and designed in Germany during the 1880s. In 1903, Henry Ford founded the Ford Motor Company and started an era of U.S. leadership in auto production that would last for most of the twentieth century. In 1908, Ford introduced the highly popular Model T, which by 1913 was being manufactured through assembly line techniques. Innovations by Ford, General Motors, and other manufacturers near Detroit made that city the manufacturing center for the U.S. car industry. By the 1920s, General Motors had become the world's largest auto manufacturer, a distinction it still held in the mid-1990s. Over time, the auto industry in all countries became increasingly concentrated in the hands of a few companies, and by 1939, the Big Three—Ford, General Motors, and Chrysler Corporation—had 90 percent of the U.S. market.

In 1929, there were roughly 5 million autos in the United States. All those cars required an infrastructure of roads, and by the end of World War II, the federal government had begun aggressively to fund highway development. With the intention of improving the nation's ability to defend itself, Congress passed the Federal-Aid Highway Act of 1944 (58 Stat. 838). It authorized construction of a system of multiple-lane, limited-access freeways, officially called the National System of Interstate and Defense Highways, designed to connect 90 percent of all U.S. cities of fifty thousand or more people. In 1956, the Federal-Aid Highway Act (23 U.S.C.A. § 103 [West 1995]) established the Federal Highway Trust Fund, which still provides 90 percent of the financing for interstate highways. By 1990, the interstate highway system was 99.2 percent complete and had cost $125 billion.

During the 1970s, the U.S. auto industry began to lose ground to Japanese and European automakers, and U.S. citizens relied to an increasing degree on imported autos. Japan, for example, surpassed the United States in auto production in the 1970s. Oil shortages and embargoes during the 1970s caused the price of gasoline to rise and put a premium on smaller autos, most of which were produced by foreign companies. Foreign cars also earned a reputation for higher quality during this period. The share of foreign-made cars in the U.S. market rose from 7.6 percent in 1960 to 24.9 percent in 1984.

In the early 1980s, the U.S. auto companies were suffering greatly, and the U.S. government bailed out the nearly bankrupt Chrysler Corporation. The U.S. government also negotiated a quota system with Japan that called for limits on Japanese autos imported into the United States, thereby raising the prices of Japanese cars. By the 1990s, the U.S. auto companies had regained much of the ground lost to foreign companies. In the mid-1990s, however, international manufacturing agreements meant that few cars, U.S. or foreign, were made entirely in one country.

Manufacture Throughout the twentieth century, automakers were required to conform to ever stricter standards regarding the manufacture of their vehicles. These rules were designed to improve the safety, fuel consumption, and emissions of the auto.

Safety Standards As autos increased in number and became larger and faster, and people traveled more miles a year in them, the number of motor vehicle deaths and injuries rose. By 1965, fifty thousand people were being killed in motor vehicle accidents every year, making automobiles the leading cause of accidental death for all age groups and the overall leading cause of death for the population below age forty-four. Between 1945 and 1995, 2 million people died and about 200 million were injured in auto accidents—many more than were wounded and injured in all the wars in the nation's history combined.

Beginning in the 1960s, consumer and automobile safety advocates began to press for federal safety standards for the manufacture of automobiles that would reduce such harrowing statistics. The most famous of these advocates was Ralph Nader, who published a 1965 book on the deficiencies of auto safety, called *Unsafe at Any Speed: The Designed-in Dangers of the American Automobile*. From 1965 to 1995, more than fifty safety standards were imposed on vehicle manufacturers, regulating the construction of windshields, safety belts, head restraints, brakes, tires, lighting, door strength, roof strength, and bumper strength.

In 1966, Congress passed the National Traffic and Motor Vehicle Act (15 U.S.C.A. § 1381 note, 1391 et seq. [1995]), which established a new federal regulatory agency, the National Highway Safety Bureau, later renamed the National Highway Traffic Safety Administration (NHTSA). The NHTSA was given a mandate to establish and enforce rules that would force manufacturers to build vehicles that could better avoid and withstand accidents. It was also given the power to require manufacturers to recall and repair defects in their motor vehicles, and the authority to coordinate state programs aimed at improving driver behavior. Also in 1966, Congress passed the Highway Safety Act (23 U.S.C.A. §§ 105, 303 note, et seq. [1995]), which provided for federal guidance and funding to states for the creation of highway safety programs.

As a result of these new laws, nineteen federal safety regulations came into effect on January 1, 1968. The regulations specified accident avoidance standards governing such vehicle features as brakes, tires, windshields, lights, and transmission controls. They also mandated more costly crash-protection standards. These included occupant-protection requirements for seat belts, energy-absorbing steering wheels and bumpers, head restraints, padded instrument panels, and stronger side doors. These auto safety standards have significantly reduced traffic fatalities. Between 1968 and 1979, the annual motor vehicle death rate decreased 35.2 percent, from 5.4 to 3.5 deaths per 100 million vehicle miles.

The seat belt requirement is usually considered the most important and effective safety

Safety devices and the use of a seat belt may have saved the driver of this crashed car from serious injury.

© TONY FREEMAN/PHOTOEDIT

Unsafe at Any Speed

For over half a century the automobile has brought death, injury, and the most inestimable sorrow and deprivation to millions of people." So Ralph Nader began his 1965 book *Unsafe at Any Speed: The Designed-in Dangers of the American Automobile,* a landmark in the history of U.S. consumer protection.

Nader's book recounts how U.S. automobile manufacturers resisted attempts to improve auto safety in the 1950s and 1960s. Even when makers of other vehicles such as planes, boats, and trains were forced to adhere to safety regulations, automakers were still largely uncontrolled in the area of safety. "The gap between existing design and attainable safety," Nader wrote, "has widened enormously in the post-war period."

Nader examined how auto companies lobbied against safety regulation and organized public relations campaigns that asserted over and over again that most injuries were the result of driver error. He argued that the best and most cost-effective way to reduce auto injuries is not to try to alter driver behavior—as honorable a goal as that might be—but to require automakers to design cars that better prevent accidents from occurring and better protect passengers if accidents do occur.

In telling his story, Nader cited sobering statistics on traffic injuries and fatalities, including the fact that auto accidents caused the deaths of 47,700 in 1964—"the extinguishment of about one and three-quarter million years of expected lifetimes," he noted—and one-third of all hospitalizations for injuries and 25 percent of all cases of partial and complete paralysis due to injury. Borrowing the zeal and spirit of the civil rights reform movement and the faith in technology of the space program, Nader looked at traffic fatalities as a public health issue that can be resolved through public action and technological innovation. Quoting Walt Whitman's epigram "If anything is sacred, the human body is sacred," Nader asserted that he was attempting to protect the "body rights" of U.S. citizens.

To protect those rights, Nader used his book to call for a number of different strategies to reduce traffic fatalities and injuries: federal safety standards; a federal facility for auto safety research, design, and testing; increased manufacturer research and development for safety technology; improved consumer information with regard to auto safety; better disclosure of auto manufacturers' safety engineering efforts; and the creation of a department of transportation. It is a mark of Nader's foresight and determination that all of those goals were achieved in the decades following the publishing of *Unsafe at Any Speed.* See also Nader, Ralph.

standard. According to one study, seat belts that attach across both the lap and the shoulder reduce the probability of serious injury in an accident by 64 percent and of fatalities by 32 percent for front-seat occupants. However, because people do not always use restraints that require their active participation, autos are now required to have passive restraint systems such as automatic seat belts and air bags. Air bags pop out instantly in a crash and form a cushion that prevents the occupants from hitting the windshield or dashboard. These devices can substantially reduce the motor vehicle death rate. Cars made after 1990 must have either automatic seat belts or air bags, for front-seat occupants.

However, many auto safety experts point out that regulations on the manufacture of automobiles can only go so far in reducing injuries. Studies indicate that only 13 percent of auto accidents result from mechanical failure, and of those that do, most are caused by poor maintenance, not inadequate design or construction. Other analysts maintain that safety regulations cause a phenomenon known as offsetting be-

havior. According to this theory, people will drive more dangerously because they know their risk of injury is lower, putting themselves, their passengers, and other drivers, passengers, and pedestrians at greater risk and thereby offsetting the gain in safety caused by stricter manufacturing standards.

The NHTSA may also authorize RECALLS of cars on the road that it deems a safety hazard. In a recall, the federal government mandates that a manufacturer must repair all the vehicles that it has made that have a specific problem. Between 1976 and 1980, the NHTSA authorized the recall of over 39 million vehicles. Recall is a controversial policy. One problem with it is that, typically, only 50 percent of auto owners respond to recall notices.

Emissions Standards   Emissions standards are intended to reduce the amount of pollution coming from a car's exhaust system. Autos are major contributors to air pollution. Some cities, such as Los Angeles, have notorious problems with smog, a situation that can cause serious health problems for those with respiratory problems such as asthma and bronchitis. Air

What to Do If You Are in an Auto Accident

Sooner or later, you are likely to have an accident. Fortunately, it will probably be a minor collision that damages only the vehicles involved. However, whether you are in a minor or major accident, behaving coolly, calmly, and properly after it occurs could save you a lot of money and trouble.

Here are some suggestions on what to do if you are in an auto accident:

1. If possible, move your car to the side of the road or out of the way of traffic.
2. Turn on your car flashers or set up flares to warn other motorists of the accident.
3. Do not make any statements concerning who was at fault, or assign blame to anyone involved.
4. Help any persons who are injured. Most states have laws requiring you to render aid to anyone injured in the accident. Call an ambulance if necessary.
5. Write down the name, address, license plate number, and driver's license number of the other driver and ask to see his or her vehicle registration certificate and proof of insurance. Write down the insurance company name and policy number of the other driver. If asked, do the same for the other driver. Do not reveal the amount of your insurance coverage.
6. Write down the names and addresses of all passengers involved and of any witnesses to the accident.
7. Notify the police, particularly if anyone is hurt or injured at the scene.
8. Write down the names and badge numbers of any police officers at the scene.
9. If possible, take a picture of the scene of the accident, including damage to cars and skid marks.
10. Draw a rough diagram of what happened in the accident, noting road conditions, weather, and lighting.
11. If you suspect you have any injuries, obtain medical care.
12. Talk to a lawyer if you intend to file a lawsuit regarding the accident.

All states require those involved in an accident to file a report with the police or bureau of motor vehicles if the accident involves a death, a personal injury, or property damage above a certain amount, such as $500. Some states require that the report be made immediately; others allow five to thirty days. Failure to file a report is a misdemeanor in most states and could result in the suspension of your driver's license.

Some insurance companies provide their policyholders with accident report forms. Such forms make it easier to obtain the necessary information if you are in an accident. If you have them, keep them handy in your vehicle.

---

pollution also damages plants, reduces crop yields, lowers visibility, and causes acid rain. In 1970, Congress passed the Clean Air Act Amendments (Pub. L. No. 91-604, 84 Stat. 1676–1713 [42 U.S.C.A. § 7403 et seq. (1995)]), which set an ambitious goal of eliminating, by 1975, 90 to 95 percent of the emissions of hydrocarbons, carbon monoxide, and oxides of nitrogen as measured in 1968 automobiles. Manufacturers did not meet the target date for achieving this goal, and the deadline was extended. Also, the new emissions standards caused problems because they reduced fuel economy and vehicle performance.

Congress modified emissions standards in the 1977 Clean Air Act Amendments (42 U.S.C.A. § 7401 et seq.) and in the Clean Air Act Amendments of 1990 (Pub. L. No. 101-549, 104 Stat. 2399 [42 U.S.C.A. § 7401 et seq. (1995)]). The modified standards, as defined and monitored by the Environmental Protection Agency (EPA), included new requirements for states with low air quality to implement inspection and maintenance programs for all cars. These inspections were designed to ensure that vehicle emissions systems were working properly. In 1992, the EPA implemented strict emissions testing requirements for eighteen states and thirty-three cities with excessive levels of carbon monoxide and ozone.

California has been a leader in the setting of air quality standards. In 1989, it announced new guidelines that called for the phasing out of gas-fueled cars in southern California by the year 2010.

Critics maintain that federal emissions regulations have been too costly and that regulators should focus on reducing the emissions of more significant polluters, such as power plants and factories.

Fuel Efficiency Standards In the 1975 Energy Policy and Conservation Act (Pub. L. No. 94-163, 89 Stat. 871 [codified as amended in scattered sections of 12 U.S.C.A., 15 U.S.C.A., and 42 U.S.C.A.]), Congress created a set of corporate average fuel economy (CAFE) standards for new cars manufactured in the United States. The secretary of transportation was empowered with overseeing these standards. The standards mandated that each car manufacturer achieve an average fuel economy of 27.5 miles per gallon (mpg) for its entire fleet of cars by 1985. Manufacturers that did not achieve these standards were to be fined. In 1980, an additional SALES TAX at purchase was placed upon "gas guzzlers" (cars that fail to achieve certain levels of fuel economy). The more a car's gas mileage is below a set standard—which was 22.5 mpg in 1986—the greater the tax. For example, a 1986 car that achieved less than 12.5 mpg was charged an additional sales tax of $3,850. Some members of Congress have lobbied for fuel efficiency standards as high as a 40 mpg fleet average for auto manufacturers.

The fleet-average fuel efficiency of cars nearly doubled between 1973 and 1984. However, detractors of fuel efficiency standards maintain that the increase in efficiency was not entirely due to federal standards. They argue that fuel efficiency would have risen without regulation, in response to higher gas prices and consumer demand for more efficient cars.

Import Quotas Faced with increasingly stiff competition from Japan and Europe, U.S. car manufacturers in the early 1980s pressed the federal government to limit the number of foreign cars imported into the United States. The administration of President Ronald Reagan responded by negotiating quotas, or limits, on Japanese car imports from 1981 to 1985. The Japanese voluntarily continued quotas on their car exports through the late 1980s, and quotas on pickup trucks from Japan remained in effect through the mid-1990s.

Tort Law and Automobile Manufacturing Courts have established that manufacturers may be held liable and sued for property damage and personal suffering caused by the products they have manufactured. Automobile manufacturers, like all manufacturers, are thus subject to PRODUCT LIABILITY law. Anyone who suffers harm, injury, or property damage from an improperly made auto may sue for DAMAGES. Actions that involve a breach of the manufacturer's responsibility to provide a reasonably safe vehicle are called TORTS.

Courts have found that auto manufacturers have a duty to reasonably design their vehicle against foreseeable accidents. The most important legal concept in this area is "crashworthiness"—a manufacturer's responsibility to make the car reasonably safe in the event of a crash.

The standard of crashworthiness makes it possible to hold manufacturers liable for a defect that causes or enhances injuries suffered in a crash, even if that defect did not cause the crash itself. Auto injuries are often the result of a "second collision," when the occupant's body strikes the interior of the car, or strikes an exterior object after being thrown from the vehicle. Second collisions can occur when the seat belt fails, for example. Other examples of failures in crashworthiness include instruments that protrude on a dashboard or a fuel tank that explodes after impact. The landmark case in this area of manufacturer liability was *Larsen v. General Motors Corp.*, 391 F.2d 495 (8th Cir. 1968), in which an individual was compensated for injuries suffered when his head struck a steering wheel in an accident. In another significant case, *Grimshaw v. Ford Motor Co.*, 119 Cal. App. Ct. 3d 757, 174 Cal. Rptr. 348 (1981), a California jury required Ford Motor Company to pay $125 million in PUNITIVE DAMAGES (later lowered to $3.5 million) to a teenager who was severely burned in a fire that resulted when his Ford Pinto was rear-ended and the fuel tank exploded.

Automakers may also be held liable for failure to warn of a product's dangerous tendencies. Manufacturers have, for example, been sued for failing to warn drivers that certain vehicles had a tendency to roll over under some conditions.

Sale, Lease, and Rental When shopping for a car, consumers generally receive their first information through advertising. States regulate automobile ads in different ways. In some states, an ad must state the number of advertised vehicles available for sale, the price, the dealer, and the factory-installed options and WARRANTY terms. Car buyers should beware of BAIT-AND-SWITCH advertising, in which a dealer advertises a specific car for sale without the intention of actually selling it. The ad lures the customer into the showroom so that she or he may be persuaded to buy a higher-priced, unadvertised vehicle. When buyers encounter this type of FRAUD, or any other type of consumer fraud, they should contact the consumer protection division of their state attorney general's office.

The STATUTE OF FRAUDS of the UNIFORM COMMERCIAL CODE (UCC) governs the sale of autos in every state except Louisiana. According to the UCC, an auto CONTRACT must be in writing in order to be considered valid in court. The purchaser and an AGENT of the seller—an authorized salesperson, supervisor, or manager—must sign the contract. Buyers should read all terms of the contract before signing. The contract should specify whether the car is new or used and include a description of the car, the car's vehicle identification number (VIN) (on the driver's side of the dashboard near the window), details of any trade-in, and the terms of financing, including the annual percentage rate.

Number of Motor Vehicles in Use in the United States, 1980 to 1993

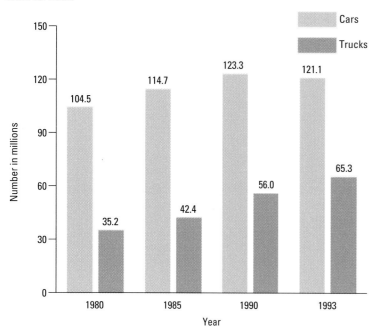

Average Age of Motor Vehicles in Use in the United States, 1980 to 1993

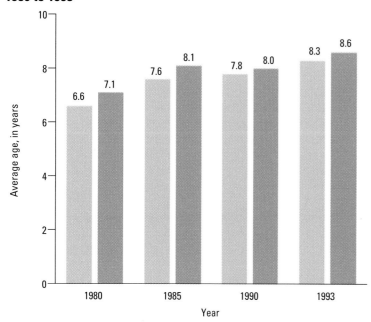

Source: American Automobile Manufacturers Association, Inc., Detroit, Mich., *Motor Vehicle Facts and Figures,* annual (copyright); and *World Motor Vehicle Data,* annual (copyright).

In most states, the TITLE for a new or used car passes to the buyer when the seller endorses the certificate of title. If the buyer does not maintain payments according to the finance agreement, the CREDITOR can repossess the car as COLLATERAL for the loan. The DEBTOR has the right to buy back the car (redeem the collateral), and can do so by paying the entire balance due plus REPOSSESSION costs. Eventually, the creditor may sell the car to another party. If the profit from the sale does not satisfy the debt, the debtor is liable for the difference. If the profit from the sale is greater than the debt, the creditor must pay the difference to the debtor. In some states, the creditor is required by the UCC to notify the debtor of the time, place, and manner of any sale of the car.

All used-car dealers must attach a buyer's guide to the side window of any car they are selling. It must state whether the car comes with a warranty; outline the specific coverage of any warranty; recommend that an independent mechanic inspect the car; state that all promises should be put in writing; and provide a list of potential problems with the car. The buyer's guide becomes part of any contract with the seller. The seller must be truthful about the car and should provide the buyer with the car's complete service records and a signed, written statement of the odometer reading and its accuracy. If the car does not perform as promised, a breach of warranty may have occurred. If an individual pays more than $500 for a used car, he or she should have a written contract and a BILL OF SALE. The latter is required in many states to register a car, and should include the date of sale; the year, make, and model of the car; the VIN; the odometer reading; the amount paid for the car and what form it took; the buyer's and seller's names, addresses, and phone numbers; and the seller's signature.

The sale of new automobiles is subject to what are popularly called lemon laws. *Lemon* is the slang term for a car that just does not work right; like a lemon, it leaves a bad taste in the mouth. Lemon laws, now in force in all states, entitle a car buyer to a replacement car or a refund if the purchased car cannot be satisfactorily repaired by the dealer. States vary in their requirements for determining whether a car is a lemon. Most define a lemon as a vehicle that has been taken in at least four times for the same repair or is out of service for a total of thirty days during the coverage period. The coverage period is usually one year from delivery or the duration of the written warranty, whichever is shorter. The owner must keep careful records of repairs and submit a written notice to the manufacturer stating the problems with the car and an intention to declare it unfit for use. Many states require that the buyer and the manufacturer or dealer submit to private ARBITRATION, a system of negotiating differences out of court. Increasingly, states are passing lemon laws for used as well as new cars.

A popular method of purchasing the use of a car is leasing. Leasing is essentially long-term rental. For persons who drive few miles a year, like to change cars often, or use their cars for business, leasing is an attractive option. A LEASE contract may or may not include other expenses such as sales tax, license fee, and insurance. In a closed-end, or "walkaway," lease contract, the car is returned at the end of the contract period and the LESSEE is free to "walk away" regardless of the value of the car. In an open-end lease, the lessee gambles that the car will be worth a stated price at the end of the lease. If the car is worth more than that price, the lessee may owe nothing or may be refunded the difference; if the car is worth less, the lessee will pay some or all of the difference. Payments are usually higher under a closed-end lease than under an open-end lease. Open-end leases more commonly have a purchase option at the end of the lease term.

To lease or rent an auto, an individual must show a valid driver's license and, usually, a major credit card. A rental business may require that a customer have a good driving record and be of a certain age, sometimes twenty-five years or older. An auto rental, as opposed to a lease, may be as short as one day. A rental company may offer a collision damage waiver (CDW) option, which provides insurance coverage for damages to the rented car. The CDW option does not cover personal injuries or personal property damage.

Operation and Maintenance The operation of an automobile on a public street or highway is a privilege that can be regulated by motor vehicle laws. The individual states derive authority to control traffic from their POLICE POWER, but often they delegate this authority to a local police force. On the national level, Congress is empowered to regulate motor vehicles that are engaged in interstate commerce.

Automobile regulations are provided for the safety and protection of the public. The laws must be reasonable and should not impose an extraordinary burden on the owners or operators. Such laws also provide a means of identifying vehicles involved in an accident or a theft and of raising revenue for the state by fees imposed on the owner or operator.

Registration and Licensing Every state requires the owner of a vehicle to possess two documents: a certificate of ownership, or title, and a certificate of registration. Through registration, the owner's name, the type of vehicle, the vehicle's license plate number, and the VIN are all registered with the state in a central government office. On payment of a fee, a certificate of registration and license plates are given to the owner as evidence of compliance with the law. The operator is required to display the license plates appropriately on the car—usually one on the front and one on the back of the vehicle—and have the certificate of registration and LICENSE in possession while driving and ready to display when in an accident or requested to do so by a police officer. If a driver moves to another state, she or he must register the vehicle in that state within a certain amount of time, either immediately or within twenty to thirty days.

A driver's license is also mandatory in every state. The age at which a state allows a person to drive varies, though it is usually at least sixteen to eighteen. Other qualifications for a driver's license include physical and mental fitness, comprehension of traffic regulations, and ability to operate a vehicle competently. Most states require a person to pass a written examination, an eye test, and a driving test before issuing a license. States generally allow an individual with a learner's permit or temporary license to operate a vehicle when accompanied by a licensed driver. This enables a person to develop the driving skills needed to qualify for a license. A license can be revoked or suspended when the motorist disregards the safety of people and property, when a physical or mental disability impairs driving ability, or if the motorist fails to accurately disclose information on the license application. When the state revokes a person's license, it permanently denies that person the right to drive; when it suspends a license, it temporarily denies the right to drive.

Traffic Laws Dozens of laws are related to the operation of an automobile, a large number of which vary by state. Minor traffic offenses include parking and speeding violations. More serious traffic offenses are reckless driving, leaving the scene of an accident, and driving without a license. Most states require motorists to file reports with the proper authorities when they are involved in accidents.

Speed limits vary by state. In 1973, during the height of the energy crisis, Congress defined a national speed limit of 55 mph in order to reduce gasoline consumption; the 55 mph limit also had the unintended effect of lowering the traffic fatality rate. Since then, most states have returned to an upper limit of 65 mph. Two types of speed limits are imposed: fixed maxi-

NO-FAULT AUTOMOBILE INSURANCE

Ever since the invention of automobiles, there have been automobile accidents. And with those accidents have come legal disputes about who was most at fault in causing them—and who should be forced to pay damages. The U.S. legal and political systems have struggled to determine the best way to handle the large number of legal disputes related to automobile accidents. Although the states vary in their procedures, two basic approaches have evolved. The first and older approach is the traditional liability litigation system, which attempts to determine, usually through jury trials, who is more liable, or more at fault, and must pay damages. The second and more recent approach is no-fault insurance, which simply allows each party to be compensated, regardless of fault, by its own insurance company for accident damages. Both approaches have their advantages and disadvantages, and the debate about which is better continues.

The traditional liability litigation system developed out of the English common law. Under this system, anyone who suffers an injury from a wrong or negligent act of another is free to sue the other party for damages. For example, someone who is paralyzed in an automobile accident and becomes confined to a wheelchair may sue the other driver or drivers involved in the accident. Whether or not the injured person receives payment for those damages is largely dependent on a determination of who was more at fault in causing the accident. If, in a court of law, it is determined that the other driver is at fault, then the injured person may collect a large sum from the other driver or, if the other driver has liability insurance, from the other driver's insurance company; if it is determined that the other driver is not at fault, the injured person may not receive any payments beyond those from her or his own insurance company.

This system of resolving disputes is also called the tort litigation process. In relation to automobile accidents, a tort is a civil (as opposed to criminal) wrong that causes an accident—for example, failure to practice caution while driving, thus causing a collision with another car and injuries to its passengers.

As time passed and auto accidents became more frequent, some people began to point out problems in the liability litigation system for resolving accident disputes. They noted that, owing to the complicated nature of many automobile accidents, it often took a great deal of time to determine who was at fault. As a result, many accident victims had to wait a considerable period before they could receive adequate compensation for their injuries. Other victims who may have been unable to work because of injuries, frequently settled for smaller amounts or even waived their right to a trial, in order to receive faster payment from insurance companies. Other critics of the liability litigation process claimed that the awards granted in auto accident cases varied greatly. Some people were overpaid, and others underpaid, for their damages. A better system, critics maintained, would make all drivers share in the cost of accidents. These critics began to press for a no-fault insurance system as an alternative to liability litigation.

As early as 1946, the Province of Saskatchewan, Canada, enacted no-fault auto insurance. Under a no-fault system, those involved in an accident are compensated for their physical injuries up to a certain limit; even the driver who causes the accident is paid for damages. In its purest form, no-fault automobile insurance does not allow those involved in an accident to sue each other, nor can any party recover damages for pain and suffering. However, no-fault plans are often combined with traditional liability systems to allow accident victims to sue when damages exceed a certain threshold. For example, in New York, it is possible to sue to recover for economic damages greater than $50,000 or for pain and suffering because of death or serious injury. No-fault insurance plans are al-

mum and prima facie. Under fixed maximum limits, it is unlawful to exceed the stated limit anywhere and at any time. Under prima facie limits, it is possible for a driver to prove in certain cases that a speed in excess of the limit was not unsafe, and therefore not unlawful, given the condition of the highway, amount of traffic, and other circumstances.

All states require children riding in automobiles to be restrained using safety belts or safety seats. Most states require adults to wear belts as well, though some require belts only for adults in the front seat. Violation of such laws results in a fine. In 1984, New York became the first state to pass a law making seat belts mandatory for adults.

Driving under the Influence Driving under the influence of alcohol or drugs is the major cause of traffic deaths in the United States. Drunk drivers kill an estimated twenty-five thousand people a year. States use different terms to describe driving under the influence of mind-altering chemicals, or what is popularly known as drunk driving. These include *driving under the influence (DUI)*, *operating under the influence (OUI)*, and *driving while intoxicated (DWI)*. To arrest someone for drunk driving, the state must have proof that the person is

ways compulsory, and every driver who wishes to register a vehicle must obtain at least the minimum standard of no-fault insurance.

In the United States, no-fault automobile insurance was first enacted by Massachusetts in 1971 (Mass. Gen. Laws Ann. ch. 90 § 34A et seq. [West 1995]) in response to public dissatisfaction with long, drawn-out, and expensive court cases for compensation of losses suffered in traffic accidents. In the same year, Congress considered no-fault as a comprehensive national automobile insurance plan, but the proposal never became law. That unsuccessful bill evolved into the National Standards for No-Fault Insurance Plans Act, which would have set federal standards for state no-fault insurance laws. It too did not pass. Opponents of the bill claimed that the states should be allowed to experiment with this new approach before a national plan was adopted. By the mid-1990s, roughly half the states had enacted no-fault insurance plans.

In arguing for no-fault insurance, advocates pointed out a number of advantages, including faster benefits payment and more equal damages awards to accident victims. They claimed that no-fault insurance would reduce the number of traffic-related court cases, thereby freeing up the courts to consider other cases. No-fault, they argued, would also reduce the cost of car insurance premiums as the legal costs associated with settling auto-related cases decreased. Since the establishment of no-fault insurance in many states, no-fault

advocates have bolstered their cause even more by pointing to statistics showing that no-fault plans increase the percentage of insurance benefits payments that go to victims rather than to lawyers and court costs. According to those statistics, in states without no-fault insurance, only forty-eight cents of each dollar spent for insurance premiums goes to those injured in accidents, whereas thirty-two cents goes to court costs and lawyers' fees. However, under the no-fault system in force in Michigan, for example, seventy-three cents of each insurance premium dollar goes to accident victims and four cents goes to court costs and lawyers' fees (Carper 1992).

On the other side of the issue, critics make a number of different points against no-fault insurance. Many, including trial lawyers and some consumer advocates, object to no-fault insurance's elimination of or substantial restrictions on the right to sue for damages. Many states, for example, allow injured parties to sue for "pain and suffering" only if they have sustained specific injuries such as dismemberment, disfigurement, or fracture. Often, "soft-tissue" injuries like whiplash are not allowed as adequate grounds for a lawsuit. Critics also maintain that no-fault insurance takes away the incentive to drive safely. Under the system of no-fault insurance, careless, negligent drivers are entitled to the same compensation in an accident as are careful, responsible drivers. In addition, critics of no-fault insurance cite evidence that the system has *not* reduced insurance

premiums. Under no-fault plans, they argue, the number of persons receiving benefits payments has increased, thus offsetting the reduction in legal costs.

It remains to be seen whether no-fault insurance will continue to spread to other states. Nevada and Pennsylvania have tried no-fault insurance plans and repealed them, with Nevada returning to a financial responsibility law and mandatory liability and property damage insurance. California has considered no-fault insurance for many years but has never adopted it. Some states are looking at compromise plans that preserve elements of both the traditional liability litigation system and the no-fault system. These plans, such as the one in New York, compensate all accident victims, regardless of fault, for basic economic losses—including medical and hospital expenses and lost wages or services—and in the process eliminate small cases where litigation is least cost-effective. At the same time, such plans preserve the right to sue for damages in cases of death or serious injury or when damages exceed a certain amount.

In the end, the question of how to handle auto accident disputes will be decided on the basis of which system—liability litigation, no-fault insurance, or a compromise between the two—is deemed better at limiting costs and at the same time preserving the value of fairness that underlies the U.S. system of justice.

See also Insurance; Torts.

---

under the influence of alcohol or drugs, and the person must be in actual physical control of a vehicle and impaired in the ability to operate it safely. Every state has "IMPLIED CONSENT" LAWS that require those with a driver's license to submit to sobriety tests if a police officer suspects they are intoxicated. These tests may include a field sobriety test (a test at the scene, such as walking a straight line), or blood, breath, or urine tests, usually administered at a police station. Refusal to take a sobriety test can result in suspension of the driver's license. Most states have "per se" laws that prohibit persons from driving if they have a blood-alcohol reading above a certain level. Several states have lowered their per se blood-alcohol limits to 0.08 percent. Penalties vary by state but can be particularly severe for repeat offenders, often involving jail sentences and revocation of driving privileges.

"DRAMSHOP" ACTS make those who sell liquor for consumption on their premises, such as bars and restaurants, liable for damages caused by an intoxicated patron's subsequent actions. In some states, individuals injured by a drunk driver have used such laws to sue bars and restaurants that served liquor to the driver. "Social host" statutes make hosts of parties who serve drugs or alcohol liable for any damages or injuries caused by guests who subsequently drive while under the influence.

Several national organizations have been formed to combat drunk driving. These include Mothers Against Drunk Driving (MADD) and Students Against Drunk Driving (SADD). The legal drinking age has been raised to twenty-one in every state, largely in an attempt to reduce drunk driving. Most states also make it illegal to transport an open alcoholic beverage container in a vehicle. Alcohol-related deaths as a proportion of all traffic deaths decreased from about 56 percent in 1982 to 47 percent in 1991.

Other Crimes Criminals both target and use automobiles in a number of different types of crime. Cars have been a favorite object of THEFT ever since their invention. As early as 1919, the Dyer Act, or National Motor Vehicle Theft Act (18 U.S.C.A. § 2311 et seq.), imposed harsh sentences on those who transported stolen vehicles across state lines. Car theft remains a serious problem in many areas of the country and is a major contributor to high insurance premiums in many urban areas. In 1994, Congress passed the Motor Vehicle Theft Prevention Act (18 U.S.C.A. § 511 et seq.; 42 U.S.C.A. § 13701 note, § 14171 [West 1995]), which established a program whereby owners can register their cars with the government, provide information on where their vehicles are usually driven, and affix a decal or marker to the cars. Owners who register their cars in the program authorize the police to stop the cars and question the occupants when the vehicles are out of their normal areas of operation.

Autos are also frequently used to commit crimes. Drivers whose NEGLIGENCE causes accidents that result in the death of other human beings may be found guilty of MANSLAUGHTER (the unlawful killing of another without malice aforethought, that is, without the intention of causing harm through an illegal act), including criminally negligent manslaughter, a crime punishable by imprisonment. Two types of crime that have received a great deal of public attention are drive-by shootings, in which occupants of a vehicle fire guns at pedestrians or at people in other cars, and car-jackings, in which criminals hijack, or take over, cars from their owners or operators, often robbing and sometimes killing the victims in the process. Because of the usually random nature of such crimes, the public has called for severe penalties for them. The Violent Crime Control and Law Enforcement Act of 1994 (Pub. L. No. 103-322, 108 Stat. 1796) made killings caused by drive-by shootings or car-jackings punishable by death.

Insurance Most states require the owner to acquire auto INSURANCE or deposit a bond before a vehicle can be properly registered. Insurance provides compensation for innocent people who suffer injuries resulting from the negligent operation of a vehicle. Other states have LIABILITY, or financial responsibility, statutes that require a motorist to pay for damages suffered in an accident resulting from his or her negligence and to furnish proof of financial capability to cover damages that he or she may cause in the future. These statutes do not necessarily require vehicle liability insurance.

About half of all states require that licensed drivers carry automobile insurance with liability, medical, and physical damage coverage. Liability insurance protects a vehicle owner against financial responsibility for damages caused by the negligence of the insured or other covered drivers. It consists of bodily injury, or personal liability, protection and property damage protection. Medical payments insurance covers the insured's household for medical and funeral expenses that result from an auto accident. Physical damage insurance consists of collision coverage, which pays for damage to a car resulting from collision, regardless of fault, and comprehensive coverage, which pays for damage from theft, fire, or vandalism. Over twenty states also require that drivers carry coverage to protect against uninsured motorists. Such coverage allows insured drivers to receive payments from their own insurer should they suffer injuries caused by an uninsured driver. Most insurance policies offer a choice of DEDUCTIBLE, which is the portion of an insurance claim that the insured must pay. The higher the deductible, the lower the annual insurance premium or payment.

Many states have laws requiring no-fault automobile insurance. Under no-fault insurance, each person's own insurance company pays for injury or damage in an auto accident, up to a certain limit, irrespective of whose fault the accident is. Each person is entitled to payment for loss of wages or salary, not exceeding a certain percentage of the value of such loss or a fixed weekly amount.

No-fault statutes provide that every person who receives PERSONAL INJURY benefits gives up the right to sue for damages. However, a person who is licensed to drive in a state that requires no-fault insurance may sue someone who has caused an accident and who is licensed in another state that does not require no-fault insur-

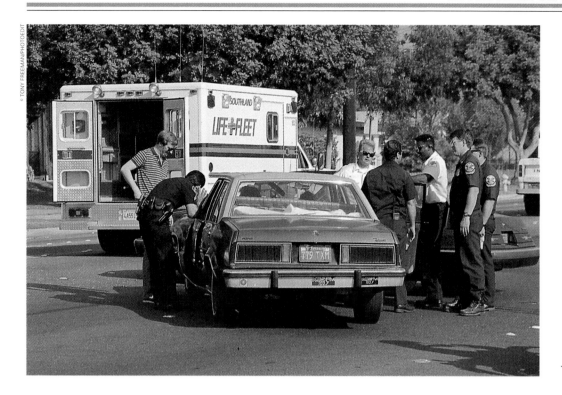

Most states require auto owners to carry insurance so that damages resulting from an accident will be covered.

ance. In some states, a person who has not obtained no-fault auto insurance is personally liable to pay damages. Some states do not abolish liability arising from the ownership, maintenance, or operation of a motor vehicle in certain circumstances, such as those in which the harm was intentionally caused, the injured person has suffered death or serious injuries, or medical expenses exceed a certain limit.

States that do not have compulsory automobile insurance typically have FINANCIAL RESPONSIBILITY ACTS. These laws are designed to ensure that negligent drivers who injure others will pay any resulting claims. They require a proof of financial responsibility from drivers involved in an accident. After reporting the accident to a state agency, drivers who do not have adequate insurance coverage must post a cash deposit or equivalent bond of up to $60,000, unless the other driver provides a written release from liability.

Disposal The last stage in the life cycle of an automobile is its disposal and recycling. In the United States, between 10 and 12 million cars are disposed of each year. In most cases, the first stage of disposal is handled by a wrecking or salvage yard. Most states require the salvage yard to have the title to an auto before the vehicle can be destroyed, and to contact a state agency regarding its destruction. This helps to prevent the destruction of cars used in crimes. Salvage yards typically must be licensed with a

state pollution control agency for hazardous waste disposal. Salvage yards remove parts and items of value that can be recycled from the vehicle, such as batteries and fluids. What is left of the automobile is then sold to a shredder, a business that breaks the car up into small parts and separates the metal from the nonmetal parts. Roughly 25 percent of the auto cannot be recycled and must be disposed of in a landfill. Auto residue to be disposed of in a landfill typically must be tested to see that it meets the standards for disposal of hazardous waste.

CROSS-REFERENCES

Alcohol; Automobile Searches; Collision; Consumer Protection; Environmental Law; Highway; Import Quotas; Nader, Ralph; Seat Belts; Transportation Department.

AUTOMOBILE SEARCHES The Fourth Amendment to the U.S. Constitution guarantees U.S. citizens freedom from "unreasonable searches and seizures." In *Katz v. United States*, 389 U.S. 347, 88 S. Ct. 507, 19 L. Ed. 2d 576 (1967), the Supreme Court established the principle that a WARRANT issued by a "neutral and detached magistrate" must be obtained before a government authority may breach the individual privacy secured by the Fourth Amendment. The *Katz* decision held that "searches conducted outside the judicial process, without prior approval by judge or magistrate, are *per se* unreasonable under the Fourth

Amendment—subject only to a few specifically established and well-delineated exceptions." Over the years, the Court has recognized a number of exceptions to this rule that allow the police in certain situations to legally conduct a search without a warrant. One of these exceptions is for automobile searches.

Warrantless Searches The automobile exception was first announced in *Carroll v. United States*, 267 U.S. 132, 45 S. Ct. 280, 69 L. Ed. 543 (1925), where the Court held that federal Prohibition agents were justified in searching, without a warrant, an automobile they stopped on a public highway because they had probable cause to believe that it contained contraband. The Court found that the search was justified by the exigency of the circumstances, noting that, unlike a dwelling, store, or other structure, an automobile can be "quickly moved out of the locality or jurisdiction in which the warrant must be sought."

After the *Carroll* decision, the Court embarked on a long and often confusing line of decisions that interpreted the automobile exception as it applied not only to automobiles but also to containers found in automobiles, to mobile homes, and to sobriety checkpoints. For several decades, the Court rarely cited *Carroll* in vehicle search cases. Instead, it relied on the "search-incident-to-arrest" doctrine, which allowed the police to search, without a warrant, areas surrounding an arrest site. Originally, the police could search areas that were outside the control of the arrested person (see, e.g., *Harris v. Stephens*, 361 F.2d 888 [8th Cir. 1966], *cert. denied*, 386 U.S. 964 [1967], in which the Court let stand a ruling by the Eighth Circuit that the search of a car parked in a driveway while the suspect was arrested at the front door of his house was valid). However, the Court restricted the search-incident-to-arrest standard in *Chimel v. California*, 395 U.S. 752, 89 S. Ct. 2034, 23 L. Ed. 2d 685 (1969), which held that a warrantless search must be limited to the area within the immediate control of the arrestee.

After the *Chimel* decision, the Court abandoned this line of reasoning and returned to the "probable-cause-accompanied-by-exigent-circumstances" rationale in *Carroll*. In *Chambers v. Maroney*, 399 U.S. 42, 90 S. Ct. 1975, 26 L. Ed. 2d 419 (1970), the justices found that *Carroll* supported a warrantless search of an impounded car. They based this finding on the theory that had the search been conducted at the time of the arrest, it would have been valid because of the exigent circumstances existing at that time. The fact that the car was impounded, and therefore immobile, by the time the search

was conducted did not affect the Court's decision. A year later, in *Coolidge v. New Hampshire*, 403 U.S. 443, 91 S. Ct. 2022, 29 L. Ed. 2d 564 (1971) (plurality opinion), the Court held that a search conducted with a warrant that was later found to be invalid fell outside the automobile exception. The Court stated that the police in *Coolidge* could not have legally conducted a warrantless search at the arrest scene because no exigent circumstances existed: at the time of arrest, the arrestee did not have access to the car and therefore could not have moved it. The *Coolidge* decision firmly established that the police must show both probable cause and exigent circumstances in order for a warrantless search to be valid.

The Court then added an alternative rationale to support automobile searches, with its decision in *Cardwell v. Lewis*, 417 U.S. 583, 94 S. Ct. 2464, 41 L. Ed. 2d 325 (1974) (plurality opinion). In *Cardwell*, the police made an impression of the tires of the suspect's car and took paint samples from the car, without a warrant. The Court held that the search was permissible because the police had probable cause and the search was conducted in a reasonable manner. No exigency existed in this case, but the Court found justification in the principle that individuals have a "lower expectation of privacy" in their automobiles. Writing for the plurality, Justice Harry A. Blackmun stated, "One has a lesser expectation of privacy in a motor vehicle because its function is transportation and it seldom serves as one's residence or as the repository of personal effects."

This "lesser-expectation-of-privacy" rationale was not sufficient to support a warrantless search in *United States v. Chadwick*, 433 U.S. 1, 97 S. Ct. 2476, 53 L. Ed. 2d 538 (1977). In *Chadwick*, the defendants were arrested immediately after they had placed a footlocker in their trunk. Federal agents, who had probable cause to believe that the footlocker contained marijuana, impounded the car and opened the footlocker without a warrant. The Court found that although the agents did have probable cause to search the footlocker, they had not proved that they had probable cause to search the car in order to find the footlocker. Since the car was impounded, no exigent circumstances existed. Furthermore, the Court held that the defendants had a greater expectation of privacy in the closed footlocker than in an automobile, which is open to public view. "The factors which diminish the privacy aspects of an automobile do not apply to the (defendants') footlocker," the Court concluded. Therefore, the lesser-expectation-of-privacy rationale did not

AUTOMOBILE SEARCHES: IS THE FOURTH AMENDMENT IN JEOPARDY?

The right to move about freely without fear of governmental interference is one of the cornerstones of democracy. Likewise, freedom from governmental intrusions into personal privacy is a cherished U.S. right. Automobiles have come to symbolize these rights in the United States. However, freedom and autonomy often conflict with law enforcement's interest in preserving domestic order.

The Fourth Amendment to the Constitution guarantees U.S. citizens freedom from "unreasonable searches and seizures." The Supreme Court, in *Katz v. United States*, 389 U.S. 347, 88 S. Ct. 507, 19 L. Ed. 2d 576 (1967), interpreted the Fourth Amendment to mean that a warrant issued by a "neutral and detached magistrate" must be obtained before police officers may lawfully search personal property. The Court in *Katz* held that "searches conducted outside the judicial process, without prior approval by judge or magistrate are *per se* unreasonable under the Fourth Amendment—subject only to a few specifically established and well-delineated exceptions."

In its struggle to balance the Fourth Amendment's personal privacy guarantees with the government's interest in effective law enforcement, the Court has allowed numerous exceptions to the warrant requirement, prompting debate over the amendment's continued viability. A particularly tricky area involves decisions regarding warrantless automobile searches.

Beginning with its decision in *Carroll v. United States*, 267 U.S. 132, 45 S. Ct. 280, 69 L. Ed. 543 (1925), the Court has granted law enforcement personnel substantial latitude when searching automobiles and their contents. *Carroll* and its progeny established that automobiles constitute a distinct class of personal property that deserves less privacy protection than other types of property. The Court has consistently held that because a car and its contents are easily and quickly moved, police

officers need not obtain a warrant to search them if they reasonably believe that doing so would result in lost evidence.

Since its decision in *Carroll*, the Supreme Court has articulated several rationales for allowing warrantless vehicle searches. First, the Court followed *Carroll* and held that a warrantless search of an automobile is valid because of the exigent circumstances involved (see, e.g., *Chambers v. Maroney*, 399 U.S. 42, 90 S. Ct. 1975, 26 L. Ed. 2d 419 [1970]). Next, the Court found that warrantless automobile searches are justified because individuals have a lower expectation of privacy in their automobiles than in their homes (see, e.g., *Cardwell v. Lewis*, 417 U.S. 583, 94 S. Ct. 2464, 41 L. Ed. 2d 325 [1974] [plurality opinion]). Finally, the Court extended the warrant exception to containers found inside a vehicle, reasoning that if the police could legally search an automobile, they could also legally search containers found in the automobile (see *United States v. Ross*, 456 U.S. 798, 102 S. Ct. 2157, 72 L. Ed. 2d 572 [1982]). However, the Court had previously ruled that where a vehicle search was illegal, a subsequent search of a suitcase found inside the trunk of the vehicle was also illegal (*Arkansas v. Sanders*, 442 U.S. 753, 99 S. Ct. 2586, 61 L. Ed. 2d 235 [1979]). The need to distinguish between a *Sanders* situation and a *Ross* situation caused some confusion, both for the police and for the courts. This need was finally addressed by the Court in 1991.

Underlying all the exceptions to the warrant requirement is the need to assist law enforcement personnel without unduly trampling on the Constitution. However, some have argued that the pendulum has swung too far in favor of police power. In 1991, the Court extended the permissible scope of the warrant exception still further with its decision in *California v. Acevedo*, 500 U.S. 565, 111 S. Ct. 1982, 114 L. Ed.

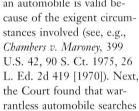

IN FOCUS

2d 619, which upheld the warrantless search of a bag found inside the defendant's vehicle. In an attempt to clarify the law regarding warrantless searches of containers found in automobiles, the justices announced that the Fourth Amendment does not require a distinction between probable cause to search an entire vehicle, including containers found inside (as in *Ross*), and probable cause to search only a container found inside an automobile (as in *Sanders*). The Court announced a new and succinct rule regarding automobile searches: "The police may search an automobile and the containers within it where they have probable cause to believe contraband or evidence is contained."

The *Acevedo* decision provides what is known as a bright-line rule, that is, a rule of law that is clear and unequivocal. But bright-line rules can obscure the important nuances that surround an issue. The *Acevedo* decision leaves little doubt in the minds of law enforcement personnel that they may now, with probable cause, search not only an automobile but also any containers found inside. But that clarity and the unfettered discretion it gives the police trouble some legal analysts. They assert that the ruling effectively guts the Fourth Amendment as it applies to automobile searches and, perhaps more disturbing, that its reasoning could and probably will be applied to searches of other types of personal property.

Justice John Paul Stevens noted in his dissent to *Acevedo* that the majority's ruling creates the paradoxical situation in which a container, such as a briefcase, is not subject to a warrantless search when it is carried in full view on a public street, but becomes subject to such a search upon being placed inside an automobile.

Critics of *Acevedo* also argue that it contradicts earlier rationales established to support exceptions to the warrant requirement. In *Acevedo*, the Court found no exigent circumstances to justify the search, as it had in *Carroll*, since

AUTOMOBILE SEARCHES: IS THE FOURTH AMENDMENT IN JEOPARDY?
(CONTINUED)

the police could have legally seized the bag and obtained a warrant for a later search. Neither, assert critics, would the defendant's expectation of privacy in the bag be diminished by virtue of his placing it into the automobile.

Lacking both exigency and the lesser expectation of privacy justifications, the Court turned to policy considerations to support its decision in *Acevedo*. The majority stated that law enforcement personnel were unnecessarily impeded by the Court's previous rulings on this issue. The Court dismissed privacy concerns by stating that protection of privacy is minimal anyway, since in many automobile search cases the police may legally search a container under the "search-incident-to-arrest" justification. Critics respond that the policy underlying that exception is that the police should be able to secure the arrest site in order to protect their safety; it does not follow that the police should be allowed to search containers even when they are not in danger.

Critics assert that by giving the police the discretion to determine what is a reasonable search, the Court ignored established precedent governing Fourth Amendment cases. Justice Robert H. Jackson wrote in *Johnson v. United States*, 333 U.S. 10 (1948),

The point of the Fourth Amendment, which is often not grasped by zealous officers, is not that it denies law enforcement the support of the usual inferences which reasonable men draw from evidence. Its protection consists in requiring that those inferences be drawn by a neutral and detached magistrate instead of being judged by the officer engaged in the often competitive enterprise of ferreting out crime.

According to Justice Stevens, the majority in *Acevedo* rejected this precedent without justification.

Justice Antonin Scalia takes a different approach. He suggests in his concurrence to *Acevedo* that the Fourth Amendment does not proscribe *warrantless* searches but rather prohibits *unreasonable* searches. Scalia opines that "the supposed 'general rule' that a warrant is always required does not appear to have any basis in the common law."

support an extension of the automobile exception to the closed footlocker.

Armed with the *Carroll-Chambers* line of cases (the probable-cause-accompanied-by-exigent-circumstances rationale) and the *Chadwick* decision (the lower-expectation-of-privacy rationale), the Court tackled the question of whether a warrantless search of a suitcase found in the trunk of a taxi fell under either justification. In *Arkansas v. Sanders*, 442 U.S. 753, 99 S. Ct. 2586, 61 L. Ed. 2d 235 (1979), the police had probable cause to believe that a suitcase picked up by the defendant at an airport contained contraband. After the defendant placed the suitcase in the trunk of a taxi and left the airport, the police stopped the taxi, opened the trunk, and searched the suitcase, which contained the contraband they expected to find. The Court evaluated the facts under each rationale and found that (a) once the taxi had been stopped, no exigency existed; and, (b) an individual's privacy expectations in a suitcase, which "serve[s] as a repository for personal items," are greater than his or her privacy expectations in an automobile. For these reasons, the Court held that the search violated the Fourth Amendment.

Later cases, however, extended the automobile exception to containers located in an automobile, where authorities have probable cause to search the automobile. For example, in *United States v. Ross*, 456 U.S. 798, 102 S. Ct. 2157, 72 L. Ed. 2d 572 (1982), the police stopped a car that they had probable cause to believe contained contraband. Without a warrant, they opened a closed paper bag they found inside the car's trunk, and discovered heroin. The Court held that the search was valid, reasoning that if the police had probable cause to conduct a warrantless search of the vehicle, they also had justification to search the bag.

The automobile exception was also extended to searches of some mobile homes, in *California v. Carney*, 471 U.S. 386, 105 S. Ct. 2066, 85 L. Ed. 2d 406 (1985). In *Carney*, the police searched a motor home parked in a public lot. The Court found the search to be valid, stating that the mobile home was being used for transportation and therefore was as readily movable as an automobile. In addition, the Court noted a reduced expectation of privacy in a mobile home, as contrasted with an ordinary residence, since mobile homes, like cars, are regulated by the state. In this case, where the mobile home was parked in a public parking lot rather than a mobile home park, and was not anchored in any way, it resembled a vehicle more than a residence. Therefore, the automobile exception applied. *Carney* established not only that the automobile exception applies to some mobile homes but also that it applies to parked vehicles as well.

Another extension of the automobile exception, called the inventory exception, was recognized by the Court in *South Dakota v. Opperman*, 428 U.S. 364, 96 S. Ct. 3092, 49 L. Ed. 2d 1000 (1976). Donald Opperman's illegally parked vehicle was ticketed and towed to an impound lot, where the police inventoried its contents. In an unlocked glove compartment, they found marijuana. The Court held that once a vehicle has been legally impounded, its contents can be inventoried. Three justifications were given: protection of the owner's property while it is in police custody, protection of the police against claims, and protection of the police against danger. Likewise, in *Colorado v. Bertine*, 479 U.S. 367, 107 S. Ct. 738, 93 L. Ed. 2d 739 (1987), the Court found that marijuana discovered in a closed backpack during an inventory of an impounded vehicle was legally seized because there was no showing that "the police, who were following standardized procedures, acted in bad faith or for the sole purpose of investigation." The Court concluded that "reasonable police regulations relating to inventory procedures administered in good faith satisfy the Fourth Amendment."

This patchwork of decisions led many, including Justice Lewis F. Powell, Jr., to conclude that "the law of search and seizure with respect to automobiles is intolerably confusing" (*Robbins v. California*, 453 U.S. 420, 101 S. Ct. 2841, 69 L. Ed. 2d 744 [1981] [Powell, J., concurring]). The Court attempted to put the confusion to rest with its decision in *California v. Acevedo*, 500 U.S. 565, 111 S. Ct. 1982, 114 L. Ed. 2d 619 (1991). In *Acevedo*, federal drug agents tracked a bag that they knew contained marijuana, as it was in transit to the defendant. They then notified police officers, who watched as the defendant put the bag into the trunk of a car and drove away. The police officers stopped the car, opened the trunk, and searched the bag, finding the marijuana. The Court held that the search was legal, stating that it is not necessary for an officer to obtain a warrant before searching a container located in an automobile when the officer has probable cause to believe that the container holds contraband or evidence. After analyzing the long and ambiguous line of automobile exception cases, the Court decided that the distinction between the *Ross* situation (where the police had probable cause to search the car) and the *Sanders* situation (where the police had probable cause only to search the container) was not supported by the requirements of the Fourth Amendment. Discarding the reasoning in *Sanders* as unworkable and an unjustified impingement on legitimate police activity, the justices announced a new and unequivocal rule: "The police may search an automobile and the containers within it where they have probable cause to believe contraband or evidence is contained."

The *Acevedo* decision was met with harsh criticism by some legal analysts, who saw it as an excessive retreat from Fourth Amendment guarantees. Supporters, however, pointed out that the police must still establish that they have probable cause to conduct a warrantless search before such a search will be found valid. Probable cause can be shown in a variety of ways, but generally it follows from a chain of events that raise police suspicions from the level of mere conjecture to the level of reasonable grounds. For example, in *Acevedo*, federal drug enforcement agents had previously seized and inspected the package that was eventually delivered to the defendant, and knew that it contained marijuana. In *Sanders*, a reliable informant had told the police that the defendant would arrive at the airport carrying a green suitcase containing marijuana. And in *Ross*, an informant had told the police that someone known as Bandit was selling drugs from the trunk of his car; when the police located the car described by the informant, they discovered through a computer check that the driver, the defendant, Albert Ross, Jr., used the alias Bandit. From these cases, the Court has shown that arbitrary searches or searches based on mere suspicion will not be supported by a spurious claim of probable cause.

Sobriety Checkpoints During the 1980s and 1990s, the Court dealt with a new line of cases, in which the automobile exception has been used to justify sobriety checkpoint programs. Under such programs, police stop motorists, typically along an interstate highway, for the purpose of apprehending drivers impaired by ALCOHOL. One such program was challenged and found to be constitutional in *Michigan Department of State Police v. Sitz*, 496 U.S. 444, 110 S. Ct. 2481, 110 L. Ed. 2d 412 (1990). The Court applied a somewhat more stringent test than that used in automobile search cases, citing as relevant authority a line of cases involving highway checkpoints for discovering illegal aliens (see, e.g., *United States v. Martinez*, 428 U.S. 543, 96 S. Ct. 3074, 49 L. Ed. 2d 1116 [1976]; *Brown v. Texas*, 443 U.S. 47, 99 S. Ct. 2637, 61 L. Ed. 2d 357 [1979]). *Brown* required "a weighing of the gravity of the public concerns served by the seizure, the degree to which the seizure advances the public interest, and the severity of the interference with individual liberty." Applying that balancing test, the majority in *Sitz* found that the intrusion on individual liberty imposed by Michigan's sobriety checkpoint program was outweighed by the advancement of the state's interest in preventing drunk driving. Therefore, it concluded that the program did not violate the Fourth Amendment.

Similar sobriety checkpoint programs have been used in other states, and, since the *Sitz* decision, all have passed constitutional muster. Less certain is the constitutionality of narcotics checkpoints. In 1992, Minnesota instituted a random narcotics checkpoint on an interstate highway exit ramp. The police stopped every third or fourth car and asked several questions of the occupants. If the answers or demeanor of the occupants aroused suspicion, the car was diverted for further investigation. A number of individuals were cited when police found marijuana, either in plain view or after a consensual search of the vehicle.

The Minnesota scheme raises serious constitutional questions. The state has a legitimate interest in curbing the use of illegal drugs. However, it is not clear that a narcotics checkpoint program is a valid means of promoting this interest, in light of the privacy interest violated by random questioning for investigation of drug possession or use. Similarly, it is unclear whether the Minnesota scheme is the type of minimal intrusion sanctioned by the Court in *Sitz*. Still, the *Sitz* and *Acevedo* decisions, both of which have been criticized as giving too much discretion to the police, indicate that the Court intends to allow a great deal of latitude to law enforcement officials in stopping and searching automobiles under most conditions.

Autopsy: Deaths, by Selected Causes, 1992*

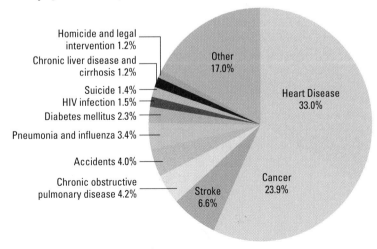

Homicide and legal intervention 1.2%
Chronic liver disease and cirrhosis 1.2%
Suicide 1.4%
HIV infection 1.5%
Diabetes mellitus 2.3%
Pneumonia and influenza 3.4%
Accidents 4.0%
Chronic obstructive pulmonary disease 4.2%
Stroke 6.6%
Cancer 23.9%
Heart Disease 33.0%
Other 17.0%

*Excludes deaths of nonresidents of the U.S.

Source: U.S. National Center for Health Statistics, *Vital Statistics of the United States,* annual.

CROSS-REFERENCES
Privacy; Drugs and Narcotics; Fourth Amendment; Probable Cause; Searches and Seizures; Search Warrant.

AUTOPSY ▨ The dissection of a dead body by a medical examiner or physician authorized by law to do so in order to determine the cause and time of a death that appears to have resulted from other than natural causes. ▨

This postmortem examination, required by law, is ordered by the local CORONER when a person is suspected to have died by violent or unnatural means. The consent of the decedent's next of kin is not necessary for an authorized autopsy to be held. The medical findings must be presented at an INQUEST and might be used as evidence in a police investigation and a subsequent criminal prosecution.

See also FORENSIC SCIENCE.

AUXILIARY ▨ Aiding; ancillary; subordinate; subsidiary. ▨

Auxiliary or ancillary administration is the management and settlement of property belonging to a decedent that is not located where he or she was domiciled. It is subordinate to the principal or DOMICILIARY ADMINISTRATION of the decedent's property that occurs in the state where the individual was domiciled. Auxiliary administration ensures that any local CREDITORS will be paid before the out-of-state property will be transferred for distribution under domiciliary administration. See also ESTATE.

AVER ▨ To specifically allege certain facts or claims in a PLEADING. ▨

AVERMENT ▨ The ALLEGATION of facts or claims in a PLEADING. ▨

The Federal Rules of Civil Procedure require that averments be simple, concise, and direct.

AVOIDABLE CONSEQUENCES ▨ The doctrine that places the responsibility of minimizing DAMAGES upon the person who has been injured. ▨

The major function of the doctrine is to reduce the damages brought about by the defendant's misconduct. Ordinarily, an individual cannot recover for losses that might have been prevented through reasonable effort by the person, particularly where the conduct causing the loss or injury is not willful, intentional, or perpetuated in BAD FAITH. The rule of avoidable consequences applies to both CONTRACT and TORT actions, but is not applicable in cases involving willful injury or where the plaintiff could not possibly have circumvented any of the harm for which he or she claims damages.

The efforts that the person who has been injured must take to avoid the consequences of the misconduct are required to be REASONABLE, based upon the circumstances of the particular case, and subject to the rules of common sense and fair dealing. That which is reasonably required is contingent upon the extent of the potential injury as compared with the cost of rectifying the situation, and the realistic likelihood of success in the protective effort. A plaintiff who neglects to mitigate damages will not be entirely barred from recovering such damages that he or she might have circumvented through reasonable efforts.

Included in the effort that the law requires is the payment of reasonable expenditures. The injured party need not, however, make extraordinary payments to prevent the consequences of the wrongdoer's conduct. The plaintiff's inability to produce funds to meet the situation presented can excuse efforts to reduce the injury.

Breach of Contract A party injured by the breach of contract generally must exercise reasonable efforts to lessen the damages. This rule has no application in an ACTION on a contract for an agreed compensation. Upon the breach of a contract to supply personal service or the use of some type of specific equipment or instrumentality, the individual who agrees to furnish such service or items must attempt to acquire a replacement contract if one can reasonably be found. The defendant can then prove, in attempting to reduce damages, that the plaintiff has procured other employment as well as the amount he or she earned or might have earned by exercising reasonable CARE and DILIGENCE. The test of the applicability of this rule is whether the employment or services of the plaintiff were personal in nature. The rule is not applicable in contracts that do not require all, or a significant portion, of the plaintiff's time, or those that do not preclude the plaintiff from becoming engaged in simultaneous performance of other contracts.

Torts A party who suffers a PERSONAL INJURY is required to exercise ordinary care and perseverance to find a cure, thereby reducing the damages to the most practicable extent. Such an individual should seek reasonable medical care if so required by the injury. It is not necessary for the person to undergo excessively painful treatment or that which involves a significant hazard of death or injury or offers a mere possibility of a cure. The pain inherent in the necessary medical care and treatment may be taken into consideration in assessing whether the plaintiff acted reasonably in declining to submit to it. Although submission to treatment is not a prerequisite to an award of damages, recovery cannot be obtained for increased dam-

ages that stem from the failure to submit to necessary medical treatment. Conversely, the mere fact that medical attention was not sought immediately, or at all, will not proscribe an award of damages where the circumstances did not reasonably indicate that medical aid and attention was necessary.

In addition, an injured party has no absolute duty to subscribe to a physician's advice to mitigate damages. The party might, however, under some circumstances, be under an obligation to exercise ordinary care in following such advice.

See also MITIGATION OF DAMAGES.

AVOIDANCE 📖 An escape from the consequences of a specific course of action through the use of legally acceptable means. Cancellation; the act of rendering something useless or legally ineffective. 📖

A taxpayer may take all legally recognized deductions in order to minimize the INCOME TAX liability. This conduct is called TAX AVOIDANCE and is legal. If, however, a taxpayer claims deductions to which he or she is not entitled so that the individual pays less income tax than is actually owed, then the taxpayer has committed TAX EVASION, a crime punishable by a fine, imprisonment, or both.

A plea in CONFESSION AND AVOIDANCE is one that admits the truth of ALLEGATIONS made in former pleading but presents new information that neutralizes or avoids the legal ramifications of those admitted facts.

AVOWAL 📖 An open declaration by an attorney representing a party in a lawsuit, made after the jury has been removed from the courtroom, that requests the admission of particular TESTIMONY from a WITNESS that would otherwise be INADMISSIBLE because it has been successfully objected to during the trial. 📖

An avowal serves two purposes. It enables an attorney to have the court learn what a witness would have replied to a question had opposing counsel not made an objection to the question sustained by the court. It also provides the interrogator with an opportunity to offer evidence that contradicts the disputed testimony. If, upon appeal, an appellate court decides that a witness should have been allowed to respond to such questions before a jury, an avowal will be a record of the witness's response.

AVULSION 📖 The immediate and noticeable addition to land caused by its removal from the property of another, by a sudden change in a water bed or in the course of a stream. 📖

When a stream that is a BOUNDARY suddenly abandons its bed and seeks a new bed, the boundary line does not change. It remains in the center of the original bed even if water no longer flows through it. This is known as the *rule of avulsion*.

Avulsion is not the same as ACCRETION or ALLUVION, the gradual and imperceptible buildup of land by the continuous activity of the sea, a river, or by other natural causes.

AWARD 📖 To concede; to give by judicial determination; to rule in favor of after an evaluation of the facts, evidence, or merits. The decision made by a panel of arbitrators or commissioners, a jury, or other authorized individuals in a controversy that has been presented for resolution. A document that memorializes the determination reached in a dispute. 📖

A jury awards damages; a municipal corporation awards a public contract to a bidder.

MILESTONES IN THE LAW

Roe v. Wade

ISSUE

Abortion

MATERIALS

Opinion of U.S. District Court, N.D. Texas,
   June 17, 1970
Briefs to the Supreme Court
Opinion of the Supreme Court, January 22,
   1973

HOW TO USE
MILESTONES IN THE LAW

This section allows readers to investigate the
facts, the arguments, and the legal reasoning
that produced the *Roe v. Wade* decision. It also
sheds light on the roles and required skills of
attorneys and judges in resolving disputes.

As you read this section, you may wish to
consider the following issues:

- How did the appellant's description of the
  issues before the Court, or questions presented, differ from the appellee's descriptions?
- How did the courts and the two parties differ in describing the meaning of particular
  prior cases to the present case?
- How did the holdings (conclusions of law)
  of the district court differ from those of the
  Supreme Court?
- On what points in the Supreme Court's majority opinion do the concurring and dissenting justices agree and disagree?
- How would you decide this case?

THIS CASE IN HISTORY

Roe versus Wade may be the most well known
and the most controversial decision of the
modern Supreme Court. With this decision,
the Court recognized a woman's right to obtain an abortion under certain circumstances.
Virtually from the moment it was handed
down, *Roe v. Wade* has divided lawyers, politicians, and the public into those who support
the decision and those who would like it overturned, either by the Supreme Court itself or
by act of the legislature. A judge's or politician's position on the subject of abortion has
played a major role in countless appointments
and elections. After the decision and for the
rest of his life, the opinion brought its author,
Justice Harry Blackmun, an unending stream
of mail both praising and villifying him for the
decision.

ROE v. WADE   1217
Cite as 314 F.Supp. 1217 (1970)

Jane ROE, Plaintiff,

v.

Henry WADE, Defendant,

v.

James Hubert HALLFORD, M.D.,
Intervenor.

John DOE and Mary Doe, Plaintiffs,

v.

Henry WADE, Defendant.

Civ. A. Nos. 3–3690–B, 3–3691–C.

United States District Court,
N. D. Texas,
Dallas Division.

June 17, 1970.

Action for judgment declaring Texas
abortion laws unconstitutional and to enjoin their enforcement. The three-judge
District Court held that laws prohibiting
abortions except for purpose of saving
life of the mother violated right secured
by the Ninth Amendment to choose
whether to have children and were unconstitutionally overbroad and vague, but
Court would abstain from issuing injunction against enforcement of the laws.

Order accordingly.

1. Constitutional Law ⟜42

Physician challenging constitutionality of Texas abortion laws had standing to raise rights of his patients, single women and married couples, as well as rights of his own. Vernon's Ann.Tex. P.C. arts. 1191–1194, 1196.

2. Constitutional Law ⟜42

Logical nexus existed between status asserted by plaintiffs, a married couple, single woman and practicing physician challenging constitutionality of Texas abortion laws, and claim sought to be adjudicated, and plaintiffs had standing. Vernon's Ann.Tex.P.C. art. 1196; 28 U.S.C.A. § 2201.

3. Courts ⟜300

Contentiousness between pregnant woman, physician and district attorney of Dallas County was sufficient to establish a "case of actual controversy" with respect to constitutionality of Texas abortion laws. 28 U.S.C.A. § 2201.

See publication Words and Phrases for other judicial constructions and definitions.

4. Courts ⟜260.4

In absence of possibility that adjudication in state courts would eliminate necessity for federal district court to pass upon plaintiffs' Ninth Amendment claim respecting constitutionality of Texas abortion laws or physician's attack on laws for vagueness, abstention as to plaintiffs' request for declaratory judgment was unwarranted. Vernon's Ann. Tex.P.C. arts. 1191–1194, 1196; U.S.C.A. Const. Amend. 9.

5. Abortion ⟜1

Texas laws prohibiting abortions except for purpose of saving life of mother deprived single women and married couples of their right, secured by the Ninth Amendment, to choose whether to have children. Vernon's Ann.Tex.P.C. arts. 1191–1194, 1196; U.S.C.A.Const. Amend. 9.

6. Constitutional Law ⟜48

District attorney had burden to demonstrate that infringement by state abortion laws upon plaintiffs' fundamental

right to chose whether to have children was necessary to support compelling state interest. Vernon's Ann.Tex.P.C. arts. 1191–1194, 1196.

7. Constitutional Law ⟜38

Fact that statutory scheme serves permissible or even compelling state interests will not save it from consequences of unconstitutional overbreadth.

8. Abortion ⟜1

While Ninth Amendment right to choose to have abortion is not unqualified or unfettered, statute designed to regulate circumstances of abortions must restrict its scope to compelling state interests. Vernon's Ann.Tex.P.C. arts. 1191–1194, 1196; U.S.C.A.Const. Amend. 9.

9. Abortion ⟜1

Texas laws prohibiting abortions except for purpose of saving life of mother are unconstitutionally overbroad in failing to limit scope to compelling state interests. Vernon's Ann.Tex.P.C. arts. 1191–1194, 1196; U.S.C.A.Const. Amend. 9.

10. Criminal Law ⟜13

Texas laws prohibiting abortions except for purpose of saving life of mother are unconstitutionally vague in failing to provide physicians with proper notice of what acts in their daily practice and consultation will subject them to criminal liability. Vernon's Ann.Tex.P.C. arts. 1191–1194, 1196.

11. Courts ⟜508(7)

Federal policy of noninterference with state criminal prosecutions must be followed except in cases where statutes are justifiably attacked on their face as abridging free expression, or where statutes are justifiably attacked as applied for the purpose of discouraging protected activities. U.S.C.A.Const. Amends. 1, 9.

12. Courts ⟜508(7)

Texas abortion laws, although unconstitutional in depriving single women and married couples of right secured by Ninth Amendment to choose whether to have children and as being vague and overbroad, could not be justifiably attacked on their face as abridging free expression or as being applied for purpose of discouraging protected activities, and federal court would abstain from enjoining enforcement of the laws. Vernon's Ann.Tex.P.C. arts. 1191–1194, 1196; U.S. C.A.Const. Amends. 1, 9.

———◆———

Linda N. Coffee, Dallas, Tex., Sarah Weddington, Austin, Tex., for plaintiffs.

Fred Bruner, Daugherty, Bruner, Lastelick & Anderson, Ray L. Merrill, Jr., Dallas, Tex., for intervenor.

John B. Tolle, Asst. Dist. Atty., Dallas, Tex., Jay Floyd, Asst. Atty. Gen., Austin, Tex., for defendant.

Before GOLDBERG, Circuit Judge, and HUGHES and TAYLOR, District Judges.

1. On March 3, 1970, plaintiff Jane Roe filed her original complaint in CA–3–3690–B under the First, Fourth, Fifth, Eighth, Ninth, and Fourteenth Amendments to the United States Constitution. She alleged jurisdiction to be conferred upon the Court by Title 28, United States Code, Sections 1331, 1343, 2201, 2202, 2281, and 2284 and by Title 42, United States Code, Section 1983. On April 22, plaintiff Roe amended her complaint to sue "on behalf of herself and all others similarly situated."

On March 23, James Hubert Hallford, M. D., was given leave to intervene. Hallford's complaint recited the same constitutional and jurisdictional grounds as the complaint of plaintiff Roe. According to his petition for intervention, Hallford seeks to represent "himself and the class of people who are physicians, licensed to practice medicine under the laws of the State of Texas and who fear future prosecution."

On March 3, 1970, plaintiffs John and Mary Doe filed their original complaint in CA–3–3691–C. The complaint of plaintiffs Doe recited the same constitutional and jurisdictional grounds as had the complaint of plaintiff Roe in CA–3–3690 and, like Roe, plaintiffs Doe subsequently amended their complaint so as to assert a class action.

Plaintiffs Roe and Doe have adopted pseudonyms for purposes of anonymity.

PER CURIAM:

Two similar cases are presently before the Court on motions for summary judgment pursuant to Rule 56 of the Federal Rules of Civil Procedure. The defendant in both cases is Henry Wade, District Attorney of Dallas County, Texas. In one action plaintiffs are John and Mary Doe, and in the other Jane Roe and James Hubert Hallford, M.D., intervenor.[1]

[1] From their respective positions of married couple, single woman, and practicing physician, plaintiffs attack Articles 1191, 1192, 1193, 1194, and 1196 of the Texas Penal Code,[2] hereinafter referred to as the Texas Abortion Laws. Plaintiffs allege that the Texas Abortion Laws deprive married couples and single women of the right to choose whether to have children, a right secured by the Ninth Amendment.

2. *Article 1191 Abortion*

If any person shall designedly administer to a pregnant woman or knowingly procure to be administered with her consent any drug or medicine, or shall use towards her any violence or means whatever externally or internally applied, and thereby procure an abortion, he shall be confined in the penitentiary not less than two nor more than five years; if it be done without her consent, the punishment shall be doubled. By "abortion" is meant that the life of the fetus or embryo shall be destroyed in the woman's womb or that a premature birth thereof be caused.

Article 1192 Furnishing the Means

Whoever furnishes the means for procuring an abortion knowing the purpose intended is guilty as an accomplice.

Article 1193 Attempt at Abortion

If the means used shall fail to produce an abortion, the offender is nevertheless guilty of an attempt to produce abortion, provided it be shown that such means were calculated to produce that result, and shall be fined not less than one hundred nor more than one thousand dollars.

Article 1194 Murder in Producing Abortion

If the death of the mother is occasioned by an abortion so produced or by an attempt to effect the same it is murder.

Article 1196 By Medical Advice

Nothing in this chapter applies to an abortion procured or attempted by medical advice for the purpose of saving the life of the mother.

Defendant challenges the standing of each of the plaintiffs to bring this action. However, it appears to the Court that Plaintiff Roe and plaintiff-intervenor Hallford occupy positions *vis-a-vis* the Texas Abortion Laws sufficient to differentiate them from the general public. Compare Pierce v. Society of Sisters, 268 U.S. 510, 45 S.Ct. 571, 69 L.Ed. 1070 (1925), and Griswold v. Connecticut, 381 U.S. 479, 85 S.Ct. 1678, 14 L.Ed.2d 510 (1965),[3] with Frothingham v. Mellon, 262 U.S. 447, 43 S.Ct. 597, 67 L. Ed. 1078 (1923). Plaintiff Roe filed her portion of the suit as a pregnant woman wishing to exercise the asserted constitutional right to choose whether to bear the child she was carrying. Intervenor Hallford alleged in his portion of the suit that, in the course of daily exercise of his duty as a physician and in order to give his patients access to what he asserts to be their constitutional right to choose whether to have children, he must act so as to render criminal liability for himself under the Texas Abortion Laws a likelihood. Dr. Hallford further alleges that Article 1196 of the Texas Abortion Laws is so vague as to deprive him of warning of what produces criminal liability in that portion of his medical practice and consultations involving abortions.

[2] On the basis of plaintiffs' substantive contentions,[4] it appears that there then exists a "nexus between the status asserted by the litigant[s] and the claim[s] [they present]." Flast v. Cohen, 392 U.S. 83, 102, 88 S.Ct. 1942, 20 L.Ed.2d 947 (1968).

[3] Further, we are satisfied that there presently exists a degree of contentiousness between Roe and Hallford and the defendant to establish a "case of actual controversy" as required by Title

28, United States Code, Section 2201. Golden v. Zwickler, 394 U.S. 103, 89 S.Ct. 956, 22 L.Ed.2d 113 (1969).

Each plaintiff seeks as relief, *first*, a judgment declaring the Texas Abortion Laws unconstitutional on their face and, *second*, an injunction against their enforcement. The nature of the relief requested suggests the order in which the issues presented should be passed upon.[5] Accordingly, we see the issues presented as follows:

I. Are plaintiffs entitled to a declaratory judgment that the Texas Abortion Laws are unconstitutional on their face?

II. Are plaintiffs entitled to an injunction against the enforcement of these laws?

I.

Defendants have suggested that this Court should abstain from rendering a decision on plaintiffs' request for a declaratory judgment. However, we are guided to an opposite conclusion by the authority of Zwickler v. Koota, 389 U.S. 241, 248–249, 88 S.Ct. 391, 19 L.Ed.2d 444 (1967):

"The judge-made doctrine of abstention * * * sanctions * * * escape only in narrowly limited 'special circumstances.' * * * One of the 'special circumstances' * * * is the susceptibility of a state statute of a construction by the state courts that would avoid or modify the constitutional question."

The Court in Zwickler v. Koota subsequently quoted from United States v. Livingston, 179 F.Supp. 9, 12–13 (E.D. S.C.1959):

"Regard for the interest and sovereignty of the state and reluctance

---

3. By the authority of *Griswold*, Dr. Hallford has standing to raise the rights of his patients, single women and married couples, as well as rights of his own.

4. "[I]n ruling on standing, it is both appropriate and necessary to look to the substantive issues * * * to determine whether there is a logical nexus between

the status asserted and the claim sought to be adjudicated." Flast v. Cohen, 392 U.S. 83, 102, 88 S.Ct. 1942, 20 L.Ed.2d 947 (1968).

5. Zwickler v. Koota, 389 U.S. 241, 254, 88 S.Ct. 391, 19 L.Ed.2d 444 (1967); Cameron v. Johnson, 390 U.S. 611, 615, 88 S.Ct. 1335, 20 L.Ed.2d 182 (1968).

ROE v. WADE   **1221**
Cite as 314 F.Supp. 1217 (1970)

needlessly to adjudicate constitutional issues may require a federal District Court to abstain from adjudication if the parties may avail themselves of an appropriate procedure to obtain state interpretation of state laws requiring construction. * * * The decision in [Harrison v. N.A.A.C.P., 360 U.S. 167, 79 S.Ct. 1025, 3 L.Ed.2d 1152], however, is not a broad encyclical commanding automatic remission to the state courts of all federal constitutional questions arising in the application of state statutes. * * * Though never interpreted by a state court, if a state statute is not fairly subject to an interpretation which will avoid or modify the federal constitutional question, it is the duty of a federal court to decide the federal question when presented to it. Any other course would impose expense and long delay upon the litigants without hope of its bearing fruit." [6]

[4] Inasmuch as there is no possibility that state question adjudication in the courts of Texas would eliminate the necessity for this Court to pass upon plaintiffs' Ninth Amendment claim or Dr. Hallford's attack on Article 1196 for vagueness, abstention as to their request for declaratory judgment is unwarranted. Compare City of Chicago v. Atchison, T. & S. F. R. Co., 357 U.S. 77, 84, 78 S.Ct. 1063, 2 L.Ed.2d 1174 (1958), with Reetz v. Bozanich, 397 U.S. 82, 90 S.Ct. 788, 25 L.Ed.2d 68 (1970).

[5] On the merits, plaintiffs argue as their principal contention [7] that the Texas Abortion Laws must be declared unconstitutional because they deprive single women and married couples of their right, secured by the Ninth Amendment,[8] to choose whether to have children. We agree.

The essence of the interest sought to be protected here is the right of choice over events which, by their character and consequences, bear in a fundamental manner on the privacy of individuals. The manner by which such interests are secured by the Ninth Amendment is illustrated by the concurring opinion of Mr. Justice Goldberg in Griswold v. Connecticut, 381 U.S. 479, 492, 85 S.Ct. 1678, 14 L.Ed.2d 510 (1965):

"[T]he Ninth Amendment shows a belief of the Constitution's authors that *fundamental* rights exist that are not expressly enumerated in the first eight amendments and intent that the list of rights included there not be deemed exhaustive." * * *

"The Ninth Amendment simply shows the intent of the Constitution's authors that other *fundamental* personal rights should not be denied such protection or disparaged in any other way simply because they are not specifically listed in the first eight constitutional amendments." (Emphasis added.) [9]

Relative sanctuaries for such "fundamental" interests have been established

6. 389 U.S. at 250–251, 88 S.Ct. at 396–397. (Citations omitted.)

7. Aside from their Ninth Amendment and vagueness arguments, plaintiffs have presented an array of constitutional arguments. However, as plaintiffs conceded in oral argument, these additional arguments are peripheral to the main issues. Consequently, they will not be passed upon.

8. "The enumeration in the Constitution, of certain rights shall not be construed to deny or disparage others retained by the people."

9. At 492, 85 S.Ct. at 1686 the opinion states: "In determining which rights are

fundamental, judges are not left at large to decide cases in light of their personal and private notions. Rather, they must look to the 'traditions and [collective] conscience of our people' to determine whether a principle is 'so rooted [there] * * * as to be ranked as fundamental'. Snyder v. [Commonwealth of] Massachusetts, 291 U.S. 97, 105 [54 S.Ct. 330, 78 L.Ed. 674]. The inquiry is whether a right involved 'is of such a character that it cannot be denied without violating those "fundamental principles of liberty and justice which lie at the base of all our civil and political institutions." * * *' Powell v. Alabama, 287 U.S. 45, 67 [53 S.Ct. 55, 77 L.Ed. 158]."

for the family,[10] the marital couple,[11] and the individual.[12]

Freedom to choose in the matter of abortions has been accorded the status of a "fundamental" right in every case coming to the attention of this Court where the question has been raised. Babbitz v. McCann, 312 F.Supp. 725 (E.D. Wis.1970); People v. Belous, 80 Cal. Rptr. 354, 458 P.2d 194 (Cal.1969); State v. Munson, (South Dakota Circuit Court, Pennington County, April 6, 1970). *Accord*, United States v. Vuitch, 305 F.Supp. 1032 (D.D.C.1969). The California Supreme Court in *Belous* stated:

"The fundamental right of the woman to choose whether to bear children follows from the Supreme Court's and this court's repeated acknowledgment of a 'right of privacy' or 'liberty' in matters related to marriage, family, and sex." 80 Cal.Rptr. at 359, 458 P.2d at 199.

The District Court in *Vuitch* wrote:

"There has been * * * an increasing indication in the decisions of the Supreme Court of the United States that as a secular matter a woman's liberty and right of privacy extends to

family, marriage and sex matters and may well include the right to remove an unwanted child at least in early stages of pregnancy." 305 F.Supp. at 1035.

Writing about Griswold v. Connecticut, *supra*, and the decisions leading up to it, former Associate Justice Tom C. Clark observed:

"The result of these decisions is the evolution of the concept that there is a certain zone of individual privacy which is protected by the Constitution. Unless the State has a compelling subordinating interest that outweighs the individual rights of human beings, it may not interfere with a person's marriage, home, children and day-to-day living habits. This is one of the most fundamental concepts that the Founding Fathers had in mind when they drafted the Constitution." [13]

[6] Since the Texas Abortion Laws infringe upon plaintiffs' fundamental right to choose whether to have children, the burden is on the defendant to demonstrate to the satisfaction of the Court that such infringement is necessary to support a compelling state interest.[14] The defendant has failed to meet this burden.

---

10. Pierce v. Society of Sisters, 268 U.S. 510, 45 S.Ct. 571, 69 L.Ed. 1070 (1925); Meyer v. Nebraska, 262 U.S. 390, 43 S.Ct. 625, 67 L.Ed. 1042 (1923); and Prince v. Commonwealth of Massachusetts, 321 U.S. 158, 64 S.Ct. 438, 88 L.Ed. 645 (1944).

11. Loving v. Commonwealth of Virginia, 388 U.S. 1, 87 S.Ct. 1817, 18 L.Ed.2d 1010 (1967); Griswold v. Connecticut, 381 U.S. 479, 85 S.Ct. 1678, 14 L.Ed.2d 510 (1965); and Buchanan v. Batchelor, 308 F.Supp. 729 (N.D.Tex.1970).

12. Skinner v. Oklahoma, 316 U.S. 535, 62 S.Ct. 1110, 86 L.Ed. 1655 (1942); and Stanley v. Georgia, 394 U.S. 557, 89 S.Ct. 1243, 22 L.Ed.2d 542 (1969).

13. Religion, Morality, and Abortion: A Constitutional Appraisal, 2 Loyola Univ. L.Rev. 1, 8 (1969). Mr. Justice Clark goes on to write, "* * * abortion falls within that sensitive area of privacy— the marital relation. One of the basic values of this privacy is birth control, as

evidenced by the *Griswold* decision. Griswold's act was to prevent formation of the fetus. This, the Court found, was constitutionally protected. If an individual may prevent contraception, why can he not nullify that conception when prevention has failed?" *Id.* at 9.

14. "In a long series of cases this Court has held that where fundamental personal liberties are involved, they may not be abridged by the States simply on a showing that a regulatory statute has some rational relationship to the effectuation of a proper state purpose. 'Where there is a significant encroachment upon personal liberty, the State may prevail only upon showing a subordinating interest which is compelling,' Bates v. [City of] Little Rock, 361 U.S. 516, 524 [80 S.Ct. 412, 4 L.Ed.2d 480]." Griswold v. Connecticut, 381 U.S. 479, 497, 85 S.Ct. 1678, 14 L.Ed.2d 510 (1965) (concurring opinion of Mr. Justice Goldberg). *See also* Kramer v. Union Free School District, 395 U.S. 621, 89 S.Ct. 1886, 23 L.Ed.2d 583 (1969).

ROE v. WADE

1223

Cite as 314 F.Supp. 1217 (1970)

To be sure, the defendant has presented the Court with several compelling justifications for state presence in the area of abortions. These include the legitimate interests of the state in seeing to it that abortions are performed by competent persons and in adequate surroundings. Concern over abortion of the "quickened" fetus may well rank as another such interest. The difficulty with the Texas Abortion Laws is that, even if they promote these interests,[15] they far outstrip these justifications in their impact by prohibiting *all* abortions except those performed "for the purpose of saving the life of the mother."[16]

[7–9] It is axiomatic that the fact that a statutory scheme serves permissible or even compelling state interests will not save it from the consequences of unconstitutional overbreadth. *E. g.*, Thornhill v. Alabama, 310 U.S. 88, 60 S.Ct. 736, 84 L.Ed. 1093 (1940); Buchanan v. Batchelor, 308 F.Supp. 729 (N.D.Tex. 1970). While the Ninth Amendment right to choose to have an abortion is not unqualified or unfettered, a statute designed to regulate the circumstances of abortions must restrict its scope to compelling state interests. There is unconstitutional overbreadth in the Texas Abortion Laws because the Texas Legislature did not limit the scope of the statutes to such interests. On the contrary, the Texas statutes, in their monolithic interdiction, sweep far beyond any areas of compelling state interest.

[10] Not only are the Texas Abortion Laws unconstitutionally overbroad, they are also unconstitutionally vague. The Supreme Court has declared that "a statute which either forbids or requires the doing of an act in terms so vague that men of common intelligence must necessarily guess at its meaning and differ as to its application violates the first essential of due process of law." Connally v.

General Construction Co., 269 U.S. 385, 391, 46 S.Ct. 126, 70 L.Ed. 322 (1926). "No one may be required at peril of life, liberty or property to speculate as to the meaning of penal statutes. All are entitled to be informed as to what the State commands or forbids." Lanzetta v. New Jersey, 306 U.S. 451, 453, 59 S.Ct. 618, 83 L.Ed. 888 (1939). *See also* Giaccio v. Pennsylvania, 382 U.S. 399, 402–403, 86 S.Ct. 518, 15 L.Ed.2d 447 (1966). Under this standard the Texas statutes fail the vagueness test.

The Texas Abortion Laws fail to provide Dr. Hallford and physicians of his class with proper notice of what acts in their daily practice and consultation will subject them to criminal liability. Article 1196 provides:

"Nothing in this chapter applies to an abortion procured or attempted by medical advice for the purpose of saving the life of the mother."

It is apparent that there are grave and manifold uncertainties in the application of Article 1196. How *likely* must death be? Must death be certain if the abortion is not performed? Is it enough that the woman could not undergo birth without an ascertainably higher possibility of death than would normally be the case? What if the woman threatened suicide if the abortion was not performed? How *imminent* must death be if the abortion is not performed? Is it sufficient if having the child will shorten the life of the woman by a number of years? These questions simply cannot be answered.

The grave uncertainties in the application of Article 1196 and the consequent uncertainty concerning criminal liability under the related abortion statutes are more than sufficient to render the Texas Abortion Laws unconstitutionally vague in violation of the Due Process Clause of the Fourteenth Amendment.

---

15. It is not clear whether the Texas laws presently serve the interests asserted by the defendant. For instance, the Court gathers from a reading of the challenged statutes that they presently would permit an abortion "for the purpose of saving the

life of the mother" to be performed *anywhere* and quite possibly by *one other than a physician.*

16. Article 1196.

II.

We come finally to a consideration of the appropriateness of plaintiffs' request for injunctive relief. Plaintiffs have suggested in oral argument that, should the Court declare the Texas Abortion Laws unconstitutional, that decision would of itself warrant the issuance of an injunction against state enforcement of the statutes. However, the Court is of the opinion that it must abstain from granting the injunction.

Clearly, the question whether to abstain concerning an injunction against the enforcement of state criminal laws is divorced from concerns of abstention in rendering a declaratory judgment. Quoting from Zwickler v. Koota,

> "[A] request for a declaratory judgment that a state statute is overbroad on its face must be considered independently of any request for injunctive relief against enforcement of that statute. We hold that a federal district court has the duty to decide the appropriateness and merits of the declaratory request irrespective of its conclusion as to the propriety of the issuance of the injunction." 389 U.S. at 254, 88 S.Ct. at 399.

[11] The strong reluctance of federal courts to interfere with the process of state criminal procedure was reflected in Dombrowski v. Pfister, 380 U.S. 479, 484–485, 85 SCt. 1116, 1120–21, 14 L.Ed. 2d 22 (1965):

> "[T]he Court has recognized that federal interference with a State's goodfaith administration of its criminal laws is peculiarly inconsistent with our federal framework. It is generally to be assumed that state courts and prosecutors will observe constitutional limitations as expounded by this Court, and that the mere possibility of erroneous initial application of constitutional standards will usually not

amount to the irreparable injury necessary to justify a disruption of orderly state proceedings."

This federal policy of non-interference with state criminal prosecutions must be followed except in cases where "statutes are justifiably attacked on their face as abridging free expression," or where statutes are justifiably attacked "as applied for the purpose of discouraging protected activities." Dombrowski v. Pfister, 380 U.S. at 489–490, 85 S.Ct. at 1122.

[12] Neither of the above prerequisites can be found here. While plaintiffs' first substantive argument rests on notions of privacy which are to a degree common to the First and Ninth Amendments, we do not believe that plaintiffs can seriously argue that the Texas Abortion Laws are vulnerable "on their face as abridging free expression." [17] Further, deliberate application of the statutes "for the purpose of discouraging protected activities" has not been alleged. We therefore conclude that we must abstrain from issuing an injunction against enforcement of the Texas Abortion Laws.

CONCLUSION

In the absence of any contested issues of fact, we hold that the motions for summary judgment of the plaintiff Roe and plaintiff-intervenor Hallford should be granted as to their request for declaratory judgment. In granting declaratory relief, we find the Texas Abortion Laws unconstitutional for vagueness and overbreadth, though for the reasons herein stated we decline to issue an injunction. We need not here delineate the factors which could qualify the right of a mother to have an abortion. It is sufficient to state that legislation concerning abortion must address itself to more than a bare negation of that right.

---

17.   "[T]he door is not open to all who would test the validity of state statutes or conduct a federally supervised pre-trial of a state prosecution by the simple expe-

dient of alleging that the prosecution somehow affects First Amendment rights." Porter v. Kimzey, 309 F.Supp. 993, 995 (N.D.Ga.1970).

1225

JUDGMENT

This action came on for hearing on motions for summary judgment before a three-judge court composed of Irving L. Goldberg, Circuit Judge, Sarah T. Hughes and W. M. Taylor, Jr., District Judges. The defendant in both cases is Henry Wade, District Attorney of Dallas County, Texas. In one action plaintiffs are John and Mary Doe, husband and wife, and in the other Jane Roe and James Hubert Hallford, M.D., intervenor.

The case having been heard on the merits, the Court, upon consideration of affidavits, briefs and arguments of counsel, finds as follows:

Findings of Fact

(1) Plaintiff Jane Roe, plaintiff-intervenor James Hubert Hallford, M.D., and the members of their respective classes have standing to bring this lawsuit.

(2) Plaintiffs John and Mary Doe failed to allege facts sufficient to create a present controversy and therefore do not have standing.

(3) Articles 1191, 1192, 1193, 1194 and 1196 of the Texas Penal Code, hereinafter referred to as the Texas Abortion Laws, are so written as to deprive single women and married persons of the opportunity to choose whether to have children.

(4) The Texas Abortion Laws are so vaguely worded as to produce grave and manifold uncertainties concerning the circumstances which would produce criminal liability.

Conclusions of Law

(1) This case is a proper one for a three-judge court.

(2) Abstention, concerning plaintiffs' request for a declaratory judgment, is unwarranted.

(3) The fundamental right of single women and married persons to choose whether to have children is protected by the Ninth Amendment, through the Fourteenth Amendment.

314 F.Supp.—77½

(4) The Texas Abortion Laws infringe upon this right.

(5) The defendant has not demonstrated that the infringement of plaintiffs' Ninth Amendment rights by the Texas Abortion Laws is necessary to support a compelling state interest.

(6) The Texas Abortion Laws are consequently void on their face because they are unconstitutionally overbroad.

(7) The Texas Abortion Laws are void on their face because they are vague in violation of the Due Process Clause of the Fourteenth Amendment.

(8) Abstention, concerning plaintiffs' request for an injunction against the enforcement of the Texas Abortion Laws, is warranted.

It is therefore ordered, adjudged and decreed that: (1) the complaint of John and Mary Doe be dismissed; (2) the Texas Abortion Laws are declared void on their face for unconstitutional overbreadth and for vagueness; (3) plaintiffs' application for injunction be dismissed.

In the
Supreme Court of the United States
October Term, 1970

No._____

Jane Roe, John Doe, and Mary Doe, Appellants,

James Hubert Hallford, M.D., Appellant-Intervenor,

v.

Henry Wade, Appellee.

On Appeal from the United States District Court for the Northern District of Texas

Brief for Appellant

Roy Lucas
The James Madison Constitutional Law Institute
Four Patchin Place
New York, N.Y. 10011

Norman Dorsen
School of Law
New York University
Washington Square South
New York, N.Y. 10003

Linda N. Coffee
2130 First National Bank Building
Dallas, Texas 75202

Sarah Weddington
3710 Lawton
Austin, Texas 78731

Roy L. Merrill, Jr.
Daugherty, Bruner, Lastelick &
Anderson
1130 Mercantile Bank Building
Dallas, Texas 75201

Attorneys for Appellants

TABLE OF CONTENTS

IN THE
SUPREME COURT OF THE
UNITED STATES
OCTOBER TERM, 1970
NO. .....

JANE ROE, JOHN DOE, AND MARY DOE,
APPELLANTS,
JAMES HUBERT HALLFORD, M.D.,
APPELLANT-INTERVENOR,
V.
HENRY WADE, APPELLEE.

ON APPEAL FROM THE UNITED
STATES DISTRICT COURT FOR THE
NORTHERN DISTRICT OF TEXAS

BRIEF FOR APPELLANT

Appellants bring this direct appeal from a judgment entered June 17, 1970, by a statutory three-judge United States District Court for the Northern District of Texas. The judgment appealed from granted these Appellants (Plaintiffs below) a declaration that the Texas anti-abortion statutes were unconstitutional on their face, by reason of overbreadth affecting fundamental individual rights, and that provisions in the statute suffered from unconstitutional uncertainty. However, the judgment denied a permanent injunction which had been sought as necessary in aid of the District Court's jurisdiction to enjoin future enforcement of the statute declared invalid. Appellants submit this Statement to show that this is a direct appeal over which this Court has jurisdiction, and that the appeal presents important and substantial federal questions which merit plenary review.

CITATION TO OPINIONS BELOW

The June 17, 1970, opinion of the statutory three-judge United States District Court for the Northern District of Texas is not yet reported. The text of the decision is set out in the Appendix, *infra*, at 7a.

JURISDICTION

(i) On March 3, 1970, Appellant Jane Roe filed her original complaint,[1] basing jurisdiction on 28 U.S.C. § 1343(3) (1964 ed.), and comple-

mentary remedial statutes, 28 U.S.C. § 2201 (1964 ed.); 42 U.S.C. § 1983 (1964 ed.). On the same day Appellants John and Mary Doe filed a complaint predicating federal jurisdiction on the same statutes. On March 23, 1970, the District Court granted leave for Appellant James H. Hallford, M.D., to intervene as a party-plaintiff, on the basis of a complaint alleging a class action and the same jurisdictional grounds set out above. Subsequently, on April 22, 1970, Appellant Jane Roe amended her complaint to sue "on behalf of herself and all others similarly situated" (App. at 8a n. 1). Appellants John and Mary Doe also amended their complaints to assert a class action (*Id.*). All Appellants, from their respective positions as married couples, pregnant single women, and practicing physicians asked that the Texas anti-abortion statutes[2] be declared unconstitutional on their face, and for an injunction against future enforcement of the statutes. A statutory three-judge United States District Court was requested and convened pursuant to 28 U.S.C. §§ 2281, 2284 (1964 ed.).

(ii) The final judgment of the statutory three-judge District Court, granting Appellants' request for a declaratory judgment, but denying any injunctive relief, was entered on June 17, 1970 (App. at 4a). On Monday, August 17, 1970, all Appellants filed with the United States District Court for the Northern District of Texas notices of appeal to this Court (App. at 1a), pursuant to 28 U.S.C. § 2101(b) (1964 ed.), and SUP. CT. RULES 11, 34 (July 1, 1970 ed.), 398 U.S. 1015, 1021, 1045 (1970). A protective appeal to the United States Court of Appeals for the Fifth Circuit was noticed on July 23, 1970, by Appellant Hallford (App. at 23a), and on July 24, 1970, by Appellant Jane Roe (App. at 21a).

(iii) Jurisdiction of this Court to review by direct appeal the three-judge District Court's final judgment denying a permanent injunction is conferred by 28 U.S.C. § 1253 (1964 ed.).

(iv) Cases which sustain the jurisdiction of this Court are: *Evans* v. *Cornman*, 398 U.S. 419, 420 (1970); *Goldberg* v. *Kelly*, 397 U.S. 254, 261 (1970); *Carter* v. *Jury Comm'n of Greene County*, 396 U.S. 320, 328 (1970); *Moore* v. *Ogilvie*, 394 U.S. 814, 815–16 (1969); *Williams* v. *Rhodes*, 393 U.S. 23, 26–28 (1968); *Dinis* v. *Volpe*, 389 U.S. 570 (1968) (per curiam); *Hale* v. *Bimco Trading Co.*, 306 U.S. 375, 376–78 (1939).

---

[1] The Complaint and all other documents referred to in this Jurisdictional Statement are part of the record on appeal.

[2] The statutes, set out verbatim, *infra*, at 4–5, are 2A TEXAS PENAL CODE arts. 1191–1194, 1196, at 429–36 (1961).

STATUTES INVOLVED

2A TEXAS PENAL CODE art. 1196, at 436 (1961):

"Nothing in this chapter applies to an abortion procured or attempted by medical advice for the purpose of saving the life of the mother."

2A TEXAS PENAL CODE art. 1191, at 429 (1961):

"If any person shall designedly administer to a pregnant woman or knowingly procure to be administered with her consent any drug or medicine, or shall use towards her any violence or means whatever externally or internally applied, and thereby procure an abortion, he shall be confined in the penitentiary not less than two nor more than five years; if it be done without her consent, the punishment shall be doubled. By 'abortion' is meant that the life of the fetus or embryo shall be destroyed in the woman's womb or that a premature birth thereof be caused."

2A TEXAS PENAL CODE art. 1192, at 433 (1961):

"Whoever furnishes the means for procuring an abortion knowing the purpose intended is an accomplice."

2A TEXAS PENAL CODE art. 1193, at 434 (1961):

"If the means used shall fail to produce an abortion, the offender is nevertheless guilty of an attempt to produce abortion, provided it be shown that such means were calculated to produce that result, and shall be fined not less than one hundred nor more than one thousand dollars."

2A TEXAS PENAL CODE art. 1194, at 435 (1961):

"If the death of the mother is occasioned by an abortion so produced or by an attempt to effect the same it is murder."

QUESTIONS PRESENTED

I. Whether the Three-Judge Court Should Have Enjoined Future Enforcement of the Texas Anti-Abortion Laws, Which the Court Had Declared Unconstitutional, Where an Injunction was Necessary in Aid of the Court's Jurisdiction, Proper to Effectuate the Declaratory Judgment, and Needed to Prevent Irreparable Injury to Important Federal Rights of the Class of Pregnant Women Who Are or Will be Seeking Abortions, and the Class of Physicians Who are Forced to Reject such Women as Patients Because of a Reasonable Fear of Prosecution.

II. Whether a Married Couple, and Others Similarly Situated, Have Standing to Challenge the Texas Anti-Abortion Laws, Where Said Laws Have a Present and Destructive Effect on their Marital Relations, They are Unable to Utilize Fully Effective Contraceptive Methods, Pregnancy Would Seriously Harm the Woman's Health, and Such a Couple Could Not Obtain Judicial Relief in Sufficient Time After Pregnancy to Prevent Irreparable Injury.

STATEMENT OF THE CASE

Appellants brought three actions on behalf of three variously situated classes of Plaintiffs.

John and Mary Doe, a childless married couple, sued on behalf of themselves and all others similarly situated. Mary Doe has a neural-chemical disorder which renders pregnancy a threat to her physical and mental health, although not to her survival. Her physician has so advised her, and has also advised against using oral contraceptives. The alternate means of contraception used by John and Mary Doe is subject to a significant risk of failure. In such event, Mary Doe would like to, but legally could not, obtain a therapeutic abortion in a suitable medical facility in Texas. The probability of contraceptive failure in the class represented by Mary Doe is unquestionably high, when the size of the class is considered. Also, the limitations of judicial relief for a pregnant woman seeking an abortion are well known.[3] For Mary Doe and others in her position, a pre-pregnancy ruling on the validity of the Texas anti-abortion laws was the only ruling that could grant her the relief she would be seeking. Any other decision would simply be too late to prevent irreparable injury. Accord-

---

[3] The period between pregnancy detection, which normally occurs after the fourth week, and the safest time for a therapeutic abortion, before the twelfth week, leaves little time for judicial deliberation. With the notable exception of the Seventh Circuit, courts have declined to render a decision on behalf of a pregnant woman in the limited time available. In the present case, the first complaint was filed March 3, 1970, and followed after fifteen full weeks by a decision on the merits, June 17, 1970. *Compare Doe* v. *Randall*, 314 F. Supp. 32 (D. Minn. 1970) (nearly five weeks between decision and complaint); *Doe* v. *Lefkowitz*, 69 Civ. 4423 (S.D.N.Y. Dec. 12, 1969) (per curiam) (preliminary injunction denied until all factual materials developed by deposition); and *California* v. *Belous*, 71 Cal. 2d ——, 458 P.2d 194, 80 Cal. Rptr. 354 (1969) (argument March 3, 1969; decision September 5, 1969); with *Doe* v. *Scott*, No. 18382 (7th Cir. Mar. 30, 1970) (per curiam), *rev'g* 310 F. Supp. 688 (N.D. Ill. Mar. 27, 1970) (order entered in three days where pregnancy caused by rape).

ingly, John and Mary Doe brought an action for declaratory and injunctive relief against the present effect of the Texas statutes on their marital relations, and the inevitable future effect the statutes would have, in the certain event that a member of the class would become pregnant and not qualify for a legal abortion in Texas.

Jane Roe, an unmarried pregnant woman, also brought an action of the same nature, on her own behalf and for all others similarly situated. Jane Roe had been unable to obtain a legal abortion in a medical facility in Texas, because her survival was not threatened by continued pregnancy, and no hospital would perform the abortion, in light of the Texas anti-abortion statutes.[4] Jane Roe was financially unable to journey to another jurisdiction with less restrictive laws on abortion, and accordingly had no recourse other than continuing an unwanted pregnancy, or risking her life and health at the hands of a non-medical criminal abortionist.

James H. Hallford, M.D., intervened as a Plaintiff, representing himself and other licensed Texas physicians similarly situated. Dr. Hallford's interest was twofold. As a physician, he is requested by patients, on a regular and recurring basis, to arrange for medically induced abortions in hospitals or other appropriate clinical facilities. This he cannot do, for several reasons. The Texas anti-abortion statutes are unclear in their potential application to the situations in which patients request abortions. Consequently, both physician and hospital must exercise special caution to avoid prosecution. Also, the potential sweep of the statutes is so drastic that the only clear case of legal abortion is one in which the patient is near to certain death. These cases are rare; hence the typical patient's case will be legally uncertain, or of certain illegality. To avoid the realistic possibility of severe penal and administrative sanctions, the physician must turn away the typical patient. Since the conscientious physician knows full well that such a patient may seek out an incompetent non-medical abortionist, thereby endangering her life or health, he will continually be forced by the statute to

breach his professional duty of care to the patient.[5] To rectify this invasion of the physician-patient relationship, Dr. Hallford brought this action to enjoin future enforcement of the Texas anti-abortion statutes, against himself, or against any other physician similarly situated.

Dr. Hallford's second interest in bringing the action was to seek relief against two indictments outstanding against him on abortion charges.[6] Under Texas law, a physician charged with abortion is presumed guilty, if the State is able to establish the fact of the abortion. The physician, in such a case, must admit complicity in the act, waive his privilege against self-incrimination, and defend on the basis that the abortion was "procured or attempted by medical advice for the purpose of saving the life of the [woman]." 2A TEXAS PENAL CODE art. 1196, at 436 (1961). Decisions such as *Veevers* v. *State*, 354 S.W.2d 161 (Tex. Ct. Crim. App. 1962), hold that the Article 1196 exception is an affirmative defense, which the physician must raise and prove. In numerous respects, this settled state-law practice deprives a physician of essential constitutional rights. Moreover, state practice invades the privacy of physician and patient by exposing intimate and confidential associations to the public glare of a criminal trial. In addition, the possibility of conviction carries with it the revocation of the physician's license before appeal. These elements of state practice render defense to criminal abortion charges a wholly inadequate means of vindicating the physician's constitutional rights. Accordingly, Dr. Hallford brought the present action as a Plaintiff-Intervenor in the main actions filed by Jane Roe, John Doe, and Mary Doe. The cases were consolidated, and argued together.

Essentially, the federal questions raised by each individual Plaintiff were raised by all. The complaints charged that the Texas anti-abortion statutes deprived physicians and patients of rights protected by the First, Fourth, Fifth, Eighth, Ninth, and Fourteenth Amendments, as construed by this Court in decisions such as

---

[4] While Texas does not punish the woman who persuades a physician to abort her, the anti-abortion statutes impose a felony sanction of up to five years for the physician. 2A TEXAS PENAL CODE art. 1191, at 429 (1961). Moreover, the physician risks cancellation of his license to practice. 12B TEXAS CIV. STAT. art. 4505, at 541 (1966); *id.* art. 4506, at 132 (Supp. 1969–70). Also, the hospital can lose its operating license for permitting an illegal abortion within its facilities. 12B TEXAS CIV. STAT. art. 4437f, § 9, at 216 (1966).

[5] If prior cases on abortion prosecutions in Texas are a reliable index, patients who are turned away by physicians have recourse only to an assortment of quacks. *See, e.g., Fletcher* v. *State*, 362 S.W.2d 845 (Tex. Ct. Crim. App. 1962) (non-physician using crude techniques in "cottage on the river"; hysterectomy necessary to prevent girl's death); *Catching* v. *State*, 364 S.W.2d 691 (Tex. Ct. Crim. App. 1962) (non-physician; police found "tool box containing several catheters, a knitting needle, and other items").

[6] *State* v. *Hallford*, Nos. C-69-2524-H & C-69-5307-IH (Tex. Crim. Ct., Dallas County).

Griswold v. *Connecticut*, 381 U.S. 479 (1965).[7] Defendants interposed objections to the standing of each Plaintiff, the propriety of adjudication versus abstention, the ripeness of the dispute for present decision, and the propriety of injunctive relief.

A statutory three-judge court, convened in response to Plaintiffs' request for injunctive relief from the Texas anti-abortion statutes, granted a declaratory judgment that the statutes were unconstitutionally vague and overbroad.

After dealing with the jurisdictional questions of standing,[8] ripeness,[9] and abstention,[10] raised by the Defendants, the three-judge court stated:

> "[T]he Texas Abortion Laws must be declared unconstitutional because they deprive single women and married couples of their right, secured by the Ninth Amendment, to choose whether to have children" (App. at 12a).

Reliance was placed on decisions by this Court establishing "[r]elative sanctuaries for such 'fundamental' interests [as] the family,[11] the marital couple,[12] and the individual."[13] Further precedent was found in similar decisions by other federal and state courts,[14] as well as a major treatment of *Griswold* in the abortion setting by Retired Justice Tom C. Clark, *see* Clark, *Religion, Morality, and Abortion: A Constitutional Appraisal,* 2 LOYOLA UNIV. (L.A.) L. REV. 1 (1969).

Not only were the statutes overbroad, and not justified by a narrowly drawn compelling State interest, but the language of the statutes was unconstitutionally vague. Although a physician might lawfully perform an abortion "for the purpose of saving the life of the [pregnant woman],"[15] the circumstances giving rise to such necessity were far from clear. The district court detailed a few of the more apparent ambiguities:

> "How *likely* must death be? Must death be certain if the abortion is not performed? Is it enough that the woman could not undergo birth without an ascertainably higher possibility of death than would normally be the case? What if the woman threatened suicide if the abortion was not performed? How *imminent* must death be if the abortion is not performed? Is it sufficient if having the child will shorten the life of the woman by a number of years? These questions simply cannot be answered." App. at 71a.

After finding the Texas anti-abortion statutes unconstitutional on two grounds, the district court considered the propriety of injunctive relief. Acting on the assumption that *Dombrowski* v. *Pfister,* 380 U.S. 479 (1965) controlled, the court refused to enjoin any present or future enforcement of the statutes. Appellants have brought this appeal to review the denial of injunctive relief.

THE QUESTIONS ARE SUBSTANTIAL

The present appeal presents important and unresolved federal questions which have not been but should be determined by this Court. A district court's refusal to enjoin present and future enforcement of a statute declared facially unconstitutional raises important issues for the vindication by federal courts of rights guaranteed by the Constitution. Decisions by this Court have not in recent years clarified the propriety of federal injunctive relief against state criminal statutes outside the pristine speech area of the First Amendment. A decision by this Court is needed, particularly where, as here, the injunction was sought by some Appellants who were total strangers to any pending prosecutions, and by one Appellant for whom defense of state court prosecution would be a

---

[7] In the brief on the merits, Appellants will more fully elaborate this complex substantive constitutional point. For purposes of this Statement, however, it is sufficient to note that *Griswold* has been applied in the abortion context by numerous state and federal courts. *See* cases cited in notes 31–37, *infra,* and accompanying text.

[8] Jane Roe, the pregnant Plaintiff, and Dr. Hallford, had standing because they "occupy positions *vis-à-vis* the Texas Abortion Laws sufficient to differentiate them from the general public." App. at 9a. Also, on the authority of *Griswold,* Dr. Hallford had standing to raise the "rights of his patients, single women and married couples, as well as rights of his own." App. at 9a n. 3. John and Mary Doe, however, were held to lack standing. App. at 5a.

[9] The district court was "satisfied that there presently exists a degree of contentiousness between Roe and Hallford and the defendant to establish a 'case of actual controversy'. . . ." App. at 10a.

[10] *Zwickler* v. *Koota,* 389 U.S. 241, 248–49 (1967), was sufficient authority to preclude abstention. App. at 11a.

[11] *See Pierce* v. *Society of Sisters,* 268 U.S. 510 (1925); *Meyer* v. *Nebraska,* 262 U.S. 390 (1923); *Prince* v. *Massachusetts,* 321 U.S. 158 (1944), all cited by the district court. App. at 13a.

[12] *See Griswold* v. *Connecticut,* 381 U.S. 479 (1965).

[13] *See Skinner* v. *Oklahoma,* 316 U.S. 535 (1942); *Stanley* v. *Georgia,* 394 U.S. 557 (1969).

[14] *See, e.g., McCann* v. *Babbitz,* 310 F. Supp. 293 (E.D. Wis.) (per curiam), *appeal docketed,* 38 U.S.L.W. 3524 (U.S. June 20, 1970) (No. 297, Oct. 1970 Term); *United States* v. *Vuitch,* 305 F. Supp. 1032 (D.D.C. 1969), *ques. of juris. postponed to merits,* 397 U.S. 1061, *further juris. questions propounded,* 399 U.S. 923 (1970); *California* v. *Belous,* 71 Cal. 2d ———, 458 P.2d 194, 80 Cal. Rptr. 354 (1969), *cert. denied,* 397 U.S. 915 (1970).

[15] 2A TEXAS PENAL CODE art. 1196, at 436 (1961).

wholly inadequate means of vindicating his federally protected rights.

In addition, the substantive issues in the case, which will surely be raised for further review by Appellee, are novel issues of profound national import, affecting the lives of many thousands of American citizens each year. Further, the same issues are presented in four appeals already docketed,[16] a variety of conflicting decisions in the lower courts,[17] and a host of pending actions in federal and state lower courts.[18]

INTRODUCTION

In the remainder of this Jurisdictional Statement, Appellants will show that the questions presented are substantial, and merit plenary review by the full Court. Because of the novelty and complexity of the issues, and the limited function of a Jurisdictional Statement, this showing will not undertake to develop all arguments in depth.

I. The three-judge court should have enjoined future enforcement of the Texas anti-abortion laws, which the court had declared unconstitutional, because an injunction was necessary in aid of the court's jurisdiction, proper to effectuate the declaratory judgment, and needed to prevent irreparable injury to important federal rights of the class of pregnant women who are or will be seeking abortions, and the class of physicians who are forced to reject such women as patients out of a reasonable fear of prosecution

A. The subject matter of the merits involves important and substantial federal constitutional questions. On the merits, Appellants argued successfully that decisions by this Court, construing the First, Fourth, Ninth, and Fourteenth Amendments supported a claim that the Texas anti-abortion statutes swept too broadly and thereby invaded rights protected by the Constitution (App. at 5a, 6a, 12a-16a).[19] Moreover, the statutes in question were held to be so vague and indefinite as to violate the Fourteenth Amendment due process guarantee of reasonably specific legislation (App. at 5a, 6a, 16a-18a). That guarantee is particularly significant where, as here, important personal rights are at stake, and an impermissibly vague statute operates to inhibit a wide range of constitutionally protected conduct.[20]

Ultimately, the substantive question presented is whether a State may enact a felony statute to punish a physician, a woman, and her husband, with five years in state prison, where the couple requests, and the physician performs, a therapeutic surgical procedure to abort a pregnancy which the couple did not want, but were unable to prevent.[21] Under *Griswold* v. *Connecticut*, 381 U.S. 479 (1965), it is clear that a husband and wife[22] are constitutionally privi-

---

[16] (1) *United States* v. *Vuitch*, No. 84, arises under a differently worded felony abortion statute, however, and poses numerous alternate grounds for affirmance other than the central questions presented here, of overbreadth and vagueness.
(2) *McCann* v. *Babbitz*, No. 297, was decided at the federal district court level on grounds virtually the same as those below in the present case. It appears in *McCann*, however, that the appeal was taken by the State solely from the granting of a declaratory judgment for Dr. Babbitz. No appeal was taken from the denial of an injunction, as 28 U.S.C. § 1253 (1964 ed.), would seem to require, and as this Court twice held last Term, *Mitchell* v. *Donovan*, 398 U.S. 427 (1970) (per curiam), *vacating* 300 F. Supp. 1145 (D. Minn. 1969), with directions to enter a fresh judgment of dismissal, to enable appellants to appeal to the Eighth Circuit; *Rockefeller* v. *Catholic Medical Center*, 397 U.S. 820 (1970) (per curiam).
(3) *Hodgson* v. *Randall*, No. 728, is an appeal from a three-judge federal court decision refusing to enjoin state court prosecution of a physician who sought federal relief before performing a hospital therapeutic abortion for German measles indications, and long before the state indictment.
(4) *Hodgson* v. *Minnesota*, No. 729, involves the same subject matter as No. 728, and is an appeal from the Supreme Court of Minnesota's denial of a writ of prohibition to a state trial court which had upheld the constitutionality of an abortion statute, where unconstitutionality was the only defense to the charges.
[17] *See* cases cited in notes 31–37, *infra*, and accompanying text.
[18] *See* cases cited in note 38, *infra*.

[19] In particular, Appellants relied upon the reasoning of *Griswold* v. *Connecticut*, 381 U.S. 479 (1965), where this Court invalidated a state law prohibiting use of contraceptive devices, because the law swept too broadly and invaded "a relationship lying within the zone of privacy created by several fundamental constitutional guarantees." 381 U.S. at 485.
[20] The most reliable estimates hold that fewer than 10,000 hospital therapeutic abortions are performed yearly, in states where there has been no abortion law reform. *See* Tietze, *Therapeutic Abortions in the United States*, 101 AM. J. OBST. & GYNEC. 784, 787 (1968). These constitute a minute proportion of all unwanted pregnancies which face American couples each year. Those excluded from hospitals have two alternatives: continuation of unwanted pregnancy, or extra-hospital, probably illegal, induced abortion.
[21] The woman is not an accomplice under Texas law, but other participants, including her husband, are fully liable. *See Willingham* v. *State*, 33 Tex. Crim. 98, 25 S.W. 424 (1894) (woman neither principal nor accomplice).
[22] *Griswold* was silent on the more significant problem of access by unmarried persons to contraceptives. A result of non-access, and failure, is the birth of over 100,000 illegitimate children yearly to girls age nineteen or younger. *See* U.S. BUREAU OF THE CENSUS: *Statistical Abstract of the United States: 1969*, Table 59, at 50 (90th ed. 1969).
Outside of the state judiciary in Massachusetts, authorities have uniformly held the *Griswold* rationale applicable to litigants who had not entered into the

leged to control the size and spacing of their family by contraception. The failure of contraception, however, is commonplace.[23] Authoritative estimates are that between 750,000 and 1,000,000 births each year are unwanted.[24] These are in addition to the 200,000 to 1,000,000 unwanted pregnancies which are estimated to end in abortions induced outside of the clinical setting.[25] Taken together, some 950,000 to 2,000,000 unwanted births plus non-clinical abortions occur yearly. Accordingly, one must conclude that restrictive anti-abortion statutes, such as the Texas law in question here, drastically affect the conduct of literally millions of American citizens.

The national significance of the issues in this case can also be inferred from increased activity within the medical profession, and in the legislatures. On June 25, 1970, the House of Delegates of the American Medical Association voted to permit licensed physicians to perform abortions in hospitals, with the sole additional qualification that two other physicians be consulted.[26] Physicians were cautioned, however,

not to violate existing state statutes, forty-seven of which are far more restrictive.[27] Three states in 1970—New York, Alaska, and Hawaii—removed, for the most part, any criminal penalties which might previously have been imposed upon physicians for performing abortions in appropriate medical facilities.[28] From 1967 to 1970, twelve states had adopted therapeutic abortion statutes similar to that of the MODEL PENAL CODE's 1962 Proposed Official Draft.[29] More recently, on August 4, the Commissioners on Uniform State Laws issued a Second Tentative Draft of a UNIFORM ABORTION ACT. The Act sanctioned abortions by licensed physicians "within 24 weeks after the commencement of the pregnancy; or if after 24 weeks . . ." under the circumstances set out in the MODEL PENAL CODE proposal.

These developments bear witness to the importance of the issues presented here.

While policy-making and legislative bodies have debated the issue of abortion, courts, confined to the constitutional framework, have been asked to resolve the questions of individual privacy and legislative power which are presented here. Although the questions framed in this case have not been decided[30] by this

---

marriage contract. *Compare Baird* v. *Eisenstadt*, —— F.2d ——, No. 7578 (1st Cir. July 6, 1970) (invalidating Massachusetts statute which outlawed distribution of contraceptives to the unmarried), *Mindel* v. *United States Civil Service Comm'n*, 312 F. Supp. 485 (N.D. Calif. 1970) (reinstating postal clerk who had been dismissed for cohabitation without benefit of marriage), *and* the present case, *Roe* v. *Wade*, —— F. Supp. ——, Civ. No. 3-3690-B (N.D. Tex. June 17, 1970) (per curiam) (Texas anti-abortion statutes "deprive single women and married couples of their right, secured by the Ninth Amendment, to choose whether to have children."), *with Sturgis* v. *Attorney General*, 260 N.E.2d 687, 690 (Mass. 1970) (directly contrary to federal decision in *Baird*).

[23] If a married couple is to have private control over numbers and spacing of children, induced abortion is absolutely necessary as a backstop to contraceptive failure. For compilation of contraceptive failure rates according to method used, see P. EHRLICH & A. EHRLICH, POPULATION RESOURCES ENVIRONMENT 218–19 & Table 9–1 (1970); N. EASTMAN & L. HELLMAN, WILLIAMS OBSTETRICS 1068–75 (13th ed. 1966); Hardin, *History and Future of Birth Control*, 10 PERSPECTIVES IN BIOLOGY & MED. 1, 7–13 (1966); Tietze, *Clinical Effectiveness of Contraceptive Methods*, 78 AM. J. OBST. & GYNEC. 650 (1959).

[24] The most recent scholarly examination of unwanted birth magnitudes will appear in a forthcoming issue of SCIENCE. A summary of these findings by Dr. Charles F. Westoff of Princeton University's Office of Population Research, analyzing the 1965 National Fertility Study, appeared in the N.Y. Times, Oct. 29, 1969, at 25, col. 3.

[25] Secret induced abortions are inherently incapable of quantification. Nonetheless, one can be certain that the number is very high. For estimates, see Fisher, *Criminal Abortion*, in ABORTION IN AMERICA 3–6 (H. Rosen ed. 1967); M. CALDERONE (ed.), ABORTION IN THE UNITED STATES 180 (1958); P. GEBHARD *et al.*, PREGNANCY, BIRTH AND ABORTION 136–37 (1958); F. TAUSSIG, ABORTION: SPONTANEOUS AND INDUCED 25 (1936); Regine, *A Study of Pregnancy Wastage*, 13 MILBANK MEM. FUND QUART. No. 4, at 347–65 (1935).

[26] *See* N.Y. Times, June 26, 1970, at 1, col. 1. The statement has not yet been published in an official A.M.A. document. A recent issue of the J.A.M.A. noted that only 26 physicians had resigned from the body because of new policy. 213 J.A.M.A. 1242 (Aug. 24, 1970).

[27] For analysis of abortion laws in the United States prior to the most recent changes, see Lucas, *Laws of the United States*, in I ABORTION IN A CHANGING WORLD 127 (R. Hall ed. 1970); George, *Current Abortion Laws: Proposals and Movements for Reform*, 17 W. RES. L. REV. 371 (1966).

[28] *See, e.g.*, N.Y. PENAL LAW § 125.05(3), at 79 (McKinney Supp. 1970–71).

[29] *See* MODEL PENAL CODE § 230.3(2) (Proposed Official Draft, 1962). The states are Arkansas, California, Colorado, Delaware, Georgia, Kansas, New Mexico, North Carolina, Oregon, South Carolina, and Virginia.

[30] On at least eight occasions this Court has declined to review state court decisions which involved restrictive anti-abortion laws.

The eight denials are: *Mucie* v. *Missouri*, 398 U.S. 938 (June 1, 1970), *denying cert. to* 448 S.W.2d 879 (Mo. 1970) (manslaughter abortion conviction where patient died); *California* v. *Belous*, 397 U.S. 915 (Feb. 24, 1970), *denying cert. to* 71 Cal. 2d ——, 458 P.2d 194, 80 Cal. Rptr. 354 (1969) (statute repealed after prosecution commenced); *Molinaro* v. *New Jersey*, 396 U.S. 365 (Jan. 19, 1970) (per curiam), *dismissing appeal from* 54 N.J. 246, 254 A.2d 792 (1969) (defendant jumped bail after appeal filed); *Knight* v. *Louisiana Bd. of Medical Examiners*, 395 U.S. 933 (June 2, 1969), *denying cert. to* 252 La. 889, 214 So.2d 716 (1968) (per curiam) (federal questions not properly raised and preserved); *Morin* v. *Garra*, 395 U.S. 935 (June 2, 1969), *denying cert. to* 53 N.J. 82 (1968) (per curiam) (same); *Moretti* v. *New Jersey*, 393 U.S. 952 (Nov. 18, 1968), *denying cert. to* 52 N.J. 182, 244 A.2d 499 (1968) (conspiracy conviction; abortion to have been performed by barber); *Fulton* v. *Illinois*, 390 U.S. 953 (Mar. 4, 1968), *denying cert. to* 84 Ill. App.2d 280, 228

Court, numerous federal and state decisions attest to the substantiality of the federal questions. Moreover, the sometimes sharp divisions in the courts below illustrate further the need for a decision at this level. In showing that the Court has jurisdiction, and that the questions are substantial, Appellants will outline the divisions among lower courts.

In September, 1969, the Supreme Court of California became the first appellate court to recognize the constitutional stature of a "fundamental right of the woman to choose whether to bear children. . . ."[31] The *Belous* court found this right implicit in this Court's "repeated acknowledgment of a 'right of privacy' or 'liberty' in matters related to marriage, family, and sex."[32]

More recently, three different decisions by statutory three-judge federal courts have invalidated restrictions on access to medical abortion in Wisconsin and Georgia, as well as in the present case from Texas. The first, *McCann* v. *Babbitz*,[33] recognized in that jurisdiction a woman's

"basic right reserved to her under the ninth amendment to decide whether she should carry or reject an embryo which has not yet quickened." 310 F. Supp. at 302.

McCann grew out of the prosecution of a physician, but the three-judge court had no difficulty holding that a physician has standing to assert the rights of pregnant patients.[34]

The second recent federal decision is the present case, *Roe* v. *Wade*,[35] declaring the Texas anti-abortion statutes unconstitutional on the similar ground that

"they deprive single women and married couples of their right, secured by the Ninth Amendment, to choose whether to have children."

A third federal decision, *Doe* v. *Bolton*,[36] followed *Belous*, *McCann*, and *Roe*, holding:

"[T]he concept of personal liberty embodies a right to privacy which apparently is also broad enough to include the decision to abort a pregnancy.
". . . [T]he reasons for an abortion may not be proscribed. . . ."

Numerous lower courts have followed this lead, in both federal and state disputes.[37] In addition, three-judge courts have been re-

---

[34] The standing of a physician to assert a patient's rights along with his own follows from *Griswold* v. *Connecticut*, 381 U.S. 479, 481 (1965), and *Barrows* v. *Jackson*, 346 U.S. 249, 257 (1953). On this standing point, lower court decisions involving abortion laws all agree. *See also Planned Parenthood Ass'n of Phoenix* v. *Nelson*, Civ. No. 70–334 PHX (D. Ariz. Aug. 24, 1970) (per curiam); *Doe* v. *Bolton*, —— F. Supp. ——, Civ. No. 13676 (N.D. Ga. July 31, 1970) (per curiam); *Roe* v. *Wade*, —— F. Supp. ——, Civ. No. 3-3690-B (N.D. Tex. June 17, 1970) (per curiam); *United States ex rel. Williams* v. *Follette*, 313 F. Supp. 269, 273 (S.D.N.Y. May 12, 1970).
[35] —— F. Supp. ——, Civ. No. 3-3690-B (N.D. Tex. June 17, 1970) (per curiam).
[36] —— F. Supp. ——, Civ. No. 13676 (N.D. Ga. July 31, 1970) (per curiam).
[37] *See, e.g., State* v. *Munson* (S.D. 7th Jud. Cir., Pennington County Apr. 6, 1970) (Clarence P. Cooper, *J.*) (recognizing the woman's " 'private decision whether to bear her unquickened child' "); *State* v. *Ketchum* (Mich. Dist. Ct. Mar. 30, 1970) (Reid, *J.*) ("the statute as written infringes on the right of privacy in the physician-patient relationship, and may violate the patient's right to safe and adequate medical advice and treatment."); *Commonwealth* v. *Page*, Centre County Leg. J. at 285 (Pa. Ct. Comm. Pl., Centre County July 23, 1970) (Campbell, *P.J.*) ("the abortion statute interferes with the individual's private right to have or not to have children."); *People* v. *Gwynne*, No. 176601 (Calif. Mun. Ct., Orange County Aug. 13, 1970) (Schwab, *J.*); *People* v. *Gwynne*, No. 173309 (Calif. Mun. Ct., Orange County June 16, 1970) (Thomson, *J.*); *People* v. *Barksdale*, No. 33237C (Calif. Mun. Ct., Alameda County Mar. 24, 1970) (Foley, *J.*); *People* v. *Robb*, Nos. 149005 & 159061 (Calif. Mun. Ct., Orange County Jan. 9, 1970) (Mast, *J.*); *People* v. *Anast*, No. 69–3429 (Ill. Cir. Ct., Cook County, 1970) (Dolezal, *J.*) (holding the Illinois abortion statute "unconstitutional (1) for vagueness; and (2) for infringing upon a woman's right to control her body."); *cf. United States* v. *Vuitch*, 305 F. Supp. 1032 (D.D.C. 1969), *ques. of juris. postponed to merits*, 397 U.S. 1061, *further juris. questions propounded*, 399 U.S. 923 (1970); *United States ex rel. Williams* v. *Follette*, 313 F. Supp. 269, 272–73 (S.D.N.Y. 1970) (questions substantial, but habeas petitioner-physician remitted to state courts).

N.E.2d 203 (1967); *Carter* v. *Florida*, 376 U.S. 648 (Mar. 30, 1964), *dismissing appeal from* 150 So.2d 787 (Fla. 1963).
[31] *California* v. *Belous*, 71 Cal. 2d ——, ——, 458 P.2d 194, 199, 80 Cal. Rptr. 354, 359 (1969), *cert. denied*, 397 U.S. 915 (1970). *Belous*, a state court appeal of a conspiracy conviction of a physician, involved a statute worded almost identically to that in the present case.
One year earlier, a California trial court had ruled that the Eighth and Fourteenth Amendments prohibited license revocation proceedings against physicians who had performed hospital approved abortions on patients exposed in early pregnancy to German measles. The opinion of the trial court, however, simply enumerated those Amendments among various conclusions of law, without supporting the conclusions with any attempt at reasoned analysis. Nonetheless, the result, and the factual similarities between that and the present case, are of interest. *See Shively* v. *Board of Medical Examiners*, No. 590333 (Calif. Super. Ct., San Fran. County Sept. 24, 1968) (not reported), *on remand from* 65 Cal. 2d 475, 421 P.2d 65, 55 Cal. Rptr. 217 (1968) (granting physicians' motions for discovery, without reference to merits).
[32] 71 Cal. 2d at ——, 458 P.2d at 199, 80 Cal. Rptr. at 359, *citing, e.g., Griswold* v. *Connecticut*, 381 U.S. 479 (1965); *Loving* v. *Virginia*, 388 U.S. 1, 12 (1967); *Skinner* v. *Oklahoma ex rel. Williamson*, 316 U.S. 535, 536 (1942).
[33] 310 F. Supp. 293 (E.D. Wis. 1970) (per curiam), *appeal docketed*, 38 U.S.L.W. 3524 (U.S. June 20, 1970) (No. 297, Oct. 1970 Term).

quested and/or convened in a number of states to consider questions quite similar to those raised here.[38] The convening of a statutory court, of course, requires that the questions presented be "substantial."[39]

Scholarly commentary also recognizes that these issues are of tremendous national importance, and "substantial" in the sense of warranting determination by this Court. Retired Justice Clark addressed himself to the applicability of *Griswold* in the abortion context more than a year ago.[40] According to Justice Clark's analysis,

> "Griswold's act[41] was to prevent formation of the fetus. This, the Court found, was constitutionally protected. If an individual may prevent conception, why can he not nullify that conception when prevention fails?"[42]

To examine Justice Clark's hypothetical question in the full constitutional context, and to decide the propriety of injunctive relief in this case, the Court should note probable jurisdiction, and set the matter down for full briefing and argument.

B. Having determined the merits in appellants' favor, the three-judge court should have enjoined future enforcement of the invalid statutes. Not only do the substantive issues in this case involve important federal questions, but the remedy following judgment also presents a novel point on which this Court has not clearly ruled.

Although no state proceedings were pending or imminently threatened against Appellants Jane Roe, John Doe, and Mary Doe, or members of their respective classes, the District Court declined to grant any injunctive relief whatever. This denial of necessary relief is contrary to decisions by this Court, and has the probable effect of inviting federal-state friction, rather than lessening such untoward interaction. Moreover, the denial of injunctive relief to Dr. Hallford was equally improper, as he had requested an injunction against the commencement of any future prosecutions. As to charges then pending against Dr. Hallford, an injunction would have been proper in addition, for reasons which shall appear more fully hereinafter.

Relying entirely on *Dombrowski* v. *Pfister*, 380 U.S. 479 (1965), the three-judge court recognized a "federal policy of non-interference with state criminal prosecutions [which] must be followed except in cases where 'statutes are justifiably attacked on their face as abridging free expression,' or where statutes are justifiably attacked 'as applied for the purpose of discouraging protected activities.' " 380 U.S. at 489–90. The quote from *Dombrowski*, however, was not pertinent, for Appellants' principal thrust was not against pending prosecutions, but against any *future* enforcement and effects of the challenged statutes. The pregnant Plaintiff, Jane Roe, for example, could never be prosecuted under Texas law regardless of the number of abortions she underwent, but the statute, unless enjoined, would have the effect of keeping her from obtaining an abortion.

For the most part, Appellants were strangers to any existing or contemplated prosecutions. Their chief controversy was over the drastic impact of the statutes on their lives, not any possibility of imminent enforcement. In *Dombrowski*, the appellants were actively threatened with prosecution, and an injunction would necessarily have abated that threat by operating directly on law officers who stood ready to go forward with existing indictments. Accordingly, "special circumstances" were necessary to justify the conclusion ultimately reached.

If, however, *Dombrowski* had been purely a challenge to quantifiable and recurring effects of a state criminal statute, without the pendency of criminal charges, the case would have been different. This is shown by the ease with which this Court has reversed lower courts that refused declaratory and injunctive relief against loyalty oath statutes backed by criminal sanctions. *See Keyishian* v. *Board of Regents*, 385 U.S. 589 (1967); *Baggett* v. *Bullitt*, 377 U.S. 360, 365–66 (1964). Injunctive relief against the statute in *Dombrowski* would have presented no special problem, if the statute had been a loyalty oath backed by the very same criminal penalties, and no indictments had been waiting in the wings.

---

[38] *See, e.g., Gwynne* v. *Hicks*, Civ. No. 70-1088-CC (C.D. Calif., filed May 18, 1970); *Arnold* v. *Sendak*, IP 70-C-217 (S.D. Ind., filed Mar. 29, 1970); *Corkey* v. *Edwards*, Civ. No. 2665 (W.D.N.C., filed May 12, 1970); *YWCA of Princeton* v. *Kugler*, Civ. No. 264–70 (D.N.J., filed Mar. 5, 1970); *Hall* v. *Lefkowitz*, 305 F. Supp. 1030 (S.D.N.Y. 1969), *dismissed as moot* Op. No. 36936 (S.D.N.Y. July 1, 1970) (per curiam) (statute repealed); *Benson* v. *Johnson*, Civ. No. 70–226 (D. Ore., filed Aug. 4, 1970); *Doe* v. *Dunbar*, Civ. No. C-2402 (D. Colo., filed July 2, 1970); *Henrie* v. *Blankenship*, Civ. No. 70-C-211 (N.D. Okla., filed July 6, 1970); *Planned Parenthood Ass'n of Phoenix* v. *Nelson*, Civ. No. 70–334 PHX (D. Ariz. Aug. 24, 1970) (per curiam); *Ryan* v. *Specter*, Civ. No. 70–2527 (E.D. Pa., filed Sept. 14, 1970); *Doe* v. *Rampton*, Civ. No. 234–70 (D. Utah, filed Sept. 16, 1970).
[39] *Idlewild Bon Voyage Corp.* v. *Epstein*, 370 U.S. 713, 715 (1962) (per curiam).
[40] Tom C. Clark, *Religion, Morality, and Abortion: A Constitutional Appraisal*, 2 LOYOLA UNIV. (L.A.) L. Rev. 1–11 (1969).
[41] Although it is a minor point, Griswold was the Executive Director of Planned Parenthood in the *Griswold* case. It was the physician, the late Dr. Buxton of the Yale Medical School who had examined the patients and prescribed contraceptive devices.
[42] Clark, *supra* note 40, at 9.

Dombrowski falls in the middle ground between (1) injunctive actions which are filed and completed prior to the commencement of any state criminal proceedings, and (2) actions which are filed after "proceedings in a State court,"[43] are underway. The *Dombrowski* case itself was filed but not completed before State proceedings began.[44] Hence, while *Dombrowski* acknowledged that "[28 U.S.C. § 2283 (1964 ed.)], and its predecessors do not preclude injunctions against the institution of state court proceedings, but only bar stays of suits already instituted,"[45] this Court nonetheless required "special circumstances" to justify interference with a criminal proceeding begun shortly after the federal complaint was filed.

The present case lies chronologically in the earliest of the categories, (1), because, as to the bulk of relief sought against future enforcement of the anti-abortion statute, state proceedings have never been contemplated. Appellants were thus in the same position as petitioners contesting a loyalty oath that was backed by criminal sanctions. Their entitlement to an injunction against future enforcement should have followed as a matter of course. Put another way, Appellants were "strangers to [any pending] state court proceedings." *Hale* v. *Bimco Trading Co.*, 306 U.S. 375, 378 (1939) (Frankfurter, J.).[46] The fact of pending prosecutions against other physicians, or against Dr. Hallford based upon alleged past conduct, had no bearing on Appellants' request for prospective injunctive relief.

Accordingly, the three-judge court should have undertaken an inquiry as to the propriety of injunctive relief without reference to *Dombrowski* v. *Pfister*, and without any greater concern for hypothetical federal-state friction than exists in the ordinary case where state judicial machinery has not entered the controversy. Indeed, denial of injunctive relief was an open invitation for Texas authorities to maintain existing enforcement policies. Should this have occurred against Dr. Hallford, or any other physician member of the class he represented, a federal injunction would have been sought from the district court as "necessary in aid of its jurisdiction, or to protect or effectuate its"[47] declaratory judgment invalidating the statute. A confrontation between federal and state judiciary might then have ensued. To avoid such a possibility, the three-judge court should have enjoined future enforcement of the statute on June 17, 1970, when it ruled the statute invalid. In other words, an injunction *ab initio* would have prevented federal-state conflict, and enhanced the very policy the three-judge court thought it was following by denying the injunction.

A further reason for having granted the injunction was to avoid irreparable injury to individuals in the class of Jane Roe, and to physicians deterred by the ongoing possibility that the State might continue to enforce the statute until the controversy was determined by *this* Court. Without a coercive order on record, Texas law enforcement authorities are free to ignore the declaratory judgment rendered below, because the judgment is subject to possible reversal here. It requires no argument to show that a declaratory judgment by this Court ends the controversy,[48] but such judgments at the

---

[43] 28 U.S.C. § 2283 (1964 ed.).

[44] While *Dombrowski* did not clarify the thorny definitional problems surrounding the concept of a "proceeding" in a state court, the Court did hold that at least an indictment must be returned. The federal complaint came before the indictments in *Dombrowski*, and was held to relate back where a district court erroneously dismissed the complaint. An almost identical situation in the abortion context is before this Court in *Hodgson* v. *Randall*, No. 728, docketed Sept. 21, 1970, where law enforcement authorities secured the dismissal of a federal action for want of a case or controversy, and proceeded within two days to obtain an indictment against a physician who had been a federal plaintiff.

[45] 380 U.S. at 484 n. 2.

[46] *Hale* teaches that strangers to state proceedings may secure federal injunctive relief against a state statute, even though the effect of the federal decision may be to confuse cases pending at the same time before the highest court of the state. *Hale* affirmed a three-judge court decision enjoining enforcement of a Florida statute although "the injunction in effect stayed proceedings in the Supreme Court of Florida." 306 U.S. at 376.

[47] 28 U.S.C. § 2283 (1964 ed.).

[48] A decision by this Court on the propriety of injunctive relief, however, is necessary for guidance of lower courts in similar future controversies. Otherwise, the law of the district courts would be final law in all cases where the merits were correctly resolved, but an injunction improperly denied. In addition, as commentators have frequently observed, this Court has not resolved a sufficient variety of cases concerning the parameters of 28 U.S.C. § 2283 (1964 ed.), to provide answers to questions such as those presented here. The criteria for commencement of "proceedings in a State court," for example, are uncertain, as is the relevance of a State proceeding brought after a federal complaint. Also, the extent to which the anti-injunction statute affects declaratory judgments is in dispute, as well as the availability of injunctions against future prosecutions where one or more indictments is outstanding, or prosecutions threatened. Similarly, the availability of injunctive relief against prosecutions which threaten to inhibit wide areas of constitutionally protected conduct outside the First Amendment context is uncertain. For a more comprehensive review of the need for further guidelines from this Court in these areas, see Stickgold, *Variations on the Theme of Dombrowski v. Pfister: Federal Intervention in State Criminal Proceedings Affecting First Amendment Rights*, 1968 Wis. L. Rev. 369; Brewer, *Dombrowski v. Pfister: Federal Injunctions Against State Prosecutions in*

district court level carry much less practical import.

Appellant Dr. Hallford sought not only an injunction against future enforcement of the Texas anti-abortion statutes, but also an injunction to bar the commencement of State proceedings against him based upon two outstanding indictments. This request for injunctive relief presents several substantial questions which merit review by this Court.

Assuming that the district court improperly denied an injunction directed generally against future enforcement of the anti-abortion laws, one question is whether that injunction, if entered, should cover the commencement of prosecution under the aforesaid indictments. Whether a bare indictment, returned from the secrecy of a grand jury, alone constitutes a "proceeding in a State court" is an open question.[49] If there is no "proceeding," as this Court found in *Dombrowski*, the degree of irreparable injury needed to justify an injunction must apparently be considered nonetheless. Here, unlike *Dombrowski*, law enforcement authorities have not to date gone forward with prosecutions; hence the degree of friction between state and federal judicial systems is considerably lessened.

Also here, as in *Griswold* v. *Connecticut*,[50] and unlike *Dombrowski*, the permissible range of leeway for State regulation of marital and personal privacy is small. While government may regulate many facets of speech coupled with conduct, there is much doubt whether government can so intrude into the domain of privacy. Thus, to allow any prosecution at all of Dr. Hallford is to permit the State to invade the privacy of physician and patient in an area where the district court concluded that the State had little business at all.

If one assumes that 28 U.S.C. § 2283 (1964 ed.), is *prima facie* a bar to an injunction on Dr. Hallford's behalf, the further question remains whether, notwithstanding § 2283, an injunction

would be "necessary in aid of [the three-judge court's] jurisdiction," or "to protect or effectuate" the outstanding declaratory judgment. On this theory, since the court had jurisdiction to grant an injunction on behalf of all parties, it would be incongruous to exclude Dr. Hallford. Indeed, the alleged patients who were aborted, according to the two indictments, might be able to enjoin the compulsion of process against them in order to protect their privacy.

In light of the above, the questions presented in this case, both on the merits, and with respect to relief, are substantial, novel, and hitherto unresolved by this Court. Accordingly, the Court should note probable jurisdiction, and set the case down for plenary review.

II. A married couple, and others similarly situated, have standing to challenge the Texas anti-abortion laws, because said laws have a present and destructive effect on their marital relations, they are unable to utilize fully effective contraceptive methods, pregnancy would seriously harm the woman's health, and such a couple could not obtain judicial relief in sufficient time after pregnancy to prevent irreparable injury

A further aspect of the judgment below is presented on this appeal. In one part of the lower court's opinion is the holding that "Dr. Hallford has standing to raise the rights of his patients, single women and married couples, as well as rights of his own" (App. at 9a n. 3). Yet, the judgment states that "[p]laintiffs John and Mary Doe failed to allege facts sufficient to create a present controversy and therefore do not have standing" (App. at 5a). Accordingly, both declaratory and injunctive relief were denied as to John and Mary Doe.

John and Mary Doe alleged a present impact of the Texas anti-abortion laws on their marital relations which, when considered in light of their assertion of the interests of a class, created a present controversy over a future right to relief in the event Mary Doe or another class member became pregnant.

This Statement has already pointed out, *supra* at 6–7, that the judicial machinery is not equipped to grant relief to a party such as Mary Doe after she becomes pregnant. The only meaningful relief must be forthcoming prior to the twelfth week of pregnancy. While twelve weeks is a lengthy period of time, pregnancy is rarely detected before the fourth week, and often not until considerably later, depending upon the degree of medical sophistication of the patient.

Civil Rights Cases—A New Trend in Federal-State Judicial Relations, 34 FORDHAM L. REV. 71 (1965); Note, *The Federal Anti-Injunction Statute and Declaratory Judgments in Constitutional Litigation,* 83 HARV. L. REV. 1870 (1970); Comment, *Federal Injunctions Against State Actions,* 35 GEO. WASH. L. REV. 744 (1967).

[49] Taken together, *Dombrowski,* 380 U.S. at 484 n. 2, and *Hill* v. *Martin,* 296 U.S. 393, 403 (1935), suggest that a "proceeding" begins at some time after indictment. Respectable authorities argue that the indictment or information is an administrative act, done *ex parte* and in secrecy; hence, no "proceeding" exists until trial or arraignment, when both parties are first before a "State court." *See* Brewer, *supra* note 48, at 92; Comment, 35 GEO. WASH. L. REV. at 766–67.

[50] 381 U.S. 479 (1965).

Based upon an assumed size of the class represented by Mary Doe, and the known failure rate of the contraceptive she used, it would not be speculative to assume that one or more members of the class would be or become pregnant during the litigation. To assume to the contrary, as the district court did, was not only medically unsound, but served to elevate "ripeness" requirements to an unnecessarily high point, namely a point which deprived the entire class of the relief sought simply because no class member stepped forward as pregnant. Indeed, Jane Roe, the pregnant plaintiff, won a judgment which proved meaningless to her, because it was too late.

Ample precedent, moreover, could have been found to conclude that a present controversy existed between the Does and Appellees. Not only should the lower court have considered " 'the hardship of denying judicial relief,' "[51] but the dilemma faced by the class of Mary Does when they become pregnant is " 'capable of repetition, yet evading review' . . ." *Moore* v. *Ogilvie*, 394 U.S. 814, 816 (1969). The situation, admittedly difficult if one ignores its uniqueness, is nonetheless one in which the "mere possibility of [recurrence] . . . serves to keep the case alive." *United States* v. *W. T. Grant Co.*, 345 U.S. 629, 633 (1953). To the extent that the lower court, almost without discussion, rejected the standing of John and Mary Doe for want of an Article III case or controversy, the court erred. To the Does the case was and is a very real one. There was never an absence of adversity. The relief requested had significant meaning for the Does throughout, and the denial of that relief could provide harmful pre-

---

[51] Friendly, J., in *Toilet Goods Ass'n* v. *Gardner*, 360 F.2d 677, 684 (2d Cir. 1966), *aff'd*, 387 U.S. 167, 170 (1967).

cedent for similar situations. Accordingly, this Court should reverse the determination below, after noting jurisdiction to consider the claim by John and Mary Doe that they too were entitled to declaratory and injunctive relief.

CONCLUSION

For the reasons set out in this Jurisdictional Statement, the Court should note probable jurisdiction, and set the case down for plenary consideration with briefs on the merits and oral argument.

Respectfully submitted,

ROY LUCAS
The James Madison Constitutional Law Institute
Four Patchin Place
New York, N. Y. 10011

NORMAN DORSEN
School of Law
New York University
Washington Square
New York, N. Y. 10003

LINDA N. COFFEE
2130 First National Bank Building
Dallas, Texas 75202

SARAH WEDDINGTON
3710 Lawton
Austin, Texas 78731

ROY L. MERRILL, JR.
DAUGHERTY, BRUNER, LASTELICK & ANDERSON
1130 Mercantile Bank Building
Dallas, Texas 75201

Attorneys for Appellants

IN THE
SUPREME COURT OF THE UNITED STATES

No. 70–18, 1971 TERM

JANE ROE, JOHN DOE, MARY DOE, AND

JAMES HUBERT HALLFORD, M.D. APPELLANTS,

VS.

HENRY WADE

DISTRICT ATTORNEY OF DALLAS COUNTY, TEXAS, APPELLEE.

ON APPEAL FROM THE UNITED STATES
DISTRICT COURT
FOR THE NORTHERN DISTRICT OF TEXAS

BRIEF FOR APPELLEE

HENRY WADE
Criminal District Attorney
Dallas County, Texas

JOHN B. TOLLE
Assistant District Attorney
Dallas County Government Center
Dallas, Texas 75202

CRAWFORD C. MARTIN
Attorney General of Texas

NOLA WHITE
First Assistant

ALFRED WALKER
Executive Assistant

ROBERT C. FLOWERS
Assistant Attorney General

JAY FLOYD
Assistant Attorney General
P.O. Box 12548
Capitol Station
Austin, Texas 78711

Attorneys for Appellee

TABLE OF CONTENTS

In the
Supreme Court of the
United States
No. 70-18, 1971 Term

Jane Roe, John Doe, Mary Doe, and
James Hubert Hallford, M.D. Appellants,
vs.
Henry Wade,
District Attorney of Dallas County,
Texas Appellee.

On Direct Appeal from the
United States District Court
for the Northern District of
Texas

BRIEF FOR APPELLEE

STATEMENT OF THE CASE

Appellant Jane Roe instituted an action, suing on behalf of herself and all others similarly situated, contending she was an unmarried pregnant female who desired to terminate her pregnancy by "abortion" and that she was unable to secure a legal abortion in the State of Texas because of the prohibitions of the Texas Penal Code, Articles 1191, 1192, 1193, 1194, and 1196.[1] She further contends she cannot *afford* to travel to another jurisdiction to secure a legal abortion.[2]

Appellants John and Mary Doe instituted their action, suing on behalf of themselves and all others similarly situated, contending they were a childless married couple and that Appellant Mary Doe's *physician had advised her to avoid pregnancy because of a neural-chemical disorder.*[3] They further contend *their physician has further advised against the use of birth control pills* and, though they are now practicing an alternative method of contraception, *they understand* there is nevertheless a significant risk of contraceptive failure.[4] They contend that *should* Appellant Mary Doe become pregnant, she would want to terminate such pregnancy by abortion and would be unable to do so in the State of Texas because of the above prohibitory statutes.[5]

Appellant James Hubert Hallford, M.D., filed his Application for Leave to Intervene in Appellant Roe's action[6] and his Application was granted.[7] He contends he is in the active practice of medicine and contends the Texas Abortion Laws are a principal deterrent to physicians and patients in their relationship in connection with therapeutic hospital and clinical abortions.[8] Appellant Hallford was under indictment in two (2) cases in Dallas County, Texas, charged with the offense of abortion in violation of the Statutes in issue.[9]

In substance, Appellants contended in their Complaints filed in the lower court that (1) the Texas Abortion Laws are unconstitutionally vague and uncertain on their face, (2) they deprive a woman of the "fundamental right to choose whether and when to bear children", (3) they infringe upon a woman's right to personal privacy and privacy in the physician-patient relationship, (4) they deprive women and their physicians of rights protected by the First, Fourth, Fifth, Ninth, and Fourteenth Amendments to the Constitution of the United States.[10]

Appellants sought declaratory relief that the Texas Abortion Laws were unconstitutional in violation of the Constitution of the United States and injunctive relief against the future enforcement of such Statutes.[11] They prayed that a three-judge court be convened to hear and determine their causes of action.[12]

Appellee Henry Wade filed his Answer to Appellant Roe's Complaint[13], his Motion to Dismiss the Complaint of Appellants John and Mary Doe[14] and his Answer to Appellant Hallford's Complaint.[15] The State of Texas was granted leave to respond to the Appellants' Complaints and filed its Motion to Dismiss all Complaints and its alternative plea for Judgment on the Pleadings.[16] Both Motions to Dismiss challenged the standing of Appellants John and Mary Doe[17] and the State of Texas' Motion to Dismiss challenged the standing of Appellants Roe and Hallford.[18] In addition, the State of Texas' Motion to Dismiss asserted that

---

[1] A. 11. (The Statutes in issue are commonly referred to as the Texas Abortion Laws and are set out verbatim, *infra*, at pp. 5–6.)

[2] A. 12.

[3] A. 16.

[4] A. 16–17.

[5] A. 17.

[6] A. 22–23.

[7] A. 36.

[8] A. 28.

[9] A. 30. (These cases are still pending.)

[10] A. 12–13, 19–20, 31–32, 34.

[11] A. 14, 20–21, 34.

[12] A. 13, 20, 34.

[13] A. 37–39.

[14] A. 40–41.

[15] A. 42–46.

[16] A. 47–49.

[17] A. 40, 48.

[18] A. 48.

Appellants (1) failed to state a claim upon which relief may be granted, (2) failed to raise a substantial Constitutional question, (3) failed to show irreparable injury and the absence of an adequate remedy at law, and (4) Appellant Hallford's Complaint was barred by 28 U.S.C. 2283.[19]

In the course of proceeding in the lower court, Appellants filed their Motions for Summary Judgment.[20] In support of Appellant Jane Doe's Motion for Summary Judgment, she filed her affidavit[21] and an affidavit of one Paul Carey Trickett, M.D.[22] Appellant Hallford filed his affidavit in support of his Motion for Summary Judgment[23] and annexed copies of the indictments pending against him.[24]

The cases were consolidated and processed to a hearing before the Honorable Irving L. Goldberg, Circuit Judge, and the Honorable Sarah T. Hughes and W. M. Taylor, Jr., District Judges.[25] Neither the Appellants nor the Appellee offered any evidence at such hearing[26] and arguments were presented by all parties. The Court tendered its Judgment[27] and Opinion[28] on June 17, 1970.

Appellants filed Notice of Appeal to this Court pursuant to the provisions of 28 U.S.C. 1253.[29] Appellants Roe and Hallford and Appellee Wade filed Notice of Appeal to the United States Court of Appeals for the Fifth Circuit.[30] Appellants filed their Motion to Hold Appeal to Fifth Circuit of Appellee Wade in Abeyance Pending Decision by the Supreme Court of the United States[31], which Motion was granted.[32]

The lower court found that Appellants Roe and Hallford and the *members of their respective classes*[33] had standing to bring their lawsuits, but that Appellants John and Mary Doe had failed to allege facts sufficient to create a present controversy and did not have standing.[34] That court held the Texas Abortion Laws unconstitutional in that they deprived single women and married persons of the right to choose whether

to have children in violation of the Ninth Amendment to the Constitution of the United States and that such Laws were void on their face for unconstitutional overbreadth and vagueness.[35] The court denied Appellants' applications for injunctive relief.[36]

STATUTES IN ISSUE

The Texas Abortion Laws and the statutes in issue are contained in the Texas Penal Code and consist of the following:

Article 1191. Abortion

If any person shall designedly administer to a pregnant woman or knowingly procure to be administered with her consent any drug or medicine, or shall use toward her any violence or means whatsoever externally or internally applied, and thereby procure an abortion, he shall be confined in the penitentiary for not less than two nor more than five years; if it be done without her consent, the punishment shall be doubled. By "abortion" is meant that the life of the fetus or embryo shall be destroyed in the woman's womb or that a premature birth shall be caused.

Art. 1192. Furnishing the Means

Whoever furnishes the means for procuring an abortion knowing the purpose intended is guilty as an accomplice.

Art. 1193. Attempt at Abortion

If the means used shall fail to produce an abortion, the offender is nevertheless guilty of an attempt to produce abortion, provided it be shown that such means was calculated to produce that result, and shall be fined not less than one hundred nor more than one thousand dollars.

Art. 1194. Murder in Producing Abortion

If the death of the mother is occasioned by an abortion so produced or by an attempt to effect the same it is murder.

Art. 1196. By Medical Advice

Nothing in this chapter applies to an abortion procured or attempted by medical advice for the purpose of saving the life of the mother.[37]

QUESTIONS PRESENTED

In Appellee's opinion the questions presented may be precisely stated as follows:

---

[19] A. 47–48.
[20] A. 50, 59–60.
[21] A. 56–60. (an alias affidavit)
[22] A. 51–55.
[23] A. 61–72.
[24] A. 73, 74.
[25] A. 75–110.
[26] A. 77.
[27] A. 124–126.
[28] A. 111–123.
[29] A. 127–129.
[30] A. 133, 134, 135.
[31] A. 136–138.
[32] A. 139–140. (The Court of Appeals has taken no further action in these cases).
[33] A. 124.
[34] A. 124.

---

[35] A. 125–126.
[36] A. 126.
[37] The omitted article, Article 1195, concerns destruction of the vitality or life of a child in a state of being born and before actual birth, which such child would otherwise have been born alive.

I. Whether appellants Jane Roe, and John and Mary Doe, present a justiciable controversy in their challenge to the Texas abortion laws?

II. Whether the court should enjoin the enforcement of the Texas abortion laws as to appellant Hallford in the light of pending state criminal charges?

III. Did the district court err in refusing to enjoin future enforcement of the Texas abortion laws after declaring such laws unconstitutional?

IV. Whether this court can consider plenary review of an entire case when a lower court grants declaratory relief holding a state statute unconstitutional, but refuses to enjoin future enforcement of such statute, and the appeal to this court is from that portion of the judgment denying injunctive relief?

V. Whether articles 1191, 1192, 1193, 1194 and 1196 of the Texas penal code are void on their face because of unconstitutional overbreadth and vagueness?

VI. Whether the constitution of the United States guarantees a woman the right to abort an unborn fetus?

VII. Whether the state of Texas has a legitimate interest in preventing abortion except under the limited exception of "an abortion procured or attempted by medical advice for the purpose of saving the life of the mother"?

SUMMARY OF ARGUMENT

Appellant Jane Roe has not presented a justiciable controversy admitting of specific relief for this Court in her challenge to the Texas Abortion Laws. She has not shown that she has sustained or is immediately in danger of sustaining some direct injury as a result of enforcement of the Texas Abortion Laws. Any cause of action that she may have had is not established by the record and has been mooted by the termination of her pregnancy.

Appellants John and Mary Doe's cause of action is based on speculation and conjecture and they also have not shown they have sustained or are immediately in danger of sustaining some direct injury as a result of enforcement of the Texas Abortion Laws essential to standing and a justiciable controversy.

Appellant Hallford is under indictment in two cases for violation of the statutes he attacks in the controversy before the Court. The Court should abstain from exercising jurisdiction under the principles enunciated in *Younger* v. *Harris*, etc. Appellant Hallford is not entitled to

assert a cause of action on behalf of his patients in the physician-patient relationship.

For a federal court to grant injunctive relief against the enforcement of a state statute, there must be a clear and persuasive showing of unconstitutionality and irreparable harm. The lower court can divorce injunctive and declaratory relief under its equity power and declare a statute unconstitutional, yet refuse to enjoin the enforcement of such statute.

Once a federal court has assumed jurisdiction of a cause, it may properly assume jurisdiction of the entire controversy and render a decision on all questions presented and involved in the case. If this Court determines that it has jurisdiction to consider the denial of injunctive relief to Appellants by the lower court, it may consider the constitutionality of the Texas Abortion Laws determined to be unconstitutional by the Court below.

The Texas Abortion Laws are not violative of the Constitution of the United States as being unconstitutionally vague and overbroad. *United States v. Vuitch* is decisive of the issues in this case as to vagueness and overbreadth.

Though the right of "marital privacy" and "personal privacy" are recognized, they have never been regarded as absolute. The "right to privacy" is a relative right that, in the matter of abortion, is not attached to an express right guaranteed under the Constitution of the United States. The right to life of the unborn child is superior to the right of privacy of the mother.

The state has a legitimate, if not compelling, interest in prohibiting abortion except under limited circumstances. In the light of recent findings and research in medicine, the fetus is a human being and the state has an interest in the arbitrary and unjustified destruction of this being.

ARGUMENT

I. Appellants Jane Roe, John and Mary Doe, have not presented a justiciable controversy in their challenge to the Texas abortion laws

A. Justiciability and standing. Article III of the Constitution of the United States limits the judicial power of Federal Courts to "cases" and "controversies". This has been construed by the courts to prohibit the giving of advisory opinions. *Flast v. Cohen*, 392 U.S. 83 (1968); *Bell v. Maryland*, 378 U.S. 226 (1964); *United States v. Fruehauf* 365 U.S. 146 (1961). There must be a real and substantial controversy admitting of specific relief as distinguished from an opinion advising what the law would be upon a hypothetical state of facts. *Aetna Life Insurance Company v. Hayworth*, 300 U.S. 227 (1937); accord, *Public Service Commission of Utah v. Wycoff Company*, 344 U.S. 237 (1952); *Baker v. Carr*, 369 U.S. 186 (1962); *Golden v. Zwickler*, 394 U.S. 103 (1969). Correlatively, a party challenging a statute as invalid must show that he has sustained or is immediately in danger of sustaining some direct injury as a result of the statute's enforcement before a three-judge court or any Federal court can entertain the action, *Frothingham v. Mellon*[38], 262 U.S. 447 (1923); *Ex parte Levitt*, 302 U.S. 633 (1937); *Fairchild v. Hughes* 258 U.S. 126 (1922); *Poe v. Ullman*, 367 U.S. 497 (1961). In a per curiam opinion this Court stated in *Ex Parte Levitt*:

> "It is an established principle that to entitle a private individual to invoke the judicial power to determine the validity of executive or legislative action he must show that he has sustained, or is immediately in danger of sustaining, a direct injury as the result of that action and *it is not sufficient that he has merely a general interest common to all members of the public*." (Emphasis added). 302 U.S. at 634.

In *Flask v. Cohen*, supra, this Court gave careful consideration to the nexus between *standing* and *justiciability* and stated that "Standing is an aspect of justiciability and, as such, the problem of standing is surrounded by the same complexities and vagaries that inhere in justiciability". 392 U.S. at 98–99. Most probably, the best known decision of this Court on standing is *Frothingham v. Mellon*, supra, in which Mrs. Frothingham claimed that she was a taxpayer of the United States and sued to restrain payments from the Treasury to the several states which chose to participate in a program created by the Maternity Act of 1921. She claimed that the Federal government lacked power to appropriate money for the reduction of maternal and infant mortality, and that such appropriations would cause an unconstitutional increase in her future taxes. After considerations of the interest of an individual taxpayer, remoteness, and other issues, this Court finally stated that its power to declare statutes unconstitutional exists only where the statute is involved in a justiciable case, and that to present such a case the plaintiff "must be able to show, not only that the statute is invalid, but that he has sustained or is immediately in danger of sustaining some direct injury as the result of its enforcement, and not merely that he suffers in some indefinite way in

common with the people generally". 262 U.S. at 488. See, *Cramp v. Board of Public Instruction*, 368 U.S. 278 (1961); *Baker v. Carr*, supra; *National Association for the Advancement of Colored People v. Button*, 371 U.S. 415 (1963).

A review and analysis of the decisions on standing indicate they are not easy to reconcile on the facts. It is frequently stated that to have standing a party must be able to demonstrate injury to a legally protected right or interest. *Tennessee Electric Power Co. v. Tennessee Valley Authority*, 306 U.S. 118 (1937); *Alabama Power Company v. Ickes*, 302 U.S. 464 (1938); *Perkins v. Lukens Steel Co.*, 310 U.S. 113 (1940).

B. Standing of Appellants John and Mary Doe. Applying the standards of justiciability and standing stated above, an examination of the cause of action asserted by Appellants John and Mary Doe discloses they do not have standing. In their Complaint they contend they are a childless married couple and Mary Doe was not pregnant at that time.[39] Their cause of action is based upon their fear of contraceptive failure resulting in pregnancy to Mary Doe at a time *when they are not properly prepared to accept the responsibilities of parenthood* and upon the *advice of their physician to avoid pregnancy until her health condition improves*.[40] The record is wholly lacking in proof of these contentions. The lower court properly and correctly denied standing to these Appellants upon finding they failed to allege facts sufficient to create a present controversy.[41]

Initially, it may be stated that neither Appellants Doe nor Roe can be prosecuted under the Texas Abortion Laws for securing an abortion or for attempted abortion. *Gray v. State*, 178 S.W. 337 (Tex.Crim. 1915); *Shaw v. State*, 165 S.W. 930 (Tex.Crim. 1914). Appellants John and Mary Doe's cause of action is based upon speculation of future contraceptive failure resulting in pregnancy of Mary Doe and the future speculation that these Appellants will not at that time be prepared for parenthood and, further, that Appellant Mary Doe's health condition at that time will be impaired by pregnancy. These speculative fears cannot support a cause of action. See, *Younger v. Harris*, 401 U.S. 37 (1971); *Golden v. Zwickler*, supra. For a court to decide the merits of Appellants John and Mary Doe's cause of action would result in giving an advisory opinion upon a hypothetical state of facts contrary to Federal Constitutional limitations and this Court's holdings in *Flask v. Cohen*, supra, and cases cited, supra, at p. 9.

---

[38] This case is usually referred to as *Massachusetts v. Mellon*.

[39] A. 16.

[40] A. 17.

[41] A. 124.

C. Standing of Appellant Jane Roe. Appellant Jane Roe occupies a more unique position in regard to standing. She filed her Amended Complaint in the District Court on April 22, 1970,[42] and an "alias affidavit" on May 21, 1970.[43] *The only support in the record for her contentions and allegations giving rise to her cause of action is found in her Amended Complaint and her "alias affidavit".* The affidavit filed after the commencement of her action indicates she did not desire an abortion at the time of its filing.[44] This affidavit further shows that Appellant Roe had been pregnant for several months prior to its filing.[45] The hearing was held before the three-judge panel on July 22, 1970,[46] some four and one-half (4½) months after the filing of her Original Complaint[47] and on November 3, 1971, some twenty (20) months will have expired since the filing of said Original Complaint. There is no indication in the record that Appellant Jane Roe was pregnant at the time of the hearing on July 22, 1970, and it can be reasonably concluded that she is not now pregnant.[48]

The argument that Appellant Jane Roe has not presented a justiciable controversy to give her standing is not intended to be fictitious or spurious. If her statements in her affidavit did not moot her cause of action, resort may be had to *Golden v. Zwickler,* supra, wherein this Court stated:

> "The District Court erred in holding that Zwickler was entitled to declaratory relief if the elements essential to that relief existed '[w]hen this action was initiated.' The proper inquiry was whether a 'controversy' requisite to relief under the Declaratory Judgment Act existed at the time of the hearing on remand." 394 U.S. at 108.[49]

Golden v. Zwickler indicates that this Court should consider an issue as to standing *at the time* it reviews the case and not when the suit was filed. This is supported to some extent by *Bryan v. Austin.* 354 U.S. 933 (1957), wherein Plaintiffs sought to have a South Carolina statute declared unconstitutional and, pending appeal, the statute in question was repealed. In a per curiam opinion this Court stated that the repeal of the statute in issue after the decision of the District Court rendered the cause moot. *Atherton Mills v. Johnston,* 259 U.S. 13 (1922), involved a suit for injunctive relief to prevent the discharge of a minor employee because of the Child Labor Act of 1919, which was challenged as being invalid. While the case was on appeal, the minor employee involved became of age. This Court held that the case became moot by the lapse of time and the case could not be considered by the Court.

Mootness deprives a federal court of its judicial power since no case or controversy exists. *Mechling Barge Lines, Inc., v. United States,* 368 U.S. 3224 (1961); *Local No.8–6 v. Missouri,* 361 U.S. 363 (1960); *Flast v. Cohen,* supra; *Parker v. Ellis,* 362 U.S. 574 (1960).

D. Class action aspects. It is questionable whether the requirements of Rule 23, Fed. Rules Civ. Proc., have been complied with in connection with Appellants Roe and John and Mary Doe's attempt to bring their suits as class actions. These Appellants have alleged the prerequisites required in Rule 23 (a),[50] but have not designated whether their actions are (b) (1) or (b) (2) actions under Rule 23. Again, the record is wholly void of any showing of the propriety of class action relief and the only other mention of this aspect of the case is found in the lower court's judgment as follows:

> "(1) Plaintiff Jane Roe, plaintiff-intervenor James Hubert Hallford, M.D. and the members of their respective classes have standing to bring this lawsuit." (A. 124).[51]

The 1966 amendments to Rule 23 require the judgment in a (b) (1) or (b) (2) class action to include and describe those whom the court finds to be members of the class. In a Rule 23 (b) (3) class action the 1966 amendments require the judgment include and specify or describe those to whom notice was directed, as required by Rule 23 (c) (2), and who have not requested exclusion, and who are found by the court to be members of the class.

In *Hall v. Beals,* 396 U.S. 45 (1969), this Court had before it on direct appeal a case involving new residents of the State of Colorado, who had moved into the State four (4) or five (5) months prior to the November, 1968, presidential election. They were refused permission to vote because of a Colorado statute

---

[42] A. 10.
[43] A. 56.
[44] "At the time I filed the lawsuit I wanted to terminate my pregnancy by means of an abortion . . ." (A. 57) and "I wanted to terminate my pregnancy because . . ." (A. 57).
[45] "Each month I am barely able to make ends meet" (A. 58).
[46] A. 77.
[47] Docket Entries in CA-3-3690-B (A. 1).
[48] The Court may desire to take judicial notice of this fact.
[49] This case was reversed and remanded with direction to enter a new judgment dismissing the complaint.

[50] A. 12, 19.
[51] Appellant Hallford's Complaint makes no mention of class action relief. (A. 24–35).

imposing a six (6) months residency requirement. They commenced a suit as a class action challenging the constitutionality of the statute. A three-judge court upheld the constitutionality of the statute. Thereafter, the election was held, and the State statute was amended to reduce the residency requirement for a presidential election to two (2) months. This Court, in a per curiam opinion, held that, aside from the fact that the election had been held, the case was rendered moot by the amendment to the statute that reduced the residency requirement to two (2) months, and under which the Appellants could vote, since the case had lost its character as a present, live controversy, notwithstanding that the Appellants had denominated their suit as a class action and had expressed opposition to residency requirements in general. In *Golden v. Zwickler*, supra, a distributor of anonymous handbills criticizing a congressman's voting record sought a declaratory judgment concerning the constitutionality of a New York statute which penalized the distributor of anonymous literature in connection with an election campaign. While the case was pending, the congressman left the House of Representatives and accepted a term as a justice on the Supreme Court of New York. The United States District Court held that the distributor was nevertheless entitled to a declaratory judgment because a genuine controversy had existed at the commencement of the action. This Court held there was no "controversy" of "sufficient immediacy and reality" to warrant a declaratory judgment and, in addition, stated as follows:

> "It is not enough to say, as did the District Court, that nevertheless Zwickler has a 'further and far broader right to a general adjudication of unconstitutionality . . . [in] [h]is *own interest as well as that of others* who would with like anonymity practice free speech in a political environment. . . .' The constitutional question, First Amendment or otherwise, must be presented in the context of a specific live grievance." (Emphasis added). 394 U.S. at 118.

See, *Burrows v. Jackson*, 346 U.S. 249 (1953).

The Federal Constitution limitations in Article III cannot be extended or limited by asserting a "class action" under Rule 23. Rule 82, Fed. Rules Civ. Proc., in referring to the preceding rules, including Rule 23, provides in part that "These rules shall not be construed to extend or limit the jurisdiction of the United States district courts or the venue of actions therein. . . ."

II. This court should refuse declaratory and injunctive relief to Appellant James Hubert Hallford, M.D.

In Indictment No. 2023 A, Appellant James Hubert Hallford stands charged by the State of Texas with performing an abortion on Frances C. King,[52] and in Indictment No. 556 J with performing an abortion on Jane Wilhelm.[53] He sought and obtained leave to intervene in Appellant Roe's action[54] seeking a permanent injunction against the enforcement of the Texas Abortion Laws,[55] but reserving a right to make an application for an interlocutory injunction.[56] In reality, Appellant Hallford is seeking to avoid criminal prosecution in the criminal cases pending against him.

Historically there has been great reluctance by the federal courts to interfere in the operations of a state court. *Stefanelli v. Minard*, 342 U.S. 117 (1951). General principles should be enough to show that an independent federal action is not an appropriate means to raise what should be a state court defense, but this does not stand alone. A statute almost as old as the Republic, the Anti-Injunction Act of 1793, has, with some variations in language over the years, provided that a court of the United States "may not grant an injunction to stay proceedings in a State court . . ." 28 U.S.C. 2283. This statute is no happenstance. It is a "limitation of the power of federal courts dating almost from the beginning of our history and expressing an important Congressional policy—to prevent friction between state and federal courts." *Oklahoma Packing Co. v. Oklahoma & Elec. Co.*, 309 U.S. 4 (1940).

Appellant Hallford's Complaint allegations do not justify the conclusion that any criminal charges have been brought against him in bad faith or under any conditions that would place his case within *Dombrowski's* "special circumstances". *Dombrowski v. Pfister*, 380 U.S. 479 (1965). There is no relationship worthy of note in the allegations contained in Paragraph 14 of this Complaint[57] to *Dombrowski's* "special circumstances." He appears to indicate that the State of Texas must negate the exception provided in Article 1196, supra,[58] and that he cannot offer medical testimony to bring him within the purview of the exception.

In *Atlantic Coast Line R. Co. v. Engineers*, 398 U.S. 281 (1970), the railroad obtained a state

---

[52] A. 73.
[53] A. 74.
[54] A. 22, 36.
[55] A. 34.
[56] A. 34 (it is submitted that Appellant Hallford reserved this right in the event the pending cases were set for trial).
[57] A. 30.
[58] See Article 1196, supra, at p. 6 containing the exception "procured or attempted by medical advice for the purpose of saving the life of the mother."

injunction against a union's picketing and the union sought and obtained in the Federal District Court an injunction against the enforcement of the state court injunction. The Court of Appeals for the Fifth Circuit affirmed the Federal District Court's judgment and, on certiorari, this Court reversed and remanded stating as follows:

"First, a federal court does not have inherent power to ignore the limitations of Section 2283 and to enjoin state court proceedings merely because those proceedings interfere with a protected federal right or invade an area preempted by federal law, even when the interference is unmistakably clear. This rule applies regardless of whether the federal court itself has jurisdiction over the controversy, or whether it is ousted from jurisdiction for the same reason that the state court is." (Omitting authority). 398 U.S. at 294.–295.

The above principle of federal abstention is further enunciated in *Spielman Motor Sales Co., Inc., v. Dodge*, 295 U.S. 89 (1935); *Cameron v. Johnson*, 390 U.S. 611 (1968); *Shaw v. Garrison*, 293 F.Supp. 937 (E.D.La. 1968), aff'd per curiam, 393 U.S. 220 (1968); *City of Greenwood v. Peacock*, 384 U.S. 808 (1966).

More recently, this Court has announced certain guidelines on the subject of federal court interference with pending state criminal proceedings in what is sometimes referred to as the "February 23rd Decisions". *Younger v. Harris*, supra, *Samuels v. Mackell*, 401 U.S. 66 (1971); *Boyle v. Landry*, 401 U.S. 77 (1971); *Dyson v. Stein*, 401 U.S. 200 (1971); *Perez v. Ledesma*, 401 U.S. 82 (1971); *Byrne v. Karalexis*, 401 U.S. 216 (1971). These cases very strongly indicate the availability of federal injunctive relief against pending state criminal prosecutions has been severely curtailed even in the area of First Amendment rights of expression. Thus, federal interference, even to the extent of granting preliminary restraining orders and convening three-judge courts is by far the exception rather than the rule.

The above cases further indicate that, independent of any obstacles posed by the federal anti-injunction statute, the primary prerequisite to federal court intervention in the present context, is a showing of irreparable injury. Even irreparable injury is insufficient unless it is "both great and immediate". In *Younger v. Harris*, supra, this Court stated as follows:

"Certain types of injury, in particular, the cost, anxiety, and inconvenience of having to defend against a single criminal prosecution, could not by themselves be considered 'irreparable' in the special legal sense of that term. Instead,

the threat to the Plaintiff's federally protected rights must be one that cannot be eliminated by his defense against a single criminal prosecution." 401 U.S. at 46.

Accord, *Byrne v. Karalexis*, supra.

Samuels v. Mackell, supra, considered declaratory relief prayed for in relation to the federal court's reluctance to interfere with pending state criminal proceedings and this Court stated:

"We therefore hold that, in cases where the state criminal prosecution was begun prior to the federal suit, same equitable principles relevant to the propriety of an injunction must be taken into consideration by federal district courts in determining whether to issue a declaratory judgment, and that *where an injunction would be impermissible under these principles, declaratory relief should be denied as well....* Ordinarily, however, the practical effect of the two forms of relief will be virtually identical, and the basic policy against federal interference with pending state criminal prosecutions will be frustrated as much by a declaratory judgment as it would be by an injunction." (Emphasis added). 401 U.S. at 73.

Nor can Appellant rely upon his patients' rights, which a statute supposedly threatens. See *Tileston v. Ullman*, 318 U.S. 44 (1943); accord, *Golden v. Zwicker*, supra; *Burrows v. Jackson*, supra.

Applying the guidelines set forth in *Younger v. Harris*, supra, and the other "February 23rd Decisions", this Court can properly conclude Appellant Hallford has not suffered, nor under the present state of the record, will suffer both great and immediate irreparable injury of the nature required to authorize federal injunctive or declaratory relief. His case is precisely the type to which this Court was addressing itself in the recent pronouncements condemning, except in very limited circumstances, federal court equitable injunctive and declaratory interference with pending state criminal prosecutions.

III. The United States District Court did not err in refusing to enjoin future enforcement of the Texas abortion laws after declaring such laws unconstitutional

This Court has been unwaivering in holding that a three-judge court cannot consider an action for injunctive relief under 28 U.S.C. 2281 on its merits without a preliminary showing of irreparable harm and no adequate legal remedy. In *Spielman Motor Sales Co. Inc., v. Dodge*, supra, a suit requesting a three-judge court to enjoin a New York district attorney from instituting criminal prosecutions against certain defendants under an alleged unconstitutional state statute, this court affirmed the lower court's dismissal of the action and stated:

> "The general rule is that equity will not interfere to prevent the enforcement of a criminal statute even though unconstitutional.... To justify such interference there must be exceptional circumstances and a clear showing that an injunction is necessary in order to afford adequate protection of constitutional rights." 295 U.S. at 95.

In *Mayo v. Lakeland Highlands Canning Co., Inc.*, 309 U.S. 310 (1940), a suit was brought before a three-judge court seeking to enjoin the Florida Agriculture Commission from enforcing an alleged unconstitutional state statute. This Court reversed the lower court's disposition on the merits and made the following observation:

> "The legislation requiring the convening of a court of three judges in cases such as this was intended to insure that the enforcement of a challenged statute should not be suspended by injunction except upon a clear and persuasive showing of unconstitutionality and irreparable injury." 309 U.S. at 318–319.

Accord, *Beal v. Missouri Pacific Railroad Corporation*, 312 U.S. 45 (1961); *Douglas v. City of Jeannette*, 319 U.S. 157 (1943); *Bryne v. Karalexis*, supra; *Dyson v. Stein*, supra; *Samuels v. Mackell*, supra; *Younger v. Harris*, supra.

The lower court cited *Dombrowski v. Pfister*, supra, and *Zwickler v. Koota*, 389 U.S. 241 (1967), as authority for the court to divorce injunctive and declaratory relief.[59] In *Powell v. McCormack*, 395 U.S. 486 (1969), this Court held that a court may grant declaratory relief even though it chooses not to issue an injunction or mandamus. 395 U.S. at 504. See, *United Public Workers v. Mitchell*, 330 U.S. 75 (1947).

IV. This court can consider plenary review of the entire case when a lower court grants declaratory relief holding a state statute unconstitutional, but refuses to enjoin future enforcement of such statute, and the appeal to this court is from that portion of the judgment denying injunctive relief

Should this Court determine that it has jurisdiction to consider the propriety of injunctive relief in this case, it can properly assume jurisdiction of this entire controversy and render a decision on all questions involved in this case, including the constitutionality of the Texas

Abortion Laws. Appellee joins Appellants in requesting this Court reach the issue of the Constitutionality of the Texas Abortion Laws. Appellee is in a somewhat awkward procedural position in that it lost on the merits in the lower court as to declaratory relief and neither the grant nor the refusal of a declaratory judgment, without more, will support a direct appeal to this Court under 28 U.S.C. 1253. *Mitchell v. Donovan*, 398 U.S. 427 (1970); *Gunn v. University Committee*, 399 U.S. 383 (1971). Appellee has the avenue of appeal to the Fifth Circuit.[60] Should this Court in the present case hold that the lower court properly granted declaratory relief but improperly denied injunctive relief, it then might be faced, at least indirectly, with the consideration and decision of the same constitutional issues that are being directly raised by the Appellee in the Court of Appeals for the Fifth Circuit.

Though not directly in point, *Public Service Commission of Utah v. Wycoff Co.*, supra, lends support to the premise that a federal court has the right, power, and authority to decide and determine the entire controversy and all the issues and questions involved in a case of which it has properly acquired jurisdiction. Accord, *Just v. Chambers*, 312 U.S. 383 (1941); *Florida Lime and Avocado Growers v. Jacobson*, 362 U.S. 73 (1960); cf, *Hartford Accident & Indemnity Company v. Southern Pacific Company*, 273 U.S. 207 (1927); *British Transport Commission v. United States*, 354 U.S. 129 (1957). In *Sterling v. Constantin*, 287 U.S. 378 (1932); this Court stated that:

> "As the validity of provisions of the state constitution and statutes, if they could be deemed to authorize the action of the Governor, was challenged, the application for injunction was properly heard by three judges. Stratton v. St. Louis S. W. R. Co., 282 U.S. 10, 75 L. Ed. 135, 51 S. Ct. 8. The jurisdiction of the District Court so constituted, and of this Court upon appeal, extends to every question involved, whether of state or federal law, and enables the *court to rest its judgment on the decisions of such of the questions as in its opinion effectively dispose of the case." (Omitting authority). 287 U.S. at 393–394.

V. Articles 1191, 1192, 1193, 1194 and 1196 of the Texas Penal Code are not unconstitutional on their face because of overbreadth and vagueness

The possible vagueness of state abortion statutes which allow for such a procedure only

---

[59] A. 121, 122.

[60] Appellee has appealed to the United States Court of Appeals for the Fifth Circuit (A. 135) and this appeal is being held in abeyance pending a decision of this Court (A. 139–140).

when the life, or in some cases, health, of the expectant mother is threatened has recently come under judicial scrutiny in a number of instances. One author, in commenting on the decision of the California Supreme Court in *People v. Belous*, 71 Cal. Rptr. 354, 458 P.2d 194 (1969), cert. denied, 397 U.S. 915 (1970), stated as follows:

"In attempting to define the phrase 'necessary to preserve . . . life . . .' the California Supreme Court first examined the isolated words of the statute, and concluded that no clear meaning of 'necessary' and 'preserve' could be ascertained. It is not surprising that a seriatim examination of the words convinced the court that the phrase was vague. Necessity is a relative concept and must refer to a particular object to be meaningful. Nor can the word 'preserve' be understood out of context. In the abstract, such words are not just vague, they are meaningless. Taken in context, however, these words do have meaning. The object of the necessity in this statute is 'to preserve life.' The term is defined by its object—life." 118 U. Penn. L. Rev. 643, 644 (1970).

There is some inherent vagueness in many homicide laws, such as laws which define justifiable homicide as self-defense, or those which differentiate between first- and second-degree murder. The courts, like society, however, have learned to live with a certain element of inevitable vagueness in all laws and have learned to apply it reasonably. See, *Lanzetta v. New Jersey*, 306 U.S. 451 (1939); *Connally v. General Construction Company*, 269 U.S. 385 (1926). In order for a statute to be unconstitutionally vague, it must be so vague and lacking in standards so as to compel men of ordinary intelligence to guess at its meaning. *Adderley v. Florida*, 385 U.S. 39 (1967); *Cameron v. Johnson*, supra.

A number of three-judge panels have been convened recently to consider the constitutionality of abortion laws which allowed for the performance of such operations only when the life of the mother was threatened by continuance of the pregnancy. While one such court, in dealing with such a law in Wisconsin, did hold the statute to be unconstitutional on other grounds, it said that whatever vagueness existed in the law was not sufficient, of itself, for a declaration of unconstitutionality. *Babbitz v. McCann*, 310 F.Supp. 293 (E.D. Wis. 1970). The court observed:

"We have examined the challenged phraseology and are persuaded that it is not indefinite or vague. In our opinion, the word 'necessary' and the expression 'to save the life of the mother' are both reasonably comprehensible in their meaning." 310 F.Supp. at 297.

Accord, *Rosen v. Louisiana State Board of Medical Examiners*, 318 F.Supp. 1217 (E.D. La. 1970).

In *United States v. Petrillo*, 332 U.S. 1 (1947), this Court stated:

"[That] there may be marginal cases in which it is difficult to determine the side of the line on which a particular fact situation falls is no sufficient reason to hold the language too ambiguous to define a criminal offense, *Robinson v. United States*, 324 U.S. 282, 285, 286, 89 L.Ed. 944, 946, 947, 65 S. Ct. 666. It would strain the requirement for certainty in criminal law standards too near the breaking point to say that it was impossible judicially to determine whether a person knew when he was willfully attempting to compel another to hire unneeded employees." (Omitting authority). 332 U.S. at 7–8.

See *Jordan v. DeGeorge*, 341 U.S. 223 (1951); *United States v. Ragen*, 314 U.S. 513 (1942); *United States v. Wurzback*, 280 U.S. 396 (1930).

The court below did not have the advantage of this Court's decision in *United States v. Vuitch*, 402 U.S. 62 (1971), at the time it handed down its decision in this case. In *Vuitch* this Court reversed the decision of a district court judge who had found that the District of Columbia abortion law was unconstitutionally vague. The exception clause in *Vuitch* stated in part "unless the same were done as necessary for the preservation of the mother's life or health".[61] Though this Court directed its attention to the word "health", its holding should be dispositive of the case at bar in that the exception clause is less certain of meaning than the exception found in the Texas Abortion Laws. This Court in *Vuitch* further disposed of the contention of the physician that once an abortion is performed he is "presumed guilty".

VI. The Constitution of the United States does not guarantee a woman the right to abort an unborn fetus

A. The interest of marital privacy. One must recognize the interest of a husband and wife in preserving their conjugal relations from state interference, an interest which, in *Griswold v. Connecticut*, 381 U.S. 479 (1965), was found to be violated by Connecticut's statute forbidding the use of contraceptives. This law interfered with the most private aspect of the marital relation, sexual intercourse, making it criminal for a couple to engage in sexual intercourse when using contraceptives. In contrast, the usual statute restricting abortions does not

---

[61] 22 D C Code 201.

affect the sexual relations of a couple except under some circumstances and only for a limited time. Prevention of abortion does not entail, therefore, state interference with the right of marital intercourse, nor does enforcement of the statute requiring invasions of the conjugal bedroom.

Assuming arguendo that there are other marital rights the state must respect, may it then be urged that the right of marital privacy includes the freedom of a married couple to raise and educate a child they do not want, or commit infanticide, incest, engage in pandering and the like. Family privacy, like personal privacy, is highly valued, but not absolute. The news media may publicize the events that occur when a family is victimized by criminals though they seek seclusion. *Time v. Hill*, 385 U.S. 374 (1967). The family may not practice polygamy,[62] may not prohibit schooling for a child,[63] or prohibit the child's labor,[64] or expose the community or a child to communicable disease.[65] In *Gleitman v. Cosgrove*, 49 N.J. 22, 227 A.2d 689 (1967), the unborn child's right to live came into conflict with family privacy. The Gleitmans contended that their doctor failed to warn that Mrs. Gleitman was suffering from German measles and this failure deprived the family of the opportunity of terminating the pregnancy. They alleged the child was born with grave defects as a result of the doctor's omission. The court stated as follows:

> "The right to life is inalienable in our society. . . .
> We are not faced here with the necessity of balancing the mother's life against that of her child. The sanctity of the single human life is the decisive factor in this suit in tort. Eugenic considerations are not controlling. We are not talking here about the breeding of prize cattle. It may have been easier for the mother and less expensive for the father to have terminated the life of their child while he was an embryo, but these alleged detriments cannot stand against the preciousness of a single human life to support a remedy in tort." 227 A.2d at 693.

B. Physician-patient relationship. Proponents of abortion-on-demand assert that anti-abortion laws unlawfully intrude into the privacy of the physician-patient relationship. They assume necessarily that the doctor treating a pregnancy owes an obligation of good medical care to only one patient, the pregnant woman.

In *Jones v. Jones*, 208 Misc. 721, 144 N.Y.S.2d 820 (Sup.Ct. 1955), the court stated (concerning an unborn child) as follows:

> ". . . became a patient of the mother's obstetrician, as well as the mother herself. In so holding, I can think of the infant as a third-party beneficiary of the mother-doctor contract or perhaps a principal for whom the mother acted as agent." 144 N.Y.S.2d at 826.

As a patient of the obstetrician, the child may recover damages for a prenatal injury suffered as the result of the negligence of his doctor. *Sylvia v. Gobeille*, 101 R.I. 76, 220 A.2d 222 (1966); *Seattle-First National Bank v. Rankin*, 59 Wash. 2d 288, 367 P.2d 835 (1962). It is elemental that a doctor cannot be freed from legal restraints in making socio-moral judgments. The state may regulate the medical profession to protect the health and welfare of all its citizens. See *Wasmuth v. Allen*, 14 N.Y.2d 391, 200 N.E.2d 756, 252 N.Y.S.2d 65 (1964), appeal dismissed, 379 U.S. 11 (1964); *Barsky v. Board of Regents*, 347 U.S. 442 (1954). Appellants' contentions of intrusion upon physician-patient relationship are not self-sustaining and must be associated with and connected to a violation of some basic right.

C. The interests of the woman. Personal privacy is an exalted right but, as in marital privacy, it has never been regarded as absolute. A person may be subjected to a "stop and frisk" though it constitutes an intrusion upon his person,[66] or a person may be required to submit to a vaccination,[67] and a blood sample may forcibly be extracted from the body of an individual arrested for suspicion of driving while intoxicated.[68] A woman has been required to submit to a blood transfusion necessary to preserve her life in order that her small child shall not be left without a mother.[69] The "right of privacy" is a highly cherished right—however one which is nowhere expressly mentioned in the Constitution of the United States or its amendments. Numerous examples in tort and criminal law indicate the right to privacy is a relative right.[70] A woman cannot in privacy, even though she harm no other person, legally utilize or even possess certain forbidden drugs,

---

[62] *Reynolds v. United States*, 98 U.S. 145 (1879).
[63] *Prince v. Massachusetts*, 321 U.S. 158 (1944).
[64] Id.
[65] Id.

[66] *Terry v. Ohio*, 392 U.S. 1 (1968).
[67] *Jacobson v. Massachusetts*, 197 U.S. 11 (1905).
[68] *Schmerber v. California*, 384 U.S. 757 (1966).
[69] *Application of President and Directors of Georgetown, Col.*, 331 F.2d 1000 (D.C. Cir. 1964), cert. denied, 377 U.S. 978 (1964).
[70] See Tort Law limitations on the Right of Privacy as outlined in *Prosser on Torts*, 3rd Edition, 1964, Chapter 22.

such as LSD or heroin. The right to privacy was considered a mere relative right by the framers of the Constitution. Had they not considered the right to privacy a mere relative right, they would have carefully defined additional protection for the small portion of the right to privacy protected by the guarantee against unreasonable search and seizure. In *Katz v. United States*, 389 U.S. 347 (1967), referring to searches and seizures, stated that the Fourth Amendment to the Constitution of the United States cannot be translated into a general constitutional "right of privacy". See, *Lewis v. United States*, 385 U.S. 206 (1966).

When the "right of privacy" is attached to an "express right" such as the "right of freedom of religion" a very strong constitutional basis exists for upholding the "right"—except when in conflict with the most basic and fundamental of all rights—the "right to life". In *Raleigh Fitkin-Paul Morgan Memorial Hospital v. Anderson*, 42 N.J. 421, 201 A.2d 537 (1964), cert. denied, 377 U.S. 985 (1964), the New Jersey Supreme Court was asked to decide just such an issue—a conflict between the mother's privacy and the life of the unborn child. The issue was whether the rights of a child *in utero* were violated by the pregnant woman's refusal on religious grounds to submit to a blood transfusion necessary to preserve the lives of both the mother and the unborn child. The Court's finding favored the right to life of the unborn child over the pregnant woman's freedom of religion and stated:

> "The blood transfusions (including transfusions made necessary by the delivery) may be administered if necessary to save her life or the life of the child, as the physician in charge at the time may determine." 201 A.2d at 538.

D. The human-ness of the fetus.   The crux of the moral and legal debate over abortion is, in essence, the right of the woman to determine whether or not she should bear a particular child versus the right of the child to life. The proponents of liberalization of abortion laws speak of the fetus as "a blob of protoplasm" and feel it has no right to life until it has reached a certain stage of development.[71] On the other hand, the opponents of liberalization maintain the fetus is human from the time of conception, and so interruption of pregnancy cannot be justified from the time of fertilization. It most

certainly seems logical that from the stage of differentiation, after which neither twinning nor re-combination will occur, the fetus implanted in the uterine wall deserves respect as a human life. If we take the definition of life as being said to be present when an organism shows evidence of individual animate existence, then from the blastocyst stage the fetus qualifies for respect. It is alive because it has the ability to reproduce dying cells. It is human because it can be distinguished from other non-human species, and once implanted in the uterine wall it requires only nutrition and time to develop into one of us.

The recent recognition of autonomy of the unborn child has led to the development of new medical specialties concerning the unborn child from the earliest stages of the pregnancy.[72*] Modern obstetrics has discarded as unscientific the concept that the child in the womb is but tissue of the mother. Dr. Liley, the New Zealand pediatrician, who perfected the intra-uterine transfusion, has said:

> "Another medical fallacy that modern obstetrics discards is the idea that the pregnant woman can be treated as a patient alone. No problem in fetal health or disease can any longer be considered in isolation. At the very least two people are involved, the mother and her child." Liley, H.M.I.: *Modern Motherhood*, Random House, Rev. Ed. 1969.

Yet the attack on the Texas statute assumes this discredited scientific concept and argues that abortions should be considered no differently than any medical measure taken to protect maternal health, (see appellant's brief pp. 94–98) thus completely ignoring the developing human being in the mother's womb.

The court has also abandoned that concept in *Kelly v. Gregory*, 282 App.Div. 542, 125 N.Y.S.2d 696 (1953), wherein the court stated:

> "We ought to be safe in this respect in saying that legal separability should begin where there is biological separability. We know something more of the actual process of conception and fetal development now than when some of the common law cases were decided; and what we know makes it possible to demonstrate clearly that separability begins at conception.
>
> "The mother's biological contribution from conception on is nourishment and protection;

---

[71] This is given variously as from 12 weeks to 28 weeks of intrauterine life, and some apparently feel it has no life at all until after full-term delivery.

[72] Gairdner, Douglas: *Fetal Medicine: Who Is To Practice It*, J. Obstet, and Gynec. Brit. Commonwealth, 75:1123–1124, Dec. 1968.
*The citations in this and the following are according to Medical Journal Practice.

but the fetus has become a separate organism and remains so throughout its life. That it may not live if its protection and nourishment are cut off earlier than the viable stage of its development is not to destroy its separability; it is rather to describe the conditions under which life will not continue." 125 N.Y.S.2d at 697.

It is our task in the next subsections to show how clearly and conclusively modern science—embryology, fetology, genetics, perinatology, all of biology—establishes the humanity of the unborn child. We submit that the data not only shows the constitutionality of the Texas legislature's effort to save the unborn from indiscriminate extermination, *but in fact suggests a duty to do so*. We submit also that no physician who understands this will argue that the law is vague, uncertain or overbroad for he will understand that the law calls upon him to exercise his art for the benefit of his *two patients:* mother *and* child.

From conception the child is a complex, dynamic, rapidly growing organism. By a natural and continuous process the single fertilized ovum will, over approximately nine months, develop into the trillions of cells of the newborn. The natural end of the sperm and ovum is death unless fertilization occurs. At fertilization a new and unique being is created which, although receiving one-half of its chromosomes from each parent, is really unlike either.[73]

About seven to nine days after conception, when there are already several hundred cells of the new individual formed, contact with the uterus is made and implantation begins. Blood cells begin at 17 days and a heart as early as 18 days. This embryonic heart which begins as a simple tube starts irregular pulsations at 24 days, which, in about one week, smooth into a rhythmic contraction and expansion.[74] It has been shown that the ECG on a 23 mm embryo (7.5 weeks) presents the existence of a functionally complete cardiac system and the possible existence of a myoneurol or humoral regulatory mechanism. All the classic elements of the adult ECG were seen.[75] Occasional contractions of the heart in a 6 mm (2 week) embryo have been observed as well as tracings exhibiting the classical elements of the ECG tracing of an adult in a 15 mm embryo (5 weeks).[76]

Commencing at 18 days the developmental emphasis is on the nervous system even though other vital organs, such as the heart, are commencing development at the same time. Such early development is necessary since the nervous system integrates the action of all other systems. By the end of the 20th day the foundation of the child's brain, spinal cord and entire nervous system will have been established. By the 6th week after conception this system will have developed so well that it is controlling movements of the baby's muscles, even though the woman may not be aware that she is pregnant. By the 33rd day the cerebral cortex, that part of the central nervous system that governs motor activity as well as intellect may be seen.[77]

The baby's eyes begin to form at 19 days. By the end of the first month the foundation of the brain, spinal cord, nerves and sense organs is completely formed. By 28 days the embryo has the building blocks for 40 pairs of muscles situated from the base of its skull to the lower end of its spinal column. By the end of the first month the child has completed the period of relatively greatest size increase and the greatest physical change of a lifetime. He or she is ten thousand times larger than the fertilized egg and will increase its weight six billion times by birth, having in only the first month gone from the one cell state to millions of cells.[78]

Shettles and Rugh describe this first month of development as follows:

"This, then, is the great planning period, when out of apparently nothing comes evidence of a well integrated individual, who will form along certain well tried patterns, but who will, in the end, be distinguishable from every other human being by virtue of ultra microscopic chro-

[73] Ingleman-Sundberg, Axel, and Wirsen, Cloes: *A Child Is Born: The Drama Of Life Before Birth*, photos by Lennart Nilsson, Dell Publishing Co., New York, 1965. Arey, Leslie B.: *Developmental Anatomy*, 6th Ed. Philadelphia W. B. Saunders Co. 1954 Chap. II VI. Patten, Bradley M.: *Human Embryology*, 3rd Ed. McGraw-Hill Book Co. New York, 1968 Chap. VII.

[74] Ingleman-Sundberg, Axel, and Wirsen, Cloes: *A Child Is Born: The Drama Of Life Before Birth*, supra.

[75] Arey, Leslie B.: *Developmental Anatomy*, supra. Patten, Bradley M.: *Human Embryology*, supra. Rugh, Robert, and Shettles, Landrum B., with Richard N. Einhorn: *From Conception To Birth: The Drama Of Life's Beginnings*,

Harper and Row, New York 1971. Straus, Reuben, et al: *Direct Electrocardiographic Recording Of A Twenty-Three Millimeter Human Embryo*, The American Journal of Cardiology, September 1961, pp. 443–447.

[76] Marcel, M.P., and Exchaquet, J.P.: *L'Electrocardiogramme Du Foetus Human Avec Un Cas De Double Rythme Auriculaire Verifie*, Arch. Mal. Couer, Paris 31: 504, 1938.

[77] Arey, Leslie B.: *Developmental Anatomy*, supra. Rugh, Robert, and Shettles, Landrum B., with Richard N. Einhorn: *From Conception To Birth: The Drama Of Life's Beginnings*, supra. Flannagan, G.L.: *The First Nine Months Of Life*, Simon and Schuster, 1962.

[78] Arey, Leslie B.: *Developmental Anatomy*, supra. Patten, Bradley M.: *Human Embryology*, supra. Rugh, Robert, and Shettles, Landrum B., with Richard N. Einhorn: *From Conception To Birth: The Drama Of Life's Beginnings*, supra. Ingleman-Sundberg, Axel, and Wirsen, Cloes: *A Child Is Born: The Drama Of Life Before Birth*, supra. Flannagan, G.L.: *The First Nine Months Of Life*, supra.

mosomal differences." Rugh, Robert, and Shettles, Landrum B., with Richard N. Einhorn: *From Conception To Birth: The Drama Of Life's Beginnings, supra* at p. 35.

By the beginning of the second month the unborn child, small as it is, looks distinctly human. Yet, by this time the child's mother is not even aware that she is pregnant.[79]

As Shettles and Rugh state:

> "And as for the question, 'when does the embryo become human?' The answer is that it *always* had human potential, and *no other*, from the instant the sperm and the egg came together because of its chromosomes." (Emphasis in original). Id at p. 40.

At the end of the first month the child is about ¼ of an inch in length. At 30 days the primary brain is present and the eyes, ears, and nasal organs have started to form. Although the heart is still incomplete, it is beating regularly and pumping blood cells through a closed vascular system.[80] The child and mother do not exchange blood, the child having from a very early point in its development its own and complete vascular system.[81]

Earliest reflexes begin as early as the 42nd day. The male penis begins to form. The child is almost ½ inch long and cartilage has begun to develop.[82]

Even at 5½ weeks the fetal heartbeat is essentially similar to that of an adult in general configuration. The energy output is about 20% that of the adult, but the fetal heart is functionally complete and normal by 7 weeks. Shettles and Rugh describe the child at this point of its development as a 1-inch miniature doll with a large head, but gracefully formed arms and legs and an unmistakably human face.[83]

By the end of the seventh week we see a well proportioned small scale baby. In its seventh week, it bears the familiar external features and all the internal organs of the adult, even though it is less than an inch long and weighs only 1/30th of an ounce. The body has become nicely rounded, padded with muscles and covered by a thin skin. The arms are only as long as printed exclamation marks, and have hands with fingers and thumbs. The slower growing legs have recognizable knees, ankles and toes.[84]

The new body not only exists, it also functions. The brain in configuration is already like the adult brain and sends out impulses that coordinate the function of the other organs. The brain waves have been noted at 43 days.[85] The heart beats sturdily. The stomach produces digestive juices. The liver manufactures blood cells and the kidney begins to function by extracting uric acid from the child's blood.[86] The muscles of the arms and body can already be set in motion.[87]

After the eighth week no further primordia will form; *everything* is already present that will be found in the full term baby.[88] As one author describes this period:

> "A human face with eyelids half closed as they are in someone who is about to fall asleep. Hands that soon will begin to grip, feet trying their first gentle kicks." Rugh, Roberts, and Shettles, Landrum B., with Richard N. Einhorn: *From Conception To Birth: The Drama of Life's Beginnings, supra* at p. 71.

From this point until adulthood, when full growth is achieved somewhere between 25 and 27 years, the changes in the body will be mainly in dimension and in gradual refinement of the working parts.[89]

The development of the child, while very rapid, is also very specific. The genetic pattern set down in the first day of life instructs the development of a specific anatomy. The ears are formed by seven weeks and are specific, and may resemble a family pattern.[90] The lines in

---

[79] Ingelman-Sundberg, Axel, and Wirsen, Cloes: *A Child Is Born: The Drama Of Life Before Birth, supra.*
[80] Arey, Leslie B.: *Developmental Anatomy, supra.*
[81] Arey, Leslie B.: *Developmental Anatomy, supra.* Patten, Bradley M.: *Human Embryology, supra.* Rugh, Robert, and Shettles, Landrum B., with Richard N. Einhorn: *From Conception To Birth: The Drama Of Life's Beginnings, supra.* Marcel, M.P., and Exchaquet, J.P.: *L'Electrocardiogramme Du Foetus Human Avec Un Cas De Double Rythme Auriculaire Verifie, supra.* Flannagan, G.L.: *The First Nine Months Of Life, supra.*
[82] Arey, Leslie B.: *Developmental Anatomy, supra.* Patten, Bradley M.: *Human Embryology, supra.*
[83] Rugh, Robert, and Shettles, Landrum B., with Richard N. Einhorn: *From Conception To Birth: The Drama Of Life's Beginnings, supra* at p. 54.
[84] Arey, Leslie B.: *Developmental Anatomy, supra.* Patten, Bradley M.: *Human Embryology, supra.* Rugh, Robert, and Shettles, Landrum B., with Richard N. Einhorn: *From Conception To Birth: The Drama Of Life's Beginnings, supra.* Ingelman-Sundberg, Axel, and Wirsen, Cloes: *A Child Is Born: The Drama Of Life Before Birth, supra.*
[85] Still, J.W.: J. Washington Acad. Sci. 59:46, 1969.
[86] Flannagan, G.L.: *The First Nine Months Of Life, supra.* Gesell, Arnold: *The Embryology of Behavior,* Harper & Bros. Publishers, 1945, Chap. IV, V, VI, X.
[87] Hooker, Davenport: *The Prenatal Origin of Behavior,* Univ. of Kansas Press, 1952.
[88] Rugh, Robert, and Shettles, Landrum B., with Richard N. Einhorn: *From Conception To Birth: The Drama Of Life's Beginnings, supra* at p. 71.
[89] Arey, Leslie B.: *Developmental Anatomy, supra.* Potter, Edith: *Pathology Of The Fetus And Infant,* Year Book Publishers Inc., Chicago, 1961.
[90] Streeter, Geo. L.: *Development Of The Auricle In The Human Embryo,* Contributions to Embryology, Vol. XIII No. 61, 1921.

the hands start to be engraved by eight weeks and remain a distinctive feature of the individual.[91]

The primitive skeletal system has completely developed by the end of six weeks.[92] This marks the end of the child's embryonic (from Greek, to swell or teem within) period. From this point, the child will be called a fetus (Latin, young one or offspring).[93]

In the third month, the child becomes very active. By the end of the month he can kick his legs, turn his feet, curl and fan his toes, make a fist, move his thumb, bend his wrist, turn his head, squint, frown, open his mouth, press his lips tightly together.[94] He can swallow and drinks the amniotic fluid that surrounds him. Thumb sucking is first noted at this age. The first respiratory motions move fluid in and out of his lungs with inhaling and exhaling respiratory movements.[95]

The movement of the child has been recorded at this early stage by placing delicate shock recording devices on the mother's abdomen and direct observations have been made by the famous embryologist, Davenport Hooker, M.D. Over the last thirty years, Dr. Hooker has recorded the movement of the child on film, some as early as six weeks of age. His films show that prenatal behavior develops in an orderly progression.[96]

The prerequisites for motion are muscles and nerves. In the sixth to seventh weeks, nerves and muscles work together for the first time.[97] If the area of the lips, the first to become sensitive to touch, is gently stroked, the child responds by bending the upper body to one side and making a quick backward motion with his arms. This is called a total pattern response because it involves most of the body, rather than a local part. Localized and more

appropriate reactions such as swallowing follow in the third month. By the beginning of the ninth week, the baby moves spontaneously without being touched. Sometimes his whole body swings back and forth for a few moments. By eight and a half weeks the eyelids and the palms of the hands become sensitive to touch. If the eyelid is stroked, the child squints. On stroking the palm, the fingers close into a small fist.[98]

In the ninth and tenth weeks, the child's activity leaps ahead. Now if the forehead is touched, he may turn his head away and pucker up his brow and frown. He now has full use of his arms and can bend the elbow and wrist independently. In the same week, the entire body becomes sensitive to touch.[99]

The twelfth week brings a whole new range of responses. The baby can now move his thumb in opposition to his fingers. He now swallows regularly. He can pull up his upper lip, the initial step in the development of the sucking reflex.[100] By the end of the twelfth week, the quality of muscular response is altered. It is no longer marionette-like or mechanical—the movements are now graceful and fluid, as they are in the newborn. The child is active and the reflexes are becoming more vigorous. All this is before the mother feels any movement.[101]

Every child shows a distinct individuality in his behavior by the end of the third month. This is because the actual structure of the muscles varies from baby to baby. The alignment of the muscles of the face, for example, follow an inherited pattern. The facial expressions of the baby in his third month are already similar to the facial expressions of his parents.[102]

Further refinements are noted in the third month. The fingernails appear. The child's face becomes much prettier. His eyes, previously far apart, now move closer together. The eyelids close over the eyes. Sexual differentiation is

[91] Miller, James, R.: *Dermal Ridge Patterns: Technique For Their Study In Human Fetuses*, J. Pediatric, Vol. 73, No. 4, Oct. 1969, pp. 614–616.

[92] Arey, Leslie B.: *Developmental Anatomy*, supra. Patten, Bradley M.: *Human Embryology*, supra.

[93] Patten, Bradley M.: *Human Embryology*, supra.

[94] Hooker, Davenport: *The Prenatal Origin Of Behavior*, supra.

[95] Flannagan, G.L.: *The First Nine Months Of Life*, supra. Hooker, Davenport: *The Prenatal Origin Of Behavior*, supra.

[96] Hooker, Davenport: *The Prenatal Origin Of Behavior*, supra. Hooker, Davenport: *Early Human Fetal Behavior With A Preliminary Note On Double Simultaneous Fetal Stimulation*, Proceedings of the Association for Research in Nervous and Mental Disease, Baltimore, The Williams & Wilkins Co., 1954. Gesell, Arnold, M.D., Amatruda, C.S., M.D.: *Developmental Diagnosis*, P. S. Hoeber, 1958 pp. 8–9.

[97] Arey, Leslie M.: *Developmental Anatomy*, supra.

[98] Hooker, Davenport: *Early Human Fetal Behavior With A Preliminary Note On Double Simultaneous Fetal Stimulation*, supra. Hooker, Davenport: *The Prenatal Origin Of Behavior*, supra. Flannagan, G.L.: *The First Nine Months Of Life*, supra. Hooker, Davenport: *The Origin Of Overt Behavior*, Ann Arbor, Univ. of Michigan Press, 1944.

[99] Hooker, Davenport: *The Prenatal Origin of Behavior*, supra.

[100] Gairdner, Douglas: *Fetal Medicine: Who Is To Practice It*, supra.

[101] Gairdner, Douglas: *Fetal Medicine: Who Is To Practice It*, supra. Hooker, Davenport: *The Origin Of Overt Behavior*, supra.

[102] Flannagan, G.L.: *The First Nine Months Of Life*, supra. Still, J.W.: J. Washington Acad. Sci., supra. Gesell, Arnold: *The Embryology Of Behavior*, supra.

apparent in both internal and external sex organs, and primitive eggs and sperm are formed. The vocal cords are completed. In the absence of air they cannot produce sound; the child cannot cry aloud until birth, although he is capable of crying long before.[103]

From the twelfth to the sixteenth week, the child grows very rapidly.[104] His weight increases six times, and he grows to eight to ten inches in height. For this incredible growth spurt the child needs oxygen and food. This he receives from his mother through the placental attachment—much like he receives food from her after he is born. His dependence does not end with expulsion into the external environment.[105] We now know that the placenta belongs to the baby, not the mother, as was long thought.[106]

In the fifth month, the baby gains two inches in height and ten ounces in weight. By the end of the month he will be about one foot tall and will weigh one pound. Fine baby hair begins to grow on his eyebrows and on his head and a fringe of eyelashes appear. Most of the skeleton hardens. The baby's muscles become much stronger, and as the child becomes larger his mother finally perceives his many activities.[107] The child's mother comes to recognize the movement and can feel the baby's head, arms and legs. She may even perceive a rhythmic jolting movement—fifteen to thirty per minute. This is due to the child hiccoughing.[108] The doctor can now hear the heartbeat with his stethoscope.[109]

The baby sleeps and wakes just as it will after birth.[110] When he sleeps he invariably settles into his favorite position called his "lie". Each baby has a characteristic lie.[111] When he awakens he moves about freely in the buoyant fluid turning from side to side, and frequently head over heel. Sometimes his head will be up and sometimes it will be down. He may sometimes be aroused from sleep by external vibrations. He may wake up from a loud tap on the tub when his mother is taking a bath. A loud concert or the vibrations of a washing machine may also stir him into activity.[112] The child hears and recognizes his mother's voice before birth.[113] Movements of the mother, whether locomotive, cardiac or respiratory, are communicated to the child.[114]

In the sixth month, the baby will grow about two more inches, to become fourteen inches tall. He will also begin to accumulate a little fat under his skin and will increase his weight to a pound and three-quarters. This month the permanent teeth buds come in high in the gums behind the milk teeth. Now his closed eyelids will open and close, and his eyes look up, down and sideways. Dr. Liley of New Zealand feels that the child may perceive light through the abdominal wall.[115] Dr. Still has noted that electroencephalographic waves have been obtained in forty-three to forty-five day old fetuses, and so conscious experience is possible after this date.[116]

In the sixth month, the child develops a strong muscular grip with his hands. He also starts to breathe regularly and can maintain respiratory response for twenty-four hours if born prematurely. He may even have a slim change of surviving in an incubator. The youngest children known to survive were between twenty to twenty-five weeks old.[117] The concept of *viability* is not a static one. Dr. Andre Hellegers of Georgetown University states that 10% of children born between twenty weeks and twenty-four weeks gestation will survive.[118] Modern medical intensive therapy has salvaged many children that would have been considered

[103] Arey, Leslie B.: *Developmental Anatomy*, supra. Flannagan, G.L.: *The First Nine Months Of Life*, supra. Patten, Bradley M.: *Human Embryology*, supra. Gairdner, Douglas: *Fetal Medicine: Who Is To Practice It*, supra.

[104] Hellman, L.M., et al.: *Growth And Development Of The Human Fetus Prior To The 20th Week of Gestation*, Am. J. Obstet. and Gynec. Vol. 103, No. 6, March 15, 1969, pp. 789–800.

[105] Arey, Leslie B.: *Developmental Anatomy*, supra. Patten, Bradley M.: *Human Embryology*, supra.

[106] Gairdner, Douglas: *Fetal Medicine: Who Is To Practice It*, supra.

[107] Arey, Leslie B.: *Developmental Anatomy*, supra.

[108] Flannagan, G.L.: *The First Nine Months Of Life*, supra. Gairdner, Douglas: *Fetal Medicine: Who Is To Practice It*, supra.

[109] Arey, Leslie B.: *Developmental Anatomy*, supra. Flannagan, G.L.: *The First Nine Months Of Life*, supra.

[110] Petre-Quadens, O., et al.: *Sleep In Pregnancy: Evidence Of Fetal Sleep Characteristics*, J. Neurologic Science, 4:600–605, May, June, 1967.

[111] Gairdner, Douglas: *Fetal Medicine: Who Is To Practice It*, supra.

[112] Flannagan, G.L.: *The First Nine Months Of Life*, supra.

[113] Wood, Carl: *Weightlessness: Its Implications For The Human Fetus*, J. Obstetrics & Gynecology of the British Commonwealth, 1970 Vol. 77, pp. 333–336. Liley, Albert W.: *Auckland MD To Measure Light And Sound Inside Uterus*, Medical Tribune Report, May 26, 1969.

[114] Wood, Carl: *Weightlessness: Its Implications For The Human Fetus*, supra.

[115] Liley, Albert W.: *Auckland MD To Measure Light And Sound Inside Uterus*, supra.

[116] Still, J.W.: Washington Acad. Sci., supra.

[117] Flannagan, G.L.: *The First Nine Months Of Life*, supra.

[118] Monroe, *Canadian Medical Association's Journal*, 1939. Hellegers, Andre, M.D.: *National Symposium On Abortion*, May 15, 1970, Prudential Plaza, Chicago, Illinois.

non-viable only a few years ago. The concept of an artificial placenta may be a reality in the near future and will push the date of viability back even further, and perhaps to the earliest stages of gestation.[119] After twenty-four to twenty-eight weeks the child's chances of survival are much greater.

This review has covered the first six months of life. By this time the individuality of this human being should be clear to all unbiased observers. When one views the present state of medical science, we find that the artificial distinction between born and unborn has vanished. The whole thrust of medicine is in support of the motion that the child in its mother is a distinct individual in need of the most diligent study and care, and that he is also a patient whom science and medicine treat just as they do any other person.[120]

This review of the current medical status of the unborn serves us several purposes. Firstly, it shows conclusively the humanity of the fetus by showing that human life is a continuum which commences in the womb. There is no magic in birth. The child is as much a child in those several days before birth as he is those several days after. The maturation process, commenced in the womb, continues through the post-natal period, infancy, adolescence, maturity and old age. Dr. Arnold Gesell points out in his work that no king ever had any other beginning than have had all of us in our mother's womb.[121] Quickening is only a relative concept which depends upon the sensitivity of the mother, the position of the placenta, and the size of the child.*

---

[119] Zapol, Warren, and Kolobow, Theodore: *Medical World News*, May 30, 1969. Alexander, D.P.; Britton, H.G.; Nixon, D.A.; *Maintenance Of Sheep Fetuses By An Extra Cororeal Circuit For Periods Up To 24 Hours*, Am. J. Obstet. and Gynec, Vol. 102, No. 7, Dec. 1968, pp. 969–975.
[120] *Fetology: The Smallest Patients. The Sciences*, published by the New York Academy of Sciences, Vol. 8 No. 10, Oct. 1968, pp. 11–15. Gairdner, Douglas: *Fetal Medicine: Who Is To Practice It*, supra.
[121] Gesell, Arnold: *The Embryology Of Behavior*, supra.
*If the court is interested in the actual medical history on nineteenth century legislative opposition to abortion, it may consult the American Medical Association, 1846–1951 *Digest of Official Actions* (edited F.J.L. Blasingame 1959), p. 66, where a list of the repeated American Medical Association attacks on abortion are compiled. It will be seen that the great medical battle of the nineteenth century was to persuade legislatures to eliminate the requirement of quickening and to condemn abortion from conception, see Isaac M. Quimby *Introduction to Medical Jurisprudence*, Journal of American Medical Association, August 6, 1887, Vol. 9, p. 164 and H. C. Markham *Foeticide and Its Prevention*, ibid. Dec. 8, 1888, Vol. 11, p. 805. It will be seen that the Association unanimously condemned abortion as the destruction of "human life", American Medical Association, *Minutes of*

VII. The state of Texas has a legitimate interest in prohibiting abortion except by medical advice for the purpose of "saving the life of the mother"

There seems little argument necessary if one can conclude the unborn child is a human being with birth but a convenient landmark in a continuing process—a bridge between two stages of life. The basic postulates from which the Appellees' arguments proceed are: (1) the pregnant woman has a right of control over her own body as a matter of privacy guaranteed to her by the Constitution of the United States; and (2) this right cannot be interfered with by the state since the state cannot demonstrate any compelling interest to justify its intrusion. The contrary position is the state's interest in preventing the arbitrary and unjustified destruction of an unborn child—a living human being in the very earliest stages of its development. Whatever personal right of privacy a pregnant woman may have with respect to the disposition and use of her body must be balanced against the personal right of the unborn child to life.

Whatever the metaphysical view of it is, or may have been, it is beyond argument that legal concepts as to the nature and rights of the unborn child have drastically changed, based on expanded medical knowledge, over the last 2,500 years.

In addition to the provisions of 22 D C Code 201,[122] the Congress of the United States has clearly indicated a firm general policy of the Federal government against abortion. 18 U.S.C. 1461 provides in part as follows:

> "Every obscene, lewd, lascivious, indecent, filthy or vile article, matter, thing, device, or substance; and—
>
> Every article or thing designed, adapted, or intended for preventing conception or producing *abortion*, or for any indecent or immoral use; and
>
> Every article, instrument, substance, drug, medicine, or thing which is advertised or described in a manner calculated to lead another to use or apply it for preventing conception or producing *abortion*, or for any indecent or immoral purpose; and
>
> Every written or printed card, letter, circular, book, pamphlet, advertisement, or notice of any kind giving information, directly or indirectly, where, or how, or from whom, or by what means any of such mentioned matters, articles, or things may be obtained or made or where or by whom any act or operation of any

---

the *Annual Meeting* 1859, The American Medical Gazette 1859, Vol. 10, p. 409.
[122] The District of Columbia abortion statute in issue in *United States v. Vuitch*.

kind for the procuring or producing of *abortion* will be done or performed, or how or by what means conception may be prevented or *abortion* produced, whether sealed or unsealed; and

Every paper, writing, advertisement, or representation that any article, instrument, substance, drug, medicine, or thing may, or can, be used or applied for preventing conception or producing *abortion*, or for any indecent or immoral purpose; and

Every description calculated to induce or incite a person to so use or apply any such article, instrument, substance, drug, medicine, or thing—

Is declared to be nonmailable matter and shall not be conveyed in the mails or delivered from any post office or by any letter carrier.

. . . ." (Emphasis added).

It is most seriously argued that the "life" protected by the Due Process of Law Clause of the Fifth Amendment includes the life of the unborn child. Further, it would be a denial of equal protection of law not to accord protection of the life of a person who had not yet been born but still in the womb of its mother. If it is a denial of equal protection for a statute to distinguish between a thief and an embezzler under a statute providing for the sterilization of the one and not the other,[123] then it is surely a denial of equal protection for either the state or federal government to distinguish between a person who has been born and one living in the womb of its mother.

In *Katz v. United States*, supra, this Court, after concluding that the Fourth Amendment cannot be translated into a general constitutional "right to privacy" and after making reference to other provisions of the Constitution of the United States protecting personal privacy from other forms of governmental intrusion,[124] stated that ". . . the protection of a person's *general* right to privacy—his right to be let alone by other people—is, like the protection of his property and of his very life, left largely to the law of the individual States". 389 U.S. at 352. Compare *Kovacs v. Cooper*, 336 U.S. 77 (1949).

If it be true that the compelling state interest in prohibiting or regulating abortion did not

exist at one time in the stage of history, under the result of the findings and research of modern medicine, a different legal conclusion can now be reached. The fact that a statute or law may originally have been enacted to serve one purpose does not serve to condemn it when the same statute, with the passage of time, serves a different but equally valid public purpose. See *McGowan v. Maryland*, 366 U.S. 420 (1961).

CONCLUSION

For the reasons above stated Appellee submits that the appeal from the judgment of the lower court denying injunctive relief to the Appellants should be affirmed; that this Court consider plenary review of this entire case and reverse the judgment of the court below declaring Articles 1191, 1192, 1193, 1194 and 1196 of the Texas Penal Code unconstitutional and enter its order accordingly.

Respectfully submitted,

Crawford C. Martin
Attorney General of Texas

Henry Wade
Criminal District Attorney
Dallas County, Texas

John B. Tolle
Assistant District Attorney
Dallas County Government Center
Dallas, Texas 75202

Nola White
First Assistant Attorney General

Alfred Walker
Executive Assistant

Robert C. Flowers
Assistant Attorney General

JAY FLOYD
Assistant Attorney General
P.O. Box 12548, Capitol Station
Austin, Texas, 78711

Attorneys for Appellee

---

[123] *Skinner v. Oklahoma*, 316 U.S. 535 (1942).
[124] Note 5 at page 510.

In the
Supreme Court of the United States

No. 70–18, 1972 Term

JANE ROE, JOHN DOE, MARY DOE, AND JAMES HUBERT HALLFORD, M.D., APPELLANTS

V.

HENRY WADE, DISTRICT ATTORNEY OF DALLAS COUNTY, TEXAS APPELLEE

On Appeal from the United States District Court for the Northern District of Texas

Supplemental Brief for Appellants

ROY LUCAS
James Madison Constitutional Law Institute
230 Twin Peaks Boulevard
San Francisco, California 94114

LINDA N. COFFEE
2130 First Nat'l Bank Bldg.
Dallas, Texas 75202

SARAH WEDDINGTON
JAMES R. WEDDINGTON
709 West 14th
Austin, Texas 78701

FRED BRUNER
ROY L. MERRILL, JR.
DAUGHERTY, BRUNER, LASTELICK & ANDERSON
1130 Mercantile Bank Bldg.
Dallas, Texas 75201

Attorneys for Appellants

September 1972.

TABLE OF CONTENTS

IN THE
SUPREME COURT OF THE
UNITED STATES
NO. 70-18, 1972 TERM

JANE ROE, JOHN DOE, MARY DOE, AND
JAMES HUBERT HALLFORD, M.D., APPELLANTS

V.

HENRY WADE, DISTRICT ATTORNEY OF
DALLAS COUNTY, TEXAS APPELLEE

ON APPEAL FROM THE UNITED
STATES DISTRICT COURT FOR THE
NORTHERN DISTRICT OF TEXAS

SUPPLEMENTAL BRIEF FOR
APPELLANTS

STATEMENT

The instant case was argued before this Court on December 13, 1971. It is a direct appeal from the decision of a three-judge federal panel declaring the Texas abortion law to be unconstitutional but refusing to grant injunctive relief and denying standing to Appellants Doe.

On June 27, 1972, the case was restored to the calendar for reargument. 40 U.S.L.W. 3617. Reargument is scheduled for October 11, 1972.

Several pertinent decisions have been rendered since the submission of Appellants' original brief. This supplemental brief is submitted to inform the Court of those decisions.

Request for injunctive relief

As to their request for injunctive relief, Appellants would once again point out that the injunction requested was one against *future* prosecutions only. Appellant Hallford had *not* requested injunctive relief to prevent continuation of the state criminal charge pending against him.

The continuing situation in Texas

Despite the District Court holding in June, 1970, that the Texas abortion law is unconstitutional, in November, 1971, the Texas Court of Criminal Appeals (Texas' highest criminal court), in *Thompson v. State*, No. 44,071 (Tex. Ct. Crim. App., Nov. 2, 1971), *petition for cert. filed*, 40 U.S.L.W. 3532 (U.S. March 20, 1972) (No. 71-1200), rendered a decision which directly contradicted that of the District Court. Without interpreting the abortion statute, the Texas court held that the Texas law was not vague. It specifi-

cally did not reach the issue of privacy but held that the State has a compelling interest in protecting the fetus through legislation.

Since the District Court refused to grant injunctive relief and since there is now a direct dichotomy between state and federal decisions, Texas physicians continue to refuse to perform abortions for fear of prosecution. During the last nine months of 1971, 1,658 Texas women travelled to New York to obtain abortions. Texas women continue to be unable to obtain abortion procedures in Texas and thereby continue to suffer irreparable injury.

Actions regarding abortion

At its 1972 Midyear Meeting, the American Bar Association House of Delegates approved the Uniform Abortion Act as drafted by the National Conference of Commissioners on Uniform State Laws. 58 A.B.A.J. 380 (1972). The Uniform Abortion Act allows termination of pregnancy up to twenty weeks of pregnancy and thereafter for reasons such as rape, incest, fetal deformity, and the mental or physical health of the woman.

The Rockefeller Commission on Population and the American Future has recommended that the matter of abortion should be left to the conscience of the individual concerned. *Abele v. Markle*, 342 F. Supp. 800, 802 (D. Conn. 1972).

ARGUMENT

I. Recent cases support appellants' contentions regarding standing

In the oral argument before the three-judge panel, the attorney for Henry Wade, the sole defendant herein, admitted that Appellant Dr. Hallford has standing and that Appellant Roe has standing as an individual and as the representative of the class. (A. 104). The defendent-appellee did not accede standing to John and Mary Doe.

Several recent cases support Appellants' arguments regarding standing.

This Court, in *Eisenstadt v. Baird*, 405 U.S. 438 (1972), held that Appellee Baird had standing to assert the rights of unmarried persons denied access to contraceptives even though he was not a physician or pharmacist and was not an unmarried person denied access to contraceptives.

Just as Baird was allowed to raise the rights of persons who were affected by the statute but who were not subject to prosecution thereunder, here Appellant Hallford should be allowed to raise, in addition to his own constitutional claims, the claims of women who are vitally affected by the Texas abortion law but not subject to prosecution thereunder.

Young Women's Christian Association v. Kugler, 342 F.Supp. 1048 (D.N.J. 1972), declared the New Jersey abortion laws unconstitutional. Such laws prohibited persons from causing miscarriage "without lawful justification."

Saying that "the alleged deprivations of constitutional rights depend upon the contingency of pregnancy," 342 F.Supp. at 1056, the Court dismissed all the women plaintiffs since none had alleged pregnancy. There is no indication that any had alleged status as persons wishing to give advice or assistance to women seeking abortions.

The Court recognized that all the physician plaintiffs, two of whom had lost their licenses to practice medicine and one of whom was incarcerated at the time of the action, had standing to raise the constitutional questions both on behalf of and pertaining to themselves and their women patients.

The plaintiff physicians alleged that they had been forced to turn away patients seeking advice and information about the possibility of obtaining abortions, as have Dr. Hallford and the class he represents in the instant case. Dr. Hallford and his fellow physicians are also subject to prosecution under the law if they should perform an abortion that a jury finds was not for the purpose of saving the life of the woman.

Dr. Hallford should be recognized to have standing to litigate the constitutional claims of his class of physicians and those of women patients.

In *Abele v. Markle,* 342 F.Supp. 800 (D. Conn. 1972), the Connecticut anti-abortion statutes were declared to be unconstitutional. Much like the Texas law, the statutes prohibited all abortions except those necessary to preserve the life of the mother or fetus. Prior to the District Court's consideration of the merits the Circuit Court held that pregnant women and medical personnel desiring to give advice and aid regarding abortions had standing to challenge the statute. *Abele v. Markle,* 452 F.2d 1121 (2 Cir. 1971).

In this Texas case, Appellant Jane Roe was pregnant when the action was filed. Appellants John and Mary Doe in their complaint outlined their desire to actively participate in organizations giving advice and counselling regarding abortions, along with information to specifically assist in securing abortion. (A. 18). Although the Connecticut abortion laws more specifically applied to giving aid, advice, and encouragement to bring about abortion, Texas law is such that Appellants Doe have been effectively stopped from giving such aid, advice, and encouragement for fear of being subjected to prosecution under either 1 TEXAS PENAL CODE art. 70 (1952) as accomplices to the crime of abortion, or 3 TEXAS PENAL CODE art. 1628 (1953) for conspiring to commit the crime of abortion. (A. 19). Like the Connecticut medical personnel desiring to give advice and aid regarding abortions, Appellants Doe should be recognized to have standing to challenge the Texas law.

In *Poe v. Menghini,* 339 F.Supp. 986 (D. Kan. 1972), the three-judge panel recognized that two women who were pregnant when the action was commenced and a doctor had standing to challenge certain restrictions applicable to the performance of abortions. In the instant case, Appellant Jane Roe, who was pregnant when the action was commenced, and Appellant Dr. Hallford would correspondingly have standing to challenge the Texas abortion laws.

Beecham v. Leahy, 287 A.2d 836 (Vt. 1972), declared unconstitutional the Vermont abortion law which, like Texas law, made abortion a criminal offense unless the same is necessary to preserve the life of the woman. The Vermont statute stated that the woman was not liable to the penalties prescribed by the section.

The plaintiffs in *Beecham* were an unmarried pregnant woman who wanted an abortion and a physician who, except for the law, was willing to terminate the pregnancy but who had not done so and who (unlike Appellant Dr. Hallford) was not the subject of pending state criminal action. The Court held that the unmarried pregnant woman had standing but that the physician did not. There is no indication in the opinion as to whether or not the physician sought to adjudicate the rights of his patients, which other cases have allowed.

Regarding the woman the Court said:

> By reducing her rights to ephemeral status without confronting them, the ability of the plaintiff to produce a case or controversy in the ordinary sense is likewise frustrated. She cannot sue the doctor for an action by him that cannot be compelled. She is not herself subject to legal action, by statutory exemption. Yet a very real wrong, in the eyes of the law, exists. . . . Therefore, . . . we declare that she is entitled to proceed in her action founded on her petition. . . . 287 A.2d at 840.

Appellant Jane Roe was similarly found by the lower court to have standing. She, too, was pregnant, had sought but been unable to find a physician to terminate the pregnancy, was not subject to state prosecution, and yet had suffered a very real wrong.

II. The right to seek and receive medical care for the protection of health and well-being is a fundamental personal liberty

As shown in the original brief of Appellants, the Texas abortion law effectively denies Appellants Jane Roe and Mary Doe access to health care.

Although under Texas case law it is not a crime for a pregnant woman to terminate her own pregnancy or to persuade someone else to perform an abortion on her, the Texas law effectively denies her the assistance of trained medical personnel in doing what she is otherwise legally allowed to do.

The Supreme Court of Vermont, in *Beecham v. Leahy, supra*, observed that:

> On the one hand the legislation, by specific reference, leaves untouched in the woman herself those rights respecting her own choice to bear children now coming to be recognized in many jurisdictions.... *Yet, tragically, unless her life itself is at stake, the law leaves her only to the recourse of attempts at self-induced abortion, uncounselled and unassisted by a doctor, in a situation where medical attention is imperative.* 287 A.2d at 839 (emphasis added).

The woman is guilty of no crime in Texas, although by case law rather than by statute. Tragically, Texas women are effectively prevented from securing the services of a doctor when medical expertise and experience are imperative to avoid such pitfalls as the piercing of the uterine wall and infection. By preventing the availability of medical assistance, the state effectively endangers the health and well-being of citizens in direct contravention of their best interests and fundamental rights.

III. The Texas abortion law violates fundamental rights of privacy

As the opinion of this Court in *Eisenstadt v. Baird, supra*, states:

> If the right of privacy means anything, it is the right of the *individual*, married or single, to be free from unwarranted governmental intrusion into matters so fundamentally affecting a person as the decision whether to bear or begat a child. 405 U.S. 438.

In *Vuitch v. Hardy*, Civil No. 71-1129-Y (D. Md. June 22, 1972), the Court stated: "However, this Court is convinced that a woman does have a constitutionally protected, 'fundamental personal right' to seek an abortion," citing *Griswold* and the above language from *Eisenstadt.*

Y.W.C.A. v. Kugler, supra, resulted in the New Jersey abortion law being declared unconstitutional in part as a violation of rights of privacy.

The scope of interests found to be constitutionally protected by the Supreme Court demonstrates that it views both the sanctity of the individual's person and his relationships within a family as so vital to our free society that they should be ranked as fundamental, or implicit in the concept of ordered liberty. 342 F.Supp. at 1071.

Accordingly, we are persuaded that the freedom to determine whether to bear a child and to terminate a pregnancy in its early stages is so significantly related to the fundamental individual and family rights already found to exist in the Constitution that it follows directly in their channel and requires recognition. Whether a constitutional right of privacy in this area is conceptualized as a family right, as in *Griswold*, as a personal and individual right, or as deriving from both sources is of no significance and applies equally to all women regardless of marital status, for the restriction on abortion by the New Jersey statutes immediately involves and interferes with the protected areas of both family and individual freedom. Hence we hold that a woman has a constitutional right of privacy recognizable under the Ninth and Fourteenth Amendments to determine for herself whether to bear a child or to terminate a pregnancy in its early stages, free from unreasonable interference by the State. 342 F.Supp at 1072.

The fundamental impact of the question of abortion on women was emphasized by the *Abele* Connecticut panel:

> The decision to carry and bear a child has extraordinary ramifications for a woman. Pregnancy entails profound physical changes. Childbirth presents some danger to life and health. Bearing and raising a child demands difficult psychological and social adjustments. The working or student mother must curtail or end her employment or educational opportunities. The mother with an unwanted child may find that it overtaxes her and her family's financial or emotional resources. *Thus, determining whether or not to bear a child is of fundamental importance to a woman.* 342 F.Supp. at 801 (emphasis added).

As the lower Court found in the instant case, the Texas abortion law must be declared unconstitutional because it deprives women of their right, secured by the Ninth and Fourteenth Amendments, to choose whether or not to carry a pregnancy to term.

IV. The Texas statute does not advance any state interest of compelling importance in a manner which is narrowly drawn

The legislative purposes that the Texas abortion law was meant to serve are not altogether clear. No legislative history specifically applicable to Texas is available.

Appellee during the oral argument before the lower court said the State has only one interest, that of protecting the unborn (A. 104–05). Appellee's brief and Dec. 13th argument before this Court advance no other State interest.

It is important to note that Appellee gives no authority whatsoever that even tends to establish that the purpose of the Texas legislature in adopting the abortion law was in fact what Appellee suggests.

On the other hand, Appellants' original brief establishes that the legislative purpose in other states was to protect the pregnant woman from the dangers of antiseptic surgery.

Further *Watson v. State*, 9 Tex. App. 237 (Tex. Crim. App. 1880), states that the *woman* is the *victim* of the crime of abortion.

People v. Nixon, Dkt. No. 9579 (Ct. App. 2 Div., Aug. 23, 1972), involved a challenge to the constitutionality of the Michigan abortion statute making criminal actions to terminate a pregnancy unless the same was necessary to preserve the life of the woman. The Court concluded that the "so-called 'abortion' statute was not intended to protect the 'rights' of the unquickened fetus" but rather that the obvious purpose was to protect the pregnant woman.

The Court pointed out that the woman was not subject to prosecution for self-induced abortion and concluded:

> . . . it must be assumed that the harm the statute was attempting to punish ran only to the woman and not to the fetus. If the statute were intended to protect the continued existence of the fetus, then there would be no reason for exempting the woman from prosecution. Opinion at 4, n.9.

Similarly, since self-abortion is not a crime in Texas, it is not logical to assume that the purpose of the legislature in passing the so-called "abortion" law was to protect the fetus. It is logical that the legislative purpose was to protect the woman and her health.

Appellants' original brief establishes that the Texas abortion law no longer serves to protect the health of the pregnant woman; in fact it is a hindrance to health.

Even if Appellee could establish that the legislative purpose of the Texas abortion law was to protect the life of the unborn, the state certainly cannot meet its burden of proving that the statute now has a compelling interest in such regulation nor that the law is sufficiently narrow.

The fetus, as such, is not and never has been protected in Texas, with the possible exception of the abortion statutes. In Texas, the so-called protections for the "unborn child" are dependent on the live birth of the child. Thus under Texas law, once born a child may have rights retroactive to the time prior to birth but such rights are meant to benefit those who have survived birth.

Under the criminal laws of Texas, the fetus is given little protection. Self-abortion is not a crime, and the pregnant woman who seeks or receives the help of others in terminating her pregnancy is guilty of no crime. Even the severity of the penalty for another having performed an abortion depends upon whether or not the woman consented to the procedure.

To destroy the life of a fetus has never been considered as homicide in Texas. In order to obtain a murder conviction, the state must ". . . prove that the child was born alive; (and) that it had an existence independent of the mother. . . ." *Harris v. State*, 28 Tex. App. 308, 309, 12 S.W. 1102, 1103 (1889). In *Wallace v. State*, 7 Tex. App. 570, 10 S.W. 255 (1880), the mother strangled her child with string. The court overturned her murder conviction, saying that the state failed to prove either that the child was born live or that the actual childbirth process had been completed before the child was killed.

Texas courts are not alone in following the common law rule that a child must be born alive to be the subject of the crime of murder. *State v. Dickinson*, 28 Ohio St. 2d 65, 275 N.E.2d 599 (1971); *Keeler v. Superior Court*, 2 Cal. 3d 619, 470 P.2d 662, 87 Cal. Rptr. 481 (1970); *Clark v. State*, 117 Ala. 1, 23 So. 671 (1898); *Abrams v. Foshee*, 3 Clark 274 (Iowa 1856). In those cases where a person has actually been convicted of a crime for causing the death of a fetus, it has not been under the regular homicide statute but under some special statutory provision, such as a feticide statute. Most feticide statutes have as one of their essential elements a *malicious intent to kill the mother. Passley v. State*, 194 Ga. 327, 21 S.E.2d 230 (1942); *State v. Harness*, 280 S.W.2d 11 (Mo. 1955). An intent to cause a miscarriage without an intent to kill the woman would not be sufficient to sustain a conviction of feticide. The penalties under such statutes are also generally lighter than those prescribed by the homicide laws.

Viewed from another angle, there are ironical contradictions between some Texas criminal laws and the abortion law. As stated in *Abele v. Markle, supra*, "(t)he statutes force a woman to carry to natural term a pregnancy that is the result of rape or incest. Yet these acts are prohibited by the state at least in part to avoid the offspring of such unions." 342 F.Supp at 804.

Similarly, Texas makes rape and incest criminal offenses, 2A TEXAS PENAL CODE, art.

1183 at 372 (1961), and 1 TEXAS PENAL CODE, art. 495, at 553 (1952), and prohibits the marriage of persons closely related, TEXAS FAMILY CODE section 2.21, at 17 (1971). Persons who have any infectious condition of syphilis or other veneral disease cannot obtain a marriage license. TEXAS FAMILY CODE, sections 1.21, at 9, and 1.31 at 11 (1972).

The fetus gets no more protection under Texas tort laws than it does under Texas criminal laws. The Texas courts did not recognize a right to recover for injuries received prior to birth until 1967 (113 years after the Texas abortion law was enacted) in *Leal v. C.C. Pitts Sand and Gravel, Inc.*, 419 S.W.2d 820 (Tex. 1967). *Leal* involved a wrongful death action brought by the parents of a child who died two days after birth as the result of pre-natal injuries received in an automobile collision. In allowing the wrongful death action, the Texas Supreme Court held that the child, *had it lived*, could have maintained an action for damages for the pre-natal injuries.

In *Delgado v. Yandell*, 468 S.W.2d 475 (Tex. Civ. App. 1971), *appr. per curiam*, 471 S.W.2d 569 (1971), the Texas Supreme Court approved the holding of the Court of Civil Appeals that a cause of action does exist for pre-natal injuries sustained at any pre-natal stage *provided the child is born alive and survives*. The damages in such a case are not paid to the fetus; they are compensation to a *living* child for having to spend all or a part of his life under a disability caused prior to birth by another's wrongful act.

Thus the claimed "rights" of the fetus in the tort area are actually rights which may only be exercised by a live child after birth or are the right of bereaved potential parents to be compensated for their loss.

Though much has been written concerning the property rights of the fetus, these rights are really legal fictions which have developed to protect the rights of living children. In order to receive the benefit of its supposed rights, the fetus must be born alive. There has never been a case in Texas where a fetus which was stillborn or destroyed through miscarriage or abortion has been treated as a person for the purpose of determining property rights. When certain kinds of inheritances are involved, even unconceived children can be considered to have some property "rights" in that they may receive a legacy on their subsequent birth. *Byrn v. New York City Health & Hospitals Corp.*, No. 210 72 (Ct. App. 1972). However, this has not prevented the United States Supreme Court from finding a constitutional right on the part of a woman to practice contraception. *Griswold v. Connecticut*, 381 U.S. 479 (1965).

There are other areas where Texas does not treat a fetus as a person. For example, under the rules of the Texas Welfare Department, a needy pregnant woman cannot get welfare payments for her unborn child. The state compels the birth of the child, yet does not provide the assistance often needed to produce a healthy child.

Texas does not regard the fetus as a person and has made no attempt to put the fetus on an equal footing with a living child.

Several courts have recently dealt directly with the question of whether the fetus is a person within the meaning of the United States Constitution. Arguably this Court's opinion in *Vuitch* implicitly rejected the claim that the fetus is a person under the Fifth and Fourteenth Amendments.

McGarvey v. Magee-Womens Hospital, Civil Action No. 71–196 (W.D.Pa. Mar. 17, 1972), held that the embryo or fetus is not a person or citizen within the meaning of the Fourteenth Amendment or the Civil Rights Act.

In *Byrn v. New York City Health & Hospitals Corp.*, *supra*, the issue was whether children in embryo are and must be recognized as legal persons or entities entitled under the State and Federal Constitutions to a right to life. The Court's conclusion was that the Constitution does not confer or require legal personality for the unborn.

The Appellee has failed to produce any authority for the proposition that the fetus is considered a person under the Constitution. There is evidence in the Constitution that "person" applies only to a live born person. The clause requiring a decennial census says "the whole Number of * * * Persons" in each state must be counted. U.S. Const. Art. I, § 2, Cl. 3. From the first census in 1790 to the present, census takers have counted only those born. Means, *The Phoenix of Abortional Freedom*, 17 N.Y.L. Forum 335, 402–03 (1971).

Although on its face, the Texas abortion law applies any time after conception, the Brief for Appellee submitted to this Court at page 30 states:

> It most certainly seems logical that from the stage of differentiation . . . the fetus implanted in the uterine wall deserves respect as a human life.

Here Appellee seems to suggest that the law should apply instead only after implantation. Yet on page 32 Appellee devotes a paragraph to describing the "child" during the seven to nine days *before* implantation. During oral argument Appellee suggested that Texas hospitals intervene to terminate pregnancy when a rape victim is brought in (Tr. 47–48), although there is no exception for rape in the Texas statute.

Appellee's ambivalence is but one indication that the statute does not evidence a compelling interest which could not be protected by less restrictive means.

V. The Texas abortion law is unconstitutionally vague

In *Thompson v. State, supra*, the Texas Court of Criminal Appeals upheld the conviction of a physician who allegedly had performed an abortion. The court held, relying on *United States v. Vuitch*, 402 U.S. 62 (1971), that the Texas abortion law was not vague.

The Court in *Thompson* erred. Whether or not a statute is vague is to be determined from the standpoint of the person who is considering performing an act. The Supreme Court in *Vuitch* emphasized that a doctor's day-to-day task was one of consideration for the *health* of his patients; the District of Columbia statute allowed physicians to act to preserve the life or *health* of patients. Texas, however, allows physicians to act only when necessary to protect *life*; that is not the sort of criteria physicians are accustomed to dealing with. From the physician's standpoint, as the District Court in this case pointed out, there are many uncertainties inherent in the language of the statute. *Vuitch* is not authority for upholding the Texas abortion law.

Further, in *Vuitch* the Court upheld the D.C. statute as interpreted by lower courts to include both mental and physical health. In Texas there has been no interpretation of the Texas statute. *Thompson* does not even discuss application of the statute.

Recent decisions have declared laws in New Jersey and Florida to be unconstitutionally vague. In *Y.W.C.A. v. Kugler, supra*, a federal panel declared vague the New Jersey statute against performing an abortion "without lawful justification." Florida's statute against performing an abortion "unless the same shall have been necessary to preserve the life of the mother" was declared unconstitutionally vague by the Florida Supreme Court in *State v. Barquet*, 262 So.2d 431 (1972).

The Florida court stated that "if the statutes contained a clause reading 'necessary to the preservation of the mother's life *or health*' instead of the clause 'necessary to preserve *the* life,' the statutes could be held constitutional. . . ." 262 So.2d at 433.

Chaney v. Indiana, No. 1171 S 321 (Ind. July 24, 1972), however, rejects the vagueness arguments as to a non-medical person.

VI. The Texas abortion law places an unconstitutional burden of proof in the physician

Appellant's original brief details the unconstitutionality of placing upon the physician charged with allegedly performing an abortion the burden of showing that the procedure was necessary for the purpose of saving the life of the woman. Although the burden of proof issue was not before them, the Texas Court of Criminal Appeals in a footnote in *Thompson, supra*, recognized that the *Vuitch* case does call into question the validity of Texas' statutory scheme as to who has the burden of proof on the exemption.

CONCLUSION

For the reasons stated in Appellants' original brief and this supplemental brief, this Court should reverse the lower court's judgment denying standing to Appellants Doe and denying injunctive relief; declare that the Texas Abortion Statutes, Arts. 1191, 1192, 1193, 1194 and 1196, TEXAS PENAL CODE, violate the United States Constitution; and remand with instructions that a permanent injunction against enforcement of said statutes be entered.

Respectfully submitted,

ROY LUCAS
James Madison Constitutional
Law Institute
230 Twin Peaks Blvd.
San Francisco, California 94114

SARAH WEDDINGTON
JAMES R. WEDDINGTON
709 West 14th
Austin, Texas 78701

LINDA N. COFFEE
2130 First Nat'l Bank Bldg.
Dallas, Texas 75202

FRED BRUNER
ROY L. MERRILL, JR.
DAUGHERTY, BRUNER, LASTELICK & ANDERSON
1130 Mercantile Bank Bldg.
Dallas, Texas 75201

Attorneys for Appellants

410 U.S. 113 ROE v. WADE **705**

Cite as 93 S.Ct. 705 (1973)

410 U.S. 113, 35 L.Ed.2d 147

Jane ROE, et al., Appellants,

v.

Henry WADE.

No. 70–18.

Argued Dec. 13, 1971.

Reargued Oct. 11, 1972.

Decided Jan. 22, 1973.

Rehearing Denied Feb. 26, 1973.

See 410 U.S. 959, 93 S.Ct. 1409.

Action was brought for a declaratory and injunctive relief respecting Texas criminal abortion laws which were claimed to be unconstitutional. A three-judge United States District Court for the Northern District of Texas, 314 F.Supp. 1217, entered judgment declaring laws unconstitutional and an appeal was taken. The Supreme Court, Mr. Justice Blackmun, held that the Texas criminal abortion statutes prohibiting abortions at any stage of pregnancy except to save the life of the mother are unconstitutional; that prior to approximately the end of the first trimester the abortion decision and its effectuation must be left to the medical judgment of the pregnant woman's attending physician, subsequent to approximately the end of the first trimester the state may regulate abortion procedure in ways reasonably related to maternal health, and at the stage subsequent to viability the state may regulate and even proscribe abortion except where necessary in appropriate medical judgment for preservation of life or health of mother.

Affirmed in part and reversed in part.

Mr. Chief Justice Burger, Mr. Justice Douglas and Mr. Justice Stewart filed concurring opinions.

Mr. Justice White filed a dissenting opinion in which Mr. Justice Rehnquist joined.

Mr. Justice Rehnquist filed a dissenting opinion.

1. Courts ⊜385(7)

Supreme Court was not foreclosed from review of both the injunctive and

93 S.Ct.—45

declaratory aspects of case attacking constitutionality of Texas criminal abortion statutes where case was properly before Supreme Court on direct appeal from decision of three-judge district court specifically denying injunctive relief and the arguments as to both aspects were necessarily identical. 28 U. S.C.A. § 1253.

2. Constitutional Law ⊜42.1(3), 46(1)

With respect to single, pregnant female who alleged that she was unable to obtain a legal abortion in Texas, when viewed as of the time of filing of case and for several months thereafter, she had standing to challenge constitutionality of Texas criminal abortion laws, even though record did not disclose that she was pregnant at time of district court hearing or when the opinion and judgment were filed, and she presented a justiciable controversy; the termination of her pregnancy did not render case moot. Vernon's Ann.Tex.P.C. arts. 1191–1194, 1196.

3. Courts ⊜383(1), 385(1)

Usual rule in federal cases is that an actual controversy must exist at stages of appellate or certiorari review and not simply at date action is initiated.

4. Action ⊜6

Where pregnancy of plaintiff was a significant fact in litigation and the normal human gestation period was so short that pregnancy would come to term before usual appellate process was complete, and pregnancy often came more than once to the same woman, fact of that pregnancy provided a classic justification for conclusion of nonmootness because of termination.

5. Federal Civil Procedure ⊜331

Texas physician, against whom there were pending indictments charging him with violations of Texas abortion laws who made no allegation of any substantial and immediate threat to any federally protected right that could not be asserted in his defense against state prosecutions and who had not alleged any harassment or bad faith prosecution, did not have standing to intervene in suit seeking declaratory and injunctive relief with respect to Texas abortion statutes which were claimed to be unconstitutional. Vernon's Ann.Tex.P. C. arts. 1191–1194, 1196.

6. Courts ⚶508(7)

Absent harassment and bad faith, defendant in pending state criminal case cannot affirmatively challenge in federal court the statutes under which state is prosecuting him.

7. Federal Civil Procedure ⚶321

Application for leave to intervene making certain assertions relating to a class of people was insufficient to establish party's desire to intervene on behalf of class, where the complaint failed to set forth the essentials of class suit.

8. Constitutional Law ⚶42.1(3)

Childless married couple alleging that they had no desire to have children at the particular time because of medical advice that the wife should avoid pregnancy and for other highly personal reasons and asserting an inability to obtain a legal abortion in Texas were not, because of the highly speculative character of their position, appropriate plaintiffs in federal district court suit challenging validity of Texas criminal abortion statutes. Vernon's Ann.Tex.P.C. arts. 1191–1194, 1196.

9. Constitutional Law ⚶82

Right of personal privacy or a guarantee of certain areas or zones of privacy does exist under Constitution, and only personal rights that can be deemed fundamental or implicit in the concept of ordered liberty are included in this guarantee of personal privacy; the right has some extension to activities relating to marriage. U.S.C.A.Const. Amends. 1, 4, 5, 9, 14, 14, § 1.

10. Constitutional Law ⚶82

Constitutional right of privacy is broad enough to encompass woman's decision whether or not to terminate her pregnancy, but the woman's right to terminate pregnancy is not absolute since state may properly assert important interests in safeguarding health, in maintaining medical standards and in protecting potential life, and at some point in pregnancy these respective interests become sufficiently compelling to sustain regulation of factors that govern the abortion decision. U.S.C.A.Const. Amends. 9, 14.

11. Constitutional Law ⚶82

Where certain fundamental rights are involved, regulation limiting these rights may be justified only by a compelling state interest and the legislative enactments must be narrowly drawn to express only legitimate state interests at stake.

12. Constitutional Law ⚶210, 252

Word "person" as used in the Fourteenth Amendment does not include the unborn. U.S.C.A.Const. Amend. 14.

See publication Words and Phrases for other judicial constructions and definitions.

13. Abortion ⚶1

Prior to approximately the end of the first trimester of pregnancy the attending physician in consultation with his patient is free to determine, without regulation by state, that in his medical judgment the patient's pregnancy should be terminated, and if that decision is reached such judgment may be effectuated by an abortion without interference by the state.

14. Abortion ⚶1

From and after approximately the end of the first trimester of pregnancy a state may regulate abortion procedure to extent that the regulation reasonably relates to preservation and protection of maternal health.

15. Abortion ⚶1

If state is interested in protecting fetal life after viability it may go so far as to proscribe abortion during that period except when necessary to preserve the life or the health of the mother.

16. Abortion ⇔1
    Constitutional Law ⇔258(3)

State criminal abortion laws like Texas statutes making it a crime to procure or attempt an abortion except an abortion on medical advice for purpose of saving life of the mother regardless of stage of pregnancy violate due process clause of Fourteenth Amendment protecting right to privacy against state action. U.S.C.A.Const. Amend. 14; Vernon's Ann.Tex.P.C. arts. 1191–1194, 1196.

17. Abortion ⇔1

State in regulating abortion procedures may define "physician" as a physician currently licensed by State and may proscribe any abortion by a person who is not a physician as so defined.

18. Statutes ⇔64(6)

Conclusion that Texas criminal abortion statute proscribing all abortions except to save life of mother is unconstitutional meant that the abortion statutes as a unit must fall, and the exception could not be struck down separately for then the state would be left with statute proscribing all abortion procedures no matter how medically urgent the case. Vernon's Ann.Tex.P.C. arts. 1191–1194, 1196.

Syllabus *

A pregnant single woman (Roe) brought a class action challenging the constitutionality of the Texas criminal abortion laws, which proscribe procuring or attempting an abortion except on medical advice for the purpose of saving the mother's life. A licensed physician (Hallford), who had two state abortion prosecutions pending against him, was permitted to intervene. A childless married couple (the Does), the wife not being pregnant, separately attacked the laws, basing alleged injury on the future possibilities of contraceptive failure, pregnancy, unpreparedness for parent-

hood, and impairment of the wife's health. A three-judge District Court, which consolidated the actions, held that Roe and Hallford, and members of their classes, had standing to sue and presented justiciable controversies. Ruling that declaratory, though not injunctive, relief was warranted, the court declared the abortion statutes void as vague and overbroadly infringing those plaintiffs' Ninth and Fourteenth Amendment rights. The court ruled the Does' complaint not justiciable. Appellants directly appealed to this Court on the injunctive rulings, and appellee cross-appealed from the District Court's grant of declaratory relief to Roe and Hallford. *Held:*

1. While 28 U.S.C. § 1253 authorizes no direct appeal to this Court from the grant or denial of declaratory relief alone, review is not foreclosed when the case is properly before the Court on appeal from specific denial of injunctive relief and the arguments as to both injunctive and declaratory relief are necessarily identical. Pp. 711–712.

2. Roe has standing to sue; the Does and Hallford do not. Pp. 712–715.

(a) Contrary to appellee's contention, the natural termination of Roe's pregnancy did not moot her suit. Litigation involving pregnancy, which is "capable of repetition, yet evading review," is an exception to the usual federal rule that an actual controversy must exist at review stages and not simply when the action is initiated. Pp. 712–713.

(b) The District Court correctly refused injunctive, but erred in granting declaratory, relief to Hallford, who alleged no federally protected right not assertable as a defense against the good-faith state prosecutions pending against him. Samuels v. Mackell, 401 U.S. 66, 91 S.Ct. 764, 27 L.Ed.2d 688. Pp. 713–714.

---

* The syllabus constitutes no part of the opinion of the Court but has been prepared by the Reporter of Decisions for the convenience of the reader. See United

States v. Detroit Timber & Lumber Co., 200 U.S. 321, 337, 26 S.Ct. 282, 287, 50 L.Ed. 499.

(c) The Does' complaint, based as it is on contingencies, any one or more of which may not occur, is too speculative to present an actual case or controversy. Pp. 714–715.

3. State criminal abortion laws, like those involved here, that except from criminality only a life-saving procedure on the mother's behalf without regard to the stage of her pregnancy and other interests involved violate the Due Process Clause of the Fourteenth Amendment, which protects against state action the right to privacy, including a woman's qualified right to terminate her pregnancy. Though the State cannot override that right, it has legitimate interests in protecting both the pregnant woman's health and the potentiality of human life, each of which interests grows and reaches a "compelling" point at various stages of the woman's approach to term. Pp. 726–732.

(a) For the stage prior to approximately the end of the first trimester, the abortion decision and its effectuation must be left to the medical judgment of the pregnant woman's attending physician. Pp. 731–732.

(b) For the stage subsequent to approximately the end of the first trimester, the State, in promoting its interest in the health of the mother, may, if it chooses, regulate the abortion procedure in ways that are reasonably related to maternal health. Pp. 731–732.

(c) For the stage subsequent to viability the State, in promoting its interest in the potentiality of human life, may, if it chooses, regulate, and even proscribe, abortion except where necessary, in appropriate medical judgment, for the preservation of the life or health of the mother. Pp. 732–733.

4. The State may define the term "physician" to mean only a physician currently licensed by the State, and may proscribe any abortion by a person who is not a physician as so defined. Pp. 732–733.

5. It is unnecessary to decide the injunctive relief issue since the Texas authorities will doubtless fully recognize the Court's ruling that the Texas criminal abortion statutes are unconstitutional. P. 733.

314 F.Supp. 1217, affirmed in part and reversed in part.

Sarah R. Weddington, Austin, Tex., for appellants. |115

Robert C. Flowers, Asst. Atty. Gen. of Texas, Austin, Tex., for appellee on reargument.

Jay Floyd, Asst. Atty. Gen., Austin, Tex., for appellee on original argument.

Mr. Justice BLACKMUN delivered |116 the opinion of the Court.

This Texas federal appeal and its Georgia companion, Doe v. Bolton, 410 U.S. 179, 93 S.Ct. 739, 35 L.Ed.2d 201, present constitutional challenges to state criminal abortion legislation. The Texas statutes under attack here are typical of those that have been in effect in many States for approximately a century. The Georgia statutes, in contrast, have a modern cast and are a legislative product that, to an extent at least, obviously reflects the influences of recent attitudinal change, of advancing medical knowledge and techniques, and of new thinking about an old issue.

We forthwith acknowledge our awareness of the sensitive and emotional nature of the abortion controversy, of the vigorous opposing views, even among physicians, and of the deep and seemingly absolute convictions that the subject inspires. One's philosophy, one's experiences, one's exposure to the raw edges of human existence, one's religious training, one's attitudes toward life and family and their values, and the moral standards one establishes and seeks to observe, are all likely to influence and to color one's thinking and conclusions about abortion.

In addition, population growth, pollution, poverty, and racial overtones tend

410 U.S. 118   ROE v. WADE   **709**

Cite as 93 S.Ct. 705 (1973)

to complicate and not to simplify the problem.

Our task, of course, is to resolve the issue by constitutional measurement, free of emotion and of predilection. We seek earnestly to do this, and, because we do, |117 we have inquired into, and in this opinion place some emphasis upon, medical and medical-legal history and what that history reveals about man's attitudes toward the abortion procedure over the centuries. We bear in mind, too, Mr. Justice Holmes' admonition in his now-vindicated dissent in Lochner v. New York, 198 U.S. 45, 76, 25 S.Ct. 539, 547, 49 L.Ed. 937 (1905):

> "[The Constitution] is made for people of fundamentally differing views, and the accident of our finding certain opinions natural and familiar, or novel, and even shocking, ought not to conclude our judgment upon the question whether statutes embodying them conflict with the Constitution of the United States."

I

The Texas statutes that concern us here are Arts. 1191–1194 and 1196 of the State's Penal Code,[1] Vernon's Ann.P.C. These make it a crime to "procure an abortion," as therein defined, or to attempt one, except with respect to "an abortion procured or attempted by medical advice for the purpose of saving the life of the mother." Similar statutes are in existence in a majority of the States.[2] |118

---

1. "Article 1191. Abortion

    "If any person shall designedly administer to a pregnant woman or knowingly procure to be administered with her consent any drug or medicine, or shall use towards her any violence or means whatever externally or internally applied, and thereby procure an abortion, he shall be confined in the penitentiary not less than two nor more than five years; if it be done without her consent, the punishment shall be doubled. By 'abortion' is meant that the life of the fetus or embryo shall be destroyed in the woman's womb or that a premature birth thereof be caused.
    "Art. 1192. Furnishing the means
    "Whoever furnishes the means for procuring an abortion knowing the purpose intended is guilty as an accomplice.
    "Art. 1193. Attempt at abortion
    "If the means used shall fail to produce an abortion, the offender is nevertheless guilty of an attempt to produce abortion, provided it be shown that such means were calculated to produce that result, and shall be fined not less than one hundred nor more than one thousand dollars.
    "Art. 1194. Murder in producing abortion
    "If the death of the mother is occasioned by an abortion so produced or by an attempt to effect the same it is murder."
    "Art. 1196. By medical advice
    "Nothing in this chapter applies to an abortion procured or attempted by medical advice for the purpose of saving the life of the mother."
    The foregoing Articles, together with Art. 1195, compose Chapter 9 of Title 15 of the Penal Code. Article 1195, not attacked here, reads:

    "Art. 1195. Destroying unborn child
    "Whoever shall during parturition of the mother destroy the vitality or life in a child in a state of being born and before actual birth, which child would otherwise have been born alive, shall be confined in the penitentiary for life or for not less than five years."

2. Ariz.Rev.Stat.Ann. § 13–211 (1956); Conn.Pub.Act No. 1 (May 1972 special session) (in 4 Conn.Leg.Serv. 677 (1972)), and Conn.Gen.Stat.Rev. §§ 53–29, 53–30 (1968) (or unborn child); Idaho Code § 18–601 (1948); Ill.Rev. Stat., c. 38, § 23–1 (1971); Ind.Code § 35–1–58–1 (1971); Iowa Code § 701.1 (1971); Ky.Rev.Stat. § 436.020 (1962); La.Rev.Stat. § 37:1285(6) (1964) (loss of medical license) (but see § 14–87 (Supp.1972) containing no exception for the life of the mother under the criminal statute); Me.Rev.Stat.Ann., Tit. 17, § 51 (1964); Mass.Gen.Laws Ann., c. 272, § 19 (1970) (using the term "unlawfully," construed to exclude an abortion to save the mother's life, Kudish v. Bd. of Registration, 356 Mass. 98, 248 N.E. 2d 264 (1969)); Mich.Comp.Laws § 750.14 (1948); Minn.Stat. § 617.18 (1971); Mo.Rev.Stat. § 559.100 (1969); Mont.Rev.Codes Ann. § 94–401 (1969); Neb.Rev.Stat. § 28–405 (1964); Nev.Rev. Stat. § 200.220 (1967); N.H.Rev.Stat. Ann. § 585:13 (1955); N.J.Stat.Ann. § 2A:87–1 (1969) ("without lawful justification"); N.D.Cent.Code §§ 12–25–01, 12–25–02 (1960); Ohio Rev.Code Ann. § 2901.16 (1953); Okla.Stat.Ann., Tit. 21, § 861 (1972–1973 Supp.); Pa.Stat. Ann., Tit. 18, §§ 4718, 4719 (1963) ("un-

|119 |Texas first enacted a criminal abortion statute in 1854. Texas Laws 1854, c. 49, § 1, set forth in 3 H. Gammel, Laws of Texas 1502 (1898). This was soon modified into language that has remained substantially unchanged to the present time. See Texas Penal Code of 1857, c. 7, Arts. 531–536; G. Paschal, Laws of Texas, Arts. 2192–2197 (1866); Texas Rev.Stat., c. 8, Arts. 536–541 (1879); Texas Rev.Crim.Stat., Arts. 1071–1076 (1911). The final article in each of these compilations provided the same exception, as does the present Article 1196, for an abortion by "medical advice for the purpose of saving the life of the mother."[3]

|120 |II

Jane Roe,[4] a single woman who was residing in Dallas County, Texas, instituted this federal action in March 1970 against the District Attorney of the county. She sought a declaratory judgment that the Texas criminal abortion statutes were unconstitutional on their face, and an injunction restraining the defendant from enforcing the statutes.

Roe alleged that she was unmarried and pregnant; that she wished to terminate her pregnancy by an abortion "performed by a competent, licensed physician, under safe, clinical conditions"; that she was unable to get a "legal" abortion in Texas because her life did not appear to be threatened by the continuation of her pregnancy; and that she could not afford to travel to another jurisdiction in order to secure a legal abortion under safe conditions. She claimed that the Texas statutes were unconstitutionally vague and that they abridged her right of personal privacy, protected by the First, Fourth, Fifth, Ninth, and Fourteenth Amendments. By an amendment to her complaint Roe purported to sue "on behalf of herself and all other women" similarly situated.

James Hubert Hallford, a licensed physician, sought and was granted leave to intervene in Roe's action. In his complaint he alleged that he had been arrested previously for violations of the Texas abortion statutes and |that two |121 such prosecutions were pending against him. He described conditions of patients who came to him seeking abortions, and he claimed that for many cases he, as a physician, was unable to de-

---

lawful"); R.I.Gen.Laws Ann. § 11–3–1 (1969); S.D.Compl.Laws Ann. § 22–17–1 (1967); Tenn.Code Ann. §§ 39–301, 39–302 (1956); Utah Code Ann. §§ 76–2–1, 76–2–2 (1953); Vt.Stat.Ann., Tit. 13, § 101 (1958); W.Va.Code Ann. § 61–2–8 (1966); Wis.Stat. § 940.04 (1969); Wyo.Stat.Ann. §§ 6–77, 6–78 (1957).

3. Long ago, a suggestion was made that the Texas statutes were unconstitutionally vague because of definitional deficiencies. The Texas Court of Criminal Appeals disposed of that suggestion peremptorily, saying only,

"It is also insisted in the motion in arrest of judgment that the statute is unconstitutional and void, in that it does not sufficiently define or describe the offense of abortion. We do not concur with counsel in respect to this question." Jackson v. State, 55 Tex.Cr.R. 79, 89, 115 S.W. 262, 268 (1908).

The same court recently has held again that the State's abortion statutes are not unconstitutionally vague or overbroad. Thompson v. State, 493 S.W.2d 913 (1971), appeal docketed, No. 71–1200.

The court held that "the State of Texas has a compelling interest to protect fetal life"; that Art. 1191 "is designed to protect fetal life"; that the Texas homicide statutes, particularly Art. 1205 of the Penal Code, are intended to protect a person "in existence by actual birth" and thereby implicitly recognize other human life that is not "in existence by actual birth"; that the definition of human life is for the legislature and not the courts; that Art. 1196 "is more definite than the District of Columbia statute upheld in [United States v.] Vuitch" (402 U.S. 62, 91 S.Ct. 1294, 28 L.Ed.2d 601); and that the Texas statute "is not vague and indefinite or overbroad." A physician's abortion conviction was affirmed.

In 493 S.W.2d, at 920 n. 2, the court observed that any issue as to the burden of proof under the exemption of Art. 1196 "is not before us." But see Veevers v. State, 172 Tex.Cr.R. 162, 168–169, 354 S.W.2d 161, 166–167 (1962). Cf. United States v. Vuitch, 402 U.S. 62, 69–71, 91 S.Ct. 1294, 1298–1299, 28 L.Ed.2d 601 (1971).

4. The name is a pseudonym.

410 U.S. 123   ROE v. WADE   **711**

Cite as 93 S.Ct. 705 (1973)

termine whether they fell within or outside the exception recognized by Article 1196. He alleged that, as a consequence, the statutes were vague and uncertain, in violation of the Fourteenth Amendment, and that they violated his own and his patients' rights to privacy in the doctor-patient relationship and his own right to practice medicine, rights he claimed were guaranteed by the First, Fourth, Fifth, Ninth, and Fourteenth Amendments.

John and Mary Doe,[5] a married couple, filed a companion complaint to that of Roe. They also named the District Attorney as defendant, claimed like constitutional deprivations, and sought declaratory and injunctive relief. The Does alleged that they were a childless couple; that Mrs. Doe was suffering from a "neural-chemical" disorder; that her physician had "advised her to avoid pregnancy until such time as her condition has materially improved" (although a pregnancy at the present time would not present "a serious risk" to her life); that, pursuant to medical advice, she had discontinued use of birth control pills; and that if she should become pregnant, she would want to terminate the pregnancy by an abortion performed by a competent, licensed physician under safe, clinical conditions. By an amendment to their complaint, the Does purported to sue "on behalf of themselves and all couples similarly situated."

The two actions were consolidated and heard together by a duly convened three-judge district court. The suits thus presented the situations of the pregnant single woman, the childless ⌐122 couple, with the wife not pregnant, and the licensed practicing physician, all joining in the attack on the Texas criminal abortion statutes. Upon the filing of affidavits, motions were made for dismissal and for summary judgment. The court held that Roe and members of her class, and Dr. Hallford, had standing to sue and presented justiciable controversies, but that the Does had failed to al-

lege facts sufficient to state a present controversy and did not have standing. It concluded that, with respect to the requests for a declaratory judgment, abstention was not warranted. On the merits, the District Court held that the "fundamental right of single women and married persons to choose whether to have children is protected by the Ninth Amendment, through the Fourteenth Amendment," and that the Texas criminal abortion statutes were void on their face because they were both unconstitutionally vague and constituted an overbroad infringement of the plaintiffs' Ninth Amendment rights. The court then held that abstention was warranted with respect to the requests for an injunction. It therefore dismissed the Does' complaint, declared the abortion statutes void, and dismissed the application for injunctive relief. 314 F.Supp. 1217, 1225 (N.D.Tex.1970).

The plaintiffs Roe and Doe and the intervenor Hallford, pursuant to 28 U. S.C. § 1253, have appealed to this Court from that part of the District Court's judgment denying the injunction. The defendant District Attorney has purported to cross-appeal, pursuant to the same statute, from the court's grant of declaratory relief to Roe and Hallford. Both sides also have taken protective appeals to the United States Court of Appeals for the Fifth Circuit. That court ordered the appeals held in abeyance pending decision here. We postponed decision on jurisdiction to the hearing on the merits. 402 U.S. 941, 91 S.Ct. 1610, 29 L.Ed.2d 108 (1971).

⌐III   ⌐123

[1] It might have been preferable if the defendant, pursuant to our Rule 20, had presented to us a petition for certiorari before judgment in the Court of Appeals with respect to the granting of the plaintiffs' prayer for declaratory relief. Our decisions in Mitchell v. Donovan, 398 U.S. 427, 90 S.Ct. 1763, 26 L. Ed.2d 378 (1970), and Gunn v. Universi-

---

5. These names are pseudonyms.

ty Committee, 399 U.S. 383, 90 S.Ct. 2013, 26 L.Ed.2d 684 (1970), are to the effect that § 1253 does not authorize an appeal to this Court from the grant or denial of declaratory relief alone. We conclude, nevertheless, that those decisions do not foreclose our review of both the injunctive and the declaratory aspects of a case of this kind when it is properly here, as this one is, on appeal under § 1253 from specific denial of injunctive relief, and the arguments as to both aspects are necessarily identical. See Carter v. Jury Comm'n, 396 U.S. 320, 90 S.Ct. 518, 24 L.Ed.2d 549 (1970); Florida Lime and Avocado Growers, Inc. v. Jacobsen, 362 U.S. 73; 80–81, 80 S.Ct. 568, 573–574, 4 L.Ed.2d 568 (1960). It would be destructive of time and energy for all concerned were we to rule otherwise. Cf. Doe v. Bolton, 410 U.S. 179, 93 S.Ct. 739, 35 L.Ed.2d 201.

IV

We are next confronted with issues of justiciability, standing, and abstention. Have Roe and the Does established that "personal stake in the outcome of the controversy," Baker v. Carr, 369 U.S. 186, 204, 82 S.Ct. 691, 703, 7 L.Ed.2d 663 (1962), that insures that "the dispute sought to be adjudicated will be presented in an adversary context and in a form historically viewed as capable of judicial resolution," Flast v. Cohen, 392 U.S. 83, 101, 88 S.Ct. 1942, 1953, 20 L.Ed.2d 947 (1968), and Sierra Club v. Morton, 405 U.S. 727, 732, 92 S.Ct. 1361, 1364, 31 L.Ed.2d 636 (1972)? And what effect did the pendency of criminal abortion charges against Dr. Hallford in state court have upon the propriety of the federal court's granting relief to him as a plaintiff-intervenor?

⌐|124 ⌐|[2] A. *Jane Roe.* Despite the use of the pseudonym, no suggestion is made that Roe is a fictitious person. For

purposes of her case, we accept as true, and as established, her existence; her pregnant state, as of the inception of her suit in March 1970 and as late as May 21 of that year when she filed an alias affidavit with the District Court; and her inability to obtain a legal abortion in Texas.

Viewing Roe's case as of the time of its filing and thereafter until as late as May, there can be little dispute that it then presented a case or controversy and that, wholly apart from the class aspects, she, as a pregnant single woman thwarted by the Texas criminal abortion laws, had standing to challenge those statutes. Abele v. Markle, 452 F.2d 1121, 1125 (CA2 1971); Crossen v. Breckenridge, 446 F.2d 833, 838–839 (CA6 1971); Poe v. Menghini, 339 F. Supp. 986, 990–991 (D.C.Kan. 1972). See Truax v. Raich, 239 U.S. 33, 36 S.Ct. 7, 60 L.Ed. 131 (1915). Indeed, we do not read the appellee's brief as really asserting anything to the contrary. The "logical nexus between the status asserted and the claim sought to be adjudicated," Flast v. Cohen, 392 U.S., at 102, 88 S.Ct., at 1953, and the necessary degree of contentiousness, Golden v. Zwickler, 394 U.S. 103, 89 S.Ct. 956, 22 L.Ed.2d 113 (1969), are both present.

The appellee notes, however, that the record does not disclose that Roe was pregnant at the time of the District Court hearing on May 22, 1970,[6] or on the following June 17 when the court's opinion and judgment were filed. And he suggests that Roe's case must now be moot because she and all other members of her class are no longer subject to any 1970 pregnancy.

⌐|[3] The usual rule in federal cases is ⌐|125 that an actual controversy must exist at stages of appellate or certiorari review, and not simply at the date the action is initiated. United States v. Munsingwear, Inc., 340 U.S. 36, 71 S.Ct. 104, 95

---

6. The appellee twice states in his brief that the hearing before the District Court was held on July 22, 1970. Brief for Appellee 13. The docket entries, App. 2, and the

transcript, App. 76, reveal this to be an error. The July date appears to be the time of the reporter's transcription. See App. 77.

ROE v. WADE   **713**
Cite as 93 S.Ct. 705 (1973)

L.Ed. 36 (1950); Golden v. Zwickler, *supra*; SEC v. Medical Committee for Human Rights, 404 U.S. 403, 92 S.Ct. 577, 30 L.Ed.2d 560 (1972).

[4] But when, as here, pregnancy is a significant fact in the litigation, the normal 266-day human gestation period is so short that the pregnancy will come to term before the usual appellate process is complete. If that termination makes a case moot, pregnancy litigation seldom will survive much beyond the trial stage, and appellate review will be effectively denied. Our law should not be that rigid. Pregnancy often comes more than once to the same woman, and in the general population, if man is to survive, it will always be with us. Pregnancy provides a classic justification for a conclusion of nonmootness. It truly could be "capable of repetition, yet evading review." Southern Pacific Terminal Co. v. ICC, 219 U.S. 498, 515, 31 S.Ct. 279, 283, 55 L.Ed. 310 (1911). See Moore v. Ogilvie, 394 U.S. 814, 816, 89 S.Ct. 1493, 1494, 23 L.Ed.2d 1 (1969); Carroll v. President and Commissioners of Princess Anne, 393 U.S. 175, 178–179, 89 S.Ct. 347, 350, 351, 21 L.Ed.2d 325 (1968); United States v. W. T. Grant Co., 345 U.S. 629, 632–633, 73 S.Ct. 894, 897–898, 97 L.Ed. 1303 (1953).

We, therefore, agree with the District Court that Jane Roe had standing to undertake this litigation, that she presented a justiciable controversy, and that the termination of her 1970 pregnancy has not rendered her case moot.

[5] B. *Dr. Hallford.* The doctor's position is different. He entered Roe's litigation as a plaintiff-intervenor, alleging in his complaint that he:

"[I]n the past has been arrested for violating the Texas Abortion Laws and at the present time stands charged by indictment with violating said laws in the Criminal District Court of Dallas County, Texas to-wit: (1) The State of Texas vs. James H. Hallford, No. C–69–5307–IH, and (2) The State of Texas vs. James H. Hallford, No. C–

|126

93 S.Ct.—45½

69–2524–H. In both cases the defendant is charged with abortion . . . ."

In his application for leave to intervene, the doctor made like representations as to the abortion charges pending in the state court. These representations were also repeated in the affidavit he executed and filed in support of his motion for summary judgment.

[6] Dr. Hallford is, therefore, in the position of seeking, in a federal court, declaratory and injunctive relief with respect to the same statutes under which he stands charged in criminal prosecutions simultaneously pending in state court. Although he stated that he has been arrested in the past for violating the State's abortion laws, he makes no allegation of any substantial and immediate threat to any federally protected right that cannot be asserted in his defense against the state prosecutions. Neither is there any allegation of harassment or bad-faith prosecution. In order to escape the rule articulated in the cases cited in the next paragraph of this opinion that, absent harassment and bad faith, a defendant in a pending state criminal case cannot affirmatively challenge in federal court the statutes under which the State is prosecuting him, Dr. Hallford seeks to distinguish his status as a present state defendant from his status as a "potential future defendant" and to assert only the latter for standing purposes here.

We see no merit in that distinction. Our decision in Samuels v. Mackell, 401 U.S. 66, 91 S.Ct. 764, 27 L.Ed.2d 688 (1971), compels the conclusion that the District Court erred when it granted declaratory relief to Dr. Hallford instead of refraining from so doing. The court, of course, was correct in refusing to grant injunctive relief to the doctor. The reasons supportive of that action, however, are those expressed in Samuels v. Mackell, *supra*, and in Younger v. Harris, 401 U.S. 37, 91 S.Ct. 746, 27 L.Ed.2d 669 (1971); Boyle v. Landry, 401 U.S. 77, 91 S.Ct. 758, 27 L.Ed.2d 696 (1971); Perez v. Ledesma,

|127

401 U.S. 82, 91 S.Ct. 674, 27 L.Ed.2d 701 (1971); and Byrne v. Karalexis, 401 U.S. 216, 91 S.Ct. 777, 27 L.Ed.2d 792 (1971). See also Dombrowski v. Pfister, 380 U.S. 479, 85 S.Ct. 1116; 14 L.Ed.2d 22 (1965). We note, in passing, that *Younger* and its companion cases were decided after the three-judge District Court decision in this case.

[7] Dr. Hallford's complaint in intervention, therefore, is to be dismissed.[7] He is remitted to his defenses in the state criminal proceedings against him. We reverse the judgment of the District Court insofar as it granted Dr. Hallford relief and failed to dismiss his complaint in intervention.

[8] C. *The Does.* In view of our ruling as to Roe's standing in her case, the issue of the Does' standing in their case has little significance. The claims they assert are essentially the same as those of Roe, and they attack the same statutes. Nevertheless, we briefly note the Does' posture.

Their pleadings present them as a childless married couple, the woman not being pregnant, who have no desire to have children at this time because of their having received medical advice that Mrs. Doe should avoid pregnancy, and for "other highly personal reasons." But they "fear . . . they may face the prospect of becoming parents." And if pregnancy ensues, they "would want to terminate" it by an abortion. They assert an inability to obtain an abortion legally in Texas and, consequently, the prospect of obtaining an illegal abortion there or of going outside Texas to some place where the procedure could be obtained legally and competently.

We thus have as plaintiffs a married couple who have, as their asserted immediate and present injury, only an alleged "detrimental effect upon [their] marital happiness" because they are forced to "the choice of refraining from normal sexual relations or of endangering Mary Doe's health through a possible pregnancy." Their claim is that sometime in the future Mrs. Doe might become pregnant because of possible failure of contraceptive measures, and at that time in the future she might want an abortion that might then be illegal under the Texas statutes.

This very phrasing of the Does' position reveals its speculative character. Their alleged injury rests on possible future contraceptive failure, possible future pregnancy, possible future unpreparedness for parenthood, and possible future impairment of health. Any one or more of these several possibilities may not take place and all may not combine. In the Does' estimation, these possibilities might have some real or imagined impact upon their marital happiness. But we are not prepared to say that the bare allegation of so indirect an injury is sufficient to present an actual case or controversy. Younger v. Harris, 401 U.S., at 41–42, 91 S.Ct., at 749; Golden v. Zwickler, 394 U.S., at 109–110, 89 S.Ct., at 960; Abele v. Markle, 452 F.2d, at 1124–1125; Crossen v. Breckenridge, 446 F.2d, at 839. The Does' claim falls far short of those resolved otherwise in the cases that the Does urge upon us, namely, Investment Co. Institute v. Camp, 401 U.S. 617, 91 S.Ct. 1091, 28 L.Ed.2d 367 (1971); Association of Data Processing Service Organizations, Inc. v. Camp, 397 U.S. 150, 90 S.Ct. 827,

7. We need not consider what different result, if any, would follow if Dr. Hallford's intervention were on behalf of a class. His complaint in intervention does not purport to assert a class suit and makes no reference to any class apart from an allegation that he "and others similarly situated" must necessarily guess at the meaning of Art. 1196. His application for leave to intervene goes somewhat further, for it asserts that plaintiff Roe does not

adequately protect the interest of the doctor "and the class of people who are physicians . . . [and] the class of people who are . . . patients . . . ." The leave application, however, is not the complaint. Despite the District Court's statement to the contrary, 314 F.Supp., at 1225, we fail to perceive the essentials of a class suit in the Hallford complaint.

410 U.S. 130   **ROE v. WADE**   **715**

Cite as 93 S.Ct. 705 (1973)

⌐129 25 L.Ed.2d 184 (1970); ⌐and Epperson v. Arkansas, 393 U.S. 97, 89 S.Ct. 266, 21 L.Ed.2d 228 (1968). See also Truax v. Raich, 239 U.S. 33, 36 S.Ct. 7, 60 L.Ed. 131 (1915).

The Does therefore are not appropriate plaintiffs in this litigation. Their complaint was properly dismissed by the District Court, and we affirm that dismissal.

V

The principal thrust of appellant's attack on the Texas statutes is that they improperly invade a right, said to be possessed by the pregnant woman, to choose to terminate her pregnancy. Appellant would discover this right in the concept of personal "liberty" embodied in the Fourteenth Amendment's Due Process Clause; or in personal, marital, familial, and sexual privacy said to be protected by the Bill of Rights or its penumbras, see Griswold v. Connecticut, 381 U.S. 479, 85 S.Ct. 1678, 14 L.Ed.2d 510 (1965); Eisenstadt v. Baird, 405 U.S. 438 (1972); *id.*, at 460, 92 S.Ct. 1029, at 1042, 31 L.Ed.2d 349 (White, J., concurring in result); or among those rights reserved to the people by the Ninth Amendment, Griswold v. Connecticut, 381 U.S., at 486, 85 S.Ct., at 1682 (Goldberg, J., concurring). Before addressing this claim, we feel it desirable briefly to survey, in several aspects, the history of abortion, for such insight as that history may afford us, and then to examine the state purposes and interests behind the criminal abortion laws.

VI

It perhaps is not generally appreciated that the restrictive criminal abortion laws in effect in a majority of States today are of relatively recent vintage. Those laws, generally proscribing abortion or its attempt at any time during pregnancy except when necessary to preserve the pregnant woman's life, are not of ancient or even of common-law origin. Instead, they derive from statutory changes effected, for the most part, in the latter half of the 19th century.

⌐1. *Ancient attitudes.* These are not ⌐130 capable of precise determination. We are told that at the time of the Persian Empire abortifacients were known and that criminal abortions were severely punished.[8] We are also told, however, that abortion was practiced in Greek times as well as in the Roman Era,[9] and that "it was resorted to without scruple."[10] The Ephesian, Soranos, often described as the greatest of the ancient gynecologists, appears to have been generally opposed to Rome's prevailing free-abortion practices. He found it necessary to think first of the life of the mother, and he resorted to abortion when, upon this standard, he felt the procedure advisable.[11] Greek and Roman law afforded little protection to the unborn. If abortion was prosecuted in some places, it seems to have been based on a concept of a violation of the father's right to his offspring. Ancient religion did not bar abortion.[12]

2. *The Hippocratic Oath.* What then of the famous Oath that has stood so

---

8. A. Castiglioni, A History of Medicine 84 (2d ed. 1947), E. Krumbhaar, translator and editor (hereinafter Castiglioni).

9. J. Ricci, The Genealogy of Gynaecology 52, 84, 113, 149 (2d ed. 1950) (hereinafter Ricci); L. Lader, Abortion 75–77 (1966) (hereinafter Lader); K. Niswander, Medical Abortion Practices in the United States, in Abortion and the Law 37, 38–40 (D. Smith ed. 1967); G. Williams, The Sanctity of Life and the Criminal Law 148 (1957) (hereinafter Williams); J. Noonan, An Almost Absolute Value in History, in The Mor-

ality of Abortion 1, 3–7 (J. Noonan ed. 1970) (hereinafter Noonan); Quay, Justifiable Abortion—Medical and Legal Foundations, (pt. 2), 49 Geo.L.J. 395, 406–422 (1961) (hereinafter Quay).

10. L. Edelstein, The Hippocratic Oath 10 (1943) (hereinafter Edelstein). But see Castiglioni 227.

11. Edelstein 12; Ricci 113–114, 118–119; Noonan 5.

12. Edelstein 13–14.

long as the ethical guide of the medical profession and that bears the name of the great Greek (460(?)–377(?) B.C.), |131 who has been described as the Father of Medicine, the "wisest and the greatest practitioner of his art," and the "most important and most complete medical personality of antiquity," who dominated the medical schools of his time, and who typified the sum of the medical knowledge of the past?[13] The Oath varies somewhat according to the particular translation, but in any translation the content is clear: "I will give no deadly medicine to anyone if asked, nor suggest any such counsel; and in like manner I will not give to a woman a pessary to produce abortion,"[14] or "I will neither give a deadly drug to anybody if asked for it, nor will I make a suggestion to this effect. Similarly, I will not give to a woman an abortive remedy."[15]

Although the Oath is not mentioned in any of the principal briefs in this case or in Doe v. Bolton, 410 U.S. 179, 93 S.Ct. 739, 35 L.Ed.2d 201, it represents the apex of the development of strict ethical concepts in medicine, and its influence endures to this day. Why did not the authority of Hippocrates dissuade abortion practice in his time and that of Rome? The late Dr. Edelstein provides us with a theory:[16] The Oath was not uncontested even in Hippocrates' day; only the Pythagorean school of philosophers frowned upon the related act of suicide. Most Greek thinkers, on the other hand, commended abortion, at least prior to viability. See Plato, Republic, V, 461; Aristotle, Politics, VII, 1335b 25. For the Pythagoreans, however, it was a matter of dog-

ma. For them the embryo was animate from the moment of conception, and abortion meant destruction of a living being. The abortion clause of the Oath, therefore, "echoes Pythagorean doctrines," and "[i]n no other stratum of |132 Greek opinion were such views held or proposed in the same spirit of uncompromising austerity."[17]

Dr. Edelstein then concludes that the Oath originated in a group representing only a small segment of Greek opinion and that it certainly was not accepted by all ancient physicians. He points out that medical writings down to Galen (A.D. 130–200) "give evidence of the violation of almost every one of its injunctions."[18] But with the end of antiquity a decided change took place. Resistance against suicide and against abortion became common. The Oath came to be popular. The emerging teachings of Christianity were in agreement with the Pythagorean ethic. The Oath "became the nucleus of all medical ethics" and "was applauded as the embodiment of truth." Thus, suggests Dr. Edelstein, it is "a Pythagorean manifesto and not the expression of an absolute standard of medical conduct."[19]

This, it seems to us, is a satisfactory and acceptable explanation of the Hippocratic Oath's apparent rigidity. It enables us to understand, in historical context, a long-accepted and revered statement of medical ethics.

3. *The common law.* It is undisputed that at common law, abortion performed *before* "quickening"—the first recognizable movement of the fetus *in utero*, appearing usually from the 16th to the 18th week of pregnancy[20]—was not an indictable offense.[21] The absence of a |133

13. Castiglioni 148.

14. *Id.,* at 154.

15. Edelstein 3.

16. *Id.,* at 12, 15–18.

17. *Id.,* at 18; Lader 76.

18. Edelstein 63.

19. *Id.,* at 64.

20. Dorland's Illustrated Medical Dictionary 1261 (24th ed. 1965).

21. E. Coke, Institutes III *50; 1 W. Hawkins, Pleas of the Crown, c. 31, § 16 (4th ed. 1762); 1 W. Blackstone, Commentaries *129–130; M. Hale, Pleas of the Crown 433 (1st Amer. ed. 1847).

common-law crime for pre-quickening abortion appears to have developed from a confluence of earlier philosophical, theological, and civil and canon law concepts of when life begins. These disciplines variously approached the question in terms of the point at which the embryo or fetus became "formed" or recognizably human, or in terms of when a "person" came into being, that is, infused with a "soul" or "animated." A loose concensus evolved in early English law that these events occurred at some point between conception and live birth.[22] This was |134 "mediate animation." Although Christian theology and the canon law came to fix the point of animation at 40 days for a male and 80 days for a female, a view that persisted until the 19th century, there was otherwise little agreement about the precise time of formation or

animation. There was agreement, however, that prior to this point the fetus was to be regarded as part of the mother, and its destruction, therefore, was not homicide. Due to continued uncertainty about the precise time when animation occurred, to the lack of any empirical basis for the 40–80-day view, and perhaps to Aquinas' definition of movement as one of the two first principles of life, Bracton focused upon quickening as the critical point. The significance of quickening was echoed by later common-law scholars and found its way into the received common law in this country.

Whether abortion of a *quick* fetus was a felony at common law, or even a lesser crime, is still disputed. Bracton, writing early in the 13th century, thought it homicide.[23] But the later and predomi-

---

For discussions of the role of the quickening concept in English common law, see Lader 78; Noonan 223–226; Means, The Law of New York Concerning Abortion and the Status of the Foetus, 1664–1968: A Case of Cessation of Constitutionality (pt. 1), 14 N.Y.L.F. 411, 418–428 (1968) (hereinafter Means I); Stern, Abortion: Reform and the Law, 59 J.Crim.L.C. & P.S. 84 (1968) (hereinafter Stern); Quay 430–432; Williams 152.

22. Early philosophers believed that the embryo or fetus did not become formed and begin to live until at least 40 days after conception for a male, and 80 to 90 days for a female. See, for example, Aristotle, Hist.Anim. 7.3.583b; Gen.Anim. 2.3.736, 2.5.741; Hippocrates, Lib. de Nat.Puer., No. 10. Aristotle's thinking derived from his three-stage theory of life: vegetable, animal, rational. The vegetable stage was reached at conception, the animal at "animation," and the rational soon after live birth. This theory, together with the 40/80 day view, came to be accepted by early Christian thinkers.

The theological debate was reflected in the writings of St. Augustine, who made a distinction between *embryo inanimatus*, not yet endowed with a soul, and *embryo animatus*. He may have drawn upon Exodus 21:22. At one point, however, he expressed the view that human powers cannot determine the point during fetal development at which the critical change occurs. See Augustine, De Origine

Animae 4.4 (Pub.Law 44.527). See also W. Reany, The Creation of the Human Soul, c. 2 and 83–86 (1932); Huser, The Crime of Abortion in Canon Law 15 (Catholic Univ. of America, Canon Law Studies No. 162, Washington, D. C., 1942).

Galen, in three treatises related to embryology, accepted the thinking of Aristotle and his followers. Quay 426–427. Later, Augustine on abortion was incorporated by Gratian into the Decretum, published about 1140. Decretum Magistri Gratiani 2.32.2.7 to 2.32.2.10, in 1 Corpus Juris Canonici 1122, 1123 (A. Friedberg, 2d ed. 1879). This Decretal and the Decretals that followed were recognized as the definitive body of canon law until the new Code of 1917.

For discussions of the canon-law treatment, see Means I, pp. 411–412; Noonan 20–26; Quay 426–430; see also J. Noonan, Contraception: A History of Its Treatment by the Catholic Theologians and Canonists 18–29 (1965).

23. Bracton took the position that abortion by blow or poison was homicide "if the foetus be already formed and animated, and particularly if it be animated." 2 H. Bracton, De Legibus et Consuetudinibus Angliae 279 (T. Twiss ed. 1879), or, as a later translation puts it, "if the foetus is already formed or quickened, especially if it is quickened," 2 H. Bracton, On the Laws and Customs of England 341 (S. Thorne ed. 1968). See Quay 431; see also 2 Fleta 60–61 (Book 1, c. 23) (Selden Society ed. 1955).

nant view, following the great common-law scholars, has been that it was, at most, a lesser offense. In a frequently cited|passage, Coke took the position that abortion of a woman "quick with childe" is "a great misprision, and no murder." [24] Blackstone followed, saying that while abortion after quickening had once been considered manslaughter (though not murder), "modern law" took a less severe view.[25] A recent review of the common-law precedents argues, however, that those precedents contradict Coke and that even post-quickening abortion was never established as a common-law crime.[26] This is of some importance because while most American courts ruled, in holding or dictum, that abortion of an unquickened fetus was not criminal under their received common law,[27] others followed Coke in stating that abortion of a quick fetus was a "misprision," a term they translated to mean "misdemeanor." [28] That their reliance on Coke on this aspect of the law was uncritical and, apparently in all the reported cases, dictum (due probably to the paucity of common-

law prosecutions for post-quickening abortion), makes it now appear doubtful that abortion was ever firmly established as a common-law crime even with respect to the destruction of a quick fetus.

4. *The English statutory law.* England's first criminal abortion statute, Lord Ellenborough's Act, 43 Geo. 3, c. 58, came in 1803. It made abortion of a quick fetus, § 1, a capital crime, but in § 2 it provided lesser penalties for the felony of abortion before quickening, and thus preserved the "quickening" distinction. This contrast was continued in the general revision of 1828, 9 Geo. 4, c. 31, § 13. It disappeared, however, together with the death penalty, in 1837, 7 Will. 4 & 1 Vict., c. 85, § 6, and did not reappear in the Offenses Against the Person Act of 1861, 24 & 25 Vict., c. 100, § 59, that formed the core of English anti-abortion law until the liberalizing reforms of 1967. In 1929, the Infant Life (Preservation) Act, 19 & 20 Geo. 5, c. 34, came into being. Its emphasis was upon the destruction of "the life of

24. E. Coke, Institutes III *50.

25. 1 W. Blackstone, Commentaries *129–130.

26. Means, The Phoenix of Abortional Freedom: Is a Penumbral or Ninth-Amendment Right About to Arise from the Nineteenth-Century Legislative Ashes of a Fourteenth-Century Common-Law Liberty?, 17 N.Y.L.F. 335 (1971) (hereinafter Means II). The author examines the two principal precedents cited marginally by Coke, both contrary to his dictum, and traces the treatment of these and other cases by earlier commentators. He concludes that Coke, who himself participated as an advocate in an abortion case in 1601, may have intentionally misstated the law. The author even suggests a reason: Coke's strong feelings against abortion, coupled with his determination to assert common-law (secular) jurisdiction to assess penalties for an offense that traditionally had been an exclusively ecclesiastical or canon-law crime. See also Lader 78–79, who notes that some scholars doubt that the common law ever was applied to abortion; that the English ecclesiastical courts seem to have lost interest in the problem after

1527; and that the preamble to the English legislation of 1803, 43 Geo. 3, c. 58, § 1, referred to in the text, *infra*, at 718, states that "no adequate means have been hitherto provided for the prevention and punishment of such offenses."

27. Commonwealth v. Bangs, 9 Mass. 387, 388 (1812); Commonwealth v. Parker, 50 Mass. (9 Metc.) 263, 265–266 (1845); State v. Cooper, 22 N.J.L. 52, 58 (1849); Abrams v. Foshee, 3 Iowa 274, 278–280 (1856); Smith v. Gaffard, 31 Ala. 45, 51 (1857); Mitchell v. Commonwealth, 78 Ky. 204, 210 (1879); Eggart v. State, 40 Fla. 527, 532, 25 So. 144, 145 (1898); State v. Alcorn, 7 Idaho 599, 606, 64 P. 1014, 1016 (1901); Edwards v. State, 79 Neb. 251, 252, 112 N.W. 611, 612 (1907); Gray v. State, 77 Tex.Cr.R. 221, 224, 178 S.W. 337, 338 (1915); Miller v. Bennett, 190 Va. 162, 169, 56 S.E.2d 217, 221 (1949). Contra, Mills v. Commonwealth, 13 Pa. 631, 633 (1850); State v. Slagle, 83 N.C. 630, 632 (1880).

28. See Smith v. State, 33 Me. 48, 55 (1851); Evans v. People, 49 N.Y. 86, 88 (1872); Lamb v. State, 67 Md. 524, 533, 10 A. 208 (1887).

410 U.S. 139   ROE v. WADE   719

Cite as 93 S.Ct. 705 (1973)

a child capable of being born alive." It made a willful act performed with the necessary intent a felony. It contained a proviso that one was not to be found guilty of the offense "unless it is proved that the act which caused the death of the child was not done in good faith for the purpose only of preserving the life of the mother."

A seemingly notable development in the English law was the case of Rex v. Bourne, [1939] 1 K.B. 687. This case apparently answered in the affirmative the question whether an abortion necessary to preserve the life of the pregnant woman was excepted from the criminal penalties of the 1861 Act. In his instructions to the jury, Judge Macnaghten referred to the 1929 Act, and observed that that Act related to "the case where a child is killed by a willful act at the time when it is being delivered in the ordinary course of nature." *Id.,* at 691. He concluded that the 1861 Act's use of the word "unlawfully," imported the same meaning expressed by the specific proviso in the 1929 Act, even though there was no mention of preserving the mother's life in the 1861 Act. He then construed the phrase "preserving the life of the mother" broadly, that is, "in a reasonable sense," to include a serious and permanent threat to the mother's *health,* and instructed the jury to acquit Dr. Bourne if it found he had acted in a good-faith belief that the abortion was necessary for this purpose. *Id.,* at 693–694. The jury did acquit.

Recently, Parliament enacted a new abortion law. This is the Abortion Act of 1967, 15 & 16 Eliz. 2, c. 87. The Act permits a licensed physician to perform an abortion where two other licensed physicians agree (a) "that the continuance of the pregnancy would involve risk to the life of the pregnant woman, or of injury to the physical or mental health of the pregnant woman or any existing children of her family, greater than if the pregnancy were terminated," or (b) "that there is a substantial risk that if the child were born it would suffer from such physical or mental abnormalities as to be seriously handicapped." The Act also provides that, in making this determination, "account may be taken of the pregnant woman's actual or reasonably foreseeable environment." It also permits a physician, without the concurrence of others, to terminate a pregnancy where he is of the good-faith opinion that the abortion "is immediately necessary to save the life or to prevent grave permanent injury to the physical or mental health of the pregnant woman."

5. *The American law.* In this country, the law in effect in all but a few States until mid-19th century was the pre-existing English common law. Connecticut, the first State to enact abortion legislation, adopted in 1821 that part of Lord Ellenborough's Act that related to a woman "quick with child." [29] The death penalty was not imposed. Abortion before quickening was made a crime in that State only in 1860. [30] In 1828, New York enacted legislation [31] that, in two respects, was to serve as a model for early anti-abortion statutes. First, while barring destruction of an unquickened fetus as well as a quick fetus, it made the former only a misdemeanor, but the latter second-degree manslaughter. Second, it incorporated a concept of therapeutic abortion by providing that an abortion was excused if it "shall have been necessary to preserve the life of such mother, or shall have been advised by two physicians to be necessary for such purpose." By 1840, when Texas had received the common law, [32] only eight American States had

29. Conn.Stat., Tit. 20, § 14 (1821).

30. Conn.Pub.Acts, c. 71, § 1 (1860).

31. N.Y.Rev.Stat., pt. 4, c. 1, Tit. 2, Art. 1, § 9, p. 661, and Tit. 6, § 21, p. 694 (1829).

32. Act of Jan. 20, 1840, § 1, set forth in 2 H. Gammel, Laws of Texas 177–178 (1898) ; see Grigsby v. Reib, 105 Tex. 597, 600, 153 S.W. 1124, 1125 (1913).

statutes dealing with abortion.[33]   It was not until after the War Between the States that legislation began generally to replace the common law.   Most of these initial statutes dealt severely with abortion after quickening but were lenient with it before quickening.   Most punished attempts equally with completed abortions.   While many statutes included the exception for an abortion thought by one or more physicians to be necessary to save the mother's life, that provision soon disappeared and the typical law required that the procedure actually be necessary for that purpose.

Gradually, in the middle and late 19th century the quickening distinction disappeared from the statutory law of most States and the degree of the offense and the penalties were increased.   By the end of the 1950's a large majority of the jurisdictions banned abortion, however and whenever performed, unless done to save or preserve the life of the mother.[34]   The exceptions, Alabama and the District of Columbia, permitted abortion to preserve the mother's health.[35]   Three States permitted abortions that were not "unlawfully" performed or that were not "without lawful justification," leaving interpretation of those standards to the courts.[36]   In the past several years, however, a trend toward liberalization of abortion statutes has resulted in adoption, by about one-third of the States, of less stringent laws, most of them patterned after the ALI Model Penal Code, § 230.3,[37] set forth as Appendix B to the opinion in Doe v. Bolton, 410 U.S. 205, 93 S.Ct. 754.

It is thus apparent that at common law, at the time of the adoption of our Constitution, and throughout the major portion of the 19th century, abortion was viewed with less disfavor than under most American statutes currently in effect.   Phrasing it another way, a woman enjoyed a substantially broader right to terminate a pregnancy than she does in most States today.   At least with respect to the early stage of preg-

33.   The early statutes are discussed in Quay 435–438.   See also Lader 85–88; Stern 85–86; and Means II 375–376.

34.   Criminal abortion statutes in effect in the States as of 1961, together with historical statutory development and important judicial interpretations of the state statutes, are cited and quoted in Quay 447–520.   See Comment, A Survey of the Present Statutory and Case Law on Abortion: The Contradictions and the Problems, 1972 U.Ill.L.F. 177, 179, classifying the abortion statutes and listing 25 States as permitting abortion only if necessary to save or preserve the mother's life.

35.   Ala.Code, Tit. 14, § 9 (1958); D.C. Code Ann. § 22-201 (1967).

36.   Mass.Gen.Laws Ann., c. 272, § 19 (1970); N.J.Stat.Ann. § 2A:87–1 (1969); Pa.Stat.Ann., Tit. 18, §§ 4718, 4719 (1963).

37.   Fourteen States have adopted some form of the ALI statute.   See Ark.Stat.Ann. §§ 41–303 to 41–310 (Supp.1971); Calif. Health & Safety Code §§ 25950–25955.5 (Supp.1972); Colo.Rev.Stat.Ann. §§ 40-2–50 to 40-2–53 (Cum.Supp.1967); Del. Code Ann., Tit. 24, §§ 1790–1793 (Supp. 1972); Florida Law of Apr. 13, 1972, c. 72–196, 1972 Fla.Sess.Law Serv., pp. 380–382; Ga.Code §§ 26–1201 to 26–1203 (1972); Kan.Stat.Ann. § 21–3407 (Supp.1971); Md.Ann.Code, Art. 43, §§ 137–139 (1971); Miss.Code Ann. § 2223 (Supp.1972); N.M.Stat.Ann. §§ 40A–5–1 to 40A–5–3 (1972); N.C.Gen. Stat. § 14–45.1 (Supp.1971); Ore.Rev. Stat. §§ 435.405 to 435.495 (1971); S.C.Code Ann. §§ 16–82 to 16–89 (1962 and Supp.1971); Va.Code Ann. §§ 18.1–62 to 18.1–62.3 (Supp.1972).   Mr. Justice Clark described some of these States as having "led the way."   Religion, Morality, and Abortion: A Constitutional Appraisal, 2 Loyola U. (L.A.) L.Rev. 1, 11 (1969).

By the end of 1970, four other States had repealed criminal penalties for abortions performed in early pregnancy by a licensed physician, subject to stated procedural and health requirements.   Alaska Stat. § 11.15.060 (1970); Haw.Rev.Stat. § 453–16 (Supp.1971); N.Y.Penal Code § 125.05, subd. 3 (Supp.1972–1973); Wash.Rev.Code §§ 9.02.060 to 9.02.080 (Supp.1972).   The precise status of criminal abortion laws in some States is made unclear by recent decisions in state and federal courts striking down existing state laws, in whole or in part.

410 U.S. 143 ROE v. WADE 721
Cite as 93 S.Ct. 705 (1973)

nancy, and very possibly without such a [141]limitation, the opportunity to make this choice was present in this country well into the 19th century. Even later, the law continued for some time to treat less punitively an abortion procured in early pregnancy.

6. *The position of the American Medical Association.* The anti-abortion mood prevalent in this country in the late 19th century was shared by the medical profession. Indeed, the attitude of the profession may have played a significant role in the enactment of stringent criminal abortion legislation during that period.

An AMA Committee on Criminal Abortion was appointed in May 1857. It presented its report, 12 Trans. of the Am.Med.Assn. 73–78 (1859), to the Twelfth Annual Meeting. That report observed that the Committee had been appointed to investigate criminal abortion "with a view to its general suppression." It deplored abortion and its frequency and it listed three causes of "this general demoralization":

"The first of these causes is a wide-spread popular ignorance of the true character of the crime—a belief, even among mothers themselves, that the foetus is not alive till after the period of quickening.

"The second of the agents alluded to is the fact that the profession themselves are frequently supposed careless of foetal life. . . .

"The third reason of the frightful extent of this crime is found in the grave defects of our laws, both common and statute, as regards the independent and actual existence of the child before birth, as a living being. These errors, which are sufficient in most instances to prevent conviction, are based, and only based, upon mistaken and exploded medical dogmas. With strange inconsistency, the law fully acknowledges the foetus in utero and its inherent rights, for civil purposes; while personally and as criminally affected, it fails to recognize it,

93 S.Ct.—46

[142]and to its life as yet denies all protection." *Id.,* at 75–76.

The Committee then offered, and the Association adopted, resolutions protesting "against such unwarrantable destruction of human life," calling upon state legislatures to revise their abortion laws, and requesting the cooperation of state medical societies "in pressing the subject." *Id.,* at 28, 78.

In 1871 a long and vivid report was submitted by the Committee on Criminal Abortion. It ended with the observation, "We had to deal with human life. In a matter of less importance we could entertain no compromise. An honest judge on the bench would call things by their proper names. We could do no less." 22 Trans. of the Am.Med.Assn. 258 (1871). It proffered resolutions, adopted by the Association, *id.,* at 38–39, recommending, among other things, that it "be unlawful and unprofessional for any physician to induce abortion or premature labor, without the concurrent opinion of at least one respectable consulting physician, and then always with a view to the safety of the child—if that be possible," and calling "the attention of the clergy of all denominations to the perverted views of morality entertained by a large class of females—aye, and men also, on this important question."

Except for periodic condemnation of the criminal abortionist, no further formal AMA action took place until 1967. In that year, the Committee on Human Reproduction urged the adoption of a stated policy of opposition to induced abortion, except when there is "documented medical evidence" of a threat to the health or life of the mother, or that the child "may be born with incapacitating physical deformity or mental deficiency," or that a pregnancy "resulting from legally established statutory or forcible rape or incest may constitute a threat to the mental or physical health of the [143]patient," two other physicians "chosen because of their recognized professional competency have examined the patient and have concurred in writing," and the procedure "is performed in a hospital accredited by the Joint Commission on Accreditation of Hospitals." The providing of medical information by physicians to state legislatures in their consideration of legislation regarding therapeutic abortion was "to be considered consistent with the principles óf ethics of the American Medical Association." This recommendation was adopted by the House of Delegates. Proceedings of the AMA House of Delegates 40–51 (June 1967).

In 1970, after the introduction of a variety of proposed resolutions, and of a report from its Board of Trustees, a reference committee noted "polarization of the medical profession on this controversial issue"; division among those who had testified; a difference of opinion among AMA councils and committees; "the remarkable shift in testimony" in six months, felt to be influenced "by the rapid changes in state laws and by the judicial decisions which tend to make abortion more freely available;" and a feeling "that this trend will continue." On June 25, 1970, the House of Delegates adopted preambles and most of the resolutions proposed by the reference committee. The preambles emphasized "the best interests of the patient,"

"sound clinical judgment," and "informed patient consent," in contrast to "mere acquiescence to the patient's demand." The resolutions asserted that abortion is a medical procedure that should be performed by a licensed physician in an accredited hospital only after consultation with two other physicians and in conformity with state law, and that no party to the procedure should be required to violate personally held moral principles.[38] Proceedings of the AMA ⌐144 House of Delegates 220 (June 1970). The AMA Judicial Council rendered a complementary opinion.[39]

7. *The position of the American Public Health Association.* In October 1970, the Executive Board of the APHA adopted Standards for Abortion Services. These were five in number:

"a. Rapid and simple abortion referral must be readily available through state and local public⌐health ⌐145 departments, medical societies, or other non-profit organizations.

"b. An important function of counseling should be to simplify and expedite the provision of abortion services; it should not delay the obtaining of these services.

---

38. "Whereas, Abortion, like any other medical procedure, should not be performed when contrary to the best interests of the patient since good medical practice requires due consideration for the patient's welfare and not mere acquiescence to the patient's demand; and

"Whereas, The standards of sound clinical judgment, which, together with informed patient consent should be determinative according to the merits of each individual case; therefore be it

"RESOLVED, That abortion is a medical procedure and should be performed only by a duly licensed physician and surgeon in an accredited hospital acting only after consultation with two other physicians chosen because of their professional competency and in conformance with standards of good medical practice and the Medical Practice Act of his State; and be it further

"RESOLVED, That no physician or other professional personnel shall be compelled to perform any act which violates

his good medical judgment. Neither physician, hospital, nor hospital personnel shall be required to perform any act violative of personally-held moral principles. In these circumstances good medical practice requires only that the physician or other professional personnel withdraw from the case so long as the withdrawal is consistent with good medical practice." Proceedings of the AMA House of Delegates 220 (June 1970).

39. "The Principles of Medical Ethics of the AMA do not prohibit a physician from performing an abortion that is performed in accordance with good medical practice and under circumstances that do not violate the laws of the community in which he practices.

"In the matter of abortions, as of any other medical procedure, the Judicial Council becomes involved whenever there is alleged violation of the Principles of Medical Ethics as established by the House of Delegates."

"c. Psychiatric consultation should not be mandatory. As in the case of other specialized medical services, psychiatric consultation should be sought for definite indications and not on a routine basis.

"d. A wide range of individuals from appropriately trained, sympathetic volunteers to highly skilled physicians may qualify as abortion counselors.

"e. Contraception and/or sterilization should be discussed with each abortion patient." Recommended Standards for Abortion Services, 61 Am.J.Pub.Health 396 (1971).

Among factors pertinent to life and health risks associated with abortion were three that "are recognized as important":

"a. the skill of the physician,

"b. the environment in which the abortion is performed, and above all

"c. the duration of pregnancy, as determined by uterine size and confirmed by menstrual history." *Id.,* at 397.

It was said that "a well-equipped hospital" offers more protection "to cope with unforeseen difficulties than an office or clinic without such resources. . . . The factor of gestational age is of overriding importance." Thus, it was recommended that abortions in the second trimester and early abortions in the presence of existing medical complications be performed in hospitals as inpatient procedures. For pregnancies in the first trimester, abortion in the hospital with or without overnight stay "is probably the safest practice." An abortion in an extramural facility, however, is an acceptable alternative "provided arrangements exist in advance to admit patients promptly if unforeseen complications develop." Standards for an abortion facility were listed. It was said that at present abortions should be performed by physicians or osteopaths who are licensed to practice and who have "adequate training." *Id.,* at 398.

⌐146

8. *The position of the American Bar Association.* At its meeting in February 1972 the ABA House of Delegates approved, with 17 opposing votes, the Uniform Abortion Act that had been drafted and approved the preceding August by the Conference of Commissioners on Uniform State Laws. 58 A.B.A. J. 380 (1972). We set forth the Act in full in the margin.[40] The ⌐Conference ⌐147

---

40. "UNIFORM ABORTION ACT

"Section 1. [*Abortion Defined; When Authorized.*]

"(a) 'Abortion' means the termination of human pregnancy with an intention other than to produce a live birth or to remove a dead fetus.

"(b) An abortion may be performed in this state only if it is performed:

"(1) by a physician licensed to practice medicine [or osteopathy] in this state or by a physician practicing medicine [or osteopathy] in the employ of the government of the United States or of this state, [and the abortion is performed [in the physician's office or in a medical clinic, or] in a hospital approved by the [Department of Health] or operated by the United States, this state, or any department, agency, or political subdivision of either;] or by a female upon herself upon the advice of the physician; and

"(2) within [20] weeks after the commencement of the pregnancy [or after [20] weeks only if the physician has reasonable cause to believe (i) there is a substantial risk that continuance of the pregnancy would endanger the life of the mother or would gravely impair the physical or mental health of the mother, (ii) that the child would be born with grave physical or mental defect, or (iii) that the pregnancy resulted from rape or incest, or illicit intercourse with a girl under the age of 16 years].

"Section 2. [*Penalty.*] Any person who performs or procures an abortion other than authorized by this Act is guilty of a [felony] and, upon conviction thereof, may be sentenced to pay a fine not exceeding [$1,000] or to imprisonment [in the state penitentiary] not exceeding [5 years], or both.

"Section 3. [*Uniformity of Interpretation.*] This Act shall be construed to effectuate its general purpose to make uniform the law with respect to the subject of this Act among those states which enact it.

has appended an enlightening Prefatory Note.[41]

VII

Three reasons have been advanced to explain historically the enactment of criminal abortion laws in the 19th century and to justify their continued existence.

[148] It has been argued occasionally that these laws were the product of a Victorian social concern to discourage illicit sexual conduct. Texas, however, does not advance this justification in the present case, and it appears that no court or commentator has taken the argument seriously.[42] The appellants and *amici* contend, moreover, that this is not a proper state purpose at all and suggest that, if it were, the Texas statutes are overbroad in protecting it since the law fails to distinguish between married and unwed mothers.

> "Section 4. [*Short Title.*] This Act may be cited as the Uniform Abortion Act.
> "Section 5. [*Severability.*] If any provision of this Act or the application thereof to any person or circumstance is held invalid, the invalidity does not affect other provisions or applications of this Act which can be given effect without the invalid provision or application, and to this end the provisions of this Act are severable.
> "Section 6. [*Repeal.*] The following acts and parts of acts are repealed:
> "(1)
> "(2)
> "(3)
> "Section 7. [*Time of Taking Effect.*] This Act shall take effect _____."

41. "This Act is based largely upon the New York abortion act following a review of the more recent laws on abortion in several states and upon recognition of a more liberal trend in laws on this subject. Recognition was given also to the several decisions in state and federal courts which show a further trend toward liberalization of abortion laws, especially during the first trimester of pregnancy.
"Recognizing that a number of problems appeared in New York, a shorter time period for 'unlimited' abortions was advisable. The time period was bracketed to permit the various states to insert a figure more in keeping with the different

A second reason is concerned with abortion as a medical procedure. When most criminal abortion laws were first enacted, the procedure was a hazardous one for the woman.[43] This was particularly true prior to the development of [149] antisepsis. Antiseptic techniques, of course, were based on discoveries by Lister, Pasteur, and others first announced in 1867, but were not generally accepted and employed until about the turn of the century. Abortion mortality was high. Even after 1900, and perhaps until as late as the development of antibiotics in the 1940's, standard modern techniques such as dilation and curettage were not nearly so safe as they are today. Thus, it has been argued that a State's real concern in enacting a criminal abortion law was to protect the pregnant woman, that is, to restrain her from submitting to a procedure that placed her life in serious jeopardy.

conditions that might exist among the states. Likewise, the language limiting the place or places in which abortions may be performed was also bracketed to account for different conditions among the states. In addition, limitations on abortions after the initial 'unlimited' period were placed in brackets so that individual states may adopt all or any of these reasons, or place further restrictions upon abortions after the initial period.
"This Act does not contain any provision relating to medical review committees or prohibitions against sanctions imposed upon medical personnel refusing to participate in abortions because of religious or other similar reasons, or the like. Such provisions, while related, do not directly pertain to when, where, or by whom abortions may be performed; however, the Act is not drafted to exclude such a provision by a state wishing to enact the same."

42. See, for example, YWCA v. Kugler, 342 F.Supp. 1048, 1074 (D.C.N.J.1972); Abele v. Markle, 342 F.Supp. 800, 805–806 (D.C.Conn.1972) (Newman, J., concurring in result), appeal docketed, No. 72–56; Walsingham v. State, 250 So.2d 857, 863 (Ervin, J., concurring) (Fla. 1971); State v. Gedicke, 43 N.J.L. 86, 90 (1881); Means II 381–382.

43. See C. Haagensen & W. Lloyd, A Hundred Years of Medicine 19 (1943).

410 U.S. 151   ROE v. WADE   **725**

Cite as 93 S.Ct. 705 (1973)

Modern medical techniques have altered this situation. Appellants and various *amici* refer to medical data indicating that abortion in early pregnancy, that is, prior to the end of the first trimester, although not without its risk, is now relatively safe. Mortality rates for women undergoing early abortions, where the procedure is legal, appear to be as low as or lower than the rates for normal childbirth.[44] Consequently, any interest of the State in protecting the woman from an inherently hazardous procedure, except when it would be equally dangerous for her to forgo it, has largely disappeared. Of course, important state interests in the areas of health and medical standards do remain.

|150| The State has a legitimate interest in seeing to it that abortion, like any other medical procedure, is performed under circumstances that insure maximum safety for the patient. This interest obviously extends at least to the performing physician and his staff, to the facilities involved, to the availability of after-care, and to adequate provision for any complication or emergency that might arise. The prevalence of high mortality rates at illegal "abortion mills" strengthens, rather than weakens, the State's interest in regulating the conditions under which abortions are performed. Moreover, the risk to the woman increases as her pregnancy continues. Thus, the State retains a definite interest in protecting the woman's own health and safety when an abortion is proposed at a late stage of pregnancy.

The third reason is the State's interest—some phrase it in terms of duty—in protecting prenatal life. Some of the argument for this justification rests on the theory that a new human life is present from the moment of conception.[45] The State's interest and general obligation to protect life then extends, it is argued, to prenatal life. Only when the life of the pregnant mother herself is at stake, balanced against the life she carries within her, should the interest of the embryo or fetus not prevail. Logically, of course, a legitimate state interest in this area need not stand or fall on acceptance of the belief that life begins at conception or at some other point prior to live birth. In assessing the State's interest, recognition may be given to the less rigid claim that as long as at least *potential* life is involved, the State may assert interests beyond the protection of the pregnant woman alone.

|Parties challenging state abortion |151 laws have sharply disputed in some courts the contention that a purpose of these laws, when enacted, was to protect prenatal life.[46] Pointing to the absence of legislative history to support the contention, they claim that most state laws were designed solely to protect the woman. Because medical advances have lessened this concern, at least with respect to abortion in early pregnancy, they argue that with respect to such abortions the laws can no longer be justified by any state interest. There is some scholarly support for this view of original purpose.[47] The few state courts

---

44. Potts, Postconceptive Control of Fertility, 8 Int'l J. of G. & O. 957, 967 (1970) (England and Wales); Abortion Mortality, 20 Morbidity and Mortality 208, 209 (June 12, 1971) (U.S. Dept. of HEW, Public Health Service) (New York City); Tietze, United States: Therapeutic Abortions, 1963–1968, 59 Studies in Family Planning 5, 7 (1970); Tietze, Mortality with Contraception and Induced Abortion, 45 Studies in Family Planning 6 (1969) (Japan, Czechoslovakia, Hungary); Tietze & Lehfeldt, Legal Abortion in Eastern Europe, 175 J.A.M.A. 1149, 1152 (April 1961). Other sources are discussed in Lader 17–23.

45. See Brief of Amicus National Right to Life Committee; R. Drinan, The Inviolability of the Right to Be Born, in Abortion and the Law 107 (D. Smith ed. 1967); Louisell, Abortion, The Practice of Medicine and the Due Process of Law, 16 U.C.L.A.L.Rev. 233 (1969); Noonan 1.

46. See, *e. g.*, Abele v. Markle, 342 F.Supp. 800 (D.C.Conn.1972), appeal docketed, No. 72–56.

47. See discussions in Means I and Means II.

called upon to interpret their laws in the late 19th and early 20th centuries did focus on the State's interest in protecting the woman's health rather than in preserving the embryo and fetus.[48] Proponents of this view point out that in many States, including Texas,[49] by statute or judicial interpretation, the pregnant woman herself could not be prosecuted for self-abortion or for cooperating in an abortion performed upon her by another.[50] They claim that adoption of the "quickening" distinction through |152 received common law and state statutes tacitly recognizes the greater health hazards inherent in late abortion and impliedly repudiates the theory that life begins at conception.

It is with these interests, and the weight to be attached to them, that this case is concerned.

VIII

[9] The Constitution does not explicitly mention any right of privacy. In a line of decisions, however, going back perhaps as far as Union Pacific R. Co. v. Botsford, 141 U.S. 250, 251, 11 S.Ct. 1000, 1001, 35 L.Ed. 734 (1891), the Court has recognized that a right of personal privacy, or a guarantee of certain areas or zones of privacy, does exist under the Constitution. In varying contexts, the Court or individual Justices have, indeed, found at least the roots of that right in the First Amendment, Stanley v. Georgia, 394 U.S. 557, 564, 89 S.Ct. 1243, 1247, 22 L.Ed.2d 542 (1969); in the Fourth and Fifth Amendments, Terry v. Ohio, 392 U.S. 1, 8–9, 88 S.Ct.

1868, 1872–1873, 20 L.Ed.2d 889 (1968), Katz v. United States, 389 U.S. 347, 350, 88 S.Ct. 507, 510, 19 L.Ed.2d 576 (1967); Boyd v. United States, 116 U.S. 616, 6 S.Ct. 524, 29 L.Ed. 746 (1886), see Olmstead v. United States, 277 U.S. 438, 478, 48 S.Ct. 564, 572, 72 L.Ed. 944 (1928) (Brandeis, J., dissenting); in the penumbras of the Bill of Rights, Griswold v. Connecticut, 381 U.S., at 484–485, 85 S.Ct., at 1681–1682; in the Ninth Amendment, id., at 486, 85 S.Ct. at 1682 (Goldberg, J., concurring); or in the concept of liberty guaranteed by the first section of the Fourteenth Amendment, see Meyer v. Nebraska, 262 U.S. 390, 399, 43 S.Ct. 625, 626, 67 L.Ed. 1042 (1923). These decisions make it clear that only personal rights that can be deemed "fundamental" or "implicit in the concept of ordered liberty," Palko v. Connecticut, 302 U.S. 319, 325, 58 S.Ct. 149, 152, 82 L.Ed. 288 (1937), are included in this guarantee of personal privacy. They also make it clear that the right has some extension to activities relating to marriage, Loving v. Virginia, 388 U.S. 1, 12, 87 S.Ct. 1817, 1823, 18 L.Ed.2d 1010 (1967); procreation, Skinner v. Oklahoma, 316 U.S. 535, 541–542, 62 S.Ct. 1110, 1113–1114, 86 L.Ed. 1655 (1942); contraception, Eisenstadt v. Baird, 405 U.S., at 453–454, 92 S.Ct., at 1038–1039; id., at 460, 463–465, 92 S. |153 Ct. at 1042, 1043–1044 (White, J., concurring in result); family relationships, Prince v. Massachusetts, 321 U.S. 158, 166, 64 S.Ct. 438, 442, 88 L.Ed. 645 (1944); and child rearing and education, Pierce v. Society of Sisters, 268 U.S. 510,

---

48. See, e. g., State v. Murphy, 27 N.J.L. 112, 114 (1858).

49. Watson v. State, 9 Tex.App. 237, 244–245 (1880); Moore v. State, 37 Tex. Cr.R. 552, 561, 40 S.W. 287, 290 (1897); Shaw v. State, 73 Tex.Cr.R. 337, 339, 165 S.W. 930, 931 (1914); Fondren v. State, 74 Tex.Cr.R. 552, 557, 169 S.W. 411, 414 (1914); Gray v. State, 77 Tex.Cr.R. 221, 229, 178 S.W. 337, 341 (1915). There is no immunity in Texas for the father who is not married to the mother. Ham-

mett v. State, 84 Tex.Cr.R. 635, 209 S.W. 661 (1919); Thompson v. State, Tex. Cr.App., 493 S.W.2d 913 (1971), appeal pending.

50. See Smith v. State, 33 Me., at 55; In re Vince, 2 N.J. 443, 450, 67 A.2d 141, 144 (1949). A short discussion of the modern law on this issue is contained in the Comment to the ALI's Model Penal Code § 207.11, at 158 and nn. 35–37 (Tent.Draft No. 9, 1959).

410 U.S. 155   ROE v. WADE   **727**

535, 45 S.Ct. 571, 573, 69 L.Ed. 1070 (1925), Meyer v. Nebraska, *supra.*

[10] This right of privacy, whether it be founded in the Fourteenth Amendment's concept of personal liberty and restrictions upon state action, as we feel it is, or, as the District Court determined, in the Ninth Amendment's reservation of rights to the people, is broad enough to encompass a woman's decision whether or not to terminate her pregnancy. The detriment that the State would impose upon the pregnant woman by denying this choice altogether is apparent. Specific and direct harm medically diagnosable even in early pregnancy may be involved. Maternity, or additional offspring, may force upon the woman a distressful life and future. Psychological harm may be imminent. Mental and physical health may be taxed by child care. There is also the distress, for all concerned, associated with the unwanted child, and there is the problem of bringing a child into a family already unable, psychologically and otherwise, to care for it. In other cases, as in this one, the additional difficulties and continuing stigma of unwed motherhood may be involved. All these are factors the woman and her responsible physician necessarily will consider in consultation.

On the basis of elements such as these, appellant and some *amici* argue that the woman's right is absolute and that she is entitled to terminate her pregnancy at whatever time, in whatever way, and for whatever reason she alone chooses. With this we do not agree. Appellant's arguments that Texas either has no valid interest at all in regulating the abortion decision, or no interest strong enough to support any limitation upon the woman's sole determination, are ⌊154 unpersuasive. The ⌊Court's decisions recognizing a right of privacy also acknowledge that some state regulation in areas protected by that right is appropriate. As noted above, a State may properly assert important interests in safeguarding health, in maintaining medical standards, and in protecting potential life. At some point in pregnan-

cy, these respective interests become sufficiently compelling to sustain regulation of the factors that govern the abortion decision. The privacy right involved, therefore, cannot be said to be absolute. In fact, it is not clear to us that the claim asserted by some *amici* that one has an unlimited right to do with one's body as one pleases bears a close relationship to the right of privacy previously articulated in the Court's decisions. The Court has refused to recognize an unlimited right of this kind in the past. Jacobson v. Massachusetts, 197 U.S. 11, 25 S.Ct. 358, 49 L.Ed. 643 (1905) (vaccination); Buck v. Bell, 274 U.S. 200, 47 S.Ct. 584, 71 L.Ed. 1000 (1927) (sterilization).

We, therefore, conclude that the right of personal privacy includes the abortion decision, but that this right is not unqualified and must be considered against important state interests in regulation.

We note that those federal and state courts that have recently considered abortion law challenges have reached the same conclusion. A majority, in addition to the District Court in the present case, have held state laws unconstitutional, at least in part, because of vagueness or because of overbreadth and abridgment of rights. Abele v. Markle, 342 F.Supp. 800 (D.C.Conn.1972), appeal docketed, No. 72–56; Abele v. Markle, 351 F.Supp. 224 (D.C.Conn.1972), appeal docketed, No. 72–730; Doe v. Bolton, 319 F.Supp. 1048 (N.D.Ga.1970), appeal decided today, 410 U.S. 179, 93 S.Ct. 739, 35 L.Ed.2d 201; Doe v. Scott, 321 F. Supp. 1385 (N.D.Ill.1971), appeal docketed, No. 70–105; Poe v. Menghini, 339 F.Supp. 986 (D.C.Kan.1972); YWCA v. Kugler, 342 F.Supp. 1048 (D.C.N.J. 1972); Babbitz v. McCann, ⌊310 F.Supp.   ⌊155 293 (E.D.Wis.1970), appeal dismissed, 400 U.S. 1, 91 S.Ct. 12, 27 L.Ed.2d 1 (1970); People v. Belous, 71 Cal.2d 954, 80 Cal.Rptr. 354, 458 P.2d 194 (1969), cert. denied, 397 U.S. 915, 90 S.Ct. 920, 25 L.Ed.2d 96 (1970); State v. Barquet, 262 So.2d 431 (Fla.1972).

Others have sustained state statutes. Crossen v. Attorney General, 344 F.

Supp. 587 (E.D.Ky.1972), appeal docketed, No. 72–256; Rosen v. Louisiana State Board of Medical Examiners, 318 F.Supp. 1217 (E.D.La.1970), appeal docketed, No. 70–42; Corkey v. Edwards, 322 F.Supp. 1248 (W.D.N.C.1971), appeal docketed, No. 71–92; Steinberg v. Brown, 321 F.Supp. 741 (N.D.Ohio 1970); Doe v. Rampton, 366 F.Supp. 189 (Utah 1971), appeal docketed, No. 71–5666; Cheaney v. State, Ind., 285 N.E. 2d 265 (1972); Spears v. State, 257 So. 2d 876 (Miss.1972); State v. Munson, S.D., 201 N.W.2d 123 (1972), appeal docketed, No. 72–631.

Although the results are divided, most of these courts have agreed that the right of privacy, however based, is broad enough to cover the abortion decision; that the right, nonetheless, is not absolute and is subject to some limitations; and that at some point the state interests as to protection of health, medical standards, and prenatal life, become dominant. We agree with this approach.

[11] Where certain "fundamental rights" are involved, the Court has held that regulation limiting these rights may be justified only by a "compelling state interest," Kramer v. Union Free School District, 395 U.S. 621, 627, 89 S. Ct. 1886, 1890, 23 L.Ed.2d 583 (1969); Shapiro v. Thompson, 394 U.S. 618, 634, 89 S.Ct. 1322, 1331, 22 L.Ed.2d 600 (1969); Sherbert v. Verner, 374 U.S. 398, 406, 83 S.Ct. 1790, 1795, 10 L.Ed.2d 965 (1963), and that legislative enactments must be narrowly drawn to express only the legitimate state interests at stake. Griswold v. Connecticut, 381 U.S., at 485, 85 S.Ct., at 1682; Aptheker v. Secretary of State, 378 U.S. 500, 508, 84 S.Ct. 1659, 1664, 12 L.Ed.2d 992 (1964); Cantwell v. Connecticut, 310 U. S. 296, 307–308, 60 S.Ct. 900, 904–905, |156 84 L.Ed. 1213 (1940); see Eisenstadt v. Baird, 405 U.S., at 460, 463–464, 92 S.Ct., at 1042, 1043–1044 (White, J., concurring in result).

In the recent abortion cases, cited above, courts have recognized these prin

ciples. Those striking down state laws have generally scrutinized the State's interests in protecting health and potential life, and have concluded that neither interest justified broad limitations on the reasons for which a physician and his pregnant patient might decide that she should have an abortion in the early stages of pregnancy. Courts sustaining state laws have held that the State's determinations to protect health or prenatal life are dominant and constitutionally justifiable.

IX

The District Court held that the appellee failed to meet his burden of demonstrating that the Texas statute's infringement upon Roe's rights was necessary to support a compelling state interest, and that, although the appellee presented "several compelling justifications for state presence in the area of abortions," the statutes outstripped these justifications and swept "far beyond any areas of compelling state interest." 314 F.Supp., at 1222–1223. Appellant and appellee both contest that holding. Appellant, as has been indicated, claims an absolute right that bars any state imposition of criminal penalties in the area. Appellee argues that the State's determination to recognize and protect prenatal life from and after conception constitutes a compelling state interest. As noted above, we do not agree fully with either formulation.

A. The appellee and certain *amici* argue that the fetus is a "person" within the language and meaning of the Fourteenth Amendment. In support of this, they outline at length and in detail the well-known facts of fetal development. If this suggestion of personhood is established, the appellant's case, of course, collapses, for the fetus' right to |157 life would then be guaranteed specifically by the Amendment. The appellant conceded as much on reargument.[51] On the other hand, the appellee conceded on reargument [52] that no case could be cited

51. Tr. of Oral Rearg. 20–21.

52. Tr. of Oral Rearg. 24.

that holds that a fetus is a person within the meaning of the Fourteenth Amendment.

The Constitution does not define "person" in so many words. Section 1 of the Fourteenth Amendment contains three references to "person." The first, in defining "citizens," speaks of "persons born or naturalized in the United States." The word also appears both in the Due Process Clause and in the Equal Protection Clause. "Person" is used in other places in the Constitution: in the listing of qualifications for Representatives and Senators, Art. I, § 2, cl. 2, and § 3, cl. 3; in the Apportionment Clause, Art. I, § 2, cl. 3;[53] in the Migration and Importation provision, Art. I, § 9, cl. 1; in the Emolument Clause, Art. I, § 9, cl. 8; in the Electors provisions, Art. II, § 1, cl. 2, and the superseded cl. 3; in the provision outlining qualifications for the office of President, Art. II, § 1, cl. 5; in the Extradition provisions, Art. IV, § 2, cl. 2, and the superseded Fugitive Slave Clause 3; and in the Fifth, Twelfth, and Twenty-second Amendments, as well as in §§ 2 and 3 of the Fourteenth Amendment. But in nearly all these instances, the use of the word is such that it has application only postnatally. None indicates, with any assurance, that it has any possible prenatal application.[54]

[12] All this, together with our observation, *supra*, that throughout the major portion of the 19th century prevailing legal abortion practices were far freer than they are today, persuades us that the word "person," as used in the Fourteenth Amendment, does not include the unborn.[55] This is in accord with the results reached in those few cases where the issue has been squarely presented. McGarvey v. Magee-Womens Hospital, 340 F.Supp. 751 (W.D.Pa.1972); Byrn v. New York City Health & Hospitals Corp., 31 N.Y.2d 194, 335 N.Y.S.2d 390, 286 N.E.2d 887 (1972), appeal docketed, No. 72–434; Abele v. Markle, 351 F. Supp. 224 (D.C.Conn.1972), appeal docketed, No. 72–730. Cf. Cheaney v. State, Ind., 285 N.E.2d, at 270; Montana v. Rogers, 278 F.2d 68, 72 (CA7 1960), aff'd sub nom. Montana v. Kennedy, 366 U.S. 308, 81 S.Ct. 1336, 6 L.Ed.2d 313 (1961); Keeler v. Superior Court, 2 Cal. 3d 619, 87 Cal.Rptr. 481, 470 P.2d 617 (1970); State v. Dickinson, 28 Ohio St. 2d 65, 275 N.E.2d 599 (1971). Indeed, our decision in United States v. Vuitch, 402 U.S. 62, 91 S.Ct. 1294, 28 L.Ed.2d 601 (1971), inferentially is to the same effect, for we there would not have indulged in statutory interpretation favorable to abortion in specified circumstances if the necessary consequence was the

53. We are not aware that in the taking of any census under this clause, a fetus has ever been counted.

54. When Texas urges that a fetus is entitled to Fourteenth Amendment protection as a person, it faces a dilemma. Neither in Texas nor in any other State are all abortions prohibited. Despite broad proscription, an exception always exists. The exception contained in Art. 1196, for an abortion procured or attempted by medical advice for the purpose of saving the life of the mother, is typical. But if the fetus is a person who is not to be deprived of life without due process of law, and if the mother's condition is the sole determinant, does not the Texas exception appear to be out of line with the Amendment's command?

There are other inconsistencies between Fourteenth Amendment status and the typical abortion statute. It has already

93 S.Ct.—46½

been pointed out, n. 49, *supra*, that in Texas the woman is not a principal or an accomplice with respect to an abortion upon her. If the fetus is a person, why is the woman not a principal or an accomplice? Further, the penalty for criminal abortion specified by Art. 1195 is significantly less than the maximum penalty for murder prescribed by Art. 1257 of the Texas Penal Code. If the fetus is a person, may the penalties be different?

55. Cf. the Wisconsin abortion statute, defining "unborn child" to mean "a human being from the time of conception until it is born alive," Wis.Stat. § 940.04(6) (1969), and the new Connecticut statute, Pub. Act No. 1 (May 1972 Special Session), declaring it to be the public policy of the State and the legislative intent "to protect and preserve human life from the moment of conception."

termination of life entitled to Fourteenth Amendment protection.

This conclusion, however, does not of itself fully answer the contentions raised by Texas, and we pass on to other considerations.

B. The pregnant woman cannot be isolated in her privacy. She carries an embryo and, later, a fetus, if one accepts the medical definitions of the developing young in the human uterus. See Dorland's Illustrated Medical Dictionary 478–479, 547 (24th ed. 1965). The situation therefore is inherently different from marital intimacy, or bedroom possession of obscene material, or marriage, or procreation, or education, with which *Eisenstadt* and *Griswold, Stanley, Loving, Skinner* and *Pierce* and *Meyer* were respectively concerned. As we have intimated above, it is reasonable and appropriate for a State to decide that at some point in time another interest, that of health of the mother or that of potential human life, becomes significantly involved. The woman's privacy is no longer sole and any right of privacy she possesses must be measured accordingly.

Texas urges that, apart from the Fourteenth Amendment, life begins at conception and is present throughout pregnancy, and that, therefore, the State has a compelling interest in protecting that life from and after conception. We need not resolve the difficult question of when life begins. When those trained in the respective disciplines of medicine, philosophy, and theology are unable to arrive at any consensus, the judiciary, at this point in the development of man's knowledge, is not in a position to speculate as to the answer.

⌐It should be sufficient to note briefly ⌐160 the wide divergence of thinking on this most sensitive and difficult question. There has always been strong support for the view that life does not begin until live birth. This was the belief of the Stoics.[56] It appears to be the predominant, though not the unanimous, attitude of the Jewish faith.[57] It may be taken to represent also the position of a large segment of the Protestant community, insofar as that can be ascertained; organized groups that have taken a formal position on the abortion issue have generally regarded abortion as a matter for the conscience of the individual and her family.[58] As we have noted, the common law found greater significance in quickening. Physicians and their scientific colleagues have regarded that event with less interest and have tended to focus either upon conception, upon live birth, or upon the interim point at which the fetus becomes "viable," that is, potentially able to live outside the mother's womb, albeit with artificial aid.[59] Viability is usually placed at about seven months (28 weeks) but may occur earlier, even at 24 weeks.[60] The Aristotelian theory of "mediate animation," that held sway throughout the Middle Ages and the Renaissance in Europe, continued to be official Roman Catholic dogma until the 19th century, despite opposition to this "ensoulment" theory from those in the Church who would recognize the existence of life from⌐the moment of conception.[61] The ⌐161 latter is now, of course, the official belief of the Catholic Church. As one brief *amicus* discloses, this is a view strongly held by many non-Catholics as well, and by many physicians. Substan-

---

56. Edelstein 16.

57. Lader 97–99; D. Feldman, Birth Control in Jewish Law 251–294 (1968). For a stricter view, see I. Jakobovits, Jewish Views on Abortion, in Abortion and the Law 124 (D. Smith ed. 1967).

58. Amicus Brief for the American Ethical Union et al. For the position of the National Council of Churches and of other denominations, see Lader 99–101.

59. L. Hellman & J. Pritchard, Williams Obstetrics 493 (14th ed. 1971); Dorland's Illustrated Medical Dictionary 1689 (24th ed. 1965).

60. Hellman & Pritchard, *supra,* n. 59, at 493.

61. For discussions of the development of the Roman Catholic position, see D. Callahan, Abortion: Law, Choice, and Morality 409–447 (1970); Noonan 1.

410 U.S. 163   ROE v. WADE   **731**

Cite as 93 S.Ct. 705 (1973)

tial problems for precise definition of this view are posed, however, by new embryological data that purport to indicate that conception is a "process" over time, rather than an event, and by new medical techniques such as menstrual extraction, the "morning-after" pill, implantation of embryos, artificial insemination, and even artificial wombs.[62]

In areas other than criminal abortion, the law has been reluctant to endorse any theory that life, as we recognize it, begins before live birth or to accord legal rights to the unborn except in narrowly defined situations and except when the rights are contingent upon live birth. For example, the traditional rule of tort law denied recovery for prenatal injuries even though the child was born alive.[63] That rule has been changed in almost every jurisdiction. In most States, recovery is said to be permitted only if the fetus was viable, or at least quick, when the injuries were |162 sustained, though few courts have squarely so held.[64] In a recent development, generally opposed by the commentators, some States permit the parents of a stillborn child to maintain an action for wrongful death because of prenatal injuries.[65] Such an action, however, would appear to be one to vindicate the parents' interest and is thus consistent with the view that the fetus, at most, represents only the potentiality of life. Similarly, unborn children have been

recognized as acquiring rights or interests by way of inheritance or other devolution of property, and have been represented by guardians *ad litem*.[66] Perfection of the interests involved, again, has generally been contingent upon live birth. In short, the unborn have never been recognized in the law as persons in the whole sense.

X

In view of all this, we do not agree that, by adopting one theory of life, Texas may override the rights of the pregnant woman that are at stake. We repeat, however, that the State does have an important and legitimate interest in preserving and protecting the health of the pregnant woman, whether she be a resident of the State or a nonresident who seeks medical consultation and treatment there, and that it has still *another* important and legitimate interest in protecting the potentiality of human life. These interests are separate and distinct. Each grows in substantiality as the woman approaches term |163 and, at a point during pregnancy, each becomes "compelling."

[13, 14] With respect to the State's important and legitimate interest in the health of the mother, the "compelling" point, in the light of present medical knowledge, is at approximately the end of the first trimester. This is so because of the now-established medical

---

62. See Brodie, The New Biology and the Prenatal Child, 9 J.Family L. 391, 397 (1970); Gorney, The New Biology and the Future of Man, 15 U.C.L.A.L. Rev. 273 (1968); Note, Criminal Law—Abortion—The "Morning-After Pill" and Other Pre-Implantation Birth-Control Methods and the Law, 46 Ore.L.Rev. 211 (1967); G. Taylor, The Biological Time Bomb 32 (1968); A. Rosenfeld, The Second Genesis 138–139 (1969); Smith, Through a Test Tube Darkly: Artificial Insemination and the Law, 67 Mich.L. Rev. 127 (1968); Note, Artificial Insemination and the Law, 1968 U.Ill.L.F. 203.

63. W. Prosser, The Law of Torts 335–338 (4th ed. 1971); 2 F. Harper & F.

James, The Law of Torts 1028–1031 (1956); Note, 63 Harv.L.Rev. 173 (1949).

64. See cases cited in Prosser, *supra*, n. 63, at 336–338; Annotation, Action for Death of Unborn Child, 15 A.L.R.3d 992 (1967).

65. Prosser, *supra*, n. 63, at 338; Note, The Law and the Unborn Child: The Legal and Logical Inconsistencies, 46 Notre Dame Law. 349, 354–360 (1971).

66. Louisell, Abortion, The Practice of Medicine and the Due Process of Law, 16 U.C.L.A.L.Rev. 233, 235–238 (1969); Note, 56 Iowa L.Rev. 994, 999–1000 (1971); Note, The Law and the Unborn Child, 46 Notre Dame Law. 349, 351–354 (1971).

fact, referred to above at 725, that until the end of the first trimester mortality in abortion may be less than mortality in normal childbirth. It follows that, from and after this point, a State may regulate the abortion procedure to the extent that the regulation reasonably relates to the preservation and protection of maternal health. Examples of permissible state regulation in this area are requirements as to the qualifications of the person who is to perform the abortion; as to the licensure of that person; as to the facility in which the procedure is to be performed, that is, whether it must be a hospital or may be a clinic or some other place of less-than-hospital status; as to the licensing of the facility; and the like.

This means, on the other hand, that, for the period of pregnancy prior to this "compelling" point, the attending physician, in consultation with his patient, is free to determine, without regulation by the State, that, in his medical judgment, the patient's pregnancy should be terminated. If that decision is reached, the judgment may be effectuated by an abortion free of interference by the State.

[15] With respect to the State's important and legitimate interest in potential life, the "compelling" point is at viability. This is so because the fetus then presumably has the capability of meaningful life outside the mother's womb. State regulation protective of fetal life after viability thus has both logical and biological justifications. If the State is interested in protecting fetal life after viability, it may go so far as to proscribe abortion|during that period, except when it is necessary to preserve the life or health of the mother.

[16] Measured against these standards, Art. 1196 of the Texas Penal Code, in restricting legal abortions to those "procured or attempted by medical advice for the purpose of saving the life of the mother," sweeps too broadly. The statute makes no distinction between abortions performed early in pregnancy and those performed later, and it limits to a single reason, "saving" the mother's life, the legal justification for the procedure. The statute, therefore, cannot survive the constitutional attack made upon it here.

This conclusion makes it unnecessary for us to consider the additional challenge to the Texas statute asserted on grounds of vagueness. See United States v. Vuitch, 402 U.S., at 67–72, 91 S.Ct., at 1296–1299.

XI

To summarize and to repeat:

1. A state criminal abortion statute of the current Texas type, that excepts from criminality only a *life-saving* procedure on behalf of the mother, without regard to pregnancy stage and without recognition of the other interests involved, is violative of the Due Process Clause of the Fourteenth Amendment.

(a) For the stage prior to approximately the end of the first trimester, the abortion decision and its effectuation must be left to the medical judgment of the pregnant woman's attending physician.

(b) For the stage subsequent to approximately the end of the first trimester, the State, in promoting its interest in the health of the mother, may, if it chooses, regulate the abortion procedure in ways that are reasonably related to maternal health.

(c) For the stage subsequent to viability, the State in promoting its interest in the potentiality of human life may, if it chooses, regulate, and even proscribe, abortion except where it is necessary, in appropriate medical judgment, for the preservation of the life or health of the mother.

[17] 2. The State may define the term "physician," as it has been employed in the preceding paragraphs of this Part XI of this opinion, to mean only a physician currently licensed by the

State, and may proscribe any abortion by a person who is not a physician as so defined.

In Doe v. Bolton, 410 U.S. 179, 93 S.Ct. 739, 35 L.Ed.2d 201, procedural requirements contained in one of the modern abortion statutes are considered. That opinion and this one, of course, are to be read together.[67]

This holding, we feel, is consistent with the relative weights of the respective interests involved, with the lessons and examples of medical and legal history, with the lenity of the common law, and with the demands of the profound problems of the present day. The decision leaves the State free to place increasing restrictions on abortion as the period of pregnancy lengthens, so long as those restrictions are tailored to the recognized state interests. The decision vindicates the right of the physician to administer medical treatment according to his professional judgment up to the |166 points where important state interests provide compelling justifications for intervention. Up to those points, the abortion decision in all its aspects is inherently, and primarily, a medical decision, and basic responsibility for it must rest with the physician. If an individual practitioner abuses the privilege of exercising proper medical judgment, the usual remedies, judicial and intra-professional, are available.

XII

[18] Our conclusion that Art. 1196 is unconstitutional means, of course, that the Texas abortion statutes, as a unit, must fall. The exception of Art. 1196 cannot be struck down separately,

for then the State would be left with a statute proscribing all abortion procedures no matter how medically urgent the case.

Although the District Court granted appellant Roe declaratory relief, it stopped short of issuing an injunction against enforcement of the Texas statutes. The Court has recognized that different considerations enter into a federal court's decision as to declaratory relief, on the one hand, and injunctive relief, on the other. Zwickler v. Koota, 389 U.S. 241, 252–255, 88 S.Ct. 391, 397–399, 19 L.Ed.2d 444 (1967); Dombrowski v. Pfister, 380 U.S. 479, 85 S. Ct. 1116, 14 L.Ed.2d 22 (1965). We are not dealing with a statute that, on its face, appears to abridge free expression, an area of particular concern under *Dombrowski* and refined in Younger v. Harris, 401 U.S., at 50, 91 S.Ct., at 753.

We find it unnecessary to decide whether the District Court erred in withholding injunctive relief, for we assume the Texas prosecutorial authorities will give full credence to this decision that the present criminal abortion statutes of that State are unconstitutional.

The judgment of the District Court as to intervenor Hallford is reversed, and Dr. Hallford's complaint in intervention is dismissed. In all other respects, the judgment of the District Court is affirmed. Costs are allowed to the appellee. |167

It is so ordered.

Affirmed in part and reversed in part.

Mr. Justice STEWART, concurring.

In 1963, this Court, in Ferguson v. Skrupa, 372 U.S. 726, 83 S.Ct. 1028, 10

---

67. Neither in this opinion nor in Doe v. Bolton, 410 U.S. 179, 93 S.Ct. 739, 35 L.Ed.2d 201, do we discuss the father's rights, if any exist in the constitutional context, in the abortion decision. No paternal right has been asserted in either of the cases, and the Texas and the Georgia statutes on their face take no cognizance of the father. We are aware that some statutes recognize the father under certain circumstances. North Car-

olina, for example, N.C.Gen.Stat. § 14–45.1 (Supp.1971), requires written permission for the abortion from the husband when the woman is a married minor, that is, when she is less than 18 years of age, 41 N.C.A.G. 489 (1971); if the woman is an unmarried minor, written permission from the parents is required. We need not now decide whether provisions of this kind are constitutional.

L.Ed.2d 93, purported to sound the death knell for the doctrine of substantive due process, a doctrine under which many state laws had in the past been held to violate the Fourteenth Amendment. As Mr. Justice Black's opinion for the Court in *Skrupa* put it: "We have returned to the original constitutional proposition that courts do not substitute their social and economic beliefs for the judgment of legislative bodies, who are elected to pass laws." *Id.*, at 730, 83 S.Ct., at 1031.[1]

Barely two years later, in Griswold v. Connecticut, 381 U.S. 479, 85 S.Ct. 1678, 14 L.Ed.2d 510, the Court held a Connecticut birth control law unconstitutional. In view of what had been so recently said in *Skrupa*, the Court's opinion in *Griswold* understandably did its best to avoid reliance on the Due Process Clause of the Fourteenth Amendment as the ground for decision. Yet, the Connecticut law did not violate any provision of the Bill of Rights, nor any other specific provision of the ⌊168 Constitution.[2] So it was clear⌊to me then, and it is equally clear to me now, that the *Griswold* decision can be rationally understood only as a holding that the Connecticut statute substantively invaded the "liberty" that is protected by the Due Process Clause of the Fourteenth Amendment.[3] As so understood, *Griswold* stands as one in a long line of pre-*Skrupa* cases decided under the doctrine of substantive due process, and I now accept it as such.

"In a Constitution for a free people, there can be no doubt that the meaning of 'liberty' must be broad indeed." Board of Regents v. Roth, 408 U.S. 564, 572, 92 S.Ct. 2701, 2707, 33 L.Ed.2d 548. The Constitution nowhere mentions a specific right of personal choice in matters of marriage and family life, but the "liberty" protected by the Due Process Clause of the Fourteenth Amendment covers more than those freedoms explicitly named in the Bill of Rights. See Schware v. Board of Bar Examiners, 353 U.S. 232, 238–239, 77 S. Ct. 752, 755–756, 1 L.Ed.2d 796; Pierce v. Society of Sisters, 268 U.S. 510, 534–535, 45 S.Ct. 571, 573–574, 69 L.Ed. 1070; Meyer v. Nebraska, 262 U.S. 390, 399–400, 43 S.Ct. 625, 626–627, 67 L.Ed. 1042. Cf. Shapiro v. Thompson, 394 U. S. 618, 629–630, 89 S.Ct. 1322, 1328–1329, 22 L.Ed.2d 600; United States v. Guest, 383 U.S. 745, 757–758, 86 S.Ct. 1170, 1177–1178, 16 L.Ed.2d 239; Carrington v. Rash, 380 U.S. 89, 96, 85 S.Ct. 775, 780, 13 L.Ed.2d 675; Aptheker v. Secretary of State, 378 U.S. 500, 505, 84 S.Ct. 1659, 1663, 12 L.Ed.2d 992; Kent v. Dulles, 357 U.S. 116, 127, 78 S.Ct. 1113, 1118, 2 L.Ed.2d 1204; Bolling v. Sharpe, 347 U.S. 497, 499–500, 74 S.Ct. 693, 694–695, 98 L.Ed. 884; Truax v. Raich, 239 U.S. 33, 41, 36 S.Ct. 7, 10, 60 L.Ed. 131.

⌊As Mr. Justice Harlan once wrote: ⌊169 "[T]he full scope of the liberty guaranteed by the Due Process Clause cannot be found in or limited by the precise

---

1 Only Mr. Justice Harlan failed to join the Court's opinion, 372 U.S., at 733, 83 S.Ct., at 1032.

2. There is no constitutional right of privacy, as such. "[The Fourth] Amendment protects individual privacy against certain kinds of governmental intrusion, but its protections go further, and often have nothing to do with privacy at all. Other provisions of the Constitution protect personal privacy from other forms of governmental invasion. But the protection of a person's *general* right to privacy—his right to be let alone by other people—is like the protection of his property and of his very life, left

largely to the law of the individual States." Katz v. United States, 389 U.S. 347, 350–351, 88 S.Ct. 507, 510–511, 19 L.Ed.2d 576 (footnotes omitted).

3. This was also clear to Mr. Justice Black, 381 U.S., at 507, (dissenting opinion); to Mr. Justice Harlan, 381 U.S., at 499, 85 S.Ct., at 1689 (opinion concurring in the judgment); and to Mr. Justice White, 381 U.S., at 502, 85 S.Ct., at 1691 (opinion concurring in the judgment). See also Mr. Justice Harlan's thorough and thoughtful opinion dissenting from dismissal of the appeal in Poe v. Ullman, 367 U.S. 497, 522, 81 S.Ct. 1752, 1765, 6 L.Ed.2d 989.

terms of the specific guarantees elsewhere provided in the Constitution. This 'liberty' is not a series of isolated points pricked out in terms of the taking of property; the freedom of speech, press, and religion; the right to keep and bear arms; the freedom from unreasonable searches and seizures; and so on. It is a rational continuum which, broadly speaking, includes a freedom from all substantial arbitrary impositions and purposeless restraints . . . and which also recognizes, what a reasonable and sensitive judgment must, that certain interests require particularly careful scrutiny of the state needs asserted to justify their abridgment." Poe v. Ullman, 367 U.S. 497, 543, 81 S.Ct. 1752, 1776, 6 L.Ed.2d 989 (opinion dissenting from dismissal of appeal) (citations omitted). In the words of Mr. Justice Frankfurter, "Great concepts like . . . 'liberty' . . . were purposely left to gather meaning from experience. For they relate to the whole domain of social and economic fact, and the statesmen who founded this Nation knew too well that only a stagnant society remains unchanged." National Mutual Ins. Co. v. Tidewater Transfer Co., 337 U.S. 582, 646, 69 S.Ct. 1173, 1195, 93 L.Ed. 1556 (dissenting opinion).

Several decisions of this Court make clear that freedom of personal choice in matters of marriage and family life is one of the liberties protected by the Due Process Clause of the Fourteenth Amendment. Loving v. Virginia, 388 U.S. 1, 12, 87 S.Ct. 1817, 1823, 18 L.Ed. 2d 1010; Griswold v. Connecticut, *supra*; Pierce v. Society of Sisters, *supra*; Meyer v. Nebraska, *supra*. See also Prince v. Massachusetts, 321 U.S. 158, 166, 64 S.Ct. 438, 442, 88 L.Ed. 645; Skinner v. Oklahoma, 316 U.S. 535, 541, 62 S.Ct. 1110, 1113, 86 L.Ed. 1655. As recently as last Term, in Eisenstadt v. Baird, 405 U.S. 438, 453, 92 S.Ct. 1029, 1038, 31 L.Ed.2d 349, we recognized "the right of the *individual*, married or single, to be free from unwarranted governmental intrusion into matters so fundamentally affecting a person as the decision whether to bear or beget a child." That right necessarily includes the right of a woman to decide whether or not to terminate her pregnancy. "Certainly the interests of a woman in giving of her physical and emotional self during pregnancy and the interests that will be affected throughout her life by the birth and raising of a child are of a far greater degree of significance and personal intimacy than the right to send a child to private school protected in Pierce v. Society of Sisters, 268 U.S. 510, 45 S.Ct. 571, 69 L.Ed. 1070 (1925), or the right to teach a foreign language protected in Meyer v. Nebraska, 262 U.S. 390, 43 S. Ct. 625, 67 L.Ed. 1042 (1923)." Abele v. Markle, 351 F.Supp. 224, 227 (D.C. Conn.1972).

Clearly, therefore, the Court today is correct in holding that the right asserted by Jane Roe is embraced within the personal liberty protected by the Due Process Clause of the Fourteenth Amendment.

It is evident that the Texas abortion statute infringes that right directly. Indeed, it is difficult to imagine a more complete abridgment of a constitutional freedom than that worked by the inflexible criminal statute now in force in Texas. The question then becomes whether the state interests advanced to justify this abridgment can survive the "particularly careful scrutiny" that the Fourteenth Amendment here requires.

The asserted state interests are protection of the health and safety of the pregnant woman, and protection of the potential future human life within her. These are legitimate objectives, amply sufficient to permit a State to regulate abortions as it does other surgical procedures, and perhaps sufficient to permit a State to regulate abortions more stringently or even to prohibit them in the late stages of pregnancy. But such legislation is not before us, and I think the Court today has thoroughly demonstrated that these state interests cannot constitutionally support the broad abridg-

₁₁₇₁ ment of personal liberty worked by the existing Texas law. Accordingly, I join the Court's opinion holding that that law is invalid under the Due Process Clause of the Fourteenth Amendment.

Mr. Justice REHNQUIST, dissenting.

The Court's opinion brings to the decision of this troubling question both extensive historical fact and a wealth of legal scholarship. While the opinion thus commands my respect, I find myself nonetheless in fundamental disagreement with those parts of it that invalidate the Texas statute in question, and therefore dissent.

I

The Court's opinion decides that a State may impose virtually no restriction on the performance of abortions during the first trimester of pregnancy. Our previous decisions indicate that a necessary predicate for such an opinion is a plaintiff who was in her first trimester of pregnancy at some time during the pendency of her lawsuit. While a party may vindicate his own constitutional rights, he may not seek vindication for the rights of others. Moose Lodge No. 107 v. Irvis, 407 U.S. 163, 92 S.Ct. 1965, 32 L.Ed.2d 627 (1972); Sierra Club v. Morton, 405 U.S. 727, 92 S.Ct. 1361, 31 L.Ed.2d 636 (1972). The Court's statement of facts in this case makes clear, however, that the record in no way indicates the presence of such a plaintiff. We know only that plaintiff Roe at the time of filing her complaint was a pregnant woman; for aught that appears in this record, she may have been in her *last* trimester of pregnancy as of the date the complaint was filed.

Nothing in the Court's opinion indicates that Texas might not constitutionally apply its proscription of abortion as written to a woman in that stage of pregnancy. Nonetheless, the Court uses her complaint against the Texas statute as a fulcrum for deciding that States ₁₁₇₂ may impose virtually no restrictions on

medical abortions performed during the *first* trimester of pregnancy. In deciding such a hypothetical lawsuit, the Court departs from the longstanding admonition that it should never "formulate a rule of constitutional law broader than is required by the precise facts to which it is to be applied." Liverpool, New York & Philadelphia S.S. Co. v. Commissioners of Emigration, 113 U.S. 33, 39, 5 S.Ct. 352, 355, 28 L.Ed. 899 (1885). See also Ashwander v. TVA, 297 U.S. 288, 345, 56 S.Ct. 466, 482, 80 L.Ed. 688 (1936) (Brandeis, J., concurring).

II

Even if there were a plaintiff in this case capable of litigating the issue which the Court decides, I would reach a conclusion opposite to that reached by the Court. I have difficulty in concluding, as the Court does, that the right of "privacy" is involved in this case. Texas, by the statute here challenged, bars the performance of a medical abortion by a licensed physician on a plaintiff such as Roe. A transaction resulting in an operation such as this is not "private" in the ordinary usage of that word. Nor is the "privacy" that the Court finds here even a distant relative of the freedom from searches and seizures protected by the Fourth Amendment to the Constitution, which the Court has referred to as embodying a right to privacy. Katz v. United States, 389 U.S. 347, 88 S.Ct. 507, 19 L.Ed.2d 576 (1967).

If the Court means by the term "privacy" no more than that the claim of a person to be free from unwanted state regulation of consensual transactions may be a form of "liberty" protected by the Fourteenth Amendment, there is no doubt that similar claims have been upheld in our earlier decisions on the basis of that liberty. I agree with the statement of Mr. Justice STEWART in his concurring opinion that the "liberty," against deprivation of which without due process the Fourteenth Amendment ₁₁₇ protects, embraces more than the rights found in the Bill of Rights. But that liberty is not guaranteed absolutely against deprivation, only against deprivation without due process of law. The test traditionally applied in the area of social and economic legislation is whether or not a law such as that challenged has a rational relation to a valid state objective. Williamson v. Lee Optical Co., 348 U.S. 483, 491, 75 S.Ct. 461, 466, 99 L.Ed. 563 (1955). The Due Process Clause of the Fourteenth Amendment undoubtedly does place a limit, albeit a broad one, on legislative power to enact laws such as this. If the Texas statute were to prohibit an abortion even where the mother's life is in jeopardy, I have little doubt that such a statute would lack a rational relation to a valid state objective under the test stated in *Williamson, supra.* But the Court's sweeping invalidation of any restrictions on abortion during the first trimester is impossible to justify under that standard, and the conscious weighing of competing factors that the Court's opinion apparently substitutes for the established test is far more appropriate to a legislative judgment than to a judicial one.

The Court eschews the history of the Fourteenth Amendment in its reliance on the "compelling state interest" test. See Weber v. Aetna Casualty & Surety Co., 406 U.S. 164, 179, 92 S.Ct. 1400, 1408, 31 L.Ed.2d 768 (1972) (dissenting opinion). But the Court adds a new wrinkle to this test by transposing it from the legal considerations associated with the Equal Protection Clause of the Fourteenth Amendment to this case arising under the Due Process Clause of the Fourteenth Amendment. Unless I misapprehend the consequences of this transplanting of the "compelling state interest test," the Court's opinion will accomplish the seemingly impossible feat of leaving this area of the law more confused than it found it.

⌐174⌐ While the Court's opinion quotes from the dissent of Mr. Justice Holmes in

Lochner v. New York, 198 U.S. 45, 74, 25 S.Ct. 539, 551, 49 L.Ed. 937 (1905), the result it reaches is more closely attuned to the majority opinion of Mr. Justice Peckham in that case. As in *Lochner* and similar cases applying substantive due process standards to economic and social welfare legislation, the adoption of the compelling state interest standard will inevitably require this Court to examine the legislative policies and pass on the wisdom of these policies in the very process of deciding whether a particular state interest put forward may or may not be "compelling." The decision here to break pregnancy into three distinct terms and to outline the permissible restrictions the State may impose in each one, for example, partakes more of judicial legislation than it does of a determination of the intent of the drafters of the Fourteenth Amendment.

The fact that a majority of the States reflecting, after all the majority sentiment in those States, have had restrictions on abortions for at least a century is a strong indication, it seems to me, that the asserted right to an abortion is not "so rooted in the traditions and conscience of our people as to be ranked as fundamental," Snyder v. Massachusetts, 291 U.S. 97, 105, 54 S.Ct. 330, 332, 78 L.Ed. 674 (1934). Even today, when society's views on abortion are changing, the very existence of the debate is evidence that the "right" to an abortion is not so universally accepted as the appellant would have us believe.

To reach its result, the Court necessarily has had to find within the Scope of the Fourteenth Amendment a right that was apparently completely unknown to the drafters of the Amendment. As early as 1821, the first state law dealing directly with abortion was enacted by the Connecticut Legislature. Conn.Stat., Tit. 22, §§ 14, 16. By the time of the adoption of the Fourteenth Amendment ⌐175 in 1868, there were at least 36 laws enacted by state or territorial legislatures limiting abortion.[1] While many States have amended or updated their laws, 21 of the ⌐176

laws on the books in 1868 remain in effect today.[2] Indeed, the Texas statute

1. Jurisdictions having enacted abortion laws prior to the adoption of the Fourteenth Amendment in 1868:

1. Alabama—Ala.Acts, c. 6, § 2 (1840).

2. Arizona—Howell Code, c. 10, § 45 (1865).

3. Arkansas—Ark.Rev.Stat., c. 44, div. III, Art. II, § 6 (1838).

4. California—Cal.Sess.Laws, c. 99, § 45, p. 233 (1849–1850).

5. Colorado (Terr.)—Colo.Gen.Laws of Terr. of Colo., 1st Sess., § 42, pp. 296–297 (1861).

6. Connecticut—Conn.Stat. Tit. 20, §§ 14, 16 (1821). By 1868, this statute had been replaced by another abortion law. Conn.Pub.Acts, c. 71, §§ 1, 2, p. 65 (1860).

7. Florida—Fla.Acts 1st Sess., c. 1637, subc. 3, §§ 10, 11, subc. 8, §§ 9, 10, 11 (1868), as amended, now Fla.Stat.Ann. §§ 782.09, 782.10, 797.01, 797.02, 782.16 (1965).

8. Georgia—Ga.Pen.Code, 4th Div., § 20 (1833).

9. Kingdom of Hawaii—Hawaii Pen. Code, c. 12, §§ 1, 2, 3 (1850).

10. Idaho (Terr.)—Idaho (Terr.) Laws, Crimes and Punishments §§ 33, 34, 42, pp. 441, 443 (1863).

11. Illinois—Ill.Rev. Criminal Code §§ 40, 41, 46, pp. 130, 131 (1827). By 1868, this statute had been replaced by a subsequent enactment. Ill.Pub.Laws §§ 1, 2, 3, p. 89 (1867).

12. Indiana—Ind.Rev.Stat. §§ 1, 3, p. 224 (1838). By 1868 this statute had been superseded by a subsequent enactment. Ind.Laws, c. LXXXI, § 2 (1859).

13. Iowa (Terr.)—Iowa (Terr.) Stat., 1st Legis., 1st Sess., § 18, p. 145 (1838). By 1868, this statute had been superseded by a subsequent enactment. Iowa (Terr.) Rev.Stat., c. 49, §§ 10, 13 (1843).

14. Kansas (Terr.)—Kan. (Terr.) Stat., c. 48, §§ 9, 10, 39 (1855). By 1868, this statute had been superseded by a subsequent enactment. Kan. (Terr.) Laws, c. 28, §§ 9, 10, 37 (1859).

15. Louisiana—La.Rev.Stat., Crimes and Offenses § 24, p. 138 (1856).

16. Maine—Me.Rev.Stat., c. 160, §§ 11, 12, 13, 14 (1840).

17. Maryland—Md.Laws, c. 179, § 2, p. 315 (1868).

18. Massachusetts—Mass.Acts & Resolves, c. 27 (1845).

19. Michigan—Mich.Rev.Stat., c. 153, §§ 32, 33, 34, p. 662 (1846).

20. Minnesota (Terr.)—Minn. (Terr.) Rev.Stat., c. 100, §§ 10, 11, p. 493 (1851).

21. Mississippi—Miss.Code, c. 64, §§ 8, 9, p. 958 (1848).

22. Missouri—Mo.Rev.Stat., Art. II, §§ 9, 10, 36, pp. 168, 172 (1835).

23. Montana (Terr.)—Mont. (Terr.) Laws, Criminal Practice Acts § 41, p. 184 (1864).

24. Nevada (Terr.)—Nev. (Terr.) Laws, c. 28, § 42, p. 63 (1861).

25. New Hampshire—N.H.Laws, c. 743, § 1, p. 708 (1848).

26. New Jersey—N.J.Laws, p. 266 (1849).

27. New York—N.Y.Rev.Stat., pt. 4, c. 1, Tit. 2, §§ 8, 9, pp. 12–13 (1828). By 1868, this statute had been superseded. N.Y.Laws, c. 260, §§ 1, 2, 3, 4, 5, 6, pp. 285–286 (1845); N.Y.Laws, c. 22, § 1, p. 19 (1846).

28. Ohio—Ohio Gen.Stat. §§ 111(1), 112(2), p. 252 (1841).

29. Oregon—Ore.Gen.Laws, Crim.Code, c. 43, § 509, p. 528 (1845–1964).

30. Pennsylvania—Pa.Laws No. 374 §§ 87, 88, 89 (1860).

31. Texas—Tex.Gen.Stat.Dig., c. VII, Arts. 531–536, p. 524 (Oldham & White 1859).

32. Vermont—Vt.Acts No. 33, § 1 (1846). By 1868, this statute had been amended. Vt.Acts No. 57, §§ 1, 3 (1867).

33. Virginia—Va.Acts, Tit. II, c. 3, § 9, p. 96 (1848).

34. Washington (Terr.)—Wash. (Terr.) Stats., c. II, §§ 37, 38, p. 81 (1854).

35. West Virginia—Va.Acts, Tit. II, c. 3, § 9, p. 96 (1848).

36. Wisconsin—Wis.Rev.Stat., c. 133, §§ 10, 11 (1849). By 1868, this statute had been superseded. Wis.Rev.Stat., c. 164, §§ 10, 11; c. 169, §§ 58, 59 (1858).

2. Abortion laws in effect in 1868 and still applicable as of August 1970:

1. Arizona (1865).
2. Connecticut (1860).
3. Florida (1868).
4. Idaho (1863).

struck down today was, as the majority
notes, first enacted in 1857 and "has remained substantially unchanged to the
present time." *Ante*, at 710.

|177

There apparently was no question concerning the validity of this provision or
of any of the other state statutes when
the Fourteenth Amendment was adopted.
The only conclusion possible from this
history is that the drafters did not intend to have the Fourteenth Amendment
withdraw from the States the power to
legislate with respect to this matter.

III

Even if one were to agree that the
case that the Court decides were here,
and that the enunciation of the substantive constitutional law in the Court's
opinion were proper, the actual disposition of the case by the Court is still difficult to justify. The Texas statute is
struck down *in toto*, even though the
Court apparently concedes that at later
periods of pregnancy Texas might impose these selfsame statutory limitations
on abortion. My understanding of past
practice is that a statute found to be invalid as applied to a particular plaintiff,
but not unconstitutional as a whole, is
not simply "struck down" but is, instead,
declared unconstitutional as applied to
the fact situation before the Court.
Yick Wo v. Hopkins, 118 U.S. 356, 6 S.
Ct. 1064, 30 L.Ed. 220 (1886); Street v.
New York, 394 U.S. 576, 89 S.Ct. 1354,
22 L.Ed.2d 572 (1969).

|178

For all of the foregoing reasons, I respectfully dissent.

5. Indiana (1838).		14. New Hampshire (1848).	
6. Iowa (1843).		15. New Jersey (1849).	
7. Maine (1840).		16. Ohio (1841).	
8. Massachusetts (1845).		17. Pennsylvania (1860).	
9. Michigan (1846).		18. Texas (1859).	
10. Minnesota (1851).		19. Vermont (1867).	
11. Missouri (1835).		20. West Virginia (1848).	
12. Montana (1864).		21. Wisconsin (1858).	
13. Nevada (1861).			

ABBREVIATIONS

A.	Atlantic Reporter
A. 2d	Atlantic Reporter, Second Series
AAA	American Arbitration Association; Agricultural Adjustment Act of 1933
AAPRP	All African People's Revolutionary Party
ABA	American Bar Association; Architectural Barriers Act, 1968
ABM Treaty	Anti-Ballistic Missile Treaty of 1972; antiballistic missile
ABVP	Anti-Biased Violence Project
A/C	Account
A.C.	Appeal Cases
ACAA	Air Carrier Access Act
ACF	Administration for Children and Families
ACLU	American Civil Liberties Union
ACS	Agricultural Cooperative Service
Act'g Legal Adv.	Acting Legal Advisor
ACUS	Administrative Conference of the United States
ACYF	Administration on Children, Youth, and Families
A.D. 2d	Appellate Division, Second Series, N.Y.
ADA	Americans with Disabilities Act of 1990
ADAMHA	Alcohol, Drug Abuse, and Mental Health Administration
ADC	Aid to Dependent Children
ADD	Administration on Developmental Disabilities
ADEA	Age Discrimination in Employment Act of 1967
ADR	alternative dispute resolution
AEC	Atomic Energy Commission
AECB	Arms Export Control Board
A.E.R.	All England Law Reports
AFDC	Aid to Families with Dependent Children
aff'd per cur.	affirmed by the court
AFIS	automated fingerprint identification system
AFL	American Federation of Labor
AFL-CIO	American Federation of Labor and Congress of Industrial Organizations
AFRes	Air Force Reserve
AFSCME	American Federation of State, County, and Municipal Employees
AGRICOLA	Agricultural Online Access
AIA	Association of Insurance Attorneys
AID	artificial insemination using a third-party donor's sperm; Agency for International Development

AIDS	acquired immune deficiency syndrome
AIH	artificial insemination using the husband's sperm
AIM	American Indian Movement
AIUSA	Amnesty International, U.S.A. Affiliate
AJS	American Judicature Society
ALEC	American Legislative Exchange Council
ALF	Animal Liberation Front
ALI	American Law Institute
ALJ	administrative law judge
All E.R.	All England Law Reports
ALO	Agency Liaison
A.L.R.	American Law Reports
AMA	American Medical Association
Am. Dec.	American Decisions
amdt.	amendment
Amer. St. Papers, For. Rels.	American State Papers, Legislative and Executive Documents of the Congress of the U.S., Class I, Foreign Relations, 1832–1859
AMVETS	American Veterans (of World War II)
ANA	Administration for Native Americans
Ann. Dig.	Annual Digest of Public International Law Cases
ANZUS	Australia–New Zealand–United States Security Treaty Organization
AOA	Administration on Aging
APA	Administrative Procedure Act of 1946
APHIS	Animal and Plant Health Inspection Service
App. Div.	Appellate Division Reports, N.Y. Supreme Court
Arb. Trib., U.S.-British Convention of 1853	Arbitration Tribunal, Claim Convention of 1853, United States and Great Britain
ARS	Advanced Record System
Art.	article
ASCS	Agriculture Stabilization and Conservation Service
ASM	available seatmile
ASPCA	American Society for the Prevention of Cruelty to Animals
Asst. Att. Gen.	Assistant Attorney General
AT&T	American Telephone and Telegraph
ATFD	Alcohol, Tobacco and Firearms Division
ATLA	Association of Trial Lawyers of America
ATTD	Alcohol and Tobacco Tax Division
ATU	Alcohol Tax Unit
AZT	azidothymidine
BALSA	Black-American Law Student Association
BATF	Bureau of Alcohol, Tobacco and Firearms
BCCI	Bank of Credit and Commerce International
BEA	Bureau of Economic Analysis
Bell's Cr. C.	Bell's English Crown Cases
Bevans	United States Treaties, etc. *Treaties and Other International Agreements of the United States of America, 1776–1949* (compiled under the direction of Charles I. Bevans) (1968–76)
BFOQ	bona fide occupational qualification
BI	Bureau of Investigation
BIA	Bureau of Indian Affairs; Board of Immigration Appeals
BJS	Bureau of Justice Statistics
Black.	Black's United States Supreme Court Reports
Blatchf.	Blatchford's United States Circuit Court Reports
BLM	Bureau of Land Management
BLS	Bureau of Labor Statistics
BMD	ballistic missile defense
BOCA	Building Officials and Code Administrators International
BPP	Black Panther Party for Self-Defense

Brit. and For.	British and Foreign State Papers
Burr.	James Burrows, *Report of Cases Argued and Determined in the Court of King's Bench during the Time of Lord Mansfield* (1766–1780)
BVA	Board of Veterans Appeals
c.	Chapter
C^{3}I	Command, Control, Communications, and Intelligence
C.A.	Court of Appeals
CAA	Clean Air Act
CAB	Civil Aeronautics Board
CAFE	corporate average fuel economy
Cal. 2d	California Reports, Second Series
Cal. 3d	California Reports, Third Series
CALR	computer-assisted legal research
Cal. Rptr.	California Reporter
CAP	Common Agricultural Policy
CATV	community antenna television
CBO	Congressional Budget Office
CCC	Commodity Credit Corporation
CCDBG	Child Care and Development Block Grant of 1990
C.C.D. Pa.	Circuit Court Decisions, Pennsylvania
C.C.D. Va.	Circuit Court Decisions, Virginia
CCEA	Cabinet Council on Economic Affairs
CCR	Center for Constitutional Rights
C.C.R.I.	Circuit Court, Rhode Island
CD	certificate of deposit
CDA	Communications Decency Act
CDBG	Community Development Block Grant Program
CDC	Centers for Disease Control and Prevention; Community Development Corporation
CDF	Children's Defense Fund
CDL	Citizens for Decency through Law
CD-ROM	compact disc read-only memory
CDS	Community Dispute Services
CDW	collision damage waiver
CENTO	Central Treaty Organization
CEQ	Council on Environmental Quality
CERCLA	Comprehensive Environmental Response, Compensation, and Liability Act of 1980
cert.	*certiorari*
CETA	Comprehensive Employment and Training Act
C & F	cost and freight
CFC	chlorofluorocarbon
CFE Treaty	Conventional Forces in Europe Treaty of 1990
C.F. & I.	Cost, freight, and insurance
CFNP	Community Food and Nutrition Program
C.F.R.	Code of Federal Regulations
CFTC	Commodity Futures Trading Commission
Ch.	Chancery Division, English Law Reports
CHAMPVA	Civilian Health and Medical Program at the Veterans Administration
CHEP	Cuban/Haitian Entrant Program
CHINS	children in need of supervision
CHIPS	child in need of protective services
Ch.N.Y.	Chancery Reports, New York
Chr. Rob.	Christopher Robinson, *Reports of Cases Argued and Determined in the High Court of Admiralty* (1801–1808)
CIA	Central Intelligence Agency
CID	Commercial Item Descriptions
C.I.F.	Cost, insurance, and freight
CINCNORAD	Commander in Chief, North American Air Defense Command
C.I.O.	Congress of Industrial Organizations

C.J.	chief justice
CJIS	Criminal Justice Information Services
C.J.S.	Corpus Juris Secundum
Claims Arb. under Spec. Conv., Nielsen's Rept.	Frederick Kenelm Nielsen, *American and British Claims Arbitration under the Special Agreement Concluded between the United States and Great Britain, August 18, 1910* (1926)
CLE	Center for Law and Education
CLEO	Council on Legal Education Opportunity
CLP	Communist Labor Party of America
CLS	Christian Legal Society; critical legal studies (movement), Critical Legal Studies (membership organization)
C.M.A.	Court of Military Appeals
CMEA	Council for Mutual Economic Assistance
CMHS	Center for Mental Health Services
C.M.R.	Court of Military Review
CNN	Cable News Network
CNO	Chief of Naval Operations
C.O.D.	cash on delivery
COGP	Commission on Government Procurement
COINTELPRO	Counterintelligence Program
Coke Rep.	Coke's English King's Bench Reports
COLA	cost-of-living adjustment
COMCEN	Federal Communications Center
Comp.	Compilation
Conn.	Connecticut Reports
CONTU	National Commission on New Technological Uses of Copyrighted Works
Conv.	Convention
Corbin	Arthur L. Corbin, *Corbin on Contracts: A Comprehensive Treatise on the Rules of Contract Law* (1950)
CORE	Congress of Racial Equality
Cox's Crim. Cases	Cox's Criminal Cases (England)
CPA	certified public accountant
CPB	Corporation for Public Broadcasting, the
CPI	Consumer Price Index
CPSC	Consumer Product Safety Commission
Cranch	Cranch's United States Supreme Court Reports
CRF	Constitutional Rights Foundation
CRS	Congressional Research Service; Community Relations Service
CRT	critical race theory
CSA	Community Services Administration
CSAP	Center for Substance Abuse Prevention
CSAT	Center for Substance Abuse Treatment
CSC	Civil Service Commission
CSCE	Conference on Security and Cooperation in Europe
CSG	Council of State Governments
CSO	Community Service Organization
CSP	Center for the Study of the Presidency
C-SPAN	Cable-Satellite Public Affairs Network
CSRS	Cooperative State Research Service
CSWPL	Center on Social Welfare Policy and Law
CTA	*cum testamento annexo* (with the will attached)
Ct. Ap. D.C.	Court of Appeals, District of Columbia
Ct. App. No. Ireland	Court of Appeals, Northern Ireland
Ct. Cl.	Court of Claims, United States
Ct. Crim. Apps.	Court of Criminal Appeals (England)
Ct. of Sess., Scot.	Court of Sessions, Scotland
CU	credit union

CUNY	City University of New York
Cush.	Cushing's Massachusetts Reports
CWA	Civil Works Administration; Clean Water Act
Dall.	Dallas' Pennsylvania and United States Reports
DAR	Daughter of the American Revolution
DARPA	Defense Advanced Research Projects Agency
DAVA	Defense Audiovisual Agency
D.C.	United States District Court
D.C. Del.	United States District Court, Delaware
D.C. Mass.	United States District Court, Massachusetts
D.C. Md.	United States District Court, Maryland
D.C.N.D.Cal.	United States District Court, Northern District, California
D.C.N.Y.	United States District Court, New York
D.C.Pa.	United States District Court, Pennsylvania
DCS	Deputy Chiefs of Staff
DCZ	District of the Canal Zone
DDT	dichlorodiphenyltricloroethane
DEA	Drug Enforcement Administration
Decl. Lond.	Declaration of London, February 26, 1909
Dev. & B.	Devereux & Battle's North Carolina Reports
Dig. U.S. Practice in Intl. Law	Digest of U.S. Practice in International Law
Dist. Ct. D.C.	United States District Court, District of Columbia
D.L.R.	Dominion Law Reports (Canada)
DNA	deoxyribonucleic acid
DNase	deoxyribonuclease
DNC	Democratic National Committee
DOC	Department of Commerce
DOD	Department of Defense
Dodson	Dodson's Reports, English Admiralty Courts
DOE	Department of Energy
DOER	Department of Employee Relations
DOJ	Department of Justice
DOS	disk operating system
DOT	Department of Transportation
DPT	diphtheria, pertussis, and tetanus
DRI	Defense Research Institute
DSAA	Defense Security Assistance Agency
DUI	driving under the influence; driving under intoxication
DWI	driving while intoxicated
EAHCA	Education for All Handicapped Children Act of 1975
EBT	examination before trial
ECPA	Electronic Communications Privacy Act of 1986
ECSC	Treaty of the European Coal and Steel Community
EDA	Economic Development Administration
EDF	Environmental Defense Fund
E.D.N.Y.	Eastern District, New York
EDP	electronic data processing
E.D. Pa.	Eastern District, Pennsylvania
EDSC	Eastern District, South Carolina
E.D. Va.	Eastern District, Virginia
EEC	European Economic Community; European Economic Community Treaty
EEOC	Equal Employment Opportunity Commission
EFF	Electronic Frontier Foundation
EFT	electronic funds transfer
Eliz.	Queen Elizabeth (Great Britain)
Em. App.	Temporary Emergency Court of Appeals

ENE	early neutral evaluation
Eng. Rep.	English Reports
EOP	Executive Office of the President
EPA	Environmental Protection Agency; Equal Pay Act of 1963
ERA	Equal Rights Amendment
ERISA	Employee Retirement Income Security Act of 1974
ERS	Economic Research Service
ESF	emergency support function; Economic Support Fund
ESRD	End-Stage Renal Disease Program
ETA	Employment and Training Administration
ETS	environmental tobacco smoke
et seq.	*et sequentes* or *et sequentia;* "and the following"
EU	European Union
Euratom	European Atomic Energy Community
Eur. Ct. H.R.	European Court of Human Rights
Ex.	English Exchequer Reports, Welsby, Hurlstone & Gordon
Exch.	Exchequer Reports (Welsby, Hurlstone & Gordon)
Eximbank	Export-Import Bank of the United States
F.	Federal Reporter
F. 2d	Federal Reporter, Second Series
FAA	Federal Aviation Administration; Federal Arbitration Act
FAAA	Federal Alcohol Administration Act
FACE	Freedom of Access to Clinic Entrances Act of 1994
FACT	Feminist Anti-Censorship Task Force
FAO	Food and Agriculture Organization of the United Nations
FAR	Federal Acquisition Regulations
FAS	Foreign Agricultural Service
FBA	Federal Bar Association
FBI	Federal Bureau of Investigation
FCA	Farm Credit Administration
F. Cas.	Federal Cases
FCC	Federal Communications Commission
FCIA	Foreign Credit Insurance Association
FCIC	Federal Crop Insurance Corporation
FCRA	Fair Credit Reporting Act
FCU	Federal credit unions
FDA	Food and Drug Administration
FDIC	Federal Deposit Insurance Corporation
FDPC	Federal Data Processing Center
FEC	Federal Election Commission
Fed. Cas.	Federal Cases
FEMA	Federal Emergency Management Agency
FFB	Federal Financing Bank
FGIS	Federal Grain Inspection Service
FHA	Federal Housing Authority
FHWA	Federal Highway Administration
FIA	Federal Insurance Administration
FIC	Federal Information Centers; Federation of Insurance Counsel
FICA	Federal Insurance Contributions Act
FIFRA	Federal Insecticide, Fungicide, and Rodenticide Act
FIP	Forestry Incentives Program
FIRREA	Financial Institutions Reform, Recovery, and Enforcement Act
FISA	Foreign Intelligence Surveillance Act of 1978
FMCS	Federal Mediation and Conciliation Service
FmHA	Farmers Home Administration
FMLA	Family and Medical Leave Act of 1993
FNMA	Federal National Mortgage Association, "Fannie Mae"
F.O.B.	free on board

FOIA	Freedom of Information Act
FPC	Federal Power Commission
FPMR	Federal Property Management Regulations
FPRS	Federal Property Resources Service
FR	Federal Register
FRA	Federal Railroad Administration
FRB	Federal Reserve Board
FRC	Federal Radio Commission
F.R.D.	Federal Rules Decisions
FSA	Family Support Act
FSLIC	Federal Savings and Loan Insurance Corporation
FSQS	Food Safety and Quality Service
FSS	Federal Supply Service
F. Supp.	Federal Supplement
FTA	U.S.-Canada Free Trade Agreement, 1988
FTC	Federal Trade Commission
FTS	Federal Telecommunications System
FUTA	Federal Unemployment Tax Act
FWPCA	Federal Water Pollution Control Act of 1948
GAO	General Accounting Office; Governmental Affairs Office
GAOR	General Assembly Official Records, United Nations
GA Res.	General Assembly Resolution (United Nations)
GATT	General Agreement on Tariffs and Trade
Gen. Cls. Comm.	General Claims Commission, United States and Panama; General Claims Commission, United States and Mexico
Geo. II	King George II (Great Britain)
Geo. III	King George III (Great Britain)
GM	General Motors
GNMA	Government National Mortgage Association, "Ginnie Mae"
GNP	gross national product
GOP	Grand Old Party (Republican)
GOPAC	Grand Old Party Action Committee
GPA	Office of Governmental and Public Affairs
GPO	Government Printing Office
GRAS	generally recognized as safe
Gr. Br., Crim. Ct. App.	Great Britain, Court of Criminal Appeals
GRNL	Gay Rights National Lobby
GSA	General Services Administration
Hackworth	Green Haywood Hackworth, *Digest of International Law* (1940–44)
Hay and Marriott	Great Britain. High Court of Admiralty, *Decisions in the High Court of Admiralty during the Time of Sir George Hay and of Sir James Marriott, Late Judges of That Court* (1801)
HBO	Home Box Office
HCFA	Health Care Financing Administration
H.Ct.	High Court
HDS	Office of Human Development Services
Hen. & M.	Hening & Munford's Virginia Reports
HEW	Department of Health, Education, and Welfare
HHS	Department of Health and Human Services
Hill	Hill's New York Reports
HIRE	Help through Industry Retraining and Employment
HIV	human immunodeficiency virus
H.L.	House of Lords Cases (England)
H. Lords	House of Lords (England)
HNIS	Human Nutrition Information Service
Hong Kong L.R.	Hong Kong Law Reports
How.	Howard's United States Supreme Court Reports
How. St. Trials	Howell's English State Trials
HUAC	House Un-American Activities Committee

HUD	Department of Housing and Urban Development
Hudson, Internatl. Legis.	Manley O. Hudson, ed., *International Legislation: A Collection of the Texts of Multipartite International Instruments of General Interest Beginning with the Covenant of the League of Nations* (1931)
Hudson, World Court Reps.	Manley Ottmer Hudson, ed., *World Court Reports* (1934–)
Hun	Hun's New York Supreme Court Reports
Hunt's Rept.	Bert L. Hunt, *Report of the American and Panamanian General Claims Arbitration* (1934)
IAEA	International Atomic Energy Agency
IALL	International Association of Law Libraries
IBA	International Bar Association
IBM	International Business Machines
ICBM	intercontinental ballistic missile
ICC	Interstate Commerce Commission
ICJ	International Court of Justice
IDEA	Individuals with Disabilities Education Act, 1975
IEP	individualized educational program
IFC	International Finance Corporation
IGRA	Indian Gaming Regulatory Act, 1988
IJA	Institute of Judicial Administration
IJC	International Joint Commission
ILC	International Law Commission
ILD	International Labor Defense
Ill. Dec.	Illinois Decisions
ILO	International Labor Organization
IMF	International Monetary Fund
INA	Immigration and Nationality Act
IND	investigational new drug
INF Treaty	Intermediate-Range Nuclear Forces Treaty of 1987
INS	Immigration and Naturalization Service
INTELSAT	International Telecommunications Satellite Organization
Interpol	International Criminal Police Organization
Int'l. Law Reps.	International Law Reports
Intl. Legal Mats.	International Legal Materials
IPDC	International Program for the Development of Communication
IPO	Intellectual Property Owners
IPP	independent power producer
IQ	intelligence quotient
I.R.	Irish Reports
IRA	individual retirement account; Irish Republican Army
IRCA	Immigration Reform and Control Act of 1986
IRS	Internal Revenue Service
ISO	independent service organization
ISSN	International Standard Serial Numbers
ITA	International Trade Administration
ITI	Information Technology Integration
ITO	International Trade Organization
ITS	Information Technology Service
ITU	International Telecommunication Union
IUD	intrauterine device
IWC	International Whaling Commission
IWW	Industrial Workers of the World
JCS	Joint Chiefs of Staff
JDL	Jewish Defense League
JOBS	Jobs Opportunity and Basic Skills
John. Ch.	Johnson's New York Chancery Reports
Johns.	Johnson's Reports (New York)
JP	justice of the peace

K.B.	King's Bench Reports (England)
KGB	Komitet Gosudarstvennoi Bezopasnosti (the State Security Committee for countries in the former Soviet Union)
KKK	Ku Klux Klan
KMT	Kuomintang
LAPD	Los Angeles Police Department
LC	Library of Congress
LD50	lethal dose 50
LDEF	Legal Defense and Education Fund (NOW)
LDF	Legal Defense Fund, Legal Defense and Educational Fund of the NAACP
LEAA	Law Enforcement Assistance Administration
L.Ed.	Lawyers' Edition Supreme Court Reports
LMSA	Labor-Management Services Administration
LNTS	League of Nations Treaty Series
Lofft's Rep.	Lofft's English King's Bench Reports
L.R.	Law Reports (English)
LSAS	Law School Admission Service
LSAT	Law School Aptitude Test
LSC	Legal Services Corporation; Legal Services for Children
LSD	lysergic acid diethylamide
LSDAS	Law School Data Assembly Service
LTBT	Limited Test Ban Treaty
LTC	Long Term Care
MAD	mutual assured destruction
MADD	Mothers against Drunk Driving
MALDEF	Mexican American Legal Defense and Educational Fund
Malloy	William M. Malloy, ed., *Treaties, Conventions, International Acts, Protocols, and Agreements between the United States of America and Other Powers* (1910–38)
Martens	Georg Friedrich von Martens, ed., *Noveau recueil général de traités et autres act es relatifs aux rapports de droit international* (Series I, 20 vols. [1843–75]; Series II, 35 vols. [1876–1908]; Series III [1909–])
Mass.	Massachusetts Reports
MCH	Maternal and Child Health Bureau
Md. App.	Maryland, Appeal Cases
M.D. Ga.	Middle District, Georgia
Mercy	Movement Ensuring the Right to Choose for Yourself
Metc.	Metcalf's Massachusetts Reports
MFDP	Mississippi Freedom Democratic party
MGT	Management
MHSS	Military Health Services System
Miller	David Hunter Miller, ed., *Treaties and Other International Acts of the United States of America* (1931–1948)
Minn.	Minnesota Reports
MINS	minors in need of supervision
MIRV	multiple independently targetable reentry vehicle
Misc.	Miscellaneous Reports, New York
Mixed Claims Comm., Report of Decs.	Mixed Claims Commission, United States and Germany, Report of Decisions
M.J.	Military Justice Reporter
MLAP	Migrant Legal Action Program
MLB	major league baseball
MLDP	Mississippi Loyalist Democratic party
Mo.	Missouri Reports
Mod.	Modern Reports, English King's Bench, etc.
Moore, Dig. Intl. Law	John Bassett Moore, *A Digest of International Law*, 8 vols. (1906)
Moore, Intl. Arbs.	John Bassett Moore, *History and Digest of the International Arbitrations to Which the United States Has Been a Party*, 6 vols. (1898)

Morison	William Maxwell Morison, *The Scots Revised Report: Morison's Dictionary of Decisions* (1908–09)
M.P.	member of Parliament
MPAA	Motion Picture Association of America
mpg	miles per gallon
MPRSA	Marine Protection, Research, and Sanctuaries Act of 1972
M.R.	Master of the Rolls
MS-DOS	Microsoft Disk Operating System
MSHA	Mine Safety and Health Administration
NAACP	National Association for the Advancement of Colored People
NAAQS	National Ambient Air Quality Standards
NABSW	National Association of Black Social Workers
NAFTA	North American Free Trade Agreement, 1993
NARAL	National Abortion Rights Action League
NARF	Native American Rights Fund
NARS	National Archives and Record Service
NASA	National Aeronautics and Space Administration
NASD	National Association of Securities Dealers
NATO	North Atlantic Treaty Organization
NAVINFO	Navy Information Offices
NAWSA	National American Woman's Suffrage Association
NBA	National Bar Association
NBC	National Broadcasting Company
NBLSA	National Black Law Student Association
NBS	National Bureau of Standards
NCA	Noise Control Act; National Command Authorities
NCAA	National Collegiate Athletic Association
NCAC	National Coalition against Censorship
NCCB	National Consumer Cooperative Bank
NCE	Northwest Community Exchange
NCJA	National Criminal Justice Association
NCLB	National Civil Liberties Bureau
NCP	national contingency plan
NCSC	National Center for State Courts
NCUA	National Credit Union Administration
NDA	new drug application
N.D. Ill.	Northern District, Illinois
NDU	National Defense University
N.D. Wash.	Northern District, Washington
N.E.	North Eastern Reporter
N.E. 2d	North Eastern Reporter, Second Series
NEA	National Endowment for the Arts
NEH	National Endowment for the Humanities
NEPA	National Environmental Protection Act; National Endowment Policy Act
NFIP	National Flood Insurance Program
NGTF	National Gay Task Force
NHRA	Nursing Home Reform Act, 1987
NHTSA	National Highway Traffic Safety Administration
Nielsen's Rept.	Frederick Kenelm Nielsen, *American and British Claims Arbitration under the Special Agreement Concluded between the United States and Great Britain, August 18, 1910* (1926)
NIEO	New International Economic Order
NIH	National Institutes of Health, the NIH
NIJ	National Institute of Justice
NIRA	National Industrial Recovery Act; National Industrial Recovery Administration
NIST	National Institute of Standards and Technology, the NIST
NITA	National Telecommunications and Information Administration
N.J.	New Jersey Reports

N.J. Super.	New Jersey Superior Court Reports
NLRA	National Labor Relations Act
NLRB	National Labor Relations Board
No.	Number
NOAA	National Oceanic and Atmospheric Administration
NOW	National Organization for Women
NOW LDEF	National Organization for Women Legal Defense and Education Fund
NOW/PAC	National Organization for Women Political Action Committee
NPDES	National Pollutant Discharge Elimination System
NPL	national priorities list
NPR	National Public Radio
NPT	Non-Proliferation Treaty
NRA	National Rifle Association; National Recovery Act
NRC	Nuclear Regulatory Commission
NSC	National Security Council
NSCLC	National Senior Citizens Law Center
NSF	National Science Foundation
NSFNET	National Science Foundation Network
NTIA	National Telecommunications and Information Administration
NTID	National Technical Institute for the Deaf
NTIS	National Technical Information Service
NTS	Naval Telecommunications System
NTSB	National Transportation Safety Board
N.W.	North Western Reporter
N.W. 2d	North Western Reporter, Second Series
NWSA	National Woman Suffrage Association
N.Y.	New York Court of Appeals Reports
N.Y. 2d	New York Court of Appeals Reports, Second Series
N.Y.S.	New York Supplement Reporter
N.Y.S. 2d	New York Supplement Reporter, Second Series
NYSE	New York Stock Exchange
N.Y. Sup.	New York Supreme Court Reports
NYU	New York University
OAAU	Organization of Afro American Unity
OAP	Office of Administrative Procedure
OAS	Organization of American States
OASDI	Old-age, Survivors, and Disability Insurance Benefits
OASHDS	Office of the Assistant Secretary for Human Development Services
OCED	Office of Comprehensive Employment Development
OCHAMPUS	Office of Civilian Health and Medical Program of the Uniformed Services
OCSE	Office of Child Support Enforcement
OEA	Organización de los Estados Americanos
OFCCP	Office of Federal Contract Compliance Programs
OFPP	Office of Federal Procurement Policy
OICD	Office of International Cooperation and Development
OIG	Office of the Inspector General
OJARS	Office of Justice Assistance, Research, and Statistics
OMB	Office of Management and Budget
OMPC	Office of Management, Planning, and Communications
ONP	Office of National Programs
OPD	Office of Policy Development
OPEC	Organization of Petroleum Exporting Countries
OPIC	Overseas Private Investment Corporation
Ops. Atts. Gen.	Opinions of the Attorneys-General of the United States
Ops. Comms.	Opinions of the Commissioners
OPSP	Office of Product Standards Policy
O.R.	Ontario Reports
OR	Official Records

OSHA	Occupational Safety and Health Administration
OSHRC	Occupational Safety and Health Review Commission
OSM	Office of Surface Mining
OSS	Office of Strategic Services
OST	Office of the Secretary
OT	Office of Transportation
OTA	Office of Technology Assessment
OTC	over-the-counter
OUI	operating under the influence
OWBPA	Older Workers Benefit Protection Act
OWRT	Office of Water Research and Technology
P.	Pacific Reporter
P. 2d	Pacific Reporter, Second Series
PAC	political action committee
Pa. Oyer and Terminer	Pennsylvania Oyer and Terminer Reports
PATCO	Professional Air Traffic Controllers Organization
PBGC	Pension Benefit Guaranty Corporation
PBS	Public Broadcasting Service; Public Buildings Service
P.C.	Privy Council (English Law Reports); personal computer
PCIJ	Permanent Court of International Justice
	Series A—Judgments and Orders (1922–30)
	Series B—Advisory Opinions (1922–30)
	Series A/B—Judgments, Orders, and Advisory Opinions (1931–40)
	Series C—Pleadings, Oral Statements, and Documents relating to Judgments and Advisory Opinions (1923–42)
	Series D—Acts and Documents concerning the Organization of the World Court (1922–47)
	Series E—Annual Reports (1925–45)
PCP	phencyclidine (no need to spell out)
P.D.	Probate Division, English Law Reports (1876–1890)
PDA	Pregnancy Discrimination Act of 1978
PD & R	Policy Development and Research
Perm. Ct. of Arb.	Permanent Court of Arbitration
Pet.	Peters' United States Supreme Court Reports
PETA	People for the Ethical Treatment of Animals
PGM	Program
PHA	Public Housing Agency
Phila. Ct. of Oyer and Terminer	Philadelphia Court of Oyer and Terminer
PHS	Public Health Service
PIC	Private Industry Council
Pick.	Pickering's Massachusetts Reports
PIK	Payment in Kind
PINS	persons in need of supervision
PIRG	Public Interest Research Group
P.L.	Public Laws
PLAN	Pro-Life Action Network
PLI	Practicing Law Institute
PLO	Palestine Liberation Organization
PNET	Peaceful Nuclear Explosions Treaty
POW-MIA	prisoner of war–missing in action
Pratt	Frederic Thomas Pratt, *Law of Contraband of War, with a Selection of Cases from the Papers of the Right Honourable Sir George Lee* (1856)
Proc.	Proceedings
PRP	potentially responsible party
PSRO	Professional Standards Review Organization
PTO	Patents and Trademark Office
PURPA	Public Utilities Regulatory Policies Act

PUSH	People United to Serve Humanity
PWA	Public Works Administration
PWSA	Ports and Waterways Safety Act of 1972
Q.B.	Queen's Bench (England)
Ralston's Rept.	Jackson Harvey Ralston, ed., *Venezuelan Arbitrations of 1903* (1904)
RC	Regional Commissioner
RCRA	Resource Conservation and Recovery Act
RCWP	Rural Clean Water Program
RDA	Rural Development Administration
REA	Rural Electrification Administration
Rec. des Decs. des Trib. Arb. Mixtes	G. Gidel, ed., *Recueil des décisions des tribunaux arbitraux mixtes, institués par les traités de paix* (1922–30)
Redmond	Vol. 3 of Charles I. Bevans, *Treaties and Other International Agreements of the United States of America, 1776–1949* (compiled by C. F. Redmond) (1969)
RESPA	Real Estate Settlement Procedure Act of 1974
RFRA	Religious Freedom Restoration Act
RICO	Racketeer Influenced and Corrupt Organizations
RNC	Republican National Committee
Roscoe	Edward Stanley Roscoe, ed., *Reports of Prize Cases Determined in the High Court of Admiralty before the Lords Commissioners of Appeals in Prize Causes and before the Judicial Committee of the Privy Council from 1745 to 1859* (1905)
ROTC	Reserve Officers' Training Corps
RPP	Representative Payee Program
R.S.	Revised Statutes
RTC	Resolution Trust Company
Ryan White CARE Act	Ryan White Comprehensive AIDS Research Emergency Act of 1990
SAC	Strategic Air Command
SACB	Subversive Activities Control Board
SADD	Students against Drunk Driving
SAF	Student Activities Fund
SAIF	Savings Association Insurance Fund
SALT I	Strategic Arms Limitation Talks of 1969–72
SAMHSA	Substance Abuse and Mental Health Services Administration
Sandf.	Sandford's New York Superior Court Reports
S and L	savings and loan
SARA	Superfund Amendment and Reauthorization Act
Sawy.	Sawyer's United States Circuit Court Reports
SBA	Small Business Administration
SCLC	Southern Christian Leadership Conference
Scott's Repts.	James Brown Scott, ed., *The Hague Court Reports*, 2 vols. (1916–32)
SCS	Soil Conservation Service
SCSEP	Senior Community Service Employment Program
S.Ct.	Supreme Court Reporter
S.D. Cal.	Southern District, California
S.D. Fla.	Southern District, Florida
S.D. Ga.	Southern District, Georgia
SDI	Strategic Defense Initiative
S.D. Me.	Southern District, Maine
S.D.N.Y.	Southern District, New York
SDS	Students for a Democratic Society
S.E.	South Eastern Reporter
S.E. 2d	South Eastern Reporter, Second Series
SEA	Science and Education Administration
SEATO	Southeast Asia Treaty Organization
SEC	Securities and Exchange Commission
Sec.	Section
SEEK	Search for Elevation, Education and Knowledge
SEOO	State Economic Opportunity Office

SEP	simplified employee pension plan
Ser.	Series
Sess.	Session
SGLI	Servicemen's Group Life Insurance
SIP	state implementation plan
SLA	Symbionese Liberation Army
SLBM	submarine-launched ballistic missile
SNCC	Student Nonviolent Coordinating Committee
So.	Southern Reporter
So. 2d	Southern Reporter, Second Series
SPA	Software Publisher's Association
Spec. Sess.	Special Session
SRA	Sentencing Reform Act of 1984
SS	Schutzstaffel (German for Protection Echelon)
SSA	Social Security Administration
SSI	Supplemental Security Income
START I	Strategic Arms Reduction Treaty of 1991
START II	Strategic Arms Reduction Treaty of 1993
Stat.	United States Statutes at Large
STS	Space Transportation Systems
St. Tr.	State Trials, English
STURAA	Surface Transportation and Uniform Relocation Assistance Act of 1987
Sup. Ct. of Justice, Mexico	Supreme Court of Justice, Mexico
Supp.	Supplement
S.W.	South Western Reporter
S.W. 2d	South Western Reporter, Second Series
SWAPO	South-West Africa People's Organization
SWAT	Special Weapons and Tactics
SWP	Socialist Workers party
TDP	Trade and Development Program
Tex. Sup.	Texas Supreme Court Reports
THAAD	Theater High-Altitude Area Defense System
TIA	Trust Indenture Act of 1939
TIAS	Treaties and Other International Acts Series (United States)
TNT	trinitrotoluene
TOP	Targeted Outreach Program
TPUS	Transportation and Public Utilities Service
Tripartite Claims Comm., Decs. and Ops.	Tripartite Claims Commission (United States, Austria, and Hungary), Decisions and Opinions
TRI-TAC	Joint Tactical Communications
TRO	temporary restraining order
TS	Treaty Series, United States
TSCA	Toxic Substance Control Act
TSDs	transporters, storers, and disposers
TTBT	Threshold Test Ban Treaty
TVA	Tennessee Valley Authority
UAW	United Auto Workers; United Automobile, Aerospace, and Agricultural Implements Workers of America
U.C.C.	Uniform Commercial Code; Universal Copyright Convention
U.C.C.C.	Uniform Consumer Credit Code
UCCJA	Uniform Child Custody Jurisdiction Act
UCMJ	Uniform Code of Military Justice
UCPP	Urban Crime Prevention Program
UCS	United Counseling Service
UDC	United Daughters of the Confederacy
UFW	United Farm Workers
UHF	ultrahigh frequency
UIFSA	Uniform Interstate Family Support Act

UIS	Unemployment Insurance Service
UMDA	Uniform Marriage and Divorce Act
UMTA	Urban Mass Transportation Administration
UNCITRAL	United Nations Commission on International Trade Law
UNCTAD	United Nations Conference on Trade and Development
UN Doc.	United Nations Documents
UNDP	United Nations Development Program
UNEF	United Nations Emergency Force
UNESCO	United Nations Educational, Scientific, and Cultural Organization
UNICEF	United Nations Children's Fund
UNIDO	United Nations Industrial and Development Organization
Unif. L. Ann.	Uniform Laws Annotated
UN Repts. Intl. Arb. Awards	United Nations Reports of International Arbitral Awards
UNTS	United Nations Treaty Series
UPI	United Press International
URESA	Uniform Reciprocal Enforcement of Support Act
U.S.	United States Reports
USAF	United States Air Force
U.S. App. D.C.	United States Court of Appeals for the District of Columbia
U.S.C.	United States Code
U.S.C.A.	United States Code Annotated
U.S.C.C.A.N.	United States Code Congressional and Administrative News
USCMA	United States Court of Military Appeals
USDA	U.S. Department of Agriculture
USES	United States Employment Service
USFA	United States Fire Administration
USICA	International Communication Agency, United States
USSC	U.S. Sentencing Commission
U.S.S.R.	Union of Soviet Socialist Republics
UST	United States Treaties
USTS	United States Travel Service
v.	*versus*
VA	Veterans Administration, the VA
VGLI	Veterans Group Life Insurance
Vict.	Queen Victoria (Great Britain)
VIN	vehicle identification number
VISTA	Volunteers in Service to America
VJRA	Veterans Judicial Review Act of 1988
V.L.A.	Volunteer Lawyers for the Arts
VMI	Virginia Military Institute
VMLI	Veterans Mortgage Life Insurance
VOCAL	Victims of Child Abuse Laws
WAC	Women's Army Corps
Wall.	Wallace's United States Supreme Court Reports
Wash. 2d	Washington Reports, Second Series
WAVES	Women Accepted for Volunteer Service
WCTU	Women's Christian Temperance Union
W.D. Wash.	Western District, Washington
W.D. Wis.	Western District, Wisconsin
WEAL	West's Encyclopedia of American Law, Women's Equity Action League
Wend.	Wendell's New York Reports
WFSE	Washington Federation of State Employees
Wheat.	Wheaton's United States Supreme Court Reports
Wheel. Cr. Cases	Wheeler's New York Criminal Cases
Whiteman	Marjorie Millace Whiteman, *Digest of International Law*, 15 vols. (1963–73)
WHO	World Health Organization
WIC	Women, Infants, and Children program
Will. and Mar.	King William and Queen Mary (Great Britain)

WIN	WESTLAW Is Natural; Whip Inflation Now; Work Incentive Program
WIU	Workers' Industrial Union
W.L.R.	Weekly Law Reports, England
WPA	Works Progress Administration
WPPDA	Welfare and Pension Plans Disclosure Act
WWI	World War I
WWII	World War II
Yates Sel. Cas.	Yates' New York Select Cases

BIBLIOGRAPHY

ABDICATION

Thornton, Michael. 1985. *Royal Feud: The Dark Side of the Love Story of the Century.* New York: Simon & Schuster.

Warwick, Christopher. 1986. *Abdication.* London: Sidgwick & Jackson.

ABINGTON SCHOOL DISTRICT V. SCHEMPP

ABC News Tonight. 1994. November 18.

American Civil Liberties Union (ACLU). 1993. *The Establishment Clause and Public Schools.*

Blanshard, Paul. 1963. *Religion and the Schools: The Great Controversy.* Boston: Beacon Press.

Castle, Marie, cochair, Minnesota Atheists. Telephone interview.

"Religion and Schools." 1994. *Congressional Quarterly,* February 18.

ABOLITION

Schwartz, Bernard. 1974. *The Law in America.* New York: American Heritage.

ABORTION

Butler, J. Douglas, and David F. Walbert, eds. 1986. *Abortion, Medicine, and the Law.* 3d ed. New York: Facts on File.

Drucker, Dan. 1990. *Abortion Decisions of the Supreme Court, 1973 through 1989: A Comprehensive Review with Historical Commentary.* Jefferson, N.C.: McFarland.

McCorvey, Norma. 1994. *I Am Roe.* New York: HarperCollins.

Reagan, Ronald. 1984. *Abortion and the Conscience of a Nation.* Nashville: Nelson.

Rubin, Eva R. 1987. *Abortion, Politics, and the Courts: Roe v. Wade and Its Aftermath.* New York: Greenwood.

ABSENTEE VOTING

Kimberling, Bill, deputy director, National Clearinghouse on Election Administration, Federal Election Commission. 1994. Telephone interview, June 30.

ABSTRACT

Johnson, Sandy, abstract supervisor, Quality Abstract, Oakdale, Mn. 1994. Telephone interview, June 29.

Minnesota State Bar Association. Continuing Legal Education. 1994. *Examination of Title in Minnesota.* March.

Ojile, Michael, attorney-at-law. 1994. Telephone interview, June 30.

ACCESSORY

BAR/BRI Multistate Review. 1982. Orlando, Fla.: Harcourt Brace Jovanovich Legal & Professional Publications.

Belli, Melvin, Sr., and Allen P. Wilkinson. 1986. *Everybody's Guide to the Law.* San Diego: Harcourt Brace Jovanovich.

ACQUIRED IMMUNE DEFICIENCY SYNDROME

ACLU. 1993. *ACLU Files AIDS Discrimination Suit; Challenges South Carolina Insurance Risk Pool.* Press release, April 6.

———. 1994. *ACLU Wins Precedent-Setting Claim in AIDS Case; Federal Court Rules That ADA Covers AIDS Discrimination.* Press release, November 21.

———. 1995a. *AIDS and Civil Liberties.* Briefing paper no. 13.

———. 1995b. *Lesbian and Gay Rights.* Briefing paper no. 18.

Health and Human Services Department. Social Security Administration. 1991. *A Guide to Social Security and SSI Disability Benefits for People with HIV Infection.* Pub. no. 05-10020, September.

White House. Office of the Press Secretary. 1994. *Proclamation for World AIDS Day, November 30, 1994.* Press release.

ADAMS, JOHN QUINCY

Kane, Joseph N. 1993. *Facts About the President.* 6th ed. New York: Wilson.

ADDAMS, JANE

Deegan, Mary Jo. 1988. *Jane Addams and the Men of the Chicago School, 1892–1918,* New Brunswick, N.J.: Transaction Books.

Hovde, Jane. 1989. *Jane Addams.* New York: Facts on File.

Mitchard, Jacquelyn. 1991. *Jane Addams.* Milwaukee: Garth Stevens Children's Books.

ADJUDICATION

Cardoza, Benjamin N. 1960. *The Nature of the Judicial Process.* New Haven, Conn.: Yale Univ. Press.

Lewis, William D., ed. 1922. *Commentaries on the Laws of England.* Philadelphia: Bisel.

Roosevelt, Theodore. 1908. Message to Congress. *Congressional Record,* December 8, pt. I:21.

ADJUDICATIVE FACTS

Carp, Robert A., and Ronald Stidham. 1990. *The Judicial Process in America.* Washington, D.C.: Congressional Quarterly Press.

Sigler, Jay A. 1968. *An Introduction to the Legal System.* Homewood, Ill.: Dorsey Press.

ADMINISTRATION, OFFICE OF

Executive Order No. 12,028, *Federal Register* 42:62,895 (1977).

Nelson, Michael, ed. 1989. *Congressional Quarterly's Guide to the Presidency.* New York: Facts on File.

The United States Government Manual, 1994–1995. Washington, D.C.: U.S. Government Printing Office.

ADMINISTRATIVE AGENCY

Barksdale, Yvette M. 1993. "The Presidency and Administrative Value Selection." *American University Law Review* 42.

Bledsoe, Delores, supervising attorney, Office of Hearings and Appeals, Social Security Administration, Minneapolis. 1994. Telephone interview, May 31.

Diver, Colin S. 1986. "The Uneasy Constitutional Status of the Administrative Agencies." Paper presented at the Symposium on Administrative Law, April 4.

———. 1987. "The Uneasy Constitutional Status of the Administrative Agencies, Part II: Presidential Oversight of Regulatory Decisionmaking: Commentary: Presidential Powers." *American University Law Review* 36.

The United States Government Manual, 1994–1995. Washington, D.C.: U.S. Government Printing Office.

ADMINISTRATIVE CONFERENCE OF THE UNITED STATES

Bledsoe, Delores, supervising attorney, Office of Hearings and Appeals, Social Security Administration, Minneapolis. 1994. Telephone interview, May 31.

Breger, Marshall J. 1992. "Symposium: The Administrative Conference of the United States: A Quarter Century Perspective." *University of Pittsburgh Law Review,* pp. 813–15.

Farrell, Margaret G. 1992. "Improving the Social Security Representative Payee Program—Recommendations of the Administrative Conference of the United States." *Mental and Physical Disability Law Reporter* (March–April): 232–37.

ADMINISTRATIVE OFFICE OF THE UNITED STATES COURTS

Circuit executive's office, U.S. Court of Appeals for the Eighth Circuit. Telephone interview.

National Archives and Records Administration. Office of the Federal Register. *The United States Government Manual, 1993–1994.* Washington, D.C.: U.S. Government Printing Office.

ADMIRALTY AND MARITIME LAW

Healy, Nicholas J., and David J. Sharpe. 1986. *Admiralty, Cases and Materials.* 2d ed. St. Paul: West.

Maraist, Frank L. 1988. *Admiralty.* 2d ed. St. Paul: West.

ADOPTION

DuPrau, Jeanne. 1990. *Adoption.* Englewood Cliffs, N.J.: Messner.

Rundberg, Gayle D. 1988. *How to Get Babies through Private Adoption.* Bend, Or.: Maverick.

Sloan, Irving J. 1988. *The Law of Adoption and Surrogate Parenting.* London: Oceana.

ADVERSARY SYSTEM

Doyle, Stephen, and Roger Haydock. 1991. *Without the Punches.* Minneapolis: Equilaw.

Editors of Nolo Press. 1990. *Legal Breakdown.* Berkeley, Cal.: Nolo Press.

"Essays: The State of the Adversary System 1993." 1993. *Valparaiso University Law Review* 27, no. 2 (spring).

Friedman, Lawrence M. 1985. *A History of American Law.* New York: Simon & Schuster.

Janosik, Robert J., ed. 1987. *Encyclopedia of the American Judicial System.* New York: Scribner.

Landsman, Stephen. 1984. *The Adversary System.* Washington, D.C.: American Institute for Public Policy Research.

Olson, Walter K. 1991. *The Litigation Explosion.* New York: Truman Talley Books.

ADVISORY OPINION

Abraham, Henry J. 1975. *The Judicial Process.* New York: Oxford Univ. Press.

Carp, Robert A., and Ronald Stidham. 1989. *Judicial Process in America.* Washington, D.C.: Congressional Quarterly Press.

Sigler, Jay A. 1968. *An Introduction to the Legal System.* Homewood, Ill.: Dorsey Press.

AFFIRMATIVE ACTION

ACLU. 1995a. *Affirmative Action.* Briefing paper no. 17, March 22.

———. 1995b. *The Case for Affirmative Action.* July 1.

"Affirmative Action." 1995. *CQ Researcher.* April 28.

Clinton, President Bill. 1995. Speech at the National Archives, July 31.

AGE DISCRIMINATION

Beyer, James R. 1993. "*Biggins* Leaves ADEA Issues Unresolved." *National Law Journal* (July 19).

Bodensteiner, Jill R. 1994. "Post OWBPA Developments in the Law Regarding Waivers to ADEA Claims." *Washington University Journal of Urban and Contemporary Law* 46 (summer).

Johns, Roger J., Jr. 1994. "Proving Pretext and Willfulness in Age Discrimination Cases After *Hazen Paper Company v. Biggins.*" *Labor Law Journal* 45, no. 4 (April).

Kulatz, Karen. 1993. "Trading Substantive Values for Procedural Values: Compulsory Arbitration and the ADEA." *University of Florida Journal of Law and Public Policy* 5, no. 2 (spring).

Lawrence, Emily J. 1992. "Clarifying the Timing Requirements for Federal Employees' Age Discrimination Claims." *Boston College Law Review* 33, no. 2 (March).

Marshall, Alison B. 1994. "Defective ADEA Releases: Void of Legal Effect or Subject to Ratification?" *Employee Relations Law Journal* 20, no. 2 (autumn).

AGENCY

Steffen, Roscoe T. 1977. *Agency-Partnership.* St. Paul: West.

AGE REQUIREMENT FOR HOLDING OFFICE

Council of the State Governments. *The Book of the States.* 1994. Lexington, Ky.: Council of the State Governments.

Farrand, Max, ed. 1966. *Records of the Federal Convention of 1787.* Rev. ed. Vol. 1. New Haven, Conn.: Yale Univ. Press.

Hamilton, Alexander, James Madison, and John Jay. 1787–88. *The Federalist Papers.*

AGRICULTURAL LAW

Barnes, Richard L. 1993. "The U.C.C.'s Insidious Preference for Agronomy over Ecology in Farm Lending Decisions." *University of Colorado Law Review* 64:458–79.

Coggins, George, and Margaret Lindeberg-Johnson. 1982. "The Law of Public Rangeland Management II: The Commons and the Taylor Act." *Environmental Law* 13:4.

Goettle, Shane, president, Agricultural Law Society, Hamline University School of Law. 1994. Telephone interview, April 4.

Hamilton, Neil D. 1990. "The Study of Agricultural Law in the United States: Education, Organization, and Practice." *Arkansas Law Review* 43:503–14.

———. 1993. "Feeding Our Future: Six Philosophical Issues Shaping Agricultural Law." *Nebraska Law Review* 72:211–23.

Looney, J. W. 1993. "The Changing Focus of Government Regulation of Agriculture in the United States." *Mercer Law Review* 44:764–74.

Meyer, Keith G., et al. 1985. *Agricultural Law: Cases and Materials.* St. Paul: West.

Prim, Richard. 1993. "Saving the Family Farm: Is Minnesota's Anti–Corporate Farm Statute the Answer?" *Hamline Journal of Public Law and Policy* 14:203–25.

AGRICULTURE DEPARTMENT

The United States Government Manual, 1991–1992. Washington, D.C.: U.S. Government Printing Office.

AGRICULTURE SUBSIDIES

Agriculture Department. 1981. *A Time to Choose: Summary Report on the Structure of Agriculture.* Washington, D.C.

Cochrane, Willard, and Mary Ryan. 1976. *American Farm Policy, 1948–1973.* Minneapolis: Univ. of Minnesota Press.

Rapp, David. 1988. *How the United States Got into Agriculture: And Why It Can't Get Out.* Washington, D.C.: Congressional Quarterly Press.

Rehka, Mehra. 1989. "Winners and Losers in the U.S. Sugar Program." *Resources* (Resources for the Future, Washington, D.C.) 94 (winter): 5–7.

AIRLINES

Nader, Ralph, and Wesley J. Smith. 1994. *Collision Course: The Truth about Airline Safety.* Blue Ridge Summit, Pa.: McGraw-Hill, Tab Books.

Sturken, Barbara Peterson, and James Glab. 1994. *Rapid Descent: Deregulation and the Shakeout in the Airlines.* New York: Simon & Schuster.

AIR POLLUTION

Findley, Roger W., and Daniel Farber. 1992. *Environmental Law.* St. Paul: West.

Rodgers, William H., Jr. 1986. *Environmental Law: Air and Water.* Vol. 2. St. Paul: West.

AKERMAN, AMOS TAPPAN

Baker, Nancy V. 1992. *Conflicting Loyalties: Law and Politics in the Attorney General's Office, 1789–1990.* Lawrence, Kan.: Univ. Press of Kansas.

ALCOHOL

Alcoholics Anonymous World Services (AAWS). *Twelve Steps and Twelve Traditions.* New York: AAWS.

Blocker, Jack S., ed. 1979. *Alcohol, Reform and Society.* Westport, Conn.: Greenwood Press.

Boyd, Steven R., ed. 1985. *The Whiskey Rebellion.* Westport, Conn.: Greenwood Press.

Cochran, Robert F., Jr. 1994. " 'Good Whiskey,' Drunk Driving, and Innocent Bystanders: The Responsibility of Manufacturers of Alcohol and Other Dangerous Hedonic Products for Bystander Injury." *South Carolina Law Review* 45.

Cordes, Rene. 1992. "Alcohol Manufacturer Held Partially Liable for Student's Death." *Trial* (December).

Goldberg, James. 1992. "Social Host Liability for Serving Alcohol." *Trial* (March).

Gorski, Terence T. 1989. *Understanding the Twelve Steps.* New York: Prentice-Hall/Parkside.

Khoury, Clarke E. 1989. "Warning Labels May Be Hazardous to Your Health: Common-Law and Statutory Responses to Alcoholic Beverage Manufacturers' Duty to Warn." *Cornell Law Review* 75.

Kyvig, David E., ed. 1985. *Law, Alcohol, and Order.* Westport, Conn.: Greenwood Press.

"*Lee v. Kiku Restaurant:* Allocation of Fault Between an Alcohol Vendor and a Patron—What Could Happen after Providing 'One More for the Road?' " *American Journal of Trial Advocacy* 17: note.

Lender, Mark E. 1987. *Drinking in America.* New York: Free Press.

"State Compelled Spiritual Revelation: The First Amendment and Alcoholics Anonymous as a Condition of Drunk Driving Probation." 1992. *William and Mary Bill of Rights Journal* 1 (fall).

ALCOHOL, TOBACCO AND FIREARMS, BUREAU OF

Congressional Digest. 1991. (June–July).

National Archives and Records Administration. Office of the Federal Register. *The United States Government Manual, 1971–1972.* Washington, D.C.: U.S. Government Printing Office.

ALIMONY

Sheldon, John C., and Nancy Diesel Mills. 1993. *In Search of a Theory of Alimony.* Orono, Me.: Univ. of Maine School of Law.

AMERICAN CIVIL LIBERTIES UNION

ACLU. *ACLU's Seventy-five Most Important Supreme Court Cases.* Briefing paper.
_____. *The ACLU Today.* Briefing paper.
_____. *Church and State.* Briefing paper.
_____. *Guardian of Liberty.* Briefing paper.
Powers, Richard. 1987. *Secrecy and Power: The Life of J. Edgar Hoover.* New York: Free Press.

AMNESTY

Barcroft, P. 1993. "The Presidential Pardon—A Flawed Solution." *Human Rights Law Journal* 31 (December): 381–94.
Damico, A. 1975. *Democracy and the Case for Amnesty.* Gainesville, Fla.: Univ. Presses of Florida.
Kane, Joseph N. 1981. *Facts about the Presidents.* New York: Wilson.
Norton, M., et al., eds. 1991. *A People and a Nation.* Boston: Houghton Mifflin.

ANARCHISM

Brailsford, Henry N. 1931. *Shelley, Godwin, and their Circle.* London Press.
Goldman, Emma. *Living My Life.* 2 vols. 1930. Reprint, New York: Dover.
Joll, James. 1964. *The Anarchists.* Boston: Little, Brown.
Nozick, Robert. 1975. *Anarchy, State and Utopia.* New York: Basic Books.

ANIMAL RIGHTS

Blum, Deborah. 1994. *The Monkey Wars.* New York: Oxford Univ. Press.
Congressional Record. 1990. July 23, vol. 136, S10289-01.

ANNUAL REPORT

Practising Law Institute. 1994a. *The Annual Report to Shareholders.* Corporate Law and Practice Course Handbook Series, January–February.
_____. 1994b. *Annual Reports to Securityholders and Disclosure in Annual Reports.* October–November.

ANSWER

James, Fleming, Jr. 1965. *Civil Procedure.* Boston: Little, Brown.
McCord, James W. H. "Drafting the Complaint: Defending and Testing the Lawsuit." *Practicing Law Institute* 447:399.
Witus, Morley. "What Is the Answer? New Guidelines on How to Draft the Answer and Affirmative Defenses." *Michigan Bar Journal* 73:1076.

ANTHONY, SUSAN BROWNELL

Barry, Kathleen. 1988. *Susan B. Anthony: A Biography of a Singular Feminist.* New York: New York Univ. Press.
Cooper, Ilene. 1984. *Susan B. Anthony.* New York: Watts.

Gurko, Miriam. 1974. *The Ladies of Seneca Falls: The Birth of the Woman's Rights Movement.* New York: Macmillan.
Peterson, Helen Stone. 1971. *Susan B. Anthony: Pioneer in Woman's Rights.* Champaign, Ill.: Garrard.
Wells, Ida B. 1970. *Crusade for Justice: The Autobiography of Ida B. Wells.* Ed. Alfreda M. Duster. Chicago: Univ. of Chicago Press.

ANTI-BALLISTIC-MISSILE TREATY OF 1972

American-Soviet Treaty on the Limitation of Anti-Ballistic Missile Systems. May 26, 1972. Moscow.
Assembly of Western European Union. 1993. Anti-Missile Defence for Europe, Symposium, Rome, April 20–21.
Blackwill, Robert D., and Albert Carnesale, eds. 1993. *New Nuclear Nations.* New York: Council on Foreign Relations.
Durch, William J. 1987. *The Future of the ABM Treaty.* London: International Institute for Strategic Studies.
_____. 1988. *The ABM Treaty and Western Security.* Cambridge, Mass.: Ballinger.
Greenville, J. A. S., and Bernard Wasserstein. 1987. *The Major International Treaties Since 1945.* London: Methuen.
Joint Chiefs of Staff. 1994. *Doctrine for Joint Theater Missile Defense.* Joint pub. no. 3-01.5, March 30.
Kartchner, Kerry M. 1992. *Negotiating START.* New Brunswick, N.J., and London: Transaction.
Mazarr, Michael J., and Alexander T. Lennon, eds., 1994. *Toward a Nuclear Peace.* New York: St. Martin's Press.
Voas, Jeanette. 1990. *Soviet Attitudes towards Ballistic Missile Defence and the ABM Treaty.* London: International Institute for Strategic Studies.

APPELLATE ADVOCACY

Arkin, Marc M. 1990. "Speedy Criminal Appeal: A Right without a Remedy." *Minnesota Law Review* 74.
_____. 1992. "Rethinking the Constitutional Right to a Criminal Appeal." *University of California at Los Angeles Law Review* 39.
Junkin, Frederick D. 1988. "The Right to Counsel in 'Frivolous' Criminal Appeals: A Reevaluation of the Guarantees of *Anders v. California.*" *Texas Law Review* 67.
Knibb, David G. 1990. *Federal Court of Appeals Manual.* 2d ed. St. Paul: West.
Rubin, Alvin B. 1989. *Advocacy in the Court of Appeal.* American Law Institute–American Bar Association (ALI-ABA). No. C380.

APPORTIONMENT

" 'Advice' from the Very Beginning, 'Consent' When the End Is Achieved." 1989. *American Journal of International Law* 83 (October).
Corpus Juris Secundum United States, vol. 91, secs. 11–12.
"Fair Representation: Meeting the Ideal of One Man, One Vote." 1984. *Michigan Law Review* 82 (February).
The Federalist Nos. 37, 38, 52, 54, 56, 57, 58, 62, and 63. 1787–88.
"A House of Our Own or a House We've Outgrown? An Argument for Increasing the Size of the House of Representatives." *Columbia Journal of Law and Social Problems* 25.

"Lies, Damn Lies and Statistics: Dispelling Some Myths Surrounding the United States Census." 1990. *Detroit College of Law Review* 1990 (spring).

"Montana's Lost Seats Begs Issue." 1992. *National Law Journal* (March 2).

"Politics and Purpose: Hide and Seek in the Gerrymandering Thicket after *Davis v. Bandmer.*" 1987. *University of Pennsylvania Law Review* 136 (November).

"Reapportionment: The Supreme Court Searches for Standards." 1989. *Urban Law* 21 (fall).

"The Thickest Thicket: Partisan Gerrymandering and Judicial Regulation of Politics." 1987. *Columbia Law Review* 87 (November).

"Understanding Dworkin." 1993. *George Mason Independent Law Review* 1 (spring).

ARBITRAGE

Boesky, Ivan. 1985. *Merger Mania.* New York: Holt, Rinehart.

ARBITRATION

Crowley, Thomas. 1994. "The Art of Arbitration Advocacy." *Hawaii Bar Journal* (September).

Culiner, Helen. 1994. "Practical Guidelines for Lawyers Representing Clients in Arbitration Proceedings Today." *Dispute Resolution Journal* (September).

Deye, James, and Lesly Britton. 1994. "Arbitration by the American Arbitration Association." *North Dakota Law Review.*

Mandell, Rick, arbitrator. 1995. On-line interview, May 25.

ARCHITECT OF THE CAPITOL

United States Government Manual, 1993–1994. Washington, D.C.: U.S. Government Printing Office.

ARMED SERVICES

Atomic Scientists. 1993. Bulletin, May.

National Journal. 1993. (October 9).

National Law Journal. 1991. (September 30).

New York Law Journal. 1995. (January 4).

ARMS CONTROL AND DISARMAMENT

Dunn, Lewis A., and Sharon A. Squassoni. 1993. *Arms Control: What Next?* Boulder, Colo.: Westview Press.

Sheehan, Michael. 1988. *Arms Control: Theory and Practice.* Oxford: Blackwell.

ARTICLES OF CONFEDERATION

Harrigan, John J. 1984. *Politics and the American Future.* Reading, Mass.: Addison-Wesley.

Levy, Michael B. 1982. *Political Thought in America: An Anthology.* Homewood, Ill.: Dorsey Press.

ART LAW

Budget of the United States. 1994.

Ellickson, Robert C., and A. Dan Tarlock. 1981. *Land-Use Controls: Cases and Materials.* Boston: Little, Brown.

Frohnmayer, John E. 1992. "A Litany of Taboo," *Kansas Journal of Law and Public Policy* 2 (spring).

Rathkopf, Charles A. *Rathkopf's Law of Zoning and Planning.* 4th ed. New York: Clark Boardman Callaghan.

U.S. Congress. *Congressional Arts Caucus.* Serial 20515.

ASSASSINATION

Sifakis, C. 1991. *Encyclopedia of Assassinations.* New York: Facts on File.

ATTORNEY-CLIENT PRIVILEGE

Freedman, Monroe H. 1990. *Understanding Lawyers' Ethics.* New York: Bender.

Gillers, Stephen. 1979. *The Rights of Lawyers and Clients.* 1979. New York: Avon Books.

Noona, John M., and Michael A. Knoerzer. 1989. "The Attorney-Client Privilege and Corporate Transactions: Counsel as Keeper of Corporate Secrets." In *The Attorney-Client Privilege Under Siege.* Tort and Insurance Practice. Lake Buena Vista, Fla., May 10–14.

Tinkham, Thomas, and William J. Wernz. 1993. *Attorney-Client Privilege, Confidentiality, and Work Product Doctrine in Minnesota.* Minneapolis: Dorsey & Whitney.

ATTORNEY GENERAL

American Enterprise Institute for Public Policy Research. 1968. *Roles of the Attorney General.* Washington: D.C.: American Enterprise Institute for Public Policy Research.

Baker, Nancy V. 1985. *Conflicting Loyalties: Law and Politics in the Attorney General's Office, 1789–1990.* Lawrence, Kan.: Univ. Press of Kansas.

ATTORNEY MISCONDUCT

American Bar Association (ABA). 1984–94. *ABA/BNA Lawyers' Manual on Professional Conduct.* Chicago: ABA.

———. Center for Professional Responsibility. 1994. *Model Rules of Professional Conduct.* Chicago: ABA.

Freedman, Monroe H. 1990. *Understanding Lawyers' Ethics.* Legal Text Series. New York: Bender.

Hazard, Geoffrey C. 1994. *The Law of Lawyering.* 2 vols. Englewood Cliffs, N.J.: Prentice-Hall.

Kane, Andrew W., et al. 1992. "Attorney Sexual Misconduct." *American Journal of Family Law* 6:191–95.

Pitulla, Joanne, assistant ethics counsel, ABA. Interview.

Powell, Sonya. 1993. "Intent as an Element of Attorney Misconduct." *Journal of the Legal Profession* 18: 407–15.

AUSTIN, JOHN

Merriam, Charles E., Jr. 1972. *History of the Theory of Sovereignty Since Rousseau.* New York: Garland.

AUTOMOBILES

American Automobile Association (AAA). 1993. *Digest of Motor Laws.* Heathrow, Fla.: AAA.

"Automobiles." 1994. In *American Bar Association Family Legal Guide.* New York: Random House.

Carper, Donald L., et al. 1995. "Owning and Operating Motor Vehicles." In *Understanding the Law.* 2d ed. St. Paul: West.

Crandall, Robert W., et al. 1986. *Regulating the Automobile.* Washington, D.C.: Brookings.

Goodman, Richard M. 1983. *Automobile Design Liability.* 2d ed. Rochester, N.Y.: Lawyers Cooperative.

Haas, Carol. 1991. *Your Driving and the Law.* Bountiful, Utah: Horizon.

Mashaw, Jerry L., and David L. Harfst. 1990. *The Struggle for Auto Safety.* Cambridge: Harvard Univ. Press.

Nader, Ralph. 1965. *Unsafe at any Speed.* New York: Grossman.

Rafferty, Mike, pollution control specialist intermediate, Ground Water Solid Waste Division, Minnesota Pollution Control Agency. Interview.

Winston, Clifford, et al. 1987. *Blind Intersection? Policy and the Automobile Industry.* Washington, D.C.: Brookings.

AUTOMOBILE SEARCHES

Blade, Bryan S. 1991. "Fourth Amendment—The Constitutionality of a Sobriety Checkpoint Program." *Journal of Criminal Law and Criminology* 81, no. 4 (winter).

Braeske, Chris. 1993. "The Drug War Comes to a Highway Near You: Police Power to Effectuate Highway 'Narcotics Checkpoints' under the Federal and State Constitutions." *Law and Inequality* 11 (June).

King, Lawrence T. 1988. "The Inventory Exception to the Fourth Amendment Warrant Requirement: Why the Last in Should Be the First Out—or, Putting *Opperman* and *Bertine* in Their Place." *American Journal of Trial Advocacy* 12, no. 2 (fall).

Kole, Edward T. 1987. "Parked Motor Home Held to Be within Scope of Automobile Exception to Warrant Requirement—*California v. Carney,* 471 U.S. 386 (1985)." *Seton Hall Law Review* 17, no. 3 (summer).

Soden, Steven D. 1992. "Expansion of the 'Automobile Exception' to the Warrant Requirement: Police Discretion Replaces the 'Neutral and Detached Magistrate.' " *Missouri Law Review* 57, no. 2 (spring).

TABLE OF
CASES CITED

INDEX

By Name

INDEX

BY SUBJECT

References that include photos or exhibits are printed in italic type.